Why You Need This New Edition

Six good reasons why you should buy this new edition of *Public Policy: The Essential Readings*!

1. Five new introductory essays written by the authors have been added to the text to provide you with a balance of readings that reflect current policy issues and up-to-date research.

2. Since the previous edition, 23 new readings have been added, making this the most comprehensive public policy reader available.

3. The text has been completely reorganized to align with the current thinking of the policy subfield and to better adhere to the textbooks available on the market. You are presented with readings in an order that mirrors the topics you're learning in class.

4. In addition to the 51 readings, a newly expanded section of additional suggested readings gives you many resources for research papers and other assignments, making this text the ultimate tool for students studying public policy.

5. A separate section devoted to the theories of the policy-making process prepares you with the skills and knowledge you'll need during your career in policy making.

6. Updated pedagogical features, including revised as well as new figures, give you an engaging, visual representation of some of the key concepts you read about.

PEARSON

PUBLIC POLICY

The Essential Readings

Second Edition

PUBLIC POLICY

The Essential Readings

Stella Z. Theodoulou
California State University, Northridge
Matthew A. Cahn
California State University, Northridge

PEARSON

Boston   Columbus   Indianapolis   New York   San Francisco   Upper Saddle River
Amsterdam   Cape Town   Dubai   London   Madrid   Milan   Munich   Paris
Montreal   Toronto   Delhi   Mexico City   São Paulo   Sydney
Hong Kong   Seoul   Singapore   Taipei   Tokyo

Assistant Editor: Stephanie Chaisson
Editorial Project Manager:
   Donna DeBenedictis
Executive Marketing Manager: Wendy Gordon
Production Project Manager: Debbie Ryan
Cover Design Manager: Jayne Conte

Cover Designer: Suzanne Duda
Cover Art: Alamy
Full-Service Project Management:
   Abinaya Rajendran
Composition: Integra

Library of Congress Cataloging-in-Publication Data
Public policy: the essential readings / Stella Z. Theodoulou, Matthew A. Cahn.—2nd ed.
   p. cm.
  ISBN-13: 978-0-205-85633-6 (alk. paper)
  ISBN-10: 0-205-85633-0 (alk. paper)
   1. Policy sciences.   I. Theodoulou, Stella Z.   II. Cahn, Matthew Alan, 1961–
H97.P83 2013
320.6—dc23

                                                        2011047104

ISBN 10: 0-205-85633-0
ISBN 13: 978-0-205-85633-6

*Much of what we do professionally goes on away from those
we love and cherish. But, without their support, love,
and humor we would never be able to do what we do. So, with
much love and affection, we dedicate this book to
Marti, Alex, Diane, Arlo, Tobin, and Jonah.*

BRIEF CONTENTS

CONTENTS

PREFACE

Public policy can be described as a public response to a perceived public problem. But, what is public policy exactly, and is the policy-making process a truly rational one through which effective policy is made in the public interest? Although these are apparently simple questions to those of us who do research and teach in the field of public policy, such questions confuse many students. Understanding the policy process necessitates an understanding of the environment within which policy is being made as well as compre-hending both who is involved and what needs to happen for policy to be enacted. The purpose of this reader is to help students comprehend both the environment and the actual policy-making process.

When we sat down to put the first edition together in 1994, we sought to provide a reference for students of policy. We included four sections ranging from the nature of policy to the strategies policy actors employed. We were delighted to see that the book fit a niche. And, after almost twenty years, we recognized the importance of updating the book to accommodate changes in the field. To that end, we expanded the book substantially, while simultaneously removing those selections that we believe either did not stand the test of time or appeared dated.

The second edition continues to provide key classic and contemporary readings on public policy that introduce readers to the underpinnings and current practices of the policy-making arena. As with any compilation, there will be disagreement on what has been included and claims that "better" or "classic" readings were omitted. However, as editors we have selected readings we view as "essential" in that some of them are gener-ally argued to be among the most influential in the field, or they are among the most frequently cited, or they highlight the link between theory and practice particularly well so as to make public policy intelligible and they help to clarify other readings and theorists who are generally acknowledged to have provided the bedrock of the field.

We believe that the reader supplements existing textbooks by providing extra insight into issues and concepts covered in such standard texts. At the same time, due to its organization, the book is suitable for use as a core text for both the beginner and more advanced student of policy and public administration.

NEW TO THIS EDITION

In order to make this the most comprehensive and up-to-date Public Policy reader available on the market, the text has undergone countless edits and extensive updates. Specifically, the text has undergone a strategic reorganization. The readings have been grouped into five broad sections that parallel both the organization of the majority of policy texts and the way many courses are designed. The new sections are divided as follows:

- The first section introduces material that deals with the nature of public policy and how it is studied. Readings in this section deal with what is generally meant by public policy and the section ends with readings that illustrate the theories and models of who makes public policy.
- The second section introduces the rules, strategies, resources, and culture that define public policy. This section identifies the influences, both formal and informal, that enable policy in some areas and constrain policy in others.

- The third section deals with the various theories that have been put forward as explanations of the policy process.
- The fourth section introduces the policy actors, both institutional and non-institutional, who are involved with policy making.
- The final section addresses the structure and making of policy. This section includes selections on agenda setting, implementation, analysis, and evaluation, as well as new selections on policy change and termination.
- The new organizational structure is complimented by over 23 new readings as well as additional resources that assist students with assignments and research papers.

ACKNOWLEDGEMENTS

Finally, texts such as these are not put together in a vacuum; thus, we would like to express our thanks and appreciation to our reviewers, our editors, and the staff in the dean's office at the College of Social and Behavioral Sciences, California State University, Northridge, who helped with the work of putting the manuscript into its final physical form.

Stella Z. Theodoulou
Matthew A. Cahn

PUBLIC POLICY

The Essential Readings

PART ONE

The Nature and Study of the What, Who, and Why of Public Policy

1

The Contemporary Language of Public Policy: Starting to Understand

Stella Z. Theodoulou

The reality of being a citizen in a modern democratic nation is that everyday life is impacted by the intended and unintended consequences of a whole series of public policies. Some of these policies we may personally be aware of and some we may not be aware of; however, the truth is public policy dictates how we as individuals and society as a whole live and interact, and because of this, the study of public policy has become an increasingly popular academic endeavor.

THE FIELD OF POLICY STUDIES

There is some debate over what the field of public policy studies actually is.[1] Palumbo declares the policy studies field as "any research that relates to or promotes the public interest."[2] Others see it as an umbrella which gathers several wide-ranging approaches to problems faced by society.[3] Many authors also note the multidisciplinary nature of the study of policy and argue that it has no overarching conceptual framework.[4] Reading the

classical texts in political theory, it would not be hard to argue that theorists have always been interested in analyzing what government does and what they should do to remedy certain problems facing the polity. In short, much of the political theory canon is a discussion of policy in some form. However, many of those interested in studying public policy consider the field to be relatively young. Many political scientists credit Charles Merriam, in 1922, as one of the first to study policy through his work connecting the theory and practice of politics as a means of understanding governmental activity.[5] However, the growth of a policy approach can best be attributed to the work of Harold Lasswell, who in 1951 argues for what he terms the establishment of the "policy sciences" which would require an applied, interdisciplinary study of the problems faced by government through a social sciences lens.[6] Lasswell wanted policy sciences to be a discipline that clarified and informed policy making. Crucial to Lasswell's definition of policy science is his belief that the field should be problem oriented, multidisciplinary, methodically and theoretically sophisticated, and value oriented. During the 1950s to 1970s, the field of policy studies greatly expanded with authors such as Aaron Wildavsky and Charles Lindblom, who began focusing research on public policy, and with this came a growing field of study that emphasized a focus on outcomes of government.[7]

As the study of policy has become more popular, it is beneficial to argue, as Smith and Larimer do, that rather than viewing public policy studies as one field, it is more useful to think of it as a loosely related set of subfields of policy study.[8] Thus there are the subfields of policy evaluation, policy analysis, policy implementation, and policy process. With the establishment of the policy studies subfields, there has been substantial transformation in the way governmental intervention through policy making is studied.

A cursory survey of the academic literature demonstrates a diversity of theories and models that act as frameworks from which to understand both the nature of public policy itself and how and who makes it. This plethora of frameworks has been accompanied by almost unwieldy and often conflicting policy vocabulary and specialist terminologies. Nowhere is this better illustrated than in the definition of public policy itself. Many

critics of the policy studies field argue that definitions of public policy are confusing and muddling because they rely on specialized language and are often full of jargon. There is, however, one thing that all authors on public policy seem to agree upon and that is public policy, no matter how it is defined, affects deeply all individuals' daily lives.

The starting point in this quest for understanding what public policy is, is for the reader to first comprehend that the fields of public policy emerge out of and within a number of theoretical concepts. When viewing policy choices, policy actors have to be concerned with issues such as equity. If a policy provides advantages to a few while disadvantaging the many, how can that policy choice be justified and how politically feasible is it? This brings into question what exactly equity means in a policy context. What do we mean by public and private? What should government provide for its citizens (which involves a discussion of citizen rights and needs)? Should we consider effectiveness and efficiency when looking at a policy as a solution to a problem or issue facing society? It is concepts such as these and others listed in Figure 1.1 that offer us an important basis for developing the necessary appreciation of the factors, dynamics, and tensions that affect public policy and the policy-making process. In the

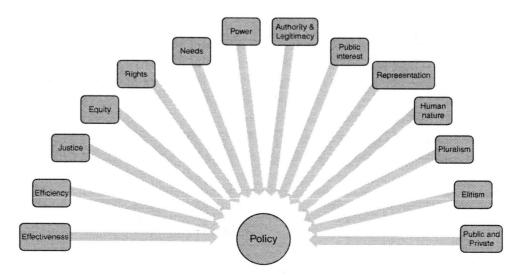

FIGURE 1.1 Theoretical Concepts Interplaying With Policy

readings that follow, authors explore how these critical concepts interplay with the making of policy.[9] Although these concepts are by no means exhaustive, they represent many of the dominant concepts found within the field of public policy and thus form the conceptual foundation of the public policy field. How an author views such concepts will determine how they define public policy and how they understand policy making.

DEFINING PUBLIC POLICY

A number of different competing definitions of public policy can be found in the literature but rather than focus on any one of these definitions, it is far more useful to discuss the common dimensions and elements that can be found within the majority of them. This will allow for a broader and less restrictive understanding of what we mean by public policy. The following represents the most common ideas and elements that are present in the majority of definitions:

- Policy is about both what governments intend to do and what they actually do: Governmental inactivity is as important as governmental activity.
- Policy is concerned with how issues and problems are defined, constructed, and placed on the political and policy agenda.
- Ideally all levels of government are involved, and one should not assume that policy is restricted to formal actors alone.
- Policy is pervasive and is not limited to simply legislation; it may also include executive orders, rules, and regulations.
- Policy is an intentional action that has an end goal as its objective.
- Policy is both long term and short term.
- Policy is an ongoing process involving formulation, implementation, enforcement, and evaluation.

It is important to keep in mind when attempting to define policy that politics cannot be divorced from public policy or the environment in which it is made. It is also important to note what public policy does and why government intervenes. Generally policy does one or more of the following: It reconciles conflicting claims on scarce resources; it establishes incentives for cooperation and collective action that would be irrational without government influence; it prohibits morally unacceptable behavior; it protects the activity of a group or an individual; and it promotes activities that are essential or important to government. Finally, policy provides direct benefits to citizens. Clearly then, for many authors, public policy focuses on the nature, causes, and effects of government action or inaction to deal with problems faced by the public.[10] Simply put, government intervenes through policy for political, moral, and economic reasons.

To summarize, public policy is a multifaceted and complex concept. Simply defined, public policy refers to a government action or inaction designed to serve a politically defined purpose. Policy should be seen as an output of government, while politics is the process by which the output is delivered. Understanding policy making requires acknowledgment that it is a series of activities involving the interaction of both formal and informal actors that cannot be divorced from the context of the political environment that it geminates from.

WHY STUDY PUBLIC POLICY

The simplest answer is we study public policy because it deals with issues, problems, and decisions that affect the public. This necessitates that we look at how issues and problems come to be defined, constructed, and placed on the political and policy agendas. In turn, this requires that the whole political system's workings be looked at— including both formal institutions such as the executive, legislature, and the judiciary and informal elements such as interest groups, the media, and public opinion.[11] Studying public policy allows us to view the entire political system and evaluate governance, including its output. In short, when we study public policy, we are concerned with what government does, why they do what they do, and who they affect by what they do. Today, those who study public policy are concerned with what consumed Harold Lasswell over seventy years ago when he wrote about politics being all about "Who gets what, when, and how."[12]

From a theoretical perspective, policy making is studied because it allows for the testing and development of explanations and generalizations that help build theories about the nature of government and politics in modern industrialized societies. On a practical level, studying policy in one setting may allow for more efficient and rational policy making in another setting. Lessons from formulation and implementation of a particular policy may lead to newer policy being more effective and appropriate. Policy making is not value-free and is surrounded by ideological debate, as is the study of policy. Theoretically, policy making should entail the use of the best reason and evidence so that the best policy is chosen from a series of alternatives;[13] however, one does not have to be a policy researcher to realize that it is often not the case. Thus, the policy-making arena should be viewed as an inherently political process that involves, often, heated conflict and struggle amongst competing actors who have conflicting interests, values, needs, and desires. For students of public policy, the goal must be analysis and not advocacy, and this should entail the use of social scientific methodology for the drawing of conclusions. Only if this is achieved reliable frameworks may be developed to understand policy making and its ramifications.

THEORIES AND MODELS ON THE NATURE OF PUBLIC POLICY

There is no one universally accepted theoretical model that helps the reader to understand the nature of policy making and why policy is developed in the way it is. There are, however, some theories and models more commonly subscribed to than others. The most common are group theory, elite theory, institutional theory, rational choice theory, systems model, and corporatist models. Each theory and model offers a different viewpoint on who makes policy and why; and which theory an individual subscribes to will influence one's view on why a certain type of policy over another is enacted. The various theories and models that attempt to answer the questions of who and why are all basically interested in explaining who controls or dominates the policy process and who benefits from policy making. Some authors have summarized this as "Who rules?"[14] It is not the purpose here to critique or compare the different theories in terms of their usefulness but rather to

outline each of them to prepare students for the relevant readings that follow.

RATIONAL CHOICE THEORY

Rational choice theorists understand policy making to be the product of policy actors taking rational actions dictated by rational policy decisions. Rationality is defined as transitivity and consistency of choice and draws heavily from microeconomic theory.[15] The model assumes that groups or individuals will act in a certain way given the environment they operate in, and their actions will always promote their self-interest. Rational choice theorists believe that we must consider what individuals value and what they perceive to be at stake in any given situation, along with their level of information and what they believe others expect.[16] Thus, actors select actions in response to what they calculate others' actions will be and then calculate the probability of possible outcomes based on what actions are taken. In doing so, it is possible to predict the propensity of individuals' behavior in a variety of settings and conditions. Thus, there is predictability to policy making.

For authors such as Herbert Simon, policy making is a sequence of rational decision stages and can be characterized as bounded rationality.[17] For Simon, by their very nature, humans are rational but real-world forces and their own cognitive capacity means they cannot always act in a rational manner. Policy decisions then might not always be ideally rational but are the best given the situation policy makers find themselves in and thus are rational. It is in policy makers' self-interest to reach agreement on what the problem is and then how to solve it. The desired solution is one which maximizes the benefits of a policy while limiting its costs. Each policy decision is made in isolation and looks at what policy makers hope to achieve in a situation, and then a decision is made on how best to achieve that outcome. Lindblom characterizes this as the "root" method of policy making, which is comprehensive in nature.[18] Policy makers are not restrained by the past decisions in the issue area and as such it's about coming up with the best decision.

Within the literature, a number of subdivisions of the rational choice model exist. The principal ones being "institutional" rational choice, public choice, game theory, and expected utility. Institutional rational choice theorists argue that the policy process can be understood as interactions between the rational actions of individuals and groups. Such theorists base their model on three main assumptions: Individuals are rational; behavior is strongly influenced by institutional rules; and those rules can change rational behavior.

Public choice theory was originally advanced by Buchanan and Tullock in the 1960s.[19] Public choice theorists understand policy to come out of a process of collective decision making by individuals and groups who have as their sole objective the maximization of their own self-interest.[20] Public choice theorists assume individuals have preferences and will always seek a course of action that maximizes the benefits of their optimal preference. Thus, individuals seek their own ends and not larger social goals. Applying neoclassical economic theory, public choice adherents argue for minimalist government intervention, with the government providing programs and services to citizens in the same way a business provides services to its customers. Citizens should be provided with a choice of programs and services and bear the costs. Government will provide citizens with the costs associated with each program and service so that efficient choices can be made.[21] In doing so, policy decisions should be ones that meet citizens' needs while protecting their natural rights, and policy making is responsive to demand. The emphasis is on governments' providing citizens the ability to influence what programs and services they are provided with. Too much intervention and extensive and far-reaching policy making intrude on citizens' personal freedom and go against what they want. In short, solutions to problems facing society should be the product of the marketplace and individual preferences. Government should only provide policy to regulate public goods such as national defense or water so that they are not destroyed or misused.

Game theory views policy making as a series of games that have strategies and payoffs and provides a mathematical framework for analyzing individuals' mutually interdependent interaction. Thus, game theorists see policy decisions as the product of the interaction of two or more rational actors, the assumption being decision makers are rational and will pursue actions that optimize their desired policy ends.[22] Theorists using game theory to explain policy making commonly do so through one of three types of game: cooperative games, where players/actors jointly benefit from the same outcomes; competitive games, in which one actor's or group of actors' gain is another actor's or groups' loss; and mixed games such as prisoner's dilemma, where there are varied motives of cooperation and competition.

Finally, theorists who use an expected utility model to explain policy making argue that policy decisions are the outcome of policy makers' need to maximize their benefits versus their costs from any choice made. The concern for such theorists is to explain how competing interests' policy position evolves over time.[23]

INCREMENTALISM

This theory argues against the idea that policy is the product of rationality and comprehensive change and views policy making as either a slowing-down or stepping-up of existing policy over time. This theory's chief architect is Charles Lindblom, who doubts whether public policies can ever be formulated through a rational and calculated process because for the most part, problems facing modern societies are too complex and multidimensional.[24] For Lindblom, any model of the policy-making process must examine power and the pluralistic interaction and mutual adaptation among multiple actors representing different interests, values, and information capacity. Policy comes then out of a complex interactive process that does not have a discernable start or an end and forces policy makers to build upon past policies.[25]

Policy making evolves over time and policy decisions are usually made on the basis of relatively small adjustments to existing situations. Hence the policy-making process is slow moving and policy changes very little; therefore, existing policies are adjusted in small ways. Policy makers do not have an ideal goal in mind as they make new policy because their focus is on past policies. There is little agreement on policy goals or how to achieve those goals and there is little interest in undertaking a comprehensive search for alternative solutions. Thus, Lindblom argues, policy makers look at how they can work within the existing policy and the influence of current political forces. Such forces would be elections, bureaucracies, elected officials, political parties, and interest groups, as well as corporations, and they in effect structure and distort the policy process. Thus, only a limited number of policy options are considered, with changes being made at the margin. In short, policy decisions naturally favor minimal over dramatic policy change, often because of the influence of politics.

Policy making is the small incremental adjustments to existing arrangements and as such can be seen as a branching-off from previous policy. Lindblom argues that the policy-making process is characterized by a process of successive limited comparisons, with each decision building upon a previous decision and as such it is easier for policy makers to find consensus.[26]

GROUP THEORY

Group theorists view public policy as the product of group struggle or specifically interest groups.[27] Group theory is largely associated with the work of David Truman and, in various formulations, with pluralist writers such as Robert Dahl.[28] Group theorists and pluralists argue that societies consist of a large number of social, ethnic, or economic groups, who are more or less well organized. These groups, in political competition with each other, put pressure on the government to produce policies favorable to them. The public interest thus tends to emerge out of the struggle among competing individual and group claims.

Specific policies reflect the relative influence of the different interests on any given issue. Therefore, each policy area involves a distinctive set of problems and separate sets of political agents and forces. Public policy is the result of a unique process of interaction. Pluralists believe within any society there are multiple centers of powers competing with each other for policy that favors their particular interest and it is through such competition that the best policy is developed. Thus, power is shared broadly among a number of groups who are all seeking access to the policy-making process. To guarantee that no one group dominates, each group that exists is counterbalanced by a group within the same interest sector but with a different agenda. For example, labor unions and organizations representing corporate interests.

ELITE THEORY

Elite theorists' basic assumption is that policies are made by a relatively small group of influential leaders who share common goals and outlooks. Public policy is not then determined by the public at large but by a minority who has political and economic power. Many elite theorists argue that society is a stratified hierarchy, with the elites being in the minority at the top of the hierarchy and the rest of society at the bottom of the hierarchy. The mass public is not particularly interested in policy until an issue affects them personally. One school of elitist theory argues that there is a diversity of elites present in the policy-making arena, and the result is diverse elites dominating different policy areas.[29] Thus, a particular elite may be influential in the area of health care but have far less influence in the area of agriculture.

A related model explaining the role of different or multiple elites is the subgovernments model, which argues that government alone does not make policy choices but endorses decisions made by sections of the government in alliance with interest groups.[30] This partnership has also been referred to as the notion of iron triangles—which are coalitions of members of Congress, the bureaucracy, and interest groups.[31] All those involved in a subgovernment have similar interests. Such structures develop around particular policy areas and involve the relevant legislators, bureaucrats, and interest groups. Policy outcomes are determined by various subgovernments and revolve around their interests. Subgovernments, therefore, tend to develop around those specialized areas of policy that have a low level of general public interest and awareness.

This perspective has in recent years expanded among political scientists, who argue that there are now much larger numbers of interested actors than the three posited by the subgovernment model.[32] A number of authors argue that the policy process is more decentralized and fragmented and that it is characterized by a series of overlapping policy subsystems of broader alliances of public and private groups such as think tanks, interest groups, and individuals.[33] Hugh Heclo builds upon the notion of policy subsystems to explain how agendas are set and policy change is achieved. He argues that one should view the policy-making process as being dominated by issue networks, all of whom have substantial expertise in the policy area.[34] Issue networks are informal coalitions of interest groups, public and private organizations, and members of the public, often having policy expertise, who come together around a particular issue. They share a mutual interest in the issue and apply pressure on the policy-making process by providing more alternatives so as to have policy reflect their interests. Such issue networks are fluid and their level of visibility will differ depending on the visibility of the issue.

However, there are elite theorists who disagree with the argument of multiple elites and argue that society is always governed by a dominant elite or ruling class. Authors such as C. Wright Mills and Ralph Miliband do not see policy as the product of group conflict and demands but rather as determined by the preferences of the dominant elite who, for the most part, control through their economic power. For Mills it's the power elite and for Miliband it's the ruling class.[35] It is the preferences of the elite or ruling class that policy makers adopt; policies reflect their values and serve their interests.

All policy making is the province of elites for it is elites who define how problems are perceived, design policy solutions to meet that problem perception, and in doing so guarantee that their interests will be served.

INSTITUTIONALISM

This framework developed as a response to group theory. Policy is seen as the product of institutional interaction. Scholars adhering to this theory believe human behavior is affected by the formal structure and its standard operating norms they are part of. Thus, for such scholars the primary focus is upon the formal and legal aspects of government as well as considering the role of nongovernmental institutions such as corporations. The policy-making process is seen as of interacting institutions which structure decision making. The concern is with analyzing institutional power, how institutions make policy decisions, how institutions and actors interact within and across institutions, the rate at which the institutions help the political system respond to problems, and the efficiency with which institutions and the political system aggregate preferences. The focus is on how institutions are arranged and how rules allow them to operate. The kind of policy making that occurs will be determined in large part by the structures and rules that policy actors operate within. Ostrom argues that the interaction of actors within and across institutions is also crucial to determining what policy emerges from a formal institution such as a legislature.[36] All policies have to be formulated, adopted, implemented, and enforced. It is the job of formal institutions such as executives, legislatures, judiciaries, and political parties to make policy through interaction with nonformal institutions.[37] Policy decisions are the output of large government organizations which function according to regular behavioral patterns and interact with other nongovernmental institutions.

In recent years, there has been an attempt to refine institutional theory and the result has been neo-institutionalism, which argues that institutional rules, processes, and structures are still significant but that they are not static, and as actors within institutions change, so can policy. Different actors bring different values and interests, and institutional rules and processes will be subject to these new priorities.

BUREAUCRATIC CORPORATISM

Corporatist theorists argue that policy making can best be understood through an acknowledgment that explicitly recognized interest groups and organizations do not merely attempt to influence policy but are incorporated into the policy-making process itself by governmental groups such as the bureaucracy.[38] Such interests negotiate policy and secure compliance from their members for the agreed-upon policy solution. In return for this participation in policy making, the groups—through the control of their members—make society more manageable for the state or government. This differs from models that argue interest groups make representations about the content of public policy. Corporatism views interests groups as having both representation and control. In return for being involved in policy formation, corporate interest groups are also seen as assisting in policy implementation. Policy is not made by rational choice but through a push–pull system of politics.

SYSTEMS THEORY

Systems theory attempts to provide a model of politics that views public policy as a political system's response to demands and supports arising from the political environment.[39] The environment is composed of general and specific factors. General factors are the structural, social, political, technological, environmental, and economic systems in which policy making occurs, while specific factors are the level of competition, cooperation, and linkages present in the political system. The political

system is thus a mechanism by which popular demands and support for the state are combined to produce those policy outputs that best ensure the long-term stability of the political system. Demands are viewed as inputs and can be seen as claims for the system to do something about a problem, while outputs are what government does about a problem. Inputs are filtered by policy actors and institutions who function as gatekeepers determining what's on the political agenda at any given point in time. Gates open and close and thus many demands never reach the agenda because they have been filtered. Policy outputs may produce new demands that lead to further outputs, and so on in a never-ending flow of public policy. This is achieved through what Easton describes as a feedback loop. The basic idea is that political systems should be seen as analogues to mechanical systems with feedback loops and clear goals, specifically a black box. Figure 1.2 adapts Easton's black box model to illustrate the policy-making process.

Systems theory is often seen as innately conservative because of its stress on stability rather

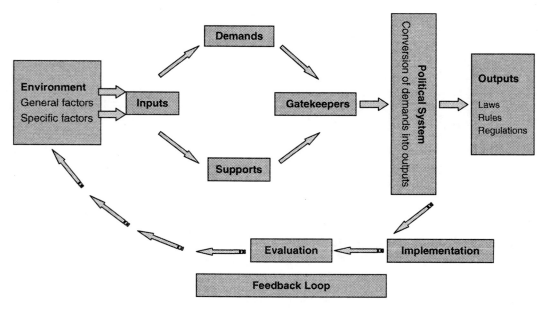

FIGURE 1.2   David Easton's Black Box Adapted to Explain the Policy-Making Process

Source: Adapted from D. Easton, *A Systems Analysis of Political Life* (New York: Wiley, 1965).

than change. However, this should not negate the theory's attempt to analyze the interrelationship of the various actors and institutions in the policy process. The systems model says little about how decisions are made or how they arrive into the decision-making structures.

CONCLUSION

The goal of this chapter has been to provide a well-balanced and broad understanding of what public policy is and how it has come to be studied. There has been no attempt to critique any of the definitions, approaches, theories, or models that are commonly found in the literature. It is hoped that such critiques will be provoked by the reading selections themselves. From this discussion, it should become clear that there is no simple way to view what public policy is, just as there can be no clear consensus on who makes policy. This is clearly supported by Paul Sabatier, who traces the development of public policy as a subfield of the political science discipline. Sabatier acknowledges that there are many sources of tension between political scientists and public policy scholars.[40] What should become clear is that policy cannot be divorced from the larger study of government and politics. The readings that follow represent a cross-section of the literature and have been selected because they are generally considered by political scientists to form the benchmark from which the discipline looks at what policy is and why it is made. What should emerge is the recognition that there exists a policy-making environment and that often an individual's understanding of that environment will be determined by one's own belief systems.

End Notes

1. Robert Goodin, Martin Rein and Michael Moran, "The Public and Its Policies," in *The Oxford Handbook of Public Policy*, eds. Michael Moran, Martin Rein and Robert E. Goodin (New York: Oxford University Press, 2006), p. 5.
2. Dennis Palumbo, "The State of Policy Studies Research and the Policy of the New Policy Studies Review," *Policy Studies Review*, 1 (August 1981), 5–10, especially p. 8.
3. Peter deLeon, *Advice and Consent: The Development of the Policy Sciences* (New York: Russel Sage Foundation, 1988), p. 219.
4. Kevin B. Smith and Christopher Larimer, *The Public Policy Theory Primer* (Philadelphia, PA: Westview Press, 2009), p. 1.
5. Daniel McCool, *Public Policy Theories, Models and Concepts: An Anthology 1995* (Englewood Cliffs, NJ: Prentice Hall, 1995), pp. 1–27.
6. Harold Lasswell, "The Policy Orientation," in *The Policy Sciences: Recent Developments in Scope and Method*, eds. Daniel Lerner and Harold Lasswell (Stanford, CA: Stanford University Press, 1951), pp. 3–15.
7. McCool, *Public Policy Theories, Models and Concepts*.
8. Smith and Larimer, *The Public Policy Theory Primer*, pp. 5–7.
9. S. I. Benn and G. F. Gaus (eds.), *Public & Private in Social Life* (London: Croom Helm, 1983); J. Habermas, *The Structural Transformation of the Public Sphere* (London: Polity Press, 1989); J. Rawls, *A Theory of Justice* (Cambridge: Harvard University Press, 1971); R. Norzick, *Anarchy, State and Utopia* (New York: Basic Books, 1974).
10. S. Nagel, "Conflicting Evaluations of Policy Studies," in *Public Administration*, eds. N. B. Lyon and A. Wildavsky (Chatham, NJ: Chatham House, 1990), p. 440; A. Heidenheimer, A. H. Heclo and C.T. Adams, *Comparative Public Policy: The Politics of Social Choice in America, Europe and Japan* (3rd ed.) (New York: St. Martins Press, 1990).
11. T. R. Dye, *Understanding Public Policy* (5th ed.) (Englewood Cliffs, NJ: Prentice Hall, 1984), pp. 5–7.
12. H. Lasswell, *Politics: Who Gets What and How* (New York: St. Martins Press, 1988). (Originally published in 1936.)
13. D. MacRae, Jr. and J. A. Wilde, *Policy Analysis for Public Decisions* (North Scituate, MA: Duxbury Press, 1979), p. 4.
14. See G. W. Domhoff (this reader, part 1, reading 10).
15. I. McLean, *Oxford Concise Dictionary of Politics* (Oxford, New York: Oxford University press, 1996), p. 421.
16. E. Ostrom, "Institutional Rational Choice: An Assessment of the Institutional Analyses and

Development Framework," in *Theories of the Policy Process*, ed. P. Sabatier (Boulder, CO: Westview Press, 2007), pp. 21–64.

17. H. Simon, *Administrative Behavior* (3rd ed.) (New York: Free Press, 1976).

18. C. Lindblom (this reader, part 1, reading 5).

19. James M. Buchanan and Gordon Tullock, *The Calculus of Consent: Logical Foundations of Constitutional Democracy* (Ann Arbor, MI: University of Michigan Press, 1962).

20. C. E. Cochran et al., *American Public Policy: An Introduction* (New York: St. Martins Press, 1999), p. 55.

21. Charles Tiebout, "A Pure Theory of Local Expenditures," *Journal of Politics*, 64 (October 1956), 416–424.

22. J. Morrow, *Game Theory for Political Scientists* (Princeton, NJ: Princeton University Press, 1994), pp. 1–2.

23. B. Buenode Mesquita, "A Decision Making Model: Its Structure and Form," *International Interactions*, 23, nos. 3–4 (1997), 236.

24. C. Lindblom, "The Science of Muddling Through," *Public Administration Review*, 19 (Spring 1959), 79–88, 114–115.

25. *Ibid.* Lindblom. *Public Administration Review.*

26. Lindblom (this reader, part 1, reading 5).

27. Alla J. Cigler and Burdett A. Loomis, *Interest Group Politics* (6th ed.) (Washington, DC: CQ Press, 2002).

28. D. B. Truman, *The Governmental Process* (2nd ed.) (New York: Knopf, 1971); R. Dahl, "Pluralism Revisited," *Comparative Politics* 10, no. 2 (January 1978), 191–204.

29. Thomas Dye and L. Harmon Zeigler, *The Irony of Democracy* (12th ed.) (Monterey, CA: Brooks Cole, 2003).

30. Frank R. Baumgartner and Bryan D. Jones (this reader, part 3, reading 25); John Kingdon (this reader, part 3, reading 26).

31. J. Leiper Freeman, *The Political Process: Executive, Bureaucratic-Legislative Committee Relations* (New York: Norton, 1979); T. L. Gais et al., "Interest Groups, Iron Triangles and Representative Institutions in American National Government," *British Journal of Political Science*, 14 (April 1984), 161–186; A. G. Jordan, "Iron Triangles, Wooly Corporations and Elastic Nets: Images of the Policy Making Process," *Journal of Public Policy*, 1 (February 1981), 95–123.

32. J. Walker, *Mobilizing Interest Groups in America* (Ann Arbor, MI: University of Michigan Press, 1991).

33. Gais et al., "Interest Groups, Iron Triangles and Representative Institutions."

34. H. Heclo (this reader, part 1, reading 9).

35. C. Wright Mills, *The Power Elite* (Oxford, UK: Oxford University Press, 1956), pp. 3–15, 276–294; R. Miliband, *The State in Capitalist Society* (New York: Basic Books, 1969), pp. 131–137 and this reader part 1 reading 7.

36. E. Ostrom (this reader, part 3, reading 28).

37. J. Anderson, *Public Policy Making: An Introduction* (Boston, MA: Houghton Mifflin, 1990), p. 31.

38. P. Schmitter and G. Lehmbruch (eds.), *Trends Toward Corporatist Intermediation* (Newbury Park, CA: Sage, 1979).

39. D. Easton, *A Systems Analysis of Political Life* (New York: Wiley, 1965).

40. See Paul A. Satatier, "Political Science and Public Policy" (this reader, part 1, reading 3).

Additional Suggested Reading

AARON, H., MANN, T., and TAYLOR, T. (eds.). *Values and Public Policy.* Washington, DC: The Brookings Institution, 1994.

AXELROD, ROBERT. "Political Science and Beyond: Presidential Address to the American Political Science Association." *Perspectives on Politics*, 6 (March 2008), 3–9.

BAUMGARTNER, F., and LEECH, B. *Basic Interests: the Importance of Groups in Politics and Political Science.* Princeton, NJ: Princeton University Press, 1998.

BERRY, C. *Human Nature.* Atlantic Highlands, NJ: Humanities Press, 1986.

CHAMPNEY, LEONARD. "Public Goods and Policy Types." *Public Administration Review*, 48 (November/December 1988), 988–994.

CRICK, BERNARD. *In Defense of Politics.* New York: Harmondworth, 1983.

DAHL, ROBERT. *Who Governs: Democracy and Power in an American City.* New Haven, CT: Yale University Press, 1963.

DANEKE, GREGORY A. "On Paradigmatic Progress in Public Policy and Administration." *Policy Studies Journal*, 17 (Winter 1988/1989), 277–296.

DOMHOFF, G. WILLIAM. "Mill's 'The Power Elite' 50 Years Later." *Contemporary Sociology*, 35, no. 6 (November 2006), 547–550.

DOWNS, ANTHONY. *An Economic Theory of Democracy.* New York: Harper and Row, 1957.

ETZONI, A. *The Monochrome Society.* Princeton, NJ: Princeton University Press, 2001.

FARR, JAMES, HACKER, JACOB, and KAZEE, NICOLE. "The Policy Scientist of Democracy: The Discipline of Harold D. Lasswell." *American Political Science Review*, 100 (November 2006), 579–587.

FRIEDMAN, JEFFREY. *The Rational Choice Controversy: Economic Models of Politics Reconsidered.* New Haven, CT: Yale University Press, 1996.

GIGERENZER, GERD, and SELTON, REINHARD. *Bounded Rationality: The Adaptive Toolbox.* Cambridge, MA: MIT Press, 2002.

GOODIN, ROBERT. "Rationality Redux: Reflections on Herbert A. Simon's Vision of Politics." In *Competition and Cooperation: Conversations with Nobelists About Economics and Political Science,* eds. James E. Alt, Margaret Levi, and Elinor Ostrom, pp. 60–84. New York: Russell Sage Foundation, 1999.

HILL, KIM QUAILE. "In Search of Policy Theory." *Policy Currents*, 7 (April 1997), 1–9.

HEYWOOD, A. *Political Ideas and Concepts: An Introduction.* New York: St. Martin's Press, 1994.

HEISLER, M. "Corporate Pluralism Revisited." *Scandinavian Political Studies*, 2 (September 1979), 277–297.

HOWELL-MORONEY, MICHAEL. "The Tiebout Hypothesis 50 Years Later: Lessons and Lingering Challenges for Metropolitan Governance in the 21st Century." *Public Administration Review* (January/February 2008), 97–109.

LASSWELL, H. D. *Politics: Who Gets What, When, and How?* New York: McGraw-Hill, 1936.

MC COOL, D. *Public Policy: Theories, Models, and Concepts.* Englewood Cliffs, NJ: Prentice Hall, 1995.

OLSON, MANCUR. *The Logic of Collective Action.* Cambridge, MA: Harvard University Press, 1965.

PETRACCA, MARK. "The Rational Choice Approach to Politics: A Challenge to Democratic Theory." *The Review of Politics*, 53, no. 2 (Spring 1991), 289–319.

RAWLS, J. *A Theory of Justice.* Cambridge, MA: Harvard University Press, 1971.

SCHATTSCHNEIDER, E. E. *The Semi-Sovereign People.* New York: Holt, Rinehart & Winston, 1969.

SCHUCHMAN, H. "The Influence of Social Values on Public Policy Determination." *The Journal of Conflict Resolution*, 6, no. 2 (June 1962), 175–182.

SCHUMPETER, J. *Capitalism, Socialism and Democracy.* London: Allen & Unwin, 1943.

SIMON, CHRISTOPHER A. *Public Policy: Preferences and Outcomes* (2nd ed.). New York: Longman, 2010.

SMITH, KEVIN B., and LARIMER, CHRISTOPHER W. *The Public Policy Theory Primer*, Boulder, CO: Westview Press, 2009.

STONE, D. A. *Policy Paradox: The Art of Political Decision Making* (2nd ed.). New York: Scott, Foresman & Co., 1997.

SUNDQUIST, JAMES L. "Political Scientists and Public Policy Research." *PS*, 24 (September 1991), 531–535.

WHITE, J. *The Values Divide: American Politics and Culture in Transition.* New York: Chatham House/Seven Bridges Press, 2003.

YANKELOVICH, D. *Coming to Public Judgement: Making Democracy Work in a Complex World.* Syracuse, NY: Syracuse University Press, 1991.

2

Enduring Political Questions and Public Policy

James J. Gosling

THE ROLE OF GOVERNMENT AND OUR LIBERAL TRADITION

Social contract theorists, such as the seventeenth century British philosophers Thomas Hobbes and John Locke, suggest that people abandon their lives as isolated individuals in the state of nature and willingly come together in a civil society that delegates power to government. They surrender to government some of the freedom they exercised in the pre-civil state of nature in exchange for government protecting them and their property, for they recognize that the absence of public restraint invites attempts by some to dominate others and to appropriate their property. Their choice is a rational one for Hobbes.

For Locke, true sovereignty resides with the people, who form a civil society and delegate power to government. If government fails to fulfill its obligations under the contract, the people may revoke that delegation of power, and then are free to reconstitute the government, entering into a contract with a new authoritative protector. Government's obligation for Locke is limited. Government exists to protect the rights of people. It provides personal security and the legal means to adjudicate wrongdoing, whether that be criminal actions against people and their property or civil breeches of contractual agreements. Otherwise, government is to exercise restraint.[1]

Yet what about the welfare of the community as a whole: What about the public interest? Are self-interest and the public interest incompatible? Do individuals acting in their self-interest undermine the broader public interest? The answer is largely no, according to the utilitarians. They view self-interested action, which seeks pleasure and avoids pain, as not only benefiting individuals but creating the greatest aggregate good possible—"the greatest good for the greatest number," as articulated by British philosopher Jeremy Bentham toward the end of the eighteenth century.[2] For Bentham, and for John Stuart Mill, an important utilitarian writer in the nineteenth century, the public interest is best approximated by the summing of self-interested individual action. In fact, it is Mill, in O*n Liberty*, who develops the operating presumption that individuals know what is best for them, and that they should be free to pursue those interests as long as they do not prevent others from exercising their liberty. Government exists fundamentally to protect that exercise of liberty and otherwise leave individuals alone in their pursuits. It is this philosophy, with its central role for individual action, that has come to be labeled classical liberalism. It is also classical liberalism that sharpens the line between the private and public spheres of life.

Mill specifically identifies three areas of private life that should be free of governmental

---

From James J. Gosling, *Understanding, Informing, and Appraising Public Policy* (New York: Pearson, 2004), pp. 1–22.

control. He refers to them as "liberty of conscience," the freedom to take positions on issues and to promulgate them; "liberty of tastes and interests," the freedom to pursue knowledge, work, and avocation; and "liberty of combination," the freedom to form associations that individuals believe advance their interests. Beyond these areas of outright proscription, the onus falls on government to make its case for intervention, to show that governmental involvement advances aggregate utility better than self-interested individual action.[3]

Adam Smith, an older contemporary of Jeremy Bentham, also focuses on self-interested behavior and its contribution to the aggregate public interest. However, his interests lie foremost in the individual as a participant in the economic life of society. Buyers purchase goods and services to satisfy their wants, and merchants sell their goods and services out of a desire to reap economic return, not out of a sense of benevolence. As Smith puts it, "It is not from the benevolence of the butcher, the brewer, or the baker that we expect our dinner, but from their regard for their own self-interest. We address ourselves, not to their humanity but to their self-love, and never talk to them of our own necessities but of their own advantages."[4]

Smith sees an economic order emerging as the unintended consequence of the actions of many, each seeking his own self-interest. Moreover, he holds that this working of "an invisible hand" promotes societal interests more effectively than do centrally directed economic choices. Still, Smith did not expect government to keep out of economic affairs altogether. He realized that private interests might not be willing to make economic investments in projects or programs that would likely fail to return a profit, even though they would benefit society or contribute to its economic well being. Here he included public works projects (such as transportation infrastructure) and public education. Nonetheless, he—like the utilitarians writing about political freedom—saw limited government intervention in the economy as the recipe for economic freedom and the economic order that flows from it.

There are those who take this position today. Milton Friedman is probably the most prominent proponent of letting individual choice in the marketplace determine the array of goods and services the economy produces. Like Adam Smith, he sees the market as making goods and services available that are wanted, as well as creating an economic order that results from the voluntary coordination of self-interested and willing buyers and sellers. He also sees the market as a force for invention and innovation that works best when not subject to government control or undue regulation.[5]

Government's role, beyond the essential of establishing a monetary system, should be largely limited to preserving the competitive market itself, by thwarting monopoly practices and ensuring that parties to economic transactions honor their contractual obligations. However, Friedman also accords government a role in protecting people from what he calls the neighborhood effects of economic activity—what economists typically refer to as negative externalities. Here pollution serves as the traditional example. An industrial plant may not control its chemical discharges because of corporate managers' concerns that the costs of abatement would too greatly weaken their firm's financial bottom line. As a result, communities downstream could find their water quality significantly deteriorated, perhaps no longer fit for swimming or fishing.

In this example, it may well be possible for governmental officials to identify the source of the pollution and to seek an injunction against further discharge, or to fine the offender until the discharge meets acceptable standards determined by government. Air pollution, in comparison, presents a thorny problem, since it is difficult for government to trace pollutants back to individual contributors. Take automobile pollution as an illustration. It becomes an overwhelming task to assess how much any person's motor vehicle is polluting the environment, and to charge the owner for costs incurred by society. That is why government has turned to regulations requiring that vehicles be equipped with pollution-control devices and that they pass emission tests, both measures to overcome neighborhood effects.

Although classical liberals such as Milton Friedman will accede to the need for government regulation to protect third parties from negative externalities, they place the burden on government to justify its intervention, seeing unsupported governmental intervention as a threat to freedom. This perception comes from their broader sense that the greater the reliance on un-fettered economic activity, the wider the range of needs and wants the economy satisfies. Friedman also argues that the wider the scope of market activities, the fewer the issues that government must decide, thus advancing individual freedom.[6] This is a position closely akin to former President Ronald Reagan's assertion that government is not a problem solver; it is the problem itself.

For Friedman, economic freedom is an "indispensable means" toward political freedom.[7] He knows of no society enjoying political freedom that fails to have a competitive market economy. He also sees growing economic freedom in authoritarian states as potentially eroding political repression over the long run, as a broadened market economy multiplies interests and disperses economic power.

An acceptance of Friedman's ideological stance leads to a corresponding belief in the need for governmental restraint. Although Friedman, like his classical liberal progenitors, accepts government's role in national defense and public safety, he raises the hurdle for government's involvement in domestic policy. Preferring competition and market outcomes, Friedman is leery of public policies that alter those outcomes. That would notably include policies that use taxation to redistribute resources. For Friedman, the tests to be met are demanding ones, for market outcomes follow the principle of just deserts—that the market rewards effort and risk, and that people get out of it about what they deserve. Moreover, Friedman's emphasis on freedom and competition leads him to support such policies as deregulation, government vouchers for parents who wish to take their children out of public schools and send them to private schools (with the vouchers approximating what government spends per child on public education), and abandonment of the present Social Security system in favor of mandatory retirement saving that allows workers to invest their savings in private sector annuities.

RETHINKING THE PUBLIC INTEREST AND GOVERNMENT'S ROLE

The market, as we have discussed, deals with wants and their satisfaction. The historic assumption here is that individuals are the best judge of their own interests. They pursue those interests through market transactions and by joining forces in organizations that pool money and effort in support of public policy positions that advance, or at least maintain, those interests.

This interpretation leaves little room for government as an advancer of the public interest, other than essentially keeping hands off, of being neutral to the ends of individual want satisfaction. Brian Barry asks if there is more to the idea of the state than merely an instrument for satisfying the wants people happen to have at any point in time, such as functioning as "a means of making good men (e.g., cultivating desirable wants or dispositions in its citizens)."[8] But classical liberalism's corollary to individuals knowing what is in their best interest is that leaders do not know what is better for the people than the people do for themselves. Americans have shown scant willingness to turn to Plato's philosopher king for enlightenment or about substantive commitments to advance the good life.

So where does this leave the public interest? Is it, again, reduced to the sum of self-interest, or is it merely what the majority says it is? In this latter sense, are the political choices that emerge from majoritarian decision making always in the public interest, by definition? In other words, can the majority make choices that are *not* in the public interest? The answer to this question comes back to how we define the public interest.

Brian Barry suggests that the public interest is those interests that people have in common as members of the public, as distinct from the narrower interests that they have as individuals or as members of organizations. These "nonassignable interests,"[9] as he calls them, transcend wants and are grounded in ideals identified with the welfare of members of the public as a whole. These ideals, about which more will be said later, become standards against which the desirability of concrete public policy choices can be evaluated. Following this reasoning, the public interest consists of making choices on behalf of the members of the public that are consistent with ideal-based standards. For Barry, it is the job of government to advance common, shared interests. If the government does not advance them, who will? Most likely, not those who are preoccupied with satisfying their personal wants.

Jean Jacques Rousseau, a French philosopher writing in the eighteenth century, offers a different perspective on the role of government than that of the British classical liberals. While classical liberalism extols the centrality of the individual, Rousseau focuses on the community and the common interests of its members. The essential role of government is to serve those interests that all people have in common—not those interests they have as self-interested individuals or as members of organizations that seek to promote narrow group interests. For Rousseau, individual self-interest is to be subordinated to the public interest, and any coincidence between the two is merely fortuitous and temporary.[10]

Modern public intellectuals have picked up on this theme. Walter Lippman suggests that the public interest is "what men would choose if they saw clearly, thought rationally, and acted disinterestedly and benevolently."[11] Building on this conception, Robert Reich accords government an important role in providing the public with "alternative visions of what is desirable and possible" as a public, rather than just tallying individual preferences.[12] For Reich, governmental leaders have the obligation to set a national agenda built on a vision of how to advance the public interest.

Other sympathetic contemporary political theorists view members of the public as welcoming of, and receptive to, governmental leadership. Gary Orren argues that values, purposes, ideas, goals, and commitments that transcend self-interest motivate people. He sees these "macromotives" as underlying successful agenda redirection, and points to the Civil Rights Movement, the Great Society social agenda, and the rise of national environmental protection policy as the products of public-spirited motives rather than aggregate self-interest.[13]

Jane Mansbridge, in her book, *Beyond Self-Interest*, addresses the question whether common interests are but a myth, invoked to provide "diversionary cover" for what is self-interest. Although she recognizes that politicians and public policy advocates are quick to clothe their preferences in the public interest, she argues that people generally take account of both self-interest and the common good when they decide "what constitutes a benefit they want to maximize."[14] In Brian Barry's parlance, want-regarding principles mix and compete with ideal-regarding principles.[15]

Deborah Stone, following this line of thought, places ideal-regarding principles at the heart of the politics of public policy. Public policy is about "communities trying to achieve something as communities,"[16] and the major debates in communities revolve around questions of goals and the ideals underpinning them. For her, the major dilemma of policy making in the *polis* (borrowing the Greek term to suggest an organic community of sorts) is how to get people to give primacy to the broader consequences of individual action when participating in goal-setting and making concrete policy choices.[17] As for Reich and Orren, political leadership plays an important role here, as political leaders offer visions of the common good that draw upon the power of public ideas.

IDEAL-REGARDING PRINCIPLES

This call for greater attention to ideal-regarding principles should not suggest that we are starting from scratch. Our American political culture includes a normative inheritance grounded in ideal-regarding principles. Yet, at the same time, it is clear that they reinforce a deeply ingrained individualism. The Declaration of Independence and the U.S. Constitution enumerate the bedrock values that shape how we view the role of government and our relationship to it and to others in society. They include popular sovereignty, or the idea that power resides in the people, not in government; liberty, or freedom; and equality. The Framers of the Constitution looked at equality through classical liberal political spectacles and worried about the potential for *government-created* inequalities that go beyond differences in individuals' talents, skills, and preparation. Thus they saw the need to check government in creating artificial privileges, such as granting charters or monopolies, or in artificially holding citizens back in their pursuit of opportunity (with slavery notoriously aside).

This combination of principles beckons individuals to seek their fortunes unhindered by government, but also protected by it. Freedom allows us to pursue our own interests, at least as long as we do not violate the right of others to pursue their interests. Equality supports equal treatment under the law and protection against government artificially constraining people in their lawful exercise of individual freedom. These fundamental principles undergird the values of individual initiative and personal responsibility—values supported by the Protestant ethic of America's early settlers, an association recognized by Alexis de Toqueville in the early nineteenth century.[18] The dicta of hard work, self-improvement, and personal advancement ring resonantly in our collective consciousness.

Americans believe in the concept of the "American dream," a term that did not get popularly coined until the early twentieth century. It holds the anticipation, if not the promise that people can get ahead through hard work. They just need an equal opportunity to be free to compete; as John Manley ironically puts it, to compete to become *unequal*.[19]

President Bill Clinton captured the essence of the American dream in a 1993 speech to the Democratic Leadership Council:

> The American dream that we were all raised on is a simple but powerful one—if you work hard and play by the rules you should be given a chance to go as far as your God-given abilities will take you.[20]

Individual enterprise lies at the heart of the American dream.

John Dewey, writing during the Progressive period in American politics of the early twentieth century, saw the exercise of individual freedom not only as an avenue to improve a person's condition but also as an opportunity for "the fullest development of human capacities to share in the good that society has produced and the ability to contribute to the common good."[21] For Dewey, that contribution comes through a cooperative effort whose quality is improved by the personal development of the collaborating participants.

Yet the question remains, borrowing a contemporary slogan from Army recruiting commercials, about how individuals can "be all that they

can be." The American dream's lure is that people can rise as far as their capabilities allow, as long as they are given the opportunity to compete. Not everybody, however, starts out in life with the same assets and resources. Differences in genetic inheritance and the social and financial standing of one's parents advantage some over others. Some will rise faster and go farther than others as they make the most of their abilities. Inequalities will exist. But liberalism views them as unobjectionable, as consistent with the principle of just deserts.

This position is not without its detractors, and criticism follows two lines of reasoning. The first focuses on equal opportunity, which critics hold is more than freedom to compete. They draw a distinction between government-ensured freedom to compete and what constitutes *effective* equality of opportunity. Critics turn their attention to the disadvantages that some individuals bring into that competition, and the debate centers on government's obligation to eliminate, or at least minimize, those disadvantages. It quickly turns to the extent of government intervention necessary to secure more effective equality of opportunity.

Traditionally, policymakers and the general public looked at America's public educational system as the vehicle for enhancing opportunity. Intellectuals such as John Dewey saw public education as the road to personal advancement and to a stronger democracy. Contemporary critics find the public schools falling short of that aim. They call for reforms to improve educational quality, while realizing that schools are only one factor, albeit a highly important one, that shapes human development and expands capabilities. They also look at how family life nurtures or impedes individuals, and to what government should do to strengthen the family and thus its contribution. The paramount question becomes *how far* should government go to ameliorate impediments that prevent some from competing on an effectively equal footing. However, the operating presumption remains that competition is to be valued, and that individual achievement should be rewarded—achievement that follows individual effort and diligence.

An alternative focus to equality of opportunity is equality of condition, and America's classical liberal ideology has held the latter suspect.

It should be made clear from the outset that in discussions of equality of condition no one advocates full equality, whether it be in income, wealth, housing, or educational attainment. Instead, the discussion turns on how large relative differences should be, and what should be government's role in using public policies to narrow them. An example would be the debate over the extent to which policymakers should use redistributive taxation policy to flatten income disparities.

Public opinion polls consistently show that the American public over-whelmingly prefers to view equality in terms of opportunity rather than condition. These polls indicate that a large majority of Americans consistently see opportunity present in the United States if one makes the effort.[22] Public opinion surveys also show that Americans are disinclined to support the proposition that government should use its taxing and legislative powers to redistribute income. As Benjamin Page and Robert Shapiro conclude, based on their fifty-year study of public opinion on policy preferences, "Surveys since the 1930s have shown that the explicit idea of income redistributing elicits very limited enthusiasm among the American public. Most Americans are content with the distributional effects of private markets."[23]

The work of sociologists James Kluegel and Eliot Smith on American public opinion comes to a similar conclusion. They report that Americans believe that everyone should count equally in moral terms and in the eyes of the law, but Americans also reject economic equality of results in favor of equality of opportunity and individual effort.[24]

Seymour Martin Lipset and Jennifer Hochschild examine whether that finding applies to African Americans, given their unique historical experience in America. Both conclude that most African Americans do believe in equal opportunity and the quest for the American dream. However, both also find that African Americans are more welcoming than whites of government intervention to help them better their condition.[25] Hochschild, in her 1995 book, *Facing Up to the American Dream: Race, Class, and the Soul of the Nation*, finds, counter to expectations, that the least advantaged blacks, including members of the working class, most strongly support the classical liberal values of individual effort, equality of opportunity, and

just deserts. Upper-income blacks, in comparison, tend to see greater obstacles in the way of upward mobility, and are more likely than lower-income blacks to invite governmental assistance in that quest. They also are more likely, in particular, to support affirmative action preferences, which conflict with the value of meritocracy....

End Notes

1. John Locke, *Second Treatise of Government*, ed. Richard H. Cox (Arlington Heights, Ill.: Harlan Davidson, 1982).
2. Jeremy Bentham, *The Theory of Legislation* (Holmes Beach, Fl.: Gaunt, 1999).
3. John Stuart Mill, *On Liberty*, ed., Currin V. Shields (New York: Bobbs-Merrill, 1956).
4. Adam Smith, *The Wealth of Nations*, ed. Edwin Cannan (Chicago: University of Chicago Press, 1976), 2:18.
5. Milton Friedman and Rose Friedman, *Free to Choose: A Personal Statement* (New York: Harcourt Brace, 1980), Chapter 1.
6. Milton Friedman, *Capitalism and Freedom* (Chicago: The University of Chicago Press, 1962).
7. *Ibid.*, 8.
8. Brian Barry, *Political Argument: A Reissue with a New Introduction* (Berkeley, Calif.: University of California Press, 1990), 66.
9. *Ibid.*, 192, 226.
10. Jean Jacques Rousseau, *Discourse on Political Economy and The Social Contract*, ed. Christopher Betts (New York: Oxford University Press, 1994).
11. Walter Lippman, *The Phantom Public* (New York: Hartcourt Brace, 1925), 16.
12. Robert B. Reich, "Introduction," in *The Power of Public Ideas*, ed. Robert B. Reich (Cambridge, Mass.: Harvard University Press, 1988), 4.
13. Garry R. Orren, "Why Public Ideas Matter," in *The Power of Public Ideas*, 31–53.
14. Jane J. Mansbridge, "Preface," in *Beyond Self-Interest*, ed. Jane J. Mansbridge (Chicago: The University of Chicago Press, 1990), x.
15. Brian Barry, *Political Argument*, 38.
16. Deborah Stone, *Policy Paradox: The Art of Political Decision Making* (New York: W.W. Norton & Co., 1997), 18.

17. *Ibid.*, 23.

18. Alexis de Toqueville, *Democracy in America,* trans. George Lawrence (New York: Harper, 1988).

19. John F. Manley, "American Liberalism and the Democratic Dream: Transcending the American Dream," *Policy Studies Review* 10 (1990): 90.

20. President Bill Clinton, *Address to Democratic Leadership Council,* November 13, 1993.

21. Terry Hoy, *The Political Philosophy of John Dewey: Toward a Constructive Renewal* (New York: Praeger Publishers, 1998), 83.

22. Jack Ludwig, "Economic Status: Americans Assess Opportunity, Fairness, and Responsibility," *Public Perspective* 10 (1999): 2–3. This source draws upon poll data from 1952 through 1998. A 2001 survey by the

Gallup Organization (January 10–14) provided further continuity, as 86 percent of respondents agreed that there is "opportunity for a person in this nation to get ahead by working hard."

23. Benjamin I. Page and Robert Y. Shapiro, *The Rational Public: Fifty Years of Trends in America's Policy Preferences* (Chicago: The University of Chicago Press, 1992), 128.

24. Jerome Kluegel and Eliot R. Smith, *Beliefs About Inequality: Americans' Views of What Is and What Ought To Be* (New York: Aldine Publishing, 1986).

25. Semour Martin Lipset, *American Exceptionalism: A Double-Edged Sword* (New York: W. W. Norton & Co., 1997, 113–150; Jennifer L. Hochschild, *Facing Up to the American Dream: Race, Class, and the Soul of the Nation* (Princeton, N.J.: Princeton University Press, 1995).

3

Political Science and Public Policy

Paul A. Sabatier

Political scientists who are policy scholars often trace their lineage back to the pioneering work of Lerner and Lasswell (1951). But public policy did not emerge as a significant subfield within the discipline of political science until the late 1960s or early 70s. This resulted from at least three important stimuli: (1) social and political pressures to apply the profession's accumulated knowledge to the pressing social problems of racial discrimination, poverty, the arms race, and environmental pollution; (2) the challenge posed by Dawson and

Robinson (1963), who argued that governmental policy decisions were less the result of traditional disciplinary concerns such as public opinion and party composition than of socioeconomic factors such as income, education, and unemployment levels; and (3) the efforts of David Easton, whose *Systems Analysis of Political Life* (1965) provided an intellectual framework for understanding the entire policy process, from demand articulation through policy formulation and implementation, to feedback effects on society.

From Paul A. Sabatier, "Political Science and Public Policy," *PS: Political Science & Politics* (June 1991), pp. 143–146. Reprinted by permission.

Over the past twenty years, policy research by political scientists can be divided into four types, depending upon the principal focus:

1. *Substantive area research.* This seeks to understand the politics of a specific policy area, such as health, education, transportation, natural resources, or foreign policy. Most of the work in this tradition has consisted of detailed, largely atheoretical, case studies. Examples would include the work of Derthick (1979) on social security, Moynihan (1970) on antipoverty programs, and Bailey and Mosher (1968) on federal aid to education. Such studies are useful to practitioners and policy activists in these areas, as well as providing potentially useful information for inductive theory building. In terms of the profession as a whole, however, they are probably less useful than theoretical case studies—such as Pressman and Wildavsky (1973) on implementation or Nelson (1984) on agenda-setting—which use a specific case to illustrate or test theories of important aspects of the policy process.

2. *Evaluation and impact studies.* Most evaluation research is based on contributions from other disciplines, particularly welfare economics (Stokey and Zeckhauser 1978; Jenkins-Smith 1990). Policy scholars trained as political scientists have made several contributions. They have broadened the criteria of evaluation from traditional social welfare functions to include process criteria, such as opportunities for effective citizen participation (Pierce and Doerksen 1976). They have focused attention on distributional effects (MacRae 1989). They have criticized traditional techniques of benefit-cost analysis on many grounds (Meier 1984; MacRae and Whittington 1988). Most importantly, they have integrated evaluation studies into research on the policy process by examining the use and non-use of policy analysis in the real world (Wildavsky 1966; Dunn 1980; Weiss 1977).

3. *Policy process.* Two decades ago, both Ranney (1968) and Sharkansky (1970) urged political scientists interested in public policy to focus on the policy process, i.e. the factors affecting policy formulation and implementation, as well as the subsequent effects of policy. In their view, focusing on substantive policy areas risked falling into the relatively fruitless realm of atheoretical case studies, while evaluation research offered little promise for a discipline without clear normative standards of good policy. A focus on the policy process would provide opportunities for applying and integrating the discipline's accumulated knowledge concerning political behavior in various institutional settings. That advice was remarkably prescient; the first paper in this symposium attempts to summarize what has been learned.

4. *Policy design.* With roots in the policy sciences tradition described by deLeon (1988), this approach has recently focused on such topics as the efficacy of different types of policy instruments (Salamon 1989; Linder and Peters 1989). Although some scholars within this orientation propose a quite radical departure from the behavioral traditions of the discipline (Bobrow and Dryzek 1987), others build upon work by policy-oriented political scientists over the past twenty years (Schneider and Ingram 1990) while Miller (1989) seeks to integrate political philosophy and the behavioral sciences.

While all have made some contributions, the third has been the most fruitful.

Before turning to a preview of the symposium, some mention should be made of tensions that have emerged between political scientists and the subfield of policy scholars.

SOURCES OF STRAIN

The first, and most subtle, concerns a difference in the fundamental conception of the purpose of government and political life (Hofferbert 1986). Virtually all policy scholars view government in *instrumental* terms: Governments are there to improve the welfare of members of society—to protect public health, provide for the common defense, correct externalities and other market failures, improve public safety, etc. Many political scientists are uncomfortable with this view. Having been schooled in Plato, Aristotle, Locke, and Mill, there is a tendency to view citizenship and political participation as ends in themselves rather than as a means of influencing policy decisions.

Fortunately, this strain need not be serious. Policy scholars can certainly acknowledge the value of solidary incentives and a sense of political efficacy arising from political participation, even if these topics hold no intrinsic interest for them. Likewise most political scientists would admit that people participate in political life at least in part to influence governmental decisions and ultimately improve social welfare. Thus both sides should be able to agree on the importance of developing theories of the policy process which focus on ascertaining the factors which affect the extent to which governmental policy decisions and their social effects are consistent with popular preferences. This is, in fact, a well-established tradition within many subfields of political science, including public opinion (Luttbeg 1968; Page and Shapiro 1983), legislative representation (Miller and Stokes 1963; Ingram et al. 1980), and administrative agencies (Meier 1975; 1987).

The second strain also involves a difference in normative assumptions which need not impede close relations. Most policy scholars have an activist bent, i.e. at some point they wish to influence policy in the area(s) in which they are specialists. Conversely, political scientists probably tend to be preoccupied with better understanding the way the world operates within their areas of specialization, with a smaller percentage seeking to use their expertise to influence political behavior. That percentage, however, is far from trivial: Henry Kissinger and Jeane Kirkpatrick are obvious exceptions, while voting scholars often serve as campaign consultants and many other political scientists have sought to improve the performance of various governmental institutions (Huntington 1988).

The third, and probably most serious, source of strain is that, in the eyes of many political scientists, policy scholars have made only modest contributions to developing reasonably clear, generalizable, and empirically verified theories of the policy process. See, for example, Eulau (1977) and Landau (1977), as well as the relatively poor performance of policy proposals in NSF's Political Science Program (Sigelman and Scioli 1987). In some respects, this indictment strikes me as quite valid. Much of what passes as policy research—particularly by substantive area specialists—shares all the defects of traditional case studies in public administration: descriptive analyses of specific institutions or decisions relying upon very subjective methods of data acquisition and analysis, virtually no attention to the theoretical assumptions underlying the research or the theoretical implications of the findings, and very little concern with the potential generalizability of those findings.

In addition, the dominant paradigm of the policy process—the stages heuristic of Jones (1970), Anderson (1975), and Peters (1986)—is not really a causal theory. Instead, it divides the policy process into several stages (agenda setting, formulation and adoption, implementation, and evaluation), but contains no coherent assumptions about what forces are driving the process from stage to stage and very few falsifiable hypotheses.[1] While the stages heuristic has helped to divide the policy process into manageable units of analysis, researchers have tended to focus exclusively on a single stage with little recognition of work in other stages. The result is weakened theoretical coherence across stages. Even within stages, such as implementation, where there has been a great deal of empirical research, disagreement exists as to how much has been learned over the past 20 years (see Sabatier 1986 and O'Toole 1986 for contrasting reviews). Finally, Nakamura (1987) and others have noted that the real world process often does not fit the sequence of stages envisaged.

On the other hand, a great deal of policy research—particularly in the policy process tradition—has been methodologically sophisticated and guided by explicit theory. Examples would include Kingdon (1984) and Nelson (1984) on agenda-setting; Pressman and Wildavsky (1973), Rodgers and Bullock (1976), Mazmanian and Sabatier (1981; 1989), and Goggin (1987) on implementation; Browning et al. (1984) on long-term policy change; and Ostrom (1990) on institutional arrangements for managing common property resources. In short, while the criticisms of Eulau and Landau were largely justified in the 1970s, they are less valid today.

None of these sources of strain should pose serious obstacles to close collaboration between "mainline" political scientists and the subfield of policy scholars. Both groups share an overwhelming common interest in developing a better understanding of the policy process, i.e. the range of factors which affect governmental policy decisions and the impacts of those decisions on society. Since at least the first part of that process has traditionally been the domain of political science, the subfield of policy scholars clearly have an interest in keeping abreast of developments in the rest of the discipline. By the same token, policy scholars can take pride in having made major contributions to our understanding of the functioning of governmental institutions which should be of interest to all political scientists, even those with no particular concerns with policy impacts.

End Notes

The participants would like to express their thanks to Robert Hauck for shepherding this symposium to publication and to Ken Meier for accepting responsibility for all errors of fact, interpretation, and logic.

1. This criticism is less valid for Anderson (1975). His first two chapters discuss a variety of socio-economic conditions and types of actors which affect the policy process, and he briefly reviews several approaches. But nowhere does he elaborate one or more frameworks and then seek to apply it/them throughout the book. Ripley (1985) proposes a somewhat similar framework, although his arguments derive primarily from Lowi's arenas of power.

On the other hand, the stages heuristic—which distinguishes a major policy decision, such as a statute, from what emerges in the implementation and reformulation stages—is one means of dealing with several of the problems mentioned by Greenberg et al. (1977).

References

ANDERSON, JAMES. 1975. *Public Policy-Making*. N.Y.: Praeger.

BAILEY, STEPHEN and MOSHER, EDITH. 1968. *ESEA: The Office of Education Administers a Law*. Syracuse: Syracuse University Press.

BORROW, DAVIS and DRYZEK, JOHN. 1987. *Policy Analysis by Design*. Pittsburgh: University of Pittsburgh Press.

BROWNING, RUFUS, MARSHALL, DALE ROGERS, and TABB, DAVID. 1984. *Protest Is Not Enough: The Struggle of Blacks and Hispanics for Equality in Urban Politics*. Berkeley: University of California Press.

DAWSON, RICHARD and ROBINSON, JAMES. 1963. "Interparty Competition, Economic Variables, and Welfare Policies in the American States," *Journal of Politics* 25 (May): 265–289.

DELEON, PETER. 1988. *Advice and Consent*. New York: Russell Sage.

DERTHICK, MARTHA. 1979. *Policymaking for Social Security*. Washington: Brookings.

DUNN, WILLIAM. 1980. "The Two-Communities Metaphor and Models of Knowledge Use," *Knowledge* 1 (June): 515–536.

EASTON, DAVID. 1965. *A Systems Analysis of Political Life*. N.Y.: John Wiley and Sons.

EULAU, HEINZ. 1977. "The Interventionist Synthesis," *American Journal of Political Science* 21 (May): 419–423.

GOGGIN, MALCOLM. 1987. *Policy Design and the Politics of Implementation*. Knoxville: University of Tennessee Press.

GREENBERG, GEORGE, JEFFREY MILLER, LAWRENCE MOHR, and BRUCE VLADECK. 1977. "Developing Public Policy Theory Perspectives from Empirical Research," *American Political Science Review* 71 (December): 1532–1543.

HOFFERBERT, RICHARD. 1974. *The Study of Public Policy*. Indianapolis: Bobbs Merrill.

———. 1986. "Policy Evaluation, Democratic Theory, and the Division of Scholarly Labor," *Policy Studies Review* 5 (Feb.): 511–519.

HUNTINGTON, SAMUEL. 1988. "One Soul at a Time: Political Science and Reform," *American Political Science Review* 82 (March): 3–10.

INGRAM, HELEN, NANCY LANEY, and JOHN McCAIN. 1980. *A Policy Approach to Political Representation: Lessons from the Four Corners States*. Baltimore: Johns Hopkins University Press.

JENKINS-SMITH, HANK. 1990. *Democratic Politics and Policy Analysis*. Pacific Grove, CA: Brooks/Cole.

JONES, CHARLES. 1970. *An Introduction to the Study of Public Policy*. Belmont, CA: Wadsworth.

KINGDON, JOHN. 1984. *Agendas, Alternatives, and Public Policies*. Boston: Little, Brown & Co.

KISER, LARRY and OSTROM, ELINOR. 1982. "The Three Worlds of Action," in *Strategies of Political Inquiry*, ed. E. Ostrom. Beverly Hills: Sage, pp. 179–222.

LANDAU, MARTIN. 1977. "The Proper Domain of Policy Analysis," *American Journal of Political Science* 21 (May): 423–427.

LERNER, DANIEL and LASSWELL, HAROLD, eds. 1951. *The Policy Sciences*. Stanford: Stanford University Press.

LINDER, STEPHEN and PETERS, B. GUY. 1989. "Instruments of Government: Perceptions and Contexts," *Journal of Public Policy* 9 (1): 35–58.

LUTTBEG, NORMAN, ed. 1968. *Public Opinion and Public Policy: Models of Political Linkages*. Homewood, IL: Dorsey.

MACRAE, DUNCAN. 1989. "Social Science and Policy Advice," Paper presented at the PSO/APSA Conference, "Advances in Policy Studies." Atlanta.

———. and WHITTINGTON, DALE. 1988. "Assessing Preferences in Cost-Benefit Analysis," *Journal of Policy Analysis and Management* 7 (Winter): 246–263.

MAZMANIAN, DANIEL and SABATIER, PAUL, eds. 1981. *Effective Policy Implementation*. Lexington, Mass.: D.C. Heath.

———. 1989. *Implementation and Public Policy*, rev. ed. Lanham, MD: University Press of America.

MEIER, KENNETH. 1975. "Representative Bureaucracy: An Empirical Analysis," *American Political Science Review* 69 (June): 526–542.

———. 1984. "The Limits of Cost-Benefit Analysis," *Decision-Making in the Public Sector*, ed. Lloyn Nigro. N.Y.: Marcel Dekker, pp. 43–63.

———. 1987. *Politics and the Bureaucracy*, 2d. ed. Monterey, CA: Brooks/Cole.

MILLER, TRUDI. 1989. "Design Science as a Unifying Paradigm," Paper presented at the PSO/APSA Conference, "Advances in Policy Studies." Atlanta.

MILLER, WARREN and STOKES, DONALD. 1963. "Constituency Influence on Congress," *American Political Science Review* 57 (March): 45–56.

MOYNIHAN, DANIEL. 1970. *Maximum Feasible Misunderstanding*. N.Y.: Free Press.

NAKAMURA, ROBERT. 1987. "The Textbook Policy Process and Implementation Research," *Policy Studies Review* 7 (1): 142–154.

NELSON, BARBARA J. 1984. *Making an Issue of Child Abuse*. Chicago: University of Chicago Press.

OSTROM, ELINOR. 1989. *Governing the Commons*. Cambridge: Cambridge University Press.

O'TOOLE, LAURENCE. 1986. "Policy Recommendations for Multi-Actor Implementation: An Assessment of the Field," *Journal of Public Policy* 6 (April): 181–210.

PAGE, BENJAMIN and SHAPIRO, ROBERT. 1983. "Effects of Public Opinion on Policy," *American Political Science Review* 77 (March): 175–190.

PETERS, B. GUY. 1986. *American Public Policy: Promise and Performance*, 2d ed. Chatham, NJ: Chatham House.

PIERCE, JOHN and DOERKSEN, eds. 1976. *Water Politics and Public Involvement*. Ann Arbor: Ann Arbor Science.

PRESSMAN, JEFFREY and WILDAVSKY, AARON. 1973. *Implementation*. Berkeley: University of California Press.

RANNEY, AUSTIN, ed. 1968. *Political Science and Public Policy*. Chicago: Markham.

4

Bounded Rationality and Rational Choice Theory

Bryan D. Jones,
Graeme Boushey, and
Samuel Workman

AN OVERVIEW

In the behavioral sciences, such as psychology and behavioral biology, the major topic of inquiry is individual behavior. In the social sciences, such as political science and economics, the aim is to understand social systems of interacting individuals. Social scientists need both a model of individual behavior and an understanding of how individuals interact to produce social outcomes, such as those produced by free markets or policymaking processes in government. As a consequence, social scientists cannot dally with the nuances of human behavior that do not impact on the interactions of people in organizations. Any model of individual choice in policymaking processes must be parsimonious, and they must link individual level actions to policymaking outcomes.

The behavioral models of *comprehensive rationality* and *bounded rationality*, which today divide the theories of public policy, were driven by a common desire to improve the rigor of political analysis. Applications of both rational choice theory and bounded rationality in the study of public policy and administration evolved from the efforts of such diverse theorists as Herbert Simon, Mancur Olson, and Anthony Downs to link individual human decision-making with broader macropolitical outcomes

(Simon 1947; Olson 1982; Downs 1957). Although the competing models of rationality disagreed about the fundamental motivations behind individual choice, they were unified in their belief that the processes and policy outcomes be most powerfully understood through exploring the role of individual behavior in collective decision-making.

A theory of rationality which anticipated individual choices in the context of the larger political process would present a significant advancement in the study of government—such a set of assumptions would act as a theoretical tool-box that could be used, not only to cut through the complexity of public decision-making, but also to locate areas of conflict within organizations, and potentially predict future political outcomes. Both rational choice theory and bounded rationality pushed the study of public policy away from case studies and atheoretical descriptions of public administration toward a generalized theory of public policy.

Despite these common aims, the theories of rationality are deeply divided over the most basic assumptions of individual choice. Rational choice theory borrows heavily from economic assumptions of individual preferences, and believes that a sufficient behavioral model could be drawn from deductions of an individual's self interested utility maximization. Bounded rationality began as a critique of comprehensive rationality, and grew from an effort to reconcile the reductionist economic assumptions of rational choice with observed psychological constraints on human decision-making. The following sections outline the distinguishing characteristics of both rational choice theory and bounded rationality as applied to the study of public policy. This critique intends not only to cast light on the major differences between the two theories, but also calls attention to exciting empirical findings which we believe are fueling increasing theoretical convergence around a single positive theory of human choice.

COMPREHENSIVE RATIONALITY AND THE THEORY OF POLICY PROCESSES

In recent decades rational choice theory has been widely applied to the study of government. This dominance extends in no small part from the model's theoretical parsimony. Rational choice theorists have explored some of the most complex aspects of politics by making relatively few core assumptions about individual behavior. As in neoclassical economic models, the theory of comprehensive rationality posits that political decision-makers are self-interested utility maximizers who hold stable preferences and objectives, and make strategic decisions to maximize the personal benefits of a given choice. To understand politics at the aggregate level, researchers need only to understand ordered preferences of individual actors who populate a specific institution or political sphere and the formal rules by which these fixed preferences are combined. In this approach, preferences + rules = policy outcomes.

Important distinctions can be drawn between rational choice models in public policy, political science, and economics; however, all rational choice models share common characteristics. First, decision-makers hold stable *ranked* and *ordered* preferences for outcomes. Given three possible alternatives—options A, B, and C, a rational chooser will form clear preferences between each of the three given alternatives. These preferences are transitive, meaning that if an individual prefers option A to B, and prefers option B to C, he also prefers option A to C. Second, a decision-maker possesses necessary *information* to connect choices to outcomes. With this information, individuals then *optimize* when making decisions—they make strategic choices in order to achieve their most preferred outcome. "Thick" rationality adds the assumption of individual *self-interest* in determining preferences. For example—preferences for a higher tax rate to fund public education over a lower overall tax rate suggest that an individual will receive greater personal *utility* for increased funding in public education than from lower taxes. Regardless of the underlying reasons for this preference, rational choice scholars reduce it to a question of self-interest. Their behaviors reflect only their effort to maximize the utility of their choice.

Even the staunchest proponents of rational choice theory regard this characterization of the model as more of an ideal type than a realistic portrayal of human behavior. Decisions made under conditions of complete certainty—when specific strategic choices are known to lead to explicit outcomes—are rarely found in political or economic life. More powerful insights have evolved from rational choice theory when theorists have examined decision-making under *risk*—where a strategy might lead to several different outcomes with known probability, or conditions of *uncertainty*—where outcomes are known but the probabilities associated with those outcomes are not, and must be estimated.

Rational choice theorists use *expected utility theory* to approximate how individuals make calculations that rank alternatives by their *expected value* (under risk or uncertainty) rather than their known value. Under conditions of risk, individuals form strategic preferences probabilistically—they compare the probability that their most preferred outcome will occur against the probability that their less preferred outcome will occur, and both against the cost of making a decision.

It is not enough that individuals calculate the probabilities that outcomes will occur if they take a particular action; they must also calculate the likelihood that their choice will yield the outcome against the probability that their choice will have no bearing on the outcome. Individuals must not only predict the probability that an event will occur, but also the chance that an event would occur without their participation, or that their less preferred outcome would occur in spite of their participation. A classic example is rational voter models, where people are predicted to vote only if their expectation that their vote will make a difference exceeds the marginal cost of voting.

Comprehensive rationality holds great appeal as a model of choice for three basic reasons. First, rational choice promises a parsimonious method for studying complex political behavior. By assuming that actors are singularly motivated to maximize gains available in political decisions, a wide range of considerations that have long complicated the study of political science—social class, partisanship, or cultural values—become peripheral to a decision-maker's preferences. The challenge of rational choice theory is to characterize accurately the payoffs available to political actors in a given arena. A classic example of this approach can be drawn from David Mayhew's study of congressional voting behavior in *Congress: the Electoral Connection*. In his analysis, democratic representation is motivated singularly by a congressman's desire to retain political power (Mayhew 1974). Ideology and policy-making matter only insomuch as they instruct a politician as to where his source of political power is located, and how to make appropriate votes to retain electoral support.

The second advantage of the rational choice method is its broad theoretical generalizability. Unlike descriptive studies of political behavior, the baseline assumptions of rational choice methods are characterized by a 'universalism that reveals generalizable implications beyond those under immediate investigation' (Levi 1997, 20). Deductions from rational choice theory are not specific to a particular time and case, but should offer insights wherever similar conditions can be observed. Mancur Olson argues that 'the persuasiveness of a theory depends not only on how many facts are explained, but also how diverse are the kinds of facts explained'. In Olson's view, the rational choice approach has the double benefit of preserving the parsimony of a theory by removing 'any inessential premises or complexities that ought to be removed from an argument,' while retaining a high degree of explanatory power (Olson 1982: 12–13). Drawing upon a

relatively small set of assumptions about human behavior, Olson is able to advance a series of predictions that serve as the basis of a theory of how the formation of interest groups in democratic societies detract economic growth. That democratic nations have sustained high levels of growth, even as interest groups have proliferated, means that Olson's theory was wrong, but that is not the point. It was clearly and cleanly stated in a generalized manner that facilitated testing against empirical observation.

This leads to the third advantage. The rational choice method is a comparably rigorous approach to the study of political processes. Rational choice researchers derive formal mathematical models from a set of assumptions about individual preferences. These models derive a set of hypotheses of anticipating a specific outcome in politics, and then test them against the self interested behavior of actors put forward in the theoretical assumptions of rational choice theory—in this regard, rational choice hypotheses are verified or falsified. This approach forces researchers to advance well-specified models of political choice. Rational choice models focus only on those most crucial elements of the political process that are necessary to explain outcomes.

Both the simplicity and the promise of theoretical generalizablity have made rational choice theory a popular tool for the study of government. The rational choice approach has been applied to such subfields as organizational behavior (Bendor and Moe 1985; Moe 1984) congress (Mayhew 1974; Arnold 1990), parties and elections (Downs 1967) and collective action problems (Olson 1982). The breadth of this research is suggestive of the theoretical power of the model. By exploring the strategic behavior of self-interested individuals, rational choice theorists have produced a rich and theoretically unified body of research in a discipline once marked by methodological eclecticism.

BOUNDED RATIONALITY AND THE THEORY OF POLICY PROCESSES

Perhaps because rational choice theory takes a decidedly reductionist approach to the study of government—one which is 'willing to sacrifice nuance for generalizability, detail for logic' (Levi 1997: 21)—dissenting researchers have long charged that these sparse assumptions of individual utility maximization distort the complexity of both individual behavior and organizational decision-making. Field researchers complain that observations of individual behavior rarely match the calculating self-interested actor posited in rational choice theory (Brehm and Gates 1997; Lipsky 1980). The behavioral norm of individual utility maximization simply does not seem to reflect accurately the actions of politicians, bureaucrats and voters, whose choices so often seem to be motivated by risk aversion, sense of mission, identity, fairness, or altruism. For these critics, rational choice theory is at best idiosyncratic—applicable only to discrete institutions such as the US congress where political behavior can be safely matched to self-interest (Rockman 2000). At worst rational choice theory is misleading, as it reduces potentially interesting social behavior such as altruism to an individual's self-interest (Monroe 1996).

Researchers who actually study individual decision making find the rational choice approach curious. Cognitive psychologists find the economic assumptions of stable ordered preferences, transitivity, and utility maximization to be a strange abstraction of human decision-making. Findings in psychology indicate that people are poor at forming preferences, generating alternatives, and making decisions (Sniderman et al. 1991; Tetlock 2000; Jones 2001). Studies show that individuals often lack even the most basic tools with which to make informed rational decisions. Preferences and choices are bounded more by emotion and environmental context than by rational analysis (Jones 2001). Research in cognitive psychology makes one wonder how people are able to form preferences or make decisions at all.

Herbert Simon (1947) developed bounded rationality as an effort to reconcile the strict economic assumptions of comprehensive rationality with actual decision-making revealed by the empirical study of organizations. Preferences and choices seemed bounded by cognitive and emotional constraints that interfered with the process of purely rational decision-making. Much like comprehensive rationality, bounded rationality offers an efficient method for moving between individual decisions and organizational outcomes. Bounded rationality retains the hallmarks of a theoretical model—it captures only those aspects of human behavior needed to understand collective decision-making.

As with so many researchers who followed him, Simon noticed that the assumptions of expected utility analysis failed to match his own observations of real world economic decision-making (Simon 1999). Looking at budgeting in Milwaukee, Simon observed that relatively little individual behavior matched 'substantive or objective rationality, that is, behavior that can be adjudged to be optimally adapted to the situation' (Simon 1985, 294). He instead found that the processes of both individual and organizational decision-making were a good deal messier than rational expectations would have us believe. Bureaucratic budgets were often adjusted incrementally, using the prior year's budgeting as a benchmark for future spending needs (Thompson and Green 2001; Simon 1991). Organizational decisions were made more through horse trading and bargaining than a process even remotely resembling fully rational decision-making (Simon 1999). Organizations and individuals proved poor at generating complex alternatives or making trade-offs. Environmental factors, such as issue salience, individual attention, and time constraints, shaped the depth of solution searches in organizations.

Simon (1985) believed the most glaring problem with comprehensive rationality was its focus on outcomes rather than the process of individual decision-making. By ignoring the procedures of choice, rational choice theory blithely accepted that 'rational' outcome emerged from self-interested behavior. Such an approach is especially dangerous when attempting to understand the broader mechanisms of collective policy-making, where the motivations for preference formation and political behavior are at least as important as the outcome itself. Simon (1985: 294) explains:

> There is a fundamental difference between substantive and procedural rationality. To deduce substantively, or objectively, rational choice in a given situation, we need to know only the choosing organism's goals

and the objective characteristics of the situation. We need know absolutely nothing else about the organism, nor would such information be of any use to us, for it could not affect the objectively rational behavior in any way.

To deduce the procedurally or boundedly rational choice in a situation, we must know the choosing organism's goals, the information and conceptualization it has of the situation, and its abilities to draw inferences from the information it possesses. We need know nothing about the objective situation in which the organism finds itself, except insofar as that situation influences the subjective representation.

Simon argued that a theoretical model oriented toward understanding procedurally or boundedly rational decision-making would provide a more realistic bridge between individual and collective choice. A 'behavioral' model of rationality would take a decidedly scientific and inductive approach to understanding decision-making. In order to make efficient generalizations connecting individual psychological processes to collective political and economic choice, research needed to follow strict scientific guidelines. Underlying theoretical assumptions of human behavior needed to be tested and retested. Those assumptions that were verified through scientific research would be preserved in the scientific model, while others would be modified or abandoned. What bounded rationality lost in parsimony it would gain in accuracy. Unlike the artificial behavioral assumptions of comprehensive rationality, bounded rationality would capture the biological, emotional, and environmental constraints that constrained the procedures of decision-making.

As with rational choice theory, bounded rationality has been widely applied in the study of public policy. While bounded rationalists might emphasize different elements of behavioral model in their research, virtually all research in bounded rationality draws from four core principles: the Principal of Intended Rationality, the Principal of Adaptation, the Principle of Uncertainty and the Principle of

Trade-offs (Jones 2003). From these principles, modern researchers have advanced a vigorous research program that explores how both people and institutions behave. As we will see, even though experimental and empirical research have improved our understanding of the behavioral model of choice, these four central tenets remain largely valid.

The Principle of Intended Rationality

The principle of intentionality suggests that we look at the goal directed behavior of people, and investigate the manner in which their cognitive and emotional constitutions either help or hinder their goal-seeking. This distinguishes bounded rationality from psychological theories, which generally focus only on the limitations of individual choice-makers. While comprehensive rationality assumes single-minded maximization, the principle of intended rationality allows researchers to distinguish between careful cost benefit analysis that closely approximates utility maximizing decision-making, quick decisions based on heuristic cues, unthinking reliance on past strategies, or even spontaneous decisions that seem to make no reference to potential gains or losses. Given the time, costs, and demands of a specific decision, humans may rely on hard-wired biological responses, generalized decision-making strategies, or full information searches. 'Cognitive architecture is most obvious when action occurs at short time scales. As one moves toward actions that take longer times, cognitive architecture is less and less evident, and the nature of the task takes on more and more importance in explaining action' (Jones 2001, 56). Humans may intend to be rational, but their decision-making capabilities break down under time constraints or very high information costs. Moreover, there is no good evidence that people are more rational when the stakes are high, as some rational choice theorists have maintained. In direct defiance of that claim, state lotteries sell more tickets when the pot is large, lowering the probabilities and the expected return.

Principle of Adaptation

The principle of adaptation is closely related to the notion of intentionality. Much of human behavior is explained by the nature of the 'task environment' surrounding a decision. With time, human decision-making adapts to the specific nature of the problems they face in a specific circumstance. The more time and learning an individual invests in a specific problem, the less constrained they become by environmental or biological constraints. This notion of adaptation accounts for changes in decision-making efficiency in a single problem space over time. When a problem is iterated over time, people learn or develop coping strategies. Even more intuitively, the principle of adaptation may explain why organizations encourage specialization in areas of complexity, and routinization in decisions under severe time constraints.

A rich tradition of research in political science and psychology explores the use of heuristics in political decision-making—attempting to identify cost-cutting cues individuals rely upon in order to limit investment costs from making complex decisions in low-information environments. The key issue is whether these heuristics are maximally adaptive (Lupia, McCubbins and Popkin 2000; Gigerenzer et al. 1999). While some have argued that heuristics invariably follow what a fully rational individual would choose, that is quite clearly not the case. 'Buy a lottery ticket when the stakes are high' is a classic heuristic that leads to lower expected returns than not buying at all, or buying when the stakes are low. It is likely that some heuristics are adaptive calculational crutches and some are misleading and even mal-adaptive.

The Principle of Uncertainty

Individuals operate in an environment of almost constant risk and uncertainty. Because of human cognitive architecture, uncertainty is far more fundamental to choice than expected utility theory admits. Not only are individuals unaware of the outcomes that will result from strategic choices, but they are uncertain of the procedures of choice themselves and are even uncertain about their own preferences. Uncertain outcomes may produce dependence on procedures, and may explain instances of extremely risk adverse behavior.

The Principle of Trade-Offs

The final notion central to models of bounded rationality is the principle of trade-offs. Unlike comprehensive rationality, which suggests that individuals are able to move seamlessly between ranked goals, bounded rationalists argue that people find it difficult to trade off one goal against another when forming preferences and making choices (Slovak 1990; Tetlock 2000). This critique is a major shift away from the transitivity assumption in rational choice theory; however it is important to capture the volatile shifts in preferences observed by both behavioral economists (Kahneman and Tversky 1986) and public opinion researchers (Zaller 1992). Preferences are determined by emotional and cognitive cues, and are rarely as stable as rational choice theorists have us believe. Because of these trade-off difficulties, Simon argued that individuals, and by extension organizations, 'satisfice,' quickly choosing an option that is 'good enough' rather than searching for one that weighs the payoff of every possible choice.

Because bounded rationality is concerned with the procedures of individual choice, the school of thought tends to approach the study of politics by looking to how individuals and organizations respond to changes in their problem environments. Because individual decision-makers have limited attention for problem solving, they must address problems serially, one-at-a-time, which means they are forever juggling inputs, prioritizing them via the allocation of attention and the sense of urgency that inputs generate. The salience of a particular problem is almost always generated by non-rational elements in politics—by scandal, by crisis, by the mobilization of critics—rather than calm decision to allocate the scarce resource of attentiveness.

In governments, as well as in all organizations, attention is allocated in a process political scientists call *agenda setting*. Organizations also suffer from limited attention spans, and must process at least major problems serially. Routine problems may be delegated and handled according to rules, but fresh problems cannot be handled this way. It is common for many problems to press forward on the governmental agenda, and whether the most severe problems receive the most attention is an empirical question. In individuals, as well as in organizations, the allocation of decision-making attention is crucial for understanding the immediate and future behavior of an organization.

Because it is explicitly oriented toward understanding the processes of decision-making, bounded rationality has been widely applied to the study of public policy and public administration. Bounded rationalists have explored a range of policy problems, ranging from agenda setting (Kingdon 1995; Baumgartner and Jones 1993), congressional decision-making (Kingdon 1973), federal budgets (Padgett 1980), incrementalism (Wildavsky 1964; Davis, Murray, Dempster and Widalsky 1966) and risk aversion (Kahneman and Tversky 2000). As a model of choice, bounded rationality is at least as broadly applicable as comprehensive rationality....

References

ALCHIAN, ARMEN A., and HAROLD DEMSETZ. 1972. Production, Information Costs, and Economic Organization. *American Economic Review* 62 (December): 777–795.

ARNOLD, R. DOUGLAS. 1990. *The Logic of Congressional Action.* Yale University Press.

BALLA, STEVEN J. 1998. Administrative Procedure and Political Control of the Bureaucracy. *The American Political Science Review* 92 (3): 663–673.

BREHM, JOHN, and SCOTT GATES. 1997. *Working, Shirking, and Sabotage: Bureaucratic Response to a Democratic Public.* Ann Arbor: University of Michigan Press.

CAMERER, COLIN and RICHARD THALER. 1995. 'Anomalies: Ultimatums, Dictators and Manners.' *Journal of Economic Perspectives* 9: 209–219.

CARPENTER, DANIEL P. 1996. Adaptive Signal Processing, Hierarchy, and Budgetary Control in Federal Regulation. *The American Political Science Review* 90 (2): 283–302.

FUDENBERG, DREW and DAVID LEVINE. 1997. 'Measuring players' losses in experimental games.' *Quarterly Journal of Economics* 112 (2): 507–536.

GARRETT, ELIZABETH. 'The Law and Economics of Elections: The Law and Economics of 'Informed Voter' Ballot Notations' (Symposium). *Virginia Law Review* 85 (November 2003): 1553.

GIGERENZER, GERD, PETER TODD, and the ABC RESEARCH GROUP. 1999. Simple Heuristics That Make Us Smart. Oxford University Press.

GOEREE, JACOB K. and CHARLES HOLT. 2000. 'Asymmetric inequality aversion and noisy behavior in alternating-offer bargaining games,' *European Economic Review* 44: 1079–1089.

GOLDEN, MARISSA MARTINO. 2000. *What Motivates Bureaucrats? Politics and Administration During the Reagan Years.* New York: Columbia University Press.

HARDIN, GARRETT. 1968. 'The Tragedy of the Commons.' *Science* 162: 1243–1248.

HENRICH, JOSEPH. 2000. 'Does Culture Matter in Economic Behavior? Ultimatum Game Bargaining among the Machiguenga of the Peruvian Amazon.' *The American Economic Review* 90: 973–980.

HINDERA, JOHN J., and CHERYL D. YOUNG. 1998. Representative Bureaucracy: The Theoretical Implications of Statistical Interaction. *Political Science Quarterly* 51 (3): 655–671.

HOFFMAN, ELIZABETH, and MATHEW L. SPITZER. 1985. 'Entitlements, Rights and Fairness: An Experimental

SNIDERMAN, PAUL, et al. 1991. *Reasoning and Choice.* Cambridge: Cambridge University Press.

SOLNICK, SARA. 2001. 'Gender Differences in the Ultimatum Game.' *Economic Inquiry* 39: 189.

TAYLOR, FREDERICK W. 1911. *The Principles of Scientific Management.* New York: W. W. Norton.

TETLOCK, PHILIP. 2000. 'Coping with Trade-offs: Psychological Constraints and Political Implications'. In Lupia, Arthur, Mathew D. McCubbins, and Samuel L. Popkin, eds., *Elements of Reason.* Cambridge: Cambridge University Press.

THALER, RICHARD H. 1992. *The Winner's Curse; Paradoxes and Anomalies of Economic Life.* Princeton University Press.

THOMPSON, FRED and MARK GREEN. 2001. Organizational Process Models of Budgeting, *Research in Public Administration*, 55–81.

WOOD, B. DAN. 1988. Principals, Bureaucrats, and Responsiveness in Clean Air Enforcements. *American Political Science Review* 82: 213–234.

WOOD, B. DAN, and RICHARD W. WATERMAN. 1991. The Dynamics of Political Control of the Bureaucracy. *The American Political Science Review* 85 (3): 801–828.

WORSHAM, JEFF, MARC ALLEN EISNER, and EVAN J. RINGQUIST. 1997. Assessing the Assumptions: A Critical Analysis of Agency Theory. *Administration and Society* 28 (4): 419–440.

5

Still Muddling, Not Yet Through

Charles E. Lindblom

For a people weary of their government, Abraham Lincoln asserted "a revolutionary right to dismember and overthrow it." Jefferson at least speculated on the possibility that occasional revolution was healthy for the body politic. It is not to dissent from them that I have been claiming that "muddling through"[1]—or incrementalism as it is more usually labeled—is and ought to be the usual method of policy making. Rather, it is that neither revolution, nor drastic policy change, nor even carefully planned big steps are ordinarily possible.

Perhaps at this stage in the study and practice of policy making the most common view (it has gradually found its way into textbooks) is that indeed no more than small or incremental steps—no more than muddling—is ordinarily possible. But most people, including many policy analysts and policy makers, want to separate the "ought" from the "is." They think we should try to do better. So do I. What remains as an issue, then? It can be clearly put. Many critics of incrementalism believe that doing better usually means turning away from incrementalism. Incrementalists believe that for complex problem solving it usually means practicing incrementalism more skillfully and turning away from it only rarely.

Of the various ways of turning away from incrementalism, two stand out. One is taking bigger steps in policy—no longer fiddling, say, with our energy problems, but dealing with them as an integrated whole. The other is more complete and scientific analysis of policy alternatives than incrementalists attempt.[2] These two—big actions and comprehensive analysis—are obviously closely related, and they come nicely together in conventional notions of "planning." Hence a choice is clearly posed. Is the general formula for better policy making one of more science and more political ambition, or, as I would argue, a new and improved muddling?

I can now analyze the choice better than I did 20 years ago.[3] I begin with an apology for sometimes confusing incremental *politics* with incremental *analysis* and for inadequately distinguishing three versions of incremental analysis. In its core meaning incrementalism *as a political pattern* is easy to specify. It is political change by small steps (regardless of method of analysis). So defined, incrementalism varies by degree. Raising or lowering the discount rate from time to time is extremely incremental. Making the original decision to use the discount rate as a method of monetary control is still modestly though not extremely incremental. Reorganizing the banking system by introducing the Federal Reserve System is still incremental, though less so.

Eliminating the use of money, as both the Soviets and the Cubans aspired in their early revolutionary years, is not incremental. Where the line is drawn is not important so long as we

From Charles E. Lindblom, "Still Muddling, Not Yet Through," *Public Administration Review*, Vol. 39, No. 6 (November–December 1979), pp. 517–526.

understand that size of step in policy making can be arranged on a continuum from small to large.

As for the three meanings of incrementalism as policy *analysis*, it now seems clear that in the literature and even in my own writing each of the following kinds of analysis sometimes takes the name of incrementalism:

1. Analysis that is limited to consideration of alternative policies all of which are only incrementally different from the status quo.

   Call this *simple incremental analysis.*

2. Analysis marked by a mutually supporting set of simplifying and focusing stratagems of which simple incremental analysis is only one, the others being those listed in my article of 20 years ago:[4] specifically,
   a. limitation of analysis to a few somewhat familiar policy alternatives;
   b. an intertwining of analysis of policy goals and other values with the empirical aspects of the problem;
   c. a greater analytical preoccupation with ills to be remedied than positive goals to be sought;
   d. a sequence of trials, errors, and revised trials;
   e. analysis that explores only some, not all, of the important possible consequences of a considered alternative;
   f. fragmentation of analytical work to many (partisan) participants in policy making.

   This complex method of analysis I have called *disjointed incrementalism.*

3. Analysis limited to any calculated or thoughtfully chosen set of stratagems to simplify complex policy problems, that is, to short-cut the conventionally comprehensive "scientific" analysis.[5]

   Such a practice I have now come to call *strategic analysis.*

Disjointed incrementalism is one of several possible forms of strategic analysis, and simple incremental analysis is one of several elements in disjointed incremental analysis. We can now examine each to see why it should be pursued as an alternative to the pursuit of conventional "scientific" analysis, which I have usually labeled "synoptic" in acknowledgement of its aspiration to be complete.[6] Let us begin with strategic analysis.

THE CASE OF STRATEGIC ANALYSIS

The case for strategic analysis as a norm or ideal is simple: No person, committee, or research team, even with all the resources of modern electronic computation, can complete the analysis of a complex problem. Too many interacting values are at stake,[7] too many possible alternatives, too many consequences to be traced through an uncertain future—the best we can do is achieve partial analysis or, in Herbert Simon's term, a "bounded rationality."[8] I need not here review the many familiar reasons by now recorded in the literature of social science for our inability to achieve a synoptic intellectual mastery of complex social problems.

Consider a continuum on which analysis is arrayed according to its *completeness* or synoptic quality. On it, we can indicate both hypothetical and real alternatives.

The continuum suggests several observations. We—policy makers, administrators, policy analysts, and researchers—usually do significantly better than the worst extreme that can be imagined. For complex problems, however, we never approach synopsis but remain instead at great distance. Some of us practice strategic analysis better than others—that is, we employ in an informed and thoughtful way a variety of simplifying stratagems, like skillfully sequenced trial and error.

Granted that, critics may ask: Doesn't the left end of the continuum, complete or synoptic analysis, represent the only defensible ideal? Should we not, therefore, continue to press toward it? To some critics the answers seem obvious, hardly worth reflecting on. Consider, however, a simple analogy. Men have always wanted to fly. Was the ambition to undertake unaided flight, devoid of any strategy for achieving it, ever a useful norm or ideal? Although the myth of Icarus stimulates the imagination, flying becomes a productive ambition only to those who accept the impossibility of flying without mechanical assistance and who entertain the thought of using fabricated wings and other devices.

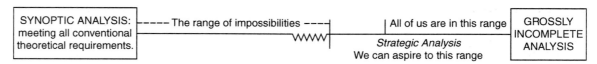

Achieving impossible feats of synopsis is a boot-less, unproductive ideal. Aspiring to improving policy analysis through the use of strategies is a *directing* or *guiding* aspiration. It points to something to be done, something to be studied and learned, and something that can be successfully approximated. What kind of aspiration, norm, or ideal gives direction and other specific guidance to a body builder—his hope to have the strength of a gorilla or his intention to exceed Arnold Schwarzenegger? For a soprano, the impossible aspiration to hit a note six octaves above the highest note ever sung, or the resolve to reach A above high-C? For a person who dislikes telephone directories, to memorize all the telephone numbers he might ever use or to memorize a still difficult smaller set of frequently called numbers? An aspiration to synopsis does not help an analyst choose manageable tasks, while an aspiration to develop improved strategies does.

I suggest that, failing to grasp this point, analysts who think in the older conventional way about problem solving pretend to synopsis; but knowing no way to approximate it, they fall into worse patterns of analysis and decision than those who, with their eyes open, entertain the

guiding ideal of strategic analysis. Again through a diagram, I can suggest what actually happens in policy analysis. We can array on the continuum a range of actually possible degrees of completeness of analysis.

For complex problems, tied to an unhelpful aspiration that simply admonishes "Be complete!", an analyst unknowingly or guiltily muddles badly. Or, pursuing a guiding ideal of strategic analysis, he knowingly and openly muddles with some skill. Hence his taking as an ideal the development of better strategic analysis will be far more helpful than his turning away from strategic analysis in an impossible pursuit of approximations to synopsis. Is the appropriate ideal for the commuter miraculously long legs or better bus service? What can actually be done in the pursuit of each of the two?

For complex social problems, even formal analytic techniques—systems analysis, operations research, management by objectives, PERT, for example—need to be developed around strategies rather than as attempts at synopsis. Some theoretical formulations of these techniques and all examples of their successful application to complex problems reflect this important point.

Ill-considered, often bumbling incompleteness in analysis.	seat-of-pants semi-strategies	seat-of-pants plus studied strategies	Strategic Analysis: informed and thoughtful choice of methods of problem simplification
	Most of us are in this broad range; some here toward the right		
		(We ought to be in this range)	

THE CASE FOR DISJOINTED INCREMENTALISM

It should now be clear why I endorse not only strategic analysis as a norm but disjointed incrementalism as one kind of it. Disjointed incrementalism is a strategy practiced with variable skill. Taking carefully considered disjointed incrementalism as a norm would improve the analytic efforts of many analysts, for the several now familiar reasons given in the article of 20 years ago. It would

set them on a productive course of analysis while turning them away from conventional attempts at formal completeness that always lapse, for complex problems, into ill-defended makeshifts. A conventional synoptic (in aspiration) attempt to choose and justify the location of a new public housing unit by an analysis of the entirety of a city's land needs and potential development patterns always degenerates at least into superficiality if not fraud. A disjointed incremental analysis can do better.

The valid objection to disjointed incrementalism as a *practical analytical method* is that one can find better kinds of strategic analysis, not that one can turn to synopsis as an alternative. The valid objection to disjointed incrementalism as a *norm or ideal* for analysis is that better strategic ideals are available, not that synopsis is a useful ideal.[9] Are there other kinds of strategic analysis, or at least other hypothetic ideals of strategic analysis? More, I would reply, than we have taken the trouble to uncover; hence much exploration remains to be undertaken. A conspicuous early alternative, tapped in a concept with which disjointed incrementalism overlaps, is Simon's "satisficing."[10] Dror and Etzioni have also investigated alternatives.[11] Given the alternative strategies often available, disjointed incrementalism is of course not always necessary in analysis.

All analysis is incomplete, and all incomplete analysis may fail to grasp what turns out to be critical to good policy. But—and this is a "but" that must be given a prominent seat in the halls of controversy over incrementalism—that means that for complex problems all attempts at synopsis are incomplete. The choice between synopsis and disjointed incrementalism—or between synopsis and any form of strategic analysis—is simply between ill-considered, often accidental incompleteness on one hand, and deliberate, designed incompleteness on the other.

Many specific weaknesses have been identified in disjointed incremental analysis: for example, that it will often do no better than find a "local" optimum, a policy better than its near and only incrementally different neighbors but possibly much inferior to a more distant alternative policy never examined. Disjointed incremental analysis is much flawed, as are all alternative possible or concretely imaginable forms of policy making and policy analysis. I think I have failed to communicate to readers just how bad I think policy analysis and policy making are, even under the best circumstances. Evidence of that failure is Langdon Winner's attribution to me of a "marvelous logic" that promises that "planners can perform effectively" and that "lack of understanding on the broad scale is not a hindrance to sound decision making."[12] Of course, it is a hindrance, and a tragic one. And that is why we need analytical

strategies like disjointed incrementalism to make the most of our limited abilities to understand.

An aspect of disjointed incrementalism which I filed away years ago as unfinished business and to which I intend shortly to return is the relation between its remedial orientation—its concern with identifiable ills from which to flee rather than abstract ends to be pursued—and what appears to be the mind's need for a broad (and some would say "higher") set of lasting ambitions or ideals. I am myself committed to some such ideals; that is, I make use of them. Yet they are often only distantly and loosely operative in the specific analysis of policy problems. At best they can only be incompletely analyzed—held in the mind loosely where they are beset by internal contradictions. They do not represent, as has been suggested, a distant synoptic guidance of incremental analysis, for synopsis on values remains impossible. Perhaps they enter into our thinking most significantly through posing trade-off problems, in which incremental gains on one front are traded against decrements on others.

THE CASE FOR SIMPLE INCREMENTAL ANALYSIS

Simple incremental analysis—which is analysis of no more than small or incremental possible departures from the status quo—cannot be defended in isolation from the more complex strategies, like disjointed incrementalism, of which it is a part. It is only an aspect of analysis and is or is not useful depending on circumstances and on the stratagem of which it is a part. Insofar, however, as we can speak of one aspect of analysis (bearing in mind its relation to the larger strategy of which it is a part), we can clear up some confusions in the literature. To begin with, the easiest point to make is that, in societies in which actual political change proceeds by incremental steps, it is difficult to deny the frequent relevance of simple incremental analysis. If political decision makers are going to choose among incremental alternatives A, B, and C, it would seem that some analysis of just those alternatives would often be helpful.

The most frequent and basic objection is not to simple incremental analysis of incremental alternatives actually on the political agenda; it is instead to the political practice of change only by increment. That is to say, the objection is not to incremental analysis but to the incremental politics to which incremental analysis is nicely suited.

Let us therefore explicitly digress from the appraisal of incremental analysis to the appraisal of incremental politics. Much can be said both for and against the latter, and I am increasingly impressed with what must be said against those forms of it that are practiced in Western Europe and North America.

Incremental Politics

Abstractly considered, incremental politics looks very good. It is intelligently exploratory when linked with sequences of trial and error. It reduces the stakes in each political controversy, thus encouraging losers to bear their losses without disrupting the political system. It helps maintain the vague general consensus on basic values (because no specific policy issue ever centrally poses a challenge to them) that many people believe is necessary for widespread voluntary acceptance of democratic government.

Moreover, incrementalism in politics is not, in principle, slow moving. It is not necessarily, therefore, a tactic of conservatism. A fast-moving sequence of small changes can more speedily accomplish a drastic alteration of the *status quo* than can an only infrequent major policy change. If the speed of change is the product of size of step times frequency of step, incremental change patterns are, under ordinary circumstances, the fastest method of change available. One might reply of course that drastic steps in policy need be no more infrequent than incremental steps. We can be reasonably sure, however, that in almost all circumstances that suggestion is false. Incremental steps can be made quickly because they are only incremental. They do not rock the boat, do not stir up the great antagonisms and paralyzing schisms as do proposals for more drastic change.

None of this line of argument defuses the deep hostility that many people quite reasonably feel toward political incrementalism. Many people see the U.S., for example, as somehow trapped in an incremental politics that leaves its government incapable of coping effectively with big problems like environmental decay, energy shortage, inflation, and unemployment. I share their concern and would like to clarify its relation to political incrementalism.

American and Western European politics suffer from serious problem-solving disabilities. One, especially pronounced in the U.S., is the dispersion of veto powers throughout the political system. In addition to those veto powers to be found in the Constitution and in legislative procedures are those even more ubiquitous veto powers that reside in property rights. I refer not to rights you and I hold in our personal possessions but to the property rights of business enterprises, which permit, with the help of judicial interpretation, the veto of many forms of government regulation that might otherwise be attempted to cope with our problems. Even business property rights in information throw obstacles in the way of regulators who cannot obtain the necessary facts.

Perhaps a better way to put the point—simultaneously enlarging it somewhat—is to note a fundamental characteristic of politics in market-oriented systems. Having assigned many or most of the great organizing and coordinating tasks of society to business enterprises, then subjecting the managers of these enterprises to market inducements rather than commands (which the constitutional rules of these systems forbid in the main), the only way to get the assigned jobs done is to give businessmen whatever inducements will in fact motivate them to perform. That renders these political systems incapable of following many lines of policy that, however attractive they might look for, say, energy conservation or environmental protection, threaten to undercut business inducements to perform.[13]

This particular structural feature of politics in market oriented societies, as well as other difficulties in policy making, is often confused with political incrementalism. To see our difficulties clearly, the problem is not incrementalism but a structure of veto powers that makes even incremental moves difficult and insufficiently frequent. (This same structure, moreover, makes drastic, less incremental moves even more difficult—ordinarily simply impossible.) If we could imagine an incremental politics without the veto powers that now abound in it, I suggest that we would find incremental politics a suitable instrument for more effectively grappling with our problems. Whether we want to buy that gain at the price we must pay—a reduced role in the system for market enterprises—is another question.

Another source of timidity in American politics is ideological conservatism having its source in the many indoctrinations that grow out of the structure of private enterprise. It is difficult for many political leaders, and for ordinary citizens as well, to open their minds to the possibility that the American Constitution, with its many curbs on the popular will, including the Fourteenth Amendment's guarantees to corporations, is not an adequate set of rules for coping with our current great problems. It is no less difficult for them to let their minds freely explore—and reconsider the traditional justifications of—the extraordinary autonomy of the business corporation and its capacities to obstruct government problem solving.[14] Yet a high degree of homogeneity of timid political opinions is not a consequence of political incrementalism. If there is any relation between the two, political incrementalism is a consequence rather than a cause.

I think these comments rise above the dubious logic that many critics of political incrementalism have employed: U.S. policy making, which is incremental, is inadequate. Let us therefore rid ourselves of incremental politics. My head, which is covered with hair, aches. I ought to shave my scalp.

At this point it would be relevant for a critic of political incrementalism to point out that even if incrementalism is not the source of our problem of widespread vetoes and governmental timidity, nevertheless incremental politics offers us no way out—specifically, no way to reduce the veto powers. To that, several responses might be made. One is that, popular as revolutionary aspiration was among a few of our brightest young people only 10 years ago, a revolutionary cause does not have enough advocates and potential activists to warrant much consideration. It is, in any case, always a treacherous method of social change that as often disappoints its movers as gratifies them. A potentially revolutionary situation—such as a Lenin, Castro, or Mao, or a Samuel Adams or Jefferson might nurture—is not now in sight.

Perhaps then, short of revolution, we should attempt a comprehensive constitutional reform of American government? Such a proposal, if it could be made effective, falls into a category of big-step policies that strain or pass beyond the limits of incremental politics. Other big step examples would be the realization in actual operation of a comprehensive energy program, to which President Carter and many Americans aspire; or at the local level, a comprehensively planned actual rebuilding of a city, socially as well as physically; or one big integrated implemented solution to environmental decay; or an actually operative development plan for a developing country. For many people these are happy visions, but except in rare circumstances they remain impossibilities. Too many vetoes are cast against them. Too many conflicting interests pull them apart. An operative, integrated solution to a problem is a vast collection of specific commitments all of which are implemented. The odds of agreement among political elites or citizens on these vast collections are extremely slim.

Moreover, among those who draw back from agreement will be many informed and thoughtful leaders and citizens who know that many of the specific elements embraced in the integrated program are bound to be mistaken. They believe that of any large sample of attempts at social problem solving, a large number will always turn out to have missed the mark or to have worsened the situation. They will prefer to see the political system act on the elements one at a time. Not that errors will be avoided, but each element will consequently receive greater attention and will be more carefully watched for feedback and correction.[15] Again, it is because we see reason to expect such big attempts to fail that we move incrementally in politics. It is not that incremental politics is the cause of our not making such attempts.

I suggest, therefore, that, poor as it is, incremental politics ordinarily offers the best chance of introducing into the political system those changes and those change-producing intermediate changes that a discontented citizen might desire. That holds out no great hope, only as much hope as can be found in any style of American politics. If we live in a system designed by the constitutional fathers to frustrate in large part the popular will, their success in doing so reminds us that even if we attempted a new constitutional convention the same consequences might follow.

Incremental politics is also a way of "smuggling" changes into the political system. Important changes in policy and in the political system often come about quite indirectly and as a surprise to many participants in the system. That life has been heavily bureaucratized by the rise of the corporation and big government is a development that sneaked up on most citizens, who never debated the issues and who did not understand at the time that such a transformation was in process. Incremental changes add up; often more happens than meets the eye. If, on one hand, this is an objection to incremental politics, this feature of it also suggests that a skilled reformer may learn paths of indirection and surprise, thus reaching objectives that would be successfully resisted were his program more fully revealed. This possibility of course raises important issues in political morality.

One last question about incremental politics: Is it true, as often suggested in the literature of political science, that democracies are for the most part committed to change by no more than incremental moves while authoritarian governments can move with bigger steps? It seems clear that authoritarian systems themselves ordinarily move by increments. Indeed, some authoritarian systems are relatively effective in suppressing political change of any kind. The pace of change in the Soviet Union, for example, incremental or other, is not demonstrably faster than in the U.S. and may be slower. On the other hand, authoritarian systems are at least occasionally capable—apparently more often than in democratic systems—of such nonincremental change as the abrupt collectivization of agriculture in the Soviet Union and the Great Leap Forward and the Cultural Revolution in China (as well as the Holocaust and the recent destruction of Cambodia's cities and much of its population).

The most common reason alleged for democratic incapacity to act with comparable vigor on an equal number of occasions is that political change must not challenge the fundamental consensus which exists on the rules of the game and other basic values without which noncoercive democratic government is impossible. Small steps do not upset the democratic applecart; big steps do.

Although that argument may be valid, we have no solid evidence on it, and I am increasingly suspicious of it. It is too simple, assigning too much effect to a single cause. Whether a political community will be split in politically dangerous ways when larger issues, posing bigger losses and gains, move onto the political agenda depends, it would seem, on at least one other variable: how rigidly participants are attached to various causes, values, and perceptions of their own interests.

In contemporary societies, political participants are attached less by the flexible or adaptable bindings of reason than by the indoctrinations through which they have been reared: by parents and school and through the ever repeated media endorsements of the American way, private enterprise, the Constitution, and the like. It is easy to imagine a body of citizens more able than ours to cope with big issues because they are less indoctrinated, less habitual, and more thoughtful in their consideration of those issues—and, in particular, more open to alternative ways in which their needs can be met.

Hence, in a very distant future, bigger political steps may be possible—not large without constraint but perhaps significantly less incremental than at present. It is worth our thinking about, even if we cannot predict it.

Simple Incremental Analysis Again

To return from our digression into incremental politics to the further appraisal of simple incremental analysis, we must meet the objection that simple incremental analysis, like disjointed incremental analysis of which it is a part, encourages political incrementalism. The analytical habit, found as it is in politicians as well as professors, encourages us all to think small, timidly, conservatively about social change. I agree, although the causation is in both directions, and the phenomenon is something like a vicious circle.

Yet the corrective is not the suppression or neglect of incremental analysis, which remains necessary and useful for all the reasons we have given above, but the supplementation of incremental analysis by broad-ranging, often highly speculative, and sometimes utopian thinking about directions and possible features, near and far in time. Skinner's *Walden Two*, Commoner's *Poverty of Power*, Fromm's *Escape from Freedom*, Shonfield's *Modern Capitalism*, Miliband's *The State in Capitalist Society*, Rawls' *Theory of Justice*, and Rousseau's *Social Contract* illustrate the variety of inputs, great and small, necessary to thinking about policy.

Some features of such analyses are especially pertinent. They are not synoptic—not even the most broadly ambitious of them, like the Platonic dialogues or Hobbes' *Leviathan*. Much is omitted; few issues are pushed to the point of exhaustion; and we take from them not closure but new insight—specifically, powerful fragments of understanding. They are methods that liberate us from both synoptic and incremental methods of analysis.

Moreover, they give us no sound basis for policy choices. They do not seek to make a contribution to policy making by assessing the pros and cons of policy alternatives. But they do greatly raise the level of intellectual sophistication with which we think about policy. Not explicitly directed to problems in policy making, many of them need a substantial interpretation and translation before they become effective, as some do, for millions of participants in policy making.

Some of these liberating analyses have the effect less of giving us information than of making us aware, and in that lies their great effect on our minds. They tell us what we know but did not know we knew; and what we know but had not before been able to make usable.[16]

Of kinds of analysis that are neither synoptic nor incremental in intention, one modest kind frequently makes a highly valuable contribution to policy making. It is the analysis of some one or a few pivotal issues or variables critical to policy choices. To research the question, Why Johnny can't read, is to attempt neither synopsis nor incremental analysis. It is simply to try to ferret out some information or develop some understanding essential to good policy making. These modest but critical or pivotal research interventions in policy making perhaps represent professional analysis in one of its most fruitful forms. They make the kind

of contribution to which professional research is well suited, and they leave most of the evaluation of policy alternatives in the hands of politicians, administrators, which is perhaps where it belongs.

PARTISAN MUTUAL ADJUSTMENT AND PLURALISM

Some critics of incrementalism have failed to catch the distinction between political incrementalism and what in *The Intelligence of Democracy* is labeled and analyzed as partisan mutual adjustment. Partisan mutual adjustment, found in varying degrees in all political systems, takes the form of fragmented or greatly decentralized political decision making in which the various somewhat autonomous participants mutually affect one another (as they always do), with the result that policy making displays certain interesting characteristics. One is that policies are resultants of the mutual adjustment; they are better described as happening than as decided upon. Another is that policies are influenced by a broad range of participants and interests (compared to those of more centralized policy making). Another is that the connection between a policy and good reasons for it is obscure, since the many participants will act for diverse reasons.

Another is that, despite the absence or weakness of central coordination of the participants, their mutual adjustments of many kinds (of which bargaining is only one) will to some degree coordinate them as policy makers. In many circumstances their mutual adjustments will achieve a coordination superior to an attempt at central coordination, which is often so complex as to lie beyond any coordinator's competence. Such a proposition does not deny the obvious failures of coordination that mark government and are especially conspicuous in Washington. It merely claims that such coordination as, with difficulty, our governments achieve will often owe more to partisan mutual adjustment than to attempts at central coordination.

One can imagine a nation practicing political incrementalism without partisan mutual adjustment, or with only a minimum of it. One can also imagine partisan mutual adjustment for nonincremental policy making. In actual fact, the two are closely linked in all national political systems; both have the effect of reducing analytical tasks.

"Partisan mutual adjustment" pins down one meaning of "pluralism." Objections to partisan mutual adjustment, often voiced as objections to pluralism, often begin with the allegation that not all interests are represented by participants in it, nor are participants influential in proportion to the numbers of citizens for whom they act. Who can deny so obvious a point? It is not, however, a persuasive objection to partisan mutual adjustment unless it can be shown that more centralized political decision making represents a fuller array of interests and does so more consistently with principles of democratic equality. In many cases it does not. For persons committed to democracy, the case for partisan mutual adjustment versus more central forms of policy making thus turns in part on which of the two can best cope with formidable inequalities in politics. A frequent opinion that the inequalities of partisan mutual adjustment are so great that more central decision making can simply be assumed to be an improvement is simply naive. Strong central authority can be—and historically is, in case after case—an instrument for protecting historically inherited inequalities.

A second major objection to partisan mutual adjustment, again expressed ordinarily as an objection to pluralism, is that it is fraudulent. The various participants do not in fact represent the variety of interests and values of the population. Instead they share dominant interests and values, and their relations with each other give the lie to those who claim to find in pluralism a healthy competition of ideas. In the extreme form, critics allege that policy is set by a ruling class with trappings of pluralist diversity.

I find it hard to deny a large core of truth in that criticism. Let us divide policy issues into two categories: those on the ordinary questions of policy, and those that constitute the grand issues pertaining to the fundamental structure of politico-economic life. The grand issues include those on the distribution of income and wealth, on the distribution of political power, and on corporate prerogatives. On the first set, the ordinary issues, partisan mutual adjustment is active (though not without defects of inequality in participation and disturbing tendencies toward corporatism). On the grand issues, partisan mutual adjustment is weak or absent. The treatment in politics of the grand issues is governed by a high degree of homogeneity of opinion—heavily indoctrinated, I would add. As has often been pointed out, the grand issues are, thanks to a homogeneity of opinion (i.e., the failure of a competition of ideas), simply left off the agenda.[17]

A third objection to partisan mutual adjustment turns out to be an objection to its particular form in many countries, the U.S. included. It is a form in which, though none of the participants can on their own initiate a change, many or all can veto it. That is not essential to partisan mutual adjustment, but it is the way we practice it in the U.S. That fact raises the possibility that a thoughtful response to the imperfections of policy making through partisan mutual adjustment might call for changing its form or its governing rules rather than trying to suppress it. Critics of partisan mutual adjustment sometimes seem to fall into no more careful a logic than: I cannot use my car because it has a flat tire; I had better sell it.

Politics and Analysis

Confusing partisan mutual adjustment with incrementalism in its various forms, Charles L. Schultze has incorrectly associated incremental analysis (specifically disjointed incrementalism) with the crudities and irrationalities of "politics" and his more conventional forms of analysis, synoptic in ambition, with "analysis."[18] If he could make that stick—that incrementalism settles issues through power, his methods by brains—it would give him an easy victory in his attack on incrementalism. But he has made at least two mistakes.

First, analytical incrementalism is analysis. It is not simply a substitution of politics for analysis. "Incrementalism" denotes the three kinds of analysis discussed above—more modest methods than he endorses, yet nevertheless methods of analysis. What he should have said is that not incrementalism but partisan mutual adjustment is to some extent a substitution of politics for analysis. The coordination of participants is in some large part left to their political interactions with each other and, in any case, is not centrally directed analyzed coordination as coordination might be in the mind of a sufficiently cerebral coordinator. Their patterns of interaction may be designed—that is, various authorities may be required to interact with each other—or the patterns may have taken form without design. In either case, their coordination arises from their reciprocating political effects on each other, not through a centrally analyzed coordination.

Incrementalism aside, Schultze's second mistake is to miss the significance of the analytical components of partisan mutual adjustment, and indeed of all "politics." In partisan mutual adjustment and all politics, participants make heavy use of persuasion to influence each other; hence they are constantly engaged in analysis designed to find grounds on which their political adversaries or indifferent participants might be converted to allies or acquiescents.

Is that kind of analysis—partisan analysis to achieve influence in mutual adjustment—an adequate way to bring information and intelligence into policy formation? The historical concept of a competition of ideas at least vaguely recognizes its importance. Adversary proceedings in courts of law show our extreme dependence on it for some kinds of decision making. Whatever contribution interest groups make to policy making is largely through partisan analysis. I should like to suggest that partisan analysis is the most characteristic analytical input into politics and also the most productive. It is in a fuller appreciation of how partisan analysis might be improved rather than, as Schultze would seem to have it, curbed, that policy making can be made more intelligent.[19]

Finally I should like to suggest the still insufficiently explored possibilities of intelligent and democratically responsive policy making that lie in improved combinations of incremental analysis (in all of its three forms), incremental politics, and partisan mutual adjustment, including partisan analysis. The possibilities are perceived, though not fully worked out, in John Stuart Mill's *Representative Government* and in other liberal expositions of a competition of ideas linked to political education through political participation. More surprising, they appear in Maoist thought, with its emphasis on achieving economic growth not by a fine-tuning of development from above

but by tapping intelligence and incentives broadly through fragmentation of responsibility and the cumulation of fast-moving incremental gains.[20] The same new or refreshed insights now have sprung out of the tradition of orthodox economics, given a new line of development by Harvey Leibenstein and his concept of X-efficiency.[21] Even more significant for skeptics of incrementalism and partisan mutual adjustment are our new insights into how science proceeds. Conventionally synoptic or "scientific" policy making turns out not to be true to science at all.

Michael Polanyi, Lakatos, and Kuhn, among others, have been revealing that in their scientific work scientific communities themselves characteristically practice both incrementalism and partisan mutual adjustment, though by other names.[22] Even Kuhn's "scientific revolutions" are the accomplishment of partisan incrementalists. Their reconsiderations of how science is practiced are, I think, conclusive objections to the synoptic ideal.

*   *   *   *   *

I have never well understood why incrementalism in its various forms has come to so prominent a place in the policy-making literature. The original *PAR* article has been reprinted in roughly 40 anthologies. I always thought that, although some purpose was served by clarifying incremental strategies of policy analysis and policy making, to do so was only to add a touch of articulation and organization to ideas already in wide circulation. Nor have I well understood the frequency with which incremental analysis as a norm is resisted. That complex problems cannot be completely analyzed and that we therefore require strategies for skillful incompleteness still seem close to obvious to me.

I thought I ventured into territory not familiar to all social scientists and administrators only when I pointed out that fragmentation of policy making and consequent political interaction among many participants are not only methods for curbing power (as they are seen to be in a long tradition of thought incorporating both Montesquieu and the founding fathers) but are methods, in many circumstances, of raising the level of information and rationality brought to bear on decisions. That led me into examining policy analysis as itself a social process not limited to what goes on in the analyst's mind and thus to the concept of the "intelligence" of partisan mutual adjustment.

I also thought that it was useful to elaborate the ways in which social problems can often be attacked (not well but with some reduction in incompetence) by "resultants" of interaction rather than "decisions" arising out of anyone's understanding of the problem at hand. If coin tossing can settle some problems better than can futile attempts at analysis of the unanalyzable (or futile attempts at analysis when information is wholly lacking), then it is not surprising that various forms of social interaction can sometimes handle problems better than analysis can when analysis at best is grossly incomplete. Understanding a social problem is not always necessary for its amelioration—a simple fact still widely over-looked.[23]

Rather than intending to stimulate a variety of attempts to question the usefulness of incremental analysis and of partisan mutual adjustment, I had earlier hoped that the *PAR* article and subsequent publications would stimulate attempts of colleagues to articulate other strategies that avoid the impossible aspiration to synopsis, to give a more precise formulation to disjointed incrementalism as one such strategy, and to model partisan mutual adjustment as a mechanism for social "rationality" rather than as, historically, a mechanism for curbing central authority. On the whole, these hopes have been disappointed.

Some of my colleagues tell me they do not understand how—or whether!—I reconcile the benign view of pluralism to be found in my work on incrementalism and partisan mutual adjustment with the skepticism about pluralism expressed in the more recent *Politics and Markets* and its emphasis on an indoctrinated citizenry and the disproportionate political power and influence of business in politics. Do I deceive myself in believing that I have followed a consistent line of thought? As I have already noted, the policy issues that come onto the political agenda in what are called the Western democracies are almost entirely secondary issues on which policy making is indeed pluralistic, though grossly lopsided. On the grand issues that rarely come on the agenda, pluralism is weak to the point of invisibility. It is true that the earlier work emphasizes what works

(though badly) in politics, the more recent work what does not work (though it persists). In both phases or steps, I have looked for half-hidden mechanisms. The only thing I see wrong about the two steps is their order. I fear that I became braver only with age, although I should like to deny that interpretation. In any case the subtle influences and pressures of one's academic colleagues are powerful in the development of a scholar's writing and teaching. If we resist yielding to them on what we believe, we often almost unknowingly yield on what we decide to study.

To a disjointed incrementalist, there is never a last word; and these words are not intended to be a "last word in incrementalism," which I have from time to time been asked to attempt. I have only a weak grasp of the concepts here discussed. Having for some years occupied myself with politics and markets and hence subordinated my interest in the further study of incrementalism, I have now returned to the study of knowledge and analysis in policy making and other forms of social problem solving.[24] I hope to muddle through—or along.

End Notes

My thanks to James W. Fesler, David R. Mayhew, and Edward W. Pauly for their helpful comments on an earlier draft.

1. I now have an opportunity to thank William B. Shore, former managing editor of this journal, for entitling my article of 20 years ago "The Science of Muddling Through" (19 *Public Administration Review*, 1959), a title that may have contributed as much to the attention the article has received as did its contents.
2. Specifically, the conventional steps, with appropriate refinements to deal with probabilities, are:
   a. Identify and organize in some coherent relation the goal and side values pertinent to the policy choice to be made.
   b. Identify all important policy alternatives that might realize the values.
   c. Analyze all important possible consequences of each of the considered alternative policies.
   d. Choose that policy the consequences of which best match the values of step a.

3. The only substantial deepening of the idea of incrementalism that I might be able to claim in the intervening period is an attempt to place incrementalism, as well as partisan mutual adjustment, in intellectual history by showing that it conforms with a long-standing half implicit model of "good" social organization and is challenged by another. See my "Sociology of Planning: Thought and Social Interaction" in Morris Bornstein (ed.), *Economic Planning, East and West* (Cambridge, Mass.: Ballinger, 1975), subsequently revised as chapters 19 and 23 of my *Politics and Markets* (New York: Basic Books, 1977).

In the intervening years, I also spelled out disjointed incrementalism in more detail, including with the extended discussion an analysis of certain problems drawn from philosophic discourse, in David Braybrooke and Lindblom, *The Strategy of Decision* (New York: Free Press, 1963). I also developed the related analysis of partisan mutual adjustment in *The Intelligence of Democracy* (New York: Free Press, 1965).

4. And more fully in Braybrooke and Lindblom, *A Strategy of Decision*, chapter 5.

5. For illustration, familiar stratagems include trial and error, bottle-neck breaking, limitation of analysis to only a few alternatives, routinization of decisions, and focusing decision making on crises, among others.

6. In the article of 20 years ago, synopsis was called the "root" method (in contrast to "branch," which was another term for incrementalism).

7. To which are added all the complications of value analysis arising out of the elusive character of values and their resistance to "scientific" verification.

8. Herbert A. Simon, *Models of Man* (New York: John Wiley, 1957), p. 198.

9. In addition, an alternative to incrementalism as practiced is more skillful incrementalism: for example, more attention to monitoring policies for feedback and correction.

10. Herbert A. Simon, "A Behavioral Model of Rational Choice," 69 *Quarterly Journal of Economics* (February 1955).

11. Yehezkel Dror, *Public Policymaking Reexamined* (San Francisco: Chandler, 1968), chapter 14; and Amitai Etzioni,

"Mixed-scanning," 27 *Public Administration Review* 1967).

12. In Todd R. LaPorte, ed., *Organized Social Complexity* (Princeton, N.J.: Princeton University Press, 1975), p. 70.

13. Developed more completely in *Politics and Markets*, Part V.

14. See *Politics and Markets*, chapters 15 and 17.

15. That I am willing to claim, despite the obvious weaknesses of monitoring of results for feedback and correction that characterize most incremental policy making.

16. On awareness as one of two forms of knowing, see the illuminating discussion in Alvin G. Gouldner, *The Coming Crisis of Western Sociology* (New York: Basic Books, 1970), pp. 491–95; also in his *Enter Plato* (New York: Basic Books, 1965), pp. 267–72.

17. Peter Bachrach and Morton S. Baratz, "The Two Faces of Power," 56 *American Political Science Review* (December 1962).

18. Charles L. Schultze, *The Politics and Economics of Public Spending* (Washington, D.C.: Brookings, 1968), chapter 3 and *passim*.

19. For a fuller statement of reasons, see Charles E. Lindblom, *The Policy-Making Process*, 2nd edition (Englewood Cliffs, N.J.: Prentice-Hall, 1979). Schultze and I agree on at least some of the benefits to be had from one kind of partisan, the research minded "partisan for efficiency." But this very special category, illustrated by the professional economist or systems analyst, is the only category of partisan that Schultze shows much appreciation for.

20. My own thinking is indebted to Albert O. Hirschman for early alerting me to the importance of problem-solving incentives, in addition to intellectual capacity, in complex problems solving. See Albert O. Hirschman and Charles E. Lindblom, "Economic Development, Research and Development, Policy Making: Some Converging Views," *Behavioral Science* (April 1962).

21. Harvey Leibenstein, "Allocative Efficiency vs. 'X-Efficiency,' " *American Economic Review* 56 (June 1966). Also his *Beyond Economic Man* (Cambridge, Mass.: Harvard University Press, 1976).

22. Michael Polanyi, "The Republic of Science," I *Minerva* (Autumn 1962); Imre Lakatos and Alan Musgrave (eds.), *Criticism and the*

Growth of Knowledge (Cambridge: Cambridge University Press, 1970); Thomas S. Kuhn, *The Structure of Scientific Revolutions*, 2nd edition (Chicago: University of Chicago Press, 1970). See also, for a detailed empirical study of incrementalism, partisan mutual adjustment, and partisan analysis—especially the latter—Ian

Mitroff, *The Subjective Side of Science* (New York: Elsevier, 1974).

23. Further developed in Charles E. Lindblom and David K. Cohen, *Usable Knowledge* (New Haven: Yale University Press, 1979), pp. 19–29.

24. As a beginning, Lindblom and Cohen, *Usable Knowledge*.

6

Group Politics and Representative Democracy

David B. Truman

"Group organization," said the late Robert Luce, momentarily dropping his usually cautious phrasing, "is one of the perils of the times."[1] The scholarly Yankee legislator's opinion has been echoed and re-echoed, sometimes in qualified and sometimes in categorical terms, by an impressive number of journalists, academicians, and politicians. The common themes running through most of these treatments are: alarm at the rapid multiplication of organized groups; an explicit or, more frequently, an implicit suggestion that the institutions of government have no alternative but passive submission to specialized group demands; and an admonition that the stability or continuance of democracy depends upon a spontaneous, self-imposed restraint in advancing group demands. Thus we are told that "there is no escape from the pressure of organized power...," that the pitiful plight of American government is that "there is nothing it can do to protect itself from pressures...," and that unless these groups "face the

kind of world they are living in...." it will be only a matter of time "until somebody comes riding in on a white horse."[2]

We have seen earlier that the vast multiplication of interests and organized groups in recent decades is not a peculiarly American phenomenon. The causes of this growth lie in the increased complexity of techniques for dealing with the environment, in the specializations that these involve, and in associated disturbances of the manifold expectations that guide individual behavior in a complex and interdependent society. Complexity of technique, broadly conceived, is inseparable from complexity of social structure. This linkage we observe in industrialized societies the world over. In the United States the multiplicity of interests and groups not only has been fostered by the extent of technical specialization but also has been stimulated by the diversity of the social patterns that these changes affect and by established political practices such as those that permit ease and freedom of association. Diversity of interests is a concomitant of specialized activity, and diversity of groups is a means of adjustment.

We have also seen that the institutions of government in the United States have reflected both the number and the variety of interests in the society and that this responsiveness is not essentially a modern feature of our politics. We have argued, in fact, that the behaviors that constitute the process of government cannot be adequately understood apart from the groups, especially the organized and potential interest groups, which are operative at any point in time. Whether we look at an individual citizen, at the executive secretary of a trade association, at a political party functionary, at a legislator, administrator, governor, or judge, we cannot describe his participation in the governmental institution, let alone account for it, except in terms of the interest with which he identifies himself and the groups with which he affiliates and with which he is confronted. These groups may or may not be interest groups, and all the interests he holds may not be represented at a given point in time by organized units. Organized interest groups, however, from their very nature bulk large in the political process. Collections of individuals interacting on the basis of shared attitudes and exerting claims upon other groups in the society usually find in the institutions of government an important means of achieving their objectives. That is, most interest groups become politicized on a continuing or intermittent basis. In this respect, therefore, such organized groups are as clearly a part of the governmental institution as are the political parties or the branches formally established by law or constitution.

The activities of political interest groups imply controversy and conflict, the essence of politics. For those who abhor conflict in any form, who long for some past or future golden age of perfect harmony, these consequences of group activity are alone sufficient to provoke denunciation. Such people look upon any groups or activities, except those to which they are accustomed, as signs of degeneration, and they view with alarm the appearance upon the political scene of new and insistent claimants. Objections from

these sources are part of the peripheral data of politics, but they offer little to an understanding of the process. There are other people, however, who do not shrink from controversy and who are ready to assume that politics inevitably emerges out of men's specialized experiences and selective perceptions. For many of these observers the kinds of activity described ... are a source of concern. They listen receptively if not with pleasure to alarms like those quoted at the opening of this chapter. They see a possibility that the pursuits of organized interest groups may produce a situation of such chaos and indecision that representative government and its values may somehow be lost. With such concerns we may appropriately reckon.

INTEREST GROUPS AND THE NATURE OF THE STATE

Predictions concerning the consequences of given political activities are based upon conceptions of the governmental process. Predictions of any sort, of course, are outgrowths of understandings concerning the process to which the anticipated events are related. When the physiologist predicts that the consumption of a quantity of alcohol will have certain effects upon an individual's reflexes, when the chemist predicts that the application of heat to a particular mixture of substances will produce an explosion, and when the astronomer predicts that on a certain date there will occur an eclipse of the sun that will be visible from particular points on the earth's surface, each is basing his anticipation on a conception or an understanding of the respective somatic, chemical, and astronomical processes. Political prediction is no different. When an observer of the governmental scene says that the activities of organized political interest groups will result in the eclipse of certain behaviors subsumed under the heading of representative government, his statement reflects a conception of the dynamics of human relationships. Other elements enter into his prediction, but some such conception is basic to it.

A major difficulty in political prediction is that, in part because the relevant processes are extremely complex, our understanding of them is often not adequate; that is, the conceptions do not always account for all the variables and specify their relative importance. Such conceptions being inadequate in these respects, predictions based upon them are not reliable. Their accuracy is in large measure a matter of chance.[3] There are many people, both laymen and professional students of government, who argue that the complexity and irregularity of the political process are such that the reliability of predictions in this area will always be of a low order. We need not enter this controversy in these pages; one's position on the issue is in any case largely a matter of faith. We cannot, however, escape the necessity to predict. Government officials and private citizens must anticipate as best they can the consequences of political actions with which they are involved, though such predictions may have to rely heavily upon hunch, intuition, or calculated risk. In a good many cases our largely unformulated conceptions of the political process in America are adequate for prediction. For example, in every presidential election except that of 1860 one could have predicted, and many people tacitly did predict, that, whichever candidate was successful, his opponents and their supporters would not appeal from the decision of the ballot box to that of open violence. In many controversial areas of political behavior, however, our conceptions are almost completely lacking in predictive value.

A second handicap in political prediction is that the underlying conceptions are often almost completely implicit. They involve an array of partial and mutually contradictory assumptions of which the prophet is only dimly aware and of which many are derived from uncritically accepted myths and folklore concerning the political process in America. Predictions that are based upon such ill-formed, incomplete, and inaccurate premises are bound to be highly unreliable. Except as these unarticulated conceptions by chance happen to conform adequately to reality, they are a treacherous foundation for predictive statements. Many, if not most, predictions about the significance and implications of organized interest groups on the American scene rest on unreliable, implicit conceptions. To the extent that such statements are intended merely

as a means of increasing or reducing the relative strength of competing interest groups, they may be evaluated wholly in terms of their effectiveness for that purpose. If they are presented, however, as systematic and responsible prognostications, they must be examined as such. In a large proportion of cases they will be found to rely on a flimsy conceptual structure, on a hopelessly inadequate and unacknowledged theory of the political process....

Men, wherever they are observed, are creatures participating in those established patterns of interaction that we call groups. Excepting perhaps the most casual and transitory, these continuing interactions, like all such interpersonal relationships, involve power. This power is exhibited in two closely interdependent ways. In the first place, the group exerts power over its members; an individual's group affiliations largely determine his attitudes, values, and the frames of reference in terms of which he interprets his experiences. For a measure of conformity to the norms of the group is the price of acceptance within it. Such power is exerted not only by an individual's present group relationships; it also may derive from past affiliations such as the childhood family as well as from groups to which the individual aspires to belong and whose characteristic shared attitudes he also holds. In the second place, the group, if it is or becomes an interest group, which any group in a society may be, exerts power over other groups in the society when it successfully imposes claims upon them.

Many interest groups, probably an increasing proportion in the United States, are politicized. That is, either from the outset or from time to time in the course of their development they make their claims through or upon the institutions of government. Both the forms and functions of government in turn are a reflection of the activities and claims of such groups. The constitution-writing proclivities of Americans clearly reveal the influence of demands from such sources, and the statutory creation of new functions reflects their continuing operation. Many of these forms and functions have received such widespread acceptance from the start or in the course of time that they appear to be independent of the overt activities of organized interest groups. The judiciary is such a form. The building of city streets and the control of vehicular traffic are examples of such a function. However, if the judiciary or a segment of it operates in a fashion sharply contrary to the expectations of an appreciable portion of the community or if its role is strongly attacked, the group basis of its structure and powers is likely to become apparent. Similarly, if street construction greatly increases tax rates or if the control of traffic unnecessarily inconveniences either pedestrians or motorists, the exposure of these functions to the demands of competing interests will not be obscure. Interests that are widely held in the society may be reflected in government without their being organized in groups. They are what we have called potential groups. If the claims implied by the interests of these potential groups are quickly and adequately represented, interaction among those people who share the underlying interests or attitudes is unnecessary. But the interest base of accepted governmental forms and functions and their potential involvement in overt group activities are ever present even when not patently operative.

The institutions of government are centers of interest-based power; their connections with interest groups may be latent or overt and their activities range in political character from the routinized and widely accepted to the unstable and highly controversial. In order to make claims, political interest groups will seek access to the key points of decision within these institutions. Such points are scattered throughout the structure, including not only the formally established branches of government but also the political parties in their various forms and the relationships between governmental units and other interest groups.

The extent to which a group achieves effective access to the institutions of government is the resultant of a complex of interdependent factors. For the sake of simplicity these may be classified in three somewhat overlapping categories: (1) factors relating to a group's strategic position in the society; (2) factors associated with the internal characteristics of the group; and (3) factors peculiar to the governmental institutions themselves. In the first category are: the group's status or prestige in the society, affecting the ease with which it commands deference from those outside its bounds; the standing it and its activities have when measured against the widely held but largely unorganized interests or "rules of the game"; the extent to which government officials are formally or informally "members" of the group; and the usefulness of the group as a source of technical and political knowledge. The second category includes: the degree and appropriateness of the group's organization; the degree of cohesion it can achieve in a given situation, especially in the light of competing group demands upon its membership; the skills of the leadership; and the group's resources in numbers and money. In the third category are: the operating structure of the government institutions, since such established features involve relatively fixed advantages and handicaps; and the effects of the group life of particular units or branches of the government.

The product of effective access, of the claims of organized and unorganized interests that achieve access with varying degrees of effectiveness, is a governmental decision. Note that these interests that achieve effective access and guide decisions need not be "selfish," are not necessarily solidly unified, and may not be represented by organized groups. Governmental decisions are the resultant of effective access by various interests, of which organized groups may be only a segment. These decisions may be more or less stable depending on the strength of supporting interests and on the severity of disturbances in the society which affect that strength.

A characteristic feature of the governmental system in the United States is that it contains a multiplicity of points of access. The federal system establishes decentralized and more or less independent centers of power, vantage points from which to secure privileged access to the national government. Both a sign and a cause of the strength of the constituent units in the federal scheme is the peculiar character of our party system, which has strengthened parochial relationships, especially those of national legislators. National parties, and to a lesser degree those in the States, tend to be poorly cohesive leagues of locally based organizations rather than unified and inclusive structures. Staggered terms for executive officials and various types of legislators accentuate differences in the effective electorates that participate in choosing these officers. Each of these different, often opposite, localized patterns (constituencies) is a channel of independent access to the larger party aggregation and to the formal government. Thus, especially at the national level, the party is an electing-device and only in limited measure an integrated means of policy determination. Within the Congress, furthermore, controls are diffused among committee chairmen and other leaders in both chambers. The variety of these points of access is further supported by relationships stemming from the constitutional doctrine of the separation of powers, from related checks and balances, and at the State and local level from the common practice of choosing an array of executive officials by popular election. At the Federal level the formal simplicity of the executive branch has been complicated by a Supreme Court decision that has placed a number of administrative agencies beyond the removal power of the president. The position of these units, however, differs only in degree from that of many that are constitutionally within the executive branch. In consequence of alternative lines of access available through the legislature and the executive and of divided channels for the control of administrative policy, many nominally executive agencies are at various times virtually independent of the chief executive.

Although some of these lines of access may operate in series, they are not arranged in a stable and integrated hierarchy. Depending upon the whole political context in a given period and upon the relative strength of contending interests, one or another of the centers of power in the formal government or in the parties may become the apex of a hierarchy of controls. Only the highly routinized governmental activities show any stability in this respect, and these may as easily be subordinated to elements in the legislature as to the chief executive. Within limits, therefore, organized interest groups, gravitating toward responsive points of decision, may play one segment of the structure against another as circumstances and strategic considerations permit. The total pattern of government over a period of time thus presents a protean complex of crisscrossing relationships that change in strength and direction with alterations in the power and standing of interests, organized and unorganized....

End Notes

1. Luce: *Legislative Assemblies*, p. 421.
2. These three quotations, taken somewhat unfairly from their contexts, are, respectively, from Harvey Fergusson: *People and Power* (New York: William Morrow & Company, 1947), p. 101; J. H. Spigelman: "The Protection of Society," *Harper's Magazine* (July, 1946), p. 6; and Stuart Chase: *Democracy Under Pressure: Special Interests vs. The Public Welfare* (New York: The Twentieth Century Fund, 1945), p. 8. Cf. Robert C. Angell: *The Integration of American Society* (New York: McGraw-Hill Book Company, 1941); Brady: *Business as a System of Power*; and John Maurice Clark: *Alternative to Serfdom* (New York: Alfred A. Knopf, Inc., 1948).
3. Cf. David B. Truman: "Political Behavior and Voting," in Mosteller *et al.*: *The Pre-election Polls of 1948*, pp. 225–50.

7

Neopluralism

Andrew S. McFarland

INTRODUCTION

"Neopluralism" has several overlapping meanings. The term can refer to one of several models of power in a local, national, or policy system: elitism, pluralism, neopluralism, corporatism, statism, clientelism, consociationism. The term can focus on the pluralist theory of political power as set forth by Robert A. Dahl in *Who Governs?* and hence refer to revived formulations of this outlook, setting forth more sophisticated methods and conclusions. Neopluralism more specifically can refer to the observation that Dahl's (1961) formulation of theoretical and methodological elements, known as pluralist theory, has been used in modified forms by researchers in the areas of public policy making, urban politics, and interest groups ever since the publication of *Who Governs?* in 1961.

Accordingly, this essay begins with an analysis of Dahl's pluralist theory. It then reviews the challenge to pluralist theory as set forth by Lowi (1964, 1969, 1979), Olson (1965), and others in the viewpoint variously described as theories of subgovernments, clientelism, and interest group liberalism, although I use the term multiple elitism. Next, the essay proceeds to the challenge posed to multiple elitism termed neopluralism, which only partially resembles Dahl's pluralism. Then I examine characteristics of neopluralism that make it something more than just another model in the line-up of models of power. A major conclusion is that this sequence of scholarship proceeding from Dahl provides the basis for a general theory of the political process.

To prevent confusion, one must first point out that there are no fewer than five usages of the term pluralism in the literatures of the social sciences and philosophy. As used herein, pluralism refers to the most common usage by political scientists since 1961, that is, referring to the theory of political power set forth by Dahl in *Who Governs?*. Dahl's usage was emulated by numerous political scientists until this pluralist theory came under serious criticism at the end of the 1960s. The usage referring to Dahl's theory differs from reference to the group theories of Truman (1951) and other political scientists in the 1950s, who stressed the primacy of interest groups in determining policy outcomes in American politics. A common error among scholars not very familiar with this literature is to assume that Dahl was also a pluralist in the group theory sense, but in truth, he was not (see below). Truman's group theory was dubbed pluralism because it was an empirical theory that stressed the role of groups, as had the political theory of the British philosopher Harold Laski a generation earlier (Laski 1921). Laski downgraded the normative role of state sovereignty in comparison to the importance of social groupings, and his theory was called pluralism (although Laski himself later became a leading Marxist). Sociologists also use the term pluralism when referring to social diversity, such as in reference to pluralist societies, perhaps containing many ethnic and religious groups. Sociologists sometimes use the term in referring to social theory that stresses the significance of social groups, as did Tocqueville. Finally, during the past 20 years, "pluralism" has come to mean political theories that emphasize the value of promoting distinctive gender and ethnic identity, implying that public policies should promote such pluralism as social diversity (Connolly 2005). Having pointed out these sources of confusion, I reiterate that pluralism and neopluralism in this essay refer to the pluralist theory of political power set forth by Dahl and to revisions of Dahl's theory by a generation of research successors.

DAHL'S PLURALISM: FOUR BASIC CONCEPTS

Dahl's pluralism is posited on four basic concepts, which have formed a template for much political science research since the publication of *Who Governs?*. They have served as assumptions for many of the subsequent critics of Dahl's theory, such as Lowi; and they are still used by neopluralists and others as a basis for a political process paradigm.

Power as Causation

A definition of power was a key element in Dahl's construction of pluralist theory. With the definition of power as causation, Dahl brought together two strands of academic discussion during the 1950s. *The Power Elite* by Mills (1956) argued that America is ruled by three connected elites: the executives of the largest corporations, those at the top of the executive branch of the U.S. government, and leading officers of the U.S. military. This book immediately was assigned in many undergraduate classes and was widely read by intellectuals outside of academia. A few years earlier, social science leaders Harold Lasswell (Lasswell & Kaplan 1950) and Herbert Simon (1953) had put forth a definition of power intended to serve as a basis for a more analytical political science discipline. Dahl picked up the Lasswell-Simon definition of power as causation and made it a basis of his *Who Governs?* study, the pluralist alternative to Mills' power-elite study.

The definition of power as causation states that *A* has power over *B* to the extent that *A* causes changes in *B*'s behavior in the direction of *A*'s intentions. For instance, when Dahl studied the urban renewal decision-making process he found that the New Haven mayor tended to realize his intentions by getting other actors to do what he wanted. Dahl (1961) defines this as political power. Power here is seen as causing changes in the behavior of others. Clearly the role of intentions is a sticky issue. Actor *A* might cause changes in the behavior of others simply by acting, but those changes might not be the ones *A* favors. In such cases, most would speak of *A* exercising "influence" by causing changes in behavior, even if *A* opposed those changes. But it seems, following Max Weber, that it is best to use "power" to refer to changes intended by the actor, and to reserve "influence" to refer to any behavioral change. Lasswell, Simon, March, and Dahl introduced the causal definition of power to American politics researchers without at first making a distinction between power and influence. Dahl and others later came to see the distinction as necessary (Weber 1946; Lasswell & Kaplan 1950; Simon 1953; March 1955; Dahl 1957, 1961, 1968; McFarland 2004).

The definition of power as causation is certainly not universal. Structural theorists tend to use "power" to refer to the control of resources, such as money and property (Polsby 1980), or, in the realm of international relations, military and economic capability (Morgenthau 1964). However, pluralists refer to these items as "resources" to be used in the pursuit of power; for example, military capability might be a resource used by one nation-state to threaten an opposing nation-state and make it comply with the policy of the first.

The Political Process Model

A second basic concept in Dahl's pluralism is the political process model. A researcher may describe a political or policy-making process or activity and then refer to the actors within that process as having power, in terms of whether the actors caused others to change their behavior. Dahl thus described political processes in *Who Governs?*. In 1961, concepts of political process were seen as empirical and innovative, as part of "the behavioral revolution" of empiricism within political science. Studies of political process relied on empirical observation of activities over time, in contrast to the preceding modes of inquiry based on textual analysis of law and constitutional traditions, description of the legal forms of state institutions, and philosophical inquiry into the nature of justice and other social values. Accordingly, two leading American exponents of empiricism in political science, Arthur F. Bentley and David B. Truman, entitled their major works *The Process of Government* and *The Governmental Process*, respectively (Bentley 1967 [1908], Truman 1951). During the 1950s, Truman's book was often regarded by scholars as the leading theoretical work on American politics, and political scientists of that era often used the term "process" in book titles and course descriptions. Dahl adopted the basic Bentley-Truman model of the political process but did not adopt the more extreme assertions of this model, in which process was claimed to be everything, and in which institutions, laws, and political culture were viewed as artifacts of the political process. Dahl described political campaigning, public policy making, bargaining among elites, and interest group behavior as political processes, but he viewed political institutions and political culture as more fixed and as responding to social changes such as economic and technical changes, cultural factors, and demography. Moreover, even within such areas as public policy making and elite bargaining, Dahl rejected the extreme Bentley-Truman viewpoint that political groups could be assumed to be the most important variable in causing outcomes, as, for instance, individual voting decisions might play an important role in elections.

Nevertheless, the political process model is a basic concept of Dahl's pluralism. Following Bentley and Truman, this model is characterized by a combination of the following elements:

1. Empirical observation indicates agents acting within a policy system.
2. These agents are seen as groups and individuals representing group interests.
3. The agents interact and affect one another's behavior.

4. The agents pursue their interests, defined according to the agents' own definitions of interest, although sometimes these must be inferred from their behavior.
5. Interests frequently change in the process of interaction among the agents over time.
6. Implicit in the foregoing, empirical observation should continue over a period sufficient to understand fluctuations in power, interest groups, and policy-making activities.

As Polsby (2006) notes, pluralist research usually tries to trace events back in time to decide who caused what to happen in the search for power. The political process model is normally complex; it normally has many units, many interrelationships that shift over time, and interests (goals) that are frequently redefined by the interacting agents. In some cases, however, there might be only a few agents, as for instance, it might be observed that one group consistently defeats a second group or just a few groups. The existence of a power elite can be empirically observed, if one group consistently defeats other groups.

Separate Domains of Political Processes

The third element of Dahl's pluralism is that power as causation and the political process model are applied to specific domains of politics and policy making. This is linked to the definition of power as causation and the empirical assumption that power might differ in different domains or fields of activity. Alternatively, of course, power might be the same in major domains, corresponding to the empirical finding that a power elite exists in a given system. In Dahl's pluralism, the political system is seen as divided into numerous separate policy areas (there may not be so many at the local level). Dahl assumed that the structure of power and the nature of the process might vary in different policy areas. One has to observe the various areas to find out. Of course, previous research may lead one to expect a particular pattern of power and process, but someone sometime had to do an empirical study to establish such a conclusion. This third assumption represents a commitment to one view of empiricism, emphasizing the need to observe (or at least study) actual political processes, and a reluctance to accept quick generalizations about power and policy making. It is a rejection of research postulating that the accumulation of wealth (Marx) or the holding of top hierarchical positions (Michels 1959) is all one needs to know about to describe the holding of political power.

Reliance on Actors' Definition of Their Own Interests

Dahl's fourth assumption is that researchers should accept the definitions of interest given by the subjects themselves, or perhaps as inferred from observations of subjects' patterns of behavior. Clearly, this assumption rules out notions of class in the Marxist sense (Balbus 1971). But this definition of interest as understood by the subjects themselves also rules out concepts of quiescence—the idea that some subjects should make an issue out of something but are not observed doing so. A writer such as John Gaventa might argue that poor coal miners should be protesting working and housing conditions, even if they are not actually doing so, and that such quiescence is the key issue in studying power. The pluralists of the 1960s called this the problem of "nonissues" and maintained that specifying a list of nonissues embodied value assumptions that could lead to biased research (Bachrach & Baratz 1962, Lukes 1974, Gaventa 1980, Polsby 1980).

WHO GOVERNS? THE PLURALIST THEORY OF POWER

From a perspective of 45 years, the statement of these interlinked four concepts is a contribution to political science as important as Dahl's refutation of Mills' power-elite theory in *Who Governs?*. The criticism of Mills and the statement of pluralist political power are of course based on the use of these four related concepts. These concepts were retained as a theoretical template by many of the critics of Dahl's pluralism and have continued to be assumed by the later writers termed neopluralists. Later in this essay I mention misinterpretations of Dahl's statement of political pluralism and discuss at greater length the better-substantiated criticisms of this pluralist theory.

In *Who Governs?* Dahl assumed a political process model for his three case studies of the urban renewal, public education, and primary elections domains for the exercise of political power. Dahl traced the recent histories of these three issue-area domains and identified individuals wielding power by gaining their way against opposition, thereby changing the course of events within the case-study issue domain. He took self-identified interests and goals for granted as the subject of research, and accepted the views of political activists that these were likely the three most important issues. As is widely remembered, Dahl found that different persons held power in the different issue domains, with the exception of the mayor, who was powerful in all three of them. There was not a single Millsian power elite. On the other hand, the urban political system was not authoritarian, because the mayor was checked by voters, who could eliminate his power in competitive primary and general elections. Accordingly, the mayor was accountable to the voters and was checked by the need to anticipate the opinions of the voters. One could then conclude that power in New Haven is not held by a power elite but is "pluralist." In other words, power is fragmented, although sometimes partially concentrated in the hands of the mayor, who is, however, held accountable through competitive elections.

Thus Dahl established this pluralist research procedure, implying the importance of doing case studies of the political process. Political issues are identified as those important to the people being studied. Power as causation implies the necessity of observing a flow of events or reconstructing a history of past events. Power is seen as divisible by issue area and so cannot be generalized from one issue area without empirical confirmation.

The techniques for case studies of politics were straightforward. Essentially, the scholar assembled a history of a sequence of political events. To do a history, one interviewed participants, collected documents issued by political participants, read newspapers and official records, and, if possible, directly observed political meetings and other events that were part of the history. The concern about causation did not rule out the communication of the ambience of political events; good writing and readability were valued.

Pluralists sometimes conducted relatively simple surveys about political participation and elections in local communities. Following Dahl, pluralists tended to pay special attention to individual politicians, their motivations, and their political strategies. Presidents, mayors, members of the U.S. Congress, state legislators, and bureaucrats were studied as political entrepreneurs assembling political resources to gain power, often to please constituents and thus to keep their jobs. City and town political organizations were another favorite topic of study; these were regarded as organizational entrepreneurs assembling resources to gain support and to win elections, sometimes thereby representing the working classes and assimilating immigrants into the American system (Wildavsky 1964a; Polsby 1971, 1980).

Such methods and concepts could be applied to most sectors of political life in America. There were pluralist studies of cities, local communities, and different issue areas both nationally and locally (Polsby 1980). Pluralist studies of the president and of mayors sometimes found them to be powerful, yet contained within a bureaucratic system of politics (Allison 1971). Political party organizations were studied in pluralistic terms (Greenstein 1963). Congress and other legislatures were studied in terms of centralization and decentralization of power (Polsby 1971). In studying federalism, pluralists assumed a political process divided into issue areas and conducted an empirical study of the relative power (causation) of central government versus state and local governments (Grodzins 1960). Pluralists studied attempts to centralize power in administrative management systems: planning, budgeting, management by objective, government reorganization, and so forth (Braybrooke & Lindblom 1963; Wildavsky 1964b, 1979; Lindblom 1965).

This pluralist theory of power did achieve some apparently permanent success. For the next 30 years, political scientists eschewed elitist or power-elite explanations of political processes. Power-elite theories of community power have been supplanted. Those interested in social elites started in the 1970s to analyze elites in terms of network theory, based on aggregating the frequency of communication among individuals or units, and then depicting such communication networks as a mathematical theory of social structure (Laumann & Knoke 1987).

MULTIPLE-ELITE THEORY

Although Dahl's pluralist theory had several major problems, most have been dealt with in subsequent neopluralist and political process research (see below). One problem in Dahl's work provided an opening for what I term "multiple-elite theory." Dahl found fragmented power in the three issue areas of *Who Governs?* except that the mayor exercised some power in all three issue areas. In turn, the mayor was controlled by voters in competitive elections. But could there not be policy systems in which a few persons or groups exercised power without any higher democratic authority to check them? Could not a particular group or coalition rule a specific issue area to the exclusion of higher democratic authority, such as chief executives, legislatures, or even higher courts? Moreover, a political system might have competitive elections for its chief executive and for its legislature, but such officials, selected by the entire citizenry, might lack control over some particular policy areas.

This was the argument made by multiple-elite theorists. Such writers sided with Dahl against Mills; they seldom observed single power elites in the United States. However, they differed from Dahl in arguing the general significance of multiple independent elites, each particular to specific policy areas, within the fragmentation of power found by Dahl. Multiple-elite theorists normally argued that this fragmentation of power led to unrepresentative government of special interests, controlling policy in a particular area to the detriment of diffused public interests.

Without using the terminology of "special interests," Dahl's colleague at Yale, Herbert Kaufman, joined Wallace Sayre of Columbia, along with research assistant Theodore Lowi, to study policy making in New York City. These authors observed islands of power within the city's policy processes, meaning that the Board of Education and the Port Authority had great power within their respective issue areas and that the mayor lacked control over these semiautonomous bodies. Sayre & Kaufman (1960) and Lowi (1964b), however, used the same research procedures as Dahl.

In a classic article, Lowi (1964a) argued that pluralism-elitism varied with the type of policy process in a discrete area. Pluralism might indeed be descriptive, Lowi argued, in policy areas focused on regulation, such as when the federal government regulates working conditions, producing an interest group politics of countervailing business and labor groups. But, Lowi argued, other policy areas might ordinarily be controlled by a narrow coalition seeking to direct the distribution of discrete benefits by government, such as the purchase of expensive military aircraft.

Multiple-elite theorists emphasized the finding that oligarchical coalitions tend to control a particular area of policy making. For instance, one might say that a coalition of trucking companies, the teamsters' union, and sympathetic Interstate Commerce Commission personnel controlled the regulation of interstate trucking. This is an example of what might be termed an "island of oligarchy." Rule by the few exists, but it is limited to a single policy area.

Such multiple-elite writers found islands of oligarchy in many areas: federal public works construction (pork barrel); the Port Authority in New York City; the antimonopoly policy of the Federal Trade Commission; and the regulation of airlines, trucking, local and long-distance telephone carriers, and railroads before their defeat by trucking interests (Maass 1951, Bernstein 1955, Sayre & Kaufman 1960, Redford 1969, Stigler 1975). Defense contracting was another area in which collaboration among defense industries, the Pentagon, and members of Congress with relevant constituencies seemed to be common. Agriculture was seen as rife with islands of oligarchy: the Farm Bureau (the center of many little governments), tobacco production, sugar production, orange production in the Sunkist cooperative, peanut production, the distribution of cheap grazing rights on federal lands, the distribution of subsidies for conservation projects such as farm ponds, the regulation of water sales from federal irrigation projects, and the distribution of benefits of the multipurpose Tennessee Valley Authority's economic development program (Selznick 1953; Foss 1960; Cater 1964; McConnell 1966; Lowi 1969, 1979). The regulation of the insurance industry by state governments was seen as another example (Orren 1974). Such research posits an alternative to Dahl's theory of political power. However, multiple-elite theory research explicitly or implicitly was based on the template of four assumptions set forth by Dahl: the need for empirical study of political process, power as causing change in the process, separability of policy domains, and interests as defined by the actors themselves.

Besides islands of oligarchy, another major new idea put forth by multiple-elite theory was Olson's (1965) logic of collective action. Olson's was the best single theory to explain the existence of islands of oligarchy. Olson based collective action theory on the sort of economic theory just considered. Oligopolies produce a collective benefit for constituent units (although not for the public), as a few units cooperate to restrict production and raise prices. But as the number of producer units increases, it becomes more difficult to collude to restrict production, because some firms will leave the production restriction to others and produce more to obtain higher profits for themselves in the short run. Similarly, Olson reasoned, a few units will contribute to support a political lobby, but as the number of units increases, they will all try to be free riders, and the lobby will get no contributions. Olson concluded that a lobby with a large number of units could exist only if an interest group offered benefits that were restricted to its members—for example, the discounts available exclusively to members of the American Association of Retired Persons—and then put some of the group's resources to work in lobbying.

The logic of collective action therefore predicted that lobbies for consumers, victims of pollution, and other constituencies of perhaps a hundred or more units would not exist unless they provided members with selective benefits worth more than the cost of joining. Collective action theory predicted, in contrast, that small groups of producers would collude to form lobbies to work in their interests, and therefore "the few would defeat the many," in Olson's terminology.

The few would defeat the many by controlling particular policy areas of regulation, for instance, through lobbying and forming a dominant coalition, whereas the more numerous constituents on the public side would be unable to organize. Such an argument would apply to much government regulation of business, such as the regulation of prices, pollution, service, and safety. It could also be applied to agricultural policy, especially insofar as local farm elites captured policy administration. It could be applied to public works construction, as beneficiaries of construction form public coalitions to maintain spending. The logic of collective action was a persuasive argument on behalf of multiple-elite theory.

Olson later published an application of his logic of collective action to explain declines in economic growth in societies other than the United States, as well as declines of growth in some areas within the United States, by positing that institutionalization of special interest political power creates oligopolistic inefficiencies (Olson 1982). Because it was tied to explaining economic growth, Olson's general work had little influence on discussions about neopluralist political power.

Along with Olson's *The Logic of Collective Action*, Lowi's *The End of Liberalism* [1979 (1969)] has been the most widely read and influential work of multiple-elite theory. Lowi did not refer to Olson's theory but alluded to about 30 case studies of political power in specific issue domains, apparently agreeing to the four assumptions used by Dahl and the pluralists in the study of political process. But Lowi's findings were quite different from those of the pluralists.

Lowi drew a general interpretation of American politics based on multiple-elite theory. He argued that the American political process had become suffused with the public philosophy of interest group liberalism, not in the sense of the Democratic Party, but in the sense of political philosophy. In its academic usage, "liberal" refers to scholars who define democracy according to some process of decision making, rather than referring to standards of justice in the substance of government action. Lowi argued that interest group liberalism in the process sense had come to permeate the values of legislative, executive, and judicial decision makers in American government, so that laws were written and interpreted without useful reference to clear standards of justice and administration. He argued that, as a consequence, lower-level executive decision makers interpreted the practical meaning of legislation after a process of bargaining with organized interest groups, thereby forming a special interest policy-making coalition specific to a particular area of public policy. Consequently, American public policy making is rife with particularistic policy coalitions, forming multiple elites within the overall system. To reform interest group liberalism, Lowi advocated institutional changes to promote the statement of clear standards in legislation and administration of public policy, such as judicial prohibition of legislation lacking such clear standards.

NEOPLURALISM VERSUS MULTIPLE-ELITE THEORY

The multiple-elite researchers observed elite coalitions controlling specific issue domains without checks from executive or legislative authority, thereby contradicting Dahl's pluralist theory. Analogously, neopluralist researchers observed that such subgovernments of multiple-elite research were not the most frequent pattern of power within issue domains, more frequently characterized by multiple opposed interest groups. Moreover, the neopluralists derived theories to deal with the implication of Olson's logic of collective action that few groups representing diffused interests would organize and maintain themselves. Neopluralists were careful to note that their observation of a proliferation of groups did not imply a fair and representative policy-making process in some issue domain. Neopluralist observations were largely based on individual studies of policy making in particular issue areas, supplemented by theories of why collective action is possible despite free riders in respect to public goods provided by lobbies. Such studies tended to appear between 1975 and 1985, in response to the research sequence set forth by Dahl's political pluralism and its critique by Lowi and Olson.

For example, in the issue domain of air pollution, studies by Jones (1975), Ornstein & Elder (1978), Ackerman & Hassler (1981), and Wenner (1982) all found that environmentalist groups have significant effects on public policy. Other authors (Berry 1977, McFarland 1984, Mitchell

1984, Nadel 1971, Vogel 1980/1981) chronicled the significant strength of public interest lobbies. Still others (Freeman 1975, Costain & Costain 1983, Klein 1984, Gelb & Palley 1982) found women's lobbies to be important. McCarthy & Zald (1977) generalized from such observations to develop the resource mobilization theory of social movements, which implies that movements frequently create lobbying organizations. Beer (1976), Haider (1974), and others described the phenomenon of governments lobbying other governments—associations of cities, counties, and so forth lobbying in Washington and elsewhere. Walker (1983) and his collaborators (Gais et al. 1984) found a great increase in lobbying by nonprofit organizations (e.g., churches, hospitals, and colleges); by professions, especially groups of government employees; and by ideological cause groups. Schlozman & Tierney (1986, pp. 55–57) found a great increase in government lobbies since 1960, although they argued that this did not substantially decrease the business domination of other lobbies.

Neopluralists thus observed a complex welter of group participation in public policy making (Jordan 1981, Jordan & Maloney 1996, Gray & Lowery 2004, Lowery & Brasher 2004). Within a single issue domain such as air pollution regulation, one might find producers of electricity, coal mining companies, auto manufacturers, the United Auto Workers, railroads (carriers of coal), environmentalist groups, the American Lung Association, the American Public Health Association, various state governments, the association of state public utility regulators, and probably other groups. Neopluralists would expect to observe this situation in numerous issue areas at the national level, rather than to observe a narrow coalition of an interest group, government agency, and legislative committee.

Concomitant with this finding of a complexity of groups active in national policy domains was the need of explaining why such groups mobilized and maintained themselves in light of Olson's persuasive theory of collective action, which stated that lobbies make public goods (public policies) available even to groups and individuals who do not contribute to the lobby and thereby act as free riders. As mentioned above, Olson posited that

groups would organize if they provided selective benefits to contributors, benefits available only to members, such as the Farm Bureau providing insurance and fuel discounts to its farmer members. But the concept of selective benefits did not provide a persuasive explanation for the existence of the full panoply of interest groups.

Why did so many interest groups exist despite the logic of collective action? Political scientists made this question a priority, particularly during 1970–1990. A number of answers received widespread acceptance and were incorporated into neopluralist views of the policy-making process.

First, a few years after the publication of *The Logic of Collective Action*, Chamberlin (1974) and Frohlich et al. (1971) pointed out that interest groups can be started and maintained by political entrepreneurs, to use economic language. One or more individuals take it upon themselves to start a group and to bear the time costs of organizing and doing the necessary fund-raising. Walker's (1991) surveys found that about half of the interest groups responding had been organized by such political entrepreneurs.

Walker then extended this mode of thought by demonstrating the key role of patrons in organizing interest groups. Patrons were particularly helpful in understanding the organizing of citizen groups, in which members contributed to lobbying for public policy issues even when such policies did not have a great immediate impact on the members' own pocketbooks. Patrons are seen as providing money and other resources to the entrepreneurs who do the organizing. Patrons include wealthy individuals, foundations, other organizations (creating spin-off groups, for instance), and governments, particularly the federal government. Walker emphasized the government as a patron, noting that the federal government actually played a key role in organizing several major groups, such as the Farm Bureau, the U.S. Chambers of Commerce, and the National Organization of Women (Walker 1983, 1991; McFarland 2004, pp. 44–45).

A third source of interest groups is social movements. Although they use non-institutionalized tactics, social movements eventually encompass supporters who prefer to work within established political institutions to attain movement goals, thus forming lobbies for large but seemingly diffused groups, such as women, environmentalists, and religious fundamentalists. Social movements are a major reason for the sudden expansion of organized lobbies occurring in Washington, DC around 1970. Although efforts have been made to explain social movements using a rational choice framework similar to that of Olson's collective action theory (Chong 1991, Lichbach 1995), most writers emphasize a variety of causes for social movements (McAdam 1982, Costain & McFarland 1998), thereby employing variables outside of Olson's theory.

A fourth theory addressing the proliferation of interest groups was provided by policy theorist Hugh Heclo (1978), whose concept of "issue networks" found immediate, widespread acceptance among political scientists. Heclo observed that although the particularistic coalitions described by multiple-elite writers do indeed exist, they are only part of a complex network of communication and interaction within some issue domain. Heclo termed such an overall network an "issue network." He argued that the subgovernments or little governments of multiple-elite theory existed in only a minority of cases, and that ordinarily such limited coalitions, only part of an issue network, are checked by other actors within the issue network (sometimes called a "policy network"). In addition, from the standpoint of collective action theory, the issue network provides a basis for mobilizing lobbies to represent interests more diffuse than the oligopolistic coalitions implied by Olson's theory.

For instance, in the case of air pollution policy, there is a potential subgovernment consisting of eastern coal mining businesses; eastern miners; legislators representing Kentucky, Ohio, Illinois, and West Virginia; and the Department of Energy. Such a subgovernment would favor the use of high-sulfur coal, which would require the purchase of expensive emissions-scrubbing equipment or regulatory variation to meet the requirements of air pollution legislation. But in addition to the electric utilities directly affected, there exists a network of communication of political, economic, and technical information within this issue area. The federal Environmental Protection Agency and state EPAs regularly communicate about air pollution issues, as do university researchers, environmental group personnel,

recreation industry personnel, American Lung Association staff, journalists, federal and state legislators specializing in environmental legislation, and the staffs of such legislators. Because of the overall issue network, the potential high-sulfur coal subgovernment cannot control information and public attention regarding policy in this area. A countervailing lobby representing widespread but diffuse interests can be organized from other elements in the issue network. A potential issue-area elite is checked by forces within the more general issue network. Heclo's viewpoint has been adopted by neopluralists and probably by most political scientists.

A fifth reason for the proliferation of interest groups follows from an expansion of Olson's concept of selective benefits, meaning that one can organize a large group on the basis of "members-only" benefits. Professional and occupational groups normally organize conventions or other members-only meetings, in which the selective benefit is valuable information about professional opportunities or the presentation of significant recent research (Moe 1980).

COUNTERVAILING POWER AND SELECTIVE ATTENTION

Neopluralists thus observe a world of political domains that normally contain competing interest groups. One is immediately reminded of the "balance of power" concept in the history of international relations. The analogous concept in domestic politics is Galbraith's (1952) "countervailing power." Balance of power or countervailing power implies initially observing a dominant power that subsequently is checked by one or several balancers of power. This is a primitive but useful concept for observing public policy making.

In the study of American policy making, the next step is to observe how the countervailing power groups communicate policy information to various political entities in the process of calling public attention to the observed policy domain. In other words, how do the countervailing power groups exercise power? They have the potential to influence the executive, legislative, judicial, and federal decision-making institutions in American government. For example, in the 1970s, when environmentalists opposed the coalition supporting nuclear power generation, they initiated lawsuits to point out the economic and safety problems of nuclear power to the public, and directly and indirectly to regulatory commissions and to legislators not on the Joint Committee on Atomic Energy. Thus, the politics of countervailing power is not usually one of group gridlock, but rather of groups maneuvering to call attention to their policy preferences as they attempt to influence decision makers in different political venues (Baumgartner & Jones 1993, Jones 1994, Jones & Baumgartner 2005). This is a politics of influencing the selective attention of decision makers, who cannot attend to the scores of potential issues that might come before them.

Two models of policy making follow from the observation of countervailing group power. The first is something of a paradox: The existence of countervailing groups prevents the capture of a government agency by a dominant group, a basic part of the multiple-elitist model of the controlling coalition of interest group, legislative committee, and government agency. In other words, countervailing power groups enhance the autonomy of government agencies, which, for instance, are more likely to design and execute policy reflective of professional norms, such as those of lawyer, economist, educator, or biologist (Wilson 1980; McFarland 2004, p. 48). More groups lead to more autonomy for government agencies (controlled in varying degrees by executive or legislative officials).

Countervailing group power is related to the theory of advocacy coalitions, as set forth by Sabatier & Jenkins-Smith (1993). In the history of international relations, one refers to bipolar systems; in American domestic politics, one frequently observes competing advocacy coalitions, such as competition between environmentalists and development interests in Western communities. An advocacy coalition is a stable alliance, probably lasting ten years or more, among actors within a policy network, including individuals representing government agencies at all levels of federalism. The concept of advocacy coalition within a policy network, often in competition with each other, has proved useful in scores of studies of policy making (Sabatier & Jenkins-Smith 1999).

CHARACTERISTICS OF NEOPLURALIST POLITICAL PROCESS

The basic meaning of neopluralism is a finding about power structure within the framework of four assumptions underlying Dahl's theory of political power (process, power as causation, domains, subjective definition of interests). Using these and perhaps other assumptions, political science has set forth seven findings about power structure: power elite theory, Dahl's pluralist theory, multiple-elite theory, neopluralism, corporatism (Schmitter 1974), statism (Krasner 1978), and consociationism (Lijphart 1969). Neopluralism was derived from a research sequence that started with Mills versus Dahl and proceeded through multiple-elite theory, finally resulting in neopluralism.

Explicitly or implicitly, these seven research findings can be based on the use of Dahl's concepts and methods. Dahl (1958) criticized Mills for not using these methods, but a scholar can readily find a single elite ruling a single issue domain, a community, or even a nation by using Dahl's methods and arguing that the same group controls the core of public policy. The multiple-elite theorists did this in respect to single policy domains. Neopluralism is thus a type of finding in research about political power. But it is more than this; neopluralism can be called a theory, because researchers assuming neopluralist power domains have begun to make other theoretical observations about political and policy-making processes.

As of 2006, according to my reading of the literature, most political scientists and other public policy researchers assume a condition of neopluralism in the policy domains they study. Dahl's pluralist theory and multiple-elite theory are normally seen to be dated as general theories, although they might provide accurate explanations for outcomes in a minority of policy domains. Disproving the existence of a power elite or a state of Dahl's pluralism within a policy domain is no longer a priority in research studies, although in urban studies, the question of political power continues to have priority, especially in dealing with the elite "growth machine" hypothesis in urban politics (Logan & Molotch 1987). The most influential type of political power study in urban politics is the regime theory of Stone (1989, 2006), who found that political norms in Atlanta, GA encourage a long-lasting alliance between the mayor's faction and organized downtown business to promote economic growth, especially in the downtown area. Stone calls this "power-to" as opposed to Dahl's "power-over." He disagrees with Dahl's definition of "power" as causing intended changes in the behavior of people, rather than bringing about some intended new state of the city.

As public policy researchers show less interest in discussing models of political power and more interest in analyzing other questions regarding the political process, the theory of political power is becoming embedded in an emerging theory of policy-making process. In other words, neopluralism is becoming the core of a political process theory (McFarland 2004). Let us examine some of the concerns and conclusions of this emerging neopluralist theory.

Neopluralist researchers find many interest groups active in most policy domains, but they clearly do not equate such group multiplicity with fair representation.

Olson's logic of collective action, in which the majority do not organize, is an important factor in public policy making, even if it is not a dominant factor. This needs to be said because in academic discussions, scholars sometimes confuse Dahl's pluralist theory of political power with the Bentley-Truman pluralist theory, which comes closer to saying that a multiplicity of groups is a basis for adequate representation. Dahl did not make this assumption, but did not make this clear to many in the scholarly community (Dahl 1982, pp. 207–209), sending many critics of pluralism in the wrong direction. A later generation of scholars, observing a multiplicity of active groups, normally also observe that business groups might have more power than others concerned, and that certain interests are still hardly represented. Such statements provide a basis to criticize the adequacy of representation within some policy domain.

In addition to incorporating Dahl's four basic assumptions for the study of political power, neopluralist theory also incorporates multiple-elite theory. It recognizes policy domains characterized by a singularity of group organization, leading to unrepresentative policy outcomes. This is now called niche theory and is incorporated into neopluralist theory. In the 1990s, Browne (1990) and Gray & Lowery (1996) began using the term policy niche to refer to a highly specific forum or type of public policy, such as the regulation of cesium or subsidies for honey production. Although a particular policy niche might seem unimportant, the total of such policy niches apparently numbers in the thousands at the federal level. Since the 1950s, policy experts have been telling us that agriculture is fragmented into separate policy systems for major commodities—wheat, corn, soybeans, beef, pork, tobacco, and so forth—and even separate systems for smaller sectors such as walnuts or almonds. Browne (1990), the leading expert on agricultural policy making of his generation, stated that there are more than 400 policy niches in national agricultural policy making.

At about the same time, Gray & Lowery (1996) stressed "interest group niches" and "group niche behavior" in their data-rich study of interest group systems and lobbying in fifty state governments. They put forth the ecological model of interest group systems. Because groups compete with one another, it is rational and "ecological" for interest groups to occupy a piece of the policy-making turf that has little or no competition from other groups trying to mobilize resources in the same policy-making space. In their study of 137 representative national policy domains, Baumgartner & Leech (2001, p. 1201) found 17 domains in which >200 groups were interested to lobby, whereas in 23 domains only a single group was interested to lobby, and 16 of those 23 policy domains apparently had significant breadth. This empirical finding combines the neopluralist insistence that a multiplicity of groups are often mobilized in power domains with the multiple elitists' finding that sometimes only a single group is significant within a domain. However, neopluralism states that the observation of a multiplicity of groups is the more general research finding.

Lipsky (1970), and perhaps a few other scholars, anticipated neopluralist conclusions but did not frame them in the debate about the extent of multiple-elitism. Lipsky's widely read *Protest in City Politics: Rent Strikes, Housing and the Power of the Poor* (1970) presented a neopluralist study ten years ahead of its time. Studying the nationally famous Harlem rent strike of 1963–1964, Lipsky used methods similar to those of the pluralists by focusing on a case study of a political process within a single domain, while assuming Dahl's definition of political power by referring to "protest as a political resource" rather than protest as "power" itself. Lipsky observed that the economic stakeholders normally were powerful in the domain of city housing rent regulation, but he found that a social movement could form organizations to challenge economic power. Such organizations, however, were quickly subject to processes of decay. In this case, collective action was furthered by a movement entrepreneur, who found the costs of organization lessened by the proximity of supporters living in the same building.

NEOPLURALISM AND THE TWO FACES OF POWER

The significance of the concept of neopluralism would be limited if discussion of Dahl's pluralism and its successors had been cut off by the classic article "The Two Faces of Power," one of the most influential articles published in political science during the past 50 years. This work by Bachrach & Baratz (1962) states that although *Who Governs?* is an adequate study of power over issues on the political agenda (the first face of power), Dahl's pluralist theory of power has little to say about the power to determine which issues appear on the political agenda (the second face of power). The two-faces-of-power refutation of Dahl's theory was immediately accepted by many political scientists, although the implications of accepting this argument were not very clear. Polsby (1980 [1963]) soon pointed out that the two-faces-of-power argument was an injunction to study "nonissues," and that this was not an empirical endeavor, being subject to the interpolation of a scholar's values in choosing which nonissues were important. But Polsby could not persuade most political scientists about the invalidity of the two-faces-of-power argument.

Bachrach & Baratz's concern about power over the agenda applies to the range of studies that accept Dahl's four assumptions in the study of power, including multiple-elite and neopluralist studies. Actually, two faces of power also applies to other theories of power insofar as such theories are based on observations of who wins and loses on certain political issues. Following the two-faces-of-power argument, some might say that neopluralism as a theory might as well be ignored. Yet researchers into power and the political process have shed much light on power over the political agenda.

Kingdon's *Agendas, Alternatives, and Public Policies* (1984) is now a standard treatment of the development of political issues among scholars of public policy. Kingdon views the policy agenda in terms of two streams: a stream of perceived problems and a stream of proposed solutions. When "a window of opportunity develops," political entrepreneurs link problems with solutions to initiate new public policies. Kingdon uses organization theory and a time frame of about seven or more years, as does Polsby (1984), who states a similar argument using historical case study materials. A second standard approach to the agenda, which can be linked to Kingdon's approach, is Baumgartner & Jones's work on the punctuated equilibrium. Clearly, a punctuation of policy involves a change in the political agenda, incorporating new issues and reinterpretation of old issues (Baumgartner & Jones 1993, Jones & Baumgartner 2005). The study of who or what is causing the punctuation is a study of power over issues. A third empirical approach to the study of issues and the agenda can be derived from Heclo's concept of the policy network. If a scholar becomes very familiar with a policy network, he or she becomes aware of persons or groups putting forth proposals rejected by others in the network. Such ideas, perhaps put forth by socialists or evangelical Christians, may not get attention in the institutional forums of policy discussion, but their defeat can be observed within the policy network. A similar idea is the concept of "hidden narratives," derived by Scott (1990) from postmodern historical studies. One can observe the powerless indicating their dissatisfaction in a disguised form, such as the freedom chants of slaves at work or the sabotage of industrial production by workers under Communism. Although not appearing on a political agenda, such nonissues can be discussed on the basis of observation and empirical data.

A fifth concept related to studying the political agenda is that of a policy regime or a political regime, guided by norms which legitimate some policies and discourage others. Stone (1989) has observed that the norms of political regimes affect the political agendas of cities, e.g., by legitimizing cooperation between African-American politicians and downtown business interests. Some policy domains can be said to have embedded norms about the proper role of government versus private interests, such as in determining the private use of public lands for grazing, forestry, and mining (Klyza 1994).

Since the mid 1990s, there has been much interest among social scientists, not just political scientists, in the concept of issue framing (Benford & Snow 2000). Calling a tax a "death tax" rather than an "estate tax" can make a big difference in the policy-making process; the first issue frame emphasizes intervention of big government into private affairs and making money from death, whereas the issue frame of "estate" emphasizes the idea of taxing the wealthy. The examination of issue framing is a valuable addition to the study of political agendas because framing the agenda in one way or another affects political outcomes. Successful issue framing says something important about political power.

Bachrach & Baratz made their point with "The Two Faces of Power," but we must now acknowledge the succeeding 40 years of research about political agendas in the policy-making process. Neopluralism incorporates a great deal of useful research about influencing the political agenda. However, I must acknowledge the "third face of power" argument put forth by Lukes (1974). The third face of power is seen when a potential issue is rendered a nonissue because the persons who might want something are socialized to be unaware of their lack. Political process or neopluralist theories assume that persons being studied are aware of their own interests, and thus neopluralism is limited in its treatment of situations some call hegemony, that is, domination through cultural indoctrination. Hegemony must be studied through comparative cultural history, but on a less grand level, neopluralism has a lot to say about power and the political agenda.

CONCLUSION: NEOPLURALISM AS A RESEARCH SEQUENCE

Neopluralism can be described as a research sequence dating back to Dahl's *Who Governs?* (Laudan 1984, McFarland 2004). I see Dahl's major contribution as joining together the four assumptions mentioned above (political process model, power as causation, issue domains, subjective definition of interest) to provide a research mode for the study of power and policy making. Although Dahl's work did have major insufficiencies in such areas as power over the agenda, islands of power, the logic of collective action, and lack of clarity about the role of the state, these questions have been well treated in the research sequence subsequent to his work.

Many political scientists now think in terms of Kuhn's brilliant *The Structure of Scientific Revolution* (1962). Kuhn argues that science is based on conceptual paradigms, and scientific progress occurs when a new paradigm is put forth to address the puzzles, anomalies, or insufficient answers that were produced by research conducted according to the old paradigm. The new concepts gain adherents among younger researchers, while older researchers either switch viewpoints or retire from research, mostly the latter. The result is a scientific revolution, a complete change in views about some subject matter.

In my opinion, Kuhn's terms do not always apply to our discipline. Scholars are tempted to say that there has been "a paradigm change" in, for example, the evaluation of Dahl's pluralist theory of political power, but in fact, succeeding researchers accepted part of Dahl's work while regarding other parts as insufficient. The study of models of political power, public policy making in complex political systems, and urban politics has thus proceeded as a research sequence. Regarding neopluralism as exemplary of a research sequence (Laudan 1984) helps to understand the development of recent political science.

In this essay, I have sometimes shifted wording from "neopluralism" to "political process theory." This is because I do believe that the paradigm concept is useful, although paradigms in political science do not operate in the manner described by Kuhn. In political science, several paradigms exist and develop simultaneously. In our field, a paradigm might emerge in a single brilliant statement (Marx, Weber) or it might emerge over generations in a research sequence, such as the one producing neopluralism. In other words, a general theory of political process has been evolving.

Literature Cited

Ackerman B, Hassler WT. 1981. *Clean Coal/Dirty Air.* New Haven, CT: Yale Univ. Press

Allison G. 1971. *Essence of Decision.* Boston: Little, Brown

Bachrach P, Baratz M. 1962. Two faces of power. *Am. Polit. Sci. Rev.* 56:947–52

Balbus ID. 1971. The concept of interest in pluralist and Marxian analysis. *Polit. Soc.* 1:151–78

Baumgartner FR, Jones BD. 1993. *Agendas and Instability in American Politics.* Chicago: Univ. Chicago Press

Baumgartner FR, Leech BL. 2001. Interest niches and policy bandwagons: patterns of interest group involvement in national politics. *J. Polit.* 63:1191–1213

Beer SH. 1976. The adoption of general revenue sharing: a case study in public sector politics. *Public Policy* 24:127–95

Benford RD, Snow DA. 2000. Framing processes and social movements: an overview and assessment. *Am. Rev. Sociol.* 26:611–39

Bentley AF. 1967 (1908). *The Process of Government.* Cambridge, MA: Belknap Press of Harvard Univ. Press

Bernstein M. 1955. *Regulating Business by Independent Commission.* Princeton, NJ: Princeton Univ. Press

Berry JM. 1977. *Lobbying for the People.* Princeton, NJ: Princeton Univ. Press

Braybrooke D, Lindblom CE. 1963. *A Strategy of Decision.* New York: Free

Browne WP. 1990. Organized interests and their issue niches: a search for pluralism in a policy domain. *J. Polit.* 52:477–509

Cater D. 1964. *Power in Washington.* New York: Random House

Chamberlin J. 1974. Provision of collective goods as a function of group size. *Am. Polit. Sci. Rev.* 68:707–16

Chong D. 1991. *Collective Action and the Civil Rights Movement.* Chicago: Univ. Chicago Press

Connolly WE. 2005. *Pluralism.* Durham, NC: Duke Univ. Press

Costain A, Costain WD. 1983. The women's lobby: impact of a movement on Congress. In *Interest Group Politics*, ed. AJ Cigler, BA Loomis, pp. 191–216. Washington, DC: Congr. Q.

Costain AN, McFarland AS. 1998. *Social Movements and American Political Institutions.* Lanham, MD: Rowman & Littlefield

Dahl RA. 1957. The concept of power. *Behav. Sci.* 2:201–15

Dahl RA. 1958. A critique of the ruling elite model. *Am. Polit. Sci. Rev.* 52:463–66

Dahl RA. 1961. *Who Governs?* New Haven, CT: Yale Univ. Press

Dahl RA. 1968. Power. In *International Encyclopedia of Social Sciences*, Vol. 12, pp. 405–15. New York: Macmillan and Free

Dahl RA. 1982. *Dilemmas of Pluralist Democracy.* New Haven, CT: Yale Univ. Press

Foss PO. 1960. *Politics and Grass.* Seattle: Univ. Wash. Press

Freeman J. 1975. *The Politics of Women's Liberation.* New York: McKay

Frohlich N, Oppenheimer J, Young O. 1971. *Political Leadership and Collective Goods.* Princeton, NJ: Princeton Univ. Press

Gais TL, Peterson MA, Walker JL. 1984. Interest groups, iron triangles, and representative institutions in American national government. *Br. J. Polit. Sci.* 14:161–85

Galbraith JK. 1952. *American Capitalism: The Concept of Countervailing Power.* Boston: Houghton Mifflin

Gaventa J. 1980. *Power and Powerlessness.* Urbana, IL: Univ. Ill. Press

Gelb J, Palley ML. 1982. *Women and Public Policies.* Princeton, NJ: Princeton Univ. Press

Gray V, Lowery D. 1996. *The Population Ecology of Interest, Representation: Lobbying Communities in the American States.* Ann Arbor: Univ. Mich. Press

Gray Y, Lowery D. 2004. A neopluralist perspective on research on organized interests. *Polit. Res. Q.* 57:163–75

Greenstein FI. 1963. *The American Party System and the American People.* Englewood Cliffs, NJ: Prentice-Hall

Grodzins M. 1960. The federal system. In *Goals for Americans*, President's Commission on National Goals, pp. 265–82. Englewood Cliffs, NJ: Prentice-Hall

Haider D. 1974. *When Governments Come to Washington*. New York: Free

Heclo H. 1978. Issue networks and the executive establishment. In *The New American Political System*, ed. A King, pp. 87–124. Washington, DC: Am. Enterp. Inst.

Jones BD. 1994. *Reconceiving Decision-Making in Democratic Politics: Attention, Choice, and Public Policy*. Chicago: Univ. Chicago Press

Jones BD, Baumgartner FR. 2005. *The Politics of Attention*. Chicago: Univ. Chicago Press

Jones CO. 1975. *Clean Air: The Policies and Politics of Pollution Control*. Pittsburgh: Univ. Pittsburgh Press

Jordan G. 1981. Iron triangles, woolly corporatism, and elastic nets: images of the policy process. *J. Public Policy* 1:95–123

Jordan G, Maloney WA. 1996. How bumble-bees fly: accounting for public interest participation. *Polit. Stud.* 44:668–85

Kingdon JW. 1984. *Agendas, Alternatives, and Public Policies*. Boston: Little, Brown

Klein E. 1984. *Gender Politics*. Cambridge, MA: Harvard Univ. Press

Klyza CM. 1994. Ideas, institutions, and policy patterns: hardrock mining, forestry, and grazing policy on United States public lands, 1870–1985. *Stud. Am. Polit. Dev.* 8:341–74

Krasner SD. 1978. *Defending the National Interest: Raw Materials Investment and U. S. Foreign Policy*. Princeton, NJ: Princeton Univ. Press

Kuhn TS. 1962. *The Structure of Scientific Revolution*. Chicago: Univ. Chicago Press

Laski HJ. 1921. *The Foundations of Sovereignty and Other Essays*. New York: Harcourt, Brace

Lasswell HD, Kaplan A. 1950. *Power and Society*. New Haven, CT: Yale Univ. Press

Laudan L. 1984. *Science and Values: The Aims of Science and Their Role in Scientific Debate*. Berkeley: Univ. Calif. Press

Laumann EO, Knoke D. 1987. *The Organizational State: Social Choice in National Policy Domains*. Madison: Univ. Wisc. Press

Lichbach MI. 1995. *The Rebel's Dilemma*. Ann Arbor: Univ. Mich. Press

Lindblom CE. 1965. *The Intelligence of Democracy*. New York: Macmillan

Lijphart A. 1969. Consociational democracy. *World Polit.* 21:207–25

Lipsky M. 1970. *Protest in City Politics: Rent Strikes, Housing and the Power of the Poor*. Chicago: Rand-McNally

Logan JR, Molotch HM. 1987. *Urban Fortunes: The Political Economy of Place*. Berkeley: Univ. Calif. Press

Lowery D, Brasher H. 2004. *Organized Interests and American Government*. New York: McGraw-Hill

Lowi TJ. 1964a. American business, public policy, case studies and political theory. *World Polit.* 16:677–715

Lowi TJ. 1964b. *At the Pleasure of the Mayor*. New York: Free

Lowi TJ. 1969. *The End of Liberalism*. New York: WW Norton

Lowi TJ. 1979. *The End of Liberalism*. New York: WW Norton. Rev. ed.

Lukes S. 1974. *Power: A Radical View*. London: Macmillan

Maass AA. 1951. *Muddy Waters*. Cambridge, MA: Harvard Univ. Press

March JG. 1955. An introduction to the theory and measurement of influence. *Am. Polit. Sci. Rev.* 49:431–51

McAdam D. 1982. *Political Process and the Development of Black Insurgency, 1930–1970*. Chicago: Univ. Chicago Press

McCarthy JD, Zald MN. 1977. Resource mobilization and social movements. *Am. J. Sociol.* 82:1212–41

McConnell G. 1966. *Private Power and American Democracy*. New York: Knopf

McFarland AS. 1984. *Common Cause: Lobbying in the Public Interest*. Chatham, NJ: Chatham House

McFarland AS. 2004. *Neopluralism: The Evolution of Political Process Theory*. Lawrence: Univ. Press Kansas

Michels R. 1959. *Political Parties*. New York: Dover

Mills CW. 1956. *The Power Elite*. New York: Oxford Univ. Press

Mitchell RC. 1984. Public opinion and environmental politics in the 1970s and 1980s. In *Environmental Politics in the 1980s: Reagan's New Agenda*, ed. NJ Vig, ME Kraft, pp. 51–74. Washington, DC: Congr. Q.

Moe TM. 1980. *The Organization of Interests: Incentives and the Internal Dynamics of Political Interest Groups*. Chicago: Univ. Chicago Press

Morgenthau HJ. 1964. *Politics among Nations*. New York: Knopf. 3rd ed.

Nadel MV. 1971. *The Politics of Consumer Protection*. Indianapolis: Bobbs-Merrill

Olson M. 1965. *The Logic of Collective Action*. Cambridge, MA: Harvard Univ. Press

Olson M. 1982. *The Rise and Decline of Nations: Economic Growth, Stagflation, and Social Rigidities.* New Haven, CT: Yale Univ. Press

Orren K. 1974. *Corporate Power and Social Change: The Politics of the Life Insurance Industry.* Baltimore, MD: Johns Hopkins Univ. Press

Ornstein N, Elder S. 1978. *Interest Groups, Lobbying, and Policymaking.* Washington, DC: Congr. Q.

Polsby NW. 1971. *Congress and the Presidency.* Englewood Cliffs, NJ: Prentice-Hall. 2nd ed.

Polsby NW. 1980 (1963). *Community Power and Political Theory.* New Haven, CT: Yale Univ. Press. 2nd enlarged ed.

Polsby NW. 1984. *Political Innovation in America: The Politics of Policy Initiation.* New Haven, CT: Yale Univ. Press

Polsby NW. 2006. Remarks for 2006 Southern Political Science Association Roundtable. Typescript, Inst. Gov. Stud., Univ. Calif., Berkeley

Redford E. 1969. *Democracy in the Administrative State.* New York: Oxford Univ. Press

Sabatier PA, Jenkins-Smith HC, eds. 1993. *Policy Change and Learning: An Advocacy Coalition Approach.* Boulder, CO: Westview

Sabatier PA, Jenkins-Smith HC. 1999. The advocacy coalition framework: an assessment. In *Theories of the Policy Process*, ed. PA Sabatier, pp. 117–66. Boulder, CO: Westview

Sayre WS, Kaufman H. 1960. *Governing New York City.* New York: Russell Sage Found.

Schlozman KL, Tierney JT. 1986. *Organized Interests and American Democracy.* New York: Harper & Row

Schmitter P. 1974. Still the century of corporatism? *Rev. Polit.* 36:85–131

Scott JC. 1990. *Domination and the Arts of Resistance.* New Haven, CT: Yale Univ. Press

Selznick P. 1953. *TVA and the Grass Roots.* Berkeley: Univ. Calif. Press

Simon HA. 1953. Notes on the observation and measurement of power. *J. Polit.* 15:500–16

Stigler GJ. 1975. *The Citizen and the State: Essays on Regulation.* Chicago: Univ. Chicago Press

Stone CN. 1989. *Regime Politics: Governing Atlanta, 1946–1988.* Lawrence: Univ. Press Kansas

Stone CN. 2006. Power, reform, and urban regime analysis. *City Community* 5:23–38

Truman DB. 1951. *The Governmental Process.* New York: Knopf

Vogel D. 1980/1981. The public interest movement and the American reform tradition. *Polit. Sci. Q.* 95:607–27

Walker JL. 1983. The origins and maintenance of interest groups in America. *Am. Polit. Sci. Rev.* 77:390–406

Walker JL. 1991. *Mobilizing Interest Groups in America.* Ann Arbor: Univ. Mich. Press

Weber M. 1946. Class, status, party. In *From Max Weber: Essays in Sociology*, ed./transl. HH Gerthe, CW Mills, pp. 180–95. New York: Oxford Univ. Press

Wenner LM. 1982. *The Environmental Decade in Court.* Bloomington: Univ. Indiana Press

Wildavsky AB. 1964a. *Leadership in a Small Town.* Bedminister, NJ: Totowa

Wildavsky AB. 1964b. *The Politics of the Budgetary Process.* Boston: Little, Brown

Wildavsky AB. 1979. *Speaking Truth to Power: The Art and Craft of Policy Analysis.* Boston: Little, Brown

Wilson JQ. 1980. *The Politics of Regulation.* New York: Basic Books

8

Imperfect Competition

Ralph Miliband

Democratic and pluralist theory could not have gained the degree of ascendancy which it enjoys in advanced capitalist societies if it had not at least been based on one plainly accurate observation about them, namely that they permit and even encourage a multitude of groups and associations to organise openly and freely and to compete with each other for the advancement of such purposes as their members may wish. With exceptions which mainly affect the Left, this is indeed the case.

What is wrong with pluralist-democratic theory is not its insistence on the fact of competition but its claim (very often its implicit assumption) that the major organised 'interests' in these societies, and notably capital and labour, compete on more or less equal terms, and that none of them is therefore able to achieve a decisive and permanent advantage in the process of competition. This is where ideology enters, and turns observation into myth. In previous chapters, it was shown that business, particularly large-scale business, did enjoy such an advantage *inside* the state system, by virtue of the composition and ideological inclinations of the state elite. In this chapter, we shall see that business enjoys a massive superiority *outside* the state system as well, in terms of the immensely stronger pressures which, as compared with labour and any other interest, it is able to exercise in the pursuit of its purposes.

1

One such form of pressure, which pluralist 'group theorists' tend to ignore, is more important and effective than any other, and business is uniquely placed to exercise it, without the need of organisation, campaigns and lobbying. This is the pervasive and permanent pressure upon governments and the state generated by the private control of concentrated industrial, commercial and financial resources. The existence of this major area of independent economic power is a fact which no government, whatever its inclinations, can ignore in the determination of its policies, not only in regard to economic matters, but to most other matters as well. The chairman of the editorial board of *Fortune* magazine said in 1952 that 'any president who wants to seek a prosperous country depends on the corporation at least as much—probably more than—the corporation depends on him. His dependence is not unlike that of King John on the landed barons at Runnymede, where Magna Carta was born'.[1] The parallel may not be perfect but the stress on the independent power of business, and on the dependence of government upon it, is altogether justified, not only for the United States but for all other advanced capitalist countries.

Of course, governments do have the formal power to impose their will upon business, to prevent it, by the exercise of legitimate authority, from doing certain things and to compel it to do certain other things. And this is in fact what governments have often done. But this, though true and important, is not at all the point at issue. Quite obviously, governments are not *completely* helpless in the face of business power, nor is it the case that businessmen, however large the concerns which they run, can openly defy the state's command, disregard its rules and flout the law. The point is rather that the control by business of large and crucially important areas of economic life makes it extremely *difficult* for governments to impose upon it policies to which it is firmly opposed. Other interests, it may well be said, are by no means helpless *vis-à-vis* their government either; they too may oppose, sometimes successfully, the purposes and policies of the state. But business, in the very nature of a capitalist system of economic organisation, is immeasurably better placed than any other interest to do so effectively, and to cause governments to pay much greater attention to its wishes and susceptibilities than to anybody else.

Writing about the United States, Professor Hacker has noted in this connection that:*

> what Parsons and other liberals like to think of as business regulation is, despite the predictable complaints of businessmen, more a paper tiger than an effective system of economic controls in the public interest … [and, he goes on] a few questions may be asked about these supposed powers of the national government. Can any public agency determine the level of wages, of prices, of profits? Can it perhaps, more important, specify the level and direction of capital investment? Can any government bureau allocate raw materials or control plant location? Can it in any way guarantee full employment or the rate of economic growth? Has any writ of the Anti-Trust Division actually broken up one of our larger corporations in any appreciable way? The simple answer is that measures such as these are neither possible under the laws nor do we know what the reaction to them would be.[2]

Even for the United States this may well underestimate the influence which governments do have, by direct and indirect intervention, on economic life;

and in many other capitalist countries, where a more positive philosophy of intervention has generally come to prevail, governments have been able to do rather more than what is here suggested as possible.

Nevertheless, the *limits* of intervention, at least in relation to business, and particularly *against* it, are everywhere much more narrow and specific than insistence on the formal powers of government would tend to suggest; and the area of decision-making which is left to private enterprise is correspondingly greater than is usually conveyed by the assiduously propagated image of a 'business community' cribbed and confined by bureaucratically meddlesome governments and their agents.

Even governments which *are* determined to 'control' private enterprise soon find that the mechanisms of intervention which they seek to super-impose upon business are extremely cumbersome and almost impossible to operate without the collaboration and help of business itself. But that collaboration and help are unlikely to be forthcoming unless a price is paid for them—the price being that governments should not be too determined in the pursuit of policies which business itself deems detrimental to it, and of course to the 'national interest'.

What is involved here is not necessarily or at all the active resistance of the controllers of economic power to the law, or the deliberate evasion of duly promulgated regulations, though there may be that as well. More important than such defiance, which may be politically damaging and even dangerous, is the *inert* power of business, the failure to do such things as are not positively commanded by the state but merely asked for, and the doing of other things which are not strictly illegal. Much is possible on this basis, and would be sufficient to present a reforming government with formidable problems, so long as it chose to operate within the framework of a capitalist regime. As Professor Meynaud notes, in a reference to Italy which is of more general application, private ownership and control

> makes it very difficult to undertake a policy of reform within the framework of established economic structures. Any government

---

*Excerpt from *The Social Theories of Talcott Parsons*, by Andrew Hacker. Copyright © 1961 by Andrew Hacker. Reprinted with permission of the author.

concerned to engineer a certain redistribution of economic power and of the social product without bringing into question the foundations of the system rapidly comes up, in the medical sense of the word, against a kind of intolerance of the regime to such changes.

This 'intolerance', it must be stressed, is not such as to prevent *any* kind of economic policy of which business disapproves. The veto power of business, in other words, is not absolute. But it is very large, and certainly larger than that of any other interest in capitalist society.

It has sometimes been argued that governments have now come to possess one extremely effective weapon in relation to business, namely the fact that they are now by far the largest customer of private enterprise and have thus an important and speedy instrument for influencing the decisions of private industry and commerce in such a way as to enable the government to achieve *on time* its major national industrial objectives....

In the abstract, governments do indeed have vast resources and powers at their command to "wield the big stick" against business. In practice, governments which are minded to use these powers and resources—and most of them are not—soon find, given the economic and political context in which they operate, that the task is fraught with innumerable difficulties and perils.

These difficulties and perils are perhaps best epitomised in the dreaded phrase "loss of confidence." It is an implicit testimony to the power of business that all governments, not least reforming ones, have always been profoundly concerned to gain and retain its "confidence". Nor certainly is there any other interest whose "confidence" is deemed so precious, or whose "loss of confidence" is so feared.

The presidency of John F. Kennedy provides some illuminating instances of this concern. Soon after he came to office, President Kennedy found himself engaged in a "spectacular power struggle" with the Business Advisory Council, "an exclusive and self-perpetuating club of top corporate executives that had enjoyed a private and special relationship with the government since 1933" and which 'from Administration to Administration...had a continuous privilege to participate in government decisions with no public record or review.'[3] The Secretary of Commerce, Luther Hartwell Hodges, though hardly a fiery radical, entertained the odd notion that the manner of appointment of BAC members, and its procedures, ought to be modified. In the event, the difficulties this produced led the BAC itself to sever its official connections and to rename itself the Business Council. "Hodges drew plans for a new BAC, one that would include a broad cross-section of American business—big, medium and small-sized. It would include representatives as well of labor, agriculture, and education".[4]

But these plans never materialised: faced with many problems which appeared to him to require business support, "and sensitive to the growing insistence that he was 'anti-business', the President turned full circle from his earlier, firm and bold posture toward the Business Advisory Council."[5] A rapprochement was engineered and arrangements were made for 'small committees of the BC to be assigned to each of several government departments and agencies—and to the White House itself.'[6] For their part, "labor leaders complained about the Kennedy campaign against 'inflationary wage increases', itself part of Kennedy's assurance to business that he was playing no favorites. But the President wanted to restore a good working relationship with the Business Council *regardless of labor's concerns.*"[7]

It was only a few months later that the President found himself 'at war' with no less a member of the business establishment than Roger Blough, the chairman of U.S. Steel, who announced a substantial increase in the price of steel produced by his company and who was soon followed by other steel giants. On this occasion, the mobilisation of various forms of presidential pressure,[8] including a spectacular display of presidential anger on television, succeeded in causing the rescinding of the increases—though only for a year. However, the episode was no loss to business in general, since it merely enhanced the President's almost obsessional concern to earn and enjoy its "confidence." Indeed, Governor Connally, who was riding in the President's car at the time of the assassination, has recalled that at least part of Kennedy's purpose in undertaking the trip to Texas was to reassure its "business community" as to his intentions; "I think it galled him," Governor Connally writes, "that conservative business people would suspect that he, a wealthy product himself of our capitalistic system, would do anything to damage that system."[9] ...

Given the degree of economic power which rests in the "business community" and the decisive importance of its actions (or of its non-actions) for major aspects of economic policy, any government with serious pretensions to radical reform must either seek to appropriate that power or find its room for radical action rigidly circumscribed by the requirements of business "confidence." So far, no government in any Western-type political system, whatever its rhetoric before assuming office, has taken up the first of these options. Instead, reform-minded governments have, sometimes reluctantly, sometimes not, curbed their reforming propensities (though never enough for the men they sought to appease) or adapted their reforms to the purposes of business (as happened in the case of the nationalisation proposals of the 1945 Labor government), and turned themselves into the allies of the very forces they had promised, while in opposition, to counter and subdue. Politics, in this context, is indeed the art of the possible. But what is possible is above all determined by what the 'business community' finds acceptable.

Nowadays, however, it is not only with the power of their own business class that reform-minded and "left-wing" governments have to reckon, or whose 'confidence' they must try and earn. Such governments must also reckon, now more than ever before, with the power and pressure of outside capitalist interests and forces—large foreign firms, powerful and conservative foreign governments, central banks, private international finance, official international credit organizations like the International Monetary Fund and the World Bank, or a formidable combination of all these. Economic and financial orthodoxy, and a proper regard for the prerogatives and needs of the free enterprise system, is not only what internal business interests expect and require from their office-holders; these internal interests are now powerfully seconded by outside ones, which may easily be of greater importance.

Capitalism, we have already noted, is now more than ever an international system, whose constituent economies are closely related and interlinked. As a result, even the most powerful capitalist countries depend, to a greater or lesser extent, upon the good will and cooperation of the rest, and of what has become, notwithstanding enduring and profound national capitalist rivalries, an interdependent international capitalist "community." The disapproval by that 'community' of the policies of one of its members, and the withdrawal of good will and co-operation which may follow from it, are obviously fraught with major difficulties for the country concerned. And so long as a country chooses to remain part of the 'community', so long must the wish *not* to incur its disapproval weigh very heavily upon its policy decisions and further reduce the impulses of reform-minded governments to stray far from the path of orthodoxy. Central bankers, enjoying a high degree of autonomy from their governments, have come to assume extraordinary importance as the guardians of that orthodoxy, and as the representatives *par excellence* of 'sound finance'. A *conservative* government in a relatively strong economic and financial position, such as the government of President de Gaulle long enjoyed, may play rogue elephant without undue risk of retribution. A radical government, on the other hand, would be unlikely to be given much shrift by these representatives of international capitalism.

Moreover, radical governments, as was also noted earlier, normally come to office in circumstances of severe economic and financial crisis, and find that credits, loans and general financial support are only available on condition that they pursue economic and foreign policies which are acceptable to their creditors and bankers and which are only marginally distinguishable, if at all, from the conservative policies they had previously denounced....

This kind of dependence and surveillance has always been characteristic of the relations between the world of advanced capitalism and those governments of the 'Third World' which have sought aid and credits from it; and the price of such aid and credits has always been the pursuit by the governments concerned of policies designed to favour, or at least not to hinder, foreign capitalist enterprise, and the adoption in international affairs of policies and attitudes not likely, at the least, to give offence to the creditors and donors.

But these external pressures do not only now affect the underdeveloped countries of the 'Third World'. They can also be directed, with considerable effect, upon the governments of advanced capitalist countries; and here, obviously, is a great source of additional strength to national capitalist interests faced with governments bent on policies unacceptable to these interests. Class conflict, in these countries, has always had an international dimension, but this is now even more directly and specifically true than in the past.

2

In the light of the strategic position which capitalist enterprise enjoys in its dealings with governments, simply by virtue of its control of economic resources, the notion, which is basic to pluralist theory, that here is but one of the many 'veto groups' in capitalist society, on a par with other 'veto groups', must appear as a resolute escape from reality.

Of these other groups, it is labour, as an 'interest' in society, whose power is most often assumed to equal (when it is not claimed to surpass) the power of capital. But this is to treat as an accomplished fact what is only an unrealised potentiality, whose realisation is beset with immense difficulties.

For labour has nothing of the power of capital in the day-to-day economic decision-making of capitalist enterprise. What a firm produces; whether it exports or does not export; whether it invests, in what, and for what purpose; whether it absorbs or is absorbed by other firms—these and many other such decisions are matters over which labour has at best an indirect degree of influence and more generally no influence at all. In this sense, labour lacks a firm basis of economic power, and has consequently that much less pressure potential *vis-à-vis* the state. This is also one reason why governments are so much less concerned to obtain the 'confidence' of labour than of business.

Moreover, labour does not have anything, by way of exercising pressure, which corresponds to the foreign influences which are readily marshalled on behalf of capital. There are no labour 'gnomes' of Zurich, no labour equivalent of the World Bank, the International Monetary Fund, or the OECD, to ensure that governments desist from taking measures detrimental to wage-earners and favourable to business, or to press for policies which are of advantage to 'lower income groups' and which are opposed to the interests of economic elites. For wage-earners in the capitalist world, international solidarity is part of a hallowed rhetoric which seldom manifests itself concretely and effectively; for business, it is a permanent reality.

The one important weapon which labour, as an 'interest', does have is the strike; and where it has been used with real determination its effectiveness as a means of pressure has often been clearly demonstrated. Again and again, employers and governments have been forced to make concessions to labour because of the latter's resolute use of the strike weapon, or even because of the credible threat of its use. On innumerable occasions, demands which, the unions and the workers were told, could not conceivably be granted since they must inevitably mean ruin for a firm or industry or inflict irreparable damage to the national economy, have somehow become acceptable when organised labour has shown in practice that it would not desist.

Determination, however, is the problem. For labour, as a pressure group, is extremely vulnerable to many internal and external influences calculated to erode its will and persistence. Because of the effectiveness of these influences, governments have generally found it unnecessary to treat labour with anything like the deference which they have accorded to business....

One important weakness which affects labour as a pressure group, as compared to business, is that the latter's national organisations are able to speak with considerably more authority than can their labour counterparts.

There are a number of reasons for this. One of them is that business organisations can truly claim to 'speak for business', either because they include a very high percentage of individual business units or because the firms which they do represent are responsible for a crucial part of economic activity. The equivalent labour organisations on the other hand nowhere include a majority of wage-earners, and mostly include far less. Business associations, in this sense, are much more representative than trade unions.

Secondly, and more important, business is nowhere as divided as labour. The point has been made before that business is neither an economic nor an ideological monolith, speaking always or even normally with one single voice on all issues. Indeed, its separate interests find everywhere expression in the different national associations which represent different sectors of the 'business community'. These divisions, notably the division between large-scale enterprise and medium or small business, are by no means negligible, either in specific or in general terms. But they do not prevent a basic ideological consensus, which is of fundamental importance in the representation and impact of business. Thus the policies advocated by the Diet of German Industry and Commerce may well be more 'moderate and liberal' than those of the Federation of German Industry;[10] and similar shades of difference may also be found among national business associations in other countries. But these differences obviously occur within a fairly narrow *conservative* spectrum of agreement which precludes major conflict. Business, it could be said, is tactically divided but strategically cohesive; over most of the larger issues of economic policy, and over other large national issues as well, it may be expected to present a reasonably united front.

This is certainly not the case for trade union movements anywhere. *Their* outstanding characteristic, in fact, is division, not unity; and the divisions from which they suffer, far from being tactical and superficial, are more often than not deep and fundamental.

Trade unions have of course always been divided from each other (and often, indeed, within themselves) in terms of the particular functions and skills of their members, sometimes by geography, often by religious, ethnic or racial factors. But, whether because of these factors or for other reasons, they are above all divided by ideology and attitudes from each other and within themselves.

In some countries, for instance France and Italy, these divisions find institutional expression in the existence of separate, distinct and often bitterly antagonistic federations—Communist, social-democratic and Christian, whose conflicts are a profoundly inhibiting factor in their encounter both with employers and with the state, and in

their effectiveness as pressure groups. Nowhere does business suffer anything remotely comparable to these divisions.

Moreover, even in countries where ideological cleavages have not found institutional expression, trade union movements have still been subject to profound divisions, which may be contained within one organisation, but which are scarcely less debilitating....

End Notes

1. Mills, *The Power Elite*, p. 169. Or, as Alfred de Grazia puts it, 'whoever controls the great industries will have awful political power' (*Politics and Government*, 1962, vol. 2, p. 56).
2. A. Hacker, 'Sociology and Ideology,' in M. Black (ed.), *The Social Theories of Talcott Parsons*, 1961, p. 302.
3. Rowen, *The Free Enterprisers. Kennedy, Johnson and the Business Establishment*, pp. 61–62. Another writer has described the Council as follows: 'Although nominally a private organisation, the BAC is publicly influential in a way in which pressure groups without the same case of access to the federal government can never be. It is apparent, for instance, that it serves as a recruiting and placement agency for personnel in many of the federal agencies. More significantly, it prepares elaborate "studies" and "reports". Although the specific import of such advisory reports is often hard to gauge, the Justice Department has found it necessary to inform the Secretary of the Interior that "fundamental questions of basic policy" are being initially settled by industry advisory committees, with the result that government action amounts to no more than giving effect to decisions already made by such committees' (Kariel, *The Decline of American Pluralism*, p. 99).
4. Rowen, op cit., p. 70.
5. *Ibid.*, p. 71.
6. *Ibid.*, p. 71.
7. *Ibid.*, p. 73 (my italics).
8. For which see *ibid.*, chapter 6.
9. J. Connally, 'Why Kennedy went to Texas', *Life*, 24 November 1967, p. 100.
10. Braunthal, *The Federation of German Industry in Politics*, p. 27.

9

Issue Networks and the Executive Establishment

Hugh Heclo

The connection between politics and administration arouses remarkably little interest in the United States. The presidency is considered more glamorous, Congress more intriguing, elections more exciting, and interest groups more troublesome. General levels of public interest can be gauged by the burst of indifference that usually greets the announcement of a new President's cabinet or rumors of a political appointee's resignation. Unless there is some White House "tie-in" or scandal (preferably both), news stories about presidential appointments are usually treated by the media as routine filler material.

This lack of interest in political administration is rarely found in other democratic countries, and it has not always prevailed in the United States. In most nations the ups and downs of political executives are taken as vital signs of the health of a government, indeed of its survival. In the United States, the nineteenth-century turmoil over one type of connection between politics and administration—party spoils—frequently overwhelmed any notion of presidential leadership. Anyone reading the history of those troubled decades is likely to be struck by the way in which political administration in Washington registered many of the deeper strains in American society at large. It is a curious switch that appointments to

the bureaucracy should loom so large in the history of the nineteenth century, when the federal government did little, and be so completely discounted in the twentieth century, when government tries to do so much.

Political administration in Washington continues to register strains in American politics and society, although in ways more subtle than the nineteenth-century spoils scramble between Federalists and Democrats, Pro- and Anti-tariff forces, Nationalists and States-Righters, and so on. Unlike many other countries, the United States has never created a high level, government-wide civil service. Neither has it been favored with a political structure that automatically produces a stock of experienced political manpower for top executive positions in government. How then does political administration in Washington work? More to the point, how might the expanding role of government be changing the connection between administration and politics?

Received opinion on this subject suggests that we already know the answers. Control is said to be vested in an informal but enduring series of "iron triangles" linking executive bureaus, congressional committees, and interest group clienteles with a stake in particular programs. A President or presidential appointee may occasionally try to muscle in, but few people doubt the capacity of these sub-governments to thwart outsiders in the long run.

Based largely on early studies of agricultural, water, and public works policies, the iron triangle concept is not so much wrong as it is disastrously incomplete. And the conventional view is especially inappropriate for understanding changes in politics and administration during recent years. Preoccupied with trying to find the few truly powerful actors, observers tend to overlook the power and influence that arise out of the configurations through which leading policy makers move and do business with each other. Looking for the closed triangles of control, we tend to miss the fairly open networks of people that increasingly impinge upon government....

Obviously questions of power are still important. But for a host of policy initiatives undertaken in the last twenty years it is all but impossible to identify clearly who the dominant actors are. Who is controlling those actions that go to make up our national policy on abortions, or on income redistribution, or consumer protection, or energy? Looking for the few who are powerful, we tend to overlook the many whose webs of influence provoke and guide the exercise of power. These webs, or what I will call "issue networks," are particularly relevant to the highly intricate and confusing welfare policies that have been undertaken in recent years.

The notion of iron triangles and subgovernments presumes small circles of participants who have succeeded in becoming largely autonomous. Issue networks, on the other hand, comprise a large number of participants with quite variable degrees of mutual commitment or of dependence on others in their environment; in fact it is almost impossible to say where a network leaves off and its environment begins. Iron triangles and subgovernments suggest a stable set of participants coalesced to control fairly narrow public programs which are in the direct economic interest of each party to the alliance. Issue networks are almost the reverse image in each respect. Participants move in and out of the networks constantly. Rather than groups united in dominance over a program, no one, as far as one can tell, is in control of the policies and issues. Any direct material interest is often secondary to

intellectual or emotional commitment. Network members reinforce each other's sense of issues as their interests, rather than (as standard political or economic models would have it) interests defining positions on issues.

Issue networks operate at many levels, from the vocal minority who turn up at local planning commission hearings to the renowned professor who is quietly telephoned by the White House to give a quick "reading" on some participant or policy. The price of buying into one or another issue network is watching, reading, talking about, and trying to act on particular policy problems. Powerful interest groups can be found represented in networks but so too can individuals in or out of government who have a reputation for being knowledgeable. Particular professions may be prominent, but the true experts in the networks are those who are issue-skilled (that is, well informed about the ins and outs of a particular policy debate) regardless of formal professional training. More than mere technical experts, network people are policy activists who know each other through the issues. Those who emerge to positions of wider leadership are policy politicians—experts in using experts, victuallers of knowledge in a world hungry for right decisions.

In the old days—when the primary problem of government was assumed to be doing what was right, rather than knowing what was right—policy knowledge could be contained in the slim adages of public administration. Public executives, it was thought, needed to know how to execute. They needed power commensurate with their responsibility. Nowadays, of course, political administrators do not execute but are involved in making highly important decisions on society's behalf, and they must mobilize policy intermediaries to deliver the goods. Knowing what is right becomes crucial, and since no one knows that for sure, going through the process of dealing with those who are judged knowledgeable (or at least continuously concerned) becomes even more crucial. Instead of power commensurate with responsibility, issue networks seek influence commensurate with their understanding of the various, complex social choices being made. Of course some participants would like nothing better than complete power over the issues in question. Others seem to want little more than the security that comes with being well informed. As the executive of one new group moving to Washington put it, "We didn't come here to change the world; we came to minimize our surprises."[1]

Whatever the participants' motivation, it is the issue network that ties together what would otherwise be the contradictory tendencies of, on the one hand, more widespread organizational participation in public policy and, on the other, more narrow technocratic specialization in complex modern policies. Such networks need to be distinguished from three other more familiar terms used in connection with political administration. An issue network is a shared-knowledge group having to do with some aspect (or, as defined by the network, some problem) of public policy. It is therefore more well-defined than, first, a shared-attention group or "public"; those in the networks are likely to have a common base of information and understanding of how one knows about policy and identifies its problems. But knowledge does not necessarily produce agreement. Issue networks may or may not, therefore, be mobilized into, second, a shared-action group (creating a coalition) or, third, a shared-belief group (becoming a conventional interest organization). Increasingly, it is through networks of people who regard each other as knowledgeable, or at least as needing to be answered, that public policy issues tend to be refined, evidence debated, and alternative options worked out—though rarely in any controlled, well-organized way.

What does an issue network look like? It is difficult to say precisely, for at any given time only one part of a network may be active and through time the various connections may intensify or fade among the policy intermediaries and the executive and congressional bureaucracies. For example, there is no single health policy network but various sets of people knowledgeable and concerned about cost-control mechanisms, insurance techniques, nutritional programs, prepaid plans, and so on. At one time, those expert in designing a nationwide insurance system may seem to be operating in relative isolation, until it becomes clear that previous efforts to control costs have already created precedents that have to be accommodated in any new system, or that

the issue of federal funding for abortions has laid land mines in the path of any workable plan.

The debate on energy policy is rich in examples of the kaleidoscopic interaction of changing issue networks. The Carter administration's initial proposal was worked out among experts who were closely tied in to conservation-minded networks. Soon it became clear that those concerned with macroeconomic policies had been largely bypassed in the planning, and last-minute amendments were made in the proposal presented to Congress, a fact that was not lost on the networks of leading economists and economic correspondents. Once congressional consideration began, it quickly became evident that attempts to define the energy debate in terms of a classic confrontation between big oil companies and consumer interests were doomed. More and more policy watchers joined in the debate, bringing to it their own concerns and analyses: tax reformers, nuclear power specialists, civil rights groups interested in more jobs; the list soon grew beyond the wildest dreams of the original energy policy planners. The problem, it became clear, was that no one could quickly turn the many networks of knowledgeable people into a shared-action coalition, much less into a single, shared-attitude group believing it faced the moral equivalent of war. Or, if it was a war, it was a Vietnam-type quagmire.

It would be foolish to suggest that the clouds of issue networks that have accompanied expanding national policies are set to replace the more familiar politics of subgovernments in Washington. What they are doing is to overlay the once stable political reference points with new forces that complicate calculations, decrease predictability, and impose considerable strains on those charged with government leadership. The overlay of networks and issue politics not only confronts but also seeps down into the formerly well-established politics of particular policies and programs. Social security, which for a generation had been quietly managed by a small circle of insiders, becomes controversial and politicized. The Army Corps of Engineers, once the picture-book example of control by subgovernments, is dragged into the brawl on environmental politics. The once quiet "traffic safety establishment" finds its own safety permanently endangered by the consumer movement. Confrontation between networks and iron triangles in the Social and Rehabilitation Service, the disintegration of the mighty politics of the Public Health Service and its corps—the list could be extended into a chronicle of American national government during the last generation.[2] The point is that a somewhat new and difficult dynamic is being played out in the world of politics and administration. It is not what has been feared for so long: that technocrats and other people in white coats will expropriate the policy process. If there is to be any expropriation, it is likely to be by the policy activists, those who care deeply about a set of issues and are determined to shape the fabric of public policy accordingly.

THE TECHNOPOLS

The many new policy commitments of the last twenty years have brought about a play of influence that is many-stranded and loose. Iron triangles or other clear shapes may embrace some of the participants, but the larger picture in any policy area is likely to be one involving many other policy specialists. More than ever, policy making is becoming an intramural activity among expert issue-watchers, their networks, and their networks of networks. In this situation any neat distinction between the governmental structure and its environment tends to break down.

Political administrators, like the bureaucracies they superintend, are caught up in the trend toward issue specialization at the same time that responsibility is increasingly being dispersed among large numbers of policy intermediaries. The specialization in question may have little to do with purely professional training. Neither is it a matter of finding interest group spokesmen placed in appointive positions. Instead of party politicians, today's political executives tend to be policy politicians, able to move among the various networks, recognized as knowledgeable about the substance of issues concerning these networks, but not irretrievably identified with highly controversial positions. Their reputations among those "in the know" make them available for presidential appointments. Their mushiness on the most sensitive issues makes them acceptable.

Neither a craft professional nor a gifted amateur, the modern recruit for political leadership in the bureaucracy is a journeyman of issues.

Approximately 200 top presidential appointees are charged with supervising the bureaucracy. These political executives include thirteen departmental secretaries, some half a dozen nondepartmental officials who are also in the cabinet, several dozen deputy secretaries or undersecretaries, and many more commission chairmen, agency administrators, and office directors. Below these men and women are another 500 politically appointed assistant secretaries, commissioners, deputies, and a host of other officials. If all of these positions and those who hold them are unknown to the public at large, there is nevertheless no mistaking the importance of the work that they do. It is here, in the layers of public managers, that political promise confronts administrative reality, or what passes for reality in Washington.

At first glance, generalization seems impossible. The political executive system in Washington has everything. Highly trained experts in medicine, economics, and the natural sciences can be found in positions where there is something like guild control over the criteria for a political appointment. But one can also find the most obvious patronage payoffs; obscure commissions, along with cultural and inter-American affairs, are some of the favorite dumping grounds. There are highly issue-oriented appointments, such as the sixty or so "consumer advocates" that the Ralph Nader groups claimed were in the early Carter administration. And there are also particular skill groups represented in appointments devoid of policy content (for example, about two-thirds of the top government public relations positions were filled during 1977 with people from private media organizations). In recent years, the claims of women and minorities for executive positions have added a further kind of positional patronage, where it is the number of positions rather than any agreed policy agenda that is important. After one year, about 11 percent of President Carter's appointees were women, mainly from established law firms, or what is sometimes referred to as the Ladies' Auxiliary of the Old Boys' Network.

How to make sense of this welter of political executives? Certainly there is a subtlety in the arrangements by which top people become top people and deal with each other. For the fact is that the issue networks share information not only about policy problems but also about people. Rarely are high political executives people who have an overriding identification with a particular interest group or credentials as leading figures in a profession. Rather they are people with recognized reputations in particular areas of public policy. The fluid networks through which they move can best be thought of as proto-bureaucracies. There are subordinate and superordinate positions through which they climb from lesser to greater renown and recognition, but these are not usually within the same organization. It is indeed a world of large-scale bureaucracies but one interlaced with loose, personal associations in which reputations are established by word of mouth. The reputations in question depend little on what, in Weberian terms, would be bureaucratically rational evaluations of objective performance or on what the political scientist would see as the individual's power rating. Even less do reputations depend on opinions in the electorate at large. What matters are the assessments of people like themselves concerning how well, in the short term, the budding technopol is managing each of his assignments in and at the fringes of government....

The emergence of the policy politicians in our national politics goes back many years, at least to the new policy commitments of the New Deal era. Policy initiatives undertaken in the last generation have only intensified the process. For example, since 1960 the selection process for presidential appointees has seen important changes.[3] Using somewhat different techniques, each White House staff has struggled to find new ways of becoming less dependent on the crop of job applicants produced by normal party channels and of reaching out to new pools of highly skilled executive manpower. The rationale behind these efforts is always that executive leadership in the bureaucracy requires people who are knowledgeable about complex policies and acceptable to the important groups that claim an interest in the ever growing number of issue areas. Not surprisingly, the policy experts within the various networks who are consulted typically end by recommending each other. Thus over half of the people

President-elect Carter identified as his outside advisers on political appointments ended up in executive jobs themselves. Similarly, while candidate Carter's political manager promised to resign if establishment figures such as Cyrus Vance and Zbigniew Brzezinski were given appointments after the election, at least half of the candidate's expert foreign policy advisers (including Vance and Brzezinski) wound up in major political positions with the administration....

What are the implications for American government and politics? The verdict cannot be one-sided, if only because political management of the bureaucracy serves a number of diverse purposes. At least three important advantages can be found in the emerging system.

First, the reliance on issue networks and policy politicians is obviously consistent with some of the larger changes in society. Ordinary voters are apparently less constrained by party identification and more attracted to an issue-based style of politics. Party organizations are said to have fallen into a state of decay and to have become less capable of supplying enough highly qualified executive manpower. If government is committed to intervening in more complex, specialized areas, it is useful to draw upon the experts and policy specialists for the public management of these programs. Moreover, the congruence between an executive leadership and an electorate that are both uninterested in party politics may help stabilize a rapidly changing society. Since no one really knows how to solve the policy puzzles, policy politicians have the important quality of being disposable without any serious political ramifications (unless of course there are major symbolic implications, as in President Nixon's firing of Attorney General Elliot Richardson).

Within government, the operation of issue networks may have a second advantage in that they link Congress and the executive branch in ways that political parties no longer can. For many years, reformers have sought to revive the idea of party discipline as a means of spanning the distance between the two branches and turning their natural competition to useful purposes. But as the troubled dealings of recent Democratic Presidents with their majorities in Congress have indicated, political parties tend to be a weak bridge.

Meanwhile, the linkages of technocracy between the branches are indeliberately growing. The congressional bureaucracy that has blossomed in Washington during the last generation is in many ways like the political bureaucracy in the executive branch. In general, the new breed of congressional staffer is not a legislative crony or beneficiary of patronage favors. Personal loyalty to the congressman is still paramount, but the new-style legislative bureaucrat is likely to be someone skilled in dealing with certain complex policy issues, possibly with credentials as a policy analyst, but certainly an expert in using other experts and their networks.

None of this means an absence of conflict between President and Congress. Policy technicians in the two branches are still working for different sets of clients with different interests. The point is that the growth of specialized policy networks tends to perform the same useful services that it was once hoped a disciplined national party system would perform. Sharing policy knowledge, the networks provide a minimum common framework for political debate and decision in the two branches. For example, on energy policy, regardless of one's position on gas deregulation or incentives to producers, the policy technocracy has established a common language for discussing the issues, a shared grammar for identifying the major points of contention, a mutually familiar rhetoric of argumentation. Whether in Congress or the executive branch or somewhere outside, the "movers and shakers" in energy policy (as in health insurance, welfare reform, strategic arms limitation, occupational safety, and a host of other policy areas) tend to share an analytic repertoire for coping with the issues. Like experienced party politicians of earlier times, policy politicians in the knowledge networks may not agree; but they understand each other's way of looking at the world and arguing about policy choices.

A third advantage is the increased maneuvering room offered to political executives by the loose-jointed play of influence. If appointees were ambassadors from clearly defined interest groups and professions, or if policy were monopolized in iron triangles, then the chances for executive leadership in the bureaucracy would be small. In fact, however, the proliferation of administrative middlemen and networks of policy watchers offers new strategic resources for public managers. These are mainly opportunities to split and recombine the many sources of support and opposition that exist on policy issues. Of course, there are limits on how far a political executive can go in shopping for a constituency, but the general tendency over time has been to extend those limits. A secretary of labor will obviously pay close attention to what the AFL-CIO has to say, but there are many other voices to hear, not only in the union movement but also minority groups interested in jobs, state and local officials administering the department's programs, consumer groups worried about wage-push inflation, employees faced with unsafe working conditions, and so on. By the same token, former Secretary of Transportation William Coleman found new room for maneuver on the problem of landings by supersonic planes when he opened up the setpiece debate between pro- and anti-Concorde groups to a wider play of influence through public hearings. Clearly the richness of issue politics demands a high degree of skill to contain expectations and manage the natural dissatisfaction that comes from courting some groups rather than others. But at least it is a game that can be affected by skill, rather than one that is predetermined by immutable forces.

These three advantages are substantial. But before we embrace the rule of policy politicians and their networks, it is worth considering the threats they pose for American government. Issue networks may be good at influencing policy, but can they govern? Should they?

The first and foremost problem is the old one of democratic legitimacy. Weaknesses in executive leadership below the level of the President have never really been due to interest groups, party politics, or Congress. The primary problem has always been the lack of any democratically based power. Political executives get their popular mandate to do anything in the bureaucracy secondhand, from either an elected chief executive or Congress. The emerging system of political technocrats makes this democratic weakness much more severe. The more closely political administrators become identified with the various specialized policy networks, the farther they become separated from the ordinary citizen. Political executives can maneuver among the already mobilized issue networks and may occasionally do a little mobilizing of their own. But this is not the same thing as creating a broad base of public understanding and support for national policies. The typical presidential appointee will travel to any number of conferences, make speeches to the membership of one association after another, but almost never will he or she have to see or listen to an ordinary member of the public. The trouble is that only a small minority of citizens, even of those who are seriously attentive to public affairs, are likely to be mobilized in the various networks.[4] Those who are not policy activists depend on the ability of government institutions to act on their behalf.

If the problem were merely an information gap between policy experts and the bulk of the population, then more communication might help. Yet instead of garnering support for policy choices, more communication from the issue networks tends to produce an "everything causes cancer" syndrome among ordinary citizens. Policy forensics among the networks yield more experts making more sophisticated claims and counterclaims to the point that the nonspecialist becomes inclined to concede everything and believe nothing that he hears. The ongoing debates on energy policy, health crises, or arms limitation are rich in examples of public skepticism about what "they," the abstruse policy experts, are doing and saying. While the highly knowledgeable have been playing a larger role in government, the proportion of the general public concluding that those running the government don't seem to know what they are doing has risen rather steadily.[5] Likewise, the more government has tried to help, the more feelings of public helplessness have grown.

No doubt many factors and events are linked to these changing public attitudes. The point is that the increasing prominence of issue networks is bound to aggravate problems of legitimacy and public disenchantment. Policy activists have little desire to recognize an unpleasant fact: that their influential systems for knowledgeable policy making tend to make democratic politics more difficult. There are at least four reasons.

Complexity. Democratic political competition is based on the idea of trying to simplify complexity into a few, broadly intelligible choices. The various issue networks, on the other hand, have a stake in searching out complexity in what might seem simple. Those who deal with particular policy issues over the years recognize that policy objectives are usually vague and results difficult to measure. Actions relevant to one policy goal can frequently be shown to be inconsistent with others. To gain a reputation as a knowledgeable participant, one must juggle all of these complexities and demand that other technocrats in the issue networks do the same.

Consensus. A major aim in democratic politics is, after open argument, to arrive at some workable consensus of views. Whether by trading off one issue against another or by combining related issues, the goal is agreement. Policy activists may commend this democratic purpose in theory, but what their issue networks actually provide is a way of processing dissension. The aim is good policy—the right outcome on the issue. Since what that means is disputable among knowledgeable people, the desire for agreement must often take second place to one's understanding of the issue. Trade-offs or combinations—say, right-to-life groups with nuclear-arms-control people; environmentalists and consumerists; civil liberties groups and anti-gun controllers—represent a kind of impurity for many of the newly proliferating groups. In general there are few imperatives pushing for political consensus among the issue networks and many rewards for those who become practiced in the techniques of informed skepticism about different positions.

Confidence. Democratic politics presumes a kind of psychological asymmetry between leaders and followers. Those competing for leadership positions are expected to be sure of themselves and of what is to be done, while those led are expected to have a certain amount of detachment and dubiety in choosing how to give their consent to be governed. Politicians are supposed to take credit for successes, to avoid any appearance of failure, and to fix blame clearly on their opponents; voters weigh these claims and come to tentative judgments, pending the next competition among the leaders.

The emerging policy networks tend to reverse the situation. Activists mobilized around the policy issues are the true believers. To survive, the newer breed of leaders, or policy politicians, must become well versed in the complex, highly disputed substance of the issues. A certain tentativeness comes naturally as ostensible leaders try to spread themselves across the issues. Taking credit shows a lack of understanding of how intricate policies work and may antagonize those who really have been zealously pushing the issue. Spreading blame threatens others in the established networks and may raise expectations that new leadership can guarantee a better policy result. Vagueness about what is to be done allows policy problems to be dealt with as they develop and in accord with the intensity of opinion among policy specialists at that time. None of this is likely to warm the average citizen's confidence in his leaders. The new breed of policy politicians are cool precisely because the issue networks are hot.

Closure. Part of the genius of democratic politics is its ability to find a non-violent decision-rule (by voting) for ending debate in favor of action. All the incentives in the policy technocracy work against such decisive closure. New studies and findings can always be brought to bear. The biggest rewards in these highly intellectual groups go to those who successfully challenge accepted wisdom. The networks thrive by continuously weighing alternative courses of action on particular policies, not by suspending disbelief and accepting that something must be done.

For all of these reasons, what is good for policy making (in the sense of involving well-informed people and rigorous analysts) may be bad for democratic politics. The emerging policy technocracy tends, as Henry Aaron has said of social science research, to "corrode any simple faiths around which political coalitions ordinarily are built."[6] Should we be content with simple faiths? Perhaps not; but the great danger is that the emerging world of issue politics and policy experts will turn John Stuart Mill's argument about the connection between liberty and popular government on its head. More informed argument about policy choices may produce more incomprehensibility. More policy intermediaries may widen participation among activists but deepen suspicions among unorganized nonspecialists. There may be more group involvement and less democratic legitimacy,

more knowledge and more Know-Nothingism. Activists are likely to remain unsatisfied with, and nonactivists uncommitted to, what government is doing. Superficially this cancelling of forces might seem to assure a conservative tilt away from new, expansionary government policies. However, in terms of undermining a democratic identification of ordinary citizens with their government, the tendencies are profoundly radical.

A second difficulty with the issue networks is the problem that they create for the President as ostensible chief of the executive establishment. The emerging policy technocracy puts presidential appointees outside of the chief executive's reach in a way that narrowly focused iron triangles rarely can. At the end of the day, constituents of these triangles can at least be bought off by giving them some of the material advantages that they crave. But for issue activists it is likely to be a question of policy choices that are right or wrong. In this situation, more analysis and staff expertise—far from helping—may only hinder the President in playing an independent political leadership role. The influence of the policy technicians and their networks permeates everything the White House may want to do. Without their expertise there are no option papers, no detailed data and elaborate assessments to stand up against the onslaught of the issue experts in Congress and outside. Of course a President can replace a political executive, but that is probably merely to substitute one incumbent of the relevant policy network for another....

Where does all this leave the President as a politician and as an executive of executives? In an impossible position. The problem of connecting politics and administration currently places any President in a classic no-win predicament. If he attempts to use personal loyalists as agency and department heads, he will be accused of politicizing the bureaucracy and will most likely put his executives in an untenable position for dealing with their organizations and the related networks. If he tries to create a countervailing source of policy expertise at the center, he will be accused of aggrandizing the Imperial Presidency and may hopelessly bureaucratize the White House's operations. If he relies on some benighted idea of collective cabinet government and on departmental executives for leadership in the bureaucracy (as Carter did in his first term), then the President does more than risk abdicating his own leadership responsibilities as the only elected executive in the national government; he is bound to become a creature of the issue networks and the policy specialists. It would be pleasant to think that there is a neat way out of this trilemma, but there is not.

Finally, there are disturbing questions surrounding the accountability of a political technocracy. The real problem is not that policy specialists specialize but that, by the nature of public office, they must generalize. Whatever an influential political executive does is done with all the collective authority of government and in the name of the public at large. It is not difficult to imagine situations in which policies make excellent sense within the cloisters of the expert issue watchers and yet are nonsense or worse seen from the viewpoint of ordinary people, the kinds of people political executives rarely meet. Since political executives themselves never need to pass muster with the electorate, the main source of democratic accountability must lie with the President and Congress. Given the President's problems and Congress's own burgeoning bureaucracy of policy specialists, the prospects for a democratically responsible executive establishment are poor at best.

Perhaps we need not worry. A case could be made that all we are seeing is a temporary commotion stirred up by a generation of reformist policies. In time the policy process may reenter a period of detumescence as the new groups and networks subside into the familiar triangulations of power.

However, a stronger case can be made that the changes will endure. In the first place, sufficient policy-making forces have now converged in Washington that it is unlikely that we will see a return to the familiar cycle of federal quiescence and policy experimentation by state governments. The central government, surrounded by networks of policy specialists, probably now has the capacity for taking continual policy initiatives. In the second place, there seems to be no way of braking, much less reversing, policy expectations generated by the compensatory mentality. To cut back on commitments undertaken in the last generation would itself be a major act of redistribution and could be

expected to yield even more turmoil in the policy process. Once it becomes accepted that relative rather than absolute deprivation is what matters, the crusaders can always be counted upon to be in business.

A third reason why our politics and administration may never be the same lies in the very fact that so many policies have already been accumulated. Having to make policy in an environment already crowded with public commitments and programs increases the odds of multiple, indirect impacts of one policy on another, of one perspective set in tension with another, of one group and then another being mobilized. This sort of complexity and unpredictability creates a hostile setting for any return to traditional interest group politics.

Imagine trying to govern in a situation where the short-term political resources you need are stacked around a changing series of discrete issues, and where people overseeing these issues have nothing to prevent their pressing claims beyond any resources that they can offer in return. Imagine too that the more they do so, the more you lose understanding and support from public backers who have the long-term resources that you need. Whipsawed between cynics and true believers, policy would always tend to evolve to levels of insolubility. It is not easy for a society to politicize itself and at the same time depoliticize government leadership. But we in the United States may be managing to do just this.

End Notes

1. Steven V. Roberts, "Trade Associations Flocking to Capital as U.S. Role Rises," *New York Times*, March 4, 1978, p. 44.
2. For a full account of particular cases, see for example Martha Derthick, *Policy-Making for Social Security* (Washington, D.C.: Brookings Institution, 1979); Daniel Mazmanian and Jeanne Nienaber, *Environmentalism, Participation and the Corps of Engineers: A Study of Organizational Change* (Washington, D.C.: Brookings Institution, 1978). For the case of traffic safety, see Jack L. Walker, "Setting the Agenda in the U.S. Senate," *British Journal of Political Science*, vol. 7 (1977), pp. 432–45.

3. Changes in the presidential personnel process are discussed in Hugh Heclo, A *Government of Strangers* (Washington, D.C.: Brookings Institution, 1977), pp. 89–95.
4. An interesting recent case study showing the complexity of trying to generalize about who is "mobilizable" is James N. Rosenau, *Citizenship Between Elections* (New York: The Free Press, 1974).
5. Since 1964 the Institute for Social Research at the University of Michigan has asked the question, "Do you feel that almost all of the people running the government are smart people, or do you think that quite a few of them don't seem to know what they are doing?" The proportions choosing the latter view have been 28 percent (1964), 38 percent (1968), 45 percent (1970), 42 percent (1972), 47 percent (1974), and 52 percent (1976). For similar findings on public feelings of lack of control over the policy process, see U.S. Congress, Senate, Subcommittee on Intergovernmental Relations of the Committee on Government Operations, *Confidence and Concern: Citizens View American Government*, committee print, 93d Cong., 1st sess., 1973, pt. 1, p. 30. For a more complete discussion of recent trends see the two articles by Arthur H. Miller and Jack Citrin in the *American Political Science Review* (September 1974).
6. Henry J. Aaron, *Politics and the Professors* (Washington, D.C.: Brookings Institution, 1978), p. 159.

10

Who Benefits, Who Governs, Who Wins?

G. William Domhoff

WHAT IS POWER?

American ideas about power have their origins in the struggle for independence. What is not so well known is that these ideas owe as much to the conflict within each colony over the role of ordinary citizens as they do to the war itself. It is often lost from sight that the average citizens were making revolutionary political demands on their leaders as well as helping in the fight against the British. Before the American Revolution, governments everywhere had been based on the power and legitimacy of religious leaders, kings, self-appointed conventions, or parliaments. The upper-class American revolutionary leaders who drafted the constitutions for the thirteen states between 1776 and 1780 expected their handiwork to be debated and voted upon by state legislatures, but they did not want to involve the general public in a direct way.

Instead, it was members of the "middling" classes of yeoman farmers and artisans who gradually developed the idea out of their own experience that power is the possession of all the people and is delegated to government with their consent. They therefore insisted that special conventions be elected to frame each colony's constitution, and that the constitutions then be ratified by the vote of all free white males without regard to their property holdings. They were steeled in their resolve by their participation in the revolutionary struggle and by a fear of the potentially onerous property laws and taxation policies that might be written into the constitutions by those who were known at the time as their "betters." So the idea of the people as the constituent power of the new United States arose from the people themselves (Palmer 1959).

In the end, the middle-level insurgents only won the right to both a constitutional convention of elected delegates and a vote on subsequent ratification in Massachusetts in 1780. From that time forth, however, it has been widely agreed that "power" in the United States belongs to "the people." Since then every liberal, leftist, populist, or ultraconservative political group has claimed that it represents "the people" in its attempt to wrest arbitrary power from the "vested interests," the "economic elite," the "cultural elite," "the media," the "bureaucrats," or the "politicians in Washington." Even the Founding Fathers of 1789, who were far removed from the general population in their wealth, income, education, and political experience, did not try to promulgate their new constitution, designed to more fully protect private property and compromise some of their fundamental disagreements, without asking for the consent of the governed. In the process they were forced to add the Bill of Rights to ensure the constitution's acceptance. In a very profound cultural sense, then, no group or class has "power" in America, but only "influence." Any small group or class that has power over the people is therefore perceived as illegitimate. This may help explain why those with power in America always deny they have any (Vogel 1978, for a full analysis).

THE SOCIAL SCIENCE VIEW OF POWER

Most social scientists believe that power has two intertwined dimensions. The first involves the degree to which a community or nation has the capacity to perform effectively in pursuing its common goals, which is called *collective power*. Here, the stress is on the degree to which a collectivity has the technological resources, organizational forms, population size, and common spirit to achieve its goals. In that sense, many nations have become more powerful in recent decades than they were in the past, including the United States. Moreover, the collective power of the United States has grown because of its ability to assimilate immigrants of varying economic and educational levels from all over the world as productive citizens. The gradual acceptance of African-Americans into mainstream social institutions also has increased the nation's collective power.

The second dimension of power concerns the ability of a group or social class within a community or nation to be successful in conflicts with its rivals on issues of concern to it. Here, the stress is on *power over*, which is also called *distributive power*. Paralleling general American beliefs, most social scientists think of distributive power in the sense of great or preponderant influence, not in the sense of complete and absolute control. More specifically, a powerful group or class is one that can realize its goals even if some other group or class is opposed (Olsen and Marger 1993; Wrong 1995). This definition captures the sense of struggle that is embodied in the everyday meaning of power and it readily encompasses the idea of class conflict defined in the Introduction. It also fits with the main goal of this book, which is to show that a social upper class of owners and high-level executives has the power to institute the policies it favors even in the face of organized opposition from the liberal-labor coalition.

Generally speaking, the ability of a group or class to prevail begins in one of the four major social networks—economic, political, military, and religious—that can be turned into a strong organizational base for wielding power (Mann 1986). Although economic and political networks have been the main power networks in the United States for historical reasons that are discussed in Chapter 8, the four power networks have combined in several different ways in other countries to create widely varying power structures. For example, military force has led to the capture of the government and control of the economic system in many countries past and present. In other countries, such as Iran in the 1970s, a well-organized religious group has been able to develop popular support and demonstrate the ability to exercise force if need be in maintaining control over the government.

Due to the variety of power outcomes that the historical record provides, most social scientists believe there is no one fundamental basis for distributive power from which the other types of power can be derived. The four basic power networks have existed since hunting and gathering societies developed and they have always been intertwined (Gendron and Domhoff 2009, pp. 194–196). This means that the concept of distributive power is a fundamental one in the social sciences, just as energy is a fundamental concept in the natural sciences for the same reason: No one form of energy or power is more basic than any other (Russell 1938; Wrong 1995).

However, a definition of distributive power does not explain how a concept is to be measured. In the case of distributive power, it is seldom possible to observe interactions that reveal its operation even in small groups, let alone to see something as large and diffuse as a social class producing effects on another social class. People and organizations are what can be seen in a power struggle within a community or nation, not rival social classes, although it may turn out that the people and organizations represent the interests of social classes. It is therefore necessary to develop what are called *indicators of power.*

Although distributive power is first and foremost a relationship between two or more contending groups or classes, for research purposes it is useful to think of distributive power as an underlying trait or property of a group or social class. As with any underlying trait that cannot be observed directly, it is measured by a series of indicators, or signs, that bear a probabilistic relationship to it. This means that not all of the indicators necessarily appear each and every time the trait is manifesting itself. It might make this point more clear to add that the personality traits studied by psychologists to understand individual behavior and the concepts developed to explain findings in the natural sciences have a similar logical structure. Whether a theorist is concerned with friendliness, as in psychology, or magnetism, as in physics, or power, as in the case of this book, the nature of the investigatory procedure is the same. In each case, there is an underlying concept whose presence can be inferred only through a series of diagnostic signs or indicators that vary in their strength under differing conditions. Research proceeds, in this view, through a series of *if-then* statements based on as many independent indicators as possible. *If* a group is powerful, *then* at least some of the indicators of power should be measurable in some circumstances (Lazarsfeld 1966, for a classic statement of this approach).

THREE POWER INDICATORS

Since an indicator of power may not necessarily appear or be measurable in each and every instance where power is operating, it is necessary to have several indicators. Working within this framework, three different types of power indicators are used in this book. They are called (1) Who benefits? (2) Who governs? and (3) Who wins? Each of these empirical indicators has its own strengths and weaknesses. However, the potential weaknesses of each indicator do not present a serious problem because all three of them have to point to the owners and managers of large income-producing property as the most powerful class for the case to be considered convincing.

Who Benefits?

Every society has material objects and experiences that are highly valued. If it is assumed that everyone would like to have as great a share of these good things of life as possible, then their distribution can be utilized as a power indicator. Those who have the most of what people want are, by inference, the powerful. Although some value distributions may be unintended outcomes that do not really reflect power, the general distribution of valued experiences and objects within a society still can be viewed as the most publicly visible and stable outcome of the operation of power.

In American society, for example, wealth and well-being are highly valued. People seek to own property, to have high incomes, to have interesting and safe jobs, to enjoy the finest in travel and leisure, and to live long and healthy lives. All of these "values" are unequally distributed, and all may be utilized as power indicators. In this book, however, the primary focus with this type of indicator is on the wealth and income distributions. This does not mean that wealth and income are the same thing as power. Instead, high income and the possession of great wealth are simply visible signs that a class has power in relation to other classes.

The argument for using value distributions as power indicators is strengthened by studies showing that such distributions vary from country to country, depending upon the relative strength of rival political parties and trade unions. One study reported that the degree of inequality in the income distribution in Western democracies varied inversely with the percentage of social democrats who had been elected to the country's legislature in the first three decades after 1945. The greater the social democratic presence, the greater the amount of income that goes to the lower classes (Hewitt 1977).[1] In a study based on eighteen Western democracies in the same era, it was found that strong trade unions and successful social democratic parties are correlated with greater equality in the income distribution and a higher level of welfare spending (Stephens 1979). Thus, there is evidence that value distributions do vary depending on the relative power of contending groups or classes.

Closer to home and the present moment, the highly concentrated wealth distribution highlighted earlier in this chapter provides the first piece of evidence that the American upper class is a dominant class. The fact that the top 1 percent of households (the upper class) own 34.3 percent of all marketable assets and that the next 9 percent, most of whom are high-level managers, professionals, successful small business owners, professional athletes, and entertainers, own 36.9 percent, means that 10 percent of the population owns 71.2 percent of all marketable assets. This leaves 28.8 percent for the 90 percent of the people who are lower-level managers, supervisors, teachers, clerical workers, production workers, and service workers (Wolff 2007, Table 2). These numbers provide a stark x-ray of the distribution of power in the United States. In addition, the increasing concentration of both the wealth and income distributions between the 1980s and 2004 implies that the upper class and corporate community gained increasing power over everyday wage earners during that time period. (You can read the document "Wealth, Income, and Power" on www.whorulesamerica.net to learn more details on the wealth and income distributions and their relationship to power.)

The ratio of average yearly income for chief executive officers (usually called CEOs) of major corporations compared to average factory workers is another excellent indicator in the *Who benefits?* category. As briefly mentioned in the Introduction, this ratio rose from 42:1 in 1960 to 344:1 in 2007. The ratio was even higher in 2007 for the managers of private investment funds, where the average annual earnings for the top officers at the fifty largest firms was $588 million—that's 19,000 times as much as the average worker (Anderson et al. 2008). At that point, Wall Street financiers truly were the rulers of the universe.

Who Governs?

Power also can be determined by studying who occupies important institutional positions and takes part in important decision-making groups. If a group or class is highly overrepresented or underrepresented in relation to its proportion of the population, it can be inferred that the group or class is relatively powerful or powerless, as the case may be. For example, if a class that contains 1 percent of the population has 30 percent of the important positions in the government, which is thirty times as many as would be expected by chance, then it can be inferred that the class is powerful. Conversely, if it is found that women are in only a small percentage of the leadership positions in government, even though they make up a majority of the population, it can be inferred that women are relatively powerless in that important sector of society. Similarly, if it is determined that a minority group has only a small percentage of its members in leadership positions, even though it comprises 10 to 20 percent of the population in a given city or state, then the basic processes of power—inclusion and exclusion—are inferred to be at work.

This indicator is not perfect because some official positions may not really possess the power they are thought to have, and some groups or classes may exercise power from "behind the scenes." Once again, however, the case for the usefulness of this indicator is strengthened by the fact that it has been shown to vary over time and place. For example, the decline of landed aristocrats and the rise of business leaders in Great Britain has been charted through their degree of representation in Parliament (Guttsman 1969). Then, too, as women, African-Americans, Latinos, and Asian-Americans joined movements to demand a greater voice in the Unites States in the 1960s and 1970s, their representation in positions of authority began to increase (Zweigenhaft and Domhoff 2006).

Who Wins?

There are many issues over which the corporate community and the liberal-labor coalition disagree, including taxation, unionization, and business regulation. Power can be inferred on the basis of these issue conflicts by determining who successfully initiates, modifies, or vetoes policy alternatives. This indicator, by focusing on relationships between the two rival coalitions, comes closest to approximating the process of power contained in the formal definition. It is the indicator preferred by most social scientists. For many reasons, however, it is also the most difficult to use in an accurate way. Aspects of a decision process may remain hidden, some informants may exaggerate or downplay their roles, and people's memories about who did what often become cloudy shortly after the event. Worse, the key concerns of the corporate community may never arise as issues on the political agenda because it has the power to keep them in the realm of *non-issues* (i.e., most people know there is a problem, but it is never addressed in the political arena)...

Despite the difficulties in using the *Who wins?* indicator of power, it is possible to provide a theoretical framework for analyzing governmental decision-making that mitigates many of the methodological problems. This framework encompasses the various means by which the corporate community attempts to influence both

the government and the general population in a conscious and planned manner, thereby making it possible to assess its degree of success very directly. More specifically, there are four relatively distinct but overlapping processes (discovered by means of membership network analysis) through which the corporate community tries to control the public agenda and win policy victories on the issues that do appear on it. These processes are based in four power networks, which are discussed in more detail in later chapters.

1. The *special-interest process* deals with the narrow and short-run policy concerns of wealthy families, specific corporations, and specific business sectors. It operates primarily through lobbyists, company lawyers, and trade associations, with a focus on congressional committees, departments of the executive branch, and regulatory agencies. The lobbyists are often former elected officials or former aides and advisers to elected officials who can command very large salaries in the private sector because their information and connections are so valuable to corporations.

2. The *policy-planning process* formulates the general interests of the corporate community. It operates through a policy-planning network of foundations, think tanks, and policy-discussion groups, with a focus on the White House, relevant congressional committees, and the high-status newspapers and opinion magazines published in New York and Washington. It is the place where corporate leaders meet with academic experts and former government officials to discuss differences and prepare themselves for government appointments.

3. The *opinion-shaping process* attempts to influence public opinion and keep some issues off the public agenda. Often drawing on policy positions, rationales, and statements developed within the policy-planning process, it operates through the public relations departments of large corporations, general public relations firms, and many small opinion-shaping organizations, which direct their attention to middle-class

voluntary organizations, educational institutions, and the mass media. Many advertising executives, former journalists, and former government officials are employed by the organizations in this network. Sometimes the process works through harsh media attacks on opponents of the corporate community.

4. The *candidate-selection process* is concerned with the election of politicians who are sympathetic to the agenda put forth in the special-interest and policy-planning processes. It operates through large campaign donations and hired political consultants; it is focused on the presidential campaigns of both major political parties and the congressional campaigns of the Republican Party.

Taken together, the people and organizations that operate in these four networks constitute the political-action arm of the corporate community and upper class....

End Notes

1. Social democrats come from a tradition that began with a socialist orientation and then moved in a more reformist direction. For the most part, social democratic parties have only slightly more ambitious goals than the liberal-labor coalition in the United States; the left wing of the liberal-labor coalition would feel at home in a strong social democratic party in Western Europe.

PART TWO

Rules, Strategies, Resources, and Culture

11

Rules, Strategies, Resources, and Culture

Matthew A. Cahn

The public policy process has been described by several observers as a game.[1] The game analogy is not intended to trivialize the process, rather, it suggests that policy actors must utilize rational strategies to maximize their interests. Policy entrepreneurs will maximize their interest to the extent that they have knowledge of the policy bureaucracy (bureaucratic knowledge), access to individuals within the bureaucracy (network), citizen backing (size of constituency), money for political contributions, and resources to mount an effective public relations (media) campaign. But these resources only explain one component of policy competition. It is also necessary to understand the rules and culture of the policy environment. The following discussion explores the context and environment of the policy process, including the constitutional basis of public policy, the culture of policy, maximizing policy strategies, and the problem of policy resources.

THE CONSTITUTIONAL BASIS OF PUBLIC POLICY

Legal scholars have long described Constitutional law as an arena of conflict resolution that, while not perfect, offers citizens a forum to redress grievances.[2] While legislation on all levels adds rules to the game at various points, the constitutional basis of policy remains the foundation. For this reason the discourse on constitutional law is of prime importance to policy observers. Rather than focus on specific court decisions, this section is concerned with the constitutional foundations of the policy process.

The classic debate over whose interests are best protected by the Constitution is best illustrated by Charles Beard[3] on the one hand, and Forrest McDonald[4] and Robert Brown[5] on the other. Beard's economic interpretation thesis argues that the Constitution was created by the economic elite at the expense of the debtor class (disenfranchised and small farmers). McDonald and Brown argue that Beard's historiography is factually flawed. They point to the existence of a large middle class, and suggest that all sectors of society benefitted from ratification. Further, they argue that while the delegates to the convention were clearly elites, self-interest was not their motivation.

What is of concern to policy scholars is where the dust settled. Rather than quibble over historical detail, contemporary scholars examine how public law has come to be structured, and whether public policy has come to favor specific sectors. Beard's thesis represents one of the most critical interpretations of the U.S. Constitution. Arguing that the Constitution was written by specific elites, for their own self-interest, Beard documents the economic interconnections of the members of the Convention in 1787. Further, he explores the specific benefits each received after ratification. Rather than argue conspiracy theory, Beard sees the framers as representing the dominant elites in American society at the time.[6]

Robert Brown and Forrest McDonald both present critiques of Beard's economic interpretation. Brown disputes Beard's central assertion that the convention delegates shared economic interests that were distinct from the agrarian interests of the debtor classes. Instead, Brown argues that the dominant wealth at the convention was also agrarian, in the form of farmland and slaves, and that the interests of the framers included the interests of society at large. While Brown may be correct in his assertion that the interests represented at the convention included agriculture, in failing to discuss the distinctly different interests held by artisans, laborers, and small farmers in comparison to large slaveholding plantations—Brown fails to consider distinctive class differences present in 1787. McDonald's work fills in the historical details for Beard, drawing a vivid picture of propertied elites interacting to create the Constitution. Similar to Brown, McDonald cites the weight of agrarian interests represented at the convention to disprove Beard. And also similar, McDonald fails to discuss that these economic elites were largely diversified and were thus to benefit from the economic system the Constitution guaranteed. In reviewing the data, McDonald fails to comment on the potential coherence of interests represented.

While the delegates of the Constitutional convention had economic interests that conflicted in some areas, their interests cohered in key areas: (a) in a strong central government that could protect commerce across state boundaries and control the "passions" of the masses; (b) in the creation of a central currency, protecting creditors from depreciation; (c) in creating protection to creditors for monies loaned at interest—at the distinct disadvantage of the debtor classes represented by people like Daniel Shays.

By failing to discuss the massive propaganda effort, best illuminated by the Federalist articles, Brown and McDonald gloss over the conflict over ratification. *The Federalist Papers*[7] focused on the structural changes the Constitution would bring, but Hamilton, Madison, and Jay were careful not to discuss the economic implications. While Brown and McDonald may correctly point out the inadequacy in Beard's historiography, it is clear that the framers were elites who stood to benefit from the adoption of the Constitution. In his classic text *The American Political Tradition*[8] Richard Hofstadter points out that to the framers of the Constitution, liberty was tied to property, not democracy. Freedom meant the freedom to own and dispose of private property, not freedom of self-government. The resulting political economy of an urbanized industrial society is the direct manifestation of the framers' principles.

The implications for public policy are significant. The early Constitution provided for republican government, with only limited citizen participation, resulting in an insulated relationship between elected officials and the populace. This suggests that the framers intentionally sought to protect the Union from "popular passions" through mechanisms such as the electoral college and indirect election of the president, the appointment of Senators by State legislators until 1913, single-member districts which preclude minority party representation, and the state-imposed gender and property requirements.

Although the American policy process has evolved since the late eighteenth century, the original constitutional framework has had serious policy consequences for those classes who were earlier excluded. African Americans and other peoples of color, women, the poor, and most recently gays and lesbians have spent the last two centuries fighting an uphill battle for parity. The policy framework continues to provide inherent advantages to economic elites. The following section explores the impact of this legacy on the policy process.

POLITICAL CULTURE AND PUBLIC POLICY

Till there be property there can be no government, the very end of which is to secure wealth, and to defend the rich from the poor. (Adam Smith, 1776)[9]

(Property is) that dominion which one man claims and exercises over the external things of the world, in exclusion of every other individual. (James Madison, 1792)[10]

All communities divide themselves into the few and the many. The first are the rich and the well-born, the other the mass of the people.... The people are turbulent and changing; they seldom judge or determine right. (Alexander Hamilton, 1787).[11]

Public policy outcomes cannot be divorced from political culture. The assumptions held by a society narrow the scope of viable policy options. As Adam Smith, James Madison, and Alexander Hamilton suggest, American political culture reflects a property-oriented legacy. American political culture is based on the natural or "inalienable" rights of individuals. Drawing from the well of Lockean liberal imagery the Declaration of Independence clearly sets forth the primacy of individual rights to life, liberty, and property. Yet, the primacy of liberal individualism creates a dilemma for public policy: Lockean individualism is nowhere manifest more strongly than in its commitment to individual property rights, and as a result, individual property rights limit the notion of communal rights, creating a problematic definition of communal good.

American political culture, true to its utilitarian roots, defines the common good as the aggregate sum of individual good. That is, the role of the community is to provide the infrastructure to make individual rights possible. No more, no less. In Lockean terms, the role of the community is to create a stable environment for the acquisition, use, and disposition of private property. Public policy, therefore, is fundamentally organized around economic interaction. The policy implications are twofold: public policy tends to create independent economic actors; and, public policy demands that any communal need be evaluated in light of individual property rights.[12]

In the classic work in this area, *Capitalism, Socialism, and Democracy*,[13] Schumpeter explains the dilemma of democracy in a capitalist political economy. Stated simply, capitalism defines freedom (rights) on the principle of ownership: one dollar, one vote.[14] Democracy defines freedom (rights) on the principle of one person, one vote. While Milton Friedman[15] and others will argue that there is no conflict here, Schumpeter sees an inherent contradiction. In examining the Schumpeter thesis, Samuel Bowles and Herbert Gintis identify the multiple spheres that make up an individual's life. In *Democracy and Capitalism*[16] Bowles and Gintis point out that liberal society is broken up into two spheres, public and private. The public sphere includes those aspects of society where both liberty and democracy apply, such as government. The private sphere includes those areas where only liberty applies. Bowles and Gintis argue that

Liberal social theory's arbitrary asymmetric treatment of state and economy stems... from the untenable notion that the capitalist economy is a private sphere—in other words, that its operation does not involve the socially consequential exercise of power.[17]

Bowles and Gintis look to the "labor commodity proposition" to explain the antidemocratic tendency within American social culture: If labor were not considered a commodity, to be bought and sold, but rather a partnership, the hierarchical organization of the workplace and the "privacy" of the economy would be untenable. The "market" is a political arena. The feminist notion that the personal is political perhaps is best understood in such a context. Any definition of politics must include the distribution of goods as well as the distribution of power. For all of us, this is regularly played out in our economic relationships.

Bowles and Gintis redevelop the utilitarian argument that people are created by the role they play in society. Our values are tied inextricably to our culture. If liberal society is characterized by limited choice and extensive spheres of domination, the chances of developing democratic values are limited. The economic system produces social values; in short, "the economy produces people."

> The economy produces people. The experience of individuals as economic actors is a major determinant of their personal capacities, attitudes, choices, interpersonal relations, and social philosophies.[18]

As Mancur Olson points out, the individualist tendency in American society is so strong that even when collective action would produce benefits to all, "self-interested individuals will not act to achieve their common or group interest."[19]

Michael Rogin[20] argues that economic domination is only one of the policy implications of American political culture. As a result of the in/out dichotomy of social contract theory, American political culture demonizes cultural and political adversaries. Social contract theory is based on the notion of a society sharing a single set of cultural and political values. That is, one is part of the social contract, either explicitly or implicitly, when he or she accepts the responsibilities of ideological homogeneity. Through a shared concept of civilization all parties of the social contract are able to live and interact with each other predictably and safely. As they are out of Locke's state of nature, the theoretical state of war is, for the duration of the social contract, over. The implications for anyone outside of the social contract are clear. They are unpredictable, dangerous, and at war with us. Consequently, any individual or group who does not share the dominant cultural and political ideology are, by definition, suspect.[21] The policy implications are that discrimination and inequality are an inherent part of the political and social environment. From the enslavement of African Americans, to the dislocation of native Americans, to the incarceration of Japanese Americans, to the exclusion of gay and lesbian Americans, Rogin argues that exclusion is a function of American political culture.

Other observers argue that while there is intolerance and antidemocratic tendencies within American society, they are not an integral part of American political culture. Louis Hartz and C.B. Macpherson[22] see the American emphasis on individual economic self-interest as the mechanism for social stability. "Possessive individualism" diverts the passions of men (laziness and self-indulgence) into a drive for economic gain, creating sober, productive citizens. Anthony Downs[23] and other "Public Choice" scholars see self-interest as the primary motivation of all people. As a consequence, such scholars argue that inequality can, and ultimately will, be addressed within the context of contemporary political culture, albeit with a renewed concern for social and political, if not economic, equality.

MAXIMIZING POLICY STRATEGIES

In *The Prince*[24] Machiavelli presents a blueprint for the effective development and maintenance of power. Machiavelli's notion of virtu'—controlling political destiny—is based on the successful manipulation of human circumstances. The virtuous prince is good, merciful, and honest, as long as expediency dictates. Yet, he must be prepared to be cruel and deceptive. Control is the primary consideration, both of one's populace, and of one's neighboring states. Virtu', ultimately, requires successful strategies to maximize policy interests. In *Presidential Power*[25] Neustadt outlines a Machiavellian strategy for the president. He, like Machiavelli, is overwhelmingly concerned with how a president expands his power, and maintains it. Since he lacks the formal power of a dictator the president must rely on his power to persuade rather than command. In examining Machiavellian influence in American politics, it is necessary to read Neustadt both as prescriptive, as he intended, and as narrative—how president's ought to gain power, and how strong ones do. The presidency, in Neustadt's analysis, is a "clerkship," based on balancing differing interests, and keeping in mind the public good.

Presidential virtue is based on the presentation of image. Every decision must take into account how it will be perceived. The reputation of a president, and his or her future power, is greatly dependent on a strong image. Charisma is essential for the smooth development of power, as the president must be identified with, respected, and even loved. The president must act quickly and decisively to criticize opponents and reward allies. And, perhaps most important for both Machiavelli and Neustadt, the president must make effective use of the political climate. Only through the successful resolution of crisis can a president truly create dependence and power. While Machiavelli's Prince can rely on respect or fear, presidents, for the most part, can only rely on respect and the successful manufacture of consent.[26] Through deception, and manipulation of the political climate, a president can essentially create consent. Favorable public opinion, Machiavelli's notion of adulation, is necessary for presidential action. But, that public opinion can be manipulated. Drawing on cultural biases, symbols, and traditions, a skilled president can maximize his power, and implement policies as he sees fit. The marriage of Locke and Machiavelli becomes clear. Locke's notion of executive prerogative and the cunning of Machiavelli's Prince each influence the successful American president.

The meaning of prerogative, in the context of American Liberalism, is that no rights are absolute, no rights are inalienable. On the one hand the constitution promises individual rights; but on the other, it denies those rights at the discretion of the executive. One of the best illustrations of executive prerogative in the United States was the suspension of constitutional protections and collective incarceration of Japanese Americans. By executive order, the president of the United States (Roosevelt) mandated the imprisonment of all persons of Japanese ancestry living on the West Coast of the nation.

Murray Edelman[27] similarly argues that those who seek to maximize their policy interests will use deceit and symbolism to manipulate the policy discourse. No one person can possibly experience the entire world. Yet, everyone has an image or "picture" of the world. Kenneth Burke suggests that however important that "sliver of reality each of us has experienced firsthand," the overall "picture" is a "construct of symbolic systems."[28] This construct is based on political cognitions which Edelman suggests are "ambivalent and highly susceptible to symbolic cues...."[29] Government, Edelman argues, influences behavior by shaping the cognitions of people in ambiguous

situations. In this way, government, or policy elites, help engineer beliefs about what is "fact" and what is "proper."

Maximizing policy strategies is critical for policy influence. Each actor, regardless of his or her position in the policy environment, seeks to influence policy outcomes. The degree to which actors utilize rational strategies, however creative, however slippery, will determine the degree to which policy success can be achieved. This is not to suggest that there are no ethical constraints on players; there are. Rather, the Machiavellian legacy in American political culture recognizes that strategy and cunning are acceptable and necessary components of the policy process.

THE PROBLEM OF POLICY RESOURCES

In *A Preface to Economic Democracy*[30] Robert Dahl redefines his thinking on American democracy. Dahl has long recognized the existence of economic elites and their influence on the policy process. His earlier work[31] argued that these elites compete with one another, creating an equilibrium within which different interests can be represented. This work argues that rather than compete, the interests of these economic elites cohere in specific areas. The result is that democratic processes are dominated by the influence of economic elites— specifically, corporate elites. E. E. Schattschneider writes, "The flaw in the pluralist heaven is that the heavenly chorus sings with a strong upper-class accent."[32] A social upper class operates as a ruling class by virtue of its dominance of economic resources. While there are other political resources—for example, expertise and bureaucratic knowledge—these other resources can and are purchased. Thus, Schattschneider points out, financial power is often the basis of policy influence.

If it is true that policy influence requires requisite political resources, inequality in resource distribution is tantamount to inequality in political representation. Thus, as Dahl, Schattschneider, and many other observers[33] argue, if Americans are serious about creating a truly pluralistic society, it is necessary to democratize political resources, specifically economic resources. In the past, civic relationships have dulled the greatest impact of resource inequality. Neighbors, churches, and even bowling leagues have provided sufficient social capital to mitigate these tensions. But, these communities are less and less able to do this. Robert Bellah and his colleagues lament the changing role of community in America, citing the increasing culture of separation.[34] Robert Putnam argues that unless community can be resurrected, the erosion of social capital will bleed over to the erosion of democratic institutions.[35]

CONCLUSION

This chapter has explored the context of rules, strategies, resources, and culture on the policy environment. Since public policy cannot be studied apart from the constraints imposed by cultural inheritances, it is necessary to investigate subtle social legacies. The following readings in this section of the book further explore these policy influences.

End Notes

1. See, for example, Peter Navarro, *The Policy Game: How Special Interests and Ideologues are Stealing America* (Lexington, KY: Lexington Books, 1984) and Larry J. Sabato, *The Rise of Political Consultants: New Ways of Winning Elections* (New York: Basic Books, 1981); as well, for a discussion on the competing games individuals play in a democratic society, see Samuel Bowles and Herbert Gintis, *Democracy and Capitalism: Property, Community, and the Contradictions of Modern Social Thought* (New York: Basic Books, Inc, 1986).
2. See, for example, Herbert Jacob, *Justice in America: Courts, Lawyers, and the Judicial Process* (4th Ed.) (Boston, MA: Little, Brown and Co., 1984).
3. Charles Beard, *An Economic Interpretation of the Constitution of the United States* (New York: MacMillan, 1936).
4. Forrest McDonald, *We the People: The Economic Origins of the Constitution* (Chicago, IL: The University of Chicago Press, 1958).
5. Robert Brown, *Charles Beard and the Constitution: A Critical Analysis of "An Economic Interpretation of the Constitution"* (Princeton, NJ: Princeton University Press, 1956).
6. Charles Beard, op. cit.
7. Alexander Hamilton, James Madison and John Jay, *The Federalist Papers*, ed. Clinton Rossiter (New York: New American Library, 1961).
8. Richard Hofstadter, *The American Political Tradition* (New York: Knopf, 1948:11).
9. Adam Smith, *An Inquiry into the Nature and Causes of the Wealth of Nations* (1776), in Michael Parenti *Democracy for the Few* (5th Ed.) (New York: St. Martins Press, 1988:21).
10. James Madison in "Essay on Property" (1792), in Alpheas Mason and D. Grier Stephenson Jr., *American Constitutional Law* (Englewood Cliffs, NJ: Prentice-Hall, 1987:271).
11. Alexander Hamilton, comments from the Constitutional Convention, in Max Farrand *Records of the Federal Convention,* vol. 1 (New Haven, CT: Yale University Press, 1927).
12. For a fuller discussion on the policy constraints imposed by the liberal legacy, see Chapter 1 of Matthew Cahn *Environmental Deceptions: The Tension between Liberalism and Environmental Policymaking in the United States* (Engelwood Cliffs, NJ: Prentice Hall, 1995).
13. Joseph Schumpeter, *Capitalism, Socialism, and Democracy* (New York: Harper and Row, 1942).
14. See also Richard Coe and Charles Wilber (eds.), *Capitalism and Democracy: Schumpeter Revisited* (Notre Dame, IN: University of Notre Dame Press, 1985).
15. Milton Friedman, *Capitalism and Freedom* (Chicago, IL: University of Chicago Press, 1972).
16. Samuel Bowles and Herbert Gintis, *Democracy and Capitalism: Property, Community, and the Contradictions of Modern Social Thought* (New York: Basic Books, Inc, 1986).
17. Bowles and Gintis, op. cit., p. 67.
18. Bowles and Gintis, op. cit., p. 131.
19. Mancur Olson, *The Logic of Collective Action.* Harvard University Press, 1971 p. 2.
20. Michael Rogin, *Ronald Reagan the Movie, and Other Episodes in Political Demonology* (Berkeley, CA: University of California Press, 1987).
21. See also Howard Zinn, *A People's History of the United States* (New York: Harper and Row, 1980).

22. Louis Hartz, *The Liberal Tradition in America* (New York: Harcourt Brace Jovanovich, 1955); C.B. Macpherson, *The Life and Times of Liberal Democracy* (New York: Oxford University Press, 1977).

23. Anthony Downs, *An Economic Theory of Democracy* (New York: Harper and Row, 1957).

24. Niccolo Machiavelli, *The Prince*, in Peter Bondanella and Mark Muse (eds.), *The Portable Machiavelli* (New York: Penguin Books, 1983).

25. Richard Neustadt, *Presidential Power* (New York: John Wiley and Sons Inc. 1980).

26. For a complete discussion, see Clinton Rossiter, *Constitutional Dictatorship* (New York: Harcourt Brace and World, Inc., 1948, 1963).

27. Murray Edelman, *Constructing the Political Spectacle* (Chicago, IL: The University of Chicago Press, 1988).

28. Kenneth Burke, *Language as Symbolic Action* (Berkeley, CA: University of California Press, 1966:5).

29. Murray Edelman, *Politics as Symbolic Action* (Chicago, IL: Markham Publishing Co., 1971:2).

30. Robert Dahl, *A Preface to Economic Democracy* (Berkeley, CA: University of California Press, 1985).

31. Robert Dahl, *A Preface to Democratic Theory* (Chicago, IL: University of Chicago Press, 1956) and *Who Governs?* (New Haven, CT: Yale University Press, 1961).

32. E.E. Schattschneider, *The Semisovereign People* (Dryden Press, 1975:35).

33. In addition to Dahl (1985) and Schattschneider, see for example, C. Wright Mills, *The Power Elite* (New York: Oxford University Press, 1956); G. William Domhoff, *Who Rules America? Challenges to Corporate and Class Dominance* (McGraw-Hill, 2009); and Bowles and Gintis, op. cit.; Matthew Cahn, op. cit.

34. Robert Bellah, Richard Madsen, William Sullivan, Ann Swidler and Steven Tipton, *Habits of the Heart: Individualism and Commitment in American Life* (UC Press, 1985).

35. Robert Putnam, *Bowling Alone: The Collapse and Revival of American Community* (Simon and Schuster 2000).

Suggested Reading

B. GUY PETERS, *American Public Policy: Promise and Performance* (3rd Ed.) (CQ Press, 8th Ed, 2009).

HAROLD LASSWELL, *Politics: Who Gets What, When, and How* (New York: St. Martin's Press, 1988).

HEDRICK SMITH, *The Power Game: How Washington Works* (New York: Ballantine Books, 1988).

MATTHEW A. CAHN, *Environmental Deceptions: The Tension between Liberalism and Environmental Policymaking in the United States* (Albany, NY: SUNY Press, 1995).

C. WRIGHT MILLS, *The Power Elite* (Oxford, UK: Oxford University Press, 1956).

G. WILLIAM DOMHOFF, *Who Rules America? Challenges to Corporate and Class Dominance* (McGraw-Hill, 2009).

RICHARD HOFSTADTER, *The American Political Tradition* (New York: Knopf, 1948).

MAX FARRAND, *Records of the Federal Convention* (New Haven, CT: Yale University Press, 1927).

MILTON FRIEDMAN, *Capitalism and Freedom* (Chicago, IL: University of Chicago Press, 1972).

HOWARD ZINN, *A People's History of the United States* (Harper Perennial Modern Classics, 2010).

NICCOLO MACHIAVELLI, *The Prince*, in Peter Bondanella and Mark Muse (eds.), *The Portable Machiavelli* (New York: Penguin Books, 1983).

CLINTON ROSSITER, *Constitutional Dictatorship* (New York: Harcourt Brace and World, Inc., 1948, 1963).

ROBERT BELLAH, RICHARD MADSEN, WILLIAM SULLIVAN, ANN SWIDLER, and STEVEN TIPTON, *Habits of the Heart: Individualism and Commitment in American Life* (UC Press, 1985).

ROBERT PUTNAM, *Bowling Alone: The Collapse and Revival of American Community* (Simon and Schuster 2000).

12

The Federalist Papers 1, 10, 15

FEDERALIST #1: GENERAL INTRODUCTION

From the *Independent Journal*.

Author: Alexander Hamilton

To the People of the State of New York:

AFTER an unequivocal experience of the inefficiency of the subsisting federal government, you are called upon to deliberate on a new Constitution for the United States of America. The subject speaks its own importance; comprehending in its consequences nothing less than the existence of the UNION, the safety and welfare of the parts of which it is composed, the fate of an empire in many respects the most interesting in the world. It has been frequently remarked that it seems to have been reserved to the people of this country, by their conduct and example, to decide the important question, whether societies of men are really capable or not of establishing good government from reflection and choice, or whether they are forever destined to depend for their political constitutions on accident and force. If there be any truth in the remark, the crisis at which we are arrived may with propriety be regarded as the era in which that decision is to be made; and a wrong election of the part we shall act may, in this view, deserve to be considered as the general misfortune of mankind.

This idea will add the inducements of philanthropy to those of patriotism, to heighten the solicitude which all considerate and good men must feel for the event. Happy will it be if our choice should be directed by a judicious estimate of our true interests, unperplexed and unbiased by considerations not connected with the public good. But this is a thing more ardently to be wished than seriously to be expected. The plan offered to our deliberations affects too many particular interests, innovates upon too many local institutions, not to involve in its discussion a variety of objects foreign to its merits, and of views, passions and prejudices little favorable to the discovery of truth.

Among the most formidable of the obstacles which the new Constitution will have to encounter may readily be distinguished the obvious interest of a certain class of men in every State to resist all changes which may hazard a diminution of the power, emolument, and consequence of the offices they hold under the State establishments; and the perverted ambition of another class of men, who will either hope to aggrandize themselves by the confusions of their country, or will flatter themselves with fairer prospects of elevation from the subdivision of the empire into several partial confederacies than from its union under one government.

It is not, however, my design to dwell upon observations of this nature. I am well aware that it would be disingenuous to resolve indiscriminately the opposition of any set of men (merely because their situations might subject them to suspicion) into interested or ambitious views. Candor will oblige us to admit that even such men may be actuated by upright intentions; and it cannot be doubted that much of the opposition which has made its appearance, or may hereafter make its appearance, will spring from sources, blameless at least, if not respectable—the honest errors of minds led astray by preconceived jealousies and fears. So numerous indeed and so powerful are the causes which serve to give a false bias to the judgment, that we, upon many occasions, see wise and good men on the wrong as well as on the right side of questions of the first magnitude to society. This circumstance, if duly attended to, would furnish a lesson of moderation to those who are ever so much persuaded of their being in the right in any controversy. And a further reason for caution, in this respect, might be drawn from the reflection that we are not always sure that those who advocate the truth are influenced by purer principles than their antagonists. Ambition, avarice, personal animosity, party opposition, and many other motives not more laudable than these, are apt to operate as well upon those who support as those who oppose the right side of a question. Were there not even these inducements to moderation, nothing could be more ill-judged than that intolerant spirit which has, at all times, characterized political parties. For in politics, as in religion, it is equally absurd to aim at making proselytes by fire and sword. Heresies in either can rarely be cured by persecution.

* * *

In the course of the preceding observations, I have had an eye, my fellow-citizens, to putting you upon your guard against all attempts, from whatever quarter, to influence your decision in a matter of the utmost moment to your welfare, by any impressions other than those which may result from the evidence of truth. You will, no doubt, at the same time, have collected from the general scope of them, that they proceed from a source not unfriendly to the new Constitution. Yes, my countrymen, I own to you that, after having given it an attentive consideration, I am clearly of opinion it is your interest to adopt it. I am convinced that this is the safest course for your liberty, your dignity, and your happiness. I affect not reserves which I do not feel. I will not amuse you with an appearance of deliberation when I have decided. I frankly acknowledge to you my convictions, and I will freely lay before you the reasons on which they are founded. The consciousness of good intentions disdains ambiguity. I shall not, however, multiply professions on this head. My motives must remain in the depository of my own breast. My arguments will be open to all, and may be judged of by all. They shall at least be offered in a spirit which will not disgrace the cause of truth.

* * *

It may perhaps be thought superfluous to offer arguments to prove the utility of the UNION, a point, no doubt, deeply engraved on the hearts of the great body of the people in every State, and one, which it may be imagined, has no adversaries. But the fact is, that we already hear it whispered in the private circles of those who oppose the new Constitution, that the thirteen States are of too great extent for any general system, and that we must of necessity resort to separate confederacies of distinct portions of the whole. This doctrine will, in all probability, be gradually propagated, till it has votaries enough to countenance an open avowal of it. For nothing can be more evident, to those who are able to take an enlarged view of the subject, than the alternative of an adoption of the new Constitution or a dismemberment of the Union. It will therefore be of use to begin by examining the advantages of that Union, the certain evils, and the probable dangers, to which every State will be exposed from its dissolution. This shall accordingly constitute the subject of my next address.

FEDERALIST #10: THE SAME SUBJECT CONTINUED: THE UNION AS A SAFEGUARD AGAINST DOMESTIC FACTION AND INSURRECTION

From the *New York Packet*.

Friday, November 23, 1787.

Author: James Madison

To the People of the State of New York:

AMONG the numerous advantages promised by a well-constructed Union, none deserves to be more accurately developed than its tendency to break and control the violence of faction. The friend of popular governments never finds himself so much alarmed for their character and fate, as when he contemplates their propensity to this dangerous vice. He will not fail, therefore, to set a due value on any plan which, without violating the principles to which he is attached, provides a proper cure for it. The instability, injustice, and confusion introduced into the public councils, have, in truth, been the mortal diseases under which popular governments have everywhere perished; as they continue to be the favorite and fruitful topics from which the adversaries to liberty derive their most specious declamations. The valuable improvements made by the American constitutions on the popular models, both ancient and modern, cannot certainly be too much admired; but it would be an unwarrantable partiality, to contend that they have as effectually obviated the danger on this side, as was wished and expected. Complaints are everywhere heard from our most considerate and virtuous citizens, equally the friends of public and private faith, and of public and personal liberty, that our governments are too unstable, that the public good is disregarded in the conflicts of rival parties, and that measures are too often decided, not according to the rules of justice and the rights of the minor party, but by the superior force of an interested and overbearing majority. However anxiously we may wish that these complaints had no foundation, the evidence, of known facts will not permit us to deny that they are in some degree true. It will be found, indeed, on a candid review of our situation, that some of the distresses under which we labor have been erroneously charged on the operation of our governments; but it will be found, at the same time, that other causes will not alone account for many of our heaviest misfortunes; and, particularly, for that prevailing and increasing distrust of public engagements, and alarm for private rights, which are echoed from one end of the continent to the other. These must be chiefly, if not wholly, effects of the unsteadiness and injustice with which a factious spirit has tainted our public administrations.

By a faction, I understand a number of citizens, whether amounting to a majority or a minority of the whole, who are united and actuated by some common impulse of passion, or of interest, adversed to the rights of other citizens, or to the permanent and aggregate interests of the community.

There are two methods of curing the mischiefs of faction: the one, by removing its causes; the other, by controlling its effects.

There are again two methods of removing the causes of faction: the one, by destroying the liberty which is essential to its existence; the other, by giving to every citizen the same opinions, the same passions, and the same interests.

It could never be more truly said than of the first remedy, that it was worse than the disease. Liberty is to faction what air is to fire, an aliment without which it instantly expires. But it could not be less folly to abolish liberty, which is essential to political life, because it nourishes faction, than it would be to wish the annihilation of air, which is essential to animal life, because it imparts to fire its destructive agency.

The second expedient is as impracticable as the first would be unwise. As long as the reason of man continues fallible, and he is at liberty to exercise it, different opinions will be formed. As long as the connection subsists between his reason and his self-love, his opinions and his passions will have a reciprocal influence on each other; and the former will be objects to which the latter will attach themselves. The diversity in the faculties of men, from which the rights of property originate, is not less an insuperable obstacle to a uniformity of interests. The protection of these faculties is the first object of government. From the protection of different and unequal faculties of acquiring property, the possession of different degrees and kinds of property immediately results; and from the influence of these on the sentiments and views of the respective proprietors, ensues a division of the society into different interests and parties.

The latent causes of faction are thus sown in the nature of man; and we see them everywhere brought into different degrees of activity, according to the different circumstances of civil society. A zeal for different opinions concerning religion, concerning government, and many other points, as well of speculation as of practice; an attachment to different leaders ambitiously contending for pre-eminence and power; or to persons of other descriptions whose fortunes have been interesting to the human passions, have, in turn, divided mankind into parties, inflamed them with mutual animosity, and rendered them much more disposed to vex and oppress each other than to co-operate for their common good. So strong is this propensity of mankind to fall into mutual animosities, that where no substantial occasion presents itself, the most frivolous and fanciful distinctions have been sufficient to kindle their unfriendly passions and excite their most violent conflicts. But the most common and durable source of factions has been the various and unequal distribution of property. Those who hold and those who are without property have ever formed distinct interests in society. Those who are creditors, and those who are debtors, fall under a like discrimination. A landed interest, a manufacturing interest, a mercantile interest, a moneyed interest, with many lesser interests, grow up of necessity in civilized nations, and divide them into different classes, actuated by different sentiments and views. The regulation of these various and interfering interests forms the principal task of modern legislation, and involves the spirit of party and faction in the necessary and ordinary operations of the government....

* * *

FEDERALIST #15: THE INSUFFICIENCY OF THE PRESENT CONFEDERATION TO PRESERVE THE UNION

For the *Independent Journal.*

Author: Alexander Hamilton

To the People of the State of New York:

IN THE course of the preceding papers, I have endeavored, my fellow-citizens, to place before you, in a clear and convincing light, the importance of Union to your political safety and happiness. I have unfolded to you a complication of dangers to which you would be exposed, should you permit that sacred knot which binds the people of America together be severed or dissolved by ambition or by avarice, by jealousy or by misrepresentation. In the sequel of the inquiry through which I propose to accompany you, the truths intended to be inculcated will receive further confirmation from facts and arguments hitherto unnoticed. If the road over which you will still have to pass

should in some places appear to you tedious or irksome, you will recollect that you are in quest of information on a subject the most momentous which can engage the attention of a free people, that the field through which you have to travel is in itself spacious, and that the difficulties of the journey have been unnecessarily increased by the mazes with which sophistry has beset the way. It will be my aim to remove the obstacles from your progress in as compendious a manner as it can be done, without sacrificing utility to dispatch.

In pursuance of the plan which I have laid down for the discussion of the subject, the point next in order to be examined is the "insufficiency of the present Confederation to the preservation of the Union." It may perhaps be asked what need there is of reasoning or proof to illustrate a position which is not either controverted or doubted, to which the understandings and feelings of all classes of men assent, and which in substance is admitted by the opponents as well as by the friends of the new Constitution. It must in truth be acknowledged that, however these may differ in other respects, they in general appear to harmonize in this sentiment, at least, that there are material imperfections in our national system, and that something is necessary to be done to rescue us from impending anarchy. The facts that support this opinion are no longer objects of speculation. They have forced themselves upon the sensibility of the people at large, and have at length extorted from those, whose mistaken policy has had the principal share in precipitating the extremity at which we are arrived, a reluctant confession of the reality of those defects in the scheme of our federal government, which have been long pointed out and regretted by the intelligent friends of the Union.

We may indeed with propriety be said to have reached almost the last stage of national humiliation. There is scarcely anything that can wound the pride or degrade the character of an independent nation which we do not experience. Are there engagements to the performance of which we are held by every tie respectable among men? These are the subjects of constant and unblushing violation. Do we owe debts to foreigners and to our own citizens contracted in a time of imminent peril for the preservation of our political existence? These remain without any proper or satisfactory provision for their discharge. Have we valuable territories and important posts in the possession of a foreign power which, by express stipulations, ought long since to have been surrendered? These are still retained, to the prejudice of our interests, not less than of our rights. Are we in a condition to resent or to repel the aggression? We have neither troops, nor treasury, nor government. Are we even in a condition to remonstrate with dignity? The just imputations on our own faith, in respect to the same treaty, ought first to be removed. Are we entitled by nature and compact to a free participation in the navigation of the Mississippi? Spain excludes us from it. Is public credit an indispensable resource in time of public danger? We seem to have abandoned its cause as desperate and irretrievable. Is commerce of importance to national wealth? Ours is at the lowest point of declension. Is respectability in the eyes of foreign powers a safeguard against foreign encroachments? The imbecility of our government even forbids them to treat with us. Our ambassadors abroad are the mere pageants of mimic sovereignty. Is a violent and unnatural decrease in the value of land a symptom of national distress? The price of improved land in most parts of the country is much lower than can be accounted for by the quantity of waste land at market, and can only be fully explained by that want of private and public confidence, which are so alarmingly prevalent among all ranks, and which have a direct tendency to depreciate property of every kind. Is private credit the friend and patron of industry? That most useful kind which relates to borrowing and lending is reduced within the narrowest limits, and this still more from an opinion of insecurity than from the scarcity of money. To shorten an enumeration of particulars which can afford neither pleasure nor instruction, it may in general be demanded, what indication is there of national disorder, poverty, and insignificance that could befall a community so peculiarly blessed with natural advantages as we are, which does not form a part of the dark catalogue of our public misfortunes?

This is the melancholy situation to which we have been brought by those very maxims and councils which would now deter us from adopting the proposed Constitution; and which, not content with having conducted us to the brink of a precipice, seem resolved to plunge us into the abyss that awaits us below. Here, my countrymen, impelled by every motive that ought to influence an enlightened people, let us make a firm stand for our safety, our tranquility, our dignity, our reputation. Let us at last break the fatal charm which has too long seduced us from the paths of felicity and prosperity.

It is true, as has been before observed that facts, too stubborn to be resisted, have produced a species of general assent to the abstract proposition that there exist material defects in our national system; but the usefulness of the concession, on the part of the old adversaries of federal measures, is destroyed by a strenuous opposition to a remedy, upon the only principles that can give it a chance of success. While they admit that the government of the United States is destitute of energy, they contend against conferring upon it those powers which are requisite to supply that energy. They seem still to aim at things repugnant and irreconcilable; at an augmentation of federal authority, without a diminution of State authority; at sovereignty in the Union, and complete independence in the members. They still, in fine, seem to cherish with blind devotion the political monster of an imperium in imperio. This renders a full display of the principal defects of the Confederation necessary, in order to show that the evils we experience do not proceed from minute or partial imperfections, but from fundamental errors in the structure of the building, which cannot be amended otherwise than by an alteration in the first principles and main pillars of the fabric.

The great and radical vice in the construction of the existing Confederation is in the principle of LEGISLATION for STATES or GOVERNMENTS, in their CORPORATE or COLLECTIVE CAPACITIES, and as contradistinguished from the INDIVIDUALS of which they consist. Though this principle does not run through all the powers delegated to the Union, yet it pervades and governs those on which the efficacy of the rest depends. Except as to the rule of appointment, the United States has an indefinite discretion to make requisitions for men and money; but they have no authority to raise either, by regulations extending to the individual citizens of America. The consequence of this is, that though in theory their resolutions concerning those objects are laws, constitutionally binding on the members of the Union, yet in practice they are mere recommendations which the States observe or disregard at their option.

It is a singular instance of the capriciousness of the human mind, that after all the admonitions we have had from experience on this head, there should still be found men who object to the new Constitution, for deviating from a principle which has been found the bane of the old, and which is in itself evidently incompatible with the idea of GOVERNMENT; a principle, in short, which, if it is to be executed at all, must substitute the violent and sanguinary agency of the sword to the mild influence of the magistracy....

* * *

13

The Anti-Federalist Papers

The Anti-Federalist Papers are a loose collection of essays written in opposition to ratification of the Constitution. The authorship of many papers is uncertain, though they clearly represent the views of the dominant critics of a strong central government.

FROM LETTERS FROM THE FEDERAL FARMER (1787)

While the *Letters from the Federal Farmer* were anonymous, Richard Henry Lee is thought by many observers to be the likely author. Lee was a Virginian farmer, a signer of the Declaration of Independence, and a former president of the Continental Congress.

From Letter I

Dear Sir,
My letters to you last winter, on the subject of a well balanced national government for the United States, were the result of free enquiry; when I passed from that subject to enquiries relative to our commerce, revenues, past administration, etc.

I anticipated the anxieties I feel, on carefully examining the plan of government proposed by the convention. It appears to be a plan retaining some federal features; but to be the first important step, and to aim strongly to one consolidated government of the United States. It leaves the powers of government, and the representation of the people, so unnaturally divided between the general and state governments, that the operations of our system must be very uncertain. My uniform federal attachments, and the interest I have in the protection of property, and a steady execution of the laws, will convince you, that, if I am under any biass at all, it is in favor of any general system which shall promise those advantages. The instability of our laws increases my wishes for firm and steady government; but then, I can consent to no government, which, in my opinion, is not calculated equally to preserve the rights of all orders of men in the community...

* * *

The first principal question that occurs, is. Whether, considering our situation, we ought to precipitate the adoption of the proposed constitution? If we remain cool and temperate, we are

The Anti-Federalist Papers, Edited with an Introduction by Morton Borden, Michigan State University Press, 1965.

in no immediate danger of any commotions; we are in a state of perfect peace, and in no danger of invasions; the state governments are in the full exercise of their powers; and our governments answer all present exigencies, except the regulation of trade, securing credit, in some cases, and providing for the interest, in some instances, of the public debts; and whether we adopt a change, three or nine months hence, can make but little odds with the private circumstances of individuals; their happiness and prosperity, after all, depend principally upon their own exertions. We are hardly recovered from a long and distressing war: The farmers, fishmen, &c. have not yet fully repaired the waste made by it. Industry and frugality are again assuming their proper station. Private debts are lessened, and public debts incurred by the war have been, by various ways, diminished; and the public lands have now become a productive source for diminishing them much more. I know uneasy men, who wish very much to precipitate, do not admit all these facts; but they are facts well known to all men who are thoroughly informed in the affairs of this country. It must, however, be admitted, that our federal system is defective, and that some of the state governments are not well administered; but, then, we impute to the defects in our governments many evils and embarrassments which are most clearly the result of the late war.

* * *

Independant of the opinions of many great authors, that a free elective government cannot be extended over large territories, a few reflections must evince, that one government and general legislation alone, never can extend equal benefits to all parts of the United States: Different laws, customs, and opinions exist in the different states, which by a uniform system of laws would be unreasonably invaded. The United States contain about a million of square miles, and in half a century will, probably, contain ten millions of people; and from the center to the extremes is about 800 miles.

Before we do away the state governments, or adopt measures that will tend to abolish them, and to consolidate the states into one entire government, several principles should be considered

and facts ascertained:—These, and my examination into the essential parts of the proposed plan, I shall pursue in my next.

Your's &c.
The Federal Farmer.

From Letter 3

Dear Sir,
The great object of a free people must be so to form their government and laws, and so to administer them, as to create a confidence in, and respect for the laws; and thereby induce the sensible and virtuous part of the community to declare in favor of the laws, and to support them without an expensive military force. I wish, though I confess I have not much hope, that this may be the case with the laws of congress under the new constitution. I am fully convinced that we must organize the national government on different principals, and make the parts of it more efficient, and secure in it more effectually the different interests in the community; or else leave in the state governments some powers propose[d] to be lodged in it—at least till such an organization shall be found to be practicable. Not sanguine in my. expectations of a good federal administration, and satisfied, as I am, of the impracticability of consolidating the states, and at the same time of preserving the rights of the people at large, I believe we ought still to leave some of those powers in the state governments, in which the people, in fact, will still be represented—to define some other powers proposed to be vested in the general government, more carefully, and to establish a few principles to secure a proper exercise of the powers given it. It is not my object to multiply objections, or to contend about inconsiderable powers or amendments; I wish the system adopted with a few alterations; but those, in my mind, are essential ones; if adopted without, every good citizen will acquiesce though I shall consider the duration of our governments, and the liberties of this people, very much dependant on the administration of the general government. A wise and honest administration, may make the people happy under any government; but necessity only can justify even our leaving open avenues to the abuse of power, by wicked, unthinking, or ambitious men....

FROM THE ESSAYS OF BRUTUS, NOVEMBER 1787

Like the Federalist Farmer, the precise identity of Brutus is uncertain, however, it is widely believed that Robert Yates is the author. Yates was a prominent leader in New York during and after the Revolution. He served as an Associate Justice of the New York Supreme Court from 1777–1790 and Chief Justice from 1790–1798.

To the Citizens of the State of New-York.

I flatter myself that my last address established this position, that to reduce the Thirteen States into one government, would prove the destruction of your liberties.

But lest this truth should be doubted by some, I will now proceed to consider its merits.

Though it should be admitted, that the argument[s] against reducing all the states into one consolidated government, are not sufficient fully to establish this point; yet they will, at least, justify this conclusion, that in forming a constitution for such a country, great care should be taken to limit and definite its powers, adjust its parts, and guard against an abuse of authority. How far attention has been paid to these objects, shall be the subject of future enquiry. When a building is to be erected which is intended to stand for ages, the foundation should be firmly laid. The constitution proposed to your acceptance, is designed not for yourselves alone, but for generations yet unborn. The principles, therefore, upon which the social compact is founded, ought to have been clearly and precisely stated, and the most express and full declaration of rights to have been made—But on this subject there is almost an entire silence.

If we may collect the sentiments of the people of America, from their own most solemn declarations, they hold this truth as self evident, that all men are by nature free. No one man, therefore, or any class of men, have a right, by the law of nature, or of God, to assume or exercise authority over their fellows. The origin of society then is to be sought, not in any natural right which one man has to exercise authority over another, but in the united consent of those who associate. The mutual wants of men, at first dictated the propriety of forming societies; and when they were established, protection and defence pointed out the necessity of instituting government. In a state of nature every individual pursues his own interest; in this pursuit it frequently happened, that the possessions or enjoyments of one were sacrificed to the views and designs of another; thus the weak were a prey to the strong, the simple and unwary were subject to impositions from those who were more crafty and designing. In this state of things, every individual was insecure; common interest therefore directed, that government should be established, in which the force of the whole community should be collected, and under such directions, as to protect and defend every one who composed it. The common good, therefore, is the end of civil government, and common consent, the foundation on which it is established. To effect this end, it was necessary that a certain portion of natural liberty should be surrendered, in order, that what remained should be preserved: how great a proportion of natural freedom is necessary to be yielded by individuals, when they submit to government, I shall not now enquire. So much, however, must be given up, as will be sufficient to enable those, to whom the administration of the government is committed, to establish laws for the promoting the happiness of the community, and to carry those laws into effect. But it is not necessary, for this purpose, that individuals should relinquish all their natural rights. Some are of such a nature that they cannot be surrendered. Of this kind are the rights of conscience, the right of enjoying and defending life, etc. Others are not necessary to be resigned, in order to attain the end for which government is instituted, these therefore ought not to be given up. To surrender them, would counteract the very end of government, to wit, the common good. From these observations it appears, that in forming a government on its true principles, the foundation should be laid in the manner I before stated, by expressly reserving to the people such of their essential natural rights, as are not necessary to be parted with. The same reasons which at first induced mankind to associate and institute government, will operate to influence them to observe this precaution.

If they had been disposed to conform themselves to the rule of immutable righteousness, government would not have been requisite. It was because one part exercised fraud, oppression, and violence on the other, that men came together, and agreed that certain rules should be formed, to regulate the conduct of all, and the power of the whole community lodged in the hands of rulers to enforce an obedience to them. But rulers have the same propensities as other men; they are as likely to use the power with which they are vested for private purposes, and to the injury and oppression of those over whom they are placed, as individuals in a state of nature are to injure and oppress one another. It is therefore as proper that bounds should be set to their authority, as that government should have at first been instituted to restrain private injuries.

This principle, which seems so evidently founded in the reason and nature of things, is confirmed by universal experience. Those who have governed, have been found in all ages ever active to enlarge their powers and abridge the public liberty. This has induced the people in all countries, where any sense of freedom remained, to fix barriers against the encroachments of their rulers. The country from which we have derived our origin, is an eminent example of this. Their magna charta and bill of rights have long been the boast, as well as the security, of that nation. I need say no more, I presume, to an American, than, that this principle is a fundamental one, in all the constitutions of our own states; there is not one of them but what is either founded on a declaration or bill of rights, or has certain express reservation of rights interwoven in the body of them. From this it appears, that at a time when the pulse of liberty beat high and when an appeal was made to the people to form constitutions for the government of themselves, it was their universal sense, that such declarations should make a part of their frames of government. It is therefore the more astonishing, that this grand security, to the rights of the people, is not to be found in this constitution...

* * *

Brutus

PATRICK HENRY: FROM THE DEBATE IN THE VIRGINA CONVENTION CALLED TO RATIFY THE CONSTITUTION (JUNE 5, 1788)

… This Constitution is said to have beautiful features; but when I come to examine these features, sir, they appear to me horribly frightful. Among other deformities, it has an awful squinting; it squints toward monarchy, and does not this raise indignation in the breast of every true American?

Your president may easily become king. Your Senate is so imperfectly constructed that your dearest rights may be sacrificed to what may be a small minority; and a very small minority may continue for ever unchangeably this government, altho horridly defective. Where are your checks in this government? Your strongholds will be in the hands of your enemies. It is on a supposition that your American governors shall be honest that all the good qualities of this government are founded; but its defective and imperfect construction puts it in their power to perpetrate the worst of mischiefs should they be bad men; and, sir, would not all the world, blame our distracted folly in resting our rights upon the contingency of our rulers being good or bad? Show me that age and country where the rights and liberties of the people were placed on the sole chance of their rulers being good men without a consequent loss of liberty! I say that the loss of that dearest privilege has ever followed, with absolute certainty, every such mad attempt.

If your American chief be a man of ambition and abilities, how easy is it for him to render himself absolute! The army is in his hands, and if he be a man of address, it will be attached to him, and it will be the subject of long meditation with him to seize the first auspicious moment to accomplish his design, and, sir, will the American spirit solely relieve you when this happens? I would rather infinitely—and I am sure most of this Convention are of the same opinion—have a king, lords, and commons, than a government so replete with such insupportable evils. If we make a king we may prescribe the rules by which he shall rule his people, and interpose such checks as shall prevent him from infringing them; but the president, in the field, at the head of his army, can prescribe the terms on which he shall reign master, so far that it will puzzle any American ever to get his neck from under the galling yoke. I can not with patience think of this idea. If ever he violate the laws, one of two things will happen: he will come at the head of the army to carry everything before him, or he will give bail, or do what Mr. Chief Justice will order him. If he be guilty, will not the recollection of his crimes teach him to make one bold push for the American throne? Will not the immense difference between being master of everything and being ignominiously tried and punished powerfully excite him to make this bold push? But, sir, where is the existing force to punish him? Can he not, at the head of his army, beat down every opposition? Away with your president! we shall have a king: the army will salute him monarch; your militia will leave you, and assist in making him king, and fight against you: and what have you to oppose this force? What will then become of you and your rights? Will not absolute despotism ensue?

14

Capitalism and Freedom

Milton Friedman

In a much quoted passage in his inaugural address, President Kennedy said, "Ask not what your country can do for you—ask what you can do for your country." It is a striking sign of the temper of our times that the controversy about this passage centered on its origin and not on its content. Neither half of the statement expresses a relation between the citizen and his government that is worthy of the ideals of free men in a free society. The paternalistic "what your country can do for you" implies that government is the patron, the citizen the ward, a view that is at odds with the free man's belief in his own responsibility for his own destiny. The organismic, "what you can do for your country" implies that government is the master or the deity, the citizen, the servant or the votary. To the free man, the country is the collection of individuals who compose it, not something over and above them. He is proud of a common heritage and loyal to common traditions. But he regards government as a means, an instrumentality, neither a grantor of favors and gifts, nor a master or god to be blindly worshipped and served. He recognizes no national goal except as it is the consensus of the goals that the citizens severally serve. He recognizes no national purpose except as it is the consensus of the purposes for which the citizens severally strive.

The free man will ask neither what his country can do for him nor what he can do for his country. He will ask rather "What can I and my compatriots do through government" to help us discharge our individual responsibilities, to achieve our several goals and purposes, and above all, to protect our freedom? And he will accompany this question with another: How can we keep the government we create from becoming a Frankenstein that will destroy the very freedom we establish it to protect? Freedom is a rare and delicate plant. Our minds tell us, and history confirms, that the great threat to freedom is the concentration of power. Government is necessary to preserve our freedom, it is an instrument through which we can exercise our freedom; yet by concentrating power in political hands, it is also a threat to freedom. Even though the men who wield this power initially be of good will and even though they be not corrupted by the power they exercise, the power will both attract and form men of a different stamp.

How can we benefit from the promise of government while avoiding the threat to freedom? Two broad principles embodied in our Constitution give an answer that has preserved our freedom so far, though they have been violated repeatedly in practice while proclaimed as precept.

First, the scope of government must be limited. Its major function must be to protect our freedom both from the enemies outside our gates and from our fellow-citizens: to preserve law and order, to enforce private contracts, to foster competitive markets. Beyond this major function, government may enable us at times to accomplish jointly what we would find it more difficult or expensive to accomplish severally. However, any such use of government is fraught with danger. We should not and cannot avoid using government in this way. But there should be a clear and large balance of advantages before we do. By relying primarily on voluntary co-operation and private enterprise, in both economic and other activities, we can insure that the private sector is a check on the powers of the governmental sector and an effective protection of freedom of speech, of religion, and of thought.

The second broad principle is that government power must be dispersed. If government is to exercise power, better in the county than in the state, better in the state than in Washington. If I do not like what my local community does,

be it in sewage disposal, or zoning, or schools, I can move to another local community, and though few may take this step, the mere possibility acts as a check. If I do not like what my state does, I can move to another. If I do not like what Washington imposes, I have few alternatives in this world of jealous nations.

The very difficulty of avoiding the enactments of the federal government is of course the great attraction of centralization to many of its proponents. It will enable them more effectively, they believe, to legislate programs that—as they see it—are in the interest of the public, whether it be the transfer of income from the rich to the poor or from private to governmental purposes. They are in a sense right. But this coin has two sides. The power to do good is also the power to do harm; those who control the power today may not tomorrow; and, more important, what one man regards as good, another may regard as harm. The great tragedy of the drive to centralization, as of the drive to extend the scope of government in general, is that it is mostly led by men of good will who will be the first to rue its consequences.

The preservation of freedom is the protective reason for limiting and decentralizing governmental power. But there is also a constructive reason. The great advances of civilization, whether in architecture or painting, in science or literature, in industry or agriculture, have never come from centralized government. Columbus did not set out to seek a new route to China in response to a majority directive of a parliament, though he was partly financed by an absolute monarch. Newton and Leibnitz; Einstein and Bohr; Shakespeare, Milton, and Pasternak; Whitney, McCormick, Edison, and Ford; Jane Addams, Florence Nightingale, and Albert Schweitzer; no one of these opened new frontiers in human knowledge and understanding, in literature, in technical possibilities, or in the relief of human misery in response to governmental directives. Their achievements were the product of individual genius, of strongly held minority views, of a social climate permitting variety and diversity.

Government can never duplicate the variety and diversity of individual action. At any moment in time, by imposing uniform standards in housing, or nutrition, or clothing, government could undoubtedly improve the level of living of many individuals; by imposing uniform standards in schooling, road construction, or sanitation, central government could undoubtedly improve the level of performance in many local areas and perhaps even on the average of all communities. But in the process, government would replace progress by stagnation, it would substitute uniform mediocrity for the variety essential for that experimentation which can bring tomorrow's laggards above today's mean.

*   *   *

An abstract statement can conceivably be complete and exhaustive, though this ideal is certainly far from realized.... The application of the principles cannot even conceivably be exhaustive. Each day brings new problems and new circumstances. That is why the role of the state can never be spelled out once and for all in terms of specific functions. It is also why we need from time to time to re-examine the bearing of what we hope are unchanged principles on the problems of the day. A by-product is inevitably a retesting of the principles and a sharpening of our understanding of them.

It is extremely convenient to have a label for the political and economic viewpoint.... The rightful and proper label is liberalism. Unfortunately, "As a supreme, if unintended compliment, the enemies of the system of private enterprise have thought it wise to appropriate its label"[1] so that liberalism has, in the United States, come to have a very different meaning than it did in the nineteenth century or does today over much of the Continent of Europe.

As it developed in the late eighteenth and early nineteenth centuries, the intellectual movement that went under the name of liberalism emphasized freedom as the ultimate goal and the individual as the ultimate entity in the society. It supported laissez faire at home as a means of reducing the role of the state in economic affairs and thereby enlarging the role of the individual; it supported free trade abroad as a means of linking the nations of the world together peacefully and democratically. In political matters, it supported the development of representative government and of parliamentary institutions, reduction in the arbitrary power of the state, and protection of the civil freedoms of individuals.

Beginning in the late nineteenth century, and especially after 1930 in the United States, the term liberalism came to be associated with a very different emphasis, particularly in economic policy. It came to be associated with a readiness to rely primarily on the state rather than on private voluntary arrangements to achieve objectives regarded as desirable. The catchwords became welfare and equality rather than freedom. The nineteenth-century liberal regarded an extension of freedom as the most effective way to promote welfare and equality; the twentieth-century liberal regards welfare and equality as either prerequisites of or alternatives to freedom. In the name of welfare and equality, the twentieth-century liberal has come to favor a revival of the very policies of state intervention and paternalism against which classical liberalism fought. In the very act of turning the clock back to seventeenth-century mercantilism, he is fond of castigating true liberals as reactionary!

The change in the meaning attached to the term liberalism is more striking in economic matters than in political. The twentieth-century liberal, like the nineteenth-century liberal, favors parliamentary institutions, representative government, civil rights, and so on. Yet even in political matters, there is a notable difference. Jealous of liberty, and hence fearful of centralized power, whether in governmental or private hands, the nineteenth-century liberal favored political decentralization. Committed to action and confident of the beneficence of power so long as it is in the hands of a government ostensibly controlled by the electorate, the twentieth-century liberal favors centralized government. He will resolve any doubt about where power should be located in favor of the state instead of the city, of the federal government instead of the state, and of a world organization instead of a national government.

Because of the corruption of the term liberalism, the views that formerly went under that name are now often labeled conservatism. But this is not a satisfactory alternative. The nineteenth-century liberal was a radical, both in the etymological sense of going to the root of the matter, and in the political sense of favoring major changes in social institutions. So too must be his modern heir. We do not wish to conserve the state interventions that have interfered so greatly with our freedom, though, of course, we do wish to conserve those that have promoted it. Moreover, in practice, the term conservatism has come to cover so wide a range of views, and views so incompatible with one another, that we shall no doubt see the growth of hyphenated designations, such as libertarian-conservative and aristocratic-conservative.

Partly because of my reluctance to surrender the term to proponents of measures that would destroy liberty, partly because I cannot find a better alternative, I shall resolve these difficulties by using the word liberalism in its original sense—as the doctrines pertaining to a free man.

End Notes

   1. Joseph Schumpeter, *History of Economic Analysis* (New York: Oxford University Press, 1954) p. 394.

15

The Logic of Collective Action

Mancur Olson

It is often taken for granted, at least where economic objectives are involved, that groups of individuals with common interests usually attempt to further those common interests. Groups of individuals with common interests are expected to act on behalf of their common interests much as single individuals are often expected to act on behalf of their personal interests. This opinion about group behavior is frequently found not only in popular discussions but also in scholarly writings. Many economists of diverse methodological and ideological traditions have implicitly or explicitly accepted it. This view has, for example, been important in many theories of labor unions, in Marxian theories of class action, in concepts of "countervailing power," and in various discussions of economic institutions. It has, in addition, occupied a prominent place in political science, at least in the United States, where the study of pressure groups has been dominated by a celebrated "group theory" based on the idea that groups will act when necessary to further their common or

Reprinted by permission of the publisher from *The Logic of Collective Action: Public Goods and The Theory of Groups* by Mancur Olson, pp. 1–3, Cambridge, Mass.: Harvard University Press, Copyright © 1965, 1971 by the President and Fellows of Harvard College.

group goals. Finally, it has played a significant role in many well-known sociological studies.

The view that groups act to serve their interests presumably is based upon the assumption that the individuals in groups act out of self-interest. If the individuals in a group altruistically disregarded their personal welfare, it would not be very likely that collectively they would seek some selfish common or group objective. Such altruism, is, however, considered exceptional, and self-interested behavior is usually thought to be the rule, at least when economic issues are at stake; no one is surprised when individual businessmen seek higher profits, when individual workers seek higher wages, or when individual consumers seek lower prices. The idea that groups tend to act in support of their group interests is supposed to follow logically from this widely accepted premise of rational, self-interested behavior. In other words, if the members of some group have a common interest or objective, and if they would all be better off if that objective were achieved, it has been thought to follow logically that the individuals in that group would, if they were rational and self-interested, act to achieve that objective.

But it is *not* in fact true that the idea that groups will act in their self-interest follows logically from the premise of rational and self-interested behavior. It does *not* follow, because all of the individuals in a group would gain if they achieved their group objective, that they would act to achieve that objective, even if they were all rational and self-interested. Indeed, unless the number of individuals in a group is quite small, or unless there is coercion or some other special device to make individuals act in their common interest, *rational, self-interested individuals will not act to achieve their common or group interests.* In other words, even if all of the individuals in a large group are rational and self-interested, and would gain if, as a group, they acted to achieve their common interest or objective, they will still not voluntarily act to achieve that common or group interest. The notion that groups of individuals will act to achieve their common or group interests, far from being a logical implication of the assumption that the individuals in a group will rationally further their individual interests, is in fact inconsistent with that assumption. ...

If the members of a large group rationally seek to maximize their personal welfare, they will *not* act to advance their common or group objectives unless there is coercion to force them to do so, or unless some separate incentive, distinct from the achievement of the common or group interest, is offered to the members of the group individually on the condition that they help bear the costs or burdens involved in the achievement of the group objectives. Nor will such large groups form organizations to further their common goals in the absence of the coercion or the separate incentives just mentioned. These points hold true even when there is unanimous agreement in a group about the common good and the methods of achieving it.

The widespread view, common throughout the social sciences, that groups tend to further their interests, is accordingly unjustified, at least when it is based, as it usually is, on the (sometimes implicit) assumption that groups act in their self-interest because individuals do. There is paradoxically the logical possibility that groups composed of either altruistic individuals or irrational individuals may sometimes act in their common or group interests. But, as later, empirical parts of this study will attempt to show, this logical possibility is usually of no practical importance. Thus the customary view that groups of individuals with common interests tend to further those common interests appears to have little if any merit.

None of the statements made above fully applies to small groups, for the situation in small groups is much more complicated. In small groups there may very well be some voluntary action in support of the common purposes of the individuals in the group, but in most cases this action will cease before it reaches the optimal level for the members of the group as a whole. In the sharing of the costs of efforts to achieve a common goal in small groups, there is however a surprising tendency for the "exploitation" of the *great* by the *small*.

16

Constructing the Political Spectacle

Murray Edelman

SOME PREMISES ABOUT POLITICS

The pervasiveness of literacy, television, and radio in the industrialized world makes frequent reports of political news available to most of the population, a marked change from the situation that prevailed until approximately the Second World War. What consequences for ideology, action, and quiescence flow from preoccupation with political news as spectacle? How does the spectacle generate interpretations? What are its implications for democratic theory?...

There is a conventional answer that can be captured in a sentence rather than a volume: citizens who are informed about political developments can more effectively protect and promote their own interests and the public interest. That response takes for granted a world of facts that have a determinable meaning and a world of people who react rationally to the facts they know. In politics neither premise is tenable, a conclusion that history continually reaffirms and that observers of the political scene are tempted to ignore. To explore that conclusion is not likely to generate an optimistic book or a reassuring view of the human condition; but I hope...will provide a realistic appreciation of the link between politics and well-being and a greater chance that political action can be effective.

The spectacle constituted by news reporting continuously constructs and reconstructs social problems, crises, enemies, and leaders and so creates a succession of threats and reassurances. These constructed problems and personalities furnish the content of political journalism and the data for historical and analytic political studies. They also play a central role in winning support and opposition for political causes and policies.

The latter role is usually masked by the assumption that citizens, journalists, and scholars are observers of "facts" whose meanings can be accurately ascertained by those who are properly trained and motivated. That positivist view is accepted rather than defended today. We are acutely aware that observers and what they observe construct one another; that political developments are ambiguous entities that mean what concerned observers construe them to mean; and that the roles and self-concepts of the observers themselves are also constructions, created at least in part by their interpreted observations.[1]

This study is an essay in applying that epistemological principle to politics. Rather than seeing political news as an account of events to which people react, I treat political developments as creations of the publics concerned with them. Whether events are noticed and what they mean depend upon observers' situations and the language that reflects and interprets those situations. A social problem, a political enemy, or a leader is both an entity and a signifier with a range of meanings that vary in ways we can at least partly understand. Similarly, I treat people who engage in political actions as constructions in two senses.

First, their actions and their language create their subjectivity, their sense of who they are. Second, people involved in politics are symbols to other observers: they stand for ideologies, values, or moral stances and they become role models, benchmarks, or symbols of threat and evil.

My focus, in short, is upon people and developments with multiple and changing meanings to one another. That perspective offers a difficult analytic challenge because entities do not remain stable while you study them and subjects and objects are continuously evolving constructions of each other. Historical evidence and psychological theory nonetheless support these assumptions. In every era and every national culture, political controversy and maneuver have hinged upon conflicting interpretations of current actions and developments: leaders are perceived as tyrannical or benevolent, wars as just or aggressive, economic policies as supports of a class or the public interest, minorities as pathological or helpful. It is precisely such differences about the referents of politically significant signs that constitute political and social history.

If political developments depended upon factual observations, false meanings would be discredited in time and a consensus upon valid ones would emerge, at least among informed and educated observers. That does not happen, even over long time periods. The characteristic of problems, leaders, and enemies that makes them political is precisely that controversy over their meanings is not resolved. Whether poverty originates in the inadequacies of its victims or in the pathologies of social institutions, whether a leader's actions are beneficial or damaging to the polity, whether a foreign, racial, religious, or ethnic group is an enemy or a desirable ally, typify the questions that persist indefinitely and remain controversial as historical issues just as they were controversial in their time. The debates over such questions constitute politics and catalyze political action. There is no politics respecting matters that evoke a consensus about the pertinent facts, their meanings, and the rational course of action.

It is just as evident that individuals' opinions on political issues change with transformations in their social situations, with cues about the probable future consequences of political actions, with information about the sources and authoritative support for policies, and with the groups with whom they identify. The meanings of the self, the other, and the social object are facets of the same transaction, changing and remaining stable as those others do. Psychological theorists as diverse as Mead, Vygotsky, Marcuse, and Festinger concur on this point with the lesson of historical observation. The radical student who becomes a conventional liberal or conservative with graduation to new jobs and new ambition, the dedicated communist who becomes a fervent anticommunist, the liberal who becomes a neoconservative, the pacifists who support war when their country is about to embark on one, are recurring examples of the principle that political self-definitions and roles reflect the conditions, constraints, and opportunities in which people find themselves: that ideology and material conditions are part of the same transaction. To understand either stability or change, it is necessary to look to the social situations people experience, anticipate, or fantasize.

The incentive to reduce ambiguity to certainty, multivalent people to egos with fixed ideologies, and the observer's predilections to the essence of rationality pervades everyday discourse and social science practice. These premises reassure observers that their own interpretations are defensible. And there is a related reason that the conventional view is appealing: its implicit promise that rationality and information will end the uninterrupted record of war, poverty, cruelty and other evils that have marked human history; that rational choice may never be optimal, but is a central influence in decision making, policy formation, and voting, and is likely to become a stronger one.

The alternative assumption denies a sharp break between the past and the future; the political language that has rationalized privileges, disadvantages, aggressions, and violence in the past is likely to continue to do so; the phrase "rational choice" is one more symbol in the process of rationalization rather than the path to enlightenment. Pessimistic conclusions are disturbing but are not reasons for rejecting the premises from which they flow. On the contrary, any political analysis that encourages belief in a secure, rational, and cooperative world fails the test of conformity to experience and to the record of history.

The kinds of empirical observations already mentioned and others to be noted later support the view that interpretations of political news construct diverse realities. Many influential social theories of the twentieth century point to the same conclusion. In his recent books Nelson Goodman has analyzed with impressive rigor and clarity the process of what he calls "making worlds." Goodman sees science, art, and other cultural forms as "ways of worldmaking."[2] So far as politics is concerned, news reporting is a major way as well, complementing scientific claims and works of art. The realities people experience, then, are not the same for every person or for all time, but rather are relative to social situations and to the signifiers to which observers pay some attention. ...

But relativism is unsettling. It leaves us without a reassuring test of what is real and of who we are; and relativist propositions cannot be verified or falsified in the positivist sense because they pose the Mannheim Paradox problem: observers who postulate that the meanings of observations vary with the social situation or with something else must take the same skeptical and tentative position with respect to their own relativism.

Belief in the verifiability (or falsifiability) of observations, the separability of facts from values, and the possibility of relying upon deduction to establish valid generalizations is a formula for self-assurance, even for dogmatism, as well as for claims to power over others. But if those assumptions are invalid, if knowledge and meanings are in any sense relative to other knowledge and to the observer's social position, then neither precision in observation nor rigor in deductive reasoning will yield acceptable "covering laws" or generalizations. They offer an appearance of doing so as long as attention is diverted from the problematic premises; but reliance upon that conceptual framework for doing social science is rather like looking under the lamppost, where the light is good, for the quarter one dropped in a dark section of the street.

Critics of relativist positions charge that the latter make it impossible to test their own assumptions and conclusions because these conclusions are *also* relative to something else; but that claim

should not be mistaken for an affirmation that relativist positions are false. The claim is only that they cannot be conclusively established as true. But the same must be said of the positivist position. There is reason for tentativeness about all forms of explanation. Relativist positions are not uniquely vulnerable with respect to verification or falsification. Reasons for support or for doubt are all mortals can hope for. Final conclusions, like final solutions, are for dogmatists.

There is a moral argument for rejecting relativism as well: the contention that it justifies any kind of behavior at all because it fails to provide an absolute ethical standard. Both logic and historical experience dispute that conclusion. A relativist posture in no way denies the need for a clear moral code; it recognizes, rather, that interpretations of actions do vary with social situations. Acceptance of that variation encourages careful examination of moral claims and tentativeness in applying them in ways that others might find objectionable or harmful; but it neither establishes nor undermines the moral code of an individual or a group.

It is moral certainty, not tentativeness, that historically has encouraged people to harm or kill others. Genocide, racial and religious persecution, and the rest of the long catalogue of political acts that have stained human history can only come from people who are sure that they are right. Only in bad novels and comic books do characters knowingly do evil and boast of it. In life, people rationalize their actions in moral terms, an observation that suggests that relativism is a buttress of the moral life because it encourages a critical and reflective stance toward others' actions and toward one's own.

Some critics contend that anyone who believes that realities are constructed and multiple must also believe that they are equally valid, but that conclusion does not follow. On the contrary, the notion of reality construction implies that some are valid and others not. There are multiple realities because people differ in their situations and their purposes. The reality an impressionist painter constructs respecting a maritime scene is not that of a sailor or that of an atomic physicist. The reality a destitute black person constructs respecting the nature of poverty has little validity for a conservative political candidate or a conservative political scientist or even for the same black when he is trying to achieve high grades in a business school. Every construction of a world is a demanding activity. It can be done well or badly and be right or wrong. To understand the multiple realities are prevalent is liberating, but such understanding in no way suggests that every construction is as good as every other.[3]

Social scientists who deny that there are many worlds cut themselves off from vital modes of observation and interpretation; but they reject their intellectual and moral obligations and their capabilities if they do not also recognize some realities as more valid than others for those who construct them and for social analysts.

Materialism, Idealism, and Indifference

Politicians, officials, journalists whose careers depend on news stories, advocates of causes, and a fair number of people who are continually concerned, shocked, entertained, or titillated by the news constitute an avid audience for the political spectacle. For them there are weekly, daily, sometimes hourly triumphs and defeats, grounds for hope and for fear, a potpourri of happenings that mark trends and aberrations, some of them historic. Political life is hyperreal: typically more portentous than personal affairs.

But most of the world's population, even most of the population of the "advanced countries," has no incentive to define joy, failure, or hope in terms of public affairs. Politics and political news are remote, not often interesting, and for the most part irrelevant. This indifference of "the masses" to the enthusiasms and fears of people who thrive on public attention to political matters is the despair of the latter group. Public indifference is deplored by politicians and by right-thinking citizens. It is the target of civics courses, oratory, and television news shows and the reiterated theme of polls that discover how little political information the public has and how low politics rates among public concerns.

Actions that show resistance to political involvement are even more persuasive than surveys. Nonvoters constitute a larger political grouping in America than the adherents of any political party.

Only a small proportion of the population contributes money for political purposes, engages in any other kind of political activity, or pays more than passing attention to political news.[4]

That indifference, which academic political science notices but treats as an obstacle to enlightenment or democracy, is, from another perspective, a refuge against the kind of engagement that would, if it could, keep everyone's energies taken up with activism: election campaigns, lobbying, repressing some and liberating others, wars, and all other political activities that displace living, loving, and creative work. Regimes and proponents of political causes know that it takes much coercion, propaganda, and the portrayal of issues in terms that entertain, distort, and shock to extract a public response of any kind. "The public" is mainly a black hole into which the political efforts of politicians, advocates of causes, the media, and the schools disappear with hardly a trace.[5] Its apathy, indifference, quiescence, and resistance to the consciousness industry[6] is especially impressive in an age of widespread literacy and virtually universal access to the media. Indifference to the enthusiasms and alarms of political activists has very likely always been a paramount political force, though only partially effective and hard to recognize because it is a nonaction. Without it, the slaughter and repression of diverse groups in the name of nationalism, morality, or rationality would certainly be even more widespread than it has been; for the claim that a political cause serves the public interest has often distorted or destroyed concern for personal wellbeing.

Recognition of the power that springs from indifference to political appeals is a precondition for understanding the effectiveness of political symbolism. Symbols, whether language or icons, that have no relevance to everyday lives, frustrations, and successes are meaningless and impotent. They are like the reactions of spectators in a museum to the icons of a culture with which they feel no empathy. In the measure that political advocates resort to appeals that do not touch the experiences of their audience, indifference is to be expected.

Symbols become that facet of experiencing the material world that gives it a specific meaning. The language, rituals, and objects to which people respond are not abstract ideas. If they matter at all, it is because they are accepted as basic to the quality of life. The term "unemployment" may evoke a yawn from an affluent person who has never feared it. It carries a more intense connotation in a depression than at other times even for workers who are always vulnerable to layoffs. A flag may be a garish piece of cloth, a reminder of the repressions and sufferings justified by appeals to patriotism, or an evocation of nostalgia for a land in which one grew up or for the stories about its history one learned as a child. A symbol always carries a range of diverse, often conflicting, meanings that are integral aspects of specific material and social situations. The material condition as experienced and the symbol as experienced stand for each other. The psychological processes by which they come to do so are doubtless subtle and complex and are certainly not fully understood. They may involve the displacement of private affect onto public objects, as Harold Lasswell suggested,[7] or a search for self-esteem[8] or a rational calculation, or a combination of functions. In any case the material basis for the symbol is critical. My references...to language or actions or objects that evoke meanings always presuppose that the "evocation" takes place only as a function of a specific material and social condition. Idealism and materialism are dichotomies as abstract concepts, but in everyday life they are facets of the same transaction. Every sign exercises its effect because of the specific context of privilege, disadvantage, frustration, aspiration, hope, and fear in which it is experienced.

The Incoherence of the Subject, the Object, and the Text

These observations about my conceptual framework foreshadow a more general point of view that grows out of the work of George Herbert Mead and Lev Vygotsky and is also explicit in the writings of the French poststructuralists, especially Michel Foucault and Jacques Derrida.

The subject cannot be regarded as the origin of coherent action, writing, or other forms of expression. As just noted, actions and interpretations hinge upon the social situation in which they begin, including the language that depicts

a social situation. The language that interprets objects and actions also constitutes the subject. Political leaders, like all other subjects, act and speak as reflections of the situations they serially confront; their diversities and inconsistencies are statements of those situations, not of a persistent "self," for the kind of stability in action that transcends situations with varying political inducements has never existed... constructed very largely by the term "leader," that identifiable officials are originators of coherent courses of action... explores the distortions in analysis implicit in the conventional assumptions about political leaders.[9]

It is probably less jarring to recognize that political objects and events are also discontinuous, sometimes contradictory, entities constituted by the signifiers and contexts that give them meanings.... Quite apart from the examples that emerge with every careful examination of a political object, entities are necessarily incoherent because the language that constructs their meaning is inherently discontinuous and in some sense undermines itself.[10] Affirmations bring to consciousness evidence for the contrary position, which the affirmations try to blunt, a form of inversion and sometimes of self deception that is especially pervasive in political language.

When an American official claims that client states like El Salvador or Guatemala are protecting human rights, the statement also reminds those who hear it of evidence that they are not doing so. Every instance of language and action resonates with the memory, the fear, or the anticipation of other signifiers, so that there are radiating networks of meaning that vary with the situations of spectators and actors.

That framework gives political action, talk, writing, and news reporting a different import from that taken for granted in politicians' statements and in conventional social science writing. Accounts of political issues, problems, crises, threats, and leaders now become devices for creating disparate assumptions and beliefs about the social and political world rather than factual statements. The very concept of "fact" becomes irrelevant because every meaningful political object and person is an interpretation that reflects and perpetuates an ideology. Taken together, they comprise a spectacle which varies with the social situation of the spectator and serves as a meaning machine: a generator of points of view and therefore of perceptions, anxieties, aspirations, and strategies. The conventional distinction between procedures and outcomes loses its salience because both are now signifiers, generators of meanings that shape political quiescence, arousal, and support or opposition to causes. The denotations of key political terms become suspect because leaders are not originators of courses of action, problems are not necessarily undesirable conditions to be solved, and enemies need not do or threaten harm. Instead, the uses of all such terms in specific situations are strategies, deliberate or unrecognized, for strengthening or undermining support for specific courses of action and for particular ideologies.

The political entities that are most influential upon public consciousness and action, then, are fetishes: creations of observers that then dominate and mystify their creators. I try here to analyze the pervasive consequences of the fetishism at the core of politics, never a wholly successful enterprise because it is tempting to exorcise a fetish by constructing a rational theory of politics.

End Notes

1. Two recent books, one by an eminent philosopher and the other by an eminent psychologist, expound the conceptual framework I apply here in some detail: Nelson Goodman, *Of Mind and Other Matters* (Cambridge: Harvard University Press, 1983); Jerome Bruner, *Actual Minds, Possible Worlds* (Cambridge: Harvard University Press, 1985).
2. Nelson Goodman, *Ways of Worldmaking* (Indianapolis: Hackett Publishing Co., 1978), and Bruner, *Actual Minds, Possible Worlds.*
3. I discussed this position in *Political Language* (New York: Academic Press, 1978), 5–20. See also Goodman, *Ways of Worldmaking*, 17–22. For a contrary view, see William Connolly's review of *Political Language in American Political Science Review* 73 (September 1979): 847.
4. For survey data on the low level of political information among adults see Robert S. Erikson, Norman R. Luttbeg, and Kent L. Tedin, *American Public Opinion*, 2nd ed. (New York: Wiley, 1980), 19.
5. Jean Baudrillard, *In the Shadow of the Silent Majorities* (New York: Semiotext, 1983), 1–64.
6. The term comes from Hans Magnus Enzensberger, *The Consciousness Industry* (New York: Seabury Press, 1974).
7. Harold D. Lasswell, *Psychopathology and Politics* (Chicago: University of Chicago Press, 1930).
8. Paul M. Sniderman, *Personality and Democratic Politics* (Berkeley: University of California Press, 1975).
9. The same lesson applies, of course, to the term "author." In writing...I also am constituted by a range of disparate sources and inducements, including such contradictory ones as the poststructuralist writers who impress me now and the conventional political scientists I read as a graduate student and whose work I may have learned too well. If the idea that language that depicts discontinuity is itself discontinuous and self-contradictory induces a sense of vertigo, that is preferable to reassuring assumptions that divert analysis from an account of the discontinuities of the social world. The vertigo may stimulate criticism and insight.
10. The point is developed in the work of Jacques Derrida, and also in Kenneth Burke's writing on political rhetoric. See Burke, *The Grammar of Motives* (New York: McGraw-Hill, 1945).

17

A Preface to Economic Democracy

Robert Dahl

Within a generation or so after the Constitutional Convention, a rough consensus appears to have been reached among Americans—among white male citizens, at any rate—that a well-ordered society would require at least three things: political equality, political liberty, and economic liberty; that circumstances in the United States made it possible for Americans to attain these ends; and that, in fact, to a reasonably satisfactory degree these three ends had already been attained in America. Such was the state of mind that Alexis de Tocqueville encountered among Americans in 1831.

At the same time, however, some eminent and philosophically minded observers of the human condition believed that the three goals might very well conflict with one another, quite possibly, indeed, *must* conflict with one another. John Adams, Thomas Jefferson, and James Madison, together with many of Madison's fellow members of the American Constitutional Convention, were deeply concerned that political equality might conflict with political liberty. This possibility forms a major theme—in my view, *the* major theme—of Tocqueville's *Democracy in America*. Echoing an already ancient idea, in the penultimate chapter of his second volume Tocqueville asserts his belief that

> it is easier to establish an absolute and despotic government amongst a people in which the conditions of society are equal, than amongst any other; and I think that if such a government were once established

amongst such a people, it would not only oppress men but would eventually strip each of them of several of the highest qualities of humanity. Despotism therefore appears to me peculiarly to be dreaded in democratic ages. I should have loved freedom, I believe, at all times, but in the time in which we live I am ready to worship it. *(Tocqueville [1835] 1961, 2:385)*[1]

While Tocqueville was mainly concerned with the threat that equality—political, social, and economic—posed for *political* liberty and personal independence, many of the Constitution's framers had been alarmed by the prospect that democracy, political equality, majority rule, and even political liberty itself would endanger the rights of property owners to preserve their property and use it as they chose. In this sense, democracy was thought to menace *economic* liberty as it was then commonly conceived—in particular, that kind of liberty represented by the right to property. Like the conflict between equality and political liberty, this potential conflict between democracy and property was also part of a much older debate. In the United States, the concern expressed at the Constitutional Convention has been frequently voiced ever since.

In considering the threat posed by equality to liberty, Tocqueville, like Jefferson and the Framers before him, observed a society in which it was by no means unreasonable to expect, and hope, that male citizens would be approximately equal in their resources—property, knowledge, social standing, and so on—and consequently in their capacities for influencing political decisions. For they saw a country that was still overwhelmingly agrarian: seven of every ten persons gainfully employed were in agriculture, and the citizen body was predominantly composed of free farmers, or farmhands who aspired to become free farmers. What no one could fully foresee, though advocates of a republic constituted by free farmers sometimes expressed worrisome anticipations, was the way in which the agrarian society would be revolutionized by the development of the modern corporation as the main employer of most Americans, as the driving force of the economy and society. The older vision of a citizen body of free farmers among whom an equality of resources seemed altogether possible, perhaps even inevitable, no longer fitted that reality of the new economic order in which economic enterprises automatically generated inequalities among citizens: in wealth, income, social standing, education, knowledge, occupational prestige and authority, and many other resources. Had Tocqueville and his predecessors fully anticipated the shape of the economic order to come, they probably would have viewed the problem of equality and liberty in a different light. For if, in the older view, an equality among citizens might endanger liberty, in the new reality the liberty of corporate enterprises helped to create a body of citizens highly unequal in the resources they could bring to political life.

The question I want to confront, therefore, is whether it would be possible for Americans to construct a society that would more nearly achieve the values of democracy and political equality and at the same time preserve as much individual liberty as we now enjoy, and perhaps even more. Or is there an inescapable trade-off between liberty and equality, so that we can only enjoy the liberties we now possess by forgoing greater equality? Would therefore the price of greater equality necessarily be less liberty?

More concretely, I propose to explore the possibility of an alternative economic structure that would, I believe, help to strengthen political equality and democracy by reducing inequalities originating in the ownership and control of firms in a system like that we now possess—a system that for want of a better term I call *corporate capitalism*. ...

In examining this possibility I have deliberately narrowed the scope of our inquiry into the problem of freedom and equality: first by focusing on *political* equality, then by focusing on the consequences of owning and controlling enterprises. Important as it is, political equality—equality among citizens engaged in governing themselves by means of the democratic process—is not the only relevant form of equality that might serve as a standard for a good society. And owning and controlling firms is not the only source of undesirable inequalities among human beings, or even of political inequalities.

Yet narrowing the focus is, I believe, justified on several grounds. For one, the *general* problem of equality is so complex that perhaps we can deal with it well only by examining parts of it. As Douglas Rae concludes at the end of his masterly analysis of the meaning, kinds, and values of equality:

> Equality is the simplest and most abstract of notions, yet the practises of the world are irremediably concrete and complex. How, imaginably, could the former govern the latter? It cannot. We are always confronted with more than one practical meaning for equality and equality itself cannot provide a basis for choosing among them. The question "Which equality?" will never be answered simply by insisting upon equality. *(Rae 1981, 150)*[2]

Moreover, of the various kinds of equality that might exist in a good society, political equality is surely one of the most crucial, not only as a means of self-protection but also as a necessary condition for many other important values, including one of the most fundamental of all human freedoms, the freedom to help determine, in cooperation with others, the laws and rules that one must obey. In a somewhat similar way, differences in ownership and control of enterprises, while certainly not at the origin of all forms of inequality, are deeply implicated in inequalities of many kinds: in esteem, respect, and status, in control over one's daily life, in income and wealth and all the opportunities associated with them, in life chances for adults and children alike. It seems to me scarcely open to doubt that a society with significantly greater equality in owning and controlling economic enterprises would produce profoundly greater equality than exists among Americans today.

Before considering whether an alternative to corporate capitalism might strengthen political equality without sacrificing liberty, we first need to search for a clearer understanding of the relationships between political equality, political liberty, and economic liberty. In my view these relationships have often been misconceived, or asserted in so general a fashion that we can scarcely judge the truth of statements about them. An enormously influential example of what I believe to be a mistaken view of these relationships is to be found in a very great work by a very great writer—Tocqueville himself, in *Democracy in America*.... Tocqueville believed that equality, desirable though it may be, poses a standing threat to liberty. But if self-government by means of the democratic process is a fundamental, even an inalienable right; if the exercise of that inalienable right necessarily requires a substantial number of more particular rights, which are therefore also fundamental and inalienable; and if a certain equality of condition is necessary to the political equality entailed in the democratic process, then the conflict, if there be one, is not simply between equality and liberty. It is, rather, a conflict between fundamental liberties of a special kind, the liberties people enjoy by virtue of governing themselves through the democratic process, and other liberties of a different kind.

Among these other liberties is economic liberty, which Americans have generally understood to include a personal and inalienable right to property. Applied to an economic enterprise, ownership carries with it a right to govern the enterprise, within broad limits, of course, set by the government of the state. Transferred from the operation of farms and small businesses to the large corporation, ownership rights have given legality and legitimacy to undemocratic governments that intrude deeply into the lives of many people, and most of all the lives of those who work under the rulership of authorities over whom they exercise scant control. Thus a system of government Americans view as intolerable in governing the state has come to be accepted as desirable in governing economic enterprises.

I have sketched here an alternative form of government for economic enterprises that holds promise of eliminating, or at least reducing, this contradiction. A system of self-governing enterprises would be one part of a system of equalities and liberties in which both would, I believe, be stronger, on balance, than they can be in a system of corporate capitalism. But whether many Americans will find this vision attractive I cannot say. For we Americans have always been torn between two conflicting visions of what American society is and ought to be. To summarize them oversimply, one is a vision of the world's first and grandest attempt to realize democracy, political equality, and political liberty on a continental scale. The other is a vision of a country where unrestricted liberty to acquire unlimited wealth would produce the world's most prosperous society. In the first, American ideals are realized by the achievement of democracy, political equality, and the fundamental political rights of all citizens in a country of vast size and diversity. In the second, American ideals are realized by the protection of property and of opportunities to prosper materially and to grow wealthy. In the first view, the right to self-government is among the most fundamental of all human rights, and, should they conflict, is superior to the right to property. In the second, property is the superior, self-government the subordinate right.

As a people we are divided among ourselves in the strength of our commitment to these conflicting ideals; and many Americans are divided within themselves. I cannot say whether a people so divided possesses the firmness of purpose and the clarity of vision to assert the priority of democracy, political equality, and the political rights necessary to self-government over established property rights, economic inequality, and undemocratic authority within corporate enterprises.

End Notes

1. Alexis de Tocqueville, *Democracy in America*, 2 vols. (New York: Schocken Books, [1835, 1840] 1961).
2. Douglas Rae, *Equalities* (Cambridge, Mass.: Harvard University Press, 1981).

18

The Semisovereign People

E. Schattschneider

... The class bias of associational activity gives meaning to the limited scope of the pressure system, because *scope and bias are aspects of the same tendency.* The data raise a serious question about the validity of the proposition that special-interest groups are a universal form of political organization reflecting *all* interests. As a matter of fact, to suppose that everyone participates in pressure-group activity and that all interests get themselves organized in the pressure system is to destroy the meaning of this form of politics. The pressure system makes sense only as the political instrument of a segment of the community. It gets results by being selective and biased; *if everybody got into the act, the unique advantages of this form of organization would be destroyed, for it is possible that if all interests could be mobilized the result would be a stalemate.*

Special-interest organizations are most easily formed when they deal with small numbers of individuals who are acutely aware of their exclusive interests. To describe the conditions of presssure-group organization in this way is, however, to say that it is primarily a business phenomenon. Aside from a few very large organizations (the churches, organized labor, farm organizations, and veterans' organizations) the residue is a small segment of the population. *Pressure politics is essentially the politics of small groups.*

The vice of the groupist theory is that it conceals the most significant aspects of the system. The flaw in the pluralist heaven is that the heavenly chorus sings with a strong upper-class accent. Probably about 90 percent of the people cannot get into the pressure system.

The notion that the pressure system is automatically representative of the whole community is a myth fostered by the universalizing tendency of modern group theories. *Pressure politics is a selective process* ill designed to serve diffuse interests. The system is skewed, loaded, and unbalanced in favor of a fraction of a minority.

On the other hand, pressure tactics are not remarkably successful in mobilizing general interests. When pressure-group organizations attempt to represent the interests of large numbers of people, they are usually able to reach only a small segment of their constituencies. Only a chemical trace of the fifteen million Negroes in the United States belong to the National Association for the Advancement of Colored People. Only one five hundredths of 1 percent of American women belong to the League of Women Voters, only one sixteen hundredths of 1 percent of the consumers belong to the National Consumers' League, and only 6 percent of American automobile drivers belong to the American Automobile Association, while about 15 percent of the veterans belong to the American Legion.

From E. E. Schattschneider, *The Semisovereign People: A Realists View of Democracy in America* (Hinsdale, IL: The Dryden Press, 1975) (originally published 1960), pp. 34–37.

The competing claims of pressure groups and political parties for the loyalty of the American public revolve about the difference between the results likely to be achieved by small-scale and large-scale political organization. Inevitably, the outcome of pressure politics and party politics will be vastly different.

A CRITIQUE OF GROUP THEORIES OF POLITICS

It is extremely unlikely that the vogue of group theories of politics would have attained its present status if its basic assumptions had not been first established by some concept of economic determinism. The economic interpretation of politics has always appealed to those political philosophers who have sought a single prime mover, a sort of philosopher's stone of political science around which to organize their ideas. The search for a single, ultimate cause has something to do with the attempt to explain *everything* about politics in terms of group concepts. The logic of economic determinism is to *identify the origins of conflict and to assume the conclusion*. This kind of thought has some of the earmarks of an illusion. The somnambulatory quality of thinking in this field appears also in the tendency of research to deal only with successful pressure campaigns or the willingness of scholars to be satisfied with having placed pressure groups on the scene of the crime without following through to see if the effect can really be attributed to the cause. What makes this kind of thinking remarkable is the fact that in political contests there are as many failures as there are successes. Where in the literature of pressure politics are the failures?

Students of special-interest politics need a more sophisticated set of intellectual tools than they have developed thus far. The theoretical problem involved in the search for a single cause is that all power relations in a democracy are reciprocal. Trying to find the original cause is like trying to find the first wave of the ocean.

Can we really assume that we know all that is to be known about a conflict if we understand its *origins?* Everything we know about politics suggests that a conflict is likely to change profoundly as it becomes political. It is a rare individual who can confront his antagonists without changing his opinions to some degree. Everything changes once a conflict gets into the political arena—*who* is involved, *what* the conflict is about, the resources available, etc. It is extremely difficult to predict the outcome of a fight by watching its beginning because we do not even know who else is going to get into the conflict. The logical consequence of the exclusive emphasis on the determinism of the private origins of conflict is to assign zero value to the political process.

The very expression "pressure politics" invites us to misconceive the role of special-interest groups in politics. The word "pressure" implies the use of some kind of force, a form of intimidation, something other than reason and information, to induce public authorities to act against their own best judgment. In Latham's famous statement already quoted the legislature is described as a "referee" who "ratifies" and "records" the "balance of power" among the contending groups.[1]

It is hard to imagine a more effective way of saying that Congress has no mind or force of its own or that Congress is unable to invoke new forces that might alter the equation.

Actually the outcome of political conflict is not like the "resultant" of opposing forces in physics. To assume that the forces in a political situation could be diagramed as a physicist might diagram the resultant of opposing physical forces is to wipe the slate clean of all remote, general, and public considerations for the protection of which civil societies have been instituted.

Moreover, the notion of "pressure" distorts the image of the power relations involved. *Private conflicts are taken into the public arena precisely because someone wants to make certain that the power ratio among the private interests most immediately involved shall not prevail.* To treat a conflict as a mere test of the strength of the private interests is to leave out the most significant factors. This is so true that it might indeed be said that the only way to preserve private power ratios is to keep conflicts out of the public arena.

*   *   *

End Notes

1. Earl Latham, *The Group Basis of Politics.* Ithaca, 1952, pp. 35 and 36, says, "The legislature referees the group struggle, ratifies the victories of the successful coalitions, and records the terms of the surrenders, compromises, and conquests in the form of statutes...." "the legislative vote on which any issue tends to represent the composition of strength, i.e., the balance of power, among the contending groups at the moment of voting."

19

Habits of the Heart: Individualism and Commitment in American Life

Robert N. Bellah,
Richard Madsen,
William M. Sullivan,
Ann Swidler, and
Steven M. Tipton

A CHANGE OF ERAS?

... [W]e have documented the latest phase of that process of separation and individuation that modernity seems to entail. John Donne, in 1611, at the very beginning of the modern era, with the prescience that is sometimes given to great poets, vividly described that process:

> 'Tis all in peeces, all cohaerence gone;
>
> All just supply, and all Relation:
>
> Prince, Subject, Father, Sonne, are things forgot,
>
> For every man alone thinkes he hath got
>
> To be a Phoenix, and that then can bee
>
> None of that kinde, of which he is, but hee.[1]

Donne lived in a world where the ties of kinship and village and feudal obligation were already loosening, though only a few perceived how radical the consequences would be.

America was colonized by those who had come loose from the older European structures, and so from the beginning we had a head start in the process of modernization. Yet the colonists brought with them ideas of social obligation and

From Robert N. Bellah, Richard Madsen, William M. Sullivan, Ann Swidler, and Steven M. Tipton, *Habits of the Heart: Individualism and Commitment in American Life.* UC Press, 1985, 1996, 2998. pp. 275–283.

group formation that disposed them to recreate in America structures of family, church, and polity that would continue, if in modified form, the texture of older European society. Only gradually did it become clear that every social obligation was vulnerable, every tie between individuals fragile. Only gradually did what we have called ontological individualism, the idea that the individual is the only firm reality, become widespread. Even in our day, when separation and individuation have reached a kind of culmination, their triumph is far from complete. The battles of modernity are still being fought.

But today the battles have become halfhearted. There was a time when, under the battle cry of "freedom," separation and individuation were embraced as the key to a marvelous future of unlimited possibility. It is true that there were always those, like Donne, who viewed the past with nostalgia and the present with apprehension and who warned that we were entering unknown and dangerous waters. It is also true that there are still those who maintain their enthusiasm for modernity, who speak of the third wave or the Aquarian Age or the new paradigm in which a dissociated individuation will reach a final fulfillment. Perhaps most common today, however, is a note of uncertainty, not a desire to turn back to the past but an anxiety about where we seem to be headed. In this view, modernity seems to be a period of enormously rapid change, a transition from something relatively fixed toward something not yet clear. Many might find still applicable Matthew Arnold's assertion that we are

Wandering between two worlds, one dead,
The other powerless to be born.[2]

There is a widespread feeling that the promise of the modern era is slipping away from us. A movement of enlightenment and liberation that was to have freed us from superstition and tyranny has led in the twentieth century to a world in which ideological fanaticism and political oppression have reached extremes unknown in previous history. Science, which was to have unlocked the bounties of nature, has given us the power to destroy all life on the earth. Progress,

modernity's master idea, seems less compelling when it appears that it may be progress into the abyss. And the globe today is divided between a liberal world so incoherent that it seems to be losing the significance of its own ideals, an oppressive and archaic communist statism, and a poor, and often tyrannical, Third World reaching for the very first rungs of modernity. In the liberal world, the state, which was supposed to be a neutral night-watchman that would maintain order while individuals pursued their various interests, has become so overgrown and militarized that it threatens to become a universal policeman.

Yet in spite of those daunting considerations, many of those we talked to are still hopeful. They realize that though the processes of separation and individuation were necessary to free us from the tyrannical structures of the past, they must be balanced by a renewal of commitment and community if they are not to end in self-destruction or turn into their opposites. Such a renewal is indeed a world waiting to be born if we only had the courage to see it.

THE CULTURE OF SEPARATION

One of the reasons it is hard to envision a way out of the impasse of modernity is the degree to which modernity conditions our consciousness. If modernity is "the culture of separation," Donne characterized it well when he said " 'Tis all in peeces, all cohaerence gone." When the world comes to us in pices, in fragments, lacking any overall pattern, it is hard to see how it might be transformed.

A sense of fragmentariness is as characteristic of high intellectual culture as of popular culture. Starting with science, the most respected and influential part of our high culture, we can see at once that it is not a whole, offering a general interpretation of reality, as theology and philosophy once did, but a collection of disciplines each having little to do with the others. As Stephen Toulmin recently put it:

From the early seventeenth century on, and increasingly so as the centuries passed, the tasks of scientific inquiry were progressively divided up between separate and distinct "disciplines." ...Every independent scientific discipline is marked by its own specialized modes of abstraction: and the issues to be considered in each discipline are so defined that they can be investigated and discussed independently—in abstraction from—the issues belonging to other disciplines. ... As a result of this first kind of abstraction, the broad and general questions about "cosmic interrelatedness" which were the focus of the earlier debates about nature have been superseded by other, more specialized, disciplinary questions.... In its actual content (that is to say) the science of the nineteenth and early twentieth centuries became an aggregate, rather than an integration, of results from its component disciplines.[3]

What Toulmin has pointed out for the natural sciences is equally true of the social sciences and, indeed, of all the "disciplines" and "fields" into which contemporary intellectual culture is divided. As the French anthropologist Louis Dumont has observed:

[I]n the modern world each of our particular viewpoints or specialized pursuits does not know very well—or does not know at all—what it is about and the reason for its existence or distinctness, which is more often a matter of fact than of consensus or rationality. Just as our rationality is mostly a matter of the relation of means and ends, while the hierarchy of ends is left out, so also our rationality manifests itself within each of our neatly distinct compartments but not in their distribution, definition and arrangement.[4]

The poet and critic Wendell Berry has described the consequences for the place of poetry in a culture of separation and specialization. Since science specializes in the external reality of the world, the poet is consigned to speak about his own feelings. He is himself his chief subject matter and "the old union of beauty, goodness and truth is broken." Such poets can no longer be public persons, so that even when, as of late,

some of them have turned to protest, it is a private protest. As Berry puts it, "In his protest, the contemporary poet is speaking publicly, but not as a spokesman; he is only one outraged citizen speaking *at* other citizens who do not know him, whom he does not know, and with whom he does not sympathize."[5] One recent poet who tried to integrate the world—politics, economics, culture—into one vast poem, taking Dante as his model, only showed how impossible such an integration is under modern conditions. According to Helen Vendler, Ezra Pound's huge *Cantos* are a "jumble of detail," a "mound of potsherds," of which Pound himself finally said, "I cannot make it cohere."[6]

These developments in the realm of high culture have had devastating consequences for education. Here, particularly in higher education, students were traditionally supposed to acquire some general sense of the world and their place in it. In the contemporary multiversity, it is easier to think of education as a cafeteria in which one acquires discrete bodies of information or useful skills. Feeble efforts to reverse these trends periodically convulse the universities, but the latest such convulsion, the effort to establish a "core curriculum," often turns into a battle between disciplines in which the idea of a substantive core is lost. The effort is thus more symptomatic of our cultural fracture than of its cure.

When we turn from intellectual culture to popular culture, particularly the mass media, the situation is, if anything, even more discouraging. Within the disciplinary and subdisciplinary "compartments" of intellectual culture, though there is little integration between them, there is still meaning and intensity in the search for truth. In popular culture, it is hard to say even that much. To take an extreme example, television, it would be difficult to argue that there is any coherent ideology or overall message that it communicates. There is a sense in which the broadcasters' defense of their role—that they are merely mirroring the culture—has a certain plausibility. They do not support any clear set of beliefs or policies, yet they cast doubt on everything. Certainly, they do not glorify "the power structure." Big business is not admirable: its leaders are frequently power-hungry bullies without any moral restraints (J. R. Ewing, for example). Government is under a cloud of suspicion: politicians are crooks. Labor is badly tarnished: labor leaders are mobsters. The debunking that is characteristic of our intellectual culture is also characteristic of the mass media. While television does not preach, it nevertheless presents a picture of reality that influences us more than an overt message could. As Todd Gitlin has described it,

> [T]elevision's world is relentlessly upbeat, clean and materialistic. Even more sweepingly, with few exceptions prime time gives us people preoccupied with personal ambition. If not utterly consumed by ambition and the fear of ending up as losers, these characters take both the ambition and the fear for granted. If not surrounded by middle-class arrays of consumer goods, they themselves are glamorous incarnations of desire. The happiness they long for is private, not public; they make few demands on society as a whole, and even when troubled they seem content with the existing institutional order. Personal ambition and consumerism are the driving forces of their lives. The sumptuous and brightly lit settings of most series amount to advertisements for a consumption-centered version of the good life, and this doesn't even take into consideration the incessant commercials, which convey the idea that human aspirations for liberty, pleasure, accomplishment and status can be fulfilled in the realm of consumption. The relentless background hum of prime time is the packaged good life.[7]

Gitlin's description applies best to daytime and prime-time soaps. It does not apply nearly so well to situation comedies, where human relations are generally more benign. Indeed, the situation comedy often portrays people tempted to dishonesty or personal disloyalty by the prospect of some private gain, who finally decide to put family or friends ahead of material aggrandizement. Yet, finally, both soaps and situation comedies are based on the same contrast: human decency versus brutal competitiveness

for economic success. Although the soaps show us that the ruthlessly powerful rich are often unhappy and the situation comedies show us that decent "little people" are often happy, they both portray a world dominated by economic competition, where the only haven is a very small circle of warm personal relationships. Thus the "reality" that looms over a narrowed-down version of "traditional morality" is the overwhelming dominance of material ambition.

Of course, in television none of these things is ever really argued. Since images and feelings are better communicated in this medium than ideas, television seeks to hold us, to hook us, by the sheer succession of sensations. One sensation being as good as another, there is the implication that nothing makes any difference. We switch from a quiz show to a situation comedy, to a bloody police drama, to a miniseries about celebrities and with each click of the dial, nothing remains.

But television operates not only with a complete disconnectedness between successive programs. Even within a single hour or half-hour program, there is extraordinary discontinuity. Commercials regularly break whatever mood has built up with their own, often very different, emotional message. Even aside from commercials, television style is singularly abrupt and jumpy, with many quick cuts to other scenes and other characters. Dialogue is reduced to clipped sentences. No one talks long enough to express anything complex. Depth of feeling, if it exists at all, has to be expressed in a word or a glance.

The form of television is intimately related to the content. Except for the formula situation comedies (and even there, divorce is increasingly common), relationships are as brittle and shifting as the action of the camera. Most people turn out to be unreliable and double-dealing. Where strong commitments are portrayed, as in police dramas, they are only between buddies, and the environing atmosphere, even within the police force, is one of mistrust and suspicion.

If popular culture, particularly television and the other mass media, makes a virtue of lacking all qualitative distinctions, and if the intellectual culture, divided as it is, hesitates to say anything about the larger issues of existence, how does our culture hold together at all? The culture of separation offers two forms of integration—or should we say pseudo-integration?—that turn out, not surprisingly, to be derived from utilitarian and expressive individualism. One is the dream of personal success. As Gitlin has observed, television shows us people who are, above all, consumed by ambition and the fear of ending up losers. That is a drama we can all identify with, at least all of us who have been (and who has not?) exposed to middle-class values. Isolated in our efforts though we are, we can at least recognize our fellows as followers of the same private dream. The second is the portrayal of vivid personal feeling. Television is much more interested in how people feel than in what they think. What they think might separate us, but how they feel draws us together. Successful television personalities and celebrities are thus people able freely to communicate their emotional states. We feel that we "really know them." And the very consumption goods that television so insistently puts before us integrate us by providing symbols of our version of the good life. But a strange sort of integration it is, for the world into which we are integrated is defined only by the spasmodic transition between striving and relaxing and is without qualitative distinctions of time and space, good and evil, meaning and meaninglessness. And however much we may for a moment see something of ourselves in another, we are really, as Matthew Arnold said in 1852, "in the sea of life enisled... / We mortal millions live *alone*."[8]

THE CULTURE OF COHERENCE

But that is not the whole story. It could not be the whole story, for the culture of separation, if it ever became completely dominant, would collapse of its own incoherence. Or, even more likely, well before that happened, an authoritarian state would emerge to provide the coherence the culture no longer could. If we are not entirely a mass of interchangeable fragments within an aggregate, if we are in part qualitatively distinct members of a whole, it is because there are still operating among us, with whatever difficulties, traditions that tell us about the nature of the world, about the nature of society, and about

who we are as people. Primarily biblical and republican, these traditions are, as we have seen, important for many Americans and significant to some degree for almost all. Somehow families, churches, a variety of cultural associations, and, even if only in the interstices, schools and universities, do manage to communicate a form of life, a *paideia*, in the sense of growing up in a morally and intellectually intelligible world.

The communities of memory of which we have spoken are concerned in a variety of ways to give a qualitative meaning to the living of life, to time and space, to persons and groups. Religious communities, for example, do not experience time in the way the mass media present it—as a continuous flow of qualitatively meaningless sensations. The day, the week, the season, the year are punctuated by an alternation of the sacred and the profane. Prayer breaks into our daily life at the beginning of a meal, at the end of the day, at common worship, reminding us that our utilitarian pursuits are not the whole of life, that a fulfilled life is one in which God and neighbor are remembered first. Many of our religious traditions recognize the significance of silence as a way of breaking the incessant flow of sensations and opening our hearts to the wholeness of being. And our republican tradition, too, has ways of giving form to time, reminding us on particular dates of the great events of our past or of the heroes who helped to teach us what we are as a free people. Even our private family life takes on a shared rhythm with a Thanksgiving dinner or a Fourth of July picnic.

In short, we have never been, and still are not, a collection of private individuals who, except for a conscious contract to create a minimal government, have nothing in common. Our lives make sense in a thousand ways, most of which we are unaware of, because of traditions that are centuries, if not millennia, old. It is these traditions that help us to know that it does make a difference who we are and how we treat one another. Even the mass media, with their tendency to homogenize feelings and sensations, cannot entirely avoid transmitting such qualitative distinctions, in however muted a form.

But if we owe the meaning of our lives to biblical and republican traditions of which we seldom consciously think, is there not the danger that the erosion of these traditions may eventually deprive us of that meaning altogether? Are we not caught between the upper millstone of a fragmented intellectual culture and the nether millstone of a fragmented popular culture? The erosion of meaning and coherence in our lives is not something Americans desire. Indeed, the profound yearning for the idealized small town that we found among most of the people we talked to is a yearning for just such meaning and coherence. But although the yearning for the small town is nostalgia for the irretrievably lost, it is worth considering whether the biblical and republican traditions that small town once embodied can be reappropriated in ways that respond to our present need. Indeed, we would argue that if we are ever to enter that new world that so far has been powerless to be born, it will be through reversing modernity's tendency to obliterate all previous culture. We need to learn again from the cultural riches of the human species and to reappropriate and revitalize those riches so that they can speak to our condition today.

We may derive modest hope from the fact that there is a restlessness and a stirring in the intellectual culture itself. Stephen Toulmin tells us that "our own natural science today is no longer 'modern' science." It is a "postmodern" science in which disciplinary boundaries are beginning to appear as the historical accidents they are and the problems that are necessarily "transdisciplinary" are beginning to be addressed. This recognition is based on the realization that we cannot, after all, finally separate who we are from what we are studying. As Toulmin puts it, "We can no longer view the world as Descartes and Laplace would have us do, as 'rational onlookers,' from outside. Our place is within the same world that we are studying, and whatever scientific understanding we achieve must be a kind of understanding that is available to participants within the processes of nature, i.e., from inside." Perhaps nature as perceived by the poet, the theologian, and the scientist may be the same thing after all. At least there is now room to talk about that possibility. And there are parallel developments in the social sciences. There, too, it appears that studying history and acting in it are not as different as we had thought. If our high culture could begin to talk about nature and history, space and time, in ways that did not disaggregate them into fragments, it might be possible for us to find connections and analogies with the older ways in which human life was made meaningful. This would not result in a neotraditionalism that would return us to the past. Rather, it might lead to a recovery of a genuine tradition, one that is always self-revising and in a state of development. It might help us find again the coherence we have almost lost.

*   *   *

End Notes

1. John Donne, "Anatomie of the World: The First Anniversary."
2. Matthew Arnold, "Stanzas from the Grand Chartreuse" (1855).
3. Stephen Toulmine, *The Return to Cosmology: Postmodern Science and Theology of Nature* (Berkeley and Los Angeles: University of California Press, 1982), pp. 228–29, 234.
4. Louis Dumont, *From Mandeville to Marx: The Genesis and Truimph of Economic Ideology* (Chicago: University of Chicago Press, 1977), p. 20.
5. Wendell Berry, *Standing by Words* (San Francisco: North Point Press, 1983), pp. 5, 20.
6. Helen Vendler, "From Fragments a World Perfect at Last," *New Yorker*, March 19, 1984, p. 143.
7. Todd Gitlin, *Inside Prime Time* (New York: Pantheon, 1983), pp. 268–69. Conversations with Todd Gitlin and Lisa Heilbronn were helpful in clarifying our views of television.
8. Matthew Arnold, "To Marguerite." Emphasis in original.

PART THREE

Theories on the Policy Process

20

In Search of a Framework to Understand the Policy Process

Stella Z. Theodoulou

Just as there is no one universally accepted definition of public policy, there is no one universally accepted theoretical model that helps the reader to understand how policy develops, is executed, or changes. What exists is a set of competing theories and models that provide different approaches to studying and understanding the policy process. One such approach is the policy cycle and process model that explains the policy process as a sequential cycle of stages of activities that needs to occur in order for government to make policy. A second approach taken by some theorists is a policy typologies framework. Theorists utilizing this approach do so because they feel the stages approach negates the output of the process thus the typologies framework looks at the different types of policies being formed and their impact on politics. A third approach is taken by theorists who argue that the stages perspective is synthetic in nature and does not explain policy change. Such theorists argue the stages approach

tends to create an oversimplified view of policy making because real-world policy making does not take place in an orderly sequential process. Such theorists believe the focus of study should be the relationship between how problems are defined, agendas are set, and the decision-making and implementation processes. The assumption being that these activities are not necessarily sequential and that policy making is the product of a complex interplay of actors, groups, institutions, and the political environment which cuts across the diverse activities of the policy process.

One may ask why the literature has diverse theories and models guiding our understanding of policy making; the answer lies in the nature of the real world. In reality, the policy-making process seldom works exactly as described by any one theory or model. No one theory is completely satisfactory in how well it describes and explains the dynamics of the policy process; each theory has strengths and weaknesses. The value of having diverse theories is that each offers evidence of the multidimensional nature of policy making. Thus the choice between theories, models, and frameworks is not an either–or proposition. The challenge is to utilize the approaches where warranted, derive analytical value from them where applicable, and understand that the policy process is intrinsically complex. It is not the purpose here to critique or compare the different theories in terms of their usefulness but rather to outline each of them to prepare students for the relevant readings that follow. In Chapter 48 an organizational map of policy making is suggested that views the policy process as distinct phases of activities that must take place, the phases being Pre-decision, Decision, and Post-decision.[1]

THE POLICY CYCLE AND PROCESS MODEL

As early as 1970, Charles Jones advocated for a policy approach that looked at all the processes necessary to complete the policy cycle.[2] He argued focus should be placed on the entire policy process from problem definition to governmental response to evaluation to assessment of whether the solution should be adjusted or terminated. The next year, Harold Lasswell identified the policy decision process as a set of common stages that are necessary for a policy decision to be arrived at: problem recognition, information gathering, problem solutions, implementation of solution, assessment of the solution, and potential termination.[3] Both Jones and Lasswell are promoting an approach that views policymaking as the by-product of a process that was linear and sequential. In essence Jones and Lasswell provided policy scholars with a conceptual foundation and framework for understanding the basic policy process. This approach is commonly referred to as the *Stages-Heuristic Model*. The model views policy making as an evolutionary cycle composed of a series of stages; policy can be understood to begin through a stimulus and end with adoption of an action. Thus, many authors utilizing this approach view the policy process as a deliberative, staged, recursive, and administrative cycle.[4] Such a perspective is based on an assumption that policy makers respond to

demands to deal with an issue or problem. Policy making is seen as a cycle made up of a series of interlocking and fluid activities composed of distinct policy stages. This approach allows for an understanding of how policies originate, develop, and are executed. Authors such as Anderson, Dye, Lester, and Stewart have applied this model to demonstrate how private issues evolve into public and political concerns.[5]

Figure 20.1 notes the commonly agreed-upon policy stages. According to Peter DeLeon, it is assumed that each stage of the policy process has "a distinctive characteristic and mannerism and process that give the individual stage a life and presence of its own."[6] Policy making is an ongoing process whereby issues evolve into problems, problems are placed on the public and political agenda, and solutions are formulated, adopted, implemented, and then evaluated. Evaluation can lead to policy maintenance, change, or termination.

The stages-heuristic model allows for analysis of both the policy actors and the institutional setting present at each stage of activity. It also allows for identification of relationships across institutions and policy actors. Most textbooks on

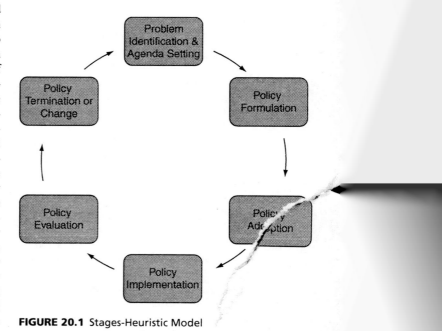

FIGURE 20.1 Stages-Heuristic Model

policy making that utilize a stages-heuristic approach present the sequential stages as a policy cycle so as to emphasize the continuous nature of policy making and that no policy decision is final. Real-world dynamics force constant reassessment and adjustment of solutions.

POLICY TYPOLOGIES

Since the great depression, all industrialized nations have witnessed a proliferation of public policies to deal with the problems that stem from modernization. The sheer number of policies has forced policy scientists to develop ways in which different policies can be categorized by type. Determining what type of policy a governmental action is allows for an understanding of the different purposes of public policy. Many theorists would argue if the basic differences among policies are identified, then it should be possible to recognize the political conditions that lead to policy types. Theodore Lowi presented one of the earliest typologies based on two premises: First, policy causes politics

and thus different types of policy produce different power relationships among actors, and second, government has coercive power. Lowi looks at the likelihood of government using its coercive power to identify four types of policy: regulatory, redistributive, distributive, and self regulatory. Such a typology differentiates policies on the basis of their impact on society and the relationship among those involved in policy formation. A number of competing typologies were developed in response to Lowi.[7] Box 20.1 summarizes Lowi's typology and some of the main rival typologies that can be found within the literature. It does not suggest that these are the only ones or the best ones, rather they are typologies commonly referred to in many policy texts. Each typology offers a different way in which the intent and purpose of a particular policy can be understood. In reality perhaps it is beneficial to see that the different types are actually not competing but rather are complimentary to one another. Thus, within a given policy domain, many policies will reflect a number of types dependent upon the particular context of time and the political

---

BOX 20.1
Policy Typologies

Lowi Typology

- **Redistributive:** Reallocating of rights, monies, property to assist a specific individual/group or segement of population
- **Distributive:** Allocation of goods and services for specific individual/group or segment of population
- **Regulatory:** Application of rules of behavior on industry, individuals or groups
- **Self regualtory:** Self monitoring by individual or group

Anderson Typology

- **Substantive:** Specific actions, with costs and benefits, advantages and disadvantages
- **Procedural:** Directions as to how substantive actions will be taken

Edelman Typology

- **Material:** Provision tangible costs or benfits, imposition of real disadvantages or advantages on a select actor or population
- **Symbolic:** Declaration or action without tangible disadvantages or advantages

Wade & Curry Typology

- **Collective:** Provides indivisible goods, if given to one individual or group must be given to all groups or individual
- **Private:** Provides divisible goods and are charged for on an individual basis

O'Hare Typology

- **Direct Actions & Indirect Actions:** Addresses issues when private or public sector don't allocate goods efficiently or when there are equity or distributional problems

environment they are part of. If one accepts policy making is political in nature, then we may also classify policies as either liberal interventionist or conservative. The former seeks governmental action to bring about social change while the latter opposes governmental intervention. However, in recent years it is difficult to distinguish between the two as in reality modern society faces a number of issues which require intervention of some sort by government. The debate today is not on whether government should intervene but in what areas, in what form, and on whose behalf. Issue areas have also been used to classify types of policy, for example, welfare policy, foreign policy, and environmental policy. Additionally some authors type policy through an institutional designation, for example, judicial policy or legislative policy.[8]

MODELS AND FRAMEWORKS LOOKING AT POLICY CHANGE AND UTILIZING A PROBLEMS, AGENDA-SETTING, DECISION-MAKING, AND IMPLEMENTATION FOCUSED APPROACH

Advocacy Coalition Framework

This framework emphasizes the importance of information and beliefs in the policy process and the role of a range of institutional and non-institutional actors. Paul Sabatier and Hank Jenkins Smith argue that policy change cannot be explained successfully if the agenda-setting phase of the policy process is separated out from the wider policy-making process.[9] The policy

process is viewed as a dynamic ongoing process with multiple actors. The framework assumes that around each policy issue a specific policy subsystem—which includes competing advocacy coalitions, power brokers, and decision makers—exists and is subject to the stability and dynamic nature of elements external to the subsystem (see Figure 20.2). Examples of stable external elements are the constitutional structure of the state or the polity's dominant socio-cultural values. Such elements are determined to be stable because they are difficult to change over time. Dynamic factors are those elements that do alter over time and thus change the political environment, for example, the election of a new government or president or an economic downturn. The actors around each policy subsystem unite and interact with "advocacy coalitions." Advocacy coalitions may be distinguished from each other by their beliefs and resources; this in turn makes them relatively cohesive because of shared belief systems which may or may not change over time. The objective of an advocacy coalition is to ensure that policy conforms to their core belief system at a given point in time.

In essence, Sabatier and his adherents are arguing that agenda setting and the policy-making process in general are dominated by elite opinion. If policy change is to be understood, then elite opinion and the factors which make it shift over time must be looked at. The policy process and policy change can best be understood by looking at the relationships within and between policy subsystems. Policy systems can be composed of journalists, academics, policy

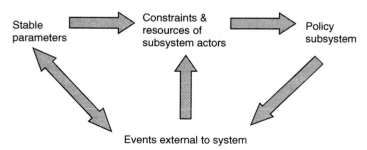

FIGURE 20.2 Sabatier's Policy Subsystem

Source: Adapted from Sabatier, "An Advocacy Coalition Framework of Policy Change," *Policy Sciences* 21(3), 1988, pp.129–168.

analysts, and governmental actors active in policy formulation. For most problems, policy making will provide policy modification because of the stability of the core beliefs of the advocacy coalition. For real change to occur, dynamic factors must change the core beliefs of the advocacy coalitions.[10] The advocacy coalition framework clearly provides a way to include all the diverse variables involved in the policy process. Clearly the advocacy coalitions framework links the problem-definition and agenda-setting stages with decision making and implementation, and thus the predecisional phase and the decisional phase in many instances blend into each other. Policy solutions are the product of one or more advocacy coalitions who form policy subsystems to advance solutions that are advantageous to the involved advocacy coalitions.

Punctuated Equilibrium Model

Baumgartner and Jones offer a further problems-focused framework that explains how the policy process can affect policy change. This model deals with the predecisional and decisional phases of the policy process and is an attempt to understand how radical policy change occurs in a policy process that is incrementally conservative in nature and relatively stable.[11] It offers a much broader way to look at agenda setting. Baumgartner and Jones view the policy process has having long periods of stability interspersed with periods of instability and policy change—punctuated equilibria. When the system is stable, there is widespread agreement on how problems are defined and on the policy-making agenda.

At certain points in time when there is significant change in the political system, such as the altering of socioeconomic or political conditions, institutional and constitutional subsystems and subsystems evident within American politics mobilize to alter the status quo. They label such periods *policy punctuation*. The outcome is change in policy and institutional arrangements, and a new point of equilibrium is set from which policy can be evaluated. These new institutional arrangements then create the foundation for a new period of stability.[12] This punctuated equilibrium is driven by two interacting forces: policy

image and institutional policy venues. A series of continuously operating policy subsystems within and across the political system surround issues.

As the number of issues confronted by a subsystem increases, policy solutions tend to be incremental, and this can fuel dissatisfaction among groups and interests. This dissatisfaction drives them to mobilize and forces the issue onto the macro-level political agenda within the legislature or executive branches of government. The mobilization is energized by changing policy images surrounding an issue. Policy image explains which subsystem remains stable. If a policy image fosters consensus over how an issue is understood, then there is stability. As the consensus breaks down and a new policy image gains support, instability and punctuated change are more likely to occur. Policy change is possible because individual and collective decisions can change.

A punctuated equilibrium model requires an acceptance that individuals have limited ability to process information and this means that similar issues are processed together rather than individually. Policy subsystems allow the political system to do this simultaneous processing. This explains why policy can for the most part be incrementalist and at other times provide sweeping change. The policy process is then characterized as having periods of incrementalist policy making and periods of punctuated equilibrium producing change in policy making.

Multiple Streams Model

Adherents of this model attempt to explain why some issues and problems are more prominent on the policy agenda and eventually have policy enacted to solve them, while other issues and problems do not. John Kingdon originated the multiple streams model as an alternative to rational models of decision making. For Kingdon, policy making is not the result of rational choice but is the product of organizational anarchy. Utilizing the garbage can model of decision making developed by Cohen, March, and Olsen, Kingdon views the agenda-setting process as a garbage can in which problems and possible solutions are "dumped" and often solutions attach to problems that they might have not necessarily been designed for.[13]

The multiple streams model views the policy process as the interplay of three streams within policy institutions and processes: the problem stream, the policy (alternatives) stream, and the politics stream.[14] The problem stream is where issues become salient to decision makers and then how they perceive them to be problems. For an issue to be a problem, there has to be a general feeling that something should be done to change the situation; this depends on how the problem is framed or brought to the forefront through a focusing event which determines whether the issue is placed on or eliminated from the agenda.[15] Thus, not all issues become problems and there are issues that decision makers can choose to ignore; thus the only issues acted upon are those that decision makers and citizens want addressed and are politically feasible.[16] Problems are brought to the policymakers' attention through three mechanisms: indicators which are measurements that assess the scale of and change in the problem; events bringing attention to the problem; and feedback which provides information on how the problem is being dealt with.

The policy stream is the constant flow of policy solutions that are floated throughout the political system as responses to identified problems. Kingdon conceptualizes this as a "soup" where ideas are floated around. Some solutions float to the top while others sink to the bottom. Policy solutions are recombined and incubated over the years in "policy communities" of specialists and experts. What determines these floating hierarchies of policy solutions are policy entrepreneurs who provide the linkage between ideas and policy decision makers. Policy entrepreneurs are individuals or groups who act as advocates for a particular action or solution and invest resources so as to get the policy solution that they favor adopted; they might be elected officials, bureaucrats, lobbyists, academics, or journalists.

The politics stream operates separately from the other two streams and serves at times to determine a problem's status on the agenda. It can be defined as the political factors influencing the agenda, such as national mood, current political climate, organized political forces, change in elected officials, and consensus on what solution is proposed and enacted. The politics stream is what the political system and policy actors are willing to place on the agenda and it is where solutions emerge as policy outcomes.

The streams are broad, separate, continuously active, and independent, and at critical given times and in certain contexts the streams converge and a solution is attached to a problem and is turned into policy. The process by which the streams converge is what Kingdon calls coupling (see Figure 20.3).[17] Coupling can be partial or pervasive and is brought about by chance events or through the work of policy entrepreneurs. Policy entrepreneurs dramatize an issue by highlighting indicators of the problem. They also push for a problem definition they favor and present specific policies as solutions to the problem as they define it. Often entrepreneurs achieve their goal through "softening up" policymakers through activities such as a public hearing and media coverage. The job of a policy entrepreneur is to convince policy makers to see a problem the way he or she sees it and then adopt the solution the entrepreneur favors. Usually what is required for coupling to occur is a focusing event that allows policy entrepreneurs to merge the streams by attaching an idea from the policy stream to an issue floating in the problem stream, which allows for the policy

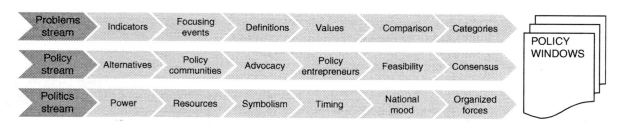

FIGURE 20.3 Kingdon's Coupling Process

opportunities Kingdom refers to as policy windows. Theorists utilizing a multiple streams model view the policy process as a series of opening and closing policy windows that are the result of the interplay between problems, policies, and politics at any given time. Windows can close easily so policy entrepreneurs must make the most of the opportunity to move the policy solution forward.

For Kingdon, it is important to look at both formal and informal actors within the policy process if we want to understand which issues are agendized. Policies emerge out of what he views as a complex political and policy environment in which multiple streams operate separately, and at times they will merge or divide to provide opportunities for policy entrepreneurs to take advantage of and push their preferred solution. When the three streams divide policy can develop through two of the streams merging through partial coupling, although, in this instance a successful outcome is harder to achieve.

In recent years, the multiple streams model has been refined by a number of theorists.[18] Such theorists have argued that any model utilizing multiple streams must take into account institutional structural factors. Additionally some altered the policy stream into a policy field by joining the problem stream and the politics stream together.[19] With these revisions, there has been a shift in focus from agenda setting to policy design and formulation.

Policy Design and Social Construction of Target Populations

This framework focuses on how attitudes about a policy's target population influence the type of policy formulated and how policy affects how target populations are viewed. The originating theorists Schneider and Ingram argue that it is important when looking at policy design to understand how a particular segment of the population will be impacted. In their article "The Social Construction of Target Populations," Schneider and Ingram illustrate what they believe to be the relationship between pervasive stereotypes and policy making.[20] They argue that the justification and substance of any policy can be understood through recognition of how groups targeted by a given

policy are socially constructed. Social construction is how society perceives a group. In short, it is the image held of a group by others within both the political arena and society in general. The theory suggests that within society there are groups of individuals (target populations) endowed with positive or negative culturally constructed images. Such images influence policymakers with respect to the types of benefits and burdens they are willing to distribute to the groups through policy design. The effects of such image construction are that in electoral periods incumbents hope to maximize their electoral advantage through prior policy choices.[21] Thus, the ideal is for positively constructed groups to receive benefits while their negative counterparts receive burdens. The danger for policymakers is they can incorrectly perceive the social construction and political power of some target populations and thus give benefits and burdens to the wrong groups. One possible consequence of such misperception is that policymakers' electoral success could be affected. Thus, policymakers ideally hope to distribute the most benefits to those groups with the most political power and most positive social construction. In order to justify this behavior, Schneider and Ingram argue that policymakers utilize a number of believable rationalizations to justify their policy actions.[22] Thus, policymakers exploit rationalizations that maximize the benefits and minimize the burdens targeted at favored groups.

Policy Diffusion

Authors utilizing a policy diffusion framework focus on policy emulation and learning across states or across nations. The framework assumes that the adoption of a policy in one setting is used as a model for policymakers in another setting to follow; basically states and nations adopt similar policies to deal with similar problems.[23] The framework has its origins in the literature on state policy innovativeness and owes much to the work of Jack Walker, who looked at why some states are quicker at adopting policy than other states.[24] However, the use of the policy diffusion framework to understand the policy process became more common after the publication of Berry and Berry's work on American state lottery policy making.[25] Using event history analysis, Berry and Berry demonstrated how policymakers in one state were influenced by prior policy choices in other states.

Studies using a policy diffusion framework are for the most part quantitative and longitudinal; thus, states or nations are tracked over a period of time until policy adoption occurs. The main drivers of policy diffusion are internal factors and external forces. Internal factors are socioeconomic markers, election cycles, partisanship, policy entrepreneurs, group conflict, and political institutions, while external forces include, but are not limited to, competition and social learning.[26] The social learning process explains why states or nations feel pressure to adopt policies that other states or nations have adopted. Sometimes nations adopt what others have implemented because it's cost and time effective or because there is a feeling that the state or nation will be left behind and viewed as less advanced than other states or nations.

Institutional Analysis and Development Framework

The Institutional Analysis and Development (IAD) framework was developed by Elinor Ostrom and her colleagues at the Indiana University Workshop in Political Theory and Policy Analysis, and it provides an understanding of the policy process by focusing on the behavior of individuals who make decisions and the way in which the institutions they are part of affect their decision making.[27] The focus is on the way in which institutions shape social interactions and decision-making processes. Social choices and decisions take place in "action arenas." IAD theorists define institutions as a set of prescriptions and constraints that are used to organize all forms of repetitive and structured interactions; prescriptions include rules, norms, and shared strategies.[28] Institutions can be formal (rules-in-form) or informal structures (rules-in-use).[29]

The action arena is affected by three categories of variables: institutions or rules that govern the action arena, the characteristics of the community or collective unit of interest, and the attributes of the physical environment within which

the community acts.[30] "Action situations" and "actors" make up the action arena. The components of an action situation are the participants in the situation, the participants' positions, the outcomes of participants' decisions, the payoffs or costs and benefits associated with outcomes, the linkages between actions and outcomes, the participants' control in the situation, and the level of participants' information. Actors can be assessed in the action arena by evaluating their information-processing capabilities, their preferences or values for different actions, their resources, and the processes they use for choosing actions.

Ostrom argues there are three levels of action explaining collective choices: the operational level, which are collective decisions about day-to-day activities; the collective-choice level, which are decisions about the choice of rules that govern operational activities; and the constitutional level, where decision makers determine how collective-choice actors are chosen and the rules governing those collective choice actors.[31] Constitutional choice actions impact collective choice decisions, which then impact operational actions. Schlager and Blomquist argue that actors can move among the three levels with the goal of obtaining the best outcomes with the given rules or changing the rule choices to their benefit.[32]

CONCLUSION

It can be concluded there are a number of theories within the public policy field that look at the policy-making process as the result of distinct activities by various actors. Some believe that the activities may be grouped as a sequence or stages, while others believe that the real world does not comply with this orderly process. However, no one theory is perfect or offers the complete explanation. Each of the theories discussed offers key insights into understanding the policy process and demonstrates that explaining the policy process requires an understanding of the relationships among a complex set of factors and systems, all of which have various interactions and uncertain inputs and outputs. Each of the theories offers a piece of the puzzle that is useful to advancing our understanding of public policy. Each theory has its advocates and detractors. It is our hope the

32. Schager and Blomquist "A Comparison of Three Emerging Theories of the Policy Process," *Political Research Quarterly,* 49 (September 1996).

Additional Suggested Readings

COHEN, MICHAEL, MARCH, JAMES, and OLSEN, JOHAN, "A Garbage Can Model of Organizational Choice," *Administrative Science Quarterly*, 17 (June 1972), pp. 1–25.

GILARDI FABRIZIO, "Who Learns from What in Policy Diffusion Processes?" *American Journal of Political science*, 54 (3) (July 2010), pp. 650–666.

HILL and KIM QUAILE, "In Search of Policy Theory." *Policy Currents*, 7 (April 1997), pp. 1–9.

JONES, BRYAN D., BAUMGARTNER, FRANK R., and TRUE, JAMES L, "Policy Punctuations: U.S. Budget Authority, 1947–1995," *Journal of Politics*, 60 (February 1998), pp. 1–33.

JONES, BRYAN D., SULKIN, TRACY, and LARSEN, HEATHER A, "Policy Punctuations in American Political Institutions." *American Political Science Review*, 97 (February 2003), pp. 151–169.

JOHN and PETER, "Is There Life after Policy Streams, Advocacy Coalitions and Punctuations: Using Evolutionary Theory to Explain Policy Change?" *Policy Studies Journal*, 31 (4) 2003, pp. 481–497.

LESTER, JAMES, and STEWART Jr., JOSEPH, *Public Policy: An Evolutionary Approach* (Belmont, CA: Wadsworth, 2000).

LINDBLOM, CHARLES E, and WOODHOUSE, L.G, *The Policy-Making Process* (3rd ed.) (Englewood Cliffs, NJ: Prentice-Hall, 1993).

MAY and PETER J, "Reconsidering Policy Design: Policies and Publics." *Journal of Public Policy*, 11 (April–June 1991), pp.187–206.

———. "Policy Learning and Failure," *Journal of Public Policy*, 12 (October–December 1992), pp. 331–354.

McCOOL and DANIEL C , "Policy Subsytems." In *Public Policy Theories, Models, and Concepts: An Anthology*, ed. Daniel C. McCool (Englewood Cliffs, NJ: Prentice Hall, 1995), pp. 251–255.

MICHAEL MINTROM and SANDRA VERGARI, "Advocacy, Coalitions, Policy Entrepreneurs, and Policy change," *Policy Studies Journal*, 24 (3) 1996, pp. 420–434.

NICHOLSON-CROTTY, SEAN, and MEIER, KENNETH, "From Perception to Public Policy: Translating Social Constructions in Policy Designs." In *Deserving and Entitled: Social Constructions and Target Populations*, (eds.) Anne L. Schneider and Helen M. Ingram (Albany, NY SUNY Press, 2005), pp. 223–242.

OSTROM and ELINOR, "Rational Choice Theory and Institutional Analysis: Toward Complementarity," *American Political Science Review*, 85 (1) (March 1991), pp. 237–243.

ROBINSON, SCOTT, CAVER, FLOUNSAY, MEIER, KENNETH J., O'TOOLE Jr., and LAURENCE J, "Explaining Policy Punctuations: Bureaucratization and Budget Change." *American Journal of Political Science*, 51 (January 1985), pp. 140–150.

ROSE and RICHARD, *Lesson-Drawing in Public Policy* (Chatham, NJ: Chatham House, 1993).

SABATIER and PAUL A, *Theories of the Policy Process* (Boulder, CO: Westview Press, 1999).

SABATIER and PAUL A, *Theories of the Policy Process* (Boulder, CO: Westview Press, 2007).

E. SCHLAGER and W. BLOMQUIST, "A Comparison of Three Emerging Theories of the Policy Process," *Political Research Quarterly*, 49, 1996.

SMITH and KEVIN B, "Typologies, Taxonomies, and the Benefits of Policy Classification," *Policy Studies Journal*, 30 (August 2002), pp. 379–395.

ZACHARIDIS and NICOLAS, "Comparing Lenses in Comparative Public Policy," *Policy Studies Journal*, 1995.

ZACHARIDES and NICOLAS, *Ambiguity and Choice in Public Policy: Political Decision Making in Modern Democracies* (Washington, DC: Georgetown University Press, 2003).

21

Theories Of and In the Policy Process

David L. Weimer

Political scientists trained in the generations of my teachers, William Riker and Aaron Wildavsky, commonly studied public administration as a field.[1] As newer bodies of knowledge pushed public administration out of its previously prominent role within political science, and public administration largely split off into its own discipline, political scientists became less well connected to the nitty-gritty questions of governance.[2] Public policy, which emerged as a field to fill that role, has not had a comfortable place in political science.[3] Research on policy processes often seems too ambitious, spanning more established fields without necessarily fertilizing them. Policy research, the practical and explicitly normative side of public policy, often seems too catholic in its disciplinary sources, yet overly narrow in its focus, as it addresses real problems of the world rather than intellectual puzzles of political science.[4] These two orientations toward public policy roughly correspond to Harold Lasswell's (1971, p. 1) distinction between *knowledge of* the policy process and *knowledge in* the policy process. Consideration of the role of theory in public policy should recognize these different types of knowledge. In this brief essay, I argue that creating and testing theories of the policy process is a desirable project for political scientists, but that theories drawn from the narrower fields of political science and other disciplines are more likely to be useful in policy research.

My own bias is that theories with actors, whether hyper or boundedly rational, are most likely to be relevant to the majority of questions of interest to political scientists. For the purpose of this discussion, however, I require only that theory offer understanding of some general phenomenon. Thus, I avoid the entire rational choice debate within political science, which has been extensive and intense (Friedman, 1996), largely because I have nothing new to add to it. Obviously, though, my view of theory certainly rejects the claim that generalization of any kind is futile.

THEORIES OF THE POLICY PROCESS

The public policy section of the American Political Science Association describes itself as "committed to producing rigorous empirical and theoretical knowledge of the processes and products of governing and the application of that knowledge to policy issues." The first part of the commitment—knowledge of the processes and products of governing—concerns theory of the policy process. Assuming we do not just govern for its own sake, the "products of governing" phrase implies attention to how people are affected. Concern about the outcomes resulting from politics is one feature that distinguishes public policy as a field within political science.[5] The other feature is considering processes broadly, rather than how they operate within

From David L. Weimer, "Theories Of and In the Policy Process," *The Policy Studies Journal,* Vol. 36, No. 4, 2008, pp. 489–495.

specific institutions (international organizations, legislatures, the executive, the courts, subnational governments, etc.) or involve specific behaviors (voting, organizational behavior, socialization, etc.) that define mainstream positive political science. It is this broad view that makes public policy desirable; it also makes theorizing especially difficult.

In an academic world with increasing pressures on scholars to speak on questions of current interest to the discipline and to specialize in narrow fields within disciplines, public policy admirably aspires to be more comprehensive in its view of political process so as to explain not just parts of the process, but how their interactions produce policy outcomes. It potentially can play a role in "integrating the discipline's accumulated knowledge concerning political behavior in various institutional settings" (Sabatier, 1991, p. 144). However, with comprehensiveness inevitably comes complexity. Theorizing and building useful models becomes inherently more difficult with complexity. So too does the problem of testing, or at least validating in some way, the hypotheses (or implications) that flow from the various models implied by any theory.

Models of complex phenomena can be useful in several ways. Perhaps the most useful models allow those employing them to make meaningful predictions about what is likely to occur. I think we have some narrow models that, over well-defined domains, are useful in this way. For example, in many legislative situations, Black's Median Voter Theorem is likely to give us a pretty good prediction of what bill will be able to command a majority over the status quo. Of course, as soon as we allow for various sorts of complexity—preferences that are not single-peaked, policy alternatives that are multidimensional, etc.—we may no longer be able to make specific predictions. I do not think that the existing models of the policy process are very useful in prediction.[6] Perhaps the advocacy coalition framework (Sabatier & Jenkins-Smith, 1993) allows some predictions about what kinds of information in what sort of fora are likely to be effective in facilitating convergence between opposing coalitions in terms of policies and the ways they are implemented. Perhaps the institutional rational choice framework allows us to predict when cooperation at the operational level is

likely to be effective in producing public goods or preserving common property resources (Ostrom, 1990). In each of these cases, however, the frameworks are offering not predictions about the policy process itself, but rather about behavior in particular segments of it.

When confronted with complex phenomena, however, models (or as their creators often more modestly call them, frameworks) can be useful in giving us a resource for cognition, allowing us to identify some important features that can serve as the basis for seeing patterns among the complexity. For example, consider the policy/problem/political streams framework of Kingdon (1995). It does not offer much in the way of specific prediction, and it only offers limited and vague prescription—policy entrepreneurs should be ready to exploit policy windows that create an opportunity to push a policy alternative that they favor onto the public agenda. Nonetheless, I think that the policy streams framework is very useful in helping bring some order to the very complex policy process. It gives one someplace to start when thinking about the policy process writ large. One can also imagine embedding the advocacy coalition framework or the institutional rational choice model into the policy stream to understand better how the policy subsystems operate.

Testing or validating poses a problem for the policy process models. It is hard for me to imagine framing a refutable hypothesis based on the Kingdon (1995) framework, though in terms of retrospection (the actual domain of almost all social science prediction except that based on experiments!), it seems to provide a basis for plausible explanation. The advocacy coalition framework does lend itself to the specification of refutable hypotheses, some of which have been qualitatively tested (Sabatier & Jenkins-Smith, 1999, pp. 125–27). Amenability to testing, however, does not necessarily imply usefulness. For example, consider the punctuated equilibrium model (Baumgartner & Jones, 1993; Jones & Baumgartner, 2005; Jones, Sulkin, & Larsen, 2003). If one accepts the null hypothesis of policy changes being drawn randomly from a normal distribution, then rejecting the normal distribution in favor of a distribution with positive kurstosis provides evidence in favor of a U.S. policy process characterized generally by incrementalism, with the occasional major shift in policy. Although there is a coherent story behind the model, it is not, I think, one that brings much useful enlightenment to our understanding of the policy process beyond more narrowly focused models.

Of course, testing becomes even more difficult when one moves to theories that seek to explain the outcomes of policy processes across different sets of political institutions (and cultures). Few scholars have sufficient knowledge of the political institutions and cultures of more than a few countries to do detailed empirical comparisons as individual scholars. This is an area of research that almost certainly requires coordinated effort by teams of scholars (Riker & Weimer, 1995). Some examples of such projects include the study of changes in property rights in post-Communist countries (Weimer, 1997), the comparison of the governance of the health, steel, and financial sectors in six Western European countries (Bovens, 't Hart, & Peters, 2001), and the design of reproductive policies in 10 developed countries (Bleiklie, Goggin, & Rothmayr, 2004).

Policy research seeks to give advice about how to achieve desired outcomes. As policy researchers seek to contribute to the realization of desired outcomes, they must necessarily be concerned with what can be attained politically— political feasibility is at least instrumental to achieving substantive goals. A powerful theory of the policy process would thus be extremely valuable to policy researchers (and especially policy analysts).[7] As I argued above, however, models of the policy process offer only limited help in predicting. Consequently, they are not likely to be very useful to policy researchers in their efforts to predict the political fate of policy alternatives.

Instead, theories and frameworks of narrow scope are more likely to be useful. Policy researchers seek to predict the outcomes of specific processes, such as legislation, regulation, and implementation as they assess concrete policy alternatives. The more closely tailored the theories, models, and frameworks to the specific decision processes at hand, the more likely they are to provide relevant predictions. As social scientists, we should value generalization; as policy researchers, we must usually deal with the specific if we are to

inform real decisions.[8] A model of legislative process may be less valuable than a model of a particular legislature, which in turn may be less valuable than a model of how that particular legislature makes decisions in the policy area of concern.

Theories that are narrow in another sense are also likely to be helpful to policy analysts. I have in mind here the implications of models that seek to understand some generic behavior. For example, the notion that one may gain a stronger bargaining position by foreclosing some possible courses of action and making threats more credible seems to me something that a policy analyst would usefully have among his or her capital stock of ideas. It would join ideas drawn from a variety of intellectual sources, such as organizational behavior (Miles' Law—where you stand depends on where you sit), path dependence (programs create constituencies), her-esthetics (making a latent policy dimension salient may disrupt an equilibrium), rhetoric (framing issues to resonate with cultural values may change public perceptions of the issues), rational choice theory of institutions (repeated interaction can support cooperation not obtainable in one-off interaction), cognitive psychology (people fear loss more powerfully than they anticipate comparable gain), and political economy (rectangles tend to be larger than triangles—rent transfers are more policy relevant than deadweight losses).

Notice that I did not include economics in the above list of sources. (If I were to select a single insight, then perhaps it would be "the scarce resource gets the rent.") If one were interested just in predicting political behavior, then one could draw on a variety of economically grounded theories, such as rent seeking. I did not include economic theory in the above list because it has such a broad influence on policy research that singling out a few insights would be grossly misleading. The influence of economic theory is both positive, in the sense of providing a starting point for prediction, and normative in the sense of providing systematic ways to assess the relative efficiency of alternatives through cost-benefit analysis. One can also point to many specific examples where economic theory and modeling played fundamental roles in policy research and analysis. For example, the design of the very successful simultaneous ascending auctions of spectrum by the Federal Communications Commission in the mid-1990s drew heavily on theory (McAfee & McMillan, 1996).[9] Political scientists who do policy research may face a disciplinary dilemma: To take full advantage of available theory, they may have to cross disciplinary lines; crossing disciplinary lines, however, may reduce the validity of their work among their political science peers.[10] If one were restructuring the social science disciplines to better support policy research, then one might very well go back to Smith's political economy as the overarching framework for both political science and economics so that disciplinary lines would be less likely to constrain the theories used and the research approaches taken.

CONCLUSION

Theories of the policy process face conflicting demands. The discipline of political science seeks theories of a general nature; policy researchers seek theories that help them predict political outcomes in specific contexts. Reconciling these demands may not be possible. Rather, we may be left with grand theories that are not helpful and helpful theories that are not grand. Political scientists who seek to promote better public policy should encourage both types of theory.

End Notes

The author thanks Hank Jenkins-Smith and the other participants in the panel on Public Policy Theories at the 2004 Midwest Political Science Meetings for comments. The opinions expressed are solely those of the author.

1. Some might find it surprising that Riker contributed to the first Harvard case book on public administration (Stein, 1952).
2. Writing about the declining relationship between public administration and political science in the postwar years, Waldo (1968, p. 478) asserted that "the present relationship of Public Administration to Political Science is in significant part one of convention and inertia and the future relationship must be regarded as problematic." He went on to argue that social psychology, sociology, and economics all had come to have greater intellectual interchange with public administration than did political science have with public administration (p. 460).
3. See, for example, Hecklo (1972) and Bobrow, Eulau, Landau, Jones, and Axelrod (1977).
4. For the purpose of discussion, I consider policy research to be scholarly work directed at informing public decisions by framing undesirable social conditions as policy problems, by evaluating the consequences of adopted policies, or by predicting and valuing the consequences of policies that might be adopted. I reserve the term "policy analysis" for professional practice, specifically the provision of "client-oriented advice relevant to public decisions and informed by social values" (Weimer & Vining, 1999, p. 27). Policy research may be policy analysis in some circumstances, though it often neither has a clear client orientation nor speaks to imminent public decisions.
5. Normative theory speaks to the valuation of outcomes, but usually does not deal in any depth with the measurement or prediction of outcomes.
6. For overviews of policy process models, see Sabatier (1999) and Schlager and Blomquist (1996).
7. An extremely powerful theory would pose what Jagdish Bhagwati calls the "determinacy paradox": Political economy models that successfully endogenize politics would leave little room for the advice of policy analysts. See O'Flaherty and Bhagwati (1997).
8. Of course, some ideas of a general nature do influence public policy in important ways (Hall, 1989; Kelman, 1990; Walsh, 2000). The impact of ideas, however, may not be immediate but rather flow like water in limestone, reappearing unexpectedly (Thomas, 1987). They may also play a general "enlightenment role," setting the context for policy discussion (Weiss, 1977). Based on the cases with which I am familiar, I would claim that such general policy ideas seem to come primarily from economists.
9. By the way, here is an example of the "limestone model" of policy ideas—auctioning spectrum was suggested by Ronald Coase in 1959.
10. The particular substance of policy problems may also necessitate drawing on theories of other disciplines, such as sociology and psychology.

References

BAUMGARTNER, FRANK R., and BRYAN D. JONES. 1993. *Agendas and Instability in American Politics.* Chicago: University of Chicago Press.

BLEIKLIE, IVAR, MALCOLM GOGGIN, and CHRISTINE ROTHMAYR, eds. 2004. *Comparative Biomedical Policy: Governing Assisted Reproductive Technologies.* London: Routledge.

BOBROW, DAVID B., HEINZ EULAU, MARTIN LANDAU, CHARLES O. JONES, and ROBERT AXELROD. 1977. "The Place of Policy Analysis in Political Science: Five Perspectives." *American Journal of Political Science* 21 (2): 415–33.

BOVENS, MARK, PAUL 'T HART, and B. GUY PETERS, eds. 2001. *Success and Failure in Public Governance: A Comparative Analysis.* Cheltenham, UK: Edward Elgar.

COASE, RONALD A. 1959. "The Federal Communications Commission." *Journal of Law and Economics* 11 (2): 1–40.

FRIEDMAN, JEFFREY, ed. 1996. *The Rational Choice Controversy: Economic Models of Politics Reconsidered.* New Haven, CT: Yale University Press.

HALL, PETER A., ed. 1989. *The Political Power of Economic Ideas.* Princeton, NJ: Princeton University Press.

HECKLO, H. HUGH. 1972. "Review Article: Policy Analysis." *British Journal of Political Science* 2 (1): 83–108.

JONES, BRYAN D., and FRANK R. BAUMGARTNER. 2005. *The Politics of Attention: How Government Prioritizes Problems.* Chicago: University of Chicago Press.

JONES, BRYAN D., TRACY SULKIN, and HEATHER A. LARSEN 2003. "Policy Punctuations in American Political Institutions." *American Political Science Review* 97 (1): 151–69.

KELMAN, STEVEN. 1990. "Why Public Ideas Matter." In *The Power of Public Ideas*, ed. Robert B. Reich. Cambridge, MA: Harvard University Press, 31–53.

KINGDON, JOHN W. 1995. *Agendas, Alternatives, and Public Policies*, 2nd ed. New York: HarperCollins College Publishers.

LASSWELL, HAROLD D. 1971. *A Pre-View of the Policy Sciences.* New York: American Elsevier.

MCAFEE, R. PRESTON, and JOHN MCMILLAN 1996. "Analyzing the Airwaves Auction." *Journal of Economic Perspectives* 10 (1): 159–75.

OSTROM, ELINOR. 1990. *Governing the Commons.* New York: Cambridge University Press.

O'FLAHERTY, BRENDAN, and JAGDISH BHAGWATI. 1997. "Will Free Trade with Political Science Put Normative Economists Out of Work?" *Economics and Politics* 9 (3): 207–19.

RIKER, WILLIAM H., and DAVID L. WEIMER 1995. "The Political Economy of Transformation: Liberalization and Property Rights." In *Modern Political Economy: Old Topics, New Directions*, ed. Jeffrey Banks and Eric Hanushek. New York: Cambridge University Press, 80–107.

SABATIER, PAUL A. 1991. "Political Science and Public Policy," *PS: Political Science and Politics* 24 (2): 144–47.

———. ed. 1999. *Theories of the Policy Process.* Boulder, CO: Westview Press.

SABATIER, PAUL A., and HANK C. JENKINS-SMITH, eds. 1993. *Policy Change and Learning: An Advocacy Coalition Approach.* Boulder, CO: Westview Press.

———. 1999. "The Advocacy Coalition Framework: An Assessment." In Theories of the Policy Process, ed. Paul A. Sabatier. Boulder, CO: Westview Press, 117–66.

SCHLAGER, EDELLA, and WILLIAM BLOMQUIST. 1996. "A Comparison of Three Emerging Theories of the Policy Process." *Political Research Quarterly* 49 (3): 651–72.

STEIN, HAROLD. 1952. *Public Administration and Policy Development: A Case Book.* New York: Harcourt, Brace and Company.

THOMAS, PATRICIA. 1987. "The Use of Social Research: Myths and Models." In *Social Science Research and Government: Comparative Essays on Britain and the United States*, ed. Martin Bulmer. New York: Cambridge University Press, 51–60.

WALDO, DWIGHT. 1968. "Public Administration." *Journal of Politics* 30 (2): 443–79.

WALSH, JAMES I. 2000. "When Do Ideas Matter? Explaining the Successes and Failures of Thatcherite Ideas." *Comparative Political Studies* 33 (4): 483–516.

WEIMER, DAVID L., ed. 1997. *Political Economy of Property Rights: Institutional Change and Credibility in the Reform of Centrally Planned Economies.* New York: Cambridge University Press.

WEIMER, DAVID L., and AIDAN R. VINING 1999. *Policy Analysis: Concepts and Practice*, 3rd ed. Upper Saddle River, NJ: Prentice Hall.

WEISS, CAROL. 1977. "Research for Policy's Sake: The Enlightenment Function of Social Research." *Policy Analysis* 3 (4): 531–45.

22

The Stages Approach to the Policy Process

Peter DeLeon

More than forty-five years ago, Harold D. Lasswell articulated the first formal usage of the concept *policy sciences.* Although informal policy advice had been offered by advisers to rulers for centuries, Lasswell was the first to define in any coherent manner what composed this "new" approach to government and its characteristics (Lasswell, 1951; also Lasswell and Kaplan, 1950). Since then, the policy sciences—largely under the derivative rubrics of policy analysis and later public management—have made tremendous strides in terms of widespread acceptance, surely in the United States and increasingly in other nations. But as the policy sciences orientation approaches half a century, one can legitimately wonder what it has produced in terms of Lasswell's original vision, its everyday operation, and, most important, its capacity for future research, in short, its overall success. More pessimistic observers would agree with Donald Schön and Martin Rein (1994, p. xvi), who—although themselves sympathetic to the policy sciences—wrote that "the policy analytic movement begun by Harold Lasswell in the early 1950s has largely failed."

In this essay, I deal with one particular aspect of Lasswell's vision of the policy sciences. Lasswell operationalized—although rather abstractly—many of his ideas about improving the quality of governance by improving the quality of the information being rendered to government. He focused particular attention on the "policy process," or the functional stages or phases that a given government policy (or program) would go through during its "policy life." As we shall see, many observers have argued against the Lasswellian approach and have strongly suggested the shortcomings of the policy process/stages approach. In this context, we can examine Lasswell's (and others') policy framework to see if it has become as antiquated (some would claim dysfunctional) as its critics have charged. Alternatively, we can see if it still offers some utility as the art and craft of policy research continue to evolve as a tool to improve the quality of the information offered government.

KNOWLEDGE IN THE POLICY PROCESS

Lasswell gave special emphasis to what he termed "knowledge *of* the policy process" and "knowledge *in* the policy process," the former being more substantive (e.g., How much CO_2 can be released into the atmosphere without evoking a disastrous global warming condition?) and the latter being more procedural (How does a democratic polity publicly intervene in reducing its CO_2 emissions?). He framed a "conceptual map [that] must provide

From Peter DeLeon, "The Stages Approach to the Policy Process: What Has It Done? Where Is It Going," In Paul Sabatier, (Boulder Westview Press), pp. 19–32, 1999.

a guide to obtaining a generalistic image of the major phases of any collective act" (Lasswell, 1971, p. 28) and nominated seven "stages" of what he was later to call "the decision process" (Lasswell, 1956):

- Intelligence
- Promotion
- Prescription
- Invocation
- Application
- Termination
- Appraisal

This listing reflects the origin of what has arguably been the most widely accepted concept of the policy sciences, that is, the policy process, the procedure by which a given policy is proposed, examined, carried out, and perhaps terminated (see Lasswell, 1956). Later, one of Lasswell's students at Yale University, Garry D. Brewer (1974), proposed a derivative list (almost certainly with Lasswell's specific approval) that (with other very similar alternatives from other authors) has shaped much of the research agenda undertaken by policy scientists since the mid-1970s, in both substantive and practical terms:[1]

- Initiation
- Estimation
- Selection
- Implementation
- Evaluation
- Termination

These stages are not simply divined from the heady atmosphere of the academy. Both individually and in combination, they offer a way to think about public policy in concept and, just as important, in operation. Although they certainly can merge with one another, each does have a distinctive characteristic and mannerism and process that give the individual stage a life and presence of its own. Without denying that the stages can (and often should) share information and procedures, few observers would confuse the distinguishing set of activities that defines program estimation with those dealing with (say) policy termination. Angela Browne and Aaron Wildavsky (1984, p. 205) made the point with great cogency as they distinguished between the mutually supportive duality of implementation and evaluation:

> The conceptual distinction between evaluation and implementation is important to maintain, however much the two overlap in practice, because they protect against the absorption of analysis into action to the detriment of both.

The idea of a delineated, sequential policy process framework apparently was much admired, for, as stated above, numerous authors have availed themselves of the framework, either explicitly or implicitly. Charles Jones's *An Introduction to the Study of Public Policy* (1970/1977/1984) and James Anderson's *Public Policy Making* (1975/1979) were among the first "policy process" volumes; Anderson references both Lasswell and Jones in his description of the policy stages (although omitting termination). In 1983, Brewer and deLeon published their volume, which completely laid out the stages of and rationales for the policy process. All three volumes (and other analogous models, such as Judith May and Aaron Wildavsky, 1978, and Dennis Palumbo, 1988) focused the reader's attentions on "knowledge *of*," that is, the workings of the policy process as a process-oriented event.

Just as important, these volumes and their advocacy (or at least their utilization) of the policy process model directed an entire generation of research by noted policy scholars, as they studied stages as stages (e.g., policy initiation) rather than as specific issue areas (e.g., energy resources).[2] These works include such unquestionable policy classics as:[3]

- Initiation: Nelson Polsby's *Political Innovation in America* (1984), John Kingdon's *Agendas, Alternatives, and Public Policy* (1984/1996), and Barbara Nelson's *Making an Issue of Child Abuse* (1984).
- Estimation: Alice Rivlin's *Systematic Thinking for Social Action* (1971), Edward Quade's *Analysis for Public Decisions* (1983), and David Weimer and Aidan Vining's *Policy Analysis* (1989).
- Implementation: Jeffrey Pressman and Aaron Wildavsky's *Implementation...* (1973),

Eugene Bardach's *The Implementation Game* (1977), and Daniel Mazmanian and Paul Sabatier's *Implementation and Public Policy* (1983).

- Evaluation: Edward Suchman's *Evaluation Research* (1967) and Richard Titmuss's *The Gift Relationship* (1971).
- Termination: Herbert Kaufman's *Are Government Organizations Immortal?* (1976) and Fred Iklè 's *Every War Must End* (1971/1991).

In his *Advice and Consent* (1988), deLeon compared the relative strengths and weaknesses of the segmentation of the policy stages/process framework as it affects the policy sciences research agenda. On the one hand, these works brought a new richness to the policy sciences, as Polsby and other policy scholars emphasized the intense complexity that theorists in political science and economics, in search of more rigorous, hypotheses-generating-models, might have overlooked. For instance, Pressman and Wildavsky's detailing of the high drama performed by the Economic Development Administration (EDA) and its incredibly cumbersome ballet with the city of Oakland, partially initiated to ward off potential urban violence (that surely was not part of the EDA's initial mission), demonstrated just how involved and actually convoluted policy implementation could be. Similarly, Titmuss's normatively oriented evaluation of comparative blood transfusion policies in *The Gift Relationship* forcefully argues against a reliance on standard benefit-cost analyses that were the growing standard of program evaluation.

Moreover, an emphasis on the policy process moved research away from a strict adherence to the study of public administration and institutions, which was increasing in political science, and of quasi-markets, which was the predilection of economics. Thus, it helped to rationalize a new problem-oriented perspective markedly different from its disciplinary predecessors. The cumulative analyses of the various stages clearly demonstrated Lasswell's insistence on a multidisciplinary approach to the policy sciences, as well as the interactive effects among the different stages. Finally, the policy process framework readily permitted the explicit inclusion of social norms and personal values, a component too often neglected or ignored in contemporary political and economic examinations.

But at the same time, these analyses of specific stages in the policy process model had a clear downside in that they oriented scholars toward looking at just one stage at a time (deLeon, 1988), thereby neglecting the entire process. Ultimately, many policy researchers (and policymakers[4]) came to view the process as a sharply differentiated set of activities: First, you define the problem; then, a completely different set of actors implements the chosen policy option; a third stage defines the evaluation; and so on. Likewise, they portrayed a disjointed, episodic process rather than a more ongoing, continuous one, as well as a policy phenomenon that seemingly took place in the relatively short term, one more suitable to the policymaker's rapidly changing schedule than the life span of a given policy. Finally, to many, the policy process/stages image implied a certain linearity—for example, first initiation, then estimation.... then (possibly) termination—as opposed to a series of feedback actions or recursive loops (e.g., estimation can lead back to initiation rather than the next step, selection, and implementation and evaluation insistently feed back and forth on each other) that characterize the operations and politics of the policy process.

Nevertheless, most (even subsequent critics) agree that the framework of the policy process and its various stages held center stage for at least the better part of the 1970s and 1980s. It was, for many, the "conventional wisdom" (Robert Nakaruma, 1987, referred to it as "the textbook policy process") that forced itself upon an emerging discipline, largely in disregard of Albert Hirschman's (1970) prescient warning that paradigms, unless closely considered, can become a hindrance to understanding. And arguably, that is exactly what happened as policy scholars began to inform their own interpretations of the policy process framework as if it were the target rather than the condition it sought to describe. Although certainly none would argue against a new statement of perspectives, one can openly question its basic assumptions. Let us therefore examine the thrust of these criticisms....

In short, before we discard a useful friend—in this instance, the policy process or policy stages framework—we need to make sure, first, that it really does warrant a place in the dustbin of abandoned paradigms; second, that we have a better, more robust framework on which to rely; and third, that even in our quest for the theoretical, we have little use for the operational. None of these criteria (or the alternative models) argues decisively or even very strongly for abandoning the policy stages framework.

The policy process paradigm has never given us everything we might have wanted from it, so we need to ask two additional questions: In lieu of alternative policy formulations, have we loaded an impossibly heroic stature upon the policy stages framework? And more centrally, exactly what are we asking it to provide? A theory of political change or occurrences? Perhaps, but what about other—and now neglected—stages of public policy? And, failing that, as we certainly must, then certainly operational insights or, as Lasswell observed, "better intelligence leading to better government" is an acceptable alternative to empty theorizing. In Lasswell's own words (quoted in Brunner, 1991, p. 81):

> It is the growth of insight, not simply of the capacity of the observer to predict the future operation of an automatic compulsion, or of a non-personal factor, that represents the major contribution of the scientific study of interpersonal relations to policy.

It was, of course, F. Scott Fitzgerald—the consummate policy analyst for the Roaring Twenties—writing about the fatally deluded Jay Gatsby, who offered what could be an appropriate paean to the troubled and maligned policy stages framework, heuristic, or model:

> Gatsby believed in the green light, the orgiastic future that year by year recedes before us. It eluded us then, but that's no matter—tomorrow we will run faster, stretch out our arms farther.... And one fine morning—

End Notes

1. In the early 1980s, when Garry Brewer and Peter deLeon were finalizing their *Foundations of Policy Analysis* (1983), they asked Lasswell if he might prepare a foreword. He chose not to, explaining that the book and its format were fine just as they were.

2. Perhaps of equal importance, these stages assisted in the design of a number of academic curricula, engendering a flurry of policy design, estimation, and evaluation courses.

3. Obviously this is meant to be a representative rather than an exhaustive listing; apologies to those missing are hereby given.

4. On 25 November 1986, President Ronald Reagan explained to the American public that although "our policy goals [in dealing with the revolutionary government of Iran] were to be well founded ... information brought to my attention yesterday convinced me that, in one aspect, the *implementation* of the policy was seriously flawed" (emphasis added), thus announcing the denouement of the Iran-Contra scandal.

References

ANDERSON, JAMES E. 1979. *Public Policy Making*, 2d ed. New Holt, Rinehart, & Winston. (Originally published in 1975.)

BARDACH, EUGENE. 1977. *The Implementation Game*. Chicago: University of Chicago Press.

BAUMGARTNER, FRANK R., and BRYAN D. JONES. 1993. *Agendas and Instability in American Politics*. Chicago: University of Chicago Press.

BELLAH, ROBERT, et al. 1985. *Habits of the Heart*. New York: Perennial Library of Harper & Row.

BOBROW, DAVIS B., and JOHN S. DRYZEK. 1987. *Policy Analysis by Design*. Pittsburgh: University of Pittsburgh Press.

BREWER, GARRY D. 1974. "The Policy Sciences Emerge: To Nurture and Structure a Discipline." *Policy Sciences* 5(3) (September): 239–244.

BREWER, GARRY D., and PETER DELEON. 1983. *The Foundations of Policy Analysis*. Monterey, Calif.: Brooks/Cole.

BROWNE, ANGELA, and AARON WILDAVSKY. 1984. "What Should Evaluation Mean to Implementation?" In Jeffrey L. Pressman and Aaron Wildavsky, eds.,

Implementation ..., 3d ed. Berkeley: University of California Press.

BRUNNER, RONALS D. 1991. "The Policy Movement as a Policy Problem, *Policy Sciences* 24(1) (February):65–98.

"DAMNED LIES." 1996. *The Economist* 341(7993) (November 23):18.

DANZIGER, MARIE. 1995. "Policy Analysis Postmodernized," *Policy Studies Journal* 23(3) (Fall):435–450.

DELEON, PETER. 1988. *Advice and Consent: The Development of the Policy Sciences.* New York: Russell Sage Foundation.

———. 1994a. "The Policy Sciences Redux: New Roads to Post-Positivism," *Policy Studies Journal* 22(2) (Summer):200–212.

———. 1994b. "Reinventing the Policy Sciences: Three Steps Back to the Future," *Policy Sciences* 27(1):77–95.

———. 1997. *Democracy and the Policy Sciences.* Albany: State University of New York Press.

DERY, DAVID. 1984. *Problem Definition in Policy Analysis.* Lawrence: University of Kansas Press.

DROR, YEHEZKEL. 1971. *Design for the Policy Sciences.* New York: American Elsevier.

ETZIONI, AMITAI. 1988. *The Moral Dimension.* New York: Free Press.

FISCHER, FRANK. 1995. *Evaluating Public Policy.* Chicago: Nelson Hall.

FISCHER, FRANK, and JOHN FORESTER, eds. 1993. *The Argumentative Turn in Policy Analysis and Planning.* Durham, N.C.: Duke University Press.

FORESTER, JOHN, ed. 1985. *Critical Thinking and Public Life.* Cambridge, Mass.: MIT Press.

———. 1993. *Critical Theory, Public Policy, and Planning Practice.* Albany: State University of New York Press.

GROGGIN, MALCOLM L. et al. 1990. *Implementation Theory and Practice.* Glenville, Ill.: Scott, Foresman/Little, Brown.

HAWKESWORTH, M. E., 1988. *Theoretical Issues in Policy Analysis.* Albany: State University of New York Press.

HIRSCHMAN, ALBERT O. 1970. "The Search for Paradigms as a Hindrance to Understanding," *World Politics* 22(3) (April):329–343.

HOFFERBERT, RICHARD. 1974. *A Study of Public Policy.* Indianapolis, Ind.: Bobbs-Merrill.

———. 1990. *The Reach and Grasp of Policy Analysis.* Tuscaloosa: University of Alabama Press.

IKLÈ, FRED CHARLES. 1991. *Every War Must End, rev. ed.* New York: Columbia University Press. (Originally published in 1971.)

JENKINS-SMITH, HANK C., and PAUL A. SABATIER. 1993. "The Study of the Public Policy Process." In Paul A. Sabatier and Hank C. Jenkins-Smith, eds., 1993. *Policy Change and Learning: An Advocacy Coalition Approach.* Boulder: Westview Press.

———. 1995. "Evaluating the Advocacy Coalition Framework," *Journal of Public Policy* 14(2):175–203.

JONES, CHARLES. 1984. *An Introduction to the Study of Public Policy, 3d ed.* Belmont, Calif.: Wadsworth. (Originally published in 1970; 2d ed., 1977.)

KAUFMAN, HERBERT. 1976. *Are Government Organizations Immortal?* Washington, D.C.: Brookings Institution.

KINGDON, JOHN. 1996. *Agendas, Alternatives, and Public Policy* (2nd ed.). Boston: Little, Brown.

KINGDON, JOHN. 1996. *Agendas, Alternatives, and Public Policy,* 2d ed. Boston: Little, Brown. (Originally published in 1984.)

KUHN, THOMAS. 1962. *The Structure of Scientific Revolutions.* Chicago: University of Chicago Press.

LASSWELL, HAROLD D. 1951. "The Policy Orientation." In Daniel Lerner and Harold D. Lasswell, eds., *The Policy Sciences.* Stanford: Stanford University Press.

———. 1956. *The Decision Process.* College Park: University of Maryland Press.

———. 1971. *A Pre-View of Policy Sciences.* New York: American Elsevier.

LASSWELL, HAROLD D., and Abraham Kaplan. 1950. *Power and Society.* New Haven: Yale University Press.

LAWLOR, EDWARD F. 1996. "Book Review." *Journal of Policy Analysis and Management* 15(1) (Winter):110–121.

LINDBLOM, CHARLES E. 1990. *Inquiry and Change.* New Haven: Yale University Press.

LINDBLOM, CHARLES E., and DAVID K. COHEN. 1971. *Usable Knowledge.* New Haven: Yale University Press.

MAY, JUDITH V., and AARON B. WILDAVSKY, eds. 1978. *The Policy Cycle.* Beverly Hills, Calif.: Sage.

MAZMANIAN DANIEL, and PAUL A. SABATIER. 1983. *Implementation and Public Policy.* Glen-view, Ill.: Scott Foresman. (Reissued in 1989 by University Press of America.)

MERTON, ROBERT K. 1968. *Social Theory and Social Structure.* New York: Free Press. (Originally published in 1949.)

NAKARUMA, ROBERT. 1987. "The Textbook Policy Process and Implementation Research," *Policy Studies Review* 7(2) (Autumn):142–154.

NELSON, BARBARA. 1984. *Making an Issue of Child Abuse*. Chicago: University of Chicago Press.

OSTROM, ELINOR. 1990. *Governing the Commons: The Evolutions of Institutions for Collective Action*. New York: Cambridge University Press.

PALUMBO, DENNIS. 1988. *Public Policy in America*. New York: Harcourt, Brace Jovanovich.

POLSBY, NELSON W. 1984. *Political Innovation in America*. New Haven: Yale University Press.

PRESSMAN, JEFFREY L., and AARON B. WILDAVSKY. 1973. *Implementation* ... Berkeley: University of California Press. (Revised in 1979 and 1984.)

PURDUM, TODD S. 1996. "Clinton Orders Expanded Agent Orange Benefits," *New York Times* (May 29), pp. A1, A12.

QUADE, EDWARD S. 1983. *Analysis for Public Decisions*. New York: American Elsevier.

RIVLIN, ALICE M. 1971. *Systematic Thinking for Social Action*. Washington, D.C.: Brookings Institution.

SABATIER, PAUL A. 1988. "An Advocacy Coalition Framework of Policy Change and the Role of Policy-Oriented Learning Therein," *Policy Sciences* 21(2–3):129–168.

_____. 1991. "Towards Better Theories of the Policy Process," *PS: Political Science and Politics* 24(2) (June): 147–156.

_____. 1993. "Policy Change over a Decade or More." In Paul A. Sabatier and Hank C. Jenkins-Smith, eds., *Policy Change and Learning: An Advocacy Coalition Approach*. Boulder: Westview Press.

SABATIER, PAUL A., and HANK C. JENKINS-SMITH, eds. 1993. *Policy Change and Learning: An Advocacy Coalition Approach*. Boulder: Westview Press.

SABATIER, PAUL A., JOHN LOOMIS, and CATHERINE MCCARTHY. 1995. "Hierarchical Controls, Professional Norms, Local Constituencies, and Budget Maximization: An Analysis of U.S. Forest Service Planning Decisions," *American Journal of Political Science* 39(1) (February):204–242.

SCHÖN, DONALD A., and MARTIN REIN. 1994. *Frame Reflection*. New York: BasicBooks.

SUCHMAN, EDWARD A. 1967. *Evaluative Research*. New York: Russell Sage Foundation.

TITMUSS, RICHARD. 1971. *The Gift Relationship*. New York: Pantheon Books of Random House.

WALDMAN, STEVEN. 1995. *The Bill*. New York: Penguin.

WEIMER, DAVID L., and AIDAN R. VINING. 1989. *Policy Analysis: Concepts and Practice*. Englewood Cliffs, N.J.: Prentice-Hall.

23

Typologies of Public Policy

Peter J. Steinberger

... Dating back to Lowi's (1964) now classic review article, the typological tradition has produced a variety of conceptions that have proven to be immensely appealing and influential. Nearly all summarizations of the policy field make reference to the typological literature, and usually do so in a favorable light, emphasizing the conceptual and theoretical insights it provides. And, indeed, there appears to be good reason for this. There can be no doubt, for example, that

First published as the article "Typologies of Public Policy: Meaning Construction and the Policy Process," by Peter J. Steinberger, in Social Science Quarterly Volume 61 Issue 2, pp. 185–196. Copyright © 1980 by the University of Texas Press. All rights reserved.

Lowi's typology of distributive, redistributive and regulatory policies seems to zero in on some useful and very fundamental distinctions. There is a certain plausibility in the formulation, and a fortuitous clarifying of common sense understandings, that has led numerous scholars to accept its accuracy and relevance virtually on the face of it. Even more importantly, Lowi's typology does indeed suggest a powerful and useful *theory* of the policy process. By arguing that different kinds of policies have different kinds of politics associated with them, Lowi provides an attractive explanatory scheme, one in which linkages between substance and process would appear to be concrete, testable and entirely credible.

Much the same can be said for several of the other typologies that have been influential in the field. Particularly notable, of course, is the "public goods/non-public goods" distinction from economics which has been enthusiastically adopted by contemporary policy analysts (see Olson, 1965). But one must also mention several other important classificatory schemes, especially Froman's (1967) "areal/segmental" distinction, Eulau and Eyestone's (1968) taxonomy of "adaptive" and "control" policies, and Edelman's (1974) emphasis on the "symbolic" dimension of politics. Each of these typologies seems to focus on a particularly salient aspect of public policy and to provide a basis for sound theorizing. It makes sense that redistributive policies will engender more conflict; or that public goods will produce the kinds of problems described by Olson; or that homogeneous cities are more likely to pursue areal policies than heterogeneous cities. As Lowi indicates, it is only through such efforts to conceptualize—to typify—that policy analysts can overcome the limitations inherent in the case-study method.

Unfortunately, this most promising of approaches has also proven to be most frustrating. What originally looked like a useful set of theories has, in fact, turned out to have serious practical limitations. There have been at least two reasons for this.

First, the various typologies may each be understood as an attempt to identify what is most fundamental, most distinctive, in public policy. Thus, in an important sense they have developed as rivals. One typology is offered, at least tacitly, as an improvement over another and, yet, there seems to be little to choose between them. The result is that policy analysis has retained at least some of its noncumulative character. An analyst interested in this approach must select one of the typologies, but the criteria for selection are by no means clear. Moreover, any particular study will be truly comparable only with other studies using the same typology. Thus, the effort to establish a general conceptual scheme has not been successful.

The second and more important difficulty has to do with the classification of actual cases. In brief, it has proved nearly impossible to confidently indentify a particular policy as being of this type or that (Line-berry and Sharkansky, 1971). Most actual policies tend, upon analysis, to overlap categories. For example, in examining the "areal-segmental" distinction, Froman (1967) classifies urban renewal policy as segmental (i.e., affecting only a section of the city) and annexation policy as areal (affecting the entire city). Yet there are numerous reasons for finding this a dubious, indeed misleading, classification. It can hardly be denied that annexation has a certain segmental quality; the area annexed, as well as adjacent areas, will likely be affected in special ways. Similarly, while urban renewal certainly is segmental in one sense, there can also be no doubt that it is likely to have a profound impact on the entire urban area. Thus, an objective classification appears to be impossible (Greenberg et al., 1977; Dornan, 1977). This problem has proved to be a general one. Few policies can be easily pigeonholed in terms of any of the typologies. Lowi himself notes, for example, that virtually every policy has a redistributive aspect of some kind.

The upshot of this has been well outlined by Hofferbert (1964): "To date, little empirical work has been fruitfully conducted with any of these typologies... The evidence is as yet incomplete regarding the typologies discussed here. It is disturbing, however, at least with respect to the Lowi scheme, that the bait has not been taken by other researchers. Lowi's insightful review is often noted in critical essays, but there is no instance in the literature I have read where his classification scheme has been examined with specific data and tested propositions" (Cf. Greenberg et al., 1977; Wilson, 1973).

This is disturbing indeed. The seemingly fruitful and enlightening conceptualizations outlined above have thus far been barren, and for very good reasons as we have seen. We appear to have a set of theories that are clearly insightful and perceptive but which seem to be, in practical terms, useless....

A PHENOMENOLOGICAL APPROACH TO POLICY ANALYSIS

Appropriately enough, our starting point is the complex and ambiguous nature of public policy. As indicated above, this frustrating complexity has made it difficult to classify policies with confidence. Such a consistent lack of success must, at some point, raise the possibility that the enterprise is not merely difficult but, in a fundamental way, impossible.

Indeed, the premise of this paper is that we should regard ambiguity not as a defect in understanding but, rather, as a salient and ineluctable characteristic of public policy. The elusiveness of policy should not be considered a nuisance, an obstacle in the way of sound analysis. Rather, it should be regarded as a fundamental, defining element. By and large, policies are not self-explanatory. Once we accept this, the way may be open for a methodological approach to typological analysis that is both feasible and fruitful.

The central hypothesis is that most particular policies can be, and are, coherently understood and defined in a wide variety of ways. Indeed, policy-related controversies rarely involve simple questions of pro and con, or good versus bad. Rather, they generally involve two (or more) entirely different and competing understandings or definitions of the very same policy, of its purpose, its substance and its potential impact. That is, for one group a particular proposal or initiative may be fundamentally a matter of (say) regulatory policy, while for another it may be a question of distribution or redistribution. The implications are that each policy is likely to have different *meanings* for different participants; that the exact meaning of a policy, then, is by no means self-evident but, rather, is ambiguous and manipulable; and that the policy process is—at least in part—a struggle to get one or another meaning established as the accepted one.

Indeed, we must go a bit further than this and suggest—again provisionally—that a particular policy has virtually *no* relevant meaning *until* one is attached to it by some kind of participant. Normally, of course, policy is initially formulated by a participant who has an explicit meaning in mind. But this meaning is by no means final or definitive. The import and significance of any particular policy is, in the most general sense, indeterminate and open to interpretation and dispute.

As indicated above, Lowi himself appears to recognize something like this when he admits, for example, that in the long run virtually all government policies have redistributive impacts, and regulatory ones as well. But he seems to think that this is the case only in a trivial sense, and that most policies are clearly more of one type than another. The present argument, on the other hand, suggests that we regard ambiguity as fundamental and unavoidable. Few policies are obviously or "objectively" distributive rather than redistributive or regulatory; few are clearly more "adaptive" than "control," or "segmental" rather than "areal." In general, we should at least consider the possibility that the meaning of a particular policy must therefore be constituted by the various participants in the policy process.

The idea of reality and meaning as a social construct is an old one in epistemology, traceable, without doubt, to Kant and to his philosophical heirs. However, it has also had a profound impact on the social sciences. Berger and Luckmann's classic work on the social construction of reality is merely a recent example of an important, if controversial, social science tradition that dates back to Dilthey, Weber, Mead and especially Schutz. According to this general view, the social world—and its institutions, roles, ideas, etc.—is essentially a series of socially constructed meanings. In the words of Berger and Luckmann (1966):

> Men *together* produce a human environment, with the totality of its socio-cultural and psychological formations ... (S)ocial order is a human product, or more precisely, an ongoing human production. It is produced by man in the course of his ongoing externalization ... Social order exists *only* as a product of human activity.

Clearly this perspective is intended to apply to all of social reality, including (we must presume) the realm of policy meanings. It is precisely here, then, that the typological tradition can be especially useful. The interpretive approach to social science relies heavily on the concept of "type." Indeed, Berger and Luckmann, following the lead of both Weber and Schutz, indicate that socially constructed meanings generally appear as "typifications." That is, meanings tend to take on a variety of basic, more-or-less agreed-upon, typical forms. Such typifications, taken together, describe not merely social meanings but also social reality, since that reality can be nothing more than structures of meaning. Thus, the central function of the social scientist is to discover and analyze these forms. In this sense, and most importantly, we can suggest that the achievement and insight of the typological tradition is not in its analysis of "objective" policy characteristics. Rather, the best of the typologies are plausible and useful in that they describe (or, rather, can be used to describe) *typifications* that are generally and commonly employed by participants in the political process to define public policies. In other words, they are insightful in elucidating and in specifying socially constructed meanings.

Thus, when we talk about distributive, redistributive and regulatory policies, for example, we are not talking about objectively different kinds of policy. Rather, we are conceptualizing some of the ways in which participants tend to define policies. The participants inevitably engage in typification, in meaning construction, and the typological tradition is useful in specifying, categorizing and conceptualizing those various typifications. It is thus that we can explain the appeal of the typological approach and can begin to show its research potential.

Most emphatically, the argument is *not* that policies have no concrete, objective characteristics. Obviously, any policy proposal specifies courses of action, allocations of resources, methods of implementation, etc. These characteristics are salient, real and, indeed, crucial. They work to shape and constrain and mold the policy's meaning (though they do so in ways we can only hypothesize about). But they are not identical with that meaning. By the *meaning* of a policy (and,

hence, of its objective characteristics) we refer essentially to the understandings that participants have regarding the policy's purpose, its potential impact and its relationship to other policies. Even when these things are somehow "spelled out" in the policy, there can—indeed must—be interpretation and reinterpretation. Thus, the meaning of a policy can only be something which has been attached to it by the various participants in the policy process (Edner, 1976).

MEANING CONSTRUCTION AND THE POLICY PROCESS

Interestingly, Lowi (1964:707) has suggested something rather like the approach here outlined. In his own words:

> … it is not the actual outcomes but the expectations as to what the outcomes *can be* that shape the issues and determine their politics. One of the most important strategies in any controversial issue is to attempt to define it in redistributive terms in order to broaden the base of opposition or support.

But unfortunately, and revealingly, Lowi relegates this comment to a footnote and does not pursue it. Nor do the other writers in the typological tradition. Thus, the perspective described above has been largely overlooked in favor of what has proven to be a less promising approach. This is particularly surprising in light of the influential literature on the *strategy* of the policy process, most notably the work of Schattschneider. Indeed, the method suggested in the present paper is largely useful in bringing together, and thereby broadening, the insights of Schattschneider (among others) and those of the typological writers. Schattschneider (1960) has taught us much about the way in which participants attempt to manipulate the scope of conflict in order to further their policy preferences. His formulation provides a good perspective on the policy process, and has been valuable as a research tool. But in at least a couple of ways, the approach here suggested can extend and improve upon Schattschneider's theory.

First, by emphasizing the social construction of reality, the present perspective helps to clarify the nature of the processes involved. For what we are concerned with is not just questions of good and bad, nor simple efforts to control the scope of conflict. Rather, we are interested in broad questions of social meaning. This emphasis tends to locate the policy process more squarely within the social world generally, helps to specify the mechanisms by which contexts are manipulated, and suggests a particular research agenda, viz., the empirical examination of typifications. Further, the present approach does away with certain pejorative connotations by demonstrating the very necessity of meaning construction. Efforts to define and redefine policies are not, as Schattschneider would have it, simply matters of strategy or distortion; they are in fact unavoidable if policies are to be at all relevant and meaningful. This, of course, implies also that various participants will define a single policy in various ways not simply out of tactical or prudential considerations but, rather, because of contrasting perspectives or worldviews. In this sense, the sociology of knowledge is obviously relevant; different groups are likely to see things differently. Conflict can therefore be a result of genuine definitional disagreements about the meaning of a policy.

Moreover, the typological tradition broadens Schattschneider's insight by demonstrating the wide variety of possible policy meanings. The typologies show that conflict or disagreement is not limited to the issue of scope, of public versus private, but may also include an entire range of other questions dealing with political impact, economic impact, motive, relationships to basic values, etc. The possibilities are numerous. And as indicated below, this greater complexity can, in turn, significantly broaden our theoretical and research opportunities.

Even a casual reexamination of the case study literature in public policy would turn up a good deal of support for the perspective outlined in this essay. The literature on the War on Poverty presents an interesting example. A reading of the numerous relevant case studies suggests that this set of policies was initially defined as "adaptive," in the sense outlined by Eulau and Eyestone. That is, proponents of the War on Poverty understood it as an attempt by government to adapt its practices to meet the special political needs of the poor (see, for example, Kramer, 1969). Thus, the establishment of community action agencies would considerably change the decision-making process so as to include representatives of the poor and give them real power over the allocation of resources. But the same literature indicates that certain key opponents thought the War on Poverty had a rather different meaning (see especially Piven and Cloward, 1971). They defined it as, perhaps, a series of "control" policies. According to this view, the government wasn't actually adapting itself in any real sense. Rather, the purpose was to control the environment, to co-opt the poor and take the sting out of social protest. No real change in the distribution of power resources was involved.

RESEARCH CONSEQUENCES

.....the primary value of the typological tradition would seem to involve analysis of the policy process itself. More specifically, it promises to provide the basis for a sound theoretical approach to the relationship between substance and process. This, of course, was Lowi's central concern in initiating typological analysis. He hypothesized that different types of policy would have different kinds of politics associated with them. Once again, little progress has been made in actually examining this thesis. But the transformation that has been suggested here can, in my view, significantly facilitate research in this regard.

In order to fully utilize the typological tradition, some coherence, some semblance of order, must be made out of the various existing schemes. The major typologies have generally been formulated in isolation from one another and, moreover, have never been adequately integrated. However, once we accept each of the major typologies as presenting a useful and enlightening perspective on public policy, then a unified approach is both possible and desirable. It would seem, most importantly, that none of the typologies are antipathetical to any of the others. Thus, we may suggest that each typology simply reflects one of the several ways in which policies can be conceptualized. Taken together, they indicate the various salient dimensions of public policy. This is illustrated in Table 23-1.

TABLE 23-1 Typologies of Public Policy			
Dimensions of Public Policy		**Categories of Public Policy**	
Substantive impact:	Distributive	Redistributive	Regulatory
Political impact:	Adaptive	Control	
Scope of impact:	Areal	Segmental	
Exhaustibility:	Public Goods	Private goods	
Tangibility:	Symbolic	Tangible	

There is, of course, no pretense that the list outlined here is definitive or final. But the implications of the table are numerous. For example, it suggests that participants in the policy process do not merely select certain meanings; they also select, or emphasize, thereby certain *dimensions* of meaning. Thus, it is entirely conceivable that two sides of any particular controversy will choose not only different meanings but also different dimensions. Further, the table suggests that the potential socially-revelant impacts of a policy are—in theoretical terms—much more numerous than previously expected. Rather than three possibilities, as Lowi has suggested, the table indicates a much more complex conceptual scheme. Indeed, if combinations of multiple meanings are considered (e.g., "distributive-areal" or "control-symbolic"), the range of possibilities is obviously enormous.

At least three different sets of substantive issues may be addressed in terms of this table, issues which, taken together, would seem to comprise a stimulating research agenda. One such group of issues concerns the *definitional process* itself. This would especially refer to the way in which particular policy meanings are developed and disseminated. Among the more specific questions that could be raised here are the following:

—Do certain policies (that is, policies having certain objective characteristics) tend to be defined in characteristic ways? For example, it seems likely that tax policies will usually be defined in terms of "substantive impact" (see, for example, Friedman, 1962). But this may not be generally true. In some circumstances, tax policies might be defined as primarily "control," or "symbolic," or even "segmental" policies. Moreover, there is the further question of (what might be called) historical paradigms. It may well be that certain policies

are defined one way in a particular era and rather differently in another. The recent history of environmental politics in America, for example, might be understandable in these terms.

—Do certain actors and groups tend to see all policies in terms of one or two specific dimensions? Rather than the policy itself being the decisive factor, here we raise the possibility that the participants' particular perspectives are crucial. For example, it seems plausible that business groups, labor organizations, environmental groups, professional associations, etc., will each have a distinctive and particular set of concepts with which to make sense out of the political world. These concepts might be usefully analyzed in terms of the typological tradition. Thus, it could be hypothesized that business groups see everything in terms of "substantive impact," environmental groups in terms of "exhaustibility," and so on.

—How are definitions actually formulated and disseminated? There is a good deal of research on interest group behavior, but little of it focuses on the question of meaning selection. It is important to understand the ways in which meanings are thought up, ratified and propagated by organized political forces. This, indeed, might well get to the crux of the entire group process.

A second set of substantive questions concerns the *decision-making process.* Here the focus would be on "politics" as Lowi understands it, that is, on the process by which policy initiatives are approved or rejected. Again, several specific questions arise:

—Are there characteristic juxtapositions of meaning? That is, does the adoption of one particular meaning by Group A tend to lead Group B to adopt a logically alternative meaning? If so, one might then be able to formulate a taxonomy of oppositions and, ultimately, of decision-making processes in general.

—Does the nature of political conflict, for example, its intensity, correlate with the juxtaposition of definitions? It may well be that certain kinds of meaning disputes are particularly conducive to rancor. In this regard, we would ask if it makes a difference whether opposed meanings are intra- or interdimensional. Controversies involving interdimensional juxtaposition might be more diffuse, less focused, hence less rancorous. Indeed, conflict may actually be most intense if opposing groups *agree* on definition but disagree on evaluation. For example, opponents on certain welfare proposals might well agree that the proposals are essentially "redistributive" but disagree violently as to whether or not redistribution is a good thing. In such a case, the controversy would perhaps be especially pointed, the issues clear, and the interest obvious.

—Are meanings likely to multiply during the course of the decision process or are they likely to become fewer? This is roughly the same as asking if things are likely to grow more complex or more simple. Since both phenomena undoubtedly do occur at various times, we would also want to know under what circumstances these changes take place.

A third and final set of substantive questions concerns the process of *implementation*. In this regard, one could ask, among other things:

—To what extent are implementors conscious of, and interested in, policy meanings? The discretion of many administrative institutions may well include leeway in terms of which particular policy meaning to adopt. This, in turn, may have a profound effect on the way a particular policy is implemented. From a research point of view, the problem is a particularly complex one, but it may be crucial in formulating a comprehensive theory of the policy process.

—A related question would be the following: to what extent do implementors ignore the meanings generated by the "political" process and redefine policies to suit themselves? Again, this is a complex problem, but it seems to put the issue of administrative discretion in a particularly interesting light.

—Does meaning ambiguity, i.e., the lack of clear-cut definitions, make implementation especially difficult? An example of this might again be the community action provision of the War on Poverty in which such crucial but vague phrases as "maximum feasible participation" made it nearly impossible for planners to decide how to proceed.

This has been an exploratory and provisional discussion. Indeed, the purpose has been merely to suggest an alternative approach to policy analysis in the hopes of generating some dialogue. Clearly, the essential question is whether or not the research agenda outlined above can amount to a feasible and valuable approach to the study of public policy.

In their intelligent and provocative article on policy analysis, Green-berg et al. (1977) offer some stimulating suggestions relating to the policy field in general and include a discussion of the typological tradition. But though they point to the usual criticisms of typological analysis, they too fail to free themselves from the limitations inherent in the older approach. Thus, for example, they show that "there is *no* a priori way for the researcher to determine which … impacts are to be considered in deciding whether a policy is 'areal' or 'segmental'" (p. 1538); but they offer nothing very tangible in the way of an alternative strategy. Similarly, they demonstrate several problems inherent in the inevitable existence of a multiplicity of "perceptions" (or meanings), but all they can tell us is that we must somehow decide whose perceptions are most important (p. 1543).

The present discussion can be usefully considered supplemental to the analysis provided by Greenberg et al. It is, in effect, an attempt to meet their challenge by placing certain conceptual insights from the existing literature on a firmer theoretical foundation. Thus, the tentative list of hypotheses outlined above can provide a starting point for policy analysts interested in pursuing more fully the insights of the typological tradition.

References

ALTSHULER, ALAN. 1965. *Locating the Intercity Freeway.* (New York: Bobbs Merrill).

ART, ROBERT. 1968. *The TFX Decision: McNamara and the Military.* (Boston: Little, Brown).

BAILEY, STEPHEN K. 1950. *Congress Makes a Law.* (New York: Columbia University Press).

BANFIELD, EDWARD. 1961. *Political Influence.* (New York: Free Press).

BERGER, PETER and THOMAS LUCKMANN. 1966. *The Social Construction of Reality* (Garden City: Doubleday).

DORNAN, PAUL. 1977. "Whither Urban Policy Analysis: A Review Essay," *Polity,* 9 (Summer): 503–27.

EDELMAN, MURRAY. 1974. *The Symbolic Uses of Politics.* (Urbana: University of Illinois Press).

EDNER, SHELDON. 1976. "Intergovernmental Policy Development: The Importance of Problem Definition," pp. 149–68 in Charles O. Jones and Robert D. Thomas, eds., *Public Policy Making in a Federal System* (Beverly Hills, Calif.: Sage Publications).

EULAU, HEINZ and ROBERT EYESTONE. 1968. "Policy Maps of City Councils and Policy Outcomes," *American Political Science Review,* 62 (March): 124–43.

FRIEDMAN, MILTON. 1962. *Capitalism and Freedom.* (Chicago: University of Chicago Press).

FROMAN, LEWIS. 1967. "An Analysis of Public Policy in Cities," *Journal of Politics,* 29 (February): 94–108.

GODWIN, R. KENNETH and W. BRUCE SHEPARD. 1976. "Political Processes and Public Expenditures: A Re-Examination Based on Theories of Representative Government," *American Political Science Review,* 70 (December): 1127–35.

GREENBERG, GEORGE et al. 1977. "Developing Public Policy Theory: Perspectives from Empirical Research," *American Political Science Review,* 71 (December): 1532–44.

GREENSTONE, J. DAVID and PAUL PETERSEN. 1973. *Race and Authority in Urban Politics.* (New York: Russell Sage).

HALPERIN, MORTON. 1972. "The Decision to Deploy the ABM," *World Politics,* 25 (October): 62–95.

HOFFERBERT, RICHARD. 1974. *The Study of Public Policy.* (New York: Bobbs Merrill).

KRAMER, RALPH. 1969. *Participation of the Poor.* (Englewood Cliffs, N.J.: Prentice Hall).

LINEBERRY, ROBERT and IRA SHARKANSKY. 1971. *Urban Politics and Public Policy.* (New York: Harper & Row).

LOWI, THEODORE. 1964. "American Business, Public Policy, Case Studies, and Political Theory," *World Politics,* 16 (July): 677–715.

OLSON, MANCUR. 1965. *The Logic of Collective Action.* (Cambridge, Mass.: Harvard University Press).

PIVEN, FRANCES FOX and RICHARD CLOWARD. 1971. *Regulating the Poor.* (New York: Vintage).

PRESSMAN, JEFFREY and AARON WILDAVSKY. 1973. *Implementation.* (Berkeley: University of California Press).

SCHATTSCHNEIDER, E. E. 1960. *The Semi-Sovereign People.* (New York: Holt, Rinehart & Winston).

WILSON, JAMES Q. 1973. *Political Organizations.* (New York: Basic Books).

24

Agendas and Instability

Frank R. Baumgartner and Bryan D. Jones

AGENDA-SETTING AND EQUILIBRIUM

Models of policymaking are generally based on the twin principles of incrementalism and negative feedback. Incrementalism can be the result of a deliberate decisional style as decision makers make limited, reversible changes in the status quo because of bounds on their abilities to predict the impact of their decisions (Lindblom 1959; Hayes

From Frank R. Baumgartner and Bryan D. Jones, *Agendas and Instability in American Politics* (Chicago: The University of Chicago press, 1993), pp. 6–25.

1992). For example, new budgets for agencies are generally based on the previous year's allocation (Wildavsky 1984). Incremental changes in political systems can also be the result of countermobilization. As one group gains political advantage, others mobilize to protect themselves. In such situations, mobilizations are subject to a negative-feedback process in which changes from the current state of the system are not large.

Both forms of change, one deliberate and the other inadvertent, result in a self-correcting system. If deliberate incremental decisions characterize policymaking, then decisions that lead to undesirable consequences can be reversed. Hence deliberate incrementalism allows a system to maintain a dynamic equilibrium with its environment. Similarly, a democratic system that allows groups to mobilize and countermobilize will display dynamic equilibrium. When the system veers away from balance, it corrects itself, always tending toward an equilibrium between the demands of democratically organized interests and the policy outputs of government. This view of a political system at balance is quite conservative, since it implies that dramatic changes from the status quo are unlikely.

Even a casual observer of the public agenda can easily note that public attention to social problems is anything but incremental. Rather, issues have a way of grabbing headlines and dominating the schedules of public officials when they were virtually ignored only weeks or months before. Policy action may or may not follow attention, but when it does, it will not flow incrementally. In the scholarly literature on agenda-setting, incrementalism plays little role. Rather, focusing events, chance occurences, public-opinion campaigns by organized interests, and speeches by public officials are seen[1] to cause issues to shoot high onto the agenda in a short period.

Herbert Simon has noted that such intermittent performance characterizes certain classes of social systems. In such cases, "the environment makes parallel demands on the system, but the system can respond only serially" (Simon 1977, 157). That is, the system is grappling with a great number of real, tangible, problems, but its leaders can attend to them only one at a time. In such situations, just how problems capture the attention of policymakers is critical. The intermittent

nature of high-level attention to a given problem builds into our system of government the possibility not only of incrementalism, but also of periodic punctuations to these temporary periods of equilibrium.

Why have students of the policy process so often ignored the nonincremental nature of the allocation of attention to problems in political systems? There are two reasons. First is the traditional division of labor among scholars. Those who have studied policy implementation typically have not emphasized the dramatic changes that often occur in the public agenda, and those who focus on the agenda often discount the strong elements of stability or incrementalism present in other parts of the policy cycle. Second is a tendency among some to view the disruptive acts of agenda access as political penumbra, either symbolic events designed to reassure the mass public (Edelman. 1964) or as furious activity that fails to solve problems (Downs 1972). Taking a broader view of the policy process forces us to consider seriously both the politics of negative feedback and the processes of agenda-setting that lead to dramatic change. ... [W]e show that both of these processes are at work simultaneously in American politics, and that they interact to produce long periods of relative stability or incrementalism interrupted by short bursts of dramatic change. Far from being penumbra, these bursts alter forever the prevailing arrangements in a policy system.

In the pluralist model of countervailing forces in the political system, "potential groups" mobilize when their interests are threatened (Truman 1951, 30). In the absence of artificial or legal barriers to organization and lobbying, social and professional groups can be expected to protect themselves, as the invisible hand of action and reaction produces a sort of equilibrium in politics just as the invisible hand of the marketplace does in economics. While few accept these notions of unfettered organization these days, especially after Olson's (1965) discussion of the inherent advantages of certain kinds of groups over others in generating the support needed to mobilize effectively, perceived threats do indeed produce increased mobilization in many cases (see Hansen 1985).

The most significant criticisms of the pluralist approach have focused on bias in the mobilization of interests. As E. E. Schattschneider wrote over thirty years ago, "The flaw in the pluralist heaven is that the heavenly chorus sings with a strong upper-class accent" (1960, 35). He noted that the essence of political conflict is the scope of participation. Because in any given issue there are always more people disinterested than those involved, competition between winners and losers in the original policy dispute gives incentives for the losers to enlarge the scope of conflict. For Schattschneider, enlargement of the scope of political conflict was essential to the democratic process. This insight remains central to all studies of agenda-setting, since it raises the question of the motivations of those seeking to put something on the public agenda or to keep something from reaching it. Roger Cobb and Charles Elder (1983) continued this line of inquiry by noting the mechanisms by which policymakers attempt to expand the sphere of participation in a given policy dispute.

Much of recent agenda research has centered on the question of where policy ideas come from. John Kingdon (1984) reinvigorated agenda research with his study of the genesis of policy ideas and the exploitation of "windows of opportunity" by policy entrepreneurs. Milward and Laird (1990), reviewing five cases of agenda-setting, found that issue definition, policy knowledge, and opportunity interacted to yield agenda success.

The question "Where does policy come from?" is interesting but misleading. There is generally a surfeit of policy ideas in society. However, alternatives are structured out of politics by the existing "winners" in the policy process, who fuse their policy to strong symbols: progress, national identity, economic growth, and so forth. New alternatives often reach the decision making stage through fresh definitions of old issues (Baumgartner 1989; Stone 1989). "Losers" can often redefine the basic dimension of conflict to their advantage, thereby attracting previously uninvolved citizens. The issue-definition perspective, then, ties the role of Schattschneider's notion of conflict expansion to the content of the ideas coming into the political system.

Neglected in this line of thought are the policy consequences of agenda-setting. What happens when new ideas become the prevailing wisdom in a policy community? Understandings of important public policy issues have clearly changed over time. As these understandings have been altered, so policy processes and policy outcomes have changed as well. We focus here on these links, tracing the effects of change in policy understandings when these occur. We also note that agenda status changes over time. Some issues are high on the governmental or public agenda at one time, then recede from it later. Issue definition and agenda-setting are related, because changes in issue definition often lead to the appearance of an issue on the public agenda. We take these studies as our starting point and focus here not on the reasons for these changes, but on their consequences.

Focusing on consequences directs our attention to institutional structures. All political institutions channel conflict in a particular way; all are related to the mobilization of bias. Noting the structure of bias inherent in any set of political institutions not only shows who is advantaged, however; it also shows what changes might come about from destruction or alteration of an existing arrangement. Those left out of the original system may not be heard there, but if the structures are changed, then dramatic changes in the mobilization of bias may result. Institutional structures in American politics are generally not easy to change, but when they do change, these changes often lead to dramatic and long-lasting changes in policy outcomes. So institutions play an important role in this analysis, since they make possible a system of periods of relative stability, where the mobilization of bias is structured by a set of institutions that remain stable for some period. However, these periods of stability may be linked by periods of rapid change during which the institutional framework is challenged. Because of this, incremental changes are less important than the dramatic alterations in the mobilization of bias during these critical periods. The result is that the American political system lurches from one point of apparent equilibrium to another, as policymakers establish new institutions to support the policies they favor or alter existing ones to give themselves greater advantage.

Searching for Equilibrium

Political science is the study of how political preferences are formed and aggregated into policy outputs by governments. Obviously the institutions of government are complex, so how preferences are aggregated by these institutions is not easy to determine. It would be nice if we could isolate the great forces acting on democratic policymaking and show that these forces reach equilibrium at some point. That is the way classical physics worked. That is the model economics has followed. Indeed, the search for equilibria and partial equilibria has been touted as the cornerstone of the scientific approach, because systems at or near equilibrium are well behaved and amenable to causal analysis (Riker 1980; see also Bentley 1908).

At equilibrium, a system of democratic policymaking would be stable in two senses. First, its essential features would not change significantly, and, second, should a force push the system away from equilibrium, it would move back toward equilibrium over time. A system can remain relatively unchanging over an extended period of time and not be at equilibrium if external forces are sufficiently weak, so one should not equate stability with equilibrium under all circumstances. If a system is not at equilibrium, even minor shifts in inputs may lead to dramatic changes in outputs. Since the behavior of systems at equilibrium is much easier to understand and to predict than systems without equilibrium, scholars have been drawn to them. However, equilibria may be less common in politics than is often thought. Systems that are not at equilibrium show greatly ranging behaviors that are not easily predictable. However, if we hope to understand them we must grapple with the causes and the consequences of their inherent instability.

Political scientists have undertaken two grand initiatives that attempt to establish the existence of equilibria in politics. These are, first, social choice theory and, second, group theory and pluralism. Social choice theory takes individual preferences as fixed and examines how they are combined to yield collective choices. In *Liberalism against Populism,* William Riker (1982) provides a survey and critique of the social choice approach. Riker's critical point is that social choice theorists have demonstrated conclusively that equilibria are rare in politics; indeed, they may not exist at all. Most fundamentally, any voting scheme is unstable with three or more voters in two or more dimensions of conflict. This

is the well-known paradox of voting, first analyzed by the French mathematician Concordet in the late eighteenth century and rediscovered by Duncan Black in the 1950s. In the three-voter, two-dimension situation, there is no policy (made up of levels from the two dimensions of conflict) that guarantees equilibrium. That is, there is always another point which can attract more support than the status quo. After reviewing much of the literature in social choice, Riker concludes: "And what we have learned is simply this: Disequilibrium, or the potential that the status quo be upset, is the characteristic feature of politics" (1980, 443).

Considering that equilibrium outcomes could not be assumed even for small groups making decisions, models of how the complex institutions of government collectively generate public policies could not possibly be at equilibrium. In any situation where voting matters, stability is dependent on the dimensions of conflict present, on the order in which decisions are made, on the number of alternatives considered at the same time, on how alternatives are paired if choices are made in sequence, on the number of voters taking part in the decision, and on a variety of other characteristics that are not related to or affected by the distribution of the preferences of those making the decision. In such a situation, strategic entrepreneurs can manipulate the voting situation to achieve their objectives, even if they cannot change the preferences of those making the decision. Most importantly, any time political actors can introduce new dimensions of conflict, they can destabilize a previously stable situation. Since this often can be done, any stability is not necessarily indicative of equilibrium (Riker 1982; see also 1980, 1983, 1984, and 1986).

Since political stability is contingent on the actions of political entrepreneurs, any hope of establishing conditions of political equilibrium must be found at the institutional level (see Shepsle 1979). But even here, equilibrium is not guaranteed, since institutions can be changed. "Institutions are no more than rules and rules are themselves the product of social decisions. ... One can expect that losers on a series of decisions under a particular set of rules will attempt (often successfully) to change institutions and hence the kind of decisions produced under them. ... Thus the only difference between values and institutions is that the revelation of institutional disequilibrium is probably a longer process than the revelation of disequilibria of taste" (Riker 1980, 444–45). ... [W]e will see numerous examples of efforts to change institutional structures in order better to reflect the preferences of those affected by the decisions they generate. Riker argues that institutions may be seen as "congealed tastes," changing more slowly than preferences, but changing nonetheless (1980, 445).

Institutional rules inevitably have policy consequences, which is why seemingly arcane decisions, concerning rules changes in Congress, for example, so often become the subject of intense debate. Changing the procedures of decision making often has unintended consequences, however; policymakers are therefore generally conservative in altering them. So institutions, procedures, and rules play a key role in determining outcomes, since (hey inevitably favor some groups more than others, but change in institutions may come about only slowly or during periods of crisis (see, for example," Krehbiel 1991).

Another area where theorists have grappled with these questions of equilibria is in group theory and pluralism. In the purest form of group theory, interest associations interacted as vectors in Euclidean space, and public policy was the net result of the struggle. In this approach, voting was less important than freedom of association, and policy was conditioned more by group action in inter-election periods than in elections. It was easy to show that this early version of group theory did not comport with reality; too many interests failed to participate or were excluded by those who did. Most sought out niches in the governmental structure where they could dominate, but where other groups would not be able (or interested) in struggling with them. The system of American governance looked more like mutual noninterference than group struggle. Political stability, then, could not be found in the balancing of interests, although it might be found in a system of noninterfering policy monopolies.

European scholars never adopted these American ideas of group politics because they attributed much greater independent powers to the state. In fact, the organization of governmental institutions plays an important role in structuring political participation, forcing some groups out while allowing other groups into the process. So institutional forces can push the system away from whatever equilibrium it might have reached if the competition among groups were the only thing that mattered.

Pluralist theorists suggested a more complex alternative: elected political leaders brokered coalitions that differed by issue areas, and democratic accountability was maintained because of the electoral sensitivities of the elected leader (Dahl 1961). But some elements of any electoral coalition seemed "more equal" than others. Political economists argued powerfully that business interests were so predominant in capitalist democracies that they could always upset democratic policymaking. Charles Lindblom (1977) has aptly termed this the "privileged position of business." Stability could well stem from the overwhelming dominance of business interests. Yet business interests themselves seem variable in their power across time, seemingly unable to establish an equilibrium point (Jones 1986; Vogel 1989). Moreover, different elements of the business community were often at odds on public policy issues.

In a democracy, an equilibrium would balance citizen preferences and public policies through a combination of elections and the open struggle of interest groups. This doesn't happen. Instead, stability is enforced through a complex system of mutually noninterfering policy monopolies buttressed by powerful supporting images. It would seem, then, that no particular arrangement in a democracy can succeed in establishing a point of equilibrium. Our models of politics are so unsatisfactory because we have insufficiently appreciated this point. In the words of Riker, this has led to great discomfort among those seeking to build general theories of politics.

Yet the realization that the search for equilibria in politics may be fruitless can liberate. While it is not often articulated by them, political scientists with a strong focus on case histories have always harbored the deep suspicion that politics was too complex, too contingent on ill-understood details, and too dependent on strategic action at the proper time to be bound by general theory. On the other hand, the general theorists are right in feeling that a better understanding of the political cannot be had through description and induction alone. It is not theory that is misplaced; it is the search for equilibria that is. An approach to the study of politics that rejects a faith in equilibria has the potential of unifying the theoretical and the descriptive.

We begin with the supposition that political systems are never in general equilibrium. But this does not imply that political systems are in continual chaos. Stability may be maintained over long periods of time by two major devices: the existing structure of political institutions and the definition of the issues processed by those institutions. Schattschneider's famous dictum that "organization is the mobilization of bias" (1960, 71) symbolizes the strong tendency of institutions to favor some interests over others. This advantage can be maintained over extended periods of time. Associated with such institutional arrangements is invariably a supporting definition of relevant policy issues. In particular, issues may be defined to include only a single dimension of conflict. The tight connection between institution and idea provides powerful support for the prevailing distribution of political advantage. But this stability cannot provide general equilibrium, because a change in issue definition can lead to destabilization and rapid change away from the old point of stability. This happens when issues are redefined to bring in new participants. Similarly a change in institutional rules of standing or of jurisdiction can rupture an old equilibrium. If a social equilibrium is induced only by the structures that determine participation in its choice, then altering the structures (or changing the rules) can cause the equilibrium quickly to disappear.

Issue definition, then, is the driving force in both stability and instability, primarily because issue definition has the potential for mobilizing the previously disinterested. The structure of political institutions offers more or fewer arenas for raising new issues or redefining old ones—opportunities to change understandings of political conflict. Issue definition and institutional control combine to make possible the alternation between stability and rapid change that characterizes political systems.

References

BAUMGARTNER, FRANK R. 1989. *Conflict and Rhetoric in French Policymaking*. Pittsburgh, Penn.: University of Pittsburgh Press.

BENTLEY, ARTHUR F. 1908. *The Process of Government*. Chicago: University of Chicago Press.

COBB, ROGER W., and Charles D. Edler. 1983. *Participation in American Poilitics: The Dynamics of Agenda-Building*. Baltimore: Johns Hopkins University Press.

DAHL, ROBERT A. 1961. *Who Governs?* New Haven: Yale University Press.

DOWNS, ANTHONY. 1972. Up and Down with Ecology: The Issue Attention Cycle. *Public Interest* 28: 38–50.

EDELMAN, MURRAY. 1964. *The Symbolic Uses of Politics*. Urbana: University of Illinois Press.

HANSEN, JOHN MARK. 1985. The Political Economy of Group Membership. *American Political Science Review* 79: 79–81.

JONES, BRYAN D. 1986. Government and Business: The Automobile Industry and the Public Sector in Michigan. *Political Geography Quarterly* 5: 369–84.

KINGDON, JOHN W. 1984. *Agendas, Alternatives, and Public Policies*. Boston: Little, Brown.

KREHBIEL, KEITH. 1991. *Information and Legislative Organization*. Ann Arbor: University of Michigan Press.

LINDBLOM, CHARLES E. 1959. The Science of Muddling Through. *Public Administration Review* 19: 79–88.

LINDBLOM, CHARLES E. 1977. *Politics and Markets*. New York: Basic Books.

MILWARD, H. BRINTON, and WENDY LAIRD. 1990. Where Does Policy Come From? Paper presented at the annual meeting of the Western Political Science Association, Newport Beach, Calif., 23–25 March.

OLSON, MANCUR. 1965. *The Logic of Collective Action: Public Goods and the Theory of Groups*. Cambridge: Harvard University Press.

RIKER, WILLIAM H. 1980. Implication from the Disequilibrium of Majority Rile for the Study of Institutions. *American Political Science Review* 74: 432–46.

RIKER, William H. 1982. *Liberalism against Populism*. Prospect Heights, Ill.: Waveland Press.

RIKER, WILLIAM H. 1983. Political Theory and the Art of Heresthetics. In Ada Finifter, ed., *Political Science: The State of Discipline*. Washington D.C.: American Enterprise Institute.

RIKER, WILLIAM H. 1984. The Heresthetics of Constitution-Making: The Presidency in 1787, with Comments on Determinism and Rational Choice. *American Political Science Review* 78: 1–16.

RIKER, WILLIAM H. 1986. *The Art of Political Manipulation*. New Haven: Yale University Press.

SCHATTSCHNEIDER, E. E. 1960. *The Semi-Sovereign People*. New York: Holt, Rinehart and Winston.

SHEPSLE, KENNETH A. 1979. Institutional Arrangements and Equilibrium in Multidimensional Voting Models. *American Journal of Political Science* 23: 27–59.

SIMON, HERBERT A. 1977. *Models of Discovery*. Boston: D. Reidel.

STONE, DEBORAH A. 1989. Causal Stories and the Formation of Policy Agendas. *Political Science Quarterly* 104: 281–300.

TRUMAN, DAVID B. 1951. *The Government Process: Political Interest and Public Opinion*. New York: Alfred A. Knopf.

VOGEL, DAVID. 1989. Fluctuation Fortunes: *The Political Power of Business in America*. New York: Basic Books.

WILDAVSKY, AARON. 1984. *The Politics of the Budgetary Process*. 4th ed. Boston: Little, Brown.

25

Why Some Issues Rise and Others Are Negated

John Kingdon

... Why do some subjects rise on agendas while others are neglected? Why do some alternatives receive more attention than others? Some of our answers to these questions concentrate on participants: We uncover who affects agendas and alternatives, and why they do. Other answers explore the processes through which these participants affect agendas and alternatives. We have conceived of three streams of processes: problems, policies, and politics. People recognize problems, they generate proposals for public policy changes, and they engage in such political activities as election campaigns and pressure group lobbying. Each participant—president, members of Congress, civil servants, lobbyists, journalists, academics, etc.—can in principle be involved in

each process (problem recognition, proposal formation, and politics). Policy is not the sole province of analysts, for instance, nor is politics the sole province of politicians. In practice, though, participants usually specialize in one or another process to a degree. Academics are more involved in policy formation than in politics, for instance, and parties are more involved in politics than in drafting detailed proposals. But conceptually, participants can be seen as different from processes.

Each of the participants and processes can act as an impetus or as a constraint. As an impetus, the participant or process boosts a subject higher on an agenda, or pushes an alternative into more active consideration. A president or congressional committee chair, for instance,

From John W. Kingdon, *Agendas, Alternatives, and Public Policies*, Second Edition (New York: Addison-Wesley, 2003), pp. 196–208.

decides to emphasize a subject. Or a problem is highlighted because a disaster occurs or because a well-known indicator changes. As a constraint, the participant or process dampens consideration of a subject or alternative. Vigorous pressure group opposition to an item, for instance, moves it down the list of priorities or even off the agenda. As an administration emphasizes its priorities, for another example, it limits people's ability to attend to other subjects. Concerns over budgetary costs of an item can also make its serious consideration quite unlikely.

AGENDA SETTING

How are governmental agendas set? Our answer has concentrated on three explanations: problems, politics, and visible participants.

Problems

Why do some problems come to occupy the attention of governmental officials more than other problems? The answer lies both in the means by which those officials learn about conditions and in the ways in which conditions become defined as problems. As to means, we have discussed indicators, focusing events, and feedback. Sometimes, a more or less systematic indicator simply shows that there is a condition out there. Indicators are used to assess the magnitude of the condition (e.g., the incidence of a disease or the cost of a program), and to discern changes in a condition. Both large magnitude and change catch officials' attention. Second, a focusing event—a disaster, crisis, personal experience, or powerful symbol—draws attention to some conditions more than to others. But such an event has only transient effects unless accompanied by a firmer indication of a problem, by a preexisting perception, or by a combination with other similar events. Third, officials learn about conditions through feedback about the operation of existing programs, either formal (e.g., routine monitoring of costs or program evaluation studies) or informal (e.g., streams of complaints flowing into congressional offices).

There is a difference between a condition and a problem. We put up with all kinds of conditions every day, and conditions do not rise to prominent places on policy agendas. Conditions come to be defined as problems, and have a better chance of rising on the agenda, when we come to believe that we should do something to change them. People in and around government define conditions as problems in several ways. First, conditions that violate important values are transformed into problems. Second, conditions become problems by comparison with other countries or other relevant units. Third, classifying a condition into one category rather than another may define it as one kind of problem or another. The lack of public transportation for handicapped people, for instance, can be classified as a transportation problem or as a civil rights problem, and the treatment of the subject is dramatically affected by the category.

Problems not only rise on governmental agendas, but they also fade from view. Why do they fade? First, government may address the problem, or fail to address it. In both cases, attention turns to something else, either because something has been done or because people are frustrated by failure and refuse to invest more of their time in a losing cause. Second, conditions that highlighted a problem may change—indicators drop instead of rise, or crises go away. Third, people may become accustomed to a condition or relabel a problem. Fourth, other items emerge and push the highly placed items aside. Finally, there may simply be inevitable cycles in attention; high growth rates level off, and fads come and go.

Problem recognition is critical to agenda setting. The chances of a given proposal or subject rising on an agenda are markedly enhanced if it is connected to an important problem. Some problems are seen as so pressing that they set agendas all by themselves. Once a particular problem is defined as pressing, whole classes of approaches are favored over others, and some alternatives are highlighted while others fall from view. So policy entrepreneurs invest considerable resources bringing their conception of problems to officials' attention, and trying to convince them to see problems their way. The recognition and definition of problems affect outcomes significantly.

Politics

The second family of explanations for high or low agenda prominence is in the political stream. Independently of problem recognition or the development of policy proposals, political events flow along according to their own dynamics and their own rules. Participants perceive swings in national mood, elections bring new administrations to power and new partisan or ideological distributions to Congress, and interest groups of various descriptions press (or fail to press) their demands on government.

Developments in this political sphere are powerful agenda setters. A new administration, for instance, changes agendas all over town as it highlights its conceptions of problems and its proposals, and makes attention to subjects that are not among its high priorities much less likely. A national mood that is perceived to be profoundly conservative dampens attention to costly new initiatives, while a more tolerant national mood would allow for greater spending. The opposition of a powerful phalanx of interest groups makes it difficult—not impossible, but difficult—to contemplate some initiatives.

Consensus is built in the political stream by bargaining more than by persuasion. When participants recognize problems or settle on certain proposals in the policy stream, they do so largely by persuasion. They marshal indicators and argue that certain conditions ought to be defined as problems, or they argue that their proposals meet such logical tests as technical feasibility or value acceptability. But in the political stream, participants build consensus by bargaining—trading provisions for support, adding elected officials to coalitions by giving them concessions that they demand, or compromising from ideal positions that will gain wider acceptance.

The combination of national mood and elections is a more potent agenda setter than organized interests. Interest groups are often able to block consideration of proposals they do not prefer, or to adapt to an item already high on a governmental agenda by adding elements a bit more to their liking. They less often initiate considerations or set agendas on their own. And when organized interests come into conflict with the combination of national mood and elected politicians, the latter combination is likely to prevail, at least as far as setting an agenda is concerned.

Visible Participants

Third, we made a distinction between visible and hidden participants. The visible cluster of actors, those who receive considerable press and public attention, include the president and his high-level appointees, prominent members of Congress, the media, and such elections-related actors as political parties and campaigners. The relatively hidden cluster includes academic specialists, career bureaucrats, and congressional staffers. We have discovered that the visible cluster affects the agenda and the hidden cluster affects the alternatives. So the chances of a subject rising on a governmental agenda are enhanced if that subject is pushed by participants in the visible cluster, and dampened if it is neglected by those participants. The administration—the president and his appointees—is a particularly powerful agenda setter, as are such prominent members of Congress as the party leaders and key committee chairs.

At least as far as agenda setting is concerned, elected officials and their appointees turn out to be more important than career civil servants or participants outside of government. To those who look for evidences of democracy at work, this is an encouraging result. These elected officials do not necessarily get their way in specifying alternatives or implementing decisions, but they do affect agendas rather substantially. To describe the roles of various participants in agenda setting, a fairly straightforward top-down model, with elected officials at the top, comes surprisingly close to the truth.

ALTERNATIVE SPECIFICATION

How is the list of potential alternatives for public policy choices narrowed to the ones that actually receive serious consideration? There are two families of answers: (1) Alternatives are generated and narrowed in the policy stream; and (2) Relatively hidden participants, specialists in the particular policy area, are involved.

Hidden Participants: Specialists

Alternatives, proposals, and solutions are generated in communities of specialists. This relatively hidden cluster of participants includes academics, researchers, consultants, career bureaucrats, congressional staffers, and analysts who work for interest groups. Their work is done, for instance, in planning and evaluation or budget shops in the bureaucracy or in the staff agencies on the Hill.

These relatively hidden participants form loosely knit communities of specialists. There is such a community for health, for instance, which includes analogous subcommunities for more specialized areas like the direct delivery of medical services and the regulation of food and drugs. Some of these communities, such as the one for transportation, are highly fragmented, while others are more tightly knit. Each community is composed of people located throughout the system and potentially of very diverse orientations and interests, but they all share one thing: their specialization and acquaintance with the issues in that particular policy area.

Ideas bubble around in these communities. People try out proposals in a variety of ways: through speeches, bill introductions, congressional hearings, leaks to the press, circulation of papers, conversations, and lunches. They float their ideas, criticize one another's work, hone and revise their ideas, and float new versions. Some of these ideas are respectable, while others are out of the question. But many, many ideas are possible and are considered in some fashion somewhere along the line.

The Policy Stream

The generation of policy alternatives is best seen as a selection process, analogous to biological natural selection. In what we have called the policy primeval soup, many ideas float around, bumping into one another, encountering new ideas, and forming combinations and recombinations. The origins of policy may seem a bit obscure, hard to predict and hard to understand or to structure.

While the origins are somewhat haphazard, the selection is not. Through the imposition of criteria by which some ideas are selected out for survival while others are discarded, order is developed from chaos, pattern from randomness. These criteria include technical feasibility, congruence with the values of community members, and the anticipation of future constraints, including a budget constraint, public acceptability, and politicians' receptivity. Proposals that are judged infeasible—that do not square with policy community values, that would cost more than the budget will allow, that run afoul of opposition in either the mass or specialized publics, or that would not find a receptive audience among elected politicians—are less likely to survive than proposals that meet these standards. In the process of consideration in the policy community, ideas themselves are important. Pressure models do not completely describe the process. Proposals are evaluated partly in terms of their political support and opposition, to be sure, but partly against logical or analytical criteria as well.

There is a long process of softening up the system. Policy entrepreneurs do not leave consideration of their pet proposals to accident. Instead, they push for consideration in many ways and in many forums. In the process of policy development, recombination (the coupling of already-familiar elements) is more important than mutation (the appearance of wholly new forms). Thus entrepreneurs, who broker people and ideas, are more important than inventors. Because recombination is more important than invention, there may be "no new thing under the sun" at the same time that there may be dramatic change and innovation. There is change, but it involves the recombination of already-familiar elements.

The long softening-up process is critical to policy change. Opportunities for serious hearings, the policy windows we explored … pass quickly and are missed if the proposals have not already gone through the long gestation process before the window opens. The work of floating and refining proposals is not wasted if it does not bear fruit in the short run. Indeed, it is critically important if the proposal is to be heard at the right time.

COUPLING AND WINDOWS

The separate streams of problems, policies, and politics each have lives of their own. Problems are recognized and defined according to processes that are different from the ways policies are developed or political events unfold. Policy proposals are developed according to their own incentives and selection criteria, whether or not they are solutions to problems or responsive to political considerations. Political events flow along on their own schedule and according to their own rules, whether or not they are related to problems or proposals.

But there come times when the three streams are joined. A pressing problem demands attention, for instance, and a policy proposal is coupled to the problem as its solution. Or an event in the political stream, such as a change of administration, calls for different directions. At that point, proposals that fit with that political event, such as initiatives that fit with a new administration's philosophy, come to the fore and are coupled with the ripe political climate. Similarly, problems that fit are highlighted, and others are neglected.

Decision Agendas

A complete linkage combines all three streams—problems, policies, and politics—into a single package. Advocates of a new policy initiative not only take advantage of politically propitious moments but also claim that their proposal is a solution to a pressing problem. Likewise, entrepreneurs concerned about a particular problem search for solutions in the policy stream to couple to their problem, then try to take advantage of political receptivity at certain points in time to push the package of problem and solution. At points along the way, there are partial couplings: solutions to problems, but without a receptive political climate; politics to proposals, but without a sense that a compelling problem is being solved; politics and problems both calling for action, but without an available alternative to advocate. But the complete joining of all three streams dramatically enhances the odds that a subject will become firmly fixed on a decision agenda.

Governmental agendas, lists of subjects to which governmental officials are paying serious attention, can be set solely in either problems or political streams, and solely by visible actors. Officials can pay attention to an important problem, for instance, without having a solution to it. Or politics may highlight a subject, even in the absence of either problem or solution. A decision agenda, a list of subjects that is moving into position for an authoritative decision, such as legislative enactment or presidential choice, is set somewhat differently. The probability of an item rising on a decision agenda is dramatically increased if all three elements—problem, policy proposal, and political receptivity—are linked in a single package. Conversely, partial couplings are less likely to rise on decision agendas. Problems that come to decisions without solutions attached, for instance, are not as likely to move into position for an authoritative choice as if they did have solutions attached. And proposals that lack political backing are less likely to move into position for a decision than ones that do have that backing.

A return to our case studies ... illustrates these points. With aviation deregulation, awareness of problems, development of proposals, and swings of national mood all proceeded separately in their own streams. Increasingly through the late 1960s and early 1970s, people became convinced that the economy contained substantial inefficiencies to which the burdens of government regulation contributed. Proposals for deregulation were formed among academics and other specialists, through a softening-up process that included journal articles, testimony, conferences, and other forums. In the 1970s, politicians sensed a change in national mood toward increasing hostility to government size and intrusiveness. All three of the components, therefore, came together at about the same time. The key to movement was the coupling of the policy stream's literature on deregulation with the political incentive to rein in government growth, and those two elements with the sense that there was a real, important, and increasing problem with economic inefficiency.

The waterway user charge case illustrates a similar coupling. A proposal, some form of user charge, had been debated among transportation specialists for years. The political stream produced an administration receptive to imposing a user charge. This combination of policy and politics was coupled with a problem—the necessity, in a time of budget stringency, to repair or replace aging facilities like Lock and Dam 26. Thus did the joining of problem, policy, and politics push the waterway user charge into position on a decision agenda.

By contrast, national health insurance during the Carter years did not have all three components joined. Proponents could argue that there were real problems of medical access, though opponents countered that many of the most severe problems were being addressed through Medicare, Medicaid, and private insurance. The political stream did produce a heavily Democratic Congress and an administration that favored some sort of health insurance initiative. It seemed for a time that serious movement was under way. But the policy stream had not settled on a single, worked-up, viable alternative from among the many proposals floating around. The budget constraint, itself a severe problem, and politicians' reading of the national mood, which seemed to be against costly new initiatives, also proved to be too much to overcome. The coupling was incomplete, and the rise of national health insurance on the agenda proved fleeting. Then the election of Ronald Reagan sealed its fate, at least for the time being.

Success in one area contributes to success in adjacent areas. Once aviation deregulation passed, for instance, government turned with a vengeance to other deregulation proposals, and passed several in short order. These spillovers, as we have called them, occur because politicians sense the payoff in repeating a successful formula in a similar area, because the winning coalition can be transferred, and because advocates can argue from successful precedent. These spillovers are extremely powerful agenda setters, seemingly bowling over even formidable opposition that stands in the way.

Policy Windows

An open policy window is an opportunity for advocates to push their pet solutions or to push attention to their special problems. Indeed, advocates in and around government keep their proposals and their problems at hand, waiting for these opportunities to occur. They have pet solutions, for instance, and wait for problems to float by to which they can attach their solutions, or for developments in the political stream that they can

use to their advantage. Or they wait for similar opportunities to bring their special problems to the fore, such as the appearance of a new administration that would be concerned with these problems. That administration opens a window for them to bring greater attention to the problems about which they are concerned.

Windows are opened by events in either the problems or political streams. Thus there are problems windows and political windows. A new problem appears, for instance, creating an opportunity to attach a solution to it. Or such events in the political stream as turnover of elected officials, swings of national mood, or vigorous lobbying might create opportunities to push some problems and proposals to the fore and dampen the chances to highlight other problems and proposals.

Sometimes, windows open quite predictably. Legislation comes up for renewal on a schedule, for instance, creating opportunities to change, expand, or abolish certain programs. At other times, windows open quite unpredictably, as when an airliner crashes or a fluky election produces an unexpected turnover in key decision makers. Predictable or unpredictable, open windows are small and scarce. Opportunities come, but they also pass. Windows do not stay open long. If a chance is missed, another must be awaited.

The scarcity and the short duration of the opening of a policy window create a powerful magnet for problems and proposals. When a window opens, problems and proposals flock to it. People concerned with particular problems see the open window as their opportunity to address or even solve these problems. Advocates of particular proposals see the open window as the opportunity to enact them. As a result, the system comes to be loaded down with problems and proposals. If participants are willing to invest sufficient resources, some of the problems can be resolved and some of the proposals enacted. Other problems and proposals drift away because insufficient resources are mobilized.

Open windows present opportunities for the complete linkage of problems, proposals, and politics, and hence opportunities to move packages of the three joined elements up on decision agendas. One particularly crucial coupling is the link of a solution to something else. Advocates of pet proposals watch for developments in the political stream that they can take advantage of, or try to couple their solution to whatever problems are floating by at the moment. Once they have made the partial coupling of proposal to either problem or politics, they attempt to join all three elements, knowing that the chances for enactment are considerably enhanced if they can complete the circle. Thus they try to hook packages of problems and solutions to political forces, packages of proposals and political incentives to perceived problems, or packages of problems and politics to some proposal taken from the policy stream.

ENTREPRENEURS

Policy entrepreneurs are people willing to invest their resources in return for future policies they favor. They are motivated by combinations of several things: their straightforward concern about certain problems, their pursuit of such self-serving benefits as protecting or expanding their bureaucracy's budget or claiming credit for accomplishment, their promotion of their policy values, and their simple pleasure in participating. We have encountered them at three junctures: pushing their concerns about certain problems higher on the agenda, pushing their pet proposals during a process of softening up the system, and making the couplings we just discussed. These entrepreneurs are found at many locations; they might be elected officials, career civil servants, lobbyists, academics, or journalists. No one type of participant dominates the pool of entrepreneurs.

As to problems, entrepreneurs try to highlight the indicators that so importantly dramatize their problems. They push for one kind of problem definition rather than another. Because they know that focusing events can move subjects higher on the agenda, entrepreneurs push to create such things as personal viewings of problems by policy makers and the diffusion of a symbol that captures their problem in a nutshell. They also may prompt the kinds of feedback about current governmental performance that affect agendas: letters, complaints, and visits to officials.

As to proposals, entrepreneurs are central to the softening-up process. They write papers, give testimony, hold hearings, try to get press coverage, and meet endlessly with important and not-so-important people. They float their ideas as trial balloons, get reactions, revise their proposals in the light of reactions, and float them again. They aim to soften up the mass public, specialized publics, and the policy community itself. The process takes years of effort.

As to coupling, entrepreneurs once again appear when windows open. They have their pet proposals or their concerns about problems ready, and push them at the propitious moments. In the pursuit of their own goals, they perform the function for the system of coupling solutions to problems, problems to political forces, and political forces to proposals. The joining of the separate streams described earlier depends heavily on the appearance of the right entrepreneur at the right time. In our case study of Health Maintenance Organizations ... Paul Ellwood appeared on the scene to link his pet proposal (HMOs) to the problem of medical care costs and to the political receptivity created by the Nixon administration casting about for health initiatives. The problems and political streams had opened a window, and Ellwood cleverly took advantage of that opportunity to push his HMO proposal, joining all three streams in the process.

The appearance of entrepreneurs when windows are open, as well as their more enduring activities of trying to push their problems and proposals into prominence, are central to our story. They bring several key resources into the fray: their claims to a hearing, their political connections and negotiating skills, and their sheer persistence. An item's chances for moving up on an agenda are enhanced considerably by the presence of a skillful entrepreneur, and dampened considerably if no entrepreneur takes on the cause, pushes it, and makes the critical couplings when policy windows open.

26

Policy Entrepreneurship

Michael Mintrom and

Phillipa Norman

In his pioneering use of the term, Kingdon (1984/1995) noted that policy entrepreneurs "…could be in or out of government, in elected or appointed positions, in interest groups or research organizations. But their defining characteristic, much as in the case of a business entrepreneur, is their willingness to invest their resources—time, energy, reputation, and sometimes money—in the hope of a future return" (p. 122). Discussions of policy entrepreneurship have evolved over time, from instances where the term was used as a loose metaphor, to more sophisticated treatments. Ironically, the early emphasis on the individual as change agent appears to have served as an inhibitor to theorization. In any given instance of policy change, it is usually possible to locate an individual or a small team that appears to have been a driving force for action. But in all such cases, the individuals, their motives, and their ways of acting will appear idiosyncratic. And idiosyncrasy does not offer propitious grounds for theorization. To break this theoretical impasse, policy entrepreneurship needed to be studied in a manner that paid attention simultaneously to contextual factors, to individual actions within those contexts, and to how context shaped such actions.

In their analysis of change agents in local government, Schneider, Teske, and Mintrom

(1995) offered a model for understanding the emergence and practices of entrepreneurial actors, given specific contexts. Applying a similar methodology, and combining it with event history analysis, Mintrom (1997a) showed how policy entrepreneurship could be studied systematically. That work, and subsequent studies (Mintrom, 2000; Mintrom & Vergari, 1998), demonstrated that the likelihood of policy change is affected by key contextual variables and by what policy entrepreneurs do within those contexts. When a range of contextual factors indicated that legislative change was likely to happen, the actions of policy entrepreneurs did not seem to have major impacts. However, in cases where contextual variables appeared to reduce the likelihood of change occurring, the actions of effective policy entrepreneurs could be decisive. Working with different sets of policy issues and different sets of policymaking contexts, Balla (2001) and Shipan and Volden (2006) reported similar findings.

Policy entrepreneurs can be identified by their efforts to promote significant policy change. Their motivations might be diverse. However, given their goal of promoting change, their actions should follow certain patterns. What does policy entrepreneurship involve? Following others, particularly Kingdon (1984/1995), Mintrom (2000), and Roberts and King (1996), we suggest

From Michael Mintrom and Phillipa Norman, "Policy Entrepreneurship and Policy Change," *Policy Studies Journal*, Vol. 37, No. 4, November 2009, pp. 649–667.

that four elements are central to policy entrepreneurship. These are: displaying social acuity, defining problems, building teams, and leading by example.[2] We next review each element in turn, noting linkages between their discussion by those who have studied policy entrepreneurs and relevant discussions in the broader literature on policymaking and policy change. In this discussion, we do not rank the relative importance of each element. Our expectation is that all policy entrepreneurs exhibit these characteristics at least to some degree. Some policy entrepreneurs will be stronger in some of these characteristics than others. For example, Mintrom observed that some policy entrepreneurs were more effective than others at operating in networks (which relates to social acuity) and promoting and maintaining advocacy coalitions (which relates to team building).

Kingdon (1984/1995) argued that within policymaking contexts, policy entrepreneurs take advantage of "windows of opportunity" to promote policy change. The metaphor holds appeal, and empirical evidence indicates the importance of context for shaping the prospects of success for advocates of policy change. However, in policymaking contexts, as in all areas of human endeavor, opportunities must be recognized before they can be seized and used to pursue desired outcomes. This suggests change agents must display high levels of social acuity, or perceptiveness, in understanding others and engaging in policy conversations.

Empirical evidence indicates that policy entrepreneurs display social acuity in two key ways. First, they make good use of policy networks. Stretching back to Mohr's (1969) studies of organizational innovation and Walker's (1969) studies of the spread of policy innovations, we find that those actors most able to promote change in specific contexts have typically acquired relevant knowledge from elsewhere. Balla (2001), Mintrom and Vergari (1998), and True and Mintrom (2001) have demonstrated that engagement in relevant policy networks spanning across jurisdictions can significantly increase the likelihood that advocates for policy change will achieve success. The second way that policy entrepreneurs display social acuity is by understanding the ideas, motives, and concerns of others in their local policy context

and responding effectively. Policy actors who get along well with others and who are well connected in the local policy context tend to achieve more success in securing policy change than do others (Kingdon, 1984/1995; Mintrom & Vergari, 1998; Rabe, 2004).

Defining Problems

The political dynamics of problem definition have been explored extensively by policy scholars (Allison, 1971; Baumgartner & Jones, 1993; Nelson, 1984; Rochefort & Cobb, 1994; Schneider & Ingram, 1993; Schön & Rein, 1994). Problems in the policy realm invariably come with multiple attributes. How those problems get defined— or what attributes are made salient in policy discussions—can determine what individuals and groups will pay attention to them. Problem definition, then, affects how people relate specific problems to their own interests. Viewed in this way, definition of policy problems is always a political act. Effective problem definition requires the combination of social acuity with skills in conflict management and negotiation (Fisher & Patton, 1991; Heifetz, 1994).

As actors who seek to promote significant policy change, policy entrepreneurs pay close attention to problem definition. Among other things, this can involve presenting evidence in ways that suggest a crisis is at hand (Nelson, 1984; Stone, 1997), finding ways to highlight failures of current policy settings (Baumgartner & Jones, 1993; Henig, 2008), and drawing support from actors beyond the immediate scope of the problem (Levin & Sanger, 1994; Roberts & King, 1991; Schattschneider, 1960).

Building Teams

Like their counterparts in business, policy entrepreneurs are team players. Individuals are often the instigators of change, but their strength does not come from the force of their ideas alone, or from their embodiment of superhuman qualities. Rather, their real strength comes through their ability to work effectively with others. The team-building activities of policy entrepreneurs can take several forms. First, it is common to find policy entrepreneurs operating within a tight-knit team composed of individuals with different knowledge and skills, who are able to offer mutual support in the pursuit of change (Meier, 1995; Mintrom, 2000; Roberts & King, 1996). Second, as noted in our discussion of social acuity, policy entrepreneurs make use of their personal and professional networks—both inside and outside the jurisdictions where they seek to promote policy change. Policy entrepreneurs understand that their networks of contacts represent repositories of skill and knowledge that they can draw upon to support their initiatives (Burt, 2000; Knoke, 1990). Finally, policy entrepreneurs recognize the importance of developing and working with coalitions to promote policy change (Mintrom & Vergari, 1996). The size of a coalition can be crucial for demonstrating the degree of support a proposal for policy change enjoys. Just as importantly, the composition of a coalition can convey the breadth of support for a proposal. That is why policy entrepreneurs often work to gain support from groups that might appear as unlikely allies for a cause. Used effectively, the composition of a coalition can help to deflect the arguments of opponents of change (Baumgartner & Jones, 1993).

Leading by Example

Risk aversion among decision makers presents a major challenge for actors seeking to promote significant policy change. Policy entrepreneurs often take actions intended to reduce the perception of risk among decision makers. A common strategy involves engaging with others to clearly demonstrate the workability of a policy proposal. For several decades, those promoting deregulation of infrastructural industries in the United States—both at the state and national level—relaxed regulatory oversight in advance of seeking legislative change (Derthick & Quirk, 1985; Teske, 2004). These preemptive actions reduced the ability of opponents to block change by engendering fears about possible consequences. For similar reasons, foundations have funded pilot projects associated with expansion of health insurance coverage (Oliver & Paul-Shaheen, 1997), the use of school vouchers (Mintrom & Vergari, 2009; Moe, 1995), and support for early childhood programs (Knott & McCarthy, 2007). In all instances,

the creation of working models of the proposed change served to generate crucial information about program effectiveness and practicality.

When they lead by example—taking an idea and turning it into action themselves—agents of change signal their genuine commitment to improved social outcomes. This can do a lot to win credibility with others and, hence, build momentum for change (Kotter, 1996; Quinn, 2000). Further, when policy entrepreneurs take action, they can sometimes create situations where legislators look out of touch (Mintrom, 1997b). In such situations, the risk calculations of legislators can switch from a focus on the consequences of action to a focus on the consequences of inaction.

Other things being equal, policy entrepreneurs who exhibit the qualities discussed here are more likely to achieve success than those who do not. However, we should also recognize that policy entrepreneurs are embedded in social contexts, and that those contexts change across space and time. Given this, it might happen that a given policy entrepreneur can realize his or her policy goals without necessarily behaving in ways that are consistent with what has been said here. When attempting to assess why any particular policy entrepreneur or team of policy entrepreneurs happened to meet with success or failure, we need to look both at the broader conditions they faced and the actions that they engaged in. The elements of policy entrepreneurship noted here offer a starting point for thinking about the things that policy entrepreneurs might do to improve their chances of achieving success. At the same time, they suggest a means by which we might diagnose failure. Noting that particular policy entrepreneurs did not act in accord with our expectations, we might then go on to deduce how their choices contributed to the observed outcome.

POLICY ENTREPRENEURSHIP IN BROADER EXPLANATIONS OF POLICY CHANGE

Having reviewed four elements central to policy entrepreneurship, we now discuss how the concept of policy entrepreneurship can be integrated into five mainstream theorizations of policy change.[3] In so doing, we seek to address a frequent limitation of previous discussions of the activities of policy entrepreneurs.

Policy Entrepreneurship and Incrementalism

In his conceptualization of the policy process, Charles Lindblom (1968) emphasized the role of proximate policymakers. These are actors with decision-making powers such as presidents, governors, legislators, council members, and bureaucrats. Proximate policymakers are subject to influence both from inside and from outside of their various policy venues. Motivated by their own interests and agendas, they interact with each other with the hope of gathering support for their policy preferences. Lindblom rejected the notion that policymakers conduct rational, comprehensive assessments of options and consequences when making policy choices. According to Lindblom, policies are often made in a reactive fashion. Among policymakers, there are often divergent views and unanimity is difficult to achieve. As a result, policies emerge as compromises. The political posturing and risk avoidance exhibited by proximate policymakers result in incrementalism. That is, policy changes occur slowly, one step at a time. This is a way of dealing with complex policy issues. The policymakers do not do anything in haste, fearing the backlash associated with a misstep.

In this conceptualization of policymaking, there is room to consider the role of the policy entrepreneur. Policy entrepreneurs might come from the ranks of proximate policymakers or they might be more on the margins of policymaking circles. According to Lindblom, the key to successfully engaging proximate policymakers is to present your argument in an appealing form. Likewise, proximate policymakers can be influenced by their assessments of the interests represented in a policy entrepreneur's coalition, and the size and strength of it. When seeking to have influence from outside the centers of policymaking, policy entrepreneurs must be careful to cultivate close contacts with those who are in decision-making positions. In this way, they can demonstrate their trustworthiness and their commitment to their ideas for policy change. Provost

(2003, 2006) has explored the systematic ways that state attorneys general have sought to influence policymaking in their jurisdictions. Rabe (2004) has shown how state-level policy analysts and others in bureaucratic positions can have influence when technical issues are at stake.

Incrementalism presents a frustrating inhibitor to dramatic change. However, patient actors who hold a clear vision of the end they are seeking can still move policy in directions they desire. The key is to see how a series of small changes could, over time, produce similar results as more dramatic, immediate change. To maintain a functioning coalition, under incrementalism, policy entrepreneurs must keep track of their small victories and explain to their supporters how those incremental steps are taking them in the right direction.

Policy Entrepreneurship and Policy Streams

John Kingdon's (1984/1995) policy streams theory is concerned with why and how certain issues get attention at certain times. Kingdon explored how ideas gain support through formal and informal routes. Within his theory, Kingdon recognized the role that policy entrepreneurs play in linking problems, policy ideas, and politics to draw attention to issues and articulate them onto government agendas. According to Kingdon, policy entrepreneurs must find effective ways to present problems and solutions within the community of relevant actors who can contribute to debate on a given issue. Often, a good sense of timing is critical; that is, the ability to perceive and take advantage of windows of opportunity.

Kingdon's theory of policy streams has informed the work of many scholars of policy change. His portrait of policy entrepreneurs as agents of change—people who make connections across disparate groups, and engaging with proximate policymakers—has also been influential. Taking Kingdon's work as a point of departure, several efforts have been made to advance discussion of timing in the policy process (Baumgartner & Jones, 1993; Geva-May, 2004; Zahariadis, 2007). In other works that have been influenced by Kingdon's theory, closer attention has been paid to the identification of policy entrepreneurs and the analysis of their actions (Mintrom, 2000; Roberts & King, 1996).

The literature comprising the new institutionalism has developed in a number of distinctive ways (Hall & Taylor, 1996; March & Olsen, 1989; Ostrom, 2007; Thelen, 1999). However, despite the differences in methodological perspective and substantive focus, contributions to the new institutionalism all share a deep interest in the interplay between structures and the agency of actors operating within or across them. Understood as the rules of the game, institutions serve to provide stability and certainty to those operating within them (Eggertsson, 1990; North, 1990). Alongside the development of formal rules, it is common to find the emergence of informal norms of behavior that further serve to guide the behaviors of actors within the institutional structures (Barzelay & Gallego, 2006; Ostrom, 1990; Scott, 2001).

Institutionalist accounts of the policy process and policy change identify considerable space for the exercise of policy entrepreneurship (Feldman and Khademian, 2002; Majone, 1996; March & Olsen, 1989; Scharpf, 1997). However, these accounts are also useful for explaining the limits of such activity. The new institutionalism highlights several attributes of actors that can significantly increase their ability to instigate change. These include having deep knowledge of relevant procedures and the local norms that serve to define acceptable behavior. An implication of the new institutionalism, then, is that efforts to secure major change must be informed by insider sensibilities. That understanding helps us appreciate why the efforts of "outsiders" to make change often come to nothing. We are brought back to the importance of social acuity. Policy entrepreneurs must be able to understand the workings of a given context without becoming so acculturated to it that they lose their critical perspective and their motivation to promote change. Evidence suggests that policy entrepreneurs can be successful in this regard when they make good use of networks (Mintrom & Vergari, 1998) or when they form teams that contain both "insiders" and "outsiders" (Brandl, 1998; Roberts & King, 1996).

Policy Entrepreneurs and Punctuated Equilibrium

A discrepancy exists between incrementalist accounts of policy change and those that discuss instances of dramatic policy shifts. In seeking to reconcile these different accounts, Baumgartner and Jones (1993) developed their theory of the policy process as one characterized by long periods of stability punctuated by moments of abrupt, significant change. In this account of policy change, the role of policy entrepreneurs is noted, although more emphasis is placed on the broader dynamics that drive stability and change. As in Lindblom's account, Baumgartner and Jones suggested that stability is the product of the limited ability for legislators to deal with more than a few issues at a time (see also Jones, 1994; Jones & Baumgartner, 2005). Stability is further supported by the development of policy monopolies, controlled by people who go to considerable lengths to promote positive images of current policy settings and deflect calls for change. In this interpretation of policymaking and policy change, the task for the policy entrepreneur is to bring the policy issues out into the public domain and attempt to invoke a swell of interest intended to induce major change. Even within stable systems, the potential for change exists. For policy entrepreneurs, the challenge is to undermine the present policy images and create new ones that emphasize major problems and a need for change.

Baumgartner and Jones (1993) noted that, particularly in federal systems of government, it is possible for policy changes to occur in multiple venues. When policy change appears blocked at one level—say, the level of state governments—it might be effectively pursued elsewhere—say, at the local level. That observation is consistent with the notion of the policy entrepreneur as a change agent who can lead by example. As we noted earlier, it is possible for policy entrepreneurs to prompt change in one policy venue by first pursuing it in another.

Drawing upon the work of Baumgartner and Jones (1993), several studies have subsequently explored linkages between the actions of policy entrepreneurs and the initiation of dynamic policy change. These include contributions by John (1999, 2003), Peters (1994), and True (2000).

Policy Entrepreneurs and Advocacy Coalitions

Paul A. Sabatier's theorization of policy change has generated the advocacy coalition framework and ongoing refinements (Sabatier, 1988; Sabatier & Jenkins-Smith, 1993; Sabatier & Weible, 2007). Advocacy coalitions are portrayed as "people from a variety of positions (e.g., elected and agency officials, interest group leaders, researchers) who share a particular belief system—that is, a set of basic values, causal assumptions, and problem perceptions—and who show a nontrivial degree of coordinated activity over time" (Sabatier, 1988, p. 139). Coalition participants seek to ensure the maintenance and evolution of policy in particular areas, such as environmental management, education, and population health. The advocacy coalition framework tells us how ideas for change emerge from dedicated people that coalesce around an issue. Policy entrepreneurship is not treated explicitly within the framework. However, there is considerable room for compatibility between explanations of policy change grounded in the advocacy coalition framework and those grounded in a focus on policy entrepreneurship. For example, within the advocacy coalition framework, change is anticipated to come from both endogenous and exogenous shocks. But, to have political effect, those shocks need to be interpreted and translated. This process of translation is directly equivalent to the process of problem definition, whereby objective social, economic, and environmental conditions are portrayed in ways that increase the likelihood that they will receive the attention desired of decision makers. Policy entrepreneurs typically display skills needed to do this kind of translational and definitional work.

Mintrom and Vergari (1996) considered the link between formation and maintenance of advocacy coalitions and the efforts of policy entrepreneurs. In that account, emphasis was given to how policy entrepreneurs define problems in ways that maximize opportunities for bringing on board coalition partners. The value to advocacy coalitions of strong team builders was also emphasized and demonstrated empirically. In subsequent studies, drawing on empirical evidence across a range of policy areas and policymaking venues, Goldfinch and Hart (2003), Hajime (1999), Litfin (2000) and Meijerink (2005), among others, have indicated the merits of incorporating a discussion of policy entrepreneurship within discussions of advocacy coalitions.

The consensus found in most discussions of policymaking is that policy change typically occurs incrementally. However, instances arise where problems are not able to be readily addressed within existing policy settings. The concept of policy entrepreneurship helps us make sense of what happens in and around policy communities during these times. But the value of policy entrepreneurship as a concept is greatly increased when it is integrated with broader theorizations of the sources of policy stability and policy change. Our purpose here has been to show how that can be achieved. We have also noted empirical studies produced in the past two decades that have started to provide this kind of joining of policy entrepreneurship with other explanations of policy change....

End Notes

1. Entrepreneurial behavior in a range of contexts has been studied by scholars across a range of disciplines. Important contributions have been made in economics, business, sociology, and psychology. Mintrom (2000) devotes two chapters to reviewing the broader literature and the history of the concept of the entrepreneur before detailing how the concept might be translated to the policy context.
2. We acknowledge that many additional entrepreneurial traits could be usefully studied to gain insights into how people promote policy change. For example, in their respective studies of entrepreneurial behavior among legislators, Thomas (1991) and Weissert (1991) placed emphasis on other entrepreneurial traits, such as assertiveness and commitment. However, for the purpose of this article, we assume that traits such as assertiveness and commitment are captured in the practice of leadership by example and effective team building.
3. The concept of policy entrepreneurship could potentially be integrated into a much broader

range of explanations of policy change than those we have chosen to review. Here, our choice of explanations was based on their prominence and breadth of application within the field of policy studies. Many other theories exist concerning policymaking processes and how policy change occurs. For an overview of such theories, see Sabatier (2007).

References

ALLISON, GRAHAM T. 1971. *Essence of Decision: Explaining the Cuban Missile Crisis*. Boston: Little, Brown.

BALLA, STEVEN J. 2001. "Interstate Professional Associations and the Diffusion of Policy Innovations." *American Politics Research* 29: 221–45.

BARZELAY, MICHAEL, and RAQUEL GALLEGO. 2006. "From 'New Institutionalism' to 'Institutional Processualism': Advancing Knowledge about Public Management Policy Change." *Governance* 19: 531–57.

BAUMGARTNER, FRANK R., and BRYAN D. JONES. 1993. *Agendas and Instability in American Politics*. Chicago: University of Chicago Press.

BRANDL, JOHN. 1998. *Money and Good Intentions Are Not Enough: Or, Why a Liberal Democrat Thinks States Need Both Competition and Community*. Washington, DC: The Brookings Institution.

Burns, James MacGregor. 1978. *Leadership*. New York: Harper and Row.

BURT, RONALD S. 2000. "The Network Structure of Social Capital." *Research in Organizational Behaviour* 22: 345–423.

CHECKEL, JEFFREY T. 2001. "Why Comply? Social Learning and European Identity Change." *International Organization* 55: 553–88.

CROWLEY, JOCELYN ELISE. 2003. *The Politics of Child Support in America*. New York: Cambridge University Press.

DERTHICK, MARTHA, and PAUL J. QUIRK. 1985. *The Politics of Deregulation*. Washington, DC: The Brookings Institution.

DOLOWITZ, DAVID P., and DAVID MARSH. 2000. "Learning from Abroad: The Role of Policy Transfer in Contemporary Policy-Making." *Governance* 13: 5–23.

DYSON, TOM. 2008. *Politics of German Defence and Security: Policy Leadership and Military Reform in the Post-Cold War Era*. Oxford: Berghahn Books.

EGGERTSSON, THRAINN. 1990. *Economic Behaviour and Institutions: Principles of Neoinstitutional Economics*. New York: Cambridge University Press.

FELDMAN, MARTHA S., and ANNE M. KHADEMIAN. 2002. "To Manage Is to Govern." *Public Administration Review* 62: 541–55.

FINNEMORE, MARTHA, and KATHRYN SIKKINK. 1998. "International Norm Dynamics and Political Change." *International Organization* 52: 887–917.

FISHER, ROGER, and BRUCE PATTON. 1991. *Getting to Yes: Negotiating Agreement Without Giving In*, 2nd ed. Boston: Houghton Mifflin.

GEVA-MAY, IRIS. 2004. "Riding the Wave of Opportunity: Termination in Public Policy." *Journal of Public Administration Research and Theory* 14: 309–33.

GOLDFINCH, SHAUN, and PAUL HART. 2003. "Leadership and Institutional Reform: Engineering Macroeconomic Policy Change in Australia." *Governance* 16: 235–70.

GRANDE, EDGAR, and ANKE PESCHKE. 1999. "Transnational Cooperation and Policy Networks in European Science Policy-Making." *Research Policy* 28: 43–61.

HAJIME, SATO. 1999. "The Advocacy Coalition Framework and the Policy Process Analysis: The Case of Smoking Control in Japan." *Policy Studies Journal* 27: 28–44.

HALL, PETER A., and Rosemary C.R. Taylor. 1996. "Political Science and the Three New Institutionalisms." *Political Studies* 44: 936–57.

HEIFETZ, RONALD. 1994. *Leadership without Easy Answers*. Cambridge, MA: Harvard University Press.

HENIG, JEFFREY R. 2008. *Spin Cycle: How Research Is Used in Policy Debates: The Case of Charter Schools*. New York: Russell Sage Foundation: The Century Foundation.

HERRICK, REBEKAH, and MICHAEL K. MOORE. 1993. "Political Ambition's Effect on Legislative Behavior: Schlesinger's Typology Reconsidered and Revisited." *The Journal of Politics* 55: 765–76.

JOHN, PETER. 1999. "Ideas and Interests; Agendas and Implementation: An Evolutionary Explanation of Policy Change in British Local Government Finance." *British Journal of Politics and International Relations* 1: 39–62.

———. 2003. "Is There Life after Policy Streams, Advocacy Coalitions, and Punctuations?: Using Evolutionary Theory to Explain Policy Change." *Policy Studies Journal* 31: 481–98.

JONES, BRYAN D., ed. 1989. *Leadership and Politics: New Perspectives in Political Science.* Lawrence: University Press of Kansas.

———. 1994. *Reconceiving Decision-Making in Democratic Politics: Attention, Choice, and Public Policy.* Chicago: University of Chicago Press.

JONES, BRYAN D., and FRANK R. BAUMGARTNER. 2005. *The Politics of Attention: How Government Prioritizes Problems.* Chicago: University of Chicago Press.

KINGDON, JOHN W. [1984] 1995. *Agendas, Alternatives, and Public Policies*, 2nd ed. Boston: Little, Brown & Company.

KNOKE, DAVID. 1990. *Political Networks: The Structural Perspective.* New York: Cambridge University Press.

KNOTT, JACK H., and DIANE MCCARTHY. 2007. "Policy Venture Capital: Foundations, Government Partnerships, and Child Care Programs." *Administration and Society* 39: 319–53.

KOTTER, JOHN P. 1996. *Leading Change.* Boston: Harvard Business School Press.

LAFFAN, BRIGID. 1997. "From Policy Entrepreneur to Policy Manager: The Challenge Facing the European Commission." *Journal of European Public Policy* 4: 422–38.

LEVIN, MARTIN A., and MARY BRYNA SANGER. 1994. *Making Government Work: How Entrepreneurial Executives Turn Bright Ideas into Real Results.* San Francisco: Jossey-Bass.

LINDBLOM, CHARLES E. 1968. *The Policymaking Process.* Englewood Cliffs, NJ: Prentice-Hall.

LITFIN, KAREN T. 2000. "Advocacy Coalitions along the Domestic-Foreign Frontier: Globalization and Canadian Climate Change Policy." *Policy Studies Journal* 28: 236–52.

MACKENZIE, CHRIS. 2004. "Policy Entrepreneurship in Australia: A Conceptual Review and Application." *Australian Journal of Political Science* 39: 367–86.

MAJONE, GIANDOMENICO. 1996. "Public Policy and Administration: Ideas, Interests and Institutions." In *A New Handbook of Political Science*, ed. Robert E. Goodin and Hans-Dieter Klingemann. New York: Oxford University Press, 610–27.

MARCH, JAMES G., and JOHAN P. OLSEN. 1989. *Rediscovering Institutions: The Organizational Basis of Politics.* New York: Free Press.

MEIER, DEBORAH. 1995. *The Power of Their Ideas.* Boston: Beacon Press.

MEIJERINK, SANDER. 2005. "Understanding Policy Stability and Change: The Interplay of Advocacy Coalitions and Epistemic Communities, Windows of Opportunity, and Dutch Coastal Flooding Policy 1945–2003." *Journal of European Public Policy* 12: 1060–77.

MINTROM, MICHAEL. 1997a. "Policy Entrepreneurs and the Diffusion of Innovation." *American Journal of Political Science* 41: 738–70.

———. 1997b. "The State-Local Nexus in Policy Innovation Diffusion: The Case of School Choice." *Publius: The Journal of Federalism* 27: 41–60.

———. 2000. *Policy Entrepreneurs and School Choice.* Washington, DC: Georgetown University Press.

———. 2006. "Policy Entrepreneurs, Think Tanks, and Trusts." In *New Zealand Government and Politics*, 4th ed., ed. Raymond Miller. Melbourne: Oxford University Press, 536–46.

MINTROM, MICHAEL, and SANDRA VERGARI. 1996. "Advocacy Coalitions, Policy Entrepreneurs, and Policy Change." *Policy Studies Journal* 24: 420–34.

———. 1998. "Policy Networks and Innovation Diffusion: The Case of State Education Reforms." *Journal of Politics* 60: 126–48.

———. 2009. "Foundation Engagement in Education Policymaking: Assessing Philanthropic Support of School Choice Initiatives." In *Foundations and Public Policy*, ed. James M. Ferris. New York: The Foundation Center, 243–78.

MOE, TERRY M., ed. 1995. *Private Vouchers.* Stanford, CA: Hoover Institution Press.

MOHR, LAWRENCE B. 1969. "Determinants of Innovation in Organizations." *American Political Science Review* 63: 111–26.

NELSON, BARBARA. 1984. *Making an Issue of Child Abuse.* Chicago: University of Chicago Press.

NORTH, DOUGLASS C. 1990. *Institutions, Institutional Change, and Economic Performance.* New York: Cambridge University Press.

OLIVER, THOMAS R., and PAMELA PAUL-SHAHEEN. 1997. "Translating Ideas into Actions: Entrepreneurial Leadership in State Health Care Reforms." *Journal of Health Politics, Policy and Law* 22: 721–88.

OSTROM, ELINOR. 1990. *Governing the Commons: The Evolution of Institutions for Collective Action.* New York: Cambridge University Press.

———. 2007. "Institutional Rational Choice: An Assessment of the Institutional Analysis and Development Framework." In *Theories of the Policy Process*, 2nd ed., ed. Paul A. Sabatier. Boulder, CO: Westview Press, 21–64.

PETCHEY, ROLAND, JACKY WILLIAMS, and YVONNE H. CARTER. 2008. "From Street-Level Bureaucrats to Street-Level Policy Entrepreneurs? Central Policy and Local Action in Lottery-Funded Community Cancer Care." *Social Policy and Administration* 42: 59–76.

PETERS, B. GUY. 1994. "Agenda-Setting in the European Community." *Journal of European Public Policy* 1: 9–26.

PROVOST, COLIN. 2003. "State Attorneys General, Entrepreneurship, and Consumer Protection in the New Federalism." *Publius: The Journal of Federalism* 33: 37–53.

———. 2006. "The Politics of Consumer Protection: Explaining State Attorney General Participation in Multi-State Lawsuits." *Political Research Quarterly* 59: 609–18.

QUINN, ROBERT E. 2000. *Change the World: How Ordinary People Can Achieve Extraordinary Results.* San Francisco: Jossey-Bass.

RABE, BARRY. 2004. *Statehouse and Greenhouse: The Stealth Politics of America Climate Change Policy.* Washington, DC: Brookings Institution Press.

REINSTALLER, ANDREAS. 2005. "Policy Entrepreneurship in the Co-Evolution of Institutions, Preferences, and Technology: Comparing the Diffusion of Totally Chlorine Free Pulp Bleaching Technologies in the US and Sweden." *Research Policy* 34: 1366–84.

RINGIUS, LASSE. 2001. *Radioactive Waste Disposal at Sea: Public Ideas, Transnational Policy Entrepreneurs, and Environmental Regimes.* Cambridge, MA: MIT Press.

ROBERTS, NANCY C., and PAULA J. KING. 1991. "Policy Entrepreneurs: Their Activity Structure and Function in the Policy Process." *Journal of Public Administration Research and Theory* 1: 147–75.

———. 1996. *Transforming Public Policy: Dynamics of Policy Entrepreneurship and Innovation.* San Francisco: Jossey-Bass.

ROCHEFORT, DAVID A., and ROGER W. COBB, eds. 1994. *The Politics of Problem Definition.* Lawrence: University of Kansas Press.

SABATIER, PAUL A. 1988. "An Advocacy Coalition Framework of Policy Change and the Role of Policy-Oriented Learning Therein." *Policy Sciences* 21: 129–68.

———. ed. 2007. *Theories of the Policy Process,* 2nd ed. Boulder, CO: Westview Press.

SABATIER, PAUL A., and HANK JENKINS-SMITH. 1993. *Policy Change and Learning: An Advocacy Coalition Approach.* Boulder, CO: Westview Press.

SABATIER, PAUL A., and CHRISTOPHER WEIBLE. 2007. "The Advocacy Coalition Framework—Innovations and Clarifications." In *Theories of the Policy Process,* 2nd ed., ed. Paul A. Sabatier. Boulder, CO: Westview Press.

SCHARPF, FRITZ W. 1997. *Games Real Actors Play: Actor-Centered Institutionalism in Policy Research.* Boulder, CO: Westview Press.

SCHATTSCHNEIDER, ELMER. 1960. *The Semi-Sovereign People.* Hinsdale: The Dryden Press.

SCHLESINGER, JOSEPH A. 1991. *Political Parties and the Winning of Office.* Ann Arbor: University of Michigan Press.

SCHNEIDER, ANNE, and HELEN INGRAM. 1993. "Social Construction of Target Populations: Implications for Politics and Policy." *The American Political Science Review* 87: 334–47.

SCHNEIDER, MARK, PAUL TESKE, and MICHAEL MINTROM. 1995. *Public Entrepreneurs: Agents for Change in American Government.* Princeton, NJ: Princeton University Press.

SCHÖN, DONALD A., and MARTIN REIN. 1994. *Frame Reflection: Toward the Resolution of Intractable Policy Controversies.* New York: Basic Books.

SCOTT, W. RICHARD. 2001. *Institutions and Organizations,* 2nd ed. Thousand Oaks, CA: Sage Publications.

SHIPAN, CHARLES R., and CRAIG VOLDEN. 2006. "Bottom-Up Federalism: The Diffusion of Antismoking Policies from U.S. Cities to States." *American Journal of Political Science* 50: 825–43.

STONE, DEBORAH. 1997. *Policy Paradox: The Art of Political Decision Making.* New York: W.W. Norton.

STONE, DIANA. 2004. "Transfer Agents and Global Networks in the 'Transnationalization' of Policy." *Journal of European Public Policy* 11: 545–66.

TEODORO, MANUEL P. 2009. "Bureaucratic Job Mobility and The Diffusion of Innovations." *American Journal of Political Science* 53: 175–89.

TESKE, PAUL E. 2004. *Regulation in the States.* Washington, DC: Brookings Institution Press.

THELEN, KATHLEEN. 1999. "Historical Institutionalism in Comparative Politics." *Annual Review of Political Science* 2: 369–404.

THOMAS, SUE. 1991. "The Impact of Women on State Legislative Policies." *The Journal of Politics* 53: 958–76.

TRUE, JACQUI, and MICHAEL MINTROM. 2001. "Transnational Networks and Policy Diffusion: The Case of Gender Mainstreaming." *International Studies Quarterly* 45: 27–57.

TRUE, JAMES L. 2000. "Avalanches and Incrementalism." *The American Review of Public Administration* 30: 3–18.

WALKER, JACK L. 1969. "The Diffusion of Innovations among the American States." *American Political Science Review* 63: 880–99.

WEISSERT, CAROL S. 1991. "Policy Entrepreneurs, Policy Opportunists, and Legislative Effectiveness." *American Politics Quarterly* 19: 262–74.

ZAHARIADIS, NIKOLAOS. 2007. "The Multiple Streams Framework: Structure, Limitations, Prospects." In *Theories of the Policy Process*, 2nd edition. Paul A. Sabatier, ed. Boulder, CO: Westview Press, 65–92.

ZHU, XUFENG. 2008. "Strategy of Chinese Policy Entrepreneurs in the Third Sector: Challenges of 'Technical Infeasibility.'" *Policy Sciences* 41: 315–34.

ZIPPEL, KATHRIN. 2004. "Transnational Advocacy Networks and Policy Cycles in the European Union: The Case of Sexual Harassment." *Social Politics* 11: 57–85.

27

Background on the Institutional Analysis and Development Framework

Elinor Ostrom

... An institutional framework should identify the major types of structural variables that are present to some extent in all institutional arrangements, but whose values differ from one type of institutional arrangement to another. The IAD framework is thus a multi-tier conceptual map. Recently, the IAD has been integrated into a broader framework for examining SESs and I will discuss this later in the article. There have, however, been a few small changes made in the earlier way the framework was represented, which I will introduce here.

The terms "action arena" and "action situation," used until recently when arraying the IAD framework, have confused many readers. I have repeatedly been asked, what in the world is the difference? In the 1980s, Workshop colleagues were concerned that "the actor" be separated from "the situation" so that diverse theories of behavior would all be consistent with the framework. Thus, it was posited that the action arena contained an action situation and actors. When integrating the IAD into a broader framework for social-ecological systems, it was not possible to keep as much detail about the difference between actors and the situation. ... [A]s discussed by McGinnis (2011), the IAD is simplified to focus on the action situation leading to interactions and outcomes. ... [T]hen one opens up the action situation and looks at the component parts of it, one can specify how one is analyzing the actor at that level.

From Elinor Ostrom, "Background on the Institutional Analysis and Development Framework," *Policy Studies Journal*, Vol. 39, No. 1, 2011, pp. 7–27.

Thus, a key part of the framework is the identification of an action situation and the resulting patterns of interactions and outcomes, and evaluating these outcomes. The problem could be at an operational tier where actors interact in light of the incentives they face to generate outcomes directly in the world. Examples of operational problems include:

- Evaluating the service production agencies serving metropolitan areas (Oakerson & Parks, 2011).
- Exploring why day care centers vary substantially in delivering child care services (Bushouse, 2011).
- The question of how to invest in irrigation infrastructures so that capital investments enhance, rather than detract from, the organizational capabilities of local farmers (Joshi, Ostrom, Shivakoti, & Lam, 2000; Shivakoti et al., 2005).

The problem could also be at a policy (or collective-choice) tier where decision makers repeatedly have to make policy decisions within the constraints of a set of collective-choice rules. The policy decisions then affect the structure of situations, or at a constitutional tier that affects who participates in policymaking. The problem could as well be at a constitutional tier where decisions are made about who is eligible to participate in policymaking and about the rules that will be used to undertake policymaking.

The first step in analyzing a problem is thus to identify a conceptual unit—called an action situation—that can be utilized to describe, analyze, predict, and explain behavior within institutional arrangements. An actor within an action situation (an individual or a firm) includes assumptions about four clusters of variables:

1. The resources that an actor brings to a situation;
2. The valuation actors assign to states of the world and to actions;
3. The way actors acquire, process, retain, and use knowledge contingencies and information; and
4. The processes actors use for selection of particular courses of action.

Action situations are the social spaces where individuals interact, exchange goods and services, solve problems, dominate one another, or fight (among the many things that individuals do in action situations). A major proportion of theoretical work stops at this level and takes the variables specifying the situation and the motivational and cognitive structure of an actor as givens. Analysis proceeds toward the prediction of the likely behavior of individuals in such a structure.

An institutional analyst can take two additional steps after making an effort to understand the initial structure of an action situation. One step digs deeper and inquires into the factors that affect the structure of the situation (Kiser & Ostrom, 1982). A second step explores how an action situation changes over time in light of how the outcomes at an earlier time affect perceptions and strategies over time (Cox & Ostrom, 2010).

DIAGNOSIS AND EXPLANATION WITHIN THE FRAME OF AN ACTION SITUATION

The term "action situation" is used to refer to an analytic concept that enables an analyst to isolate the immediate structure affecting a process of interest to the analyst for the purpose of explaining regularities in human actions and results, and potentially to reform them. ... [A] common set of variables used to describe the structure of an action situation includes (i) the set of actors, (ii) the specific positions to be filled by participants, (iii) the set of allowable actions and their linkage to outcomes, (iv) the potential outcomes that are linked to individual sequences of actions, (v) the level of control each participant has over choice, (vi) the information available to participants about the structure of the action situation, and (vii) the costs and benefits—which serve as incentives and deterrents—assigned to actions and outcomes. In addition, whether a situation will occur once, a known finite number of times, or indefinitely affects the strategies of individuals. When one is explaining actions and cumulated results within the framework of an action situation, these variables are the "givens" that one works with to describe the structure of the situation.

These are also the common elements used in game theory to construct formal game models.

To illustrate the relation of IAD, let us use the working parts of an action situation to help organize an analysis of the appropriation (harvesting) activities related to natural resources (see E. Ostrom, Gardner, & Walker, 1994; E. Ostrom, Schroeder, & Wynne, 1993). In an analysis of appropriation problems concerning overharvesting from a common-pool resource situation, for example, answers to the following questions are needed before one can proceed far with analysis:

- The set of actors: Who and how many individuals withdraw resource units (e.g., fish, water, fodder) from this resource system?
- The positions: What positions exist (e.g., members of an irrigation association, water distributors-guards, and a chair)?
- The set of allowable actions: Which types of harvesting technologies are used? (e.g., are chainsaws used to harvest timber? Are there open and closed seasons? Do fishers return fish smaller than some limit to the water?)
- The potential outcomes: What geographic region and what events in that region are affected by participants in these positions? What chain of events links actions to outcomes?
- The level of control over choice: Do appropriators take the above actions on their own initiative, or do they confer with others? (e.g., before entering the forest to cut fodder, does an appropriator obtain a permit?)
- The information available: How much information do appropriators have about the condition of the resource itself, about other appropriators' cost and benefit functions, and about how their actions cumulate into joint outcomes?
- The costs and benefits of actions and outcomes: How costly are various actions to each type of appropriator, and what kinds of benefits can be achieved as a result of various group outcomes?

The Actor

The actor in a situation can be thought of as a single individual or as a group functioning as a corporate actor. The term "action" refers to those behaviors to which the acting individual or group attaches a subjective and instrumental meaning. All analysts of microbehavior use an implicit or explicit theory or model of the actors in situations in order to derive inferences about the likely behavior in a situation (and thus about the pattern of joint results that may be produced). The analyst must make assumptions about how and what participants value; what resources, information, and beliefs they have; what their information-processing capabilities are; and what internal mechanisms they use to decide upon strategies.

For many problems, it is useful to accept the classical political economy view that an individual's choice of strategy in any particular situation depends on how he or she perceives and weighs the benefits and costs of various strategies and their likely outcomes (Radnitzky, 1987). The most well-established formal model of the individual used in institutional analysis is *homo economicus* as developed in neoclassical economics and game theory. To use *homo economicus*, one assumes that actors have complete and well-ordered preferences and complete information, and that they maximize the net value of expected returns to themselves. All of these assumptions are controversial and are being challenged on many fronts. Many institutional analysts tend to use a broader conception of individual actors. Many stress that perceived costs and benefits include the time and resources devoted to establishing and maintaining relationships (Williamson, 1979), as well as the value that individuals attach to establishing a reputation for being reliable and trustworthy (Breton & Wintrobe, 1982).

Alternatively, one could assume that the individuals who calculate benefits and costs are fallible learners who vary in terms of the number of other persons whose perceived benefits and costs are important to them and in terms of their personal commitment to keeping promises and honoring forms of reciprocity extended to them (E. Ostrom, 1998; 2010; Simon, 1972). Fallible learners can, and often do, make mistakes. Settings differ, however, in whether the institutional incentives involved encourage people to learn from these mistakes. Fallibility and the capacity to learn can thus be viewed as assumptions of a more general theory of the individual. One can then presume that the various institutional arrangements that individuals use in governing and managing public goods, common-pool resources, toll goods (or other problematic situations) offer them different incentives and opportunities to learn. In some settings, the incentives lead them to repeat the mistakes of the past. In others, the rate of effective learning about how to improve performance over time is rapid.

When fallible, learning individuals interact in frequently repeated and simple situations, it is possible to model them as if they had complete information about the variables relevant to making choices in those situations. In highly competitive environments, a further assumption can be made that the individuals who survive the selective pressure of the environment act as if they are maximizers of a key variable associated with survival in that environment (e.g., profits or fitness) (Alchian, 1950; Dosi & Egidi, 1991). When individuals face a relatively simple decision situation where institutions generate accurate information about the variables relevant to a particular problem, that problem can be adequately represented as a straightforward, constrained maximization problem.

The most fully developed, explicit theories of individual choice compatible with the IAD framework—game theory and neoclassical economic theory—involve strong assumptions such as unlimited computational capability and full maximization of net benefits. For some field settings, these theories generate empirically confirmed explanatory and diagnostic results. When analyzing commodity auction markets that are run repeatedly in a setting where property rights are well defined and enforced at a relatively low cost to buyers and sellers, theories of market behavior and outcome based on complete information and maximization of profits predict outcomes well (Banks, Plott, & Porter, 1988; Kagel, Levin, & Harstad, 1995). Using these assumptions about individual choice turns out to be a very useful way of doing institutional analysis when the problematic settings closely approximate this type of very constrained and competitive choice.

Many of the situations of interest in understanding social dilemmas, however, are uncertain and complex. Therefore, one needs to substitute the assumption of bounded rationality—that persons are intendedly rational but only limitedly so—for the assumptions of perfect information and utility maximization used in axiomatic choice theory (see Jones, 2003; Simon, [1947], 1965, 1972; Williamson, 1985). Information search is costly, and the information-processing capabilities of human beings are limited. Individuals therefore often must make choices based on incomplete knowledge of all possible alternatives and their likely outcomes. With incomplete information and imperfect information-processing capabilities, individuals may make mistakes in choosing strategies designed to realize a set of goals (V. Ostrom, 2010). Over time, however, they can acquire a greater understanding of their situation and adopt strategies that result in higher returns. Reciprocity may develop, rather than strictly narrow, short-term pursuit of self-interest (Hyden, 1990; Oakerson, 1993; Walker & Ostrom, 2009).

Individuals rarely have access to the same information known by others with whom they interact. For example, how much any one individual contributes to a joint undertaking is often difficult for others to judge. When joint outcomes depend on multiple actors contributing inputs that are costly and difficult to measure, incentives exist for individuals to behave opportunistically (Williamson, 1975). Opportunism—deceitful behavior intended to improve one's own welfare at the expense of others—may take many forms, from inconsequential, perhaps unconscious, shirking to a carefully calculated effort to defraud others with whom one is engaged in ongoing relationships. The opportunism of individuals who may say one thing and do something else further compounds the problem of uncertainty in a given situation. The level of opportunistic behavior that may occur in any setting is affected by the norms and rules used to govern relationships in that setting, as well as by attributes of the decision environment itself.

Predicting Outcomes Within an Action Situation

Depending upon the analytical structure of a situation and the particular assumptions about the actor used, the analyst makes strong or weak inferences about results. In tightly constrained, one-shot, action situations under conditions of complete information, where participants are motivated to select particular strategies or chains of actions that jointly lead to stable equilibria, an analyst can frequently make strong inferences and predict the likely patterns of behavior and outcomes.

When no limit exists on the number of appropriators from a common-pool resource or on the amount of harvesting activities they undertake, for example, one can develop a mathematical model of an open-access, common-pool resource (see, for example, E. Ostrom et al., 1994). When the net benefits of harvesting increase for the initial set of resource units withdrawn and decrease thereafter, each appropriator acting independently tends to make decisions that jointly yield a deficient equilibrium. A model of an open-access, common-pool resource generates a clear prediction of a race to use up the resource, leading to high social costs. Both field research and laboratory experimental research strongly support the predictions of overuse and potential destruction of open-access, common-pool resources where appropriators cannot communicate and learn about each other's behavior and/or do not share access to collective-choice situations in which to change the open-access structure they face (Janssen, Holahan, Lee, & Ostrom, 2010; E. Ostrom et al., 1994).

Many situations, however, do not generate such unambiguous results. Instead of making completely independent or autonomous decisions, individuals may be embedded in communities where initial norms of fairness and conservation may change the structure of the situation dramatically. Within these situations, participants may adopt a broader range of strategies. Further, they may change their strategies over time as they learn about the results of past actions (Boyd & Richerson, 1985). The institutional analyst examining these more open, less-constrained situations makes weaker inferences and predicts the patterns of outcomes that are more-or-less likely to result from a particular type of situation. In laboratory experiments, for example, giving subjects in a public good or common-pool resource situation opportunities to communicate generally increases the joint outcomes they achieve (Isaac & Walker, 1988;

E. Ostrom & Walker, 1991). In field settings, enabling individuals to engage in face-to-face discussions for only a few meetings will usually not increase the probability of improved outcomes, but repeated opportunities will (Ghate, 2004; Mwangi, 2007; Shivakumar, 2005). Many factors affect the likelihood of successful long-term governance of resources.

In field settings, it is hard to tell where one action situation starts and another stops. Life continues in what appears to be a seamless web as individuals move from home to market to work (action situations typically characterized by reciprocity, by exchange, or by team problem solving or command). Further, within situations, choices of actions within a set of rules as contrasted to choices among future rules are frequently made without a recognition that the level of action has shifted. So, when a "boss" says to an "employee," "How about changing the way we do X?" and the two discuss options and jointly agree upon a better way, they have shifted from taking actions within previously established rules to making decisions about the rules structuring future actions. In other words, in IAD language, they have shifted to a collective-choice situation.

Evaluating Outcomes

In addition to predicting outcomes, the institutional analyst may evaluate the outcomes that are being achieved as well as the likely set of outcomes that could be achieved under alternative institutional arrangements. Evaluative criteria are applied to both the outcomes and the processes of achieving outcomes. Although analysts may use many evaluative criteria, let us briefly focus on (i) economic efficiency, (ii) equity through fiscal equivalence, (iii) redistributional equity, (iv) accountability, (v) conformance to values of local actors, and (vi) sustainability.

ECONOMIC EFFICIENCY. Economic efficiency is determined by the magnitude of net benefits associated with an allocation of resources. The concept of efficiency plays a central role in studies estimating the benefits and costs or rates of return to investments, which are often used to determine the economic feasibility or desirability of public policies. When considering alternative institutional arrangements, therefore, it is crucial to consider how revisions in the rules will alter behavior and hence the allocation of resources.

FISCAL EQUIVALENCE. Two principal means exist for assessing equity: (i) on the basis of the equality between individuals' contributions to an effort and the benefits they derive and (ii) on the basis of differential abilities to pay. The concept of equity that underlies an exchange economy holds that those who benefit from a service should bear the burden of financing that service. Perceptions of fiscal equivalence or a lack thereof can affect the willingness of individuals to contribute toward the development and maintenance of resource systems.

REDISTRIBUTIONAL EQUITY. Policies that redistribute resources to poorer individuals are of considerable importance. Thus, although efficiency would dictate that scarce resources be used where they produce the greatest net benefit, equity goals may temper this objective, and the result is the provision of facilities that benefit particularly needy groups. Redistributional objectives may in some settings conflict with the goal of achieving fiscal equivalence.

ACCOUNTABILITY. In a democratic polity, officials should be accountable to citizens concerning the development and use of public facilities and natural resources. Concern for accountability need not conflict greatly with efficiency and equity goals. Indeed, achieving efficiency requires that information about the preferences of citizens be available to decision makers. Institutional arrangements that effectively aggregate this information assist in realizing efficiency at the same time that they serve to increase accountability and to promote the achievement of redistributional objectives.

CONFORMANCE TO VALUES OF LOCAL ACTORS. In addition to accountability, one may wish to evaluate how those outcomes fit the values of those involved. Are public officials or local leaders able to cheat and go undetected to obtain very high payoffs? Are those who keep promises more likely to be rewarded and advanced in their careers? How do those who repeatedly interact within a set of institutional arrangements learn to relate to one another over the long term?

SUSTAINABILITY. Finally, unless institutional arrangements are able to respond to ever-changing environments, the sustainability of situations is likely to suffer. Rural areas of developing countries are often faced with natural disasters and highly localized special circumstances. If an institutional arrangement is too inflexible to cope with these unique conditions, it is unlikely to prosper. For example, if an irrigation system is centrally controlled and allocates only a specific amount of resources to annual and periodic maintenance, it may not be able to meet the special needs associated with a major flood that destroys a section of the canal system.

Trade-offs are often necessary in using performance criteria as a basis for selecting from alternative institutional arrangements. It is particularly difficult to choose between the goals of efficiency and redistributional equity. The trade-off issue arises most explicitly in considerations of alternative methods of funding public projects. Economically efficient pricing of the use of an existing resource or facility should reflect only the incremental maintenance costs and any external or social costs associated with its use. This is the well-known, efficiency-pricing principle that requires that prices equal the marginal costs of usage. The principle is especially problematic in the case of public goods where the marginal cost of another user utilizing the good is zero; hence, the efficient price is also zero. Zero user prices, however, require that all sources of resource mobilization be tax-based and thereby induce other kinds of perverse incentives and potential inefficiencies. Evaluating how institutional arrangements compare across overall criteria is a challenge. Analytical examination of the likely trade-offs between intermediate costs is valuable in attempts to understand comparative institutional performance (see Eggertsson, 2005; E. Ostrom et al., 1993, chap. 5; Webb & Shivakoti, 2008).

VIEWING ACTION SITUATIONS AS PARTIALLY DEPENDENT ON RULES

Underlying the way analysts conceptualize action situations are assumptions about the rules individuals use to order their relationships, about attributes of states of the world and their transformations, and about the attributes of the community within which the situation occurs. Some analysts are not interested in the role of these underlying variables and focus only on a particular situation whose structure is given. On the other hand, analysts may be more interested in one factor affecting the structure of situations than they are interested in others. Sociologists tend to be more interested in how shared value systems affect the ways humans organize their relationships with one another. Environmentalists tend to focus on a wide diversity of physical and biological variables as these interact and create opportunities or constraints on the situations human beings face. Given the importance of rules for policy analysis, let us dig deeper into this important set of variables.

The Concept of Rules

Rules are shared understandings among those involved that refer to enforced prescriptions about what actions (or states of the world) are required, prohibited, or permitted. All rules are the result of implicit or explicit efforts to achieve order and predictability among humans by creating classes of persons (positions) that are then required, permitted, or forbidden to take classes of actions in relation to required, permitted, or forbidden states of the world (Crawford & Ostrom, 2005; V. Ostrom, 1997; Siddiki, Weible, Basurto, & Calanni, 2011).

In an open and democratic governance system, many sources exist for the rules and norms that individuals use in everyday life. It is not considered illegal or improper for individuals to organize themselves and craft their own rules, if the activities they engage in are legal. In addition to the legislation and regulations of a formal central government, there are apt to be laws passed by regional, local, and special governments. Within private firms and voluntary associations, individuals are authorized to adopt many

different rules about who is a member of the firm or association, how profits (benefits) are to be shared, and how decisions will be made. Each family constitutes its own rule-making body.

When individuals genuinely participate in the crafting of multiple layers of rules, some of that crafting will occur using pen and paper. Thus, the IAD can be used to analyze formal laws (Basurto, Kingsley, McQueen, Smith, & Weible, 2010; Heikkila, Schlager, & Davis, 2011; Loveman, 1993). Much of it, however, will occur as problem-solving individuals try to figure out how to do a better job in the future than they have done in the past. Colleagues in a work team are crafting their own rules when they might say to one another, "How about if you do A in the future, and I will do B, and before we ever make a decision about C again, we both discuss it and make a joint decision?" In a democratic society, problem-solving individuals do this all the time. They also participate in less fluid decision-making arrangements, including elections to select legislators, committee structures, and bureaucratic teams.

Thus, a deeper institutional analysis first attempts to understand the working rules and norms that individuals use in making decisions. Working rules are the set of rules to which participants would make reference if asked to explain and justify their actions to fellow participants. Although following a rule may become a "social habit," it is possible to make participants consciously aware of the rules they use to order their relationships. Individuals can consciously decide to adopt a different rule and change their behavior to conform to such a decision. Over time, behavior in conformance with a new rule may itself become habitual (see Harré, 1974; Shimanoff, 1980; Toulmin, 1974). The capacity of humans to use complex cognitive systems to order their own behavior at a relatively subconscious level frequently makes it difficult for empirical researchers to ascertain what working rules underlie an ongoing action situation.

Scholars frequently try to understand where working rules come from. In a system governed by a "rule of law," the general legal framework in use will have its source in actions taken in constitutional, legislative, and administrative settings augmented by decisions taken by individuals in many different particular settings. In other words, the rules-in-form are consistent with the rules-in-use (Sproule-Jones, 1993). In a system that is not governed by a "rule of law," there may be central laws and considerable effort made to enforce them, but individuals attempt to evade rather than obey the law (Guha-Khasnobis, Kanbur, & Ostrom, 2006; Sawyer, 2005).

Rule-following or conforming actions by humans are not as predictable as biological or physical behavior governed by scientific laws. All rules are formulated in human language. Therefore, rules share the problems of lack of clarity, misunderstanding, and change that typify any language-based phenomenon (Allen, 2005; Gellar, 2005; V. Ostrom, 1980, 1997, 2008). Words are always simpler than the phenomenon to which they refer.

The stability of rule-ordered actions depends upon the shared meaning assigned to words used to formulate a set of rules. If no shared meaning exists when a rule is first formulated, confusion will exist about what actions are required, permitted, or forbidden. Regularities in actions cannot result if those who must repeatedly interpret the meaning of a rule within action situations arrive at multiple interpretations. Because "rules are not self-formulating, self-determining, or self-enforcing" (V. Ostrom, 1980, p. 312), it is human agents who formulate them, apply them in particular situations, and attempt to enforce performance consistent with them (Aligica & Boettke, 2009, 2011). Even if shared meaning exists at the time of the acceptance of a rule, transformations in technology, in shared norms, and in circumstances more generally change the events to which rules apply: "Applying language to changing configurations of development increases the ambiguities and threatens the shared criteria of choice with an erosion of their appropriate meaning" (V. Ostrom, 1980, p. 312).

What rules are important for institutional analysis? A myriad of specific rules are used in structuring complex action situations. Scholars have been trapped into endless cataloging of rules not related to a method of classification most useful for theoretical explanations. But classification is a necessary step in developing a science. Anyone attempting to define a useful typology of rules must be concerned that the classification is more than a method for imposing superficial order onto an extremely large set of seemingly disparate rules.

The way this problem has been tackled using the IAD framework is to classify rules according to their impact on the elements of an action situation.

Rule Configurations

A first step toward identifying the working rules can be made by overtly examining how rules affect each of the variables of an action situation. A set of working rules that affect these variables should constitute the minimal but necessary set of rules needed to offer an explanation of actions and results based on the working rules used by participants to order their relationships within an action situation. Working rules alone, however, never provide a necessary and sufficient explanation of the structure of an action situation and results. The action situation is also affected by a diversity of biophysical variables as well as by the structure of a community in which it operates.

Seven types of working rules can affect the structure of an action situation. ... [T]hese are boundary rules, position rules, scope rules, choice rules, aggregation rules, information rules, and payoff rules. The cumulative effect of these seven types of rules affects the seven elements of an action situation.

Boundary rules affect the number of participants, their attributes and resources, whether they can enter freely, and the conditions they face for leaving. Position rules establish positions in the situation. Choice rules assign sets of actions that actors in positions at particular nodes may, must, or must not take. Scope rules delimit the potential outcomes that can be affected and, working backward, the actions linked to specific outcomes. Choice rules, combined with the scientific laws about the relevant states of the world being acted upon, determine the shape of the decision tree that links actions to outcomes. Aggregation rules affect the level of control that a participant in a position exercises in the selection of an action at a node. Information rules affect the knowledge-contingent information sets of participants. Payoff rules affect the benefits and costs that will be assigned to particular combinations of actions and outcomes, and they establish the incentives and deterrents for action. The set of working rules is a configuration in the sense that the effect of a change in one rule may depend upon the other rules-in-use.

Let us return to the example of conducting an analysis of common-pool resources (see Gibson, McKean, & Ostrom, 2000). Now I will focus on a series of questions that are intended to help the analyst get at the rules-in-use that help structure an action situation. Thus, to understand these rules, one would begin to ask questions such as:

- *Boundary rules:* Are the appropriators from this resource limited to local residents; to one group defined by ethnicity, race, caste, gender, or family structure; to those who win a lottery; to those who have obtained a permit; to those who own required assets (such as a fishing berth or land); or in some other way limited to a class of individuals that is bounded? Is a new participant allowed to join a group by some kind of entry fee or initiation? Must an appropriator give up rights to harvest upon migrating to another location?
- *Position rules:* How does someone move from being just a "member" of a group of appropriators to someone who has a specialized task, such as the chair of a management committee or a water distributor-guard?
- *Scope rules:* What understandings do these appropriators and others have about the authorized or forbidden geographic or functional domains? Do any maps exist showing who can appropriate from which region? Are there understandings about resource units that are "off-limits" (e.g., the historical rules in some sections of Africa that particular acacia trees could not be cut down even on land owned privately or communally)?
- *Choice rules:* What understandings do appropriators have about mandatory, authorized, or forbidden harvesting technologies? For fishers, must net size be of a particular grossness? Must forest users use some cutting tools and not others? What choices do various types of monitors have related to the actions they can take?
- *Aggregation rules:* What understandings exist concerning the rules affecting the choice of harvesting activities? Do certain

actions require prior permission from, or agreement of, others?
- *Information rules:* What information must be held secret, and what information must be made public?
- *Payoff rules:* How large are the sanctions that can be imposed for breaking any of the rules identified above? How is conformance to rules monitored? Who is responsible for sanctioning nonconformers? How reliably are sanctions imposed? Are any positive rewards offered to appropriators for any actions they can take? (e.g., is someone who is an elected official relieved of labor duties?)

The problem for the field researcher is that many rules-in-use are not written down. Nor can the field researcher simply be a survey worker asking a random sample of respondents about their rules. Many of the rules-in-use are not even conceptualized by participants as rules. In settings where the rules-in-use have evolved over long periods of time and are understood implicitly by participants, obtaining information about rules-in-use requires spending time at a site and learning how to ask nonthreatening, context-specific questions about rule configurations.[1]

End Notes

This article was originally presented at the Institutional Analysis and Development Symposium, University of Colorado, Denver, April 9–10, 2010. It draws on and extends a chapter on "Institutional Rational Choice: An Assessment of the Institutional Analysis and Development Framework," in *Theories of the Policy Process,* 2nd ed., Paul Sabatier. Boulder, CO: Westview Press, 2009. The author appreciates the support provided by the National Science Foundation, the Ford Foundation, and the MacArthur Foundation. Comments by the other participants at the IAD Symposium were extremely helpful as were the comments by two anonymous reviewers. The thoughtful editing of Patty Lezotte and David Price has helped improve the manuscript.

1. The International Forestry Resources and Institutions research program has faced this problem in developing research protocols that enable a network of research scholars to

gather the "same" information from a sample of forestry sites located in multiple countries of the world. To obtain reliable information about rules-in-use, one has to have several discussions with users where one slowly develops an understanding of the rules-in-use at a particular site. One cannot use a structured survey of respondents to obtain reliable information. Reliability results from coding information about rules-in-use after repeated discussions with users and discussions among members of the research team (see Moran & Ostrom, 2005; E. Ostrom & Wertime, 2000).

References

ALCHIAN, ARMEN A. 1950. "Uncertainty, Evolution, and Economic Theory." *Journal of Political Economy* 58 (3): 211–21.

ALIGICA, PAUL DRAGOS, and PETER BOETTKE. 2009. *Challenging Institutional Analysis and Development: The Bloomington School.* New York: Routledge.

———. 2011. "The Two Social Philosophies of Ostroms' Institutionalism." *Policy Studies Journal* 39 (1): 23–43.

ALLEN, BARBARA. 2005. *Tocqueville, Covenant, and the Democratic Revolution: Harmonizing Earth with Heaven.* Lanham, MD: Lexington Books.

BANKS, JEFFREY, CHARLES R. PLOTT, and DAVID P. PORTER. 1988. "An Experimental Analysis of Unanimity in Public Goods Provision Mechanisms." *Review of Economic Studies* 55: 301–22.

BASURTO, XAVIER, GORDON KINGSLEY, KELLY MCQUEEN, MSHADONI SMITH, and CHRISTOPHER WEIBLE. 2010. "A Systematic Approach to Institutional Analysis: Applying Crawford and Ostrom's Grammar." *Political Research Quarterly* 63 (3): 523–37.

BASURTO, XAVIER, and ELINOR OSTROM. 2009. "Beyond the Tragedy of the Commons." *Economia delle fonti di energia e dell'ambiente* 52 (1): 35–60.

BOYD, ROBERT, and PETER J. RICHERSON. 1985. *Culture and the Evolutionary Process.* Chicago: University of Chicago Press.

BRETON, ALBERT, and RONALD WINTROBE. 1982. *The Logic of Bureaucratic Conduct: An Economic Analysis of Competition, Exchange, and Efficiency in Private and Public Organizations.* Cambridge: Cambridge University Press.

BUSHOUSE, BRENDA K. 2011. "Governance Structures: Using IAD to Understand Variation in Service Delivery for Club Goods with Information Asymmetry." *Policy Studies Journal* 39 (1): 99–113.

CARDENAS, JUAN-CAMILO, MARCO A. JANSSEN, and FRANCOIS BOUSQUET. 2011. "Dynamics of Rules and Resources: Three New Field Experiments on Water, Forests and Fisheries." In *Handbook on Experimental Economics and the Environment,* ed. John A. List, and Michael Price. Cheltenham, UK: Edward Elgar Publishers, in press.

COX, MICHAEL, and ELINOR OSTROM. 2010. "Applying A Social-Ecological System Framework to the Study of the Taos Valley Irrigation System Over Time." Paper presented at the 13th Economics of Infrastructures Conference, Delft University of Technology, May 27–28, 2010, Delft, the Netherlands.

COX, JAMES C., ELINOR OSTROM, and JAMES M. WALKER. 2010. "Bosses and Kings: Asymmetric Power in Paired Common-Pool and Public Good Games." Paper presented at the Biennial Social Dilemmas Conference, Rice University, September 23–25, 2010, Houston, TX.

CRAWFORD, SUE E.S., and ELINOR OSTROM. 2005. "A Grammar of Institutions." In *Understanding Institutional Diversity,* Elinor Ostrom. Princeton, NJ: Princeton University Press, pp. 137–74. Originally published in *American Political Science Review* 89 (3) (1995): 582–600.

DOSI, GIOVANNI, and MASSIMO EGIDI. 1991. "Substantive and Procedural Uncertainty: An Exploration of Economic Behaviours in Changing Environments." *Journal of Evolutionary Economics* 1 (2): 145–68.

EGGERTSSON, THRÁINN. 2005. *Imperfect Institutions: Possibilities and Limits of Reform.* Ann Arbor: University of Michigan Press.

GARDNER, ROY, and ELINOR OSTROM. 1991. "Rules and Games." *Public Choice* 70 (2): 121–49.

GELLAR, SHELDON. 2005. *Democracy in Senegal: Tocquevillian Analytics in Africa.* New York: Palgrave Macmillan.

GHATE, RUCHA. 2004. *Uncommons in the Commons: Community Initiated Forest Resource Management.* New Delhi: Concept Publishing.

GIBSON, CLARK, MARGARET MCKEAN, and ELINOR OSTROM, eds. 2000. *People and Forests: Communities, Institutions, and Governance.* Cambridge, MA: MIT Press.

GUHA-KHASNOBIS, BASUDEB, RAVI KANBUR, and ELINOR OSTROM, eds. 2006. *Linking the Formal and*

Informal Economy: Concepts and Policies. Oxford, UK: Oxford University Press.

HARRÉ, ROM. 1974. "Some Remarks on 'Rule' As A Scientific Concept." In *Understanding Other Persons,* ed. Theodore Mischel. Oxford: Basil Blackwell, 143–84.

HEIKKILA, TANYA, EDELLA SCHLAGER, and MARK W. DAVIS. 2011. "The Role of Cross-Scale Institutional Linkages in Common Pool Resource Management: Assessing Interstate River Compacts." *Policy Studies Journal* 39 (1): 115–39.

HYDEN, GORAN. 1990. "Reciprocity and Governance in Africa." In *The Failure of the Centralized State: Institutions and Self-Governance in Africa,* ed. James Wunsch, and Dele Olowu. Boulder, CO: Westview Press, 245–69.

ISAAC, R. MARK, and JAMES M. WALKER. 1988. "Communication and Free-Riding Behavior: The Voluntary Contributions Mechanism." *Economic Inquiry* 26 (4): 585–608.

JANSSEN, MARCO, ROBERT HOLAHAN, ALLEN LEE, and ELINOR OSTROM. 2010. "Lab Experiments for the Study of Social-Ecological Systems." *Science* 328 (5978): 613–17.

JONES, ERIC C. 2003. "Building on Ostrom's 'The Rudiments of A Theory of the Origins, Survival and Performance of Common-Property Institutions.'" *Journal of Ecological Anthropology* 7 (1): 65–72.

JOSHI, NEERAJ N., ELINOR OSTROM, GANESH P. SHIVAKOTI, and WAI FUNG LAM. 2000. "Institutional Opportunities and Constraints in the Performance of Farmer-Managed Irrigation Systems in Nepal." *Asia-Pacific Journal of Rural Development* 10 (2): 67–92.

KAGEL, JOHN H., DAN LEVIN, and RONALD M. HARSTAD. 1995. "Comparative Static Effects of Number of Bidders and Public Information on Behavior in Second-Price Common Value Auctions." *International Journal of Game Theory* 24: 293–319.

KISER, LARRY L., and ELINOR OSTROM. 1982. "The Three Worlds of Action: A Metatheoretical Synthesis of Institutional Approaches." In *Strategies of Political Inquiry,* ed. Elinor Ostrom. Beverly Hills, CA: Sage, 179–222.

LOVEMAN, BRIAN. 1993. *The Constitution of Tyranny: Regimes of Exception in Spanish America.* Pittsburgh: University of Pittsburgh Press.

MCGINNIS, MICHAEL D. 2000. *Polycentric Games and Institutions.* Ann Arbor: University of Michigan Press.

———. 2011. "Networks of Adjacent Action Situations in Polycentric Governance." *Policy Studies Journal* 39 (1): 45–72.

MEINZEN-DICK, RUTH S., ANDRÉ DEVAUX, and IVONNE ANTEZANA. 2009. "Underground Assets: Potato Biodiversity to Improve the Livelihoods of the Poor." *International Journal of Agricultural Sustainability* 7 (4): 235–48.

MORAN, EMILIO, and ELINOR OSTROM, eds. 2005. *Seeing the Forest and the Trees: Human-Environment Interactions in Forest Ecosystems.* Cambridge, MA: MIT Press.

MWANGI, ESTHER. 2007. *Socioeconomic Change and Land Use in Africa: The Transformation of Property Rights in Maasailand.* New York: Palgrave Macmillan.

OAKERSON, RONALD J. 1993. "Reciprocity: A Bottom-Up View of Political Development." In *Rethinking Institutional Analysis and Development: Issues, Alternatives, and Choices,* eds. Vincent Ostrom, David Feeny, and Hartmut Picht. San Francisco, CA: ICS Press, 141–58.

OAKERSON, RONALD J., and ROGER B. PARKS. 2011. "The Study of Local Public Economies: Multi-organizational, Multi-level Institutional Analysis and Development." *Policy Studies Journal* 39 (1): 141–61.

OLOWU, DELE, and JAMES S. WUNSCH. 2004. *Local Governance in Africa: The Challenges of Democratic Decentralization.* Boulder, CO: Lynne Rienner.

OSTROM, ELINOR. 1998. "A Behavioral Approach to the Rational Choice Theory of Collective Action." *American Political Science Review* 92 (1): 1–22.

———. 2005. *Understanding Institutional Diversity.* Princeton, NJ: Princeton University Press.

———. 2007. "A Diagnostic Approach for Going Beyond Panaceas." *Proceedings of the National Academy of Sciences* 104 (39): 15181–87.

———. 2009. "Institutional Rational Choice: An Assessment of the Institutional Analysis and Development Framework." In *Theories of the Policy Process,* 2nd ed., ed. Paul Sabatier. Boulder, CO: Westview Press, 21–64.

———. 2010. "Beyond Markets and States: Polycentric Governance of Complex Economic Systems." *American Economic Review* 100 (3): 641–72.

———. 2011. "Reflections on 'Some Unsettled Problems of Irrigation'." *American Economic Review* 101 (1): 1–17.

OSTROM, ELINOR, and JAMES WALKER. 1991. "Communication in A Commons: Cooperation without External Enforcement." In *Laboratory Research in Political Economy,* ed. Thomas R. Palfrey. Ann Arbor: University of Michigan Press, 287–322.

OSTROM, ELINOR, and MARY BETH WERTIME. 2000. "IFRI Research Strategy." In *People and Forests: Communities, Institutions, and Governance,* ed. Clark Gibson, Margaret McKean, and Elinor Ostrom. Cambridge, MA: MIT Press, 243–68.

OSTROM, ELINOR, LARRY SCHROEDER, and SUSAN WYNNE. 1993. *Institutional Incentives and Sustainable Development: Infrastructure Policies in Perspective.* Boulder, CO: Westview Press.

OSTROM, ELINOR, ROY GARDNER, and JAMES WALKER. 1994. *Rules, Games, and Common-Pool Resources.* Ann Arbor: University of Michigan Press.

OSTROM, ELINOR, MARCO JANSSEN, and JOHN ANDERIES. 2007. "Going Beyond Panaceas." *Proceedings of the National Academy of Sciences* 104 (38): 15176–78.

OSTROM, VINCENT 1980. "Artisanship and Artifact." *Public Administration Review* 40: 309–17.

———. 1997. *The Meaning of Democracy and the Vulnerability of Democracies: A Response to Tocqueville's Challenge.* Ann Arbor: University of Michigan Press.

———. 2008. *The Intellectual Crisis in American Public Administration,* 3rd ed. Tuscaloosa: University of Alabama Press.

———. 2010. In *The Quest to Understand Human Affairs: Natural Resources Policy and Essays on Community and Collective Action,* Vol. 1 edited by Barbara Allen. Lanham, MD: Lexington Books.

PAHL-WOSTL, CLAUDIA. 2010. "Disentangle the Action Box: A Framework for Representing Collective Action in Resource Governance and Management Contexts." Working Paper. Osnabrück, Germany: University of Osnabrück.

POTEETE, AMY, MARCO JANSSEN, and ELINOR OSTROM. 2010. *Working Together: Collective Action, the Commons, and Multiple Methods in Practice.* Princeton, NJ: Princeton University Press.

RADNITZKY, GERARD. 1987. "Cost-Benefit Thinking the Methodology of Research: The 'Economic Approach' Applied to Key Problems to the Philosophy of Science." In *Economic Imperialism: The Economic Approach Applied Outside the Field of Economics,* ed. Gerard Radnitzky, and Peter Bernholz. New York: Paragon House, 283–334.

SAWYER, AMOS. 2005. *Beyond Plunder: Toward Democratic Governance in Liberia.* Boulder, CO: Lynne Rienner.

SHIMANOFF, SUSAN B. 1980. *Communication Rules: Theory and Research.* Beverly Hills, CA: Sage.

SHIVAKOTI, GANESH, DOUGLAS VERMILLION, WAI-FUNG LAM, ELINOR OSTROM, UJJWAL PRADHAN, and ROBERT YODER, eds. 2005. *Asian Irrigation in Transition: Responding to Challenges.* New Delhi: Sage.

SHIVAKUMAR, SUJAI. 2005. *The Constitution of Development: Crafting Capabilities for Self-Governance.* New York: Palgrave Macmillan.

SIDDIKI, SABA, CHRISTOPHER M. WEIBLE, XAVIER BASURTO, and JOHN CALANNI. 2011. "Dissecting Policy Designs: An Application of the Institutional Grammar Tool." *Policy Studies Journal* 39 (1): 73–97.

SIMON, HERBERT A. [1947] 1965. *Administrative Behavior: A Study of Decision-Making Processes in Administrative Organization.* New York: Free Press.

———. 1972. "Theories of Bounded Rationality." In *Decision and Organization: A Volume in Honor of Jacob Marschak,* ed. C. B. McGuire, and Roy Radner. Amsterdam: North Holland, 161–76.

SPROULE-JONES, MARK. 1993. *Governments at Work: Canadian Parliamentary Federalism and Its Public Policy Effects.* Toronto: University of Toronto Press.

TOULMIN, S. 1974. "Rules and Their Relevance for Understanding Human Behavior." In *Understanding Other Persons,* ed. Theodore Mischel. Oxford: Basil Blackwell, 185–215.

WALKER, JAMES, and ELINOR OSTROM. 2009. "Trust and Reciprocity As Foundations for Cooperation." In *Whom Can We Trust?: How Groups, Networks, and Institutions Make Trust Possible,* ed. Karen Cook, Margaret Levi, and Russell Hardin. New York: Russell Sage Foundation, 91–124.

WEBB, EDWARD L., and Ganesh P. Shivakoti, eds. 2008. *Decentralization, Forests and Rural Communities: Policy Outcomes in South and Southeast Asia.* New Delhi: Sage.

WEISSING, FRANZ J., and ELINOR OSTROM. 1991. "Irrigation Institutions and the Games Irrigators Play: Rule Enforcement without Guards." In *Game Equilibrium Models II: Methods, Morals, and Markets,* ed. Reinhard Selten. Berlin: Springer-Verlag, 188–262.

WILLIAMSON, OLIVER E. 1975. *Markets and Hierarchies: Analysis and Antitrust Implications.* New York: Free Press.

———. 1979. "Transaction Cost Economics: The Governance of Contractual Relations." *Journal of Law and Economics* 22 (2): 233–61.

———. 1985. *The Economic Institutions of Capitalism.* New York: Free Press.

28

The Mechanisms of Policy Diffusion

Charles R. Shipan and

Craig Volden

Policy innovation occurs whenever a government—a national legislature, a state agency, a city—adopts a new policy (Mintrom 1997a; Walker 1969). The impetus for this policy innovation can come from within the polity, such as when interest groups within a state push for the adoption of a new policy, or when electoral and institutional forces within a legislature affect the likelihood of adoption. Pressure for policy innovation also can come from outside the polity, with the spread of innovations from one government to another, a process known as *policy diffusion.*

The literature on policy diffusion is vast and expanding rapidly. Building on a series of classic early studies (e.g., Crain 1966; Gray 1973; Walker 1969), as well as more recent significant theoretical and methodological advances (e.g., Berry and Berry 1990; Berry and Baybeck 2005), scholars have conducted a number of studies of diffusion during the past decade. These studies have focused on the diffusion of a range of policies, including same-sex marriage bans (Haider-Markel 2001), education reform (Mintrom 1997a), abortion (Mooney and Lee 1995), the death penalty (Mooney and Lee 1999), and HMO reforms (Balla 2001), among many others. In addition, these and other studies have shed light on the processes by which diffusion takes place, focusing on factors that enable or hinder diffusion, including the

policy's success (Volden 2006), policy entrepreneurs (Balla 2001; Mintrom 1997a, 1997b), and the initiative process (Boehmke 2005).

Although these works have uncovered a great deal of evidence that policies do diffuse, much less is understood about the specific *mechanisms* that cause a policy to spread from one government to another. That is, if a second government adopts a policy because a first government has already done so, what explains that second government's action? Here we focus on four mechanisms of diffusion: *learning, economic competition, imitation*, and *coercion*. While these mechanisms are also relevant to diffusion across states and countries (e.g., Simmons, Dobbin, and Garrett 2006), our focus on city-to-city diffusion allows us to examine each mechanism individually as well as in conjunction with one another. Previous scholarship has often referred to multiple mechanisms of diffusion, but with few exceptions (e.g., Berry and Baybeck 2005; Boehmke and Witmer 2004; Weyland 2005, 2007) these studies have not tested one explanation against another.

Throughout this discussion, for the purpose of simplicity, we often write of the "city" taking action—learning or competing, for example. In reality, individual decision makers—mayors, managers, council members, bureaucrats, and others—are the critical actors in these cities.

From Charles R. Shipan and Craig Volden, "The Mechanisms of Policy Diffusion," *American Journal of Political Science*, Vol. 52, No. 4, October 2008, pp. 840–857.

Because of this large number of individuals and forms of government, we rely on the shorthand of referring to cities as actors. As is common in the diffusion literature, we believe the individual decision makers within these cities are interested in adopting beneficial policies, either as a means to reelection or reappointment or as an end in themselves. Such motivations are at work across all four mechanisms explored here.

The first mechanism of diffusion that we explore—learning—is the process that leads states to be called laboratories of democracy (Brandeis 1932). By observing the politics of policy adoption and the impact of those policies, policymakers can learn from the experiences of other governments. We follow most previous studies in adopting a general definition of learning: as Berry and Baybeck note, for example, "[w]hen confronted with a problem, decision makers simplify the task of finding a solution by choosing an alternative that has proven successful elsewhere" (2005, 505). Most generally, then, learning involves a determination of whether a policy adopted elsewhere has been successful. If the policy is deemed to be successful, then a city is more likely to adopt it.

Ideally, political and policy success would be readily observable to decision makers and researchers alike. When success is difficult to measure (as it is at the city level for antismoking policies), various shortcuts that are consistent with learning are taken. For instance, policymakers may interpret the broad adoption of a policy without subsequent abandonment over time as evidence of the success of the policy, or at least as evidence of maintained political support. Researchers, in turn, may explore the effect of the "opportunity to learn" on policy choice as a substitute for direct evidence of learning. Put simply, policymakers cannot learn about policies that have not yet been tried. They can learn more when multiple governments try the policy, and even more when such policies affect larger segments of society. The reliance of researchers on opportunity to learn is more appropriate for policies that are eventually clearly identified as successes, both politically (as evidenced by lack of repeals) and on policy grounds (as evidenced by studies of effectiveness in general). The antismoking policies studied here meet both of these criteria. If they did not—for

example, if evidence of success were limited or not found—then it would be more difficult to discern exactly what cities learn from the experiments of others. For our case, this "opportunity to learn" idea is expressed as follows.

> *Learning Hypothesis:* The likelihood of a city adopting a policy *increases* when the same policy is adopted broadly by other cities throughout the state.

A second mechanism—economic competition—is often raised in conjunction with learning, and these two mechanisms are viewed, at least implicitly, as the most common processes explaining policy diffusion. Two recent state politics studies have sought to disentangle these two mechanisms. Boehmke and Witmer (2004) explore state adoption of Indian gaming compacts, arguing that learning and economic competition are both important in explaining *initial* adoptions, whereas only economic competition explains *subsequent* compacts because previous experience with one's own compacts removes the need to learn from the experience of others. Berry and Baybeck (2005) argue that learning can take place across states generally, while economic competition is typically confined to individuals living near state borders. Using geographic information systems (GIS) technology, they isolate the effects of learning and of competition to explain lottery adoptions and welfare benefit levels.

Like these studies and others, we contend that economic competition can lead to the diffusion of policies with economic spillovers across jurisdictions. State welfare policy is a classic example. Fearful of becoming "welfare magnets" (Peterson and Rom 1990), states may face incentives to engage in a "race to the bottom" in welfare benefits due to competitive federalism (e.g., Bailey and Rom 2004; Volden 2002). Such competition may also take place at national or local levels of government, in policy areas ranging from education and the environment to infrastructure, minimum wages, and antismoking policies. In each instance, policymakers consider the economic effects of adoption (or lack of adoption) by other governments. If there are negative economic spillovers, where the government will be hurt if it adopts a policy that its neighbors lack, then it will be less likely to adopt the policy itself. On the other hand, if there are positive spillovers, such as are found by establishing uniformity in infrastructure, then governments will be more likely to adopt the policy of others. Consistent with both theoretical and empirical approaches to economic competition, we offer the following hypothesis.

> *Economic Competition Hypothesis:* The likelihood of a city adopting a policy *decreases* when there are negative economic spillovers from that adoption to nearby cities and *increases* with positive spillovers from nearby cities.

A third diffusion mechanism—imitation—has received much less attention in the state politics literature, but arises more frequently in comparative politics (e.g., Meseguer 2006; Simmons, Dobbin, and Garrett 2006) and has roots in social psychology and in studies of the diffusion of innovations across a multitude of fields of study (Rogers 1995). Sometimes also referred to as emulation, imitation involves copying the actions of another in order to look like that other. The nature of imitation can be understood in contrast to learning. In learning, policymakers focus on the policy itself—how was it adopted, was it effective, what were its political consequences? In contrast, imitation involves a focus on the other government—what did that government do and how can we appear to be the same? The crucial distinction is that learning focuses on the *action* (i.e., the policy being adopted by another government), while imitation focuses on the *actor* (i.e., the other government that is adopting the policy). Outside of the policy adoption context, a classic example of learning is avoiding touching the hot burner after observing someone doing so with bad effects, whereas imitation is jumping off the garage roof after observing your older brother doing so, without regard for the consequences. In the former case, it is the action that matters; in the latter, the actor. In the former, you learn about consequences; in the latter you simply aspire to be like the other actor.

Although imitation sometimes has been ignored or even mislabeled in the policy diffusion literature, it is wholly consistent with early studies of local and state policy adoptions. This literature focused on which states and cities were "leaders" or "laggards" (e.g., Crain 1966, Grupp and Richards 1975; Walker 1969). Innovative leaders were found to be larger, wealthier, and more cosmopolitan. Smaller communities aspire to be like these leaders, and therefore adopt the same policies as these leaders without necessarily thinking about the consequences of such adoptions. Clearly, policymakers in these smaller cities also may learn from the policy experiences of those in larger cities. And they also may worry about competition, leading them to adopt policies in an attempt to stem the flight of citizens and businesses to these larger cities. But above and beyond learning and competition, decision makers in smaller cities also may adopt policies simply because they want their communities to be as favorably viewed as the cities that are seen as leaders. They hope that such imitation will raise their profile and make them more attractive places to live, like their larger, wealthier, and more cosmopolitan neighbors. In our context, therefore, imitation may appear as smaller cities copying the policies of their larger neighbors.

> *Imitation Hypothesis:* The likelihood of a city adopting a policy *increases* when its nearest bigger neighbor adopts the same policy.

The fourth mechanism of diffusion—coercion—differs from the previous three. Like imitation, it is more commonly raised in the comparative politics literature (e.g., Simmons, Dobbin, and Garrett 2006) than in American politics. In the international setting, for example, countries can coerce one another through trade practices and economic sanctions. They can attempt to coerce others directly, or can do so through international institutions like the United Nations and the International Monetary Fund, which encourage or pressure governments to take actions that meet common expectations. Coercion was such a major concern to the founders of the U.S. Constitution that they established the commerce clause to minimize trade barriers and other coercive mechanisms across the states.

Although horizontal coercion across states or localities in the American federal system is therefore limited, vertical (or top-down) coercion is still quite possible. This should be of no surprise to scholars of policy diffusion, who have long noted that grants from the federal government to states and localities often stimulate policy adoptions (e.g., Allen, Pettus, and Haider-Markel 2004; Karch 2006; Shipan and Volden 2006; Walker 1973; Welch and Thompson 1980). For instance, the threat of lost highway funds coerced states into adopting lower speed limits and higher drinking ages. In addition to their influence through intergovernmental grants, higher levels of government can coercively influence the actions of lower levels by taking the lead in that policy area, setting their own minimum wage or antismoking restrictions, for example.

Even more coercive are *preemptive* policies. Because cities are creatures of the state, with no constitutionally specified sovereignty, state governments can pass laws that disallow any city action contrary to state law. In the area of antismoking policy, for example, such state-level preemptive policies were commonplace and were an explicit strategy of the tobacco industry to fight back increasingly stringent local laws (e.g., Givel and Glantz 2001). A locality still might pass weaker laws that ensure the continuance of the policy if the state were to reverse its stance; or it could enact alternative laws in order to provoke a court challenge; but, in either case, the usefulness and hence the likelihood of passage of such laws are greatly diminished.

> *Coercion Hypothesis:* The likelihood of a city adopting a policy *decreases* when the state adopts a similar policy that covers the city. This decrease is even more substantial when the state law *preempts* either future local laws on the same policy or future stronger laws.

We acknowledge that the theoretical distinctions among these four categories are starker than are the realworld empirical classifications of these diffusion mechanisms. For example, when a neighboring city restricts smoking in its restaurants, this provides an opportunity to learn, raises

some economic spillover considerations, *and* may induce imitation. Separating these effects from one another is difficult. Nevertheless, we believe that raising these theoretical and archetypal mechanisms as distinct from one another provides guidance for scholars to begin to disentangle these diffusion processes. Moreover, we argue that our focus on cities provides the variance necessary to explore these distinct mechanisms. For instance, whereas learning can take place over quite a distance, economic spillovers are geographically limited. Whereas one can learn from the experiences of smaller or larger cities, imitation is focused only on the larger leader cities. And whereas larger cities may be imitated, both smaller and larger cities alike may present economic competitive concerns if sufficiently proximate. Thus, despite overlap across diffusion mechanisms, we can distinguish among them conceptually. Such conceptual distinctions guide the variable operationalizations we use to empirically test our hypotheses.

THE TEMPORAL AND CONDITIONAL NATURE OF POLICY DIFFUSION MECHANISMS

Although a major goal of this article is to differentiate, both theoretically and empirically, among multiple mechanisms of diffusion, it is equally important to explore when each of these mechanisms takes place and why one mechanism may affect some cities more than would another mechanism. Therefore we advance two additional hypotheses.

First, we consider the *temporal* nature of each mechanism, which allows us to further distinguish among mechanisms and also to gain additional perspective on whether the operationalizations that we use are appropriate. Our starting point here is the realization that some mechanisms of diffusion should be short-lived, while others should have longer lasting effects. In the former category, we would expect to find imitation. When one city imitates another, it does so fairly quickly, as policymakers in that city imitate the actions of cities that are leaders and do so in order to look like those leaders. Because imitation involves no concern about the effects of policies, but rather only a desire to do whatever a leader city has done, the response to a policy adoption should be almost immediate. If the response does not come quickly, it becomes less likely over time, as policymakers will decide whether to imitate an action or not and then will move on to other ways to imitate the leader.

In contrast to imitation, the other two mechanisms of horizontal diffusion—learning and competition—should exhibit longer-term effects. First, consider learning. If policymakers are concerned only about how to navigate through the public policy process in order to bring about a policy adoption, then all the relevant information is revealed at the time of adoption. But if policymakers are interested in knowing the political and policy consequences of an adoption, then it may take months or years to evaluate the effectiveness of a particular policy. Regardless of what is being learned, the learning effect is unlikely to fade quickly—indeed, evidence of the effects of policies, once known, is likely to remain relevant to policymakers for a considerable period of time. Second, economic competition also should exhibit long-term effects. If governments are worried about the economic spillovers from another government's policies, that competitive pressure will remain for as long as the policy is in place.

Overall, then, we should expect to find different temporal effects for imitation than for learning and competition. For imitation, we would expect a strong initial effect that then should fade over time. For the other horizontal mechanisms, we should expect both an initial effect *and* an effect into the future (e.g., a city will continue to learn from other cities two or three years after those other cities have adopted a policy). Finally, for the coercion involved in vertical diffusion, the temporal effects are less clear. Preemptive laws may immediately influence local adoptions and those effects may persevere. Yet, localities may over time adopt laws testing whether the state restrictions still have teeth. Exploratory work below examines these alternatives, while our main temporal effects hypothesis spells out our predictions for the horizontal diffusion mechanisms.

> *Temporal Effects Hypothesis*: The effects of imitation are likely to be short-lived. Learning and economic competition, on the other hand, are likely to exhibit longer-term effects.

Second, we consider the *conditional* nature of each mechanism. Some cities are better equipped to learn from others; some are more susceptible to economic competition than are others. Some are more likely to follow leaders; and some are more likely to resist coercive actions. Although there may be many criteria that divide cities along these lines, one straightforward and broadly relevant city characteristic is simply the size of its population, which is likely to matter for each of the diffusion mechanisms we are exploring. Because larger cities tend to have bigger and more professional governments, they are more capable of learning from others. Larger cities are less likely to be influenced by local economic spillovers, partly because of their economic diversity and partly because their smaller neighbors are less economically threatening. Because they are already the leaders that others look up to (e.g., Crain 1966), larger cities also are less likely to engage in imitative behavior than are smaller cities. Finally, larger cities are more likely than smaller cities to confront the coercive power of the state. We present these ideas in the following Conditional Diffusion Hypotheses.

> *Conditional Learning Hypothesis*: Larger cities are more likely to learn from other cities.
> *Conditional Competition Hypothesis*: Larger cities are less susceptible to economic competition.
> *Conditional Imitation Hypothesis*: Larger cities are less likely to engage in imitation.
> *Conditional Coercion Hypothesis*: Larger cities are less likely to be coerced effectively....

29

Advocacy Coalition Framework, Social Construction, Policy Design & Emerging Trends

Matthew Nowlin

ADVOCACY COALITION FRAMEWORK

The Advocacy Coalition Framework (ACF) was initially devised by Paul Sabatier and Hank Jenkins-Smith (Jenkins-Smith, 1990; Sabatier, 1987, 1988; Sabatier & Jenkins-Smith, 1988), and was later expanded and clarified by Sabatier and Jenkins-Smith (1993, 1999) and Sabatier and Weible (2007). The focus of the ACF is on policy learning and policy change within a policy subsystem. Policy change was initially thought to occur as a result of policy learning or external shocks. External shocks include public opinion, changes in governing coalitions, and outputs from other subsystems (Sabatier & Jenkins-Smith, 1999). More recent iterations of the ACF have added internal (subsystem) shocks, and negotiated agreements between coalitions as factors influencing policy change (Sabatier & Weible, 2007).

Central to advocacy coalitions are shared policy core beliefs that are shaped by more abstract core beliefs. The ACF argues that shared beliefs result in coalitions that are homogenous (with regard to beliefs and patterns of coordination) and stable overtime. Weible, Sabatier, and McQueen (2009) examined over 80 applications of the ACF and found that coalitions are largely stable, particularly among "principal" members. However, coalition defections occur and coalitions are not necessarily homogenous in their beliefs. Some coalition members can vary in their policy core and secondary aspect beliefs and sub-coalitions may also exist.

Coalition homogeneity may be undermined by the political and/or self-interests of coalition members (Nohrstedt, 2010; Szarka, 2010). A long line of research in the ACF has examined the possible importance of interests with regard to coalition homogeneity and stability (see Szarka, 2010, pp. 8380 for a review). More recently, Nohrstedt (2010) finds that interests played a large role in nuclear policy making in Sweden. Political parties often made policy decisions based on strategic political concerns rather than normative beliefs. Another important aspect of coalition stability may be trust (Lubell, 2007). Lubell (2007) finds that shared policy core beliefs are predictive of the level of trust that coalition member's exhibit. Other work however, has noted that narrow coalitions based on normative beliefs may not be broad-based enough to encourage substantial policy change (Ansell, Reckhow, & Kelly, 2009). In sum, coalitions have been demonstrated as stable, however political or material interest may undermine their homogeneity. On the other hand, homogeneity may weaken the ability of a coalition to bring about policy change.

From Matthew Nowlin, "Policy Process Theory," *Policy Studies Journal*, Vol. 39, No. S1, 2011, pp. 41–60.

In addition to coalitions, the ACF has traditionally been concerned with subsystem dynamics. However, work by Jones and Jenkins-Smith (2009) argues that ACF scholars should examine more macro-level, trans-subsystem features of the policymaking system. These macro-level features include clusters of linked subsystems, public opinion, and policymaking venues. These features constitute the policy topography in which policy actors operate. Jones and Jenkins-Smith (2009) argue that public opinion, underutilized in ACF applications, is the foundation of the policy topography. They contend that shifts in public opinion can act as an exogenous shock and shift the policy topography and/or act as an endogenous shock, causing shifts within a particular subsystem.

Apart from public opinion, Jones and Jenkins-Smith (2009) offer two other types of possible shocks; salience disruptions and dimension-shifts. Focusing events and events within proximate subsystems can act as exogenous shocks to a subsystem causing a salience disruption. The 9/11 terrorist attacks are offered as an example of a salience disruption. A type of internal shock mentioned by Jones and Jenkins-Smith (2009) are policy dimension-shifts. Policy dimension-shifts occur when strategic policy entrepreneurs import arguments from another proximate linked subsystem. The scientific consensus regarding anthropogenic climate change is given as an example of an issue that could possibly be used to cause a dimension-shift within one of the subsystems linked to climate change (e.g., coal energy, air quality and pollution, and nuclear energy). The paper by Jones and Jenkins-Smith (2009) offer two important expansions to the ACF; the first is the role of public opinion as both a constraint on coalition strategy and a resource, and the second is the expansion of the ACF beyond subsystems (traditionally assumed to be independent and self-contained) to a policy topography model.

Recent work summarizing over 80 applications of the ACF (Weible et al., 2009) demonstrated that the ACF has developed into a strong research program; with a growing number of applications outside the United States and across several policy areas. The work discussed above examined one of the ACF's key assumptions; the stability and homogeneity of advocacy coalitions. Overall, coalitions have been found to be relatively stable overtime, but not consistently homogenous. Stability and homogeneity may be undermined by the interest considerations of some coalition members. Weible et al. note that future work should differentiate between principal and auxiliary coalition members (2009, 130). The conjecture would be that principal coalition members are more likely to be both stable and homogenous, whereas auxiliary members may demonstrate stability but are less likely to be homogenous. Apart from coalitions, Jones and Jenkins-Smith (2009) argue that ACF scholars should examine the trans-subsystem dynamics of the policy topography model. This model offers insights based on public opinion and strategic policy entrepreneurs that can be incorporated into a fuller understanding of policy learning and change.

SOCIAL CONSTRUCTION AND POLICY DESIGN

The social construction and policy design framework is focused on the way that attitudes regarding the target population of a policy can influence the type of policy that is created. In addition, the framework is also focused on the reciprocal— how policy can impact the way that target populations are viewed. The social construction framework was initially developed by Schneider and Ingram (1993, 1997) and later clarifications were made by Ingram, Schneider, and DeLeon (2007).

A recent review of 47 applications of the social construction and policy design framework found that the framework possessed "broad utility" for both scholars and practitioners (Pierce, Schumacher, Siddiki, & Pattison, 2010, p. 20). The review examined applications by substantive policy domain and by data collection and analysis methods (Pierce et al.). Pierce et al. find that the majority of applications of the social construction and policy design framework were in the areas of health and welfare policy. Other areas included homeland security /defense, the environment, fiscal, education, immigration/race relations, and criminal justice. In terms of data collection and analysis, the majority of applications (69 percent) used qualitative methods, 20 percent were quantitative, and the remaining used mixed methods (Pierce et al.).

Recent work by Reich and Barth (2010), apply the social construction framework to policies regarding in-state tuition for undocumented college students. The authors compare in-state tuition policies across two states; Kansas and Arkansas. The states enacted different policies even though they are similar in terms of demographics and political institutions. Kansas adopted a policy that allows undocumented residents to pay in-state tuition, while similar legislation in Arkansas was not successful. Reich and Barth (2010) compared the policy deliberations that occurred in both states and found that undocumented students in Kansas where constructed as "proto-citizens", whereas the debate in Arkansas focused on questions about jurisdictional authority. They concluded that one of the key factors was the positive construction of the students in Kansas. This construction added a dimension to the debate (students, brought here as children, attempting to better their situation through education) that was able to garner enough Republican support to allow the legislation to pass. Reich and Barth (2010) provide valuable empirical and quantitative support for the importance of social constructions for policy design and adoption.

The social construction and policy design framework employs policy design as both a dependent variable and an independent variable (Ingram et al., 2007; Schneider & Sidney, 2009). PoUcy design consists of nine elements that include (1) problem definition and goals, (2) benefits and burdens to be distributed, (3) target population, (4) rules, (5) tools, (6) implementation structures, (7) social constructions, (8) rationales, and (9) underlying casual assumptions (Schneider & Sidney, 2009, pp. 104–105).

Some recent work has argued that policy design should be incorporated as a dependent variable in policy process theories and frameworks (James & Jorgensen, 2009; Real-Dato, 2009). James and Jorgensen (2009) argue that future work should examine the role of policy knowledge (i.e., policy analysis and policy evaluation) in determining policy design. In addition to being a dependent variable, policy design can be an independent variable in a feed-forward process. Schneider and Sidney (2009) identify four types of feed-forward effects that further work should develop. The first is the way that poUcy designs "create target populations," the second includes "specific rules or allocation of resources that differentially impact citizens," the third is the way that policies "embed many aspects of the rhetoric in the policy debate" specifically casual assumptions and rationales, and finally the impact of policy on pressing issues such as political participation, public cynicism, income inequality, and political rhetoric (Schneider & Sidney, 2009, p. 111).

Traditional research on policy design focused on the way in which problems were defined. The social construction and policy design framework argues scholars should also focus on the way in which target populations of a policy are defined. Building on this insight, the work by Reich and Barth (2010) found that the way that undocumented students were defined (i.e., socially constructed) played a large role in determining whether in-state tuition legislation was successful. In addition, other research brought into view considerations of the importance of policy design as both a dependent variable and an independent variable in models of the policy process. The majority of policy process research attempts to explain policy change. Scholars should be encouraged to examine issues of policy design as well.

While the limited time scale (2008 to 2010) of this essay makes identifying "trends" somewhat difficult, the following themes have emerged recently and I expect will continue to be studied by scholars of the policy process.

NARRATIVE POLICY FRAMEWORK

Recent work on the role of narratives in the policy process has offered new insight into how individuals process political and/or policy-relevant information (Jones & McBeth, 2010; McBeth et al., 2007, 2010). According to the narrative policy framework (NPF), individuals understand policy issues in terms of "stories" that include a setting or context, a plot, characters (heroes and villains), and a moral to the story (Jones & McBeth, 2010). The authors also argue that policy narratives need not be "relative" (i.e., context specific) but can be generalizable if "anchored" to normative beliefs. The authors suggest partisanship, ideology, and Cultural Theory (CT) as possible anchors that could guide the interpretation of policy narratives.

Jones and McBeth (2010) lay out several hypotheses, at both the micro and meso levels, that can be empirically tested. The micro level hypotheses posit predictions about individual level public opinion and the possibility of narratives to shift opinion. They hypothesize four ways that narratives can move individual opinion; (i) if a narrative alters how an individual views the world, (ii) if an individual identifies with the hero in the narrative, (iii) the degree to which the narrative is congruent with the individual's prior beliefs, and (iv) the amount of trust that the individual places in the source of the narrative. At the meso level, Jones and McBeth (2010) offer three hypotheses regarding the strategic use of narratives by groups and/or coalitions. These hypotheses are tied to classic ideas regarding conflict expansion by strategic policy actors. Jones and McBeth (2010) posit that (i) "losers" in the policy debate will use narratives to expand conflict, (ii) "winners" will employ narratives to contain conflict, and (iii) policy actors will use narratives to split opposing coalitions.

The NPF offers a way for policy scholars to empirically measure how policy relevant information is transmitted and interpreted by both policy elites and the mass public. It could possibly stand on its own as a policy process theory, or could be incorporated into existing frameworks and theories. For example, narratives can be used to explain policy-oriented learning between and across coalitions in the ACF. Narratives could also be employed by policy entrepreneurs to merge streams or hasten policy diffusion and adoption. Finally, narratives could possibly shed light on how and why information is weighted and processed by governments when making policy choices.

SUBSYSTEMS AND BEYOND

Policy subsystems have been the dominant level of analysis for many policy process theories and frameworks;[1] particularly the ACF and PE. Recent work has brought new insights regarding subsystems. Two recent papers by Peter May and his colleagues argue that policy subsystems remain stable even after significant external disruptions (May, Sapotichne, & Workman, 2009a,b). This insight confirms long held assumptions about how subsystems bring stability to the policymaking process. In addition, recent research has begun to focus on various types of subsystems. These types include unitary, collaborative, and adversarial (Weible, 2008). The type of subsystem can have a direct bearing on the types of coalitions within that subsystem. For example, a unitary subsystem is based on a single cooperative coalition, while collaborative subsystems could have multiple coalitions, and finally an adversarial subsystem would contain multiple competing coalitions (Weible, 2008). In addition, these different subsystems are likely to use policy information and utilize policy learning in different ways (Weible & Sabatier, 2009). Finally, subsystem dynamics can help explain how policy change occurs (or doesn't) following a focusing event or crisis (Nohrstedt, 2008; Nohrstedt & Weible, 2010).

Other recent work has begun to move beyond the subsystem as the level of analysis in policymaking. PE has expanded from a model of subsystem dynamics to a system wide model of policy choice (Jones & Baumgartner, 2005a,b). In addition, recent work has argued that the ACF should move beyond the subsystem level to a more macro level policy topography (Jones & Jenkins-Smith, 2009). Other research has argued that policy problems typically encompass more than one subsystem and could be better understood as a "policy regime" (Jochim & May, 2010). Policy regimes are "governing arrangements that foster integrative actions across elements of multiple subsystems" (Jochim & May, 2010, p. 304). These regimes often emerge as a result of messy policy problems that span multiple policy areas or a crisis which can cause large scale policy disruption (May et al., 2009a, 2009b).

POLICYMAKING AND THE BUREAUCRACY

In large part, the bureaucracy has not been a major feature of policy process theories.[2] Several recent papers have assumed a larger role for the bureaucracy and individual bureaucrats in the policymaking process. In a paper regarding information processing by governments, Workman et al. (2009) argue that Congress delegates, not only policymaking authority but also information processing to the bureaucracy. This delegation occurs as a result of the oversupply of information in the political system. Additional research regarding bureaucratic structures and information processing, argues that delegated authority and formal routines within the bureaucracy can dampen signals from political principals (Congress and the President) while centralized authority and informal procedures can amplify those signals (May, Workman, & Jones, 2008). In addition, Robinson et al. (2007) finds that bureaucratic centralization[3] can make budget punctuations more likely, while punctuations are less likely in larger organizations. A final paper argues that theories of delegation to the bureaucracy should be put alongside other policy process theories or incorporated within Jones and Baumgartner's (2005a,b) policy choice model (Lavertu & Weimer, 2009). Lavertu and Weimer argue that theories of delegation contain a, "clear causal mechanism and empirically falsifiable predictions regarding the interests, information, and institutions that affect delegated policymaking," specifically delegation "explains the level of detail and the types of administrative procedures specified in statute" (2009, p. 100).

In addition to the bureaucracy, recent work has discussed the importance of individual bureaucrats in the policymaking process. Teodoro (2009) imagines bureaucrats as policy entrepreneurs and bureaucratic mobility as a causal mechanism for policy diffusion. In addition to policy entrepreneurs, recent research equates bureaucrats and public managers and argues that their role in the policy process is underdeveloped; particularly with regard to policy implementation (Hicklin & Godwin, 2009; Meier, 2009). Meier (2009) argues that there exists an overemphasis on policy design without regard to the bureaucrats that implement those policies. As Meier notes, "one of the basic facts about of implementation is that individuals, not institutions, make the majority of decisions that drive policy" (2009, p. 14).

The importance of the bureaucracy in the policymaking process has not been sufficiently considered by current policy theory. The work discussed here offer suggestions for future work that should be explored. The role of delegated information processing to the bureaucracy has important implications for policy designs and the conditions necessary for policy change. In addition, theories of delegation could be integrated into the ACF, as well as the policy choice model. It is likely that delegation patterns would vary depending on whether bureaucrats where members of the dominant coalition or the minority coalition.

SYNTHETIC FRAMEWORK OF THE POLICY PROCESS

Recent work regarding the policy process has largely proceeded within the established theories and frameworks. However, some work has called for integrating the various frameworks (Real-Dato, 2009; Schlager, 2007). Schlager (2007) argues that "Over the past several years, the family resemblance among the policy process theories and comparative policy models has become more pronounced, to the point where they probably belong under a single roof and that roof is the currently entitled advocacy coalition framework" (p. 317).

Along similar lines, Real-Dato (2009) argues that MS, PE, and the ACF can be joined into a single "synthetic explanatory framework." In addition, he states that the IAD could serve as theoretical "baseline" that can incorporate the synthetic framework. Using the IAD imbeds the other frameworks within a structure that accounts for the importance of institutions in the policy process, and allows for multiple levels of analysis. Real-Dato (2009) goes on to argue that the synthetic framework would incorporate three mechanisms of policy change; endogenous change, conflict expansion, and exogenous impacts. Endogenous change is change that occurs within the policy subsystem, largely as a result of policy learning. Change due to conflict expansion results from policy actors looking outside the subsystem for potential allies. Conflict expansion is based on venue-shopping by dissatisfied subsystem actors, and/or change brought about by policy actors altering the policy image of those outside of the subsystem and creating a punctuation (Real-Dato, 2009). Finally, policy change can occur as a result of exogenous impacts. Exogenous impacts can indirectly impact policy through causing an endogenous change in the subsystem or through a direct impact by causing policy change "independent of internal processes within the subsystem" (Real-Dato, 2009, p. 136).

Following Schlager (2007) and Real-Dato (2009) and focusing on merging the various theories and frameworks into a unified framework of the policy process certainly seems worth pursuing.[4] The main advantage of such a unified framework is that it would allow scholars to take advantage of the cumulative knowledge of each of the frameworks.

Both before and since Sabatier's (1991) call for better theories of the policy process, multiple theories and frameworks have offered important insights into the policy process. This essay briefly outlined some recent work that has expanded those frameworks. While this essay only scratches the surface of the thriving field of policy process theory, it is my hope that one can conclude that the work examined here is of a high value and the larger field is producing interesting and exciting research. The field has generated several frameworks and theories that continue to be empirically tested and revised to sharpen our understanding of the policy process.

End Notes

1. See McCool 1998 for a review of subsystems and related concepts.
2. Bureaucrats are assumed to members of advocacy coalitions and government institutions play a role in PE. However, there aren't explicit hypotheses about the bureaucracy and its role in policymaking.
3. Measured by the "percentage of spending on central administration" in a school district (Robinson et al., 2007, p. 145).
4. An alternative approach may be a comparative one in which multiple frameworks are examined and tested in the same study to see which provides more explanatory power (Meier, 2009).

References

ANSELL, CHRIS, SARAH RECKHOW, and ANDREW KELLY. 2009. "How to Reform a Reform Coalition: Outreach, Agenda Expansion, and Brokerage in Urban School Reform." *Policy Studies Journal* 37 (4): 717–43.

BASURTO, XAVIER, GORDON KINGSLEY, KELLY MCQUEEN, MSHADONI SMITH, and Christopher Weible. 2010. "A Systematic Approach to Institutional Analysis: Applying Crawford and Ostrom's Grammar." *Political Research Quarterly* 63 (3): 523–37.

BAUMGARTNER, FRANK R., and BRYAN D. JONES. 1991. "Agenda Dynamics and Policy Subsystems." *The Journal of Politics* 53 (4): 1044–74.

———. 1993. *Agendas and Instability in American Politics.* Chicago: University of Chicago Press.

———. 2009. *Agendas and Instability in American Politics*, 2nd ed., Chicago: University of Chicago Press.

BAUMGARTNER, FRANK R., CHRISTIAN BREUNIG, CHRISTOFFER GREEN-PEDERSEN, BRYAN D. JONES, PETER B. MORTENSEN, MICHIEL NUYTEMANS, and Stefaan Walgrave. 2009. "Punctuated Equilibrium in Comparative Perspective." *American Journal of Political Science* 53 (3): 603–20.

BERRY, FRANCES STOKES, and William D. Berry. 1990. "State Lottery Adoptions As Policy Innovations: An Event History Analysis." *The American Political Science Review* 84 (2): 395–415.

———. 2007. "Innovation and Diffusion Models in Policy Research." In *Theories of the Policy Process*, ed. Paul A. Sabatier. Boulder, CO: Westview Press, 223–60.

BOSCARINO, JESSICA E. 2009. "Surfing for Problems: Advocacy Group Strategy in U.S. Forestry Policy." *Policy Studies Journal* 37 (3): 415–34.

BREUNIG, CHRISTIAN, CHRIS KOSKI, and Peter B. Mortensen. 2010. "Stability and Punctuations in Public Spending: A Comparative Study of Budget Functions." *Journal of Public Administration Research and Theory* 20 (3): 703–22.

CASHORE, BENJAMIN, and Michael Howlett. 2007. "Punctuating Which Equilibrium? Understanding Thermostatic Policy Dynamics in Pacific Northwest Forestry." *American Journal of Political Science* 51 (3): 532–51.

CRAWFORD, SUE E. S., and ELINOR OSTROM. 1995. "A Grammar of Institutions." *The American Political Science Review* 89 (3 September): 582–600.

DeLeon, Peter. 1999. "The Stages Approach to the Policy Process: What Has It Done? Where Is It Going?" *Theories of the Policy Process*, ed. Paul Sabatier. Boulder, CO: Westview, 19–32.

Gilardi, Fabrizio. 2010. "Who Learns from What in Policy Diffusion Processes?" *American Journal of Political Science* 54 (3): 650–66.

Givel, Michael. 2008. "Assessing Material and Symbolic Variations in Punctuated Equilibrium and Public Policy Output Patterns." *Review of Policy Research* 25 (6): 547–61.

Hardy, Scott D., and Tomas M. Koontz. 2009. "Rules for Collaboration: Institutional Analysis of Group Membership and Levels of Action in Watershed Partnerships." *Policy Studies Journal* 37 (3): 393–414.

Hicklin, Alisa, and Erik Godwin. 2009. "Agents of Change: The Role of Public Managers in Public Policy." *Policy Studies Journal* 37 (1): 13–20.

Ingram, Helen, Anne L. Schneider, and Peter deLeon. 2007. "Social Construction and Policy Design." In *Theories of the Policy Process*, ed. Paul A. Sabatier. Boulder, CO: Westview Press, 93–126.

James, Thomas E., and Paul D. Jorgensen. 2009. "Policy Knowledge, Policy Formulation, and Change: Revisiting A Foundational Question." *Policy Studies Journal* 37 (1): 141–62.

Jenkins-Smith, Hank C. 1990. *Democratic Politics and Policy Analysis*. Pacific Grove, CA: Brooks/Cole Publishing Company.

Jochim, Ashley E., and Peter J. May. 2010. "Beyond Subsystems: Policy Regimes and Governance." *Policy Studies Journal* 38 (2): 303–27.

John, Peter, and Will Jennings. 2010. "Punctuations and Turning Points in British Politics: The Policy Agenda of the Queen's Speech, 1940–2005." *British Journal of Political Science* 40 (3): 561–86.

Jones, Bryan D., and Frank R. Baumgartner. 2005a. "A Model of Choice for Public Policy." *Journal of Public Administration Research and Theory* 15 (3): 325–51.

———. 2005b. *The Politics of Attention: How Government Prioritizes Problems*. Chicago: University of Chicago Press.

Jones, Michael D., and Hank C. Jenkins-Smith. 2009. "Trans-Subsystem Dynamics: Policy Topography, Mass Opinion, and Policy Change." *Policy Studies Journal* 37 (1): 37–58.

Jones, Michael D., and Mark K. McBeth. 2010. "A Narrative Policy Framework: Clear Enough to be Wrong?" *Policy Studies Journal* 38 (2): 329–53.

Kingdon, John W. 1984. *Agendas, Alternatives and Public Policies*. New York: Longman.

Kiser, Larry L., and Elinor Ostrom. 1982. "The Three Worlds of Action: A Metatheorectical Synthesis of Institutional Approaches." In *Strategies of Political Inquiry*, ed. Elinor Ostrom. Beverly Hills, CA: SAGE Publications, 179–222.

Koski, Chris. 2010. "Greening America's Skylines: The Diffusion of Low-Salience Policies." *Policy Studies Journal* 38 (1): 93–117.

Lasswell, Harold. 1971. *A Pre-View of the Policy Sciences*. New York: American Elsevier.

Lavertu, Stephane, and David L. Weimer. 2009. "Integrating Delegation into the Policy Theory Literature." *Policy Studies Journal* 37 (1): 93–102.

Lowi, Theodore J. 1972. "Four Systems of Policy, Politics, and Choice." *Public Administration Review* 32 (4): 298–310.

Lubell, Mark. 2007. "Familiarity Breeds Trust: Collective Action in a Policy Domain." *The Journal of Politics* 69 (01): 237–50.

Lubell, Mark, Adam Douglas Henry, and Mike McCoy. 2010. "Collaborative Institutions in An Ecology of Games." *American Journal of Political Science* 54 (2): 287–300.

Madison, Michael J., Brett M. Frischmann, and Katherine J. Strandburg. 2010. "Constructing Commons in the Cultural Environment." *Cornell Law Review* 95: 657–710.

May, Peter J., Joshua Sapotichne, and Samuel Workman. 2009a. "Widespread Policy Disruption and Interest Mobilization." *Policy Studies Journal* 37 (4): 793–815.

———. 2009b. "Widespread Policy Disruption: Terrorism, Public Risks, and Homeland Security." *Policy Studies Journal* 37 (2): 171–94.

May, Peter J., Samuel Workman, and Bryan D. Jones. 2008. "Organizing Attention: Responses of the Bureaucracy to Agenda Disruption." *Journal of Public Administration Research and Theory* 18 (4): 517–41.

McBeth, Mark K., Elizabeth Shanahan, Ruth J. Arnell, and Paul L. Hathaway. 2007. "The Intersection of Narrative Policy Analysis and Policy Change Theory." *Policy Studies Journal* 35 (1): 87–108.

McBeth, Mark, Elizabeth Shanahan, Paul Hathaway, Linda Tigert, and Lynette Sampson. 2010. "Buffalo Tales: Interest Group Policy Stories in Greater Yellowstone." *Policy Sciences* 43 (4): 391–409.

MEIER, KENNETH J. 2009. "Policy Theory, Policy Theory Everywhere: Ravings of a Deranged Policy Scholar." *Policy Studies Journal* 37 (1): 5–11.

MINTROM, MICHAEL, AND PHILLIPA NORMAN. 2009. "Policy Entrepreneurship and Policy Change." *Policy Studies Journal* 37 (4): 649–67.

MINTROM, MICHAEL, AND SANDRA VERGARI. 1996. "Advocacy Coalitions, Policy Entrepreneurs, and Policy Change." *Policy Studies Journal* 24 (3): 420–34.

MORTENSEN, PETER B. 2009. "Political Attention and Public Spending in the United States." *Policy Studies Journal* 37 (3): 435–55.

NAKAMURA, ROBERT. 1987. "The Textbook Policy Process and Implementation Research." *Policy Studies Review* 7 (1): 142–54.

NESS, ERIK. 2010. "The Politics of Determining Merit Aid Eligibility Criteria: An Analysis of the Policy Process." *The Journal of Higher Education* 81 (1): 33–60.

NESS, ERIK C., and MOLLY A. MISTRETTA. 2009. "Policy Adoption in North Carolina and Tennessee: A Comparative Case Study of Lottery Beneficiaries." *The Review of Higher Education* 32 (4): 489–514.

NOHRSTEDT, DANIEL. 2008. "The Politics of Crisis Policymaking: Chernobyl and Swedish Nuclear Energy Policy." *Policy Studies Journal* 36 (2): 257–78.

———. 2010. "Do Advocacy Coalitions Matter? Crisis and Change in Swedish Nuclear Energy Policy." *Journal of Public Administration Research Theory* 20 (2): 309–33.

NOHRSTEDT, DANIEL, and CHRISTOPHER M. WEIBLE. 2010. "The Logic of Policy Change after Crisis: Proximity and Subsystem Interaction." *Risk, Hazards & Crisis in Public Policy* 1 (2).

OSTROM, ELINOR. 2007a. "A Diagnostic Approach for Going Beyond Panaceas." *Proceedings of the National Academy of Sciences* 104 (39): 15181–7.

———. 2007b. "Institutional Rational Choice: An Assessment of the Institutional Analysis and Development Framework." In *Theories of the Policy Process*, ed. Paul A. Sabatier. Boulder, CO: Westview Press, 21–64.

———. 2009. "A General Framework for Analyzing Sustainability of Social-Ecological Systems." *Science* 325 (5939): 419–22.

PIERCE, JONATHAN, KRISTIN SCHUMACHER, SABA SIDDIKI, and Andrew Pattison. 2010. "Understanding What Is Inside the Box: Analysis of Policy Design and Social Construction." *Annual Meeting of the Midwest Political Science Association*.

POTEETE, AMY R., MARCO A. JANSSEN, and ELINOR OSTROM. 2010. *Working Together: Collective Action, the Commons, and Multiple Methods in Practice.* Princeton, NJ: Princeton University Press.

REAL-DATO, JOSE. 2009. "Mechanisms of Policy Change: A Proposal for a Synthetic Explanatory Framework." *Journal of Comparative Policy Analysis* 11 (1): 117–43.

REICH, GARY, and JAY BARTH. 2010. "Educating Citizens Or Defying Federal Authority? A Comparative Study of In-State Tuition for Undocumented Students." *Policy Studies Journal* 38 (3): 419–45.

ROBINSON, SCOTT E., and WARREN S. ELLER. 2010. "Participation in Policy Streams: Testing the Separation of Problems and Solutions in Subnational Policy Systems." *Policy Studies Journal* 38 (2): 199–216.

ROBINSON, SCOTT E., FLOUN'SAY CAVER, KENNETH J. MEIER, and Laurence J. O'Toole. 2007. "Explaining Policy Punctuations: Bureaucratization and Budget Change." *American Journal of Political Science* 51 (1): 140–50.

RYU, JAY EUNGHA. 2009. "Exploring the Factors for Budget Stability and Punctuations: A Preliminary Analysis of State Government Sub-Functional Expenditures." *Policy Studies Journal* 37 (3): 457–73.

SABATIER, PAUL A. 1987. "Knowledge, Policy-Oriented Learning, and Policy Change: An Advocacy Coalition Framework." *Knowledge: Creation, Diffusion, Utilization* 8 (4): 649–92.

———. 1988. "An Advocacy Coalition Framework of Policy Change and the Role of Policy-Oriented Learning Therein." *Policy Sciences* 21 (2): 129–68.

———. 1991. "Toward Better Theories of the Policy Process." *PS: Political Science and Politics* 24 (2): 147–56.

———. 2007. *Theories of the Policy Process*, 2nd ed., Boulder, CO: Westview Press.

SABATIER, PAUL A., and Hank C. Jenkins-Smith, eds. 1988. "Policy Change and Policy-Oriented Learning: Exploring An Advocacy Coalition Framework." *Policy Sciences* 21: 2–3.

———. 1993. *Policy Change and Learning: An Advocacy Coalition Approach.* Boulder, CO: Westview Press.

———. 1999. "The Advocacy Coalition Framework: An Assessment." In *Theories of the Policy Process*, ed. Paul A. Sabatier. Boulder, CO: Westview, 117–66.

SABATIER, PAUL A., and Christopher M. Weible. 2007. "The Advocacy Coalition Framework: Innovations and Clarifications." In *Theories of the Policy Process*, ed. Paul A. Sabatier. Boulder, CO: Westview Press, 189–222.

SCHLAGER, EDELLA. 2007. "A Comparison of Frameworks, Theories, and Models of Policy Processes." In *Theories of the Policy Process*, ed. Paul A. Sabatier. Boulder, CO: Westview Press, 293–320.

SCHLAGER, EDELLA, and Tanya Heikkila. 2009. "Resolving Water Conflicts: A Comparative Analysis of Interstate River Compacts." *Policy Studies Journal* 37 (3): 367–92.

SCHNEIDER, ANNE, and Helen Ingram. 1993. "Social Construction of Target Populations: Implications for Politics and Policy." *The American Political Science Review* 87 (2): 334–47.

SCHNEIDER, ANNE L., and HELEN M. INGRAM. 1997. *Policy Design for Democracy*. Lawrence: University of Kansas Press.

SCHNEIDER, ANNE, and MARA SIDNEY. 2009. "What Is Next for Policy Design and Social Construction Theory?" *Policy Studies Journal* 37 (1): 103–19.

SHIPAN, CHARLES R., and CRAIG VOLDEN. 2008. "The Mechanisms of Policy Diffusion." *American Journal of Political Science* 52 (4): 840–57.

SMITH, KEVIN B., and CHRISTOPHER W. LARIMER. 2009. *The Public Policy Theory Primer*. Boulder, CO: Westview Press.

SZARKA, JOSEPH. 2010. "Bringing Interests Back In: Using Coalition Theories to Explain European Wind Power Policies." *Journal of European Public Policy* 17 (6): 836–53.

TEODORO, MANUEL P. 2009. "Bureaucratic Job Mobility and The Diffusion of Innovations." *American Journal of Political Science* 53 (1): 175–89.

TRUE, JAMES L., BRYAN D. JONES, and Frank R. Baumgartner. 2007. "Punctuated-Equilibrium Theory: Explaining Stability and Change in Public Policymaking." In *Theories of the Policy Process*, ed. Paul A. Sabatier. Boulder, CO: Westview Press, 155–88.

WALKER, JACK L. 1969. "The Diffusion of Innovations among the American States." *The American Political Science Review* 63 (3): 880–99.

WEIBLE, CHRISTOPHER M. 2008. "Expert-Based Information and Policy Subsystems: A Review and Synthesis." *Policy Studies Journal* 36 (4): 615–35.

WEIBLE, CHRISTOPHER M., and PAUL A. SABATIER. 2009. "Coalitions, Science, and Belief Change: Comparing Adversarial and Collaborative Policy Subsystems." *Policy Studies Journal* 37 (2): 195–212.

WEIBLE, CHRISTOPHER M., PAUL A. SABATIER, and Kelly McQueen. 2009. "Themes and Variations: Taking Stock of the Advocacy Coalition Framework." *Policy Studies Journal* 37 (1): 121–40.

WEIMER, DAVID L. 2008. "Theories of and in the Policy Process." *Policy Studies Journal* 36 (4): 489–95.

WORKMAN, SAMUEL, BRYAN D. JONES, and Ashley E. Jochim. 2009. "Information Processing and Policy Dynamics." *Policy Studies Journal* 37 (1): 75–92.

ZAHARIADIS, NIKOLAOS. 2007. "The Multiple Streams Framework: Structure, Limitations, Prospects." In *Theories of the Policy Process*, ed. Paul A. Sabatier. Boulder, CO: Westview Press, 65–92.

PART FOUR

Institutional and Noninstitutional Actors

30

Institutional and Noninstitutional Actors in the Policy Process

Matthew A. Cahn

As discussed earlier, public policy has been defined in different ways by different observers. Peters defines policy as "the sum of government activities... (that have) an influence on the lives of citizens."[1] Lasswell[2] pointed out that public policy determines "who gets what, when, and how." Contemporary policy analysts might also include "why?" Ripley and Franklin define policy and the policy process more specifically:

> Policy is what the government says and does about perceived problems. Policy making is how the government decides what will be done about perceived problems. Policy making is a process of interaction among governmental and nongovernmental actors; policy is the outcome of that interaction.[3]

In a real world context, public policy can be understood as the public solutions which are implemented in an effort to solve public problems.

Policy actors are those individuals and groups, both formal and informal, which seek to influence the creation and implementation of these public solutions.

This chapter explores the function and influence that policy actors exert in the policy process. It begins with an overview of the policy process and then moves on to explore each actor within the process, including the institutional actors—Congress, the president, executive agencies, and the courts—and the noninstitutional actors—parties, interest groups, political consultants, and the media.

The policy process is significantly more subtle than many realize. While the Constitution provides for a legislature that makes laws, an executive that enforces laws, and a judiciary that interprets laws, the policy process has evolved into a confusing web of state and federal departments, agencies, and committees that make up the institutional policy bureaucracy. In addition, the vast network of organized citizen groups (parties, interest groups, and PACs), as well as the rise of the electronic media, political consultants, and other image making professionals, further complicates the process. The role each actor plays, and the relationship between actors, is what determines policy outcomes.

INSTITUTIONAL ACTORS

Congress

Congress is a central institution in the policy process because of its legislative authority. Article I, section 8 of the Constitution defines the various powers of Congress, including the power to

- tax
- borrow money on the credit of the United States
- regulate interstate commerce
- regulate commerce with other nations
- produce currency and determine its value
- fix and regulate weights and measures
- establish a postal system
- establish a network of roads
- issue patents and copyrights
- declare war
- make any law that is "necessary and proper" in the implementation of the other powers

While congressional power is diffused among the 435 voting members of the House and 100 voting members of the Senate, there are specific points where power is focused. It is these points that are points of access for those seeking policy influence.

The vast majority of legislative decisions are made in committees. Between standing committees, special committees, joint committees, conference committees, and all of their associated sub-committees, there are several hundred committees in a typical congressional session. As Fenno[4] describes, committees and sub-committees are responsible for the initial review of draft legislation. Committees can report positively or negatively on any bill, or they can report amended bills. Rather than report negatively on bills, however, committees typically ignore bills that lack favor. This precludes

the necessity of debating and voting on the bill on the full floor, since bills that are not acted upon die at the close of the congressional session.[5]

Committee chairs have disproportionate influence over policy as a consequence of their power to determine committee agendas. Similarly, certain committees have more policy influence than others. The House Rules Committee, for example, is responsible for determining which bills will be heard and in what order. The Appropriation Committees in both the House and Senate are responsible for reviewing any legislation that requires funding. The power that members of such committees hold and the powers of committee chairs make them key players in the policy process.

Congressional staffers are another source of influence that is often overlooked. In *The Power Game*[6] Hedrick Smith describes staffers as "policy entrepreneurs." Staffers are important in two areas. First, as Fiorina[7] points out, the increasing use of staff in district offices to service constituents strengthens the Congress member's position among local voters, perhaps explaining in part the strength of incumbency. Second, staffers are the real expertise behind the legislator. With over six thousand bills introduced in an average session, legislators rely more and more on staff to analyze legislation, negotiate compromises, research issues, and meet with lobbyists.[8] In their roles as legislative analyst and policy negotiators, as well as their role as political confidant and counselor, senior staffers have significant policy influence.

There are several explanations of congressional behavior. What appears to be consistent between analyses is the observation that members of Congress are primarily concerned with achieving reelection. Mayhew[9] argues that the organization of Congress itself evolved to maximize the re-electability of members. Since congressional power is tied to seniority, this is not surprising. But, it does have negative policy implications. If members are acting to maximize their individual political futures, their ability to govern in the national interest is severely limited. The need to satisfy constituent interests over national interests has led to dangerously high levels of pork in legislative outcomes. The election connection has other impacts which are similarly troubling. In 2008, the average cost to run a successful congressional campaign was over $1 million for a House seat and over $6.5 million for a Senate seat.[10] As a consequence, members of Congress are in a constant state of fundraising. Those interests with greater financial resources may thus achieve greater access. With limited time to meet with members of the public, legislators have a built-in incentive to meet with those individuals who can best benefit their reelection efforts.

Committee decisions, compromises between committees and executive agencies, the influence of staffers, and the cozy relationships between legislators and deep pocket lobbyists have even greater policy importance because they all take place outside of the public eye. Although, as a consequence of political reform in the 1970s, committee meetings are open, staff reports are available for public review, lobbyists are required to register with the government, and all financial contributions are public record, few people have the time to closely follow the intricacies of the policy process. As a consequence, members of Congress and those whose business it is to influence them—and thus have the time—are generally free to act without concern of public attention.

The President and The Executive Bureaucracy

Like Congress, the president is mandated by the Constitution as a partner in the policy process. But, unlike Congress, the president can only approve or disapprove legislation, he or she has no power to amend. Thus, the policy priorities of the president cannot be directly legislated. Rather, presidents must rely on legislative partners in both houses, and on, what Neustadt[11] called, the power to persuade.

In *The Presidential Policy Stream,* Paul Light suggests that presidential policy is a result of the "stream of people and ideas that flow through the White House."[12] If public policy is a process of identifying problems, identifying solutions, and implementing those solutions, the identification of problems and solutions, Light argues, is tied to the assumptions held by players in that stream. The policy stream must accommodate the issues that percolate up through the systemic agenda, as well as those issues that may be on the presidential agenda.

In addition to balancing the demands of the systemic agenda with presidential policy objectives, the president also must balance domestic policy concerns with foreign policy concerns. Wildavsky[13] suggests that there are in fact two presidencies: the domestic presidency and the foreign policy presidency. Each has different responsibilities and different policy objectives. The foreign policy president has much more power, Wildavsky argues, than the domestic president. As Richard Neustadt suggests, the domestic president may have to rely more on his or her ability to persuade Congress and members of the executive bureaucracy to implement presidential policy objectives than on any specific domestic power. The foreign policy president, on the other hand, has the power to move troops into combat, negotiate executive agreements and treaties, and controls a vast international intelligence network.

The implementation of presidential policy objectives involves a different set of problems than those of Congress. While Congress makes laws, the president can only recommend laws. Yet, the president, as chief executive, may do whatever is necessary to enforce legislation. That enforcement, typically, involves discretionary policy decisions. Article II, sections 2 and 3 define the powers of the president:

- to recommend policy proposals to Congress
- of Commander-in-Chief of the Armed Services (the power to move and control troops, but not to declare war)
- to grant pardons and reprieves for federal offenses except in cases of impeachment
- to make treaties with advice and consent of Senate
- to appoint federal judges, ambassadors, and consuls, and the heads of cabinet-level departments and regulatory agencies with the advice and consent of the Senate
- to "faithfully" enforce all laws

While the president is often looked upon to set the national policy agenda, he or she can only do so as long as he or she holds an ability to persuade. With the expressed powers of the president limited to specific areas, effective presidents must rely on their power to persuade members of Congress, the bureaucracy, the media, and the public.

When expressed powers are insufficient, presidents can rely on executive prerogative. Executive orders have the power of law but have no statutory basis. Roosevelt's 1942 executive order #9066 authorized the incarceration of 110,000 Japanese Americans without warrants, indictments, or hearings. Submitting to anti-Asian hysteria following the bombing of Pearl Harbor, Roosevelt lifted the constitutional protections of a specific class of American citizens.

Reagan's 1981 executive order #12291 required a benefit–cost calculation be performed prior to implementing any policy. If the costs outweighed the benefits, the policy would not be implemented. Aside from the obvious problem in quantifying benefits—what is the value of clean air, for example?—EO 12291 redefines the policy relationship between the executive and the legislature. Rather than fulfilling the constitutional imperative to "faithfully execute all laws," EO 12291 claims for the executive the right to evaluate whether laws should be enforced, and how extensively.

Effective presidents use the powers and perks of their office to maximize their policy agendas. Appointments are a major source of policy influence. By appointing individuals who share his or her political perspective and agenda, a president is able to extend influence throughout the executive and judicial bureaucracies. Cabinet officers and heads of regulatory agencies establish policy priorities within their agencies. And, since most legislation allows for a significant measure of discretion among implementing and enforcement agencies, the Cabinet officers and agency heads have wide latitude in defining, implementing, and enforcing policy. This was well illustrated by Reagan's appointment of Anne Burford as EPA administrator. Burford, a corporate attorney who often represented clients in suits against the government over environmental regulations, sought to bring Reagan's anti-regulatory philosophy into the EPA. In order to sidestep the legislative mandate that defined EPA's mission, Burford instituted a variety of mechanisms intended to reduce environmental enforcement. She held unannounced meetings with regulated industries, effectively precluding public participation.[14] Further, she centralized all decision making in her office, effectively paralyzing staff activities.[15] Ultimately, discretionary policy enforcement fell to an all-time low.[16]

The ability to control the executive bureaucracy is critical for the development and maintenance of presidential power. The tendency to organize bureaucratically is best described by Max Weber, who suggests that "modern officialdom" seeks the efficiency of specificity and hierarchy.[17] Bureaucratic government incorporates a vast network of interrelated offices, each of which has a specific jurisdiction and a specific task (task differentiation); there is a set hierarchy; and authority is subservient to the rule of law. In "The Rise of the Bureaucratic State," Wilson explores the evolution of the American bureaucracy.[18] While bureaucratic organization is necessary to administer a society of 300 million people, the size of the bureaucracy itself represents certain hazards. Weber warned that bureaucracies inevitably become insensitive to individual concerns. With the executive bureaucracy employing over 4.5 million people, it may often appear sluggish and unresponsive. Still, specialization is critical for effective government; the Department of Defense clearly has different needs and concerns than the Department of Agriculture. There may, as a result, be little alternative to bureaucratic organization.

The policy influence of regulatory agencies within the executive bureaucracy is substantial. Kenneth Meier and Sheila Jasonoff[19] identify key influences of administrative agencies. Meier describes the regulatory process as a combination of regulatory bureaucracies (values, expertise, agency subculture, bureaucratic entrepreneurs) and public interaction (interest groups, economic issues, legislative committees and sub-committees). Jasonoff observes that regulatory outcomes often reflect the key influence of nonelected and nonappointed science advisors. Regulatory outcomes are a consequence of subsystem interaction between all of these influences. Those who are best able to influence these subsystems are best able to maximize their interests. As a result, policy subsystems are major points of access for policy influence.

The Courts

The influence of judges in interpreting laws has an equally significant impact on policy. The

Brown v. Topeka Board of Education decision in 1955, for example, initiated antisegregation policies and acted as a catalyst for the voting rights acts of the 1960s and civil rights policies through the 1980s. Similarly, the 1973 *Roe v. Wade* decision virtually defined abortion policy thereafter. But, judicial policy influence is not restricted to Supreme Court decisions. Lawrence Baum and Gerald Rosenberg have different views of this.[20] Baum points out that appellate courts are significant, if often ignored, partners in policy making. Appellate courts have had critical policy influence in several areas, including abortion and civil rights policy. Rosenberg observes that in spite of the heavy influence of *Brown* or *Roe*, in many areas court decisions have actually had very little policy influence.

The policy role of the judiciary is not universally appreciated. The current debate over judicial activism and judicial restraint is only the most recent in a long discourse. In "Towards an Imperial Judiciary?"[21] Nathan Glazer argues that judicial activism infringes on democratic policy institutions, and that an activist court erodes the respect and trust people hold for the judiciary. Still, whether a court is active or passive, there are significant policy implications. While the *Brown* decision may be considered "activist," for example, had the court chosen to remain passive, civil rights policy might have remained nonexistent for many more years. Nonaction is in itself a policy decision with substantial policy implications.

NONINSTITUTIONAL ACTORS

Public policy is not merely the result of independent policy-making institutions. Noninstitutional actors also play a significant role: the public elects legislators and executives; the media influences policy through its inherent agenda setting function; parties, in their role in drafting and electing candidates, influence policy through influencing the composition of legislative and executive bodies; and, organized interest groups lobby elected officials and nonelected policy makers (e.g., agency staff). Policy, then, is a result of institutional processes influenced by noninstitutional actors.

Media

The media are influential to policy outcomes because they help define social reality.[22] The work of McCombs and Shaw[23] supports the assertion that the media influence the salience of issues. As Lippmann[24] observed in 1922, perceptions of reality are based on a tiny sampling of the world around us. No one can be everywhere, no one can experience everything. Thus, to a greater or lesser extent, all of us rely on media portrayals of reality.

Graber[25] argues that the way people process information makes them especially vulnerable to media influence. First, people tend to pare down the scope of information they confront. Second, people tend to think schematically. When confronted with information, individuals will fit that information into pre-existing schema. And, since news stories tend to lack background and context, schemata allow the individual to give the information meaning. In such a way, individuals recreate reality in their minds.

The data collected by Iyengar and Kinder[26] show that television news, to a great extent, defines which problems the public considers most serious. Iyengar and Kinder refine the agenda-setting dynamic to include what they call "priming." Priming refers to the selective coverage of only certain events and the selective way in which those events are covered. Since there is no way to cover all events, or cover any event completely, selective decisions must be made. But, there are consequences.

By priming certain aspects of national life while ignoring others, television news sets the terms by which political judgments are rendered and political choices made (Iyengar and Kinder 1987:4). The implications for public policy are serious. If policy is a result of the problem recognition model that Theodoulou[27] summarized earlier, then the problems that gain media recognition are much more likely to be addressed.

Parties

Political parties are distinct from other citizen organizations. Rather than attempting to influence existing policy makers, parties seek to get their own members elected to policy-making positions.

While interest groups seek influence on specific policy issues, parties seek influence on a wide spectrum of policy issues. Parties develop issue platforms, draft candidates, campaign on behalf of candidates, and work to get out the vote. In short, parties work to bring together citizens under a common banner.

While most people may think of parties only during election cycles, their policy influence extends beyond campaigns. While the rise of the media over the last thirty years has de-emphasized the power of parties in electoral politics, Eldersveld[28] accurately points out that parties continue to play a dominant role in policy outcomes. First and foremost, the party that emerges dominant determines the direction policy will take.

The president is responsible to the party that got him or her elected and therefore must pursue at least some of the policy objectives articulated at the party convention. Congress continues to distribute committee membership and chairmanships according to party affiliation. While negotiation and compromise is typically necessary, the general direction of congressional policy is directly tied to the ideology of the larger party. The strength of political parties has waned over the past three decades, but parties maintain policy influence in critical areas. Elections, patronage appointments, legislative committees, and national policy discourses all reflect the influence of parties.

Interest Groups

Interest groups are a fundamental partner in policy making. Citizens participate in the policy process through communication with policy makers. Such communication takes place individually (e.g., letters to elected representatives) and collectively. Interest groups facilitate collective communication. James Madison recognized the propensity for individuals to factionalize in an effort to maximize political influence.[29] Robert Dahl further refined the analysis of Madisonian democracy, arguing that in an open society all persons have the right to press their interests. To the extent others share these interests, collective pressure may allow greater policy influence. Indeed, Dahl argued, those issues that

have greater salience have greater interest group representation.[30]

The interest group dynamic, however, is not so simple. While it may be true that many salient issues have interest group representation, the strength of that representation is not tied to the strength of the issue's salience. Further, the salience itself may be a consequence of interest group action. When studying policy outcomes, it is necessary to identify the policy actors and the political resources they use. Maximizing policy requires specific political resources. The most common resources include bureaucratic knowledge, a network of contacts, citizen backing (size of constituency), an ability to make political contributions, and an ability to mount a public relations (media) campaign. Clearly, no group utilizes all of these resources. But, the ability of an organized group to utilize one or more of these resources is critical for policy influence.

The pluralist model of counterbalancing elites mediating interests is inadequate. The theoretical work done by Mills and empirical work done by Schattschneider, Domhoff, and Presthus, among others, suggest that rather than competing, the interests of economic elites tend to cohere in key policy areas.[31] Lowi's *The End of Liberalism*[32] argues that this interest group influence threatens the democratic basis of government. If interest groups provide the framework for government–citizen interaction, and these groups are based on individual self-interest, there is little opportunity for pursuing a meaningful national interest.

Not only are corporate interest groups and PACs at an all-time high, but the structure of the policy-making establishment has come to accept private think tanks as democratic institutions. The Brookings Institute, RAND Corporation, Council for Economic Development (CED), Council on Foreign Relations (CFR), and others form a bridge between corporate interests and government. The think tanks are considered by many policy makers to be neutral policy consultants and are thus extended great access to the policy-making arena. Yet, virtually all of them have strong foundations in the corporate community. The RAND Corporation was created as a joint venture between the U.S. Airforce and the aerospace industry as a think tank devoted to the theory and technology of deterrence. The CED was founded in the early 1940s by a consortium of corporate leaders to influence specific policy formation. The CFR was founded in 1921 by corporate executives and financiers to help shape foreign policy. As a result, economic elites are able to influence policy through what are essentially interest group think tanks.[33]

Political Consultants

Increasingly, political expertise is purchased by those with the need and the resources. In reviewing the rise and structure of the political consulting industry, Sabato[34] exposes the fragile relationship between articulating ideas in a political marketplace and manipulating public opinion. It is virtually impossible to win at the policy game without the marketing skills held by consultants and strategists. Like many other policy resources, political consultants are costly. As a consequence, those with greater economic resources enjoy a policy advantage.

CONCLUSION

This chapter has explored the role and influence of actors in the policy process—both institutional (Congress, the president and executive bureaucracy, and the Courts) and noninstitutional (media, parties, interest groups, and political consultants). From the discussion it can be seen that policy outcomes are typically a result of institutional processes *and* noninstitutional influence.

End Notes

1. B. Guy Peters, *American Public Policy: Promise and Performance* (3rd ed.) (Chatham, NJ: Chatham House Publishers, 1993), p. 4.
2. Harold Lasswell, *Politics: Who Gets What, When, and How* (New York: St. Martin's Press, 1988).
3. Randall B. Ripley and Grace A. Franklin, *Congress, the Bureaucracy, and Public Policy* (4th ed.) (Chicago: The Dorsey Press, 1987), p. 1.
4. Richard Fenno, Jr., *Congressmen in Committees* (Boston: Little, Brown, 1973).
5. Barbara Hinckley and Sheldon Goldman, *American Politics and Government: Structure, Processes, Institutions, and Policies* (Glenview, IL: Scott, Foresman and Co., 1990).
6. Hedrick Smith, *The Power Game: How Washington Works* (New York: Ballantine Books, 1988).
7. Morris P. Fiorina, *Congress: Keystone of the Washington Establishment* (New Haven: Yale University Press, 1977).
8. James Q. Wilson, *American Government* (5th ed.) (Lexington, MA: D.C. Heath and Co., 1992).
9. David Mayhew, *Congress: the Electoral Connection* (New Haven: Yale University Press, 1974).
10. Center for Responsive Journalism http://www.opensecrets.org/news/2008/11/money-wins-whitehouse-and.html.
11. Richard Neustadt, *Presidential Power* (NY: John Wiley and Sons Inc., 1980).
12. Paul Light, "The Presidential Policy Stream" in *The Presidency and the Political System,* ed. Michael Nelson (Washington, DC: CQ Press, 1984).
13. Aaron Wildavsky, "The Two Presidencies," *Transaction,* 4: Number 2 (December 1966).
14. Walter Rosenbaum, *Environmental Politics and Policy* (2nd ed.) (Washington, DC: CQ Press, 1991).
15. Steven Cohen, "EPA: A Qualified Success," in *Controversies in Environmental Policy,* eds. Sheldon Kamieniecki, Robert O'Brien, and Michael Clark (Albany, NY: State University of New York Press, 1986).
16. Matthew A. Cahn, *Environmental Deceptions: The Tension between Liberalism and Environmental Policymaking in the United States* (Albany, NY: SUNY Press, forthcoming).
17. Max Weber, "Bureaucracy," in *From Max Weber: Essays in Sociology,* eds. H.H. Gerth and C. Wright Mills (NY: Oxford University Press, 1946).
18. James Q. Wilson, "The Rise of the Bureaucratic State," *Public Interest,* 41 (Fall 1975).
19. Kenneth J. Meier, *Regulation: Politics, Bureaucracy, and Economics* (NY: St. Martin's Press, 1985); Sheila Jasonoff, *The Fifth Branch* (Cambridge, MA: Harvard University Press, 1990).
20. Lawrence Baum, *American Courts: Process and Policy* (NY: Houghton Mifflin Co., 1990); Gerald Rosenberg, *The Hollow Hope* (University of Chicago Press, 1991).

21. Nathan Glazer, "Towards an Imperial Judiciary," *Public Interest*, 41 (Fall 1975).

22. Denis McQuail, "The Influence and Effects of Mass Media," in *Mass Communication and Society*, eds. J. Curran, M. Gurevitch, and J. Woolacott (Beverly Hills: Sage Publications, Inc., 1979).

23. Maxwell E. McCombs and Donald L. Shaw, *The Emergence of American Political Issues: The Agenda Setting Function of the Press* (Eagan, MN: West Publishing Company, 1977).

24. Walter Lippmann, *Public Opinion* (NY: The Free Press, 1922).

25. Doris Graber, *Processing the News: How People Tame the Information Tide* (2nd ed.) (NY: Longman, 1988).

26. Shanto Iyengar and Donald Kinder, *News That Matters: Television and American Opinion* (Chicago: The University of Chicago Press, 1987).

27. See Stella Z. Theodoulou (this reader, part 3, reading 20).

28. Samuel J. Eldersveld, *Political Parties in American Society* (NY: Basic Books, 1982).

29. James Madison, "Federalist #10," in Alexander Hamilton, James Madison, and John Jay, *The Federalist Papers* (NY: New American Library, 1961).

30. Robert Dahl, *Who Governs* (New Haven: Yale University Press, 1961).

31. See C. Wright Mills, *The Power Elite* (Oxford: Oxford University Press, 1956); E.E. Schattschneider, *The Semi-Sovereign People* (NY: Holt, Rinehart and Winston, 1969); Thomas Dye, *Who's Running America? The Conservative Years* (4th ed.) (Engelwood Cliffs, NJ: Prentice-Hall, 1986); G. William Domhoff, *Who Rules America Now?* (NY: Simon and Schuster, Inc., 1983); Robert Prestus, *Elites in the Policy Process* (Cambridge: Cambridge University Press, 1974).

32. Theodore Lowi, *The End of Liberalism* (2nd ed.) (NY: W.W. Norton, 1979).

33. Matthew A. Cahn, op. cit.

34. Larry J. Sabato, *The Rise of Political Consultants: New Ways of Winning Elections* (NY: Basic Books, 1981).

Suggested References

JAMES DAVID BARBER, *The Presidential Character* (4th ed.) (Engelwood Cliffs, NJ: Prentice Hall, 1992).

EDWARD CORWIN, *The Presidency: Office and Powers* (NY: NYU Press, 1957).

THOMAS CRONIN, *The State of the Presidency* (2nd ed.) (Boston: Little Brown, 1980).

RICHARD FENNO, *Homestyle: House Members in their Districts* (Boston: Little Brown, 1978).

HUGH HECLO, *A Government of Strangers* (DC: Brookings Institute, 1977).

GARY JACOBSON, *The Politics of Congressional Elections* (6th ed.) (NY: Longman, 2004).

SHEILA JASONOFF, *The Fifth Branch* (Cambridge, MA: Harvard University Press, 1990).

WILLIAM LASSER, *The Limits of Judicial Power* (Chaperl Hill, NC: University of North Carolina Press, 1988).

KAY LAWSON and PETER MERKL, *When Parties Fail: Emerging Alternative Organizations* (Princeton: Princeton University Press, 1988).

MARTIN LINSKY, *How the Press Affects Federal Policymaking* (NY: W.W. Norton, 1986).

C. WRIGHT MILLS, *The Power Elite* (NY: Oxford University Press, 1961).

DAVID M. O'BRIEN, *Storm Center: The Supreme Court and American Politics* (NY: Norton, 1986).

RANDALL RIPLEY, *Congress: Process and Policy* (NY: W.W. Norton, 1983).

GERALD ROSENBERG, *The Hollow Hope* (Chicago, IL: University of Chicago, 1991).

FRANCIS ROURKE, *Bureaucracy, Politics, and Public Policy* (3rd ed.) (Boston: Little Brown, 1984).

E.E. SCHATTSCHNEIDER, *The Semi-Sovereign People* (NY: Holt, Rinehart and Winston, 1969).

MARTIN WATTENBERG, *The Decline of American Political Parties* (Cambridge, MA: Harvard University Press, 1986).

31

Congress: Keystone of the Washington Establishment

Morris Fiorina

In this chapter... I will set out a theory of the Washington establishment(s). The theory is quite plausible from a commonsense standpoint, and it is consistent with the specialized literature of academic political science. Nevertheless, it is still a theory, not proven fact. Before plunging in let me bring out in the open the basic axiom on which the theory rests: the self-interest axiom.

I assume that most people most of the time act in their own self-interest. This is not to say that human beings seek only to amass tangible wealth but rather to say that human beings seek to achieve their own ends—tangible and intangible—rather than the ends of their fellow men. I do not condemn such behavior nor do I condone it (although I rather sympathize with Thoreau's comment that "if I knew for a certainty that a man was coming to my house with the conscious design of doing me good. I should run for my life.").[1] I only claim that political and economic theories which presume self-interested behavior will prove to be more widely applicable than those which build on more altruistic assumptions.

What does the axiom imply when used in the specific context ... a context peopled by congressmen, bureaucrats, and voters? I assume that the primary goal of the typical congressman is reelection. Over and above the $45,000 salary plus "perks" and outside money, the office of congressman carries with it prestige, excitement, and power. It is a seat in the cockpit of government. But in order to retain the status, excitement, and power (not to mention more tangible things) of office, the congressman must win reelection every two years. Even those congressmen genuinely concerned with good public policy must achieve reelection in order to continue their work. Whether narrowly self-serving or more publicly oriented, the individual congressman finds reelection to be at least a necessary condition for the achievement of his goals.[2]

Moreover, there is a kind of natural selection process at work in the electoral arena. On average, those congressmen who are not primarily interested in reelection will not achieve reelection as often as those who are interested. We, the people, help to weed out congressmen whose primary motivation is not reelection. We admire politicians who courageously adopt the aloof role of the disinterested statesman, but we vote for those politicians who follow our wishes and do us favors.

What about the bureaucrats? A specification of their goals is somewhat more controversial—those who speak of appointed officials as public servants obviously take a more benign view than those who speak of them as bureaucrats. The literature provides ample justification for asserting that most bureaucrats wish to protect and nurture their agencies. The typical bureaucrat can be expected to seek to expand his agency in terms of personnel, budget, and mission. One's status in Washington (again, not to mention more tangible things) is roughly proportional to the importance of the operation one oversees. And the sheer size of the operation is taken to be a measure of importance. As with congressmen, the specified goals apply even to those bureaucrats who genuinely believe in their agency's mission. If they believe in the efficacy of their programs, they naturally wish to expand them and add new ones. All of this requires more money and more people. The genuinely committed bureaucrat is just as likely to seek to expand his agency as the proverbial empire-builder.[3]

And what of the third element in the equation, us? What do we, the voters who support the Washington system, strive for? Each of us wishes to receive a maximum of benefits from government for the minimum cost. This goal suggests maximum government efficiency, on the one hand, but it also suggests mutual exploitation on the other. Each of us favors an arrangement in which our fellow citizens pay for our benefits.

With these brief descriptions of the cast of characters in hand, let us proceed.

TAMMANY HALL GOES TO WASHINGTON

What should we expect from a legislative body composed of individuals whose first priority is their continued tenure in office? We should expect, first, that the normal activities of its members are those calculated to enhance their chances of reelection. And we should expect, second, that the members would devise and maintain institutional arrangements which facilitate their electoral activities....

For most of the twentieth century, congressmen have engaged in a mix of three kinds of activities: lawmaking, pork barreling, and casework. Congress is first and foremost a lawmaking body, at least according to constitutional theory. In every postwar session Congress "considers" thousands of bills and resolutions, many hundreds of which are brought to a record vote (over 500 in

each chamber in the 93rd Congress). Naturally the critical consideration in taking a position for the record is the maximization of approval in the home district. If the district is unaffected by and unconcerned with the matter at hand, the congressman may then take into account the general welfare of the country. (This sounds cynical, but remember that "profiles in courage" are sufficiently rare that their occurrence inspires books and articles.) Abetted by political scientists of the pluralist school, politicians have propounded an ideology which maintains that the good of the country on any given issue is simply what is best for a majority of congressional districts. This ideology provides a philosophical justification for what congressmen do while acting in their own self-interest.

A second activity favored by congressmen consists of efforts to bring home the bacon to their districts. Many popular articles have been written about the pork barrel, a term originally applied to rivers and harbors legislation but now generalized to cover all manner of federal largesse.[4] Congressmen consider new dams, federal buildings, sewage treatment plants, urban renewal projects, etc. as sweet plums to be plucked. Federal projects are highly visible, their economic impact is easily detected by constituents, and sometimes they even produce something of value to the district. The average constituent may have some trouble translating his congressman's vote on some civil rights issue into a change in his personal welfare. But the workers hired and supplies purchased in connection with a big federal project provide benefits that are widely appreciated. The historical importance congressmen attach to the pork barrel is reflected in the rules of the House. That body accords certain classes of legislation "privileged" status: they may come directly to the floor without passing through the Rules Committee, a traditional graveyard for legislation. What kinds of legislation are privileged? Taxing and spending bills, for one: the government's power to raise and spend money must be kept relatively unfettered. But in addition, the omnibus rivers and harbors bills of the Public Works Committee and public lands bills from the Interior Committee share privileged status. The House will allow a civil rights or defense procurement or environmental bill to languish in the Rules Committee, but it takes special precautions to insure that nothing slows down the approval of dams and irrigation projects.

A third major activity takes up perhaps as much time as the other two combined. Traditionally, constituents appeal to their congressman for myriad favors and services. Sometimes only information is needed, but often constituents request that their congressman intervene in the internal workings of federal agencies to affect a decision in a favorable way, to reverse an adverse decision, or simply to speed up the glacial bureaucratic process. On the basis of extensive personal interviews with congressmen, Charles Clapp writes:

> Denied a favorable ruling by the bureaucracy on a matter of direct concern to him, puzzled or irked by delays in obtaining a decision, confused by the administrative maze through which he is directed to proceed, or ignorant of whom to write, a constituent may turn to his congressman for help. These letters offer great potential for political benefit to the congressman since they affect the constituent personally. If the legislator can be of assistance, he may gain a firm ally; if he is indifferent, he may even lose votes.[5]

Actually congressmen are in an almost unique position in our system, a position shared only with high-level members of the executive branch. Congressmen possess the power to expedite and influence bureaucratic decisions. This capability flows directly from congressional control over what bureaucrats value most: higher budgets and new program authorizations. In a very real sense each congressman is a monopoly supplier of bureaucratic unsticking services for his district.

Every year the federal budget passes through the appropriations committees of Congress. Generally these committees make perfunctory cuts. But on occasion they vent displeasure on an agency and leave it bleeding all over the Capitol. The most extreme case of which I am aware came when the House committee took away the entire budget of the Division of Labor Standards in 1947 (some of the budget was restored elsewhere

in the appropriations process). Deep and serious cuts are made occasionally, and the threat of such cuts keeps most agencies attentive to congressional wishes. Professors Richard Fenno and Aaron Wildavsky have provided extensive documentary and interview evidence of the great respect (and even terror) federal bureaucrats show for the House Appropriations Committee.[6] Moreover, the bureaucracy must keep coming back to Congress to have its old programs reauthorized and new ones added. Again, most such decisions are perfunctory, but exceptions are sufficiently frequent that bureaucrats do not forget the basis of their agencies' existence. For example, the Law Enforcement Assistance Administration (LEAA) and the Food Stamps Program had no easy time of it this last Congress (94th). The bureaucracy needs congressional approval in order to survive, let alone expand. Thus, when a congressman calls about some minor bureaucratic decision or regulation, the bureaucracy considers his accommodation a small price to pay for the goodwill its cooperation will produce, particularly if he has any connection to the substantive committee or the appropriations subcommittee to which it reports.

From the standpoint of capturing voters, the congressman's lawmaking activities differ in two important respects from his porkbarrel and casework activities. First, programmatic actions are inherently controversial. Unless his district is homogeneous, a congressman will find his district divided on many major issues. Thus when he casts a vote, introduces a piece of nontrivial legislation, or makes a speech with policy content he will displease some elements of his district. Some constituents may applaud the congressman's civil rights record, but others believe integration is going too fast. Some support foreign aid, while others believe it's money poured down a rathole. Some advocate economic equality, others stew over welfare cheaters. On such policy matters the congressman can expect to make friends as well as enemies. Presumably he will behave so as to maximize the excess of the former over the latter, but nevertheless a policy stand will generally make some enemies.

In contrast, the pork barrel and casework are relatively less controversial. New federal projects bring jobs, shiny new facilities, and general economic prosperity, or so people believe. Snipping ribbons at the dedication of a new post office or dam is a much more pleasant pursuit than disposing of a constitutional amendment on abortion. Republicans and Democrats, conservatives and liberals, all generally prefer a richer district to a poorer one. Of course, in recent years the river damming and stream-bed straightening activities of the Army Corps of Engineers have aroused some opposition among environmentalists. Congressmen happily reacted by absorbing the opposition and adding environmentalism to the pork barrel: water treatment plants are currently a hot congressional item.

Casework is even less controversial. Some poor, aggrieved constituent becomes enmeshed in the tentacles of an evil bureaucracy and calls upon Congressman St. George to do battle with the dragon. Again Clapp writes;

> A person who has a reasonable complaint or query is regarded as providing an opportunity rather than as adding an extra burden to an already busy office. The party affiliation of the individual even when known to be different from that of the congressman does not normally act as a deterrent to action. Some legislators have built their reputations and their majorities on a program of service to all constituents irrespective of party. Regularly, voters affiliated with the opposition in other contests lend strong support to the lawmaker whose intervention has helped them in their struggle with the bureaucracy.[7]

Even following the revelation of sexual improprieties, Wayne Hays won his Ohio Democratic primary by a two-to-one margin. According to a *Los Angeles Times* feature story, Hays's constituency base was built on a foundation of personal service to constituents:

> They receive help in speeding up bureaucratic action on various kinds of federal assistance—black lung benefits to disabled miners and their families, Social Security payments, veterans' benefits and passports.
>
> Some constituents still tell with pleasure of how Hays stormed clear to the

seventh floor of the State Department and into Secretary of State Dean Rusk's office to demand, successfully, the quick issuance of a passport to an Ohioan.[8]

Practicing politicians will tell you that word of mouth is still the most effective mode of communication. News of favors to constituents gets around and no doubt is embellished in the process.

In sum, when considering the benefits of his programmatic activities, the congressman must tote up gains and losses to arrive at a net profit. Pork barreling and casework, however, are basically pure profit.

A second way in which programmatic activities differ from casework and the pork barrel is the difficulty of assigning responsibility to the former as compared with the latter. No congressman can seriously claim that he is responsible for the 1964 Civil Rights Act, the ABM, or the 1972 Revenue Sharing Act. Most constituents do have some vague notion that their congressman is only one of hundreds and their senator one of an even hundred. Even committee chairmen may have a difficult time claiming credit for a piece of major legislation, let alone a rank-and-file congressman. Ah, but casework, and the pork barrel. In dealing with the bureaucracy, the congressman is not merely one vote of 435. Rather, he is a nonpartisan power, someone whose phone calls snap an office to attention. He is not kept on hold. The constituent who receives aid believes that his congressman and his congressman alone got results. Similarly, congressmen find it easy to claim credit for federal projects awarded their districts. The congressman may have instigated the proposal for the project in the first place, issued regular progress reports, and ultimately announced the award through his office. Maybe he can't claim credit for the 1965 Voting Rights Act, but he can take credit for Littletown's spanking new sewage treatment plant.

Overall then, programmatic activities are dangerous (controversial), on the one hand, and programmatic accomplishments are difficult to claim credit for, on the other. While less exciting, casework and pork barreling are both safe and profitable. For a reelection-oriented congressman the choice is obvious.

The key to the rise of the Washington establishment (and the vanishing marginals) is the following observation: *the growth of an activist federal government has stimulated a change in the mix of congressional activities.* Specifically, a lesser proportion of congressional effort is now going into programmatic activities and a greater proportion into pork-barrel and casework activities. As a result, today's congressmen make relatively fewer enemies and relatively more friends among the people of their districts.

To elaborate, a basic fact of life in twentieth-century America is the growth of the federal role and its attendant bureaucracy. Bureaucracy is the characteristic mode of delivering public goods and services. Ceteris paribus, the more the government attempts to do for people, the more extensive a bureaucracy it creates. As the scope of government expands, more and more citizens find themselves in direct contact with the federal government. Consider the rise in such contacts upon passage of the Social Security Act, work relief projects and other New Deal programs. Consider the millions of additional citizens touched by the veterans' programs of the postwar period. Consider the untold numbers whom the Great Society and its aftermath brought face to face with the federal government. In 1930 the federal bureaucracy was small and rather distant from the everyday concerns of Americans. By 1975 it was neither small nor distant.

As the years have passed, more and more citizens and groups have found themselves dealing with the federal bureaucracy. They may be seeking positive actions—eligibility for various benefits and awards of government grants. Or they may be seeking relief from the costs imposed by bureaucratic regulations—on working conditions, racial and sexual quotas, market restrictions, and numerous other subjects. While not malevolent, bureaucracies make mistakes, both of commission and omission, and normal attempts at redress often meet with unresponsiveness and inflexibility and sometimes seeming incorrigibility. Whatever the problem, the citizen's congressman is a source of succor. The greater the scope of government activity, the greater the demand for his services.

Private monopolists can regulate the demand for their product by raising or lowering the price.

Congressmen have no such (legal) option. When the demand for their services rises, they have no real choice except to meet that demand—to supply more bureaucratic unsticking services—so long as they would rather be elected than unelected. This vulnerability to escalating constituency demands is largely academic, though. I seriously doubt that congressmen resist their gradual transformation from national legislators to errand boy-ombudsmen. As we have noted, casework is all profit. Congressmen have buried proposals to relieve the casework burden by establishing a national ombudsman or Congressman Reuss's proposed Administrative Counsel of the Congress. One of the congressmen interviewed by Clapp stated:

> Before I came to Washington I used to think that it might be nice if the individual states had administrative arms here that would take care of necessary liaison between citizens and the national government. But a congressman running for reelection is interested in building fences by providing personal services. The system is set to reelect incumbents regardless of party, and incumbents wouldn't dream of giving any of this service function away to any subagency. As an elected member I feel the same way.[9]

In fact, it is probable that at least some congressmen deliberately stimulate the demand for their bureaucratic fixit services. (See the exhibit at the end of this chapter.) Recall that the new Republican in district A travels about his district saying:

> I'm your man in Washington. What are your problems? How can I help you?

And in district B, did the demand for the congressman's services rise so much between 1962 and 1964 that a "regiment" of constituency staff became necessary? Or, having access to the regiment, did the new Democrat stimulate the demand to which he would apply his regiment?

In addition to greatly increased casework, let us not forget that the growth of the federal role has also greatly expanded the federal pork barrel. The creative pork barreler need not limit himself to dams and post offices—rather old-fashioned interests. Today, creative congressmen can cadge LEAA money for the local police, urban renewal and housing money for local politicians, educational program grants for the local education bureaucracy. And there are sewage treatment plants, worker training and retraining programs, health services, and programs for the elderly. The pork barrel is full to overflowing. The conscientious congressman can stimulate applications for federal assistance (the sheer number of programs makes it difficult for local officials to stay current with the possibilities), put in a good word during consideration, and announce favorable decisions amid great fanfare.

In sum, everyday decisions by a large and growing federal bureaucracy bestow significant tangible benefits and impose significant tangible costs. Congressmen can affect these decisions. Ergo, the more decisions the bureaucracy has the opportunity to make, the more opportunities there are for the congressman to build up credits.

The nature of the Washington system is now quite clear. Congressmen (typically the majority Democrats) earn electoral credits by establishing various federal programs (the minority Republicans

typically earn credits by fighting the good fight). The legislation is drafted in very general terms, so some agency, existing or newly established, must translate a vague policy mandate into a functioning program, a process that necessitates the promulgation of numerous rules and regulations and, incidentally, the trampling of numerous toes. At the next stage, aggrieved and/or hopeful constituents petition their congressman to intervene in the complex (or at least obscure) decision processes of the bureaucracy. The cycle closes when the congressman lends a sympathetic ear, piously denounces the evils of bureaucracy, intervenes in the latter's decisions, and rides a grateful electorate to ever more impressive electoral showings. Congressmen take credit coming and going. They are the alpha and the omega.

The popular frustration with the permanent government in Washington is partly justified, but to a considerable degree it is misplaced resentment. *Congress is the linchpin of the Washington establishment.* The bureaucracy serves as a convenient lightning rod for public frustration and a convenient whipping boy for congressmen. But so long as the bureaucracy accommodates congressmen, the latter will oblige with ever larger

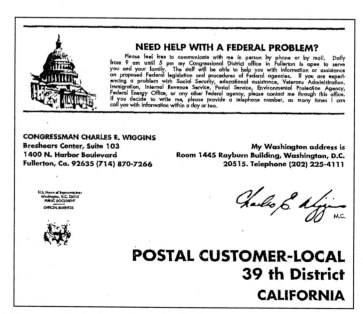

EXHIBIT: How the Congressman-as-Ombudsman Drums up Business

budgets and grants of authority. Congress does not just react to big government—it creates it. All of Washington prospers. More and more bureaucrats promulgate more and more regulations and dispense more and more money. Fewer and fewer congressmen suffer electoral defeat. Elements of the electorate benefit from government programs, and all of the electorate is eligible for ombudsman services. But the general, long-term welfare of the United States is no more than an incidental by-product of the system.

End Notes

1. Henry David Thoreau, *Walden* (London: Walter Scott Publishing Co., no date) p. 72.
2. For a more extended discussion of the electoral motivation see Fiorina, *Representatives, Roll Calls, and Constituencies,* chap. 2; David R. Mayhew, *Congress: The Electoral Connection* (New Haven: Yale University Press, 1974).
3. For a discussion of the goals of bureaucrats see William Niskanen, *Bureaucracy and Representative Government* (Chicago: Aldine-Atherton, 1971).
4. The traditional pork barrel is the subject of an excellent treatment by John Ferejohn. See his *Pork Barrel Politics: Rivers and Harbors Legislation 1947–1968,* (Stanford: Stanford University Press, 1974).
5. Charles Clapp, *The Congressman: His Job As He Sees It* (Washington: Brookings Institution, 1963), p. 84.
6. Richard Fenno, *The Power of the Purse* (Boston: Little, Brown, 1966); Aaron Wildavsky, *The Politics of the Budgetary Process,* 2d ed. (Boston: Little, Brown, 1974).
7. Clapp, *The Congressman: His Job As His Sees It,* p. 84.
8. "Hays Improves Rapidly from Overdose," *Los Angeles Times*, June 12, 1976, part I, p. 19. Similarly, Congressman Robert Leggett (D., Calif.) won reelection in 1976 even amid revelations of a thirteen-year bigamous relationship and rumors of other affairs and improprieties. The *Los Angeles Times* wrote:

   > Because of federal spending, times are good here in California's 4th Congressional District, and that is a major reason why local political leaders in both parties, as well as the man on the street, believe that Leggett will still be their congressman next year....
   >
   > Leggett has concentrated on bringing federal dollars to his district and on acting as an ombudsman for constituents having problems with their military pay or Social Security or GI benefit checks. He sends out form letters to parents of newborn children congratulating them.

   Traditionally, personal misbehavior has been one of the few shoals on which incumbent congressmen could founder. But today's incumbents have so entrenched themselves by personal service to constituents that even scandal does not harm them mortally. See David Johnson, "Rep. Leggett Expected to Survive Sex Scandal," *Los Angeles Times,* July 26, 1976, part I, p. 1.
9. Clapp, *The Congressman: His Job As He Sees It,* p. 94.

32

Congress: The Electoral Connection

David Mayhew

How to study legislative behavior is a question that does not yield a consensual answer among political scientists. An ethic of conceptual pluralism prevails in the field, and no doubt it should. If there is any consensus, it is on the point that scholarly treatments should offer explanations—that they should go beyond descriptive accounts of legislators and legislatures to supply general statements about why both of them do what they do. What constitutes a persuasive explanation? In their contemporary quest to find out, legislative students have ranged far and wide, sometimes borrowing or plundering explanatory styles from the neighboring social sciences.

The most important borrowing has been from sociology. In fact it is fair to say that legislative research in the 1950s and 1960s had a dominant sociological tone to it. The literature abounded in terms like *role, norm, system*, and *socialitation.* We learned that some United States senators adopt an "outsider" role;[1] that the House Appropriations Committee can usefully be viewed as a self-maintaining system;[2] that legislators can be categorized as "trustees," "politicos," or "delegates";[3] that the United States Senate has "followays."[4] These findings and others like them grew out of research based for the first time on systematic elite interviewing.

From no other social science has borrowing been so direct or so important. But it is possible to point to writings that have shared—or partly shared—a root assumption of economics. The difference between economic and sociological explanation is sharp. As Niskanen puts it, "the 'compositive' method of economics, which develops hypotheses about social behavior from models of purposive behavior by individuals, contrasts with the 'collectivist' method of sociology, which develops hypotheses about social behavior from models of role behavior by aggregative ideal types."[5] To my knowledge no political scientist has explicitly anchored his legislative research in economics, but a number have in one way or another invoked "purposive behavior" as a guide to explanation. Thus there are three articles by Scher in which he posits the conditions under which congressmen will find it in their interest to engage in legislative oversight.[6] Other examples are Wildavsky's work on bargaining in the budgetary process[7] and Riker's general work on coalition building with its legislative applications.[8] More recently Manley and Fenno have given a clear purposive thrust to their important committee studies.[9] Fenno's thinking has evolved to the point where he now places a strong emphasis on detecting why congressmen join specific committees and what they get out of being members of them.

There is probably a disciplinary drift toward the purposive, a drift, so to speak, from the sociological toward the economic. If so, it occurs at a time when some economists are themselves edging over into the legislative field. There is

---

Lindblom's writing on the politics of partisan mutual adjustment, with its legislative ramifications.[10] More generally there are recent writings of economists in the public finance tradition.[11] Public finance has its normative and empirical sides, the former best exemplified here in the discussion of legislative decision making offered by Buchanan and Tullock.[12] Niskanen develops the empirical side in his work positing bureaus as budget maximizers—an effort that leads him to hypothesize about the relations between bureaus and legislative committees.[13] Public finance scholars seem to have become interested in legislative studies as a result of their abandoning the old idea of the Benthamite legislator; that is, they have come to display a concern for what public officials actually do rather than an assumption that officials will automatically translate good policy into law once somebody finds out what it is.[14] With political scientists exploring the purposive and economists the legislative, there are at least three forms that future relations between writers in the two disciplines could take. First, scholars in both could continue to disregard each other's writings. Second, they could engage in an unseemly struggle over turf. Third, they could use each other's insights to develop collectively a more vigorous legislative scholarship in the style of political economy.

All this is an introduction to a statement of what I intend to do in the following essay. Mostly through personal experience on Capitol Hill, I have become convinced that scrutiny of purposive behavior offers the best route to an understanding of legislatures—or at least of the United States Congress. In the fashion of economics, I shall make a simple abstract assumption about human motivation and then speculate about the consequences of behavior based on that motivation. Specifically, I shall conjure up a vision of United States congressmen as single-minded seekers of reelection, see what kinds of activity that goal implies, and then speculate about how congressmen so motivated are likely to go about building and sustaining legislative institutions and making policy. At all points I shall try to match the abstract with the factual.

I find an emphasis on the reelection goal attractive for a number of reasons. First, I think

it fits political reality rather well. Second, it puts the spotlight directly on men rather than on parties and pressure groups, which in the past have often entered discussions of American politics as analytic phantoms. Third, I think politics is best studied as a struggle among men to gain and maintain power and the consequences of that struggle. Fourth—and perhaps most important—the reelection quest establishes an accountability relationship with an electorate, and any serious thinking about democratic theory has to give a central place to the question of accountability. The abstract assumption notwithstanding, I regard this venture as an exercise in political science rather than economics. Leaving aside the fact that I have no economics expertise to display, I find that economists who study legislatures bring to bear interests different from those of political scientists. Not surprisingly the public finance scholars tend to look upon government as a device for spending money. I shall give some attention to spending, but also to other governmental activities such as the production of binding rules. And I shall touch upon such traditional subjects of political science as elections, parties, governmental structure, and regime stability. Another distinction here is that economics research tends to be infused with the normative assumption that policy decisions should be judged by how well they meet the standard of Pareto optimality. This is an assumption that I do not share and that I do not think most political scientists share. There will be no need here to set forth any alternative assumption. I may say, for the record, that I find the model of proper legislative activity offered by Rawls a good deal more edifying than any that could be built on a foundation of Pareto optimality.[15]

My subject of concern here is a single legislative institution, the United States Congress. In many ways, of course, the Congress is a unique or unusual body. It is probably the most highly "professionalized" of legislatures, in the sense that it promotes careerism among its members and gives them the salaries, staff, and other resources to sustain careers.[16] Its parties are exceptionally diffuse. It is widely thought to be especially "strong" among legislatures as a checker of executive power. Like most Latin American legislatures but unlike most European ones, it labors in the shadow of a separately elected executive. My decision to focus on the Congress flows from a belief that there is something to be gained in an intensive analysis of a particular and important institution. But there is something general to be gained as well, for the exceptionalist argument should not be carried too far. In a good many ways the Congress is just one in a large family of legislative bodies. I shall find it useful at various points in the analysis to invoke comparisons with European parliaments and with American state legislatures and city councils. I shall ponder the question of what "functions" the Congress performs or is capable of performing—a question that can be answered only with the records of other legislatures in mind. Functions to be given special attention are those of legislating, overseeing the executive, expressing public opinion, and servicing constituents. No functional capabilities can be automatically assumed.[17] Indeed the very term *legislature* is an unfortunate one because it confuses structure and function. Accordingly I shall from here on use the more awkward but more neutral term *representative assembly* to refer to members of the class of entities inhabited by the United States House and Senate. Whatever the noun, the identifying characteristics of institutions in the class have been well stated by Loewenberg: it is true of all such entities that (1) "their members are formally equal to each other in status, distinguishing parliaments from hierarchically ordered organizations," and (2) "the authority of their members depends on their claim to representing the rest of the community, in some sense of that protean concept, representation."[18]...

End Notes

1. Ralph K. Huitt, "The Outsider in the Senate: An Alternative Role," ch. 4 in Huitt and Robert L. Peabody (eds.), *Congress: Two Decades of Analysis* (New York: Harper and Row, 1969).
2. Richard F. Fenno, Jr., *The Power of the Purse* (Boston: Little, Brown and Co., 1966), ch. 5.
3. John C. Wahlke et al., *The Legislative System* (New York: Wiley, 1962), ch. 12; Roger H. Davidson, *The Role of the Congressman* (New York: Pegasus, 1969), ch. 4.
4. Donald R. Matthews, *U.S. Senators and Their World* (Chapel Hill: University of North Carolina Press, 1960), ch. 5.
5. William A. Niskanen, *Bureaucracy and Representative Government* (New York: Aldine-Atherton, 1971), p. 5.
6. Seymour Scher, "Congressional Committee Members as Independent Agency Overseers: A Case Study," 54 *American Political Science Review* 911–20 (1960); "The Politics of Agency Organization," 15 *Western Political Quarterly* 328–44 (1962); "Conditions for Legislative Control," 25 *Journal of Politics* 526–51 (1963).
7. Aaron Wildavsky, *The Politics of the Budgetary Process* (Boston: Little, Brown and Co., 1964).
8. William H. Riker, *The Theory of Political Coalitions* (New Haven: Yale University Press, 1962), with ch. 7 specifically on Congress; also William H. Riker and Donald Niemi, "The Stability of Coalitions in the House of Representatives," 56 *American Political Science Review* 58–65 (1962).
9. John F. Manley, *The Politics of Finance: The House Committee on Ways and Means* (Boston: Little, Brown and Co., 1970); Richard F. Fenno, Jr., *Congressmen in Committees* (Boston: Little, Brown and Co., 1973).
10. Charles E. Lindblom, *The Intelligence of Democracy* (New York: Free Press, 1965).
11. A suitable characterization of this tradition: "The theory of public finance has addressed itself to the questions of how much money should be spent on public expenditures, how these expenditures should be distributed among different public wants, and how the costs should be distributed between present and future, and among the members of the society." James S. Coleman, "Individual Interests and Collective Action," in Gordon Tullock (ed.), *Papers on Non-Market Decision-Making* (Charlottesville; Thomas Jefferson Center for Political Economy, University of Virginia, 1966).
12. James M. Buchanan and Gordon Tullock, *The Calculus of Consent* (Ann Arbor: University of Michigan Press, 1967), part III.
13. Niskanen, *Bureaucracy and Representative Government*.
14. There is a discussion of this point in Nathan Rosenberg, "Efficiency in the Government Sector: Discussion," 54 *American Economic Review* 251–52 (May 1954); and in James M.

Buchanan, *Public Finance in Democratic Process* (Chapel Hill: University of North Carolina Press, 1967), p. 173.

15. John Rawls, *A Theory of Justice* (Cambridge: Harvard University Press, 1971), chs. 4 and 5, and especially pp. 274–84.

16. The term is from H. Douglas Price, "Computer Simulation and Legislative 'Professionalism': Some Quantitative Approaches to Legislative Evolution," paper presented to the annual convention of the American Political Science Association, 1970.

17. "But it is equally true, though only of late and slowly beginning to be acknowledged, that a numerous assembly is as little fitted for the direct business of legislation as for that of administration." John Stuart Mill, *Considerations on Representative Government* (Chicago: Regency, 1962), p. 104.

18. Gerhard Loewenberg, "The Role of Parliaments in Modern Political Systems," in Loewenberg (ed.), *Modern Parliaments: Change or Decline?* (Chicago: Aldine-Atherton, 1971), p. 3.

33

Presidential Power

Richard Neustadt

1

In the United States we like to "rate" a President. We measure him as "weak" or "strong" and call what we are measuring his "leadership." We do not wait until a man is dead; we rate him from the moment he takes office. We are quite right to do so. His office has become the focal point of politics and policy in our political system. Our commentators and our politicians make a specialty of taking the man's measurements. The rest of us join in when we feel "government" impinging on our private lives. In the third quarter of the twentieth century millions of us have that feeling often.

... Although we all make judgments about presidential leadership, we often base our judgments upon images of office that are far removed from the reality. We also use those images when we tell one another whom to choose as President. But it is risky to appraise a man in office or to choose a man for office on false premises about the nature of his job. When the job is the Presidency of the United States the risk becomes excessive. ...

We deal here with the President himself and with his influence on governmental action. In institutional terms the Presidency now includes 2000 men and women. The President is only one of them. But *his* performance scarcely can be measured without focusing on *him*. In terms of party, or of country, or the West, so-called, his leadership involves far more than governmental action. But the sharpening of spirit and of values and of purposes is not done in a vacuum. Although governmental action may not be the whole of leadership, all else is nurtured by it and gains meaning from it. Yet if we treat the Presidency as the President, we cannot measure him as though he were the government. Not action as an outcome but his impact on the outcome is the measure of the man. His strength or weakness, then, turns on his personal capacity to influence the conduct of the men who make up government. His influence becomes the mark of leadership. To rate a President according to these rules, one looks into the man's own capabilities as seeker and as wielder of effective influence upon the other men involved in governing the country...

"Presidential" on the title page means nothing but the President. "Power" means *his* influence. It helps to have these meanings settled at the start.

There are two ways to study "presidential power." One way is to focus on the tactics, so to speak, of influencing certain men in given situations: how to get a bill through Congress, how to settle strikes, how to quiet Cabinet feuds, or how to stop a Suez. The other way is to step back from tactics on those "givens" and to deal with influence in more strategic terms: what is its nature and what are its sources? What can *this* man accomplish to improve the prospect that he will have influence when he wants it? Strategically, the question is not how he masters Congress in a peculiar instance, but what he does to boost his chance for mastery in any instance, looking toward tomorrow from today...

2

To look into the strategy of presidential influence one must decide at whom to look. Power problems vary with the scope and scale of government, the state of politics, the progress of technology, the pace of world relationships. Power in the Nineteen-sixties cannot be acquired or employed on the same terms as those befitting Calvin Coolidge, or Theodore Roosevelt, or Grover Cleveland, or James K. Polk. But there is a real likelihood that in the next decade a President will have to reach for influence and use it under much the same conditions we have known since the Second World War. If so, the men whose problems shed most light on the White House

prospects are Dwight David Eisenhower and Harry S. Truman. It is at them, primarily, that we shall look. To do so is to see the shadow of another, Franklin D. Roosevelt. They worked amidst the remnants of his voter coalition, and they filled an office that his practice had enlarged.

Our two most recent Presidents have had in common something that is likely to endure into our future: the setting for a great deal of their work. They worked in an environment of policy and politics marked by a high degree of continuity. To sense the continuity from Truman's time through Eisenhower's one need only place the newspapers of 1959 alongside those of 1949. Save for the issue of domestic communists, the subject matter of our policy and politics remains almost unchanged. We deal as we have done in terms of cold war, of an arms race, of a competition overseas, of danger from inflation, and of damage from recession. We skirmish on the frontiers of the Welfare State and in the borderlands of race relations. Aspects change, but labels stay the same. So do dilemmas. Everything remains unfinished business. Not in this century has there been comparable continuity from a decade's beginning to its end; count back from 1949 and this grows plain. There even has been continuity in the behavior of our national electorate; what Samuel Lubell nine years ago called "stalemate" in our partisan alignments has not broken yet.

The similarities in Truman's setting and in Eisenhower's give their years a unity distinct from the War Years, or the Depression Era, or the Twenties, or before. In governmental terms, at least, the fifteen years since V-J Day deserve a designation all their own. "Mid-century" will serve for present purposes. And what distinguishes mid-century can be put very briefly: emergencies in policy with politics as usual.

"Emergency" describes mid-century conditions only by the standards of the past. By present standards what would once have been emergency is commonplace. Policy dilemmas through the postwar period resemble past emergencies in one respect, their difficulty and complexity for government. Technological innovation, social and political change abroad, population growth at home impose enormous strains not only on the managerial equipment of our policy-makers but also on their intellectual resources. The groupings of mature men at mid-century remind one of the intellectual confusions stemming from depression, thirty years ago, when men were also pushed past comprehension by the novelty of their condition. In our time innovation keeps us *constantly* confused; no sooner do we start to comprehend than something new is added, and we grope again. But unlike the Great Difficulties of the past, our policy dilemmas rarely produce what the country feels as "crisis." Not even the Korean War brought anything approaching sustained national "consensus." Since 1945 innumerable situations have been felt as crises inside government; there rarely has been comparable feeling outside government. In the era of the Cold War we have practiced "peacetime" politics. What else could we have done? Cold War is not a "crisis"; it becomes a way of life.

Our politics has been "as usual," but only by the standard of past *crises*. In comparison with what was once normality, our politics has been *un*usual. The weakening of party ties, the emphasis on personality, the close approach of world events, the changeability of public moods, and above all the ticket-splitting, none of this was "usual" before the Second World War. The symbol of mid-century political conditions is the White House in one party's hands with Congress in the other's—a symbol plainly visible in eight of the past fifteen years and all but visible in four of the remaining seven. Nothing really comparable has been seen in this country since the Eighteen-eighties. And the Eighties were not troubled by emergencies in policy.

As for politics and policy combined, we have seen some precursors of our setting at mid-century. Franklin Roosevelt had a reasonably comparable setting in his middle years as President, though not in his first years and not after Pearl Harbor. Indeed, if one excepts the war, mid-century could properly be said to start with Roosevelt's second term. Our recent situation is to be compared, as well, with aspects of the Civil War. Abraham Lincoln is much closer to us in condition than in time, the Lincoln plagued by Radicals and shunned by Democrats amidst the managerial and intellectual confusions of twentieth-century warfare in the nineteenth century.

And in 1919 Woodrow Wilson faced and was defeated by conditions something like our own. But save for these men one can say of Truman and of Eisenhower that they were the first who had to fashion presidential influence out of mid-century materials. Presumably they will not be the last.

3

We tend to measure Truman's predecessors as though "leadership" consisted of initiatives in economics, or diplomacy, or legislation, or in mass communication. If we measured him and his successors so, they would be leaders automatically. A striking feature of our recent past has been the transformation into routine practice of the actions we once treated as exceptional. A President may retain liberty, in Woodrow Wilson's phrase, "to be as big a man as he can." But nowadays he cannot be as small as he might like.

Our two most recent Presidents have gone through all the motions we traditionally associate with strength in office. So will the man who takes the oath on January 20, 1961. In instance after instance the exceptional behavior of our earlier "strong" Presidents has now been set by statute as a regular requirement. Theodore Roosevelt once assumed the "steward's" role in the emergency created by the great coal strike of 1902; the Railway Labor Act and the Taft-Hartley Act now make such interventions mandatory upon Presidents. The other Roosevelt once asserted personal responsibility for gauging and for guiding the American economy; the Employment Act binds his successors to that task. Wilson and F.D.R. became chief spokesmen, leading actors, on a world stage at the height of war; now UN membership, far-flung alliances, prescribe that role continuously in times termed "peace." Through both world wars our Presidents grappled experimentally with an emergency-created need to "integrate" foreign and military policies; the National Security Act now takes that need for granted as a constant of our times. F.D.R. and Truman made themselves responsible for the development and first use of atomic weapons; the Atomic Energy Act now puts a comparable burden on the back of every President. And what has escaped statutory recognition has mostly been accreted into presidential common law, confirmed by custom, no less binding: the "fireside chat" and the press conference, for example, or the personally presented legislative program, or personal campaigning in congressional elections.

In form all Presidents are leaders, nowadays. In fact this guarantees no more than that they will be clerks. Everybody now expects the man inside the White House to do something about everything. Laws and customs now reflect acceptance of him as the Great Initiator, an acceptance quite as widespread at the Capitol as at his end of Pennsylvania Avenue. But such acceptance does not signify that all the rest of government is at his feet. It merely signifies that other men have found it practically impossible to do *their* jobs without assurance of initiatives from him. Service for themselves, not power for the President, has brought them to accept his leadership in form. They find his actions useful in their business. The transformation of his routine obligations testifies to their dependence on an active White House. A President, these days, is an invaluable clerk. His services are in demand all over Washington. His influence, however, is a very different matter. Laws and customs tell us little about leadership in fact.

4

Why have our Presidents been honored with this clerkship? The answer is that no one else's services suffice. Our Constitution, our traditions, and our politics provide no better source for the initiatives a President can take. Executive officials need decisions, and political protection, and a referee for fights. Where are these to come from but the White House? Congressmen need an agenda from outside, something with high status to respond to or react against. What provides it better than the program of the President? Party politicians need a record to defend in the next national campaign. How can it be made except by "their" Administration? Private persons with a public axe to grind may need a helping hand or they may need a grinding stone. In either case who gives more satisfaction than a President? And outside the United States, in every country where our policies and postures influence home

politics, there will be people needing just the "right" thing said and done or just the "wrong" thing stopped *in Washington*. What symbolizes Washington more nearly than the White House?

A modern President is bound to face demands for aid and service from five more or less distinguishable sources: from Executive officialdom, from Congress, from his partisans, from citizens at large, and from abroad. The Presidency's clerkship is expressive of these pressures. In effect they are constituency pressures and each President has five sets of constituents. The five are not distinguished by their membership; membership is obviously an overlapping matter. And taken one by one they do not match the man's electorate; one of them, indeed, is outside his electorate. They are distinguished, rather, by their different claims upon him. Initiatives are what they want, for five distinctive reasons. Since government and politics have offered no alternative, our laws and customs turn those wants into his obligations.

Why, then, is the President not guaranteed an influence commensurate with services performed? Constituent relations are relations of dependence. Everyone with any share in governing this country will belong to one (or two, or three) of his "constituencies." Since everyone depends on him why is he not assured of everyone's support? The answer is that no one else sits where he sits, or sees quite as he sees; no one else feels the full weight of his obligations. Those obligations are a tribute to his unique place in our political system. But just because it is unique they fall on him alone. *The same conditions that promote his leadership in form preclude a guarantee of leadership in fact.* No man or group at either end of Pennsylvania Avenue shares his peculiar status in our government and politics. That is why his services are in demand. By the same token, though, the obligations of all other men are different from his own. His Cabinet officers have departmental duties and constituents. His legislative leaders head *congressional* parties, one in either House. His national party organization stands apart from his official family. His political allies in the States need not face Washington, or one another. The private groups that seek him out are not compelled to govern. And friends abroad are not compelled to run in our elections. Lacking his position and prerogatives, these men cannot regard his obligations as their own. They have their jobs to do; none is the same as his. As they perceive their duty they may find it right to follow him, in fact, or they may not. Whether they will feel obliged *on their responsibility* to do what he wants done remains an open question....

34

The Presidential Policy Stream

Paul Light

Presidential policy is the product of a stream of people and ideas that flows through the White House. At the start of the term, the stream is often swollen with campaign promises and competing issues. The president's major task is to narrow the stream into a manageable policy agenda. By the end of the term, the stream is reduced to a trickle and the president's major task is to pass the initial programs and get re-elected.

The stream itself is composed of four currents that come together in the White House. The first current carries the *problems* that confront an administration during its term: budget deficits, energy shortages, international crises. The second current carries the different *solutions* that emerge as answers to the problems: tax and spending cuts, solar energy research, summit diplomacy. The third current carries the *assumptions* that define the problems and solutions: economic forecasts, missile tests, guesses about Soviet intentions. The fourth current carries the *players* who participate in the presidential policy debate: presidents, their staffs, cabinet members, commissions.

Although these four currents carry the essential ingredients of presidential policy, they are narrowed into final decisions by two filters: *resources* and *opportunities*. Resources are needed to make and market the president's agenda; they include time and energy to make decisions, information and expertise to evaluate choices, public approval and party seats in Congress to win passage, and money and bureaucrats to implement final legislation. Opportunities are needed to present the national agenda to Congress and the public; these depend upon the ebb and flow of the major policy calendars and upon presidential cycles of increasing effectiveness and decreasing influence.

The four currents—problems, solutions, assumptions, and players—often flow together before they reach the presidency: problems find players: solutions find assumptions, problems find solutions, and so on. In theory, all potential problems, solutions, players, and assumptions exist somewhere in the presidential policy stream. In reality, presidents see only a fraction of the problems and solutions that merit attention. Most presidents deliberately structure the policy stream to limit the flow of problems and solutions to a manageable level, leaving the filtering decisions to the White House staff. Presidents who will not

From Paul Light, "The Presidential Policy Stream," in *The Presidency and the Political System*, ed. Michael Nelson (Washington, DC: CQ Press, 1984), pp. 423–448. Reprinted by permission.

delegate (Jimmy Carter) or do not watch the evolving process (Ronald Reagan) are sometimes overwhelmed. The key to narrowing the policy stream to a final agenda of presidential priorities—and to winning reelection or a place in history—is to combine the "right" problems with the "right" solutions, assumptions, and players. Presidents differ, of course, in their ability to make these matches.

Before looking at each policy current separately, it is important to recognize that, like a stream, the policy process is extremely fluid. A change of problems—from economics to defense, from foreign affairs to domestic programs—has a rippling effect on the rest of the stream. A change of players—from Alexander Haig to George Shultz, from Edwin Meese to James Baker—significantly affects the kinds of problems and solutions that emerge from the filtering process. A change of assumptions—from optimistic to pessimistic, from best-case to worst-case—has a major influence on players who control the winnowing decisions. And a change of solutions—from supply-side to tax-side, from MX race-track to MX dense-pack—affects assumptions and problems.

Moreover, because the process is so fluid, few fixed rules apply. There is no required sequence for channeling the four currents into a policy agenda; no rule on where to start. Although the filtering process generally begins with the selection of a problem and continues with a search for a solution, some decisions start with a solution and only then move to the problem. Still other decisions start with a pessimistic forecast or an ambitious staff player. The presidential policy stream often transcends constitutional and legal boundaries, taking on a life of its own. The very notion that there is a presidential policy stream suggests a dynamic, often unpredictable process that is much less mechanical and orderly than our civics books have led us to believe.

CURRENTS OF PRESIDENTIAL POLICY

Problems

Over time, the current of problems changes, and different issues merit presidential attention. The current includes old problems that have been discussed for decades and new problems that have just been noticed, large problems that appear to be virtually unsolvable and small problems that border on the routine. Although some problems seem to demand presidential action because of their seriousness, presidents retain considerable discretion over the choice of issues for their policy agendas. In 1969, Richard Nixon concentrated on foreign problems—détente with the Soviet Union, the Vietnam War, a new China policy—while largely ignoring domestic policy. In 1977, Jimmy Carter concentrated on domestic problems—energy, hospital cost containment, electoral reform, welfare reform—at the expense of foreign policy. In 1981, Ronald Reagan concentrated on economic problems—inflation, budget deficits, tax rates—while largely avoiding foreign and domestic policy.

Although presidents have wide leeway, some problems move through the presidential policy stream with more visibility than others. Medical care for the aged was a prominent problem long before President John F. Kennedy selected it for his domestic agenda in 1961; welfare reform was a problem on at least two presidential agendas before Carter tackled it in 1977. The rise and fall of problems within the presidential policy stream involves the combined interests of Congress, lobbyists, bureaucrats, and presidents, all looking for problems that match their political and policy goals.

Once a problem is "discovered," it may produce intense activity for several years. But hot issues usually cool off quickly. During the past decade, civil rights and education virtually disappeared from the domestic problem list, only to return as campaign issues for 1984. They were replaced by energy, welfare reform, social security deficits, and deregulation—issues that were not in the current 20 years ago.

The movement of problems within the presidential policy stream involves two simple patterns.[1] First, some problems surface so quickly and involve such controversy that all other issues are submerged. In 1981, Reagan's tax and spending cuts dominated the presidential agenda; little room was left for competing issues, including school prayer and abortion, until 1982. Other issues may dominate the problem current, not because of their controversial nature, but because of their appeal as easy targets for presidential success. In the late 1970s and early 1980s, economic deregulation greatly interested presidents: first railroad, then airline and trucking, now telecommunications. Second, some problems exhaust themselves over time, dropping from the policy currents. Often a problem proves so difficult that presidents and other policy makers finally let it drop. Richard Nixon, Gerald Ford, and Jimmy Carter all tried to tackle welfare reform and all eventually gave up.

On the other hand, some problems disappear from the presidential agenda because they appear to be resolved. One reason education dropped from the problem current is that Kennedy and Lyndon B. Johnson were remarkably successful in winning passage of their legislative agenda. Between 1961 and 1968, Congress passed a long string of education programs: aid to primary and secondary education, aid to higher education, Headstart, the Teacher Corps, library and school construction, school lunches, teacher education. For a decade after Johnson, many policy makers believed that the problems were solved. When education returned to the agenda in 1977, the problem was to build an executive department to house the programs as well as to find the money in a tight budget to pay for them. When education returned once more in 1983, however, the problem was defined as a decline in school quality, an implicit criticism of the Kennedy and Johnson programs. Perhaps some problems can never be completely resolved, returning at uncertain intervals in the policy stream.

Although individual problems come and go within the current, presidents generally think in terms of problem clusters: domestic, economic, defense and foreign affairs. Domestic and economic issues concern what happens *inside* the nation—even if the causes are international— while defense and foreign problems are about what happens *outside* the nation—even if the results are felt within the United States. These problem clusters are treated differently in the institutional presidency. Domestic problems usually move through the Office of Policy Development (known as the Domestic Council under Nixon and Ford, then as the Domestic Policy Staff under Carter); economic problems through the Council of Economic Advisers and the Office of Management and Budget; and foreign and defense problems through the National Security Council. The players in each cluster are generally separate (domestic policy aides rarely interact with national security staff), and the lines of communication radiate to different corners of the executive branch. Yet even if presidents think in terms of these "subpresidencies,"[2] the distinctions frequently are blurred in reality. Foreign crises may cause severe economic problems at home; defense problems outside the United States may cause domestic problems, particularly if the solutions call for deep domestic spending cuts (Reagan) or draft registration (Carter).

Once the problem current enters the White House policy stream, the critical question is why some problems are selected and others ignored. Why did Carter pick energy shortages and welfare reform but neglect national health insurance? Why did Kennedy choose education and medical care for the aged but delay civil rights? Why did Reagan mention school prayer and tuition tax credits in his 1983 State of the Union address but not abortion? All problems carry some level of benefits that make them attractive to presidents. Although the levels vary from problem to problem, president to president, and year to year, they exist nonetheless. Theoretically, presidents could assign specific values to every problem in the policy stream, then choose the problems with the highest returns. Realistically, they can estimate only the rough rewards of one problem over another, either through public opinion or their own political instincts.

Ultimately, then, benefits are in the eye of the beholder. School prayer was an inviting problem for Ronald Reagan but of no interest to liberal Democrats; equal rights for women was an attractive problem for Gerald Ford but not for more conservative Republicans. The reason why one president will see value in a problem when another does not is goals. Presidents want to be reelected, because they care about their place in history, or because they truly believe the problems are important....

Solutions

Solutions to problems take the form of legislation, executive orders, regulations, symbolic maneuvers, vetoes, or commissions. Even doing nothing is a possible solution in the presidential policy stream....

The solution current has two basic features. First, each problem can have a number of potential solutions. As one Carter domestic policy aide told me: "There's never any shortage of people telling you what to do. They come out from under every rock with their own answer to the problems. Energy is a great example. We got ideas ranging from solar to geothermal to coal gasification to offshore drilling to conservation. It was more an exercise in picking the right ones."

Second, and more important, most solutions are designed to answer more than one problem. Indeed, when solutions are designed to solve multiple problems, the chances for legislative passage increase. Carter's hospital cost containment plan was advertised as a solution to four different problems: inflation, by holding down medical costs; deficits, by holding down Medicare and Medicaid spending; social security bankruptcy, by freeing up room for higher payroll taxes; and urban health shortages, by providing more doctors for inner cities. That the program did not pass is a tribute to the combined efforts of the American Medical Association and the hospital lobbies, who did not agree that hospital cost containment was the proper solution to the various problems....

Solutions are actually the product of a string of decisions. First, presidents must decide whether to act. A president may understand the importance of a problem but still be unable or unwilling to propose a solution. A president may want the acclaim that comes from finding the problem but not the costs of winning a solution. Second, presidents then must decide just what to put into the solution. The choices are many. Should it involve legislation or executive action; include a specific proposal to Congress or an effort to veto a bill already passed; be new and innovative or a simple modification of past legislation; center on a large, complicated package or a small, modest bill; rely on spending or regulation to accomplish its ends; be short-term or leave more time for full implementation; be sent to Congress as a "take-it-or-leave-it" omnibus package or as a series of smaller, self-contained proposals? Although the list of questions is rarely so straightforward, each choice must be made at some point in the current of solutions.

Once the president decides to act, costs determine why some solutions are adopted and others ignored. Just as presidents weigh benefits in selecting problems, they measure costs in adopting solutions. First, presidents are very aware of *budget costs*. In an era of tight budgets and high deficits, new programs must pass the budget test before presidents will adopt them. Second, presidents assess *political costs*. Although presidents are interested in public reactions, they are concerned most directly with the question "Will it fly on Capitol Hill?" Presidents try to reduce their political costs in Congress by bargaining over pet projects, trading votes on other bills, assigning credit or blame, timing their requests to avoid overloading in important committees, lobbying to direct congressional attention to their priorities, and using the power of the presidency to stimulate public pressure. Certainly, trips to Camp David and invitations to White House dinners do not sway votes on major bills, but they do make it easier for members of Congress to stay in the habit of supporting the president longer.

Third, presidents are aware—sometimes only dimly—of *technical costs*. Unfortunately, the question "Will it work?" is asked only occasionally. Presidents appear much less concerned with workability than with budget and political costs. According to Martin Anderson, a domestic policy aide under Nixon and director of the Office of Policy Development under Reagan, Nixon's 1969 welfare reform plan never passed the technical hurdle: "No one seemed to clearly comprehend that there was, in fact, no way out of the dilemma presented by the conflicting goals of reasonably high welfare payments, low tax rates, and low cost. To some it seemed that the plan was 'such a good thing' that the possibility of it not being possible was never seriously considered."[3]

Presidents view costs, like benefits, differently. Among recent presidents, Reagan may be the most preoccupied with budget costs, while Johnson may have been overconcerned with politics. Since 1970, however, budget costs have become the dominant influence in the search for solutions. This major change in presidential policy making was evident in the Ford, Carter, and Reagan administrations: if a solution could not pass the budget hurdle, it was dropped. Concern with budgetary effects is, of course, a product of staggering deficits since the early 1970s. Yet, as the budget has grown in importance, the attention to technical issues has declined. Reagan's supply-side economic program and defense expansion surmounted both the budget and political hurdles, but as Office of Management and Budget Director David Stockman acknowledged in an interview in *The Atlantic*, they never passed the test of workability.[4] The critical issue is whether the three costs can ever be compatible. Do budget questions rule out potentially workable solutions? Do political costs conflict with budget considerations? And, if they are incompatible, which cost should come first?

Assumptions

Assumptions tell presidents what the world is like. They help presidents to understand the causes of problems and the effects of solutions. Some assumptions are based on complicated models of how the economy behaves; others are simple guesses about what the Soviets believe. Because there is always some uncertainty about how the world works, presidents often must make choices among competing assumptions. The president must decide, for example, whether the Soviets are basically evil (Reagan's assumption in a 1983 speech to evangelical Christians) or somewhat more humane (Carter's assumption until the invasion of Afghanistan).

As presidents make choices among competing problems and solutions, they must rely on the best available assumptions, which are themselves the results of subjective and sometimes conflicting estimates: How bad is the problem? Can it be solved? What are the benefits? How much will it cost? Will it work? What will the public think? When will the economy improve? Most of these questions cannot be answered in any objective sense. Presidents are no more gifted at fortunetelling than other human beings; they must rely on the best assumptions available. In early 1983, for example, Reagan was forced to choose between an optimistic economic forecast backed by supply-siders and a pessimistic forecast supported by more traditional advisers.

Assumptions may be the most important but least understood current in the presidential policy stream. Assumptions help presidents to predict the future, understand the present, and analyze the past. They help players recognize problems and work out solutions. Because assumptions are not always based on a complete knowledge of objective reality, conflict in the White House over which assumptions should be made can be intense. Indeed, assumptions are sometimes designed after the fact to build support or undermine opposition. Presidents may select a problem and adopt a solution for political, philosophical, or personal reasons, and only then prepare the evidence of need. Moreover, because presidents often see the world as they want it to be, not as it actually is, assumptions can become the critical flaw in a presidential program. For example, Reagan's overly optimistic assumption of economic recovery early in his term made change more difficult later on.

The role of assumptions in the presidential policy stream has become increasingly important during the last decade. In the 1970s, spending on federal programs, including Social Security, was increased automatically with rises in the Consumer Price Index (CPI). Thus, assumptions about future inflation became crucial for forecasting budget deficits. Much of what government now does is "uncontrollable" in the normal legislative process; thus assumptions have become the central element in telling policy makers when and where to act.

Players

Several thousand people actively engage in presidential policy making: White House staffers, cabinet secretaries, OMB analysts, bureaucrats, old friends, pollsters, the first lady, the vice president, and a host of lesser lights. Certainly the most important player is the president. As Abraham Lincoln once said to his cabinet after a heated debate: "One Aye, Seven Nays. The Ayes have it." Yet the mix of players can have an important bearing on the president's final decisions. When Shultz replaced Haig as Reagan's secretary of state, the constellation of advice changed immediately. As a former director of OMB and secretary of the Treasury, Shultz brought a much stronger economic background to his foreign policy views. Suddenly international trade was elevated as a problem in the Reagan White House. Shultz also began to participate in White House debates on the economy. He was widely seen as a powerful force in persuading Reagan of the need for a pessimistic budget forecast in 1983, as well as deeper defense cuts. There is no question that Shultz changed the direction of the Reagan agenda. Nor is there any doubt that Shultz had to compete with and against other players for the president's support.

At least four major offices fight to influence the president's policy agenda. The largest is the *Office of Management and Budget*, which has primary control over the president's annual budget and the legislative clearance process. Each year federal departments are required to submit detailed budgets and legislative priorities to OMB, which reviews all of the requests, makes "final" budget decisions, and assigns priorities to each piece of legislation. Budget and clearance responsibilities give OMB considerable leverage in dealing with the president and the executive branch, and in Stockman's first months as Reagan's budget director they were skillfully manipulated.

The second major policy office is the *Council of Economic Advisers*, which is responsible for preparing the president's annual economic report and thereby has an important role in developing the most important set of forecasts and projections. However, unlike OMB, CEA has no formal power over the budget or legislation. The OMB director is guaranteed access to the White House, but the CEA chairman must battle for a chance to speak. Reagan's first CEA chairman, Murray Weidenbaum, was unable to crack Stockman's control of economic advice; his replacement, Martin Feldstein, was initially more successful.

The third major policy agency is the *Office of Policy Development*, which originally was named the Domestic Council in 1970. OPD is primarily responsible for the review of domestic policy issues for possible elevation to the president's agenda. Unlike OMB, which reviews all executive branch requests, OPD can be more selective, performing an important role in bringing major problems and solutions to the president's attention. OPD is the domestic counterpart of the fourth major policy office, the *National Security Council*. The NSC staff acts as a much smaller version of the departments of State and Defense and has evolved into a powerful alternative source of advice.[5]

Perhaps the most important feature of these four offices is their competition *against* the executive branch for White House influence. CEA competes with the Treasury Department; OPD competes with Health and Human Service, Housing and Urban Development, and Transportation, among others; NSC competes with State and Defense; OMB competes with almost all of the departments. Although departments sometimes gain a measure of influence through a skillful secretary, the White House policy offices have an important advantage in their proximity to the president. In the "us-versus-them" mentality that often dominates the White House, presidents frequently conclude that the executive branch simply cannot be trusted to follow the presidential point of view faithfully.

Within the White House, however, the four policy offices are not the only competitors. The Congressional Relations Office, Public Liaison Office, Vice President's Office, Office of the Trade Representative, Counsel's Office, and Press Office participate in the policy debate, usually through the device of a "paper loop" that circulates proposals within the White House. At the very top, the president's chief of staff exercises the ultimate control over the movement of ideas in and out of the Oval Office. H. R. Haldeman (Nixon), Donald Rumsfeld (Ford), Hamilton Jordan (Carter), and Edwin Meese, James Baker, and Michael Deaver (Reagan) all became powerful "gate keepers" in the presidential policy stream. . . .

THE FILTERING PROCESS

As the policy stream flows through the White House, presidents must choose among the competing problems, solutions, assumptions, and players that make up the policy agenda. Because presidents cannot do everything, they must narrow the stream to a rather short list of priorities.

This presidential filtering process must serve two often competing demands in the policy stream. First, the filtering process must *merge* problems, solutions, assumptions, and players into final decisions. When the process fails, presidential proposals may face immediate defeat.

Reagan's 1981 Social Security package, rejected by the Senate 96 to 0, is an example of a decision that moved through the filtering process without being matched with the political players. Second, the filtering process must *regulate* the flow of problems and solutions into the Oval Office. If too few items reach the president, important problems, solutions, assumptions, and players may be neglected. If too many items come to his attention, serious overloading may result....

In the search for the best match of problems, solutions, assumptions, and players, the policy stream expands to include a wider current of ideas. In regulating the flow into the president, however, the stream must narrow. Here the important question is "How much is enough?" How many problems should a president tackle? How many solutions should be reviewed? How many players should be involved? While Carter spread himself over too many problems, perhaps Reagan limited himself to too few. While Kennedy opened the stream to too many players, perhaps Nixon did not listen to enough …

As presidents try to both merge and regulate the policy stream, they rely on two filters: resources and opportunities. As problems, solutions, assumptions, and players pass through these two filters, final decisions are set.

Resources

Resources "pay" for the final decisions presidents make. Some resources pay the costs of arriving at the decisions; others pay the costs of winning congressional passage; still others pay the costs of implementing the policies. Three basic kinds of resources are used for decision making, political marketing, and program implementation. These resources finance the presidential agenda.

DECISION-MAKING RESOURCES.   The most basic decision-making resource is *time*. Players need time to digest new ideas, form coalitions to influence the president, and review solutions. Similarly, problems need time to find sponsors, build public support, and locate solutions. In theory, each presidential term starts with 1,461 days. In reality, the start of the reelection campaign early in the third year limits the available policy time to

approximately 700 days. For particular policies, time can be much shorter. According to Stockman, there were only 20 to 25 days to build the Reagan economic program at the start of 1981.

Energy is a second decision-making resource. One only has to look at the "before" and "after" pictures of presidents to notice the wearing effect of the office on the individual. Similarly, some problems, solutions, and assumptions consume more energy than others. Few Carter staff members would equate the stress of the Iranian hostage crisis with the lesser demands of routine domestic policy.

A third decision-making resource is *information*. Knowledge about problems, solutions, and assumptions often varies significantly. Presidents can predict the accuracy of an MX missile within 200 yards on a normal East-to-West flight range but do not know the accuracy on the North-South arctic path to the Soviet Union. What would the magnetic fields at the North Pole do to the complex MX-guidance system? Presidents still have few proven theories on how the Social Security program affects the economy. As one economist warned the National Commission on Social Security Reform, "relatively little good evidence" is available to policy makers on the subject. Using the "best that economic theory and statistical techniques have to offer," economists "have produced a series of studies that can be selectively cited by the true believers of conflicting hunches or by people with political agendas that they seek to advance."[6]

A final decision-making resource is *expertise*. This resource applies specifically to the players, who must know how to bring problems, solutions, and assumptions together into final decisions. Policy expertise is more than the sum of an individual's experience in government. It is the skill that comes from learning.

POLITICAL RESOURCES.   The policy stream also absorbs political resources. As Vice President Mondale noted on leaving office, "a president … starts out with a bank full of good will and slowly checks are drawn on that, and it's very rare that it's replenished. It's a one-time deposit."[7] This political capital is composed of public approval and seats in Congress. For several reasons, among them the simple decay of support and presidential mistakes, capital is depleted during the term. At least since 1960, all presidents have experienced a loss in public support over time; since 1934, all presidents have lost party seats in Congress in every midterm election. Like Mondale, many White House players see political capital as a finite resource that is spent with each choice of a problem, solution, or assumption. Clearly, some problems, solutions, and assumptions are more "expensive" politically than others.

PROGRAM RESOURCES.   Just as presidents need resources to make and sell final decisions, they need them for implementation, that is, for converting legislation into actual government activity. The most basic program resources are federal dollars and employees. However, program resources also can include supplies, land, computer time, and new equipment. Carter's MX missile "racetrack" plan had a staggering list of resource needs. Designed as an elaborate shell game in the Nevada-Utah desert, the program required 200 MX missiles, numerous decoy missiles, 4,600 hardened concrete shelters, 8,500 miles of heavy-duty roadbed, huge new trucks to carry the missiles, new launchers, new computers, and 40,000 square miles of land. Each of the 200 missiles cost $50 million in the Carter budget, but construction and maintenance expenses of the entire program would have boosted the final price tag to $500 million per missile. Moreover, construction required 50,000 workers, 190 billion gallons of water, and 100 million tons of concrete—all to be transported somehow to the desert. Critics argued that construction alone would have caused a decade-long concrete shortage....

Opportunities

Once the filtering process has merged a problem with a solution, a set of assumptions, and a collection of players, and has found the decision-making, political, and program resources to pay for the combination, the White House must decide when to present the idea to Congress and the public. With the steady increase in its workload, in particular more committee and subcommittee meetings and greater constituency demands,

Congress offers fewer opportunities for presidential influence. Indeed, one of Carter's critical mistakes in filtering his legislative agenda was to flood the congressional tax-writing committees with proposals. Most of Carter's program had to move through the Senate Finance Committee and House Ways and Means Committee. His economic stimulus package (January 1977), hospital cost containment plan (April 1977), Social Security financing proposal (May 1977), welfare reform bill (August 1977), urban assistance plan (January 1978), and tax reform measure (January 1978) all moved through Congress with little thought of the opportunities for legislative review.

POLICY CALENDAR.   The timing of the president's requests to Congress is critical to their success. According to John Kessel, there is a presidential policy cycle that begins sometime "after Labor Day when programs to be proposed to Congress are readied. Fall is probably the time of the heaviest work load for the policy-staffer in the White House, because work is still progressing on Capitol Hill on the present year's program at the same time preparations for the next year are being made."[8] The calendar continues with basic choices on the budget in December, major messages to Congress in January and February (including the State of the Union address, the budget message, and the economic report), congressional decision making in the spring and summer, vacations in August, and a return to planning in September and October....

CYCLES OF INFLUENCE.   Although presidents are guaranteed a certain number of opportunities to introduce policy when they enter office—four State of the Unions, four budgets, etc.—they can create additional opportunities through the *cycle of increasing effectiveness.* Whatever the initial level of information and expertise, presidents and their staffs learn over time, becoming more effective in managing their scarce opportunities. Carter, for example, became more adept at handling Congress as his term wore on and he learned how to use his limited policy opportunities. Presidents can create opportunities for new ideas through carefully staged public events or through skillful manipulation of the press. A president's effectiveness in using these informal opportunities always grows over time, as a simple byproduct of learning the ropes.

Just as presidents can create opportunities through the cycle of increasing effectiveness, they can lose opportunities through the *cycle of decreasing influence.* As public approval and party seats drop during the term—one month-to-month, the other at the midterm election—presidents lose opportunities for influence. Even though they become more effective at finding opportunities for ideas, Congress and the public become less interested. Moreover, even the formal opportunities lose effectiveness later in the term. Major messages, televised addresses, and press conferences carry less weight.

Filtering and Policy

Why are resources and opportunities so important as policy filters? The reason is that presidents enter office with different amounts of each. Ford had only two years in his brief term, Johnson had five. Ford had fewer than 150 party faithful in the House, Johnson once had more than 290. Carter and Reagan had little expertise in national policy making, Nixon had little in domestic affairs. Carter's Georgia staff had little background in national policy, too, which left considerable room for learning, while Reagan's legislative staff had considerable expertise in legislative lobbying. These kinds of differences tell a great deal about the policy stream as it flows through an administration. The resources and opportunities at the start of a term determine both the quantity and quality of the president's policy agenda.

CONCLUSION

If presidential policy is the product of a highly dynamic stream, the final issue is whether the stream has changed its course during the past decades. The problems have changed, but have they become more difficult? Is cutting government spending more difficult than increasing it? Kennedy and Johnson selected problems that seemed to demand expanded government, while Carter and Reagan picked problems that seemed to require contracted government. Nor did Kennedy and Johnson have to tackle any of the

new "single issues" such as abortion and school prayer. Perhaps the most important change in the past 20 years has been the rise of a new class of "constituentless" issues—problems, such as energy conservation, which have few supporters but many potential enemies.

The solutions also have changed. Spending and regulation are no longer the popular response to national problems, but it is not yet clear what kinds of solutions will replace them. The players have changed, too. The rise of the National Security Council staff and the Office of Policy Development has shaped a new pool of players who compete for the president's attention and support. Moreover, most White House aides argue that interest groups are penetrating further into the policy process in recent years. As presidents reach out to interest groups to help pass their programs, interest groups reach further in to draft legislation and influence decisions.

Perhaps the most important area of change—or lack of change—is in assumptions. Despite new methods of forecasting and computer analysis, presidents do not seem much closer to being able to predict problems or solutions accurately. Much of the policy process still rests on best guesses about what will or will not happen. Even in the very short-term, players have difficulty predicting what will happen. Stockman was willing to admit in early 1983 that we cannot predict even the next year, let alone five years out. That may be the most serious obstacle to presidents as they continue to search for problems and solutions. If problems are more controversial in this era of single-issue politics, if solutions are more constrained by tight budgets and personnel shortages, if players are more competitive for presidential influence, there is even greater need for accurate assumptions. Unfortunately, presidents still look into their crystal balls and see pretty much what they want to see.

End Notes

1. See Jack L. Walker, "Setting the Agenda in the U.S. Senate: A Theory of Problem Selection," *British Journal of Political Science* (1977): 438.
2. Thomas E. Cronin, *The State of the Presidency* (Boston: Little, Brown & Co., 1980), 143–186.

3. Martin Anderson, *Welfare: The Political Economy of Welfare Reform in the United States* (Stanford, Cal.: Hoover Institution Press, 1978), 143–144.

4. William Greider, "The Education of David Stockman," *The Atlantic*, 248 (December 1981): 38, 44–47.

5. I. M. Destler, "National Security II: The Rise of the Assistant (1961–1981)," in *The Illusion of Presidential Government*, ed. Hugh Heclo and Lester M. Salamon (Boulder, Colo.: Westview Press, 1982.)

6. Henry Aaron, *Economic Effects of Social Security* (Washington: The Brookings Institution, 1983), 51, 82.

7. *Washington Post*, January 21, 1981, A-24.

8. John Kessel, *The Domestic Presidency* (Boston: Duxbury Press, 1975), 9.

35

The Rise of the Bureaucratic State

James Q. Wilson

During its first 150 years, the American republic was not thought to have a "bureaucracy," and thus it would have been meaningless to refer to the "problems" of a "bureaucratic state." There were, of course, appointed civilian officials: Though only about 3,000 at the end of the Federalist period, there were about 95,000 by the time Grover Cleveland assumed office in 1881, and nearly half a million by 1925. Some aspects of these numerous officials were regarded as problems—notably, the standards by which they were appointed and the political loyalties to which they were held—but these were thought to be matters of proper character and good management. The great political and constitutional struggles were not over the power of the administrative apparatus, but over the power of the President, of Congress, and of the states.

The Founding Fathers had little to say about the nature or function of the executive branch of the new government. The Constitution is virtually silent on the subject and the debates in the Constitutional Convention are almost devoid of reference to an administrative apparatus. This reflected no lack of concern about the matter, however. Indeed, it was in part because of the Founders' depressing experience with chaotic and inefficient management under the Continental Congress and the Articles of Confederation that they had assembled in Philadelphia. Management by committees composed of part-time amateurs had cost the colonies dearly in the War of Independence and few, if any, of the Founders wished to return to that system. The argument was only over how the heads of the necessary departments of government were to be selected, and whether these heads should be wholly subordinate to the President or whether instead they should form some sort of council that would advise the President and perhaps share in his authority. In the end, the Founders left it up to Congress to decide the matter.

From James Q. Wilson, "The Rise of the Bureaucratic State," *The Public Interest*, No. 41 (Fall 1975). Reprinted by permission.

There was no dispute in Congress that there should be executive departments, headed by single appointed officials, and, of course, the Constitution specified that these would be appointed by the President with the advice and consent of the Senate. The only issue was how such officials might be removed. After prolonged debate and by the narrowest of majorities, Congress agreed that the President should have the sole right of removal, thus confirming that the infant administrative system would be wholly subordinate—in law at least—to the President. Had not Vice President John Adams, presiding over a Senate equally divided on the issue, cast the deciding vote in favor of Presidential removal, the administrative departments might conceivably have become legal dependencies of the legislature, with incalculable consequences for the development of the embryonic government.

THE "BUREAUCRACY PROBLEM"

The original departments were small and had limited duties. The State Department, the first to be created, had but nine employees in addition to the Secretary. The War Department did not reach 80 civilian employees until 1801; it commanded only a few thousand soldiers. Only the Treasury Department had substantial powers—it collected taxes, managed the public debt, ran the national bank, conducted land surveys, and purchased military supplies. Because of this, Congress gave the closest scrutiny to its structure and its activities.

The number of administrative agencies and employees grew slowly but steadily during the 19th and early 20th centuries and then increased explosively on the occasion of World War I, the Depression, and World War II. It is difficult to say at what point in this process the administrative system became a distinct locus of power or an independent source of political initiatives and problems. What is clear is that the emphasis on the sheer *size* of the administrative establishment—conventional in many treatments of the subject—is misleading.

The government can spend vast sums of money—wisely or unwisely—without creating that set of conditions we ordinarily associate with the bureaucratic state. For example,

there could be massive transfer payments made under government auspices from person to person or from state to state, all managed by a comparatively small staff of officials and a few large computers. In 1971, the federal government paid out $54 billion under various social insurance programs, yet the Social Security Administration employs only 73,000 persons, many of whom perform purely routine tasks.

And though it may be harder to believe, the government could in principle employ an army of civilian personnel without giving rise to those organizational patterns that we call bureaucratic. Suppose, for instance, that we as a nation should decide to have in the public schools at least one teacher for every two students. This would require a vast increase in the number of teachers and school rooms, but almost all of the persons added would be performing more or less identical tasks, and they could be organized into very small units (e.g., neighborhood schools). Though there would be significant overhead costs, most citizens would not be aware of any increase in the "bureaucratic" aspects of education—indeed, owing to the much greater time each teacher would have to devote to each pupil and his or her parents, the citizen might well conclude that there actually had been a substantial reduction in the amount of "bureaucracy."

To the reader predisposed to believe that we have a "bureaucracy problem," these hypothetical cases may seem farfetched. Max Weber, after all, warned us that in capitalist and socialist societies alike, bureaucracy was likely to acquire an "overtowering" power position. Conservatives have always feared bureaucracy, save perhaps the police. Humane socialists have frequently been embarrassed by their inability to reconcile a desire for public control of the economy with the suspicion that a public bureaucracy may be as immune to democratic control as a private one. Liberals have equivocated, either dismissing any concern for bureaucracy as reactionary quibbling about social progress, or embracing that concern when obviously nonreactionary persons (welfare recipients, for example) express a view toward the Department of Health, Education, and Welfare indistinguishable from the view businessmen take of the Internal Revenue Service.

POLITICAL AUTHORITY

There are at least three ways in which political power may be gathered undesirably into bureaucratic hands: by the growth of an administrative apparatus so large as to be immune from popular control, by placing power over a governmental bureaucracy of any size in private rather than public hands, or by vesting discretionary authority in the hands of a public agency so that the exercise of that power is not responsive to the public good. These are not the only problems that arise because of bureaucratic organization. From the point of view of their members, bureaucracies are sometimes uncaring, ponderous, or unfair; from the point of view of their political superiors, they are sometimes unimaginative or inefficient; from the point of view of their clients, they are sometimes slow or unjust. No single account can possibly treat of all that is problematic in bureaucracy; even the part I discuss here—the extent to which political authority has been transferred undesirably to an unaccountable administrative realm—is itself too large for a single essay. But it is, if not the most important problem, then surely the one that would most have troubled our Revolutionary leaders, especially those that went on to produce the Constitution. It was, after all, the question of power that chiefly concerned them, both in redefining our relationship with England and in finding a new basis for political authority in the Colonies.

To some, following in the tradition of Weber, bureaucracy is the inevitable consequence and perhaps necessary concomitant of modernity. A money economy, the division of labor, and the evolution of legal-rational norms to justify organizational authority require the efficient adaptation of means to ends and a high degree of predictability in the behavior of rulers. To this, Georg Simmel added the view that organizations tend to acquire the characteristics of those institutions with which they are in conflict, so that as government becomes more bureaucratic, private organizations—political parties, trade unions, voluntary associations—will have an additional reason to become bureaucratic as well.

By viewing bureaucracy as an inevitable (or, as some would put it, "functional") aspect of society, we find ourselves attracted to theories that explain the growth of bureaucracy in terms of some inner dynamic to which all agencies respond and which makes all barely governable and scarcely tolerable. Bureaucracies grow, we are told, because of Parkinson's Law: Work and personnel expand to consume the available resources. Bureaucracies behave, we believe, in accord with various other maxims, such as the Peter Principle: In hierarchical organizations, personnel are promoted up to that point at which their incompetence becomes manifest—hence, all important positions are held by incompetents. More elegant, if not essentially different, theories have been propounded by scholars. The tendency of all bureaus to expand is explained by William A. Niskanen by the assumption, derived from the theory of the firm, that "bureaucrats maximize the total budget of their bureau during their tenure"—hence, "all bureaus are too large." What keeps them from being not merely too large but all-consuming is the fact that a bureau must deliver to some degree on its promised output, and if it consistently underdelivers, its budget will be cut by unhappy legislators. But since measuring the output of a bureau is often difficult—indeed, even *conceptualizing* the output of the State Department is mind-boggling—the bureau has a great deal of freedom within which to seek the largest possible budget.

Such theories, both the popular and the scholarly, assign little importance to the nature of the tasks an agency performs, the constitutional framework in which it is embedded, or the preferences and attitudes of citizens and legislators. Our approach will be quite different: Different agencies will be examined in historical perspective to discover the kinds of problems, if any, to which their operation gave rise, and how those problems were affected—perhaps determined—by the tasks which they were assigned, the political system in which they operated, and the preferences they were required to consult. What follows will be far from a systematic treatment of such matters, and even farther from a rigorous testing of any theory of bureaucratization: Our knowledge of agency history and behavior is too sketchy to permit that....

BUREAUCRACY AND CLIENTELISM

After 1861, the growth in the federal administrative system could no longer be explained primarily by an expansion of the postal service and other traditional bureaus. Though these continued to expand, new departments were added that reflected a new (or at least greater) emphasis on the enlargement of the scope of government. Between 1861 and 1901, over 200,000 civilian employees were added to the federal service, only 52 per cent of whom were postal workers. Some of these, of course, staffed a larger military and naval establishment stimulated by the Civil War and the Spanish-American War. By 1901 there were over 44,000 civilian defense employees, mostly workers in government-owned arsenals and shipyards. But even these could account for less than one fourth of the increase in employment during the preceding 40 years.

What was striking about the period after 1861 was that the government began to give formal, bureaucratic recognition to the emergence of distinctive interests in a diversifying economy. As Richard L. Schott has written, "whereas earlier federal departments had been formed around specialized governmental functions (foreign affairs, war, finance, and the like), the new departments of this period—Agriculture, Labor, and Commerce—were devoted to the interests and aspirations of particular economic groups."

The original purpose behind these clientele-oriented departments was neither to subsidize nor to regulate, but to promote, chiefly by gathering and publishing statistics and (especially in the case of agriculture) by research. The formation of the Department of Agriculture in 1862 was to become a model, for better or worse, for later political campaigns for government recognition. A private association representing an interest—in this case the United States Agricultural Society—was formed. It made every President from Fillmore to Lincoln an honorary member, it enrolled key Congressmen, and it began to lobby for a new department. The precedent was followed by labor groups, especially the Knights of Labor, to secure creation in 1888 of a Department of Labor. It was broadened in 1903 to be a Department of Commerce and Labor, but 10 years later, at the insistence of the American Federation of Labor,

the parts were separated and the two departments we now know were formed.

There was an early 9th-century precedent for the creation of these client-serving departments: the Pension Office, then in the Department of the Interior. Begun in 1833 and regularized in 1849, the Office became one of the largest bureaus of the government in the aftermath of the Civil War, as hundreds of thousands of Union Army veterans were made eligible for pensions if they had incurred a permanent disability or injury while on military duty; dependent widows were also eligible if their husbands had died in service or of service-connected injuries. The Grand Army of the Republic (GAR), the leading veterans' organization, was quick to exert pressure for more generous pension laws and for more liberal administration of such laws as already existed. In 1879 Congressmen, noting the number of ex-servicemen living (and voting) in their states, made veterans eligible for pensions retroactively to the date of their discharge from the service, thus enabling thousands who had been late in filing applications to be rewarded for their dilatoriness. In 1890 the law was changed again to make it unnecessary to have been injured in the service—all that was necessary was to have served and then to have acquired a permanent disability by any means other than through "their own vicious habits." And whenever cases not qualifying under existing law came to the attention of Congress, it promptly passed a special act making those persons eligible by name.

So far as is known, the Pension Office was remarkably free of corruption in the administration of this windfall—and why not, since anything an administrator might deny, a legislator was only too pleased to grant. By 1891 the Commissioner of Pensions observed that his was "the largest executive bureau in the world." There were over 6,000 officials supplemented by thousands of local physicians paid on a fee basis. In 1900 alone, the Office had to process 477,000 cases. Fraud was rampant as thousands of persons brought false or exaggerated claims; as Leonard D. White was later to write, "pensioners and their attorneys seemed to have been engaged in a gigantic conspiracy to defraud their own government." Though the Office struggled to be honest, Congress was indifferent—or more accurately, complaisant: The GAR was a powerful electoral force and it was ably and lucratively assisted by thousands of private pension attorneys. The pattern of bureaucratic clientelism was set in a way later to become a familiar feature of the governmental landscape—a subsidy was initially provided, because it was either popular or unnoticed, to a group that was powerfully benefited and had few or disorganized opponents; the beneficiaries were organized to supervise the administration and ensure the funding of the program; the law authorizing the program, first passed because it seemed the right thing to do, was left intact or even expanded because politically it became the only thing to do. A benefit once bestowed cannot easily be withdrawn.

PUBLIC POWER AND PRIVATE INTERESTS

It was at the state level, however, that client-oriented bureaucracies proliferated in the 19th century. Chief among these were the occupational licensing agencies. At the time of Independence, professions and occupations either could be freely entered (in which case the consumer had to judge the quality of service for himself) or entry was informally controlled by the existing members of the profession or occupation by personal tutelage and the management of reputations. The latter part of the 19th century, however, witnessed the increased use of law and bureaucracy to control entry into a line of work. The state courts generally allowed this on the grounds that it was a proper exercise of the "police power" of the state, but as Morton Keller has observed, "when state courts approved the licensing of barbers and blacksmiths, but not of horse-shoers, it was evident that the principles governing certification were—to put it charitably—elusive ones." By 1952, there were more than 75 different occupations in the United States for which one needed a license to practice, and the awarding of these licenses was typically in the hands of persons already in the occupation, who could act under color of law. These licensing boards—for plumbers, dry cleaners, beauticians, attorneys, undertakers, and the like—frequently have been criticized

as particularly flagrant examples of the excesses of a bureaucratic state. But the problems they create—of restricted entry, higher prices, and lengthy and complex initiation procedures—are not primarily the result of some bureaucratic pathology but of the possession of public power by persons who use it for private purposes. Or more accurately, they are the result of using public power in ways that benefited those in the profession in the sincere but unsubstantiated conviction that doing so would benefit the public generally.

The New Deal was perhaps the high water mark of at least the theory of bureaucratic clientelism. Not only did various sectors of society, notably agriculture, begin receiving massive subsidies, but the government proposed, through the National Industrial Recovery Act (NRA), to cloak with public power a vast number of industrial groupings and trade associations so that they might control production and prices in ways that would end the depression. The NRA's Blue Eagle fell before the Supreme Court—the wholesale delegation of public power to private interests was declared unconstitutional. But the piecemeal delegation was not, as the continued growth of specialized promotional agencies attests. The Civil Aeronautics Board, for example, erroneously thought to be exclusively a regulatory agency, was formed in 1938 "to promote" as well as to regulate civil aviation and it has done so by restricting entry and maintaining above-market rate fares.

Agriculture, of course, provides the leading case of clientelism. Theodore J. Lowi finds "at least 10 separate, autonomous, local self-governing systems" located in or closely associated with the Department of Agriculture that control to some significant degree the flow of billions of dollars in expenditures and loans. Local committees of farmers, private farm organizations, agency heads, and committee chairmen in Congress dominate policymaking in this area—not, perhaps, to the exclusion of the concerns of other publics, but certainly in ways not powerfully constrained by them....

SELF-PERPETUATING AGENCIES

If the Founding Fathers were to return to examine bureaucratic clientelism, they would, I suspect, be deeply discouraged. James Madison clearly foresaw that American society would be "broken into many parts, interests and classes of citizens" and that this "multiplicity of interests" would help ensure against "the tyranny of the majority," especially in a federal regime with separate branches of government. Positive action would require a "coalition of a majority"; in the process of forming this coalition, the rights of all would be protected, not merely by self-interested bargains, but because in a free society such a coalition "could seldom take place on any other principles than those of justice and the general good." To those who wrongly believed that Madison thought of men as acting only out of base motives, the phrase is instructive: Persuading men who disagree to compromise their differences can rarely be achieved solely by the parceling out of relative advantage; the belief is also required that what is being agreed to is right, proper, and defensible before public opinion.

Most of the major new social programs of the United States, whether for the good of the few or the many, were initially adopted by broad coalitions appealing to general standards of justice or to conceptions of the public weal. This is certainly the case with most of the New Deal legislation—notably such programs as Social Security—and with most Great Society legislation—notably Medicare and aid to education; it was also conspicuously the case with respect to post-Great Society legislation pertaining to consumer and environmental concerns. State occupational licensing laws were supported by majorities interested in, among other things, the contribution of these statutes to public safety and health.

But when a program supplies particular benefits to an existing or newly created interest, public or private, it creates a set of political relationships that make exceptionally difficult further alteration of that program by coalitions of the majority. What was created in the name of the common good is sustained in the name of the particular interest. Bureaucratic clientelism becomes self-perpetuating, in the absence of some crisis or scandal, because a single interest group to which the program matters greatly is highly motivated and well-situated to ward off the criticisms of other groups that have a broad but weak interest in the policy.

In short, a regime of separated powers makes it difficult to overcome objections and contrary interests sufficiently to permit the enactment of a new program or the creation of a new agency. Unless the legislation can be made to pass either with little notice or at a time of crisis or extraordinary majorities—and sometimes even then—the initiation of new programs requires public interest arguments. But the same regime works to protect agencies, once created, from unwelcome change because a major change is, in effect, new legislation that must overcome the same hurdles as the original law, but this time with one of the hurdles—the wishes of the agency and its client—raised much higher. As a result, the Madisonian system makes it relatively easy for the delegation of public power to private groups to go unchallenged and, therefore, for factional interests that have acquired a supportive public bureaucracy to rule without submitting their interests to the effective scrutiny and modification of other interests....

36

Regulation: Politics, Bureaucracy, and Economics

Kenneth J. Meier

The study of regulatory policymaking is dominated by two perspectives (Weingast and Moran, 1983).[1] One view holds that regulatory agencies are vested with vast discretion and are the major force in regulatory policy. Among the agency characteristics that affect policy outputs are professional values, policy expertise, bureaucratic entrepreneurs, and agency structure (e.g., see Wilson, 1980; Katzman, 1980).[2] A second view suggests that regulatory agencies are dominated by their environment. Interest groups, legislative committees, economic forces, and technological change are among the determinants of policy (e.g., see Stigler, 1971; Lowi, 1969; Mazmanian and Sabatier, 1980).[3] Both views are essentially incomplete. Regulatory policy is a product of both regulatory bureaucracies and environmental forces. This chapter develops an outline of the regulatory process that integrates both these explanations. Although the conceptual framework developed is moderately complex, so is regulatory policy. Little is gained by introducing simple views of regulation that are not linked to the real world.

REGULATORY POLICY OUTPUTS

The study of regulation is important because it is part of the policy process that allocates values among members of society. It is, as Lasswell[4]

(1936) described politics, a determination of "Who gets what, when and how." In short, what is important about regulatory policy from a political perspective is, Who benefits from regulation?

Although much regulation literature has focused on who benefits from regulation, this focus has been muddied by relying on the concept of the public interest. Bernstein's (1955)[5] theory that regulatory agencies in the long run were captured by the regulated industries contrasted reality with an ideal standard of regulation in the public interest (see also Stigler, 1971; Peltzman, 1976).[6] Unfortunately, defining the public interest in regulatory policy has been as elusive as it has been in other areas of politics (see Schubert, 1960).[7] Even the most self-serving appeal by a regulated group is now phrased as a quest for the public interest.

In a perceptive essay, Paul Sabatier (1977)[8] proposed an alternative to the public interest theory of regulation; regulatory policy can be arrayed on a continuum from self-regulation (regulation in the interests of the regulated) to aggressive regulation (regulation of one individual in the interests of another).[9] Sabatier's thesis can be divided into two separate dimensions—the degree to which regulation benefits the regulated industry and the degree to which it benefits nonregulated individuals such as consumers. These are two separate dimensions rather than poles on a single continuum.

As figure 36.1 reveals, the two dimensions of beneficiaries produce four extreme types of regulation. Cell 1 contains policies designed to benefit the regulated but not the nonregulated, the traditional "captured" regulation. Regulation by state occupational regulators is a classic example of cell 1 regulation. Cell 3 contains those policies whereby an industry is regulated for the benefit of another party. Occupational safety and health regulation, for example, restricts industry behavior in an attempt to benefit workers. Cell 4 contains those policies that benefit both the regulated and some portion of the nonregulated. Bank regulation and deposit insurance following the Great Depression benefited both depositors by guaranteeing the safety of their funds and the banks by encouraging the use of banks. Finally, cell 2 includes policies that benefit no one. Current antitrust policy concerning price discrimination appears to harm both businesses that wish to compete and consumers.

Although who benefits from regulatory policy is not always easy to discover, the question provides a focal point for comparing unlike regulatory policies. This text will examine two aspects of regulatory policy—what is the current set of regulatory policies, and who benefits from them? The conceptual framework in this chapter permits us to explain why regulatory agencies act as they do and why regulatory policies benefit whom they do.

SUBSYSTEM POLITICS

Although regulatory policies can be produced directly by legislatures, the chief executive, or the courts, in general, regulatory policy is implemented via bureaucracy. Typically, broad areas of regulatory discretion are granted to a regulatory agency by these political institutions of government. The Interstate Commerce Commission, for example, is charged with regulating interstate commerce with only a vague goal (the "public interest") as a guide. The policymaking activities

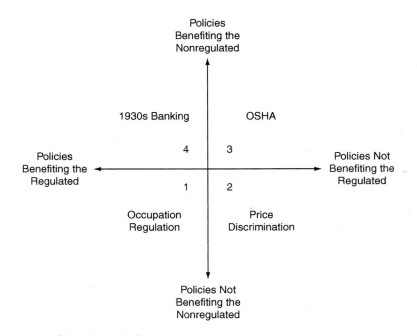

FIGURE 36.1 Dimensions of Regulatory Policy

of bureaucratic agencies can best be understood by examining the subsystem in which these agencies operate.

That public policy is made in semiautonomous subsystems composed of government bureaus, congressional committees, and interest groups has been a basic tenet of political analysis since the 1950s (see Freeman, 1965; McConnell, 1966).[10] Subsystems exist because the American political system fragments political power (Long, 1962).[11] With its division of federal authority into three branches—executive, legislative, and judicial—each operating with constraints on the other two, political power at the national level is fragmented among numerous political actors. Power is further divided by the federal system and informally kept that way by broker political parties that seek electoral success rather than unified political government. As a result, political power is not concentrated enough to dominate the policy process.

The fragmentation is exacerbated by the numerous policy issues that compete for attention on the policy agenda. Major political institutions must constantly jump from crisis to crisis—social security today, gasoline user fees tomorrow, MX missiles next week. Power in a given issue area flows to those who retain a continuing interest in it. In American politics a continuing interest usually means the permanent bureaucracy, specialized congressional committees, and the interest groups affected by the issue.

Policy subsystems can operate in a relatively independent fashion from the major political institutions *if* the members of the policy subsystem can satisfy each others' needs. The bureaucracy makes policy. It issues the permits, exceptions, and punishments; but to do so it needs resources and legislative authority. Congressional committees can provide the funds and authority needed by the bureau to operate, but the committee members need to be reelected. Reelection requires political support and campaign contributions. The interest groups affiliated with the regulated industry need the outputs that the bureaucracy is creating, especially if the outputs are favorable; and they have the political resources to commit to members of congressional committees. In combination, the members of the subsystem can often supply the needs of the other members.

If all the needs of the subsystem members are satisfied, then subsystem members make no major demands on the macropolitical system. In turn, the subsystem is given autonomy.

Although subsystems have been fruitfully applied to numerous areas of political research (see Ripley and Franklin, 1980),[12] recent work suggests that subsystems are not the homogeneous "iron triangles" that they are portrayed to be (see Heclo, 1978; Sabatier, 1983).[13] First, interest groups, even industry groups, rarely agree completely about regulatory policy. Dissension among airline companies permitted deregulation of airline fares in the 1970s (Behrman, 1980);[14] broadcasting interests are fragmented into several groups with vastly different goals, including groups representing networks, independent stations, religious broadcasters, ultrahigh frequency (UHF) stations, frequency modulation (FM) stations, and countless others (Krasnow, Longley, and Terry, 1982).[15] Second, interest groups other than industry groups actively participate in the regulatory subsystem. Consumer groups are active in the auto safety, drug regulation, and consumer products subsystems; labor unions are active in safety regulation and sometimes in environmental regulation. Rarely do industry groups have the opportunity to operate without opposition.

Third, subsystems are often divided among several different subcommittees each with different policy objectives. Environmental protection programs, for example, are under the jurisdiction of seven committees in the House and five in the Senate (Kenski and Kenski, 1984: 111).[16] Even with only a single committee involved in a subsystem, policy conflict occurs. Conflicting positions by the Commerce Committees at different times during the 1970s resulted in a series of policy changes by the Federal Trade Commission (Weingast and Moran, 1982).[17] Fourth, a variety of other actors penetrate the subsystem to urge policy actions, including journalists and scholars who generate important information on policy options. Such issues as acid rain, pesticide regulation, drug safety, and others were placed on the agenda by such actors.

Fifth, one subsystem will sometimes overlap one or more other subsystems, thus adding additional actors to the political battles and creating greater conflict. Environmental protection subsystems collided with energy subsystems following the Arab oil embargo; insurance subsystems and automobile regulation subsystems came into conflict following the Reagan administration's relaxation of automobile safety regulations.

Finally, the subsystems concept ignores the vital role of state and local government officials in the regulatory process. In many areas, federal regulatory programs are implemented by state governments; environmental protection and workplace health and safety are prominent examples. In a variety of other areas such as consumer protection, antitrust, and equal employment opportunity policies, both the federal government and state governments operate programs. Often the policy goals of state regulators can differ significantly from those of federal regulators (see Rowland and Marz, 1982),[18] resulting in policy outputs different from those intended by the federal government. This conflict can result in either more vigorous regulation or

less vigorous regulation depending on state objectives. California's aggressive mobile source air pollution regulation in the 1960s and 1970s, for example, often preceded federal efforts, but state-run workplace safety programs lag behind federal-run programs.

In figure 36.2 an expanded version of the subsystem is shown that includes other (i.e., non-industry) interest groups, significant others (e.g., researchers, journalists), and state governments in addition to the "iron" triangle. Paul Sabatier (1983) argues that policy subsystems can best be viewed as opposing advocacy coalitions; a coalition of industry and its allies (members of Congress, other groups, and so on) is opposed by other interest groups and their allies. Under such a conceptualization, the traditional iron triangle becomes a special case of a policy subsystem with only one advocacy coalition.

Among the most important aspects of policy subsystems is how open the subsystems are to outside influences via the chief executive,

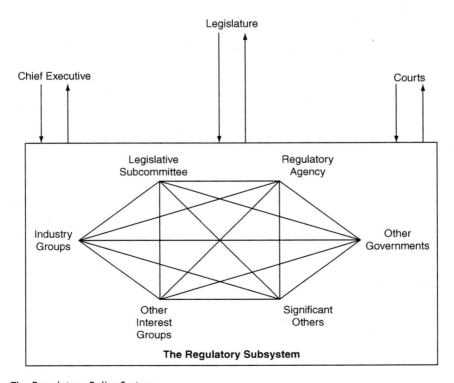

FIGURE 36.2 The Regulatory Policy System

the legislature, and other nonsubsystem actors. Policy subsystems are perceived as fairly consensual, and in areas of distributive politics—health care research, agricultural policy, and educational aid—they are (Ripley and Franklin, 1980). The distribution of tangible benefits paid for by general tax revenues ties the members of the subsystems closely together. Consensual subsystems resolve policy issues internally and present a unified front to the larger political system. As a result, consensual subsystems are usually allowed to operate without outside interference.

Regulatory subsystems are not as consensual as those in distributive policy and, therefore, are more likely to be affected by outside influences for several reasons. First, regulatory policy restricts choice so that an industry is likely to see regulation as a mixed blessing. Regulated industries may defend their regulator when it is attacked by other political actors (e.g., the airlines and the Civil Aeronautics Board (CAB) circa 1976); but they are slower to come to the defense and less committed when they do so. Second, members of Congress are likely to be less committed to a regulatory subsystem than to a distributive subsystem. Unlike other policies, regulation often imposes direct costs. A member of Congress from a rural district will receive far more credit from constituents if he or she is on the soil conservation subcommittee distributing benefits than if he or she is on the environmental committee limiting pesticide use. Third, regulatory subsystems are likely to have more nonindustry groups that want to participate in the subsystem. The Federal Communications Commission (FCC), for example, cannot operate in a consensual, autonomous subsystem because numerous interests other than the television industry are also interested in regulating television. Politicians, the movie industry, cable operators, the phone company, and many others see television as important to their interests; accordingly, they will seek to participate in FCC decisions.

REGULATORY AGENCIES: INSIDE THE BLACK BOX

Government agencies are not passive actors pushed along at the whim of other subsystem members. They shape as well as respond to pressures from the subsystem (Rourke, 1984).[19] The U.S. Department of Agriculture (USDA), for example, played a role in creating and developing the American Farm Bureau; Farm Bureau members, in turn, assisted the USDA in crop regulation. The Environmental Protection Agency funds academic research on pollution; such research is then used in debates over environmental protection. In a sense, both agencies helped create a portion of the subsystem. If bureaus can take an active role in structuring their environments, they need not passively respond to subsystem pressures. They can actively seek to influence the forces impinging on regulatory policy. To understand the policy actions of regulatory agencies, two variables—goals and resources—must be discussed.

Agency Goals

Every regulatory agency has goals including policy goals that agency employees wish to attain. Environmental Protection Agency employees seek cleaner air and water; FDA personnel pursue safe and effective drugs. Although this contention may seem trivial, many treatments of bureaucracy either assume an organization's sole goal is to survive or that the bureaucrats' goal is to maximize their income (e.g., see Niskanen, 1971).[20] Both approaches provide a misleading view of regulatory agencies.

This distinction merits some discussion. If we assume, as Niskanen does, that bureaucrats are rational utility maximizers, regulators clearly seek goals other than income maximization. Because incomes are higher in the regulated industry, an income maximizer would choose to work for the regulated industry rather than the regulatory agency. The choice to enter the public sector is not dictated by inferior skills because studies show that public sector employees in jobs similar to private sector ones have greater skills and better training (Guyot, 1979).[21] A public sector bureaucrat, therefore, must be maximizing something other than income; the most logical thing to maximize is policy goals.

Ascribing regulatory policy goals to bureaucrats is consistent with motivation theory (e.g., Maslow, 1970)[22] and empirical evidence. Employees work for the Office of Civil Rights because they believe in racial equality (Romzek and Hendricks, 1982).[23] Individuals work for OSHA because they desire to improve workplace safety (Kelman, 1980).[24] In the long run, most agency employees become advocates of the agency and its goals (Downs, 1967).[25] Those interested in higher incomes or in the goals of the regulated industry will probably leave the agency.

Having policy goals does not mean that bureaucrats would not like to see their organization survive, all things being equal. Survival, after all, is necessary to obtain most policy goals. In some cases, the present Civil Aeronautics Board bureaucrats, for example, are content to accomplish policy objectives that will eventually eliminate the agency. In sum then, regulators regulate because they wish to attain policy goals; without understanding that regulators are goal-seeking and without determining what those goals are, regulatory behavior will appear random to the outside observer.

Also important in terms of regulatory goals is the potential for goal conflict within an agency. Such lack of consensus might result from several different conflicts within the organization: central staff versus field personnel, professionals versus administrators, one profession versus another profession, career staff versus political appointees. The last source of conflict is especially important. Career staff are more likely to identify with the agency and be strongly committed to its programs (Heclo, 1977).[26] Political appointees are more likely to see themselves as the president's representative (Welborn, 1977)[27] and, therefore, hold different views.

Resources

In pursuit of policy goals, regulatory agencies have access to five resources—expertise, cohesion, legislative authority, policy salience, and leadership.[28] Access to such resources determines the value of the agency's participation to other subsystem members. The greater a regulatory agency's resources, the more likely the agency will be able to resist industry pressures for regulation solely in the interests of the industry.

EXPERTISE. Bureaucratic organizations are designed to develop and store knowledge. To a degree

greater than legislatures or courts, bureaucracies can divide tasks and gain knowledge via specialization (Rourke, 1984: 16). An EPA employee, for example, could spend an entire career dealing with the intricacies of regulating the pesticide mirex. As part of specialization, American government bureaucracies recruit skilled technocrats as employees, and the agencies become professionalized. A professionalized agency often adopts the values of the predominant profession; the values of safety and health professionals in the Occupational Safety and Health Administration, for example, are the reason why OSHA relies on engineering standards (Kelman, 1980).

Professionalization and specialization permit an agency to develop independent sources of knowledge so that the agency need not rely on the industry (or others) for its information. Although the levels of professionalism and specialization in regulatory agencies cannot rival those of such agencies as the National Institutes of Health, they are a factor. The Nobel laureate Glenn Seaborg's appointment to head the Atomic Energy Commission (AEC; now the Nuclear Regulatory Commission) increased the AEC's reputation for expertise. Similarly, the creation of a separate research arm for the Environmental Protection Agency provided the EPA with expertise it could use in its political battles (Davies and Davies, 1975).[29]

Professionalism does not mean that an agency is dominated by a single profession. At times one or more professions may be struggling for control of the agency. In the Federal Trade Commission (FTC), for example, economists and lawyers have long fought over control of the FTC's antitrust functions. The professional conflict, in fact, has major policy implications. Lawyers prefer cases that can be quickly brought to trial like Robinson-Patman cases. Economists favor either major structural monopoly cases that will significantly increase competition or cases against collusion.

COHESION. A second resource permitting the agency to affect public policy is the cohesiveness of the bureau's personnel. If agency personnel are united in pursuit of their goals, coalitions opposed to agency actions will need to develop their own sources of information to challenge agency decisions. A cohesive agency is far more difficult to resist than an agency that engages in public disputes over policy direction. Cohesion, in turn, is a function of an agency's goals and its ability to socialize members to accept these goals. Some public agencies such as the Marine Corps or the Forest Service even go so far as to create an organizational ideology for their members. Although no regulatory agency engages in the same degree of socialization that the Marine Corps does, they do seek consciously or unconsciously to influence the values of employees. Bureaucrats in the Environmental Protection Agency, for example, show much greater concern for environmental protection than for compliance costs. The Office of Education in the 1960s was a zealous advocate of school desegregation.

LEGISLATIVE AUTHORITY.   All regulatory agencies must have legislative authority to operate, but all grants of legislative authority are not equal (see Sabatier, 1977: 424–431). Five important differences in legislative authority exist and contribute to agency resources. First, policy goals as expressed in legislation can be specific or vague. Before 1973, Congress specified agricultural price support levels exactly, leaving little discretion for Agriculture Department regulators. In contrast, the Interstate Commerce Commission regulates interstate commerce with the general goal that regulation should be in the public interest. The more vague the legislative expression of goals, the greater the agency's ability to set regulatory policy. Specific policy goals should be correlated with regulation in the interests of whichever group has the best access to Congress. Consequently, specific goals are associated both with the regulation in the interests of the regulated (e.g., agriculture) and with regulation for the benefit of the nonregulated (e.g., environmental protection; see Marcus, 1980).[30]

Second, legislative delegations vary in the scope of authority they grant. Some agencies have jurisdiction over every firm in the industry (e.g., EPA). Other agencies might be denied jurisdiction over portions of their industry; OSHA's law, for example, exempts small farms. An agency with limited authority cannot affect the behavior of those outside its jurisdiction. The greater the limitations and restrictions on a regulatory agency, the more likely such an agency will regulate in the interest of the regulated industry.

Third, legislative delegations vary in the sanctions permitted to an agency. Bank regulators possess a wide variety of sanctions that can greatly influence the profits and viability of financial institutions. In contrast, the Equal Employment Opportunity Commission (EEOC) has no sanctions and must rely on court action to extract compliance. The greater the range of sanctions available to a regulatory agency, the more likely the agency will regulate in the interests of the nonregulated.

Fourth, regulatory agencies differ in their organizational structure. The two most common structural forms are the department regulatory agency (an agency headed by one person within a larger executive department) and the independent regulatory commission (a multimember board that reports directly to the legislature). Although the different structures do not appear related to performance (see Meier, 1980; Welborn, 1977),[31] often independent regulatory commissions are subjected to other restraints. At the state level, regulatory commissions are often by law composed of members of the regulated industry. When selection restrictions such as this occur, regulation in the interests of the regulated is a given.

Fifth, legislative grants of authority often specify agency procedures. The FTC must follow the lengthy *formal* rule-making process to issue rules, and the Consumer Product Safety Commission was handicapped until recently with a cumbersome "offeror" procedure. Other agencies such as the EEOC and the antitrust regulators are limited further because they must use the courts to set policy and resolve disputes. The more restrictive an agency's procedures are, the less likely the agency will be able to regulate the industry closely.

POLITICAL SALIENCE.   The salience of a regulatory issue (i.e., its perceived importance by the public) can be used as a resource in the agency's regulatory battles. Regulatory issues vary greatly in salience. Nuclear plant regulation after the Three Mile Island accident was a highly salient issue to political elites and the general public.

State regulation of barbers, on the other hand, is rarely salient. Not only does salience vary across issue areas, it also varies across time within an issue area. Banking regulation was highly salient in 1933 but not so in 1973.

According to William Gormley (1983),[32] salience determines the willingness of political elites to intervene in the regulatory process. When issues become salient, the rewards for successful intervention are greater for elected officials. In salient issue areas, therefore, regulators will find their actions closely watched by political elites whereas in nonsalient areas regulatory discretion is likely to go unchecked. A lack of salience should be to the advantage of the regulated industry because it will have little opposition to its demands.

LEADERSHIP. The final regulatory resource is the agency's leadership. Unlike the career bureaucracy, which is fairly stable, leadership positions turn over frequently. Two elements of leadership are important—quality and the leader's goals. Quality of leadership is a nebulous resource that, though difficult to define, is clearly a factor. The leadership abilities of Alfred Kahn as Civil Aeronautics Board chairperson were instrumental in deregulating airlines; the absence of strong leadership in Federal Trade Commission chairman Paul Rand Dixon was often cited as a reason for poor performance by the pre-1969 FTC.

Essential to understanding the impact of leadership are the policy goals of regulatory agency heads. Through the leadership of Caspar Weinberger, Miles Kirkpatrick, and Michael Pertschuk, the Federal Trade Commission became less tied to the interests of the regulated industry and more interested in consumer issues. The appointment of Reese Taylor to head the Interstate Commerce Commission in 1981 signaled an end to the rapid movement toward deregulation of the trucking industry.

Leadership is especially important because the agency head is the focal point for interaction with the subsystem. In such interactions, the agency head is constrained by the expertise, cohesion, legislative authority, issue salience, and policy goals of the agency. An agency head who acts in opposition to the values and normal policy activities of the career staff risks political opposition from within the agency. Anne Burford's effort to alter environmental policy in the 1980s and the response of the EPA career staff is a classic example of this.

Agency Discretion: A Recapitulation

Regulatory agencies, therefore, exercise some discretion in regulatory policy. This discretion is not limitless, however. The amount of discretion accorded an agency is a function of its resources (expertise, cohesion, legislative authority, policy salience, and leadership) and the tolerances of other actors in the political system. Each actor has a zone of acceptance (see Simon, 1957); and if agency decisions fall within that zone, no action will be taken. Because regulatory policy is more important to subsystem actors, the zone of acceptance for subsystem actors is probably narrower than that for macropolitical system actors (e.g., the president). Consequently, subsystem actors will be more active.

As long as the regulatory subsystem produces policies within the zone of acceptance of Congress, the president, and the courts, then these actors will permit the subsystem some autonomy. Actions outside the zone of acceptance will bring attempts to intervene. The size of the zones of acceptance should vary with both salience and complexity (see Gormley, 1983). Salience increases the benefits of successful intervention to a political actor, and complexity increases the costs of intervention. All things being equal, therefore, political actors will be more likely to intervene in policies that are salient but not complex (Gormley, 1983).

End Notes

1. B. Weingast and M. Moran, "Bureaucratic Discretion or Congressional Control? Regulatory Policymaking by the Federal Trade Commission," *Journal of Political Economy*, 91, no. 5 (1983) 765–800.
2. James Q. Wilson, *The Politics of Regulation* (New York: Basic Books, 1980); Robert Katzman, *Regulatory Bureaucracy* (Cambridge, Mass.: MIT Press, 1980).

3. George J. Stigler, "The Theory of Economic Regulation," *Bell Journal of Economics and Management Science*, 2 (Spring 1971), 3–21; Theodore Lowi, *The End of Liberalism* (New York: Norton, 1969); Daniel Mazmanian and Paul Sabatier, "A Multivariate Model of Public Policy-Making," *American Journal of Political Science*, 24 (August 1980), 439–468.

4. Harold Lasswell, *Politics: Who Gets What, When, How* (New York: McGraw-Hill, 1936).

5. Marver Bernstein, *Regulating Business by Independent Commission* (Princeton, N.J.: Princeton University Press, 1955).

6. George Stigler, "The Theory of Economic Regulation," *Bell Journal of Economics and Management Science*, 2 (Spring 1971), 3–21; Sam Peltzman, "Toward a More General Theory of Regulation," *Journal of Law and Economics*, 19 (August 1976), 211–240.

7. Glendon Schubert, *The Public Interest* (New York: Free Press, 1960).

8. Paul Sabatier, "Regulatory Policy Making: Toward a Framework of Analysis," *National Resources Journal*, 17 (July 1977), 415–460.

9. I have taken some liberties with Sabatier's (1977) work here. His intent was to distinguish between managerial and policing types of regulation. His work results in three types of regulation along a single dimension rather than four types along two.

10. J. Lieper Freeman, *The Political Process* (New York: Random House, 1965); Grant McConnell, *Private Power and American Democracy* (New York: Knopf, 1966).

11. Norton Long, *The Polity* (Chicago: Rand McNally, 1962).

12. Randall Ripley and Grace Franklin, *Congress, the Bureaucracy, and Public Policy* (Homewood, Ill.: Dorsey Press, 1980).

13. Hugh Heclo, "Issue Networks and the Executive Establishment," *The New American Political System*, ed. Anthony King (Washington, D.C.: American Enterprise Institute, 1978); Paul Sabatier, "Toward a Strategic Interaction Framework of Policy Evaluation and Learning," Paper presented at the annual meeting of the Western Political Science Association, 1983.

14. Bradley Behrman, "Civil Aeronautics Board," in *The Politics of Regulation*, ed. James Q. Wilson (New York: Basic Books, 1980), pp. 75–121.

15. Erwin Krasnow, Lawrence Longley, and Herbert Terry, *The Politics of Broadcast Regulation* (3rd ed.) New York: St. Martin's Press, 1982).

16. Henry Kenski and Margaret Corgan Kenski, "Congress against the President: The Struggle over the Environment," in *Environmental Policy in the 1980s*, eds. Norman Vig and Michael Kraft (Washington, D.C.: CQ Press, 1984), pp. 97–120.

17. Barry Weingast and Mark Moran, "The Myth of the Runaway Bureaucracy: The Case of the FTC," *Regulation*, 6 (May/June, 1982) 33–38.

18. C. K. Rowland and Roger Marz, "Gresham's Law: The Regulatory Analogy," *Policy Studies Review*, 1 (February 1982), 572–580.

19. Francis Rourke, *Bureaucracy, Politics, and Public Policy* (3rd ed.) (Boston: Little, Brown, 1984).

20. William Niskanen, *Bureaucracy and Representative Government* (Chicago: Aldine, 1971).

21. James Guyot, "The Convergence of Public and Private Sector Bureaucracies." Paper presented at the annual meeting of the American Political Science Association, 1979.

22. Abraham Maslow, *Motivation and Personality* (2nd ed.) (New York: HarperCollins, 1970).

23. Barbara Romzek and J. Stephen Hendricks, "Organizational Involvement and Representative Bureaucracy," *American Political Science Review*, 76 (March 1982), 75–82.

24. Steven Kelman, "Occupational Safety and Health Administration," in *The Politics of Regulation*, ed. James Q. Wilson (New York: Basic Books, 1980), pp. 236–266.

25. Anthony Downs, *Inside Bureaucracy* (Boston: Little, Brown, 1967).

26. Hugh Heclo, *Government of Strangers* (Washington, D.C.: Brookings Institution, 1977).

27. David Welborn, *The Governance of Federal Regulatory Agencies* (Knoxville: University of Tennessee Press, 1977).

28. The section on bureaucratic variables relies heavily on Rourke (1984) and Sabatier (1977). The most applicable parts of the writings of each are used. In some cases, the impact of the variables reflects my interpretation of their work rather than their interpretation.

29. J. Clarence Davies and Barbara S. Davies, *The Politics of Pollution* (2nd ed.) (Indianapolis, Ind.: Pegasus, 1975).

30. Alfred Marcus, "Environmental Protection Agency," in *The Politics of Regulation*, ed. James Q. Wilson (New York: Basic Books, 1980).

31. Kenneth Meier, "The Impact of Regulatory Agency Structure: IRCs or DRAs," *Southern Review of Public Administration*, 3 (March

1980), 427–443; David Welborn, *The Governance*, 1977.

32. William Gormley, "Regulatory Issue Networks in a Federal System." Paper presented at the annual meeting of the American Political Science Association, 1983.

37

Appellate Courts as Policy Makers

Lawrence Baum

Appellate courts differ from trial courts in their roles as policy makers. The primary task of trial courts is to apply existing legal rules to specific cases. In contrast, appellate courts have more opportunities to establish new rules, to make decisions whose implications extend far beyond individual cases. In this chapter, I will examine what appellate courts do with these opportunities, what kinds of parts they play in the making of government policy.

The chapter's primary concern is the significance of appellate courts as policy makers. As many commentators have noted, appellate courts in the United States are very active as policy makers. Over the past few decades their decisions have transformed government policy on such issues as abortion, civil rights, and compensation for personal injuries. Yet the roles of appellate courts in policy making are limited by judges' own restraint. And when courts do intervene in the making of public policy, the impact of their decisions frequently is narrowed by the reactions of other government institutions and of people outside government.

A secondary concern is the content of the policies made by appellate courts, particularly their ideological direction. At any given time, the decisions of appellate courts are mixed, ranging from some that we would characterize as quite liberal to others that appear to be quite conservative. But the federal and state appellate courts seemed to be predominantly conservative institutions until at least the 1930s; today, in contrast, many appellate courts show strong liberal tendencies.

These concerns and other characteristics of appellate courts as policy makers will be examined in two parts. The first section of the chapter will look at appellate court decisions as government policies. The second will discuss the actual impact of the policies made by appellate courts.

APPELLATE COURT DECISIONS AS POLICIES

We can think of appellate court decisions as having two components, which correspond to the functions of these courts.... The first is a review of the way that the lower court treated the parties to the case. The second is the appellate court's judgment about the principles of law that are applicable to the case, a judgment that is expressed in the opinion accompanying the decision. I will consider the policy outputs of appellate courts in terms of these two components of the decision, giving primary attention to the second.

Appellate Review of Lower Court Decisions

In each case that an appellate court hears, its most specific task is to review the treatment of the parties by the court below it. The two levels of appellate courts take somewhat different approaches to this task.

REVIEW BY FIRST-LEVEL COURTS.   First-level appellate courts—which are intermediate courts in the federal system and in most states—review trial court decisions. They review a fairly high percentage of decisions by major state trial courts and federal district courts because of the general right to appeal adverse trial decisions and the growing tendency to exercise this right.

Most often, they ratify trial decisions by affirming them. It appears that every first-level court approves well over half the trial decisions it reviews. A California court of appeal in the mid-1970s affirmed lower-court decisions 84 percent of the time, and the affirmance rate for the federal courts of appeals in 1987 was also 84 percent.[1] Furthermore, many decisions that are not affirmances (which I will call disturbances of trial decisions) are actually relatively minor modifications of decisions rather than general overturnings. For instance, an appellate court will sometimes eliminate one of several sentences given to a criminal defendant, but in doing so it may not affect that defendant's actual prison time at all.[2]

These high affirmance rates can be explained in three ways.[3] The first is in terms of generally accepted legal doctrines. One of these is the rule that a trial court's interpretation of the facts in a case will not be questioned if there is any *substantial evidence* for that interpretation. On the basis of this rule, appellate courts generally do not take a fresh look at the evidence as a whole in order to weigh it independently; rather, they seek out a basis in the evidence for upholding the trial court's ruling. Another important doctrine is the *harmless error* rule, which holds that even if a trial judge has erred in applying legal rules, an appellate court can still affirm the decision if it concludes the error was harmless, that it probably did not affect the trial court judgment.

High affirmance rates can also be explained in terms of the institutional interests of appellate courts. Frequent reversals of trial court decisions would increase conflict between the two levels of courts, because many trial judges resent reversals as negative reviews of their work. And, more important, to proceed with full and thorough reviews of trial decisions, with no preconceptions, would consume the time and energy of appellate judges at an unacceptable rate, particularly when their work loads have grown in recent years. Moreover, high reversal rates might encourage more litigants to appeal, increasing the burdens of appellate judges even more.

Finally, the past experience of appellate judges also helps to account for their tendency to affirm. Because most appeals in the past have seemed suitable for affirmance, judges expect that this will continue to be true. In combination with the substantial evidence and harmless error rules and with the institutional interests of appellate courts, a judge's past experience tends to create a strong presumption in favor of affirmance. That presumption is reflected in a 1988 opinion by a judge on the federal court of appeals in Chicago; in his view, a decision should not be overturned when it is "just maybe or probably wrong" but only when it is "wrong with the force of a five-week-old, unrefrigerated dead fish."[4]

Affirmance rates are especially high in criminal cases. Thomas Davies' study of a California court of appeal in the 1970s found that only 14 percent of the appeals from criminal convictions resulted in any disturbance of the trial decision, and only 5 percent involved a full reversal. In contrast, 31 percent of the trial decisions in civil cases were disturbed. Similarly, in the federal courts of appeals in 1987, the reversal rate was 8 percent in criminal cases and 18 percent in civil cases.[5]

One reason for this difference lies in patterns of appeals. Civil appeals carry significant monetary costs for most litigants, and civil litigants are ordinarily advised by attorneys. As a result, most appellants probably have fairly strong grounds on which to challenge trial decisions. In contrast, criminal defendants have considerable incentive to appeal when they have received substantial prison sentences, a high proportion of defendants do appeal, and a good many such appeals have little legal basis.

Nevertheless, as Davies has argued, it misses the point simply to assume that most criminal appeals are frivolous, because frivolousness is a subjective concept. Indeed, Davies found in his California study that the court of appeal cited trial court errors in about a quarter of the decisions in which it affirmed convictions.[6] Hence the concept of the frivolous criminal appeal may be as much a justification for affirmance—and for limited judicial scrutiny of trials—as it is an explanation of high affirmance rates.

Of course, the inclination to affirm is linked with the growing use of abbreviated procedures in first-level appellate courts. The establishment of such procedures has been encouraged by the belief that a high proportion of appeals are easy affirmances that staff attorneys can identify and handle. At the same time, when certain cases are labeled as requiring only abbreviated consideration, court personnel are encouraged to treat them as easy affirmances. Thus the use of abbreviated procedures may raise an affirmance rate that already is high.

REVIEW BY SECOND-LEVEL COURTS. Unlike first-level appellate courts, those at the second level disturb lower court decisions in a high proportion of the cases they decide. In its 1987–88 term, for instance, the U.S. Supreme Court affirmed the lower court in only 42 percent of the decisions for which it provided full opinions.[7]

Such a high disturbance rate suggests that second-level appellate courts are quite willing to substitute their own judgments for those of the courts below them. But in this sense, it is quite deceptive. As we have seen, judges on second-level courts are inclined to accept cases for hearings when they think that the lower court has erred in its decision. This means that they approach many of the cases they have accepted with a

presumption of reversal, rather than the presumption of affirmance that prevails in first-level courts, and a high reversal rate is virtually guaranteed.

Yet if we take into account all the cases that are brought to the second-level courts, and not just those that are accepted for review, the disturbance of lower-court decisions is in fact quite limited. Of the cases that the Supreme Court receives, for example, it disturbs decisions only in about 5 percent.[8] Thus appellate courts at both levels allow most decisions that they review to remain standing.

OVERVIEW. Because appellate courts uphold most decisions that are brought to them and because some decisions are not appealed, the overwhelming majority of decisions by trial courts and intermediate appellate courts become final. One study indicated that in the late 1960s the federal courts of appeals disturbed only about 4 percent of all the decisions made by the district courts; in turn, the Supreme Court disturbed about 1 percent of all court of appeals decisions.[9] Almost surely, the rates are lower today. Furthermore, if disturbance rates were calculated for the decisions of state trial courts, they would be even lower than those for the federal courts because a relatively small proportion of decisions by minor trial courts are appealed.[10] In this respect, then, appellate courts intervene rather little into the work of the courts below them.

Of course, this is only one aspect of the relationship between higher and lower courts. Even though appellate courts overturn relatively few decisions, the opinions they write influence what the courts below them do in a much larger number of cases. For example, one state supreme court decision on liability rules in auto accident cases can shape hundreds of trial court decisions. For this reason, we must examine the activity of the appellate courts as makers of legal rules and analyze the responses to their decisions in order to get a fuller sense of their roles within the judiciary.

Appellate Court Agendas

Through their opinions, appellate courts lay down interpretations of law that are generally regarded as binding on both lower courts and administrative bodies under their jurisdiction. These interpretations can alter existing legal rules, and they can reshape or even overturn policies made by the legislature and the executive branch. It is primarily through their legal interpretations, rather than through their treatment of individual litigants, that appellate courts exert influence as policy makers.

We can begin to sketch out this role by examining the sets of cases that appellate courts hear and decide with opinions—what I will call their agendas. The more that a court concentrates on cases in a particular field, the greater its potential to shape public policy in that field. ...[T]he agendas of appellate courts are the products of rules of jurisdiction, patterns of litigation and appeals, and the judges' choices of cases in which to write opinions. The 1987 agendas of three appellate courts at different levels are summarized in Table 37.1.

The agendas of state supreme courts reflect the work of state courts generally.[11] Thus, because state court litigation is quite diverse, so too is state supreme court business. In recent

years, several areas have been frequent subjects of supreme court opinions: torts, particularly cases arising from accidents; criminal law and procedure; contract disputes, most often between debtors and creditors; government economic regulation; and family and estate issues, primarily concerning divorce and inheritance. As a result, state supreme courts make legal rulings in a broad range of policy areas.

The agendas of the federal courts of appeals show both similarities and differences with those of the state supreme courts.[12] Their opinions, of course, are primarily on issues of federal law, but they also deal with a good many state law issues in cases brought under the diversity jurisdiction. The two policy areas that stand out on their agendas are government economic regulation and criminal law and procedure, with regulation cases considerably more numerous than they are in state appellate courts. Also common are torts, tax cases, and contract cases.

The agenda of the U.S. Supreme Court is rather distinctive.[13] Broadly speaking, the Court

TABLE 37.1   Subject Matter of Cases Decided with Published Opinions in 1987, Selected Appellate Courts, in Percentages

Category of Cases[a]	Pennsylvania Supreme Court	Federal Court of Appeals, Sixth Circuit[b]	U.S. Supreme Court[c]
Debt and contract	10.5	11.1	4.1
Real property	4.4	0.4	1.4
Business organization	0.5	3.2	2.1
Torts	18.2	7.9	5.5
Family and estates	7.7	0.0	0.0
Public Law:			
Criminal	34.8	19.8	21.4
Governmental regulation of economic activity	7.7	22.1	19.3
Other	16.0	35.6	46.2

[a]Many cases could have fit into multiple categories; different coding rules would have produced substantially different results. For this reason, the percentages shown should be viewed as illustrations of differences in the agendas of the three courts rather than as exact depictions of each court's agenda.

[b]The time period from which cases were drawn was January–June 1987.

[c]The time period from which cases were drawn was the 1987 term of the Court.

devotes itself overwhelmingly to public law issues; as the table shows, all other cases account for only a small minority of its opinions. Within this category, the Court is primarily a civil liberties specialist; indeed, in recent years about half its opinions have involved civil liberties issues. The largest number of these cases concern criminal procedure, but the Court also writes a great many opinions on the right to equal treatment under the law and such personal rights as freedom of expression and freedom of religion. Another significant part of the Court's agenda concerns economic regulation by federal and state governments. A third major area, which overlaps the first two, is federalism—that is, the constitutional relationship between national and state governments.

Even this brief discussion suggests two conclusions about the potential roles of appellate courts as policy makers. The first concerns the agendas of appellate courts taken as a whole. While the various state and federal courts cover a broad range of issues, there are some important areas of public policy in which appellate courts are largely inactive. The outstanding example is foreign policy, which state courts barely touch and in which federal courts make relatively few decisions. Even in fields where they are active, the courts may not deal with the most fundamental issues. In economic regulation, for instance, courts focus primarily on the details of regulatory policy rather than on the general form and scope of regulation.

The second conclusion concerns differences among courts. Some issue areas, such as criminal procedure, are important to appellate courts at all levels, but others are concentrated in certain courts. Property disputes and divorce are primarily the domain of state courts, while the Supreme Court gives civil liberties much greater emphasis than does any set of lower appellate courts. Thus different appellate courts have different domains in which to make policy.

Ideological Patterns in Appellate Court Policy

The discussion of agendas indicates the areas to which appellate courts devote the most attention. To get a sense of what they do in these areas, we need to examine the ideological direction and activism of appellate policies.

Ideologically, the policies of the appellate courts at any given time are certain to be quite diverse. But diversity is not the same as randomness. During particular periods in American history, liberal or conservative policies have been dominant. In the broadest terms, appellate courts traditionally were fairly conservative in their policies, by the current definition of that term, whereas a strong element of liberalism has developed in the past half century.

THE TRADITIONAL CONSERVATISM OF APPELLATE COURTS. For most of American history, the policies of appellate courts were primarily conservative. Federal and state courts addressed a wide range of legal issues involving the interests of economically powerful groups, and the dominant theme in their decisions was support for those interests.

This theme is fairly clear in the work of the U.S. Supreme Court. In the nineteenth and early twentieth centuries the Court worked to protect property rights and the freedom of business enterprises from restrictions by state and federal governments. As legislation to regulate and restrict business practices proliferated, the Court became increasingly hostile to this legislation, frequently ruling that state and federal laws violated the Constitution. These attacks culminated in the Court's decisions of the 1930s which struck down much of President Franklin Roosevelt's New Deal economic program. Meanwhile, the Court gave little support to the civil liberties of black citizens, unpopular political groups, or criminal defendants. Viewing the Court's record, Attorney General Robert Jackson, who was shortly to join the Court himself, wrote in 1941 that "never in its entire history can the Supreme Court be said to have for a single hour been representative of anything except the relatively conservative forces of its day."[14]

Scholars have disagreed about the historical record of state courts, and this disagreement reflects the diversity in their decisions.[15] But the most important elements in their policies through most of our history were primarily conservative. As the industrial economy developed, state courts did much to protect the business sector from threats to its economic well-being. In the nineteenth century, they devised rules in contract and property law that supported industrial and commercial growth. In their building of tort law in the nineteenth century, state courts created rules that "favored defendants over plaintiffs, businesses over individuals."[16] One example was the contributory negligence rule, which prevented the recovery of money for injuries if the person bringing suit was even slightly negligent. Another was the fellow-servant rule, under which a worker could not sue an employer for injuries caused by another employee. The courts also held that a family could not recover for the death of the person who was their support, because the right to sue had died with the person who was killed.

Of course, there were numerous exceptions to the conservative thrust of judicial policy. Liberal policies and even liberal courts existed throughout the long period when conservatism was predominant. The U.S. Supreme Court, for instance, varied in its hostility to government economic regulation, and some state supreme courts rejected in part or altogether the doctrines that protected businesses against lawsuits. But until fairly recently the general conservatism of appellate courts was pronounced.

This conservatism is not difficult to understand. Judges came primarily from economically advantaged segments of society and were imbued with the values of the elite. Trained in a legal profession in which conservative values predominated, they often embarked on legal careers that involved service to business enterprises. Furthermore, the most skilled advocates who came before their courts generally represented businesses and other institutions with conservative goals. Because of all these factors, it may have been almost inevitable that conservatism became the dominant theme in judicial policy.

A GROWTH IN LIBERALISM.   In the past half century, the dominant conservatism of the past has been replaced by an ideologically mixed pattern of policy in which the liberal element often has been more prominent. Across a range of issues, the courts have given more support to the interests of relatively weak groups in society, groups that possess far fewer social and economic resources and far less conventional political power than the business interests that courts tended to favor in the past.

The most visible change has been in the Supreme Court. Beginning in 1937 the Court quickly abandoned its earlier support for business interests that sought protection from government regulation. It also began to provide support for the civil liberties of relatively powerless groups in American society, support that peaked in the 1960s. It applied the constitutional rights of criminal defendants to state proceedings and established new controls on police investigations and trial procedures. It required the desegregation of Southern public schools and protected the rights of racial minority groups in other areas of life. It strengthened freedom of expression both for the mass media and for people who express their views through vehicles such as pamphlets and marches.

In the 1970s and 1980s the Supreme Court supported civil liberties with less consistency. It narrowed the rights of criminal defendants, and it became more reluctant to establish new rights in any area. But, compared with most of its past history, the Court of the past twenty years has remained relatively liberal in its support for civil liberties and its acceptance of government regulation of business.

In the past few decades the federal courts of appeals have differed a good deal in their ideological positions, but in general they too have moved away from their traditional conservatism. The court of appeals for the District of Columbia stood out for its strong liberalism from the 1960s through the mid-1980s, as evidenced in its support for the rights of criminal defendants and the mentally ill, for the interests of consumers, and for protection of the environment. Standing out in another way was the Fifth Circuit Court of Appeals in the Deep South, which gave strong support to black civil rights on school desegregation and other issues in the 1950s and 1960s despite the anti-civil rights pressures in that region.

Early in this century, state supreme courts began to reduce their long standing support for business in tort law, expanding the ability of people who suffer injuries to recover compensation.[17] This trend gradually gained momentum, as courts increasingly eliminated old rules that had favored defendants. Most dramatically, supreme courts in the 1960s and 1970s largely eliminated the requirement that those who are injured by defective products must prove that the manufacturer was negligent. Some other examples of changes in tort law since the 1950s are shown in Table 37.2.

State courts were slower to take liberal positions in civil liberties; indeed, in the 1950s and 1960s some supreme courts resisted the Supreme Court's expansions of liberties, interpreting the Court's decisions narrowly. Since the 1970s, however, state courts increasingly have undertaken their own expansions through their interpretations of state constitutions, finding broader rights in those constitutions than the Supreme Court has found in the U.S. Constitution.[18] The largest part of this activity has focused on criminal justice, but it has extended to areas such as freedom of expression and sex discrimination. Not all states have participated in this development, which is concentrated heavily in the West and Northeast, but it has become increasingly widespread.

The relative liberalism of appellate courts in recent years is more difficult to explain than was their traditional conservatism. Undoubtedly the recent liberalism is at least partially rooted in a changing pattern of social values. In this century, support by the general public and political leaders for the autonomy of business enterprises has declined. Meanwhile, some civil liberties—especially those related to equality—have gained more support. This change in values is reflected in judges' own attitudes as well as in the kinds of litigation and arguments that come to the appellate courts.

Another source of this ideological change is the kinds of people who become judges. Like judges in the past, members of the current judiciary tend to come from families with high status. But there are more exceptions to this tendency today; as a result, the attitudes of judges on economic and social issues are less likely to be conservative. Furthermore, at the federal level liberal Democratic presidents have sought out appellate judges who shared their liberalism. Franklin Roosevelt's appointments turned the Supreme Court away from its traditional conservatism. Similarly, Roosevelt, Johnson, and Carter all used their appointments to move the lower federal courts in a liberal direction. At the state level, the growing strength of the Democratic party in the North from the 1930s on brought more liberal governors into office; in turn, these governors influenced the direction of state appellate courts with their own appointments.

TABLE 37.2 Some Changes in Tort Law Doctrine Initiated by State Supreme Courts Since the 1950s		
Doctrinal Change	**Innovating State**	**How Many States?**
Abolishing the general immunity of municipalities from lawsuits.	Florida, 1957	Many
Allowing parents and children to sue each other for torts.	Wisconsin, 1963	Most
Allowing a person to sue for emotional distress without accompanying physical injury.	Hawaii, 1970	Several
Allowing a person injured by a drug product whose manufacturer is unknown to sue all the manufacturers of that product on the basis of their market shares.	California, 1980	A few

Note: The identity of the state that first adopted a legal doctrine and the number of states that have adopted it are ambiguous for some doctrines.

Sources: Some information obtained from W. Page Keeton, Dan B. Dobbs, Robert E. Keeton, and David G. Owen, *Prosser and Keeton on Torts*, 5th ed. (St. Paul: West Publishing, 1984).

To some extent, this shift to greater liberalism has been self-reinforcing. The courts' support for civil liberties encouraged interest groups to bring new cases, seeking further expansions of liberties. When the Supreme Court in the 1960s played a strong role in expanding civil liberties, many lawyers gained an appreciation for that role, and those who reached the bench themselves sought to follow it. As I suggested for torts in the state courts, a trend in judicial policy tends to gain a certain momentum of its own.

But this is not to say that the liberal trend is irreversible; unquestionably, it could be reversed, particularly with major changes in the kinds of people who are selected as judges. Indeed, this process is well under way in the federal courts. The appointments by Richard Nixon and Ronald Reagan have turned a strongly liberal Supreme Court into one that could be characterized as moderately conservative by current standards, and appointments by George Bush almost surely would move the Court further to the right. Reagan's numerous appointments to the courts of appeals made some of those courts considerably more conservative, and here too that process is likely to continue. This prospect is a reminder that the ideological stance of the courts, no matter how strong the forces behind it, is always subject to change. ...

End Notes

1. Administrative Office of the United States Courts, *Annual Report of the Administrative Office of the United States Courts, 1987* (Washington, D.C.: Government Printing Office, 1988), p. 155; Thomas Y. Davies, "Affirmed: A Study of Criminal Appeals and Decision-Making Norms in a California Court of Appeal," *American Bar Foundation Research Journal*, Summer 1982, p. 574. The figure for federal courts was calculated in a somewhat different way from the figure for the California court, so the two are not entirely comparable.
2. Davies, "Affirmed," p. 576.
3. Sources of information for this discussion include Davies, "Affirmed."
4. *Parts and Electric Motors v. Sterling Electric*, No. 88–1609 (7th Circuit 1988), p. 10.
5. Administrative Office of the United States Courts, *Annual Report 1987*, p. 155. The data for civil cases were calculated by the author.
6. Davies, "Affirmed," pp. 582–83.
7. "The Supreme Court, 1987 Term," *Harvard Law Review*, 102 (November 1988), 354.
8. This figure is estimated from the Court's rates of acceptance of cases and of disturbances in the cases it accepts. See "Statistical Recap of Supreme Court's Workload during Last Three Terms," *United States Law Week*, 57 (July 26, 1988), 3074; and J. Woodford Howard, Jr., *Courts of Appeals in the Federal Judicial System: A Study of the Second, Fifth, and District of Columbia Circuits* (Princeton, N.J.: Princeton University Press, 1981), p. 59.
9. These figures are estimated from data in Howard, *Courts of Appeals*, pp. 39, 74.
10. See, for instance, Judicial Council of California, *1984 Annual Report* (San Francisco: Judicial Council of California, 1984), pp. 211, 216.
11. Sources of information for this discussion include Robert A. Kagan, Bliss Cartwright, Lawrence M. Friedman, and Stanton Wheeler, "The Business of State Supreme Courts, 1870–1970," *Stanford Law Review*, 30 (November 1977), 132–51; and Burton M. Atkins and Henry R. Glick, "Environmental and Structural Variables as Determinants of Issues in State Courts of Last Resort," *American Journal of Political Science*, 20 (February 1976), 98–101.
12. Sources of information for this discussion include Howard, *Courts of Appeals*, pp. 315–18; and Lawrence Baum, Sheldon Goldman, and Austin Sarat, "The Evolution of Litigation in the Federal Courts of Appeals, 1895–1975," *Law & Society Review*, 16 (1981–82), 291–309.
13. Sources of information for this discussion include Richard Pacelle, "The Supreme Court Agenda across Time: Dynamics and Determinants of Change" (Ph.D. diss., Ohio State University, 1985), ch. 3.
14. Robert M. Jackson, *The Struggle for Judicial Supremacy* (New York: Alfred A. Knopf, 1941), p. 187.
15. See Lawrence M. Friedman, *A History of American Law*, rev. ed. (New York: Simon & Schuster, 1985); Stanton Wheeler, Bliss Cartwright, Robert A. Kagan, and Lawrence M. Friedman, "Do the 'Haves' Come Out Ahead? Winning and Losing in State Supreme Courts,

1870–1970," *Law & Society Review*, 21 (1987), 403–45; Melvin I. Urofsky, "State Courts and Progressive Legislation during the Progressive Era: A Reevaluation," *Journal of American Law*, 72 (June 1985), 63–91; and Gary T. Schwartz, "Tort Law and the Economy in Nineteenth-Century America: A Reinterpretation," *Yale Law Journal*, 90 (July 1981), 1717–75.

16. Lawrence M. Friedman, *Total Justice* (New York: Russell Sage Foundation, 1985), p. 54.

17. Lawrence Baum and Bradley C. Canon, "State Supreme Courts as Activists: New Doctrines in the Law of Torts," in Mary Cornelia Porter and G. Alan Tarr, eds., *State Supreme Courts: Policymakers in the Federal System* (Westport, Conn.: Greenwood Press, 1982), pp. 83–108.

18. See Ronald K. L. Collins, Peter J. Galie, and John Kincaid, "State High Courts, State Constitutions, and Individual Rights Litigation since 1980: A Judicial Survey," *Publius*, 16 (Summer 1986), 141–61; and Stanley H. Friedelbaum, ed., *Human Rights in the States: New Directions in Constitutional Policymaking* (New York: Greenwood Press, 1988).

38

The Hollow Hope: Can Courts Bring About Social Change?

Gerald Rosenberg

THE PROBLEM

JUSTICE JACKSON: "I suppose that realistically the reason this case is here was that action couldn't be obtained from Congress. Certainly it would be here much stronger from your point of view if Congress did act, wouldn't it?"

MR. RANKIN: "That is true, but ... if the Court would delegate back to Congress from time to time the question of deciding what should be done about rights ... the parties [before the Court] would be deprived by that procedure from getting their constitutional rights because of the present membership or approach of Congress to that particular question." (Oral argument in *Briggs* v. *Elliott*, quoted in Friedman 1969, 244)

When Justice Jackson and Assistant U.S. Attorney General J. Lee Rankin exchanged these thoughts during oral argument in a companion case to *Brown*, they acknowledged that the Supreme Court is part of a larger political system. As their colloquy overtly demonstrates, American courts are political institutions. Though unique in their organization and operation, they are a crucial cog in the machinery of government. But this exchange rests on a more interesting premise that is all the more influential because it is implicit and unexamined: court decisions produce change. Specifically, both Jackson and Rankin assumed that it mattered a great deal how the Court decided the issue of school segregation. If their assumption is correct, then one may ask sensibly to what extent and in what ways courts can be consequential in effecting political and social change. To what degree, and under what conditions, can judicial processes be used to produce political and social change? What are the constraints that operate on them? What factors are important and why?

These descriptive or empirical questions are important for understanding the role of any political institution, yet they are seldom asked of courts. Traditionally, most lawyers and legal scholars have focused on a related normative issue: whether courts *ought* to act. From the perspective of democratic theory, that is an important and useful question. Yet since much of politics is about who gets what, when, and how, and how that distribution is maintained, or changed, understanding to what extent, and under what conditions, courts can produce political and social change is of key importance.

The answer to the questions raised above might appear obvious if it rests on Rankin's and Jackson's implied premise that courts produce a great deal of social change. In the last several decades movements and groups advocating what I will shortly define as significant social reform have turned increasingly to the courts. Starting with the famous cases brought by the civil rights movement and spreading to issues raised by women's groups, environmental groups, political reformers, and others, American courts seemingly have become important producers of political and social change. Cases such as *Brown* (school desegregation) and *Roe* (abortion) are heralded as having produced major change. Further, such litigation has often occurred, and appears to have been most successful, when the other branches of government have failed to act. While officious government officials and rigid, unchanging institutions represent a real social force which may frustrate popular opinion, this litigation activity

suggests that courts can produce significant social reform even when the other branches of government are inactive or opposed. Indeed, for many, part of what makes American democracy exceptional is that it includes the world's most powerful court system, protecting minorities and defending liberty, in the face of opposition from the democratically elected branches. Americans look to activist courts, then, as fulfilling an important role in the American scheme.[1] This view of the courts, although informed by recent historical experience, is essentially functional. It sees courts as powerful, vigorous, and potent proponents of change. I refer to this view of the role of the courts as the "Dynamic Court" view.

As attractive as the Dynamic Court view may be, one must guard against uncritical acceptance. Indeed, in a political system that gives sovereignty to the popular will and makes economic decisions through the market, it is not obvious why courts should have the effects it asserts. Maybe its attractiveness is based on something more than effects? Could it be that the self-understanding of the judiciary and legal profession leads to an overstatement of the role of the courts, a "mystification" of the judiciary? If judges see themselves as powerful; if the Bar views itself as influential, and insulated; if professional training in law schools inculcates students with such beliefs, might these factors inflate the self-importance of the judiciary? The Dynamic Court view may be supported, then, because it offers psychological payoffs to key actors by confirming self-images, not because it is correct.[2] And when this "mystification" is added to a normative belief in the courts as the guardian of fundamental rights and liberties—what Scheingold (1974) calls the "myth of rights"—the allure of the Dynamic Court view may grow.

Further, for all its "obviousness," the Dynamic Court view has a well-established functional and historical competitor. In fact, there is a long tradition of legal scholarship that views the federal judiciary, in Alexander Hamilton's famous language, as the "least dangerous" branch of government. Here, too, there is something of a truism about this claim. Courts, we know, lack both budgetary and physical powers. Because, in Hamilton's words, they lack power over either the "sword or the purse," their ability to produce political and social change is limited. In contrast to the first view, the "least dangerous" branch can do little more than point out how actions have fallen short of constitutional or legislative requirements and hope that appropriate action is taken. The strength of this view, of course, is that it leaves Americans free to govern themselves without interference from non-elected officials. I refer to this view of the courts as weak, ineffective, and powerless as the "Constrained Court" view.

The Constrained Court view fully acknowledges the role of popular preferences and social and economic resources in shaping outcomes. Yet it seems to rely excessively on a formal-process understanding of how change occurs in American politics. But the formal process doesn't always work, for social and political forces may be overly responsive to unevenly distributed resources. Bureaucratic inertia, too, can derail orderly, processional change. There is room, then, for courts to effectively correct the pathologies of the political process. Perhaps accurate at the founding of the political system, the Constrained Court view may miss growth and change in the American political system.

Clearly, these two views, and the aspirations they represent, are in conflict on a number of different dimensions. They differ not only on both the desirability and the effectiveness of court action, but also on the nature of American democracy. The Dynamic Court view gives courts an important place in the American political system while the older view sees courts as much less powerful than other more "political" branches and activities. The conflict is more than one of mere definition, for each view captures a very different part of American democracy. We Americans want courts to protect minorities and defend liberties, *and* to defer to elected officials. We want a robust political life *and* one that is just. Most of the time, these two visions do not clash. American legislatures do not habitually threaten liberties, and courts do not regularly invalidate the acts of elected officials or require certain actions to be taken. But the most interesting and relevant cases, such as *Brown* and *Roe*, occur when activist courts overrule and invalidate the actions of elected officials, or order actions beyond what elected officials are willing

to do. What happens then? Are courts effective producers of change, as the Dynamic Court view suggests, or do their decisions do little more than point the way to a brighter, but perhaps unobtainable future? Once again, this conflict between two deeply held views about the role of the courts in the American political system has an obvious normative dimension that is worth debating.... Relying heavily on empirical data, I ask under what conditions can courts produce political and social change? When does it make sense for individuals and groups pressing for such change to litigate? What do the answers mean about the nature of the American regime?

Political and social change are broad terms. Specifically, conflict between the two views is more sharply focused when courts become involved in social reform, the broadening and equalizing of the possession and enjoyment of what are commonly perceived as basic goods in American society. What are these basic goods? Rawls (1971, 42) provides a succinct definition: "Rights and liberties, powers and opportunities, income and wealth." Later he adds self-respect (Rawls 1971, 440). Fleshed out, these include political goods such as participation in the political process and freedom of speech and association; legal goods such as equal and non-discriminatory treatment of all people; material goods; and self-respect, the opportunity for every individual to lead a satisfying and worthy life. Contributions to political and social change bring these benefits to people formerly deprived of them.

Yet, so defined, social reform is still too broad a term to capture the essence of the difference between the two views. At the core of the debate lies those specific social reforms that affect large groups of people such as blacks, or workers, or women, or partisans of a particular political persuasion; in other words, *policy change with nationwide impact*. Litigation aimed at changing the way a single bureaucracy functions would not fit this definition, for example, while litigation attempting to change the functioning of a whole set of bureaucracies or institutions nationwide would. Change affecting groups of this size, as well as altering bureaucratic and institutional practice nationwide can be called *significant* social reform. So, for example, in the

Brown litigation, when civil rights litigators sued to end school segregation nationwide, not just in the school systems in which the complaints arose, they were attempting to use the courts to produce significant social reform. Similarly, when abortion activists mounted a constitutional challenge to restrictive abortion laws, aimed at affecting all women, they were attempting to use the courts to produce significant social reform. Although the relevant boundary line cannot be drawn precisely, there is no doubt that the aim of modern litigation in the areas of civil rights, women's rights, and the like, is to produce significant social reform.[3]

This definition of significant social reform does not take much note of the role of the courts in individual cases. Due process and court procedures offer at least some protection to the individual from arbitrary action. Interposing courts and set procedures between government officials and citizens has been a hard fought-for and great stride forward in human decency.[4] However, the protection of individuals, in individual cases, tells us little about the effectiveness of courts in producing nationwide policy change. In addition, there is no clash between the two views in dealing with individuals.

There is good reason to focus solely on the effectiveness of courts in producing significant social reform. Other possibilities, such as courts acting as obstacles to significant social reform, can be excluded because adequate work has been done on them. Studies of the role of the courts in the late nineteenth and early twentieth centuries, for example, show that courts can effectively block significant social reform.[5] Further, since the mid-twentieth century litigants have petitioned American courts with increasing frequency to produce significant social reform. Reform-minded groups have brought cases and adopted strategies that assumed courts could be consequential in furthering their goals. To narrow the focus is to concentrate on an important aspect of recent political activity.

The attentive reader will have noticed that I have written of courts being consequential in effecting significant social reform, of courts producing significant social reform, or of courts being of help to reformers. All of these formulations

suggest that courts can sometimes make a difference. The question, then, is whether, and under what conditions, this occurs. When does it makes sense to litigate to help bring about significant social reform? If the judiciary lacks power, as the Constrained Court view suggests, then courts cannot make much difference. Perhaps only when political, social, and economic forces have already pushed society far along the road to reform will courts have any independent effect. And even then their decisions may be more a reflection of significant social reform already occurring than an independent, important contribution to it. But if the Dynamic Court view is the more accurate, if courts are effective producers of significant social reform, then they will be able to produce change. And if each view is partly right, if courts are effective under some conditions and not others, then I want to know when and where those conditions exist.

There is a danger that I have set up a straw man. Given the incremental nature of change in American politics, one might wonder if there is ever significant social reform in the U.S. In fact, if there is not, then asking whether and under what conditions courts produce it won't tell me anything about courts and change. I run the danger of "finding" that courts don't produce significant social reform because it doesn't exist! Fortunately, there are numerous examples of significant social reform in the U.S.: the introduction of social security, medicaid and medicare; increased minority participation in the electoral process; the increasing racial integration of American institutions and society; the increasing breakdown of gender barriers and discrimination against women; enhanced protection of the environment and reduction of pollution; protection for working men and women who organize to improve their lot; and so on. Clearly, then, there is significant social reform in the U.S. And, of course, proponents of the Dynamic Court view claim that both *Brown* and *Roe* produced significant social reform.

In order to determine whether and under what conditions courts can produce significant social reform ... on two key areas of significant social reform litigation, civil rights and women's rights. These two movements and their leading, symbolic cases (*Brown* and *Roe*) are generally considered the prime examples of the successful use of a court-based strategy to produce significant social reform. Proponents of the Dynamic Court view generally credit *Brown* with having revolutionized American race relations while *Roe* is understood as having guaranteed legal abortions for all. Defenders of the Constrained Court view, however, might suggest that neither interpretation is correct. Rather, they would point to changes in the broader political system to explain such major social and political changes. Clearly, the two views are in conflict.

It should be emphasized that an examination of civil rights, abortion, and women's rights avoids the pitfalls of simple case studies. Each movement spans a sufficient length of time to allow for variance. Covering decades, the debate over these issues has been affected by political, social, and economic variables. Besides the importance of these cases for politics (and for law and social science), they are cases in which claims about court effectiveness should be most clearly highlighted, cases which should most likely falsify one of the two views. If the constraints and conditions developed ... hold in these studies, they should illuminate the broader question under what conditions courts are capable of producing significant social reform. And, for those readers who are uncomfortable with only three case studies ... I expand the coverage to examine briefly three other modern uses of the courts to produce significant social reform.

In order to proceed, while not ignoring state and lower federal courts, I will concentrate on the U.S. Supreme Court. Like the Congress and the presidency, the Supreme Court, while not the only institution of its kind in the American political system, is the most visible and important one. It sits atop a hierarchical structure, and decisions of lower courts involving significant social reform seldom escape its scrutiny. Also, because it is the most authoritative U.S. court, it is the most concerned with public policy. Hypotheses that concern the courts and social reform must first deal with the Supreme Court and then turn to the ramifications of its decisions elsewhere in the judiciary.

There remains the question of how to deal with complicated issues of causation. Because it is difficult to isolate the effects of court decisions from other events in producing significant social reform, special care is needed in specifying how courts can be effective. On a general level, one can distinguish two types of influence courts could exercise. Court decisions might produce significant social reform through a *judicial* path that relies on the authority of the court. Alternatively, court influence could follow an *extra-judicial* path that invokes court powers of persuasion, legitimacy, and the ability to give salience to issues. Each of these possible paths of influence is different and requires separate analysis.

The *judicial* path of causal influence is straight-forward. It focuses on the direct outcome of judicial decisions and examines whether the change required by the courts was made. In civil rights, for example, if a Supreme Court decision ordering an end to public segregation was the cause of segregation ending, then one should see lower courts ordering local officials to end segregation, those officials acting to end it, the community at large supporting it, and, most important, segregation actually ending. Similarly, with abortion, if the Court's invalidation of state laws restricting or prohibiting abortion produced direct change, it should be seen in the removal of barriers to abortion and the provision of abortion services where requested. Proponents of the Dynamic Court view believe that the courts have powerful direct effects, while partisans of the Constrained Court view deny this.

End Notes

1. Not everyone, however, thinks such liberal judicial activism is a good thing. It has spawned a wave of attacks on the judiciary ranging from Nathan Glazer's warning of the rise of an "imperial judiciary" to a spate of legislative proposals to remove court jurisdiction over a number of issues. See Glazer (1975); *An Imperial Judiciary* (1979). And, of course, Presidents Nixon and Reagan pledged to end judicial activism by appointing "strict constructionists" to the federal courts.

2. As McCann (1986, 114) suggests, in the public-interest movement, lawyers are "quite

naturally the most ardent spokespersons" for the use of courts to produce change.

3. A major study of public-interest law takes a similar "focus on policy-oriented cases, where a decision will affect large numbers of people or advance a major law reform objective" (Council for Public Interest Law 1976, 7).

4. See, for example, Thompson (1975), particularly chapter 10, and Hay et al. (1975). Though the focus of both works is on the role of the criminal law in the eighteenth century in sustaining the hegemony of the English ruling class, both view law as affording some protection to individuals.

5. A simple example is child labor, where the Supreme Court twice overturned congressional legislation prohibiting it, delaying its eventual outlawing for several decades. For a careful study of the ability of courts to effectively block significant social reform, see Paul (1960). However, it should be noted that given the appointment power, and the general dependence of courts on political elites, such blocking cannot continue indefinitely. On this point, see Dahl (1957).

39

Parties, the Government, and the Policy Process

Samuel J. Eldersveld

The influence of parties on the policy decisions of governmental leaders is one of the most important questions for democratic societies. It is the "governing function" which affects us all. Does it make any difference how well parties organize, how carefully they recruit candidates, how well they are led, how effectively they campaign, how persuasively they mobilize voters and win elections—for policy outcomes? This is not the only process parties are involved in or the only basic function they perform. Parties engage in a variety of other functions—leadership selection, socialization, communication, agenda setting, government monitoring, and consensus building. But certainly their role in determining policy is a central concern. If they have no policy

function, they may still meet other needs of the system, but they could then share, or yield, center stage in the governmental arena to other groups which are important in governmental action. As V. O. Key said, "There are two radically different kinds of politics: the politics of getting into office and the politics of governing."[1]

OBSTACLES TO PARTY INFLUENCE IN THE UNITED STATES

The traditional view is that American parties are too fragmented, dispersed, and undisciplined to have much influence over policy determination. This view argues that if one wants to explain the

From Samuel J. Eldersveld, *Political Parties in American Society* (New York: Basic Books, 1982), Chapter 16. Reprinted by permission.

basis for the legislative decisions of members of Congress, United States senators, state legislators, or local policy makers one cannot explain them primarily on the basis of party influence. Even when strong mayors, governors, or presidents dominate the policy process, it is not their party roles so much as their personal appeals, personal bases of electoral support, and personal attractiveness and expertise which is important in explaining their success in getting new laws adopted. In this traditional view parties are not considered as policy leadership structures which can mobilize support to determine or significantly influence, legislative, executive, judicial, and bureaucratic decisions.

One of the major reasons for this alleged policy impotence of parties, it is argued, is the structural character of the American governmental system. The principles of our constitutional system theoretically do not facilitate a role for parties; indeed, they were designed originally to make it difficult for parties to have such a role. In *The Federalist* James Madison argued that the proposed constitution would make majority control by a party group virtually impossible. The key principles he had in mind, of course, were separation of powers, federalism, and bicameralism. The dispersion of governmental power under these principles constitutes a major challenge to parties seeking to control government for the purposes of policy initiation and innovation. Obstruction is more likely under such principles than the translation of new ideas into new laws. Structural principles, thus, can be critical for the policy process. Our peculiar principles pose a challenge to party leadership seeking to bridge and coordinate the different arenas of governmental authority.

It is not these constitutional principles alone, however, which are obstacles to party influence in the policy process. It is also the fragmentation of authority within the legislative body itself. The United States House of Representatives, up to 1910, was a body with strong leadership, with a speaker who had considerable power. But in that year there was a revolt against Speaker Joe Cannon, and in the seventy years since there has been no return to anything like the centralization of authority which Cannon had. The committee

chairmen, the floor leader, the party policy committees, the whips, the party caucus—all these agencies of House operations have divided up the party's power. In addition special groups such as the Democratic Study Group (DSG), with 200 liberal Democrats, or the Republican special group, the "Chowder and Marching Club," have contributed to the decentralization of power in the House and made leadership and policy coordination difficult. Further, as William J. Keefe points out:

> Congress is an institution vulnerable to invasion by others. The three principal external forces that interact with Congress, seeking to move it along lines congenial to their interests, are the chief executive (including the bureaucracy), interest groups, and the constituencies.[2]

Rather than moving in harmony, these actors in the policy process are often in dissonance. There is legislative-executive conflict, a struggle among opposing lobbies, and pressures from different types of constituencies. As Keefe says, on certain issues the party often seems "to fly apart."[3] *It appears* that what we have in the United States—and perhaps want, but certainly tolerate—is "a shared, multiple-leadership form of government."[4]

The traditional model, then, is one which plays down the role of parties in the policy process because constitutional principles disperse power, internal party organization in legislative bodies is not cohesive, and external pressures produce conflicts. The implicit argument is that parties cannot overcome these features of the system—parties as organizations or as leadership groups do not coordinate policy making, parties in fact are secondary to other influences on policy making, and partisan considerations and motivations do not explain policy actions.

This model, further, is usually contrasted to the parliamentary model, such as is found in Britain. It is argued that party plays a much more important role there because there is party discipline in the House of Commons, there is centralized party leadership which determines the party's position on policy questions, there is no dispersion of power as in the American constitutional system (Parliament is supreme), and external pressures play no such negative role (indeed constituency influences facilitate the relevance of party in the policy process). The majority in the party caucus (Labour, Conservative, or Liberal) in the House of Commons selects its leadership, together they decide on policy, defections from these majority decisions are not sanctioned but punished, and thus normally the party as an organization makes policy. There is, thus, *theoretically* a sharp contrast between the United States "fragmentation of party power" model and the parliamentary (British) "party dominance" model.

EVIDENCE OF PARTY INFLUENCE ON NATIONAL POLICY DECISIONS

Despite the negative expectations about the role of American parties on policy decisions, research suggests caution in reaching that conclusion. True, parties are organizationally fragmented, power is dispersed, leadership is not centralized and party discipline of the parliamentary system doesn't exist in the United States. Nevertheless, policies do change as the strength of parties ebbs and flows.

The economic policies of the national government are one important substantive area where it may indeed make a great deal of difference which party wins the election. Edward Tufte has studied this matter and concludes that "the real force of political influence on macroeconomic performance comes in the determination of economic priorities." He then argues, "Here the ideology and platform of the political party in power dominate ... the ideology of political leaders shapes the substance of economic policy."[5] Indeed, his position is that one can generalize for modern democratic societies, including the United States, as follows: Parties of the Right (including the Republicans) favor "low rates of taxation and inflation with modest and balanced government budgets; oppose income equalization; and will trade greater unemployment for less inflation most of the time." Parties of the Left (including the Democrats) favor "income equalization and lower unemployment, larger government budgets; and will accept increased rates of inflation in order to reduce unemployment." The platforms of the national parties reveal these differences. Thus, in 1976 the Democratic platform pledged "a government which will be committed to a fairer distribution of wealth, income and power." The Republican platform in 1976 pledged "less government, less spending, less inflation." In 1980 the Democratic platform promised to fight inflation but not by increasing interest rates or unemployment. The Republicans said that "our fundamental answer to the economic problem is ... full employment without inflation through economic growth."

The public's expectations concerning the performance of the two parties are clearly illustrated by their attitudes on the unemployment issue in 1976. When asked to assess the job which President Gerald Ford and the Republicans had done in dealing with unemployment, only 11 percent of the sampling responded that it had been a "good" performance, 57 percent a "fair" job, and 32 percent a "poor" one. Table 39.1 reveals the results of a study asking which presidential candidate and party would do the best job of reducing unemployment. The public clearly expected Carter to do more about unemployment. Similar results emerged when the sample was asked, "Do you think the problems of unemployment would be handled better by the Democrats, by Republicans, or about the same by both?" The results were: 39 percent Democrats, 10 percent by the Republicans, and 52 percent the same for both parties. The 1980 results were different, however: 19 percent Democrats, 23 percent Republicans, and 58 percent about the same for both parties.

Tufte demonstrates that the actual employment statistics over time reveal a linkage between presidential elections and unemployment and inflation rates. These data point to the following "rules":[6]

1. Both Democrats and Republicans will reduce inflation or unemployment if there is an economic crisis and an election is approaching.
2. If there is no real crisis, the Republicans will do much better in reducing inflation than unemployment; the Democrats will do better in reducing unemployment.

Whether Carter's actions in 1980 supported these observations is an arguable matter!

TABLE 39.1 Public's Opinion on Which Party Will Best Deal with Unemployment (as a percentage)		
Public View	**President Ford**	**Candidate Carter**
Candidate will reduce unemployment	31	52
Candidate will not reduce unemployment	46	24
Difference	−15	+28

Source: University of Michigan CPS/NES, 1976.

Another scholar, Douglas Hibbs, has also explored this problem. He concludes that "inter-party differences in government-induced unemployment levels is 2.36 percent"—a sizeable difference in national employment levels as a result of a Democratic or Republican administration. Thus, "the Kennedy-Johnson administration posture toward recession and unemployment stands in sharp contrast to Eisenhower's, ... the basic economic priorities associated with the Eisenhower era were re-established during the Nixon and Ford administrations" and were "deliberately induced." Hibbs concludes, "The real winners of elections are perhaps best determined by examining the policy consequences of partisan change rather than simply by tallying the votes."[7]

A study of the policies of our government over the years finds that whichever party is in power for a longer or shorter period of time is crucial for the content of public policy. In an exhaustive study of laws adopted by the United States government from 1800 to 1968 (requiring analysis of 60,000 pieces of legislation) Benjamin Ginsberg was able to determine when the peak points in the adoption of new policies and new laws occurred. He concluded that the peak points were 1805, 1861, 1881, and 1933. These were years after major elections in which a shift in the power of the political parties occurred, called in some instances major "realigning elections." His basic interpretation is that "clusters of policy change" do come as a result of partisan change in electoral choices. He summarized as follows:

Our findings suggest that voter alignments are, in effect, organized around substantive issues of policy and support the continued dominance in government of a party committed to the principal elements of the choice

made by voters during critical eras…. Partisan alignments form the constituent bases for governments committed to the translation of the choices made by the electorate…. The policy-making role of the electorate is, in effect, a continuing one.[8]

In other words, the voters' decision on what party should govern determines the basic direction of public policy! …

End Notes

1. V. O. Key, Jr., *Politics, Parties and Pressure Groups*, 4th ed. (New York: T. Y. Crowell, 1958), p. 702.
2. William J. Keefe, *Congress and the American People* (Englewood Cliffs, N.J.: Prentice Hall, 1980), p. 101.
3. Ibid., p. 105.
4. Thomas E. Cronin, *The State of the Presidency* (Boston: Little, Brown, 1975), p. 107.
5. Edward R. Tufte, *Political Control of the Economy* (Princeton: Princeton University Press, 1980), p. 71.
6. Ibid., pp. 101–102.
7. Douglas Hibbs, "Political Parties and Macroeconomic Policy," *American Political Science Review* 71 (1977): 1486. Other scholars disagree with this position in part, at least the implication of presidential manipulation of the economy for electoral gain. See Thad A. Brown and Arthur A. Stein, "The Political Economy of National Elections," unpublished paper, University of California at Los Angeles, November, 1980.
8. Benjamin Ginsberg, "Elections and Public Policy," *The American Political Science Review* 70, no. 1 (1976): 49.

40

The Advocacy Explosion

Jeffrey M. Berry

This is not the first period of American history in which an apparent increase in the numbers and influence of interest groups has heightened anxiety.[1] Uneasiness over the power and influence of interest group politics is part of the American political tradition. Yet today's widespread concern contrasts with fairly recent American attitudes. The New Deal, for example, was known for its positive acceptance of interest groups because of the greater role trade associations came to have in the policy making of newly established regulatory agencies. As recently as the 1960s, scholars were arguing that interest group polities contributed to democratic politics.

Currently, a pervasive, popular perception is of an unprecedented and dangerous growth in the number of interest groups and that this growth continues unabated. This view is echoed constantly in the press. *Time* tells us that "at times the halls of power are so glutted with special pleaders that government itself seems to be gagging."[2] Bemoaning the growing lobbying industry, the *New Republic* notes, "What dominates Washington is not evil and immorality, but a parasite culture. Like Rome in decline, Washington is bloated, wasteful, pretentious, myopic, decadent, and sybaritic. It is the paradise of the overpaid hangers-on."[3] The normally staid *Atlantic* thinks things have deteriorated so much that even the First Amendment right to petition the government should not stand in the way of remedial action. "Lobbyists should be denied access to the

Capitol," says an *Atlantic* writer, because they are ruining the legislative process.[4]

Journalists might be allowed a bit of literary license, but politicians ring the fire alarm too. After returning to Congress in 1987 after a twelve year absence, Representative Wayne Owens (D-Utah) lamented that "in those twelve years I was gone, basically every group you can think of has developed a Washington office or a national association aimed at presenting their case to Congress,"[5] President Jimmy Carter, in his farewell address to the nation, blamed interest groups for many shortcomings of his administration:

> ... We are increasingly drawn to single-issue groups and special interest organizations to insure that whatever else happens our own personal views and our own private interests are protected. This is a disturbing factor in American political life. It tends to distort our purpose because the national interest is not always the sum of all our single or special interests.[6]

Some scholars find interest groups to be at the heart of this country's problems as well. Economist Lester Thurow states unequivocally that "our economic problems are solvable," but adds that "political paralysis" stands in the way. The source of that paralysis, in Thurow's eyes, is an expanding system of effective interest groups that makes it impossible for government to allocate

---

the pain that comes with realistic economic solutions.[7] Political scientist Everett Ladd blames special interest politics for our economic woes as well. "The cumulative effect of this pressure has been the relentless and extraordinary rise of government spending and inflationary deficits."[8]

In short, the popular perception is that interest groups are a cancer, spreading unchecked throughout the body politic, making it gradually weaker, until they eventually kill it.

Political rhetoric aside, has there really been a significant expansion of interest group politics? Or are interest groups simply playing their familiar role as whipping boy for the ills of society?

The answer to both questions is yes. Surely nothing is new about interest groups being seen as the bane of our political system. The muckrakers at the turn of the century voiced many of the same fears that show up today in *Time* or the *Atlantic*. Yet even if the problem is familiar, it is no less troubling. The growth of interest group politics in recent years should not simply be dismissed as part of a chronic condition in American politics. Of particular concern is that this growth took place during a period of party decline. The United States is not just a country with an increasing number of active interest groups, but a country whose citizens look more and more to interest groups to speak for them in the political process.

Before addressing the larger problems that arise from this trend, we must document the increasing number of interest groups. The available statistics show an unmistakable increase in interest group activity in Washington. Jack Walker's survey of 564 lobbying organizations in Washington (Figure 40.1)[9] shows a clear pattern

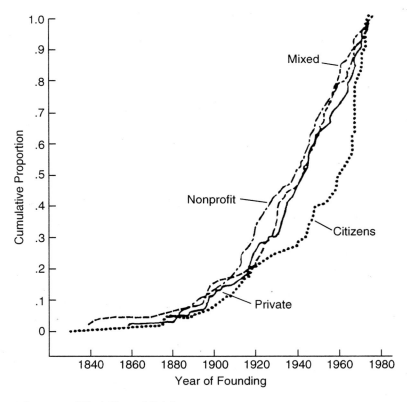

FIGURE 40.1 Interest Groups and Their Year of Origin

Source: Survey of voluntary associations by Jack L. Walker, "The Origins and Maintenance of Interest Groups in America," *American Political Science Review* 77 (June 1983), p. 395. The "mixed" category represents groups that have members from both the public and private sectors.

of growth, with approximately 30 percent of the groups originating between 1960 and 1980.[10] The figures do not, however, indicate precisely how many new groups have been started in different eras because we cannot calculate how many were started in earlier periods but have since ceased to exist. A second study, by Kay Schlozman and John Tierney, shows a similar pattern. Their examination of groups listed in a lobbying directory shows that 40 percent were founded after 1960 and 25 percent after 1970.[11] Both surveys show that citizen groups were the most likely to have formed recently. In short, we can be confident that the increase in lobbying organizations is real and not a function of overblown rhetoric about the dangers of contemporary interest groups.

The rate of growth of interest groups seems to be tapering off though. Given the rather sizable boom in the growth of groups during the 1960s and 1970s, this is hardly surprising. At some point the market for different types of interest groups becomes saturated, and new entrants will find it more difficult to gain a foothold. There will always be new constituencies developing and existing constituencies recognizing that they need greater representation, but rapid expansion of one sector of an interest group community reduces the amount of available resources for potential new groups....

THE RISE OF CITIZEN GROUPS

The growth of interest group advocacy in different sectors of society comes from many of the same roots. At the same time, the sharp growth in numbers of interest groups also reflects different sectors of society responding to each other. As one segment of the interest community grew and appeared to prosper, it spurred growth in other segments eager to equalize the increasing strength of their adversaries. This spiral of interest group activity began in large part in the civil rights and antiwar movements of the 1960s....

DEMYSTIFYING INTEREST GROUP ADVOCACY

The advocacy explosion came from many sources. Different kinds of groups responded to particular events: the growth of adversary groups, changes in the law, and evolutionary changes in the political environment. These stimuli were enhanced by a cumulative learning process as well.

In recent years there has been a "demystification" of interest group politics. A broader segment of the population has come to believe that interest group advocacy has great potential. More and more people have come to understand that interest groups are vital to protecting and furthering their own interests. And more and more people have come to understand how interest groups operate in practice and how new groups could be formed.

Interest group leaders (and prospective organizers) learned by watching other interest groups; lobbying organizations are inveterate copiers. The way in which citizen groups copied the successful civil rights and antiwar organizations is an illustration of this process. Not only did other minorities copy the black civil rights organizations, but new liberal citizen groups were started to appeal to middle-class interests as well.

Conservative citizen groups that arose in the 1970s responded directly to the success of liberal citizen groups. There was a sense that everyone was represented *except* the conservatives. Liberal citizen groups appeared to be enormously successful, with major victories such as establishing regulatory agencies like the Consumer Product Safety Commission and the EPA, the constant media attention given to Ralph Nader and Common Cause, and a stream of successful environmental lawsuits. Most important, liberal groups seemed to have the ear of government and thus were influencing its agenda.

Business in turn was influenced by the liberal citizen groups' growing advocacy. Even though the most direct stimulus was increased regulation, the public interest movement was seen as the primary instigator of "excessive" government regulation. Business has made great use of all major strategies of effective lobbying. It has formed the most PACs and donates the most money, though PACs have multiplied on all fronts. No segment of the interest group population wants to be at a disadvantage in gaining access to congressional offices.

No automatic mechanism in politics exists whereby new groups cause opposing groups to form as a countervailing power; the reality is much more complicated. In recent years, though, proliferation of groups has been facilitated by rapidly increasing knowledge about interest groups. From academic works to the omnipresent eye of the mass media, both laymen and elites have learned how these groups operate. The development of public policy and the interest groups' role in that process have been reported and analyzed in excruciating detail. Thus the costs of acquiring information about interest groups became cheaper. People found it easier to find out what they needed to know to form groups, and once they were formed, what they needed to know to operate them effectively.

More specifically, the growth of interest groups was furthered by increasing knowledge about three subjects.

ORGANIZATIONAL MAINTENANCE. Interest group leaders have become more effective at raising money and broadening their base of support. Their growing utilization of direct mail is the most obvious example; leaders of newly forming or existing groups can buy lists of likely prospects. Foundations and government became more important sources of money for interest groups during their greatest expansion period. Businesses moved quickly to use the newly acquired right to form PACs to collect money from corporate executives. For interest group leaders who feel they need help in maintaining their organization, many consultants in Washington have expertise in direct mail and how to secure government grants.

LOBBYING SKILLS. Through the years, lobbying has had an unsavory behind-the-scenes image of unctuous group representatives using their contacts in government to do the groups' bidding. Yet today's typical lobbyist will often try to gain recognition and publicity for what he or she is doing rather than hide it. Lobbying has quickly become an anyone-can-do-it activity, and little mystery is left as to what successful lobbyists do. One does not have to have close friends in high places (though it certainly doesn't hurt), but other attributes are commonly accepted as vital to effective lobbying. Chief among these is policy expertise. The ability to "network" (form coalitions), to utilize the media, and to develop lasting

professional relationships with staffers and policymakers are other well-known fundamentals of lobbying. It is much harder to raise the resources for lobbying than it is to figure out what to do with those resources.

COMMUNICATIONS. Lobbying has been furthered by a growing recognition that information is power and that the best lobbyists are the people back home. The Washington newsletter is now a staple of Washington politics. Constituents back home receive frequent mailings on the issues that are being decided by government and what they need to do to influence them. Computerized lists of constituents facilitate mailings to members in key congressional districts when a critical vote is coming. Some groups have special networks of activists, who can be instructed to contact those in government when the need arises.

The growth of interest group politics thus comes in part from learning: Successful groups set the example for others. Washington is really a town of few secrets, and what works for one group is quickly copied by others. Consultants, lawyers, and public relations specialists who work for different clients, the huge Washington media establishment, and the lobbyists who interact constantly with one another make learning about what interest groups do ever easier.

CONCLUSION

By any standard, the amount of lobbying in Washington has expanded significantly. Interests previously unrepresented are now represented before the government by recently formed organizations. Interests that were already represented in Washington tend to be even better represented today.

Although the reasons for lobbying's rise in different sectors of society vary, some common threads appear in the broad movement toward interest group politics. Pluralist theory put forward the idea that interest group involvement in policy making contributed to democratic government. Expanding governmental activity in the 1960s and 1970s, usually at the behest of interest groups, directly affected more and more constituencies and helped catalyze increased advocacy.

Finally, as new interest groups form, they stimulate other constituencies to organize because new groups increase awareness about what various interests are doing and, further, their formation threatens their natural adversaries. The success of the public interest movement, for example, resonates through this 1978 plea in the *Wall Street Journal*: "Businessmen of the World Unite." Readers were told that "we need a businessman's liberation movement and a businessman's liberation day and a businessman's liberation rally on the monument grounds of Washington, attended by thousands of businessmen shouting and carrying signs."[12]

While the advocacy explosion created new groups and expanded resources devoted to lobbying, this heightened competition between groups did not bring about a perfect balance of interests represented in Washington. Business was by far the best represented sector of American society before this upsurge in lobbying, and it remains in that position now that the growth in the numbers of interest groups is finally slowing down. Business responded to the challenge of the public interest movement with ample resources and a fierce determination to maintain its advantages in Washington. It now faces potent competition from an array of liberal public interest groups, although its traditional rival, organized labor, is on the decline. ... It is tempting to make interest groups the scapegoat for the ills of American society, believing that we would have politically acceptable solutions to public policy dilemmas if lobbies didn't exist.[13] However, differing interests will always abound. The attitudes and potential reactions of various constituencies must be considered by policymakers when decisions are made. Yet the organization of interests into an ever-increasing number of lobbying groups adds to the power of those constituencies.

The growth of interest group politics can be applauded for expanding the range of lobbying organizations represented in the political system. A related benefit of this proliferation is that it was instrumental in the replacement of many narrow subgovernments with more open, more participatory, and more conflictual issue networks. If there are to be lobbying organizations, it is best that they be as representative as possible of all segments of American society. Yet it would be naive to assume that interest groups will ever fairly reflect the different interests of all Americans. Upper- and middle-class interests will always be better represented by lobbying organizations.

Government is realistically limited in what it can do to address this imbalance, but it must try to ensure representation for the chronically underrepresented. Financial support for advocacy groups for the poor should be expanded, not decreased, as part of the overall move to cut back government funding of welfare and social services. Such cuts actually create a greater need for this kind of surrogate representation. Citizen participation programs, which have had mixed success, ought to be continued and improved. They make government more accountable to the people it serves and create a potential channel of influence for those who may not be adequately represented by interest groups.[14] The federal government can do little aside from the reforms discussed here, however, to curb the activities of interest groups. Worrisome as the spiraling growth of interest group politics may be, it is not desirable to have the government trying generally to inhibit the efforts of various constituencies to find more effective representation in the political system.

Because government's role will always be limited, prospects for further curbing the influence of faction must come from the political parties. They are the natural counterweight to interest groups, offering citizens the basic means of pursuing the nation's collective will. Only political parties can offer citizens broad choices about the major directions of public policy. Strengthening our parties is a widely shared goal, though there is little consensus over what actions need to be taken to accomplish this.[15] Whatever the future of party renewal, though, interest groups will continue to play their traditional role of articulating this nation's multitude of interests. Interest groups offer a direct link to government on the everyday issues that concern a particular constituency but not the nation as a whole. The role interest groups play is not ideal, but they remain a fundamental expression of democratic government.

End Notes

1. Some arguments here were first published in Jeffrey M. Berry, "Public Interest vs. Party System," *Society* 17 (May/June 1980), pp. 42–48.
2. Evan Thomas, "Peddling Influence," *Time*, March 3, 1986, p. 26.
3. Fred Barnes, "The Parasite Culture of Washington," *New Republic*, July 28, 1986, p. 17.
4. Gregg Easterbrook, "What's Wrong with Congress," *Atlantic*, December, 1984, p, 84.
5. Jeffrey H. Birnbaum, "Congressman Who Returned After Twelve Years Notes Changes Including More Lobbying, Budget Fights," *Wall Street Journal*, June 15, 1987.
6. "Prepared Texts of Carter's Farewell Address on Major Issues Facing the Nation," *The New York Times*, January 15, 1981.
7. Lester C. Thurow, *The Zero-Sum Society* (New York: Penguin Books, 1981), pp. 11–15.
8. Everett C. Ladd, "How to Tame the Special Interest Groups," *Fortune*, October 20, 1980, p. 66ff.
9. Jack L. Walker, "The Origins and Maintenance of Interest Groups in America," *American Political Science Review* 77 (June 1983), pp. 390–406.
10. See an earlier version of the Walker article, similarly titled, presented at the annual meeting of the American Political Science Association, New York, September 1981, p. 14.
11. Kay Lehman Schlozman and John T. Tierney, *Organized Interests and American Democracy* (New York: Harper and Row, 1986), pp. 75–76.
12. Cited in Michael Useem, *The Inner Circle* (New York: Oxford University Press, 1984), pp. 17–18.
13. See Mancur Olson, *The Rise and Decline of Nations* (New Haven: Yale University Press, 1982); and Lester C. Thurow, *The Zero-Sum Society* (New York: Penguin, 1981). See also Robert H. Salisbury, "Are Interest Groups Morbific Forces?," paper presented to the Conference Group on the Political Economy of Advanced Industrial Societies, Washington, D.C., August 1980.
14. See Benjamin Barber, *Strong Democracy* (Berkeley: University of California Press, 1984).
15. For a comprehensive program of party reform, see Larry J. Sabato, *The Party's Just Begun* (Glenview, Ill.: Scott, Foresman/Little, Brown, 1988).

41

The Consultant Corps

Larry Sabato

Controversy is raging about the role and influence of the political consultant in American elections, and properly so. There is no more significant change in the conduct of campaigns than the consultant's recent rise to prominence, if not preeminence, during the election season. Political consultants, answerable only to their client-candidates and independent of the political parties, have inflicted severe damage upon the party system and masterminded the modern triumph of personality cults over party politics in the United States. All the while they have gradually but steadily accumulated almost unchecked and unrivaled power and influence in a system that is partly their handiwork.

For a group of political elites so prominent and powerful, consultants have been remarkably little investigated and understood. Indeed, the argument about their role and influence in the electoral system has operated essentially in a vacuum.... Until now far more misinformation than fact has surfaced in the debate about politicians' use of political consultants, and there are many reasons for this. The consultants themselves make the task of separating fact from fiction and image from reality as difficult as possible. They enhance their own images and increase the fees they can command by keeping their campaign techniques as mysterious and bewildering as possible. Most consultants have been intimately involved with politics for decades, and they know better than most elected officials that, in politics, style is closely intertwined with substance. Fame and fortune—not to mention electoral success—come to those who can adjust the mirrors in just the right way and produce sufficient quantities of blue smoke in the public arena.

In using the blue smoke and mirrors of politics to cloud the view of their profession, consultants have found a valuable ally, the working press. Not only do many journalists fail to understand what it is consultants do and how they do it; those same print and television journalists are responsible in good measure for the glow of expertise and omniscience that surrounds the consultant's every pronouncement. Consultants have become prime and semipermanent sources of information and insight for political reporters, and the election professionals are rewarded with an uncritical press and frequent, beatific headlines.

No one reads these headlines more closely than the prospective candidates, and as a consequence virtually no nominee for public office at any level thinks he can survive without a consultant or two. Remarkably, though, if reporters are ignorant of the consultant trade and technology, candidates are far more so. President Gerald Ford, for instance, would admit almost total ignorance of his 1976 direct-mail operation and even

decry "junk mail" after leaving the Oval Office, despite the fact that direct mail had been one of the most successful aspects of his campaign for the Republican presidential nomination. Many other candidates have hired media and polling consultants at great cost without even a superficial comprehension of their techniques or their real worth—taking on faith what they had read and heard about these election wizards, believing all the while that consultants were essential for victory without knowing whether or why the common wisdom was true. Understandably, candidates lack the specialized training in election technology that their consultants possess and have little time to learn in a demanding, pressure-cooker campaign. This leaves the consultant a seemingly indispensable commodity, someone with immense leverage not merely during the election but also after the campaign is over. Few are the politicians who never seek office again, and their relationships with consultants are as permanent as their campaigns. Pollster Patrick Caddell's and media man Gerald Rafshoon's extraordinary alliance with President Carter is by no means exceptional any more.

If a thorough examination of the consultants' profession is in order, so too is an exhaustive study of their much-acclaimed techniques. A glance at any election-year newspaper or political trade journal tells why. In the praise being heaped upon the media masters and soothsayers and direct-mail artists, all sorts of wondrous things are being attributed to them. Upon actually meeting these political wizards, after preparatory reading of hundreds of articles by awe-struck commentators, one inevitably is reminded of Dorothy's disappointment when she unmasked the Wizard of Oz. For, despite their clever public posturings, consultants have no potions or crystal balls, and most of them will admit it forthrightly, at least in private. "If I knew the successful formula," conceded one long-time professional, "I would patent it."

It is reassuring (perhaps deceptively so) to hear one of the most widely experienced generalist consultants, Stuart Spencer, proclaim that "There are good politicians and there are bad politicians, and all the computers and all the research in the world are not going to make the campaign situation any better when bad politicians are involved." Spencer may well be right that consultants cannot turn a sow's ear into a silk purse (although at least a couple of exceptions come to mind). ... [W]ill certainly provide some evidence that a less radical transformation at the consultant's hand is possible, that a black sheep can become a white one upon application of a little dye and a corroded silver dollar can be transformed into a shiny one with a chemical and a bit of polish. Consultants and the new campaign technology have not changed the essence of politics. Politics is still persuasion, still a firm, friendly handshake. But the media of persuasion are no longer the same, and the handshake may be a projection or even an illusion.

Whatever the degree of their electoral influence, consultants—most of them—have talent and enormous experience. One hastens to add that a few well-publicized consultants do not live up even vaguely to their advance billing. As one top professional observed: "The only thing that keeps some of them alive is luck and being in the right place at the right time. They don't really affect anything in a dramatic way because they don't have the political instinct to do it." By and large, however, consultants are hard-working professionals: very bright and capable, politically shrewd and calculating, and impressively articulate. They travel tens of thousands of miles every year, work on campaigns in a dozen or more states simultaneously, and eat, breathe, and live politics. They are no less political junkies than the candidates they serve. For the most part, they are even less concerned with issues, the parties, and the substance of politics than their clients. They are businessmen, not ideologues.

While admired for their abilities and acumen, consultants also suffer an unsavory reputation in some quarters, and certainly among the general public, whose distrust of seamy, "smoke-filled-room" political operatives is traditional and enduring. At best consultants are seen as encouraging the natural instincts of plastic politicians. ("Gripp, Grinn, Waffle, & Faykit" is the sign cartoonist Jeff MacNelly hangs outside his fictional consulting firm.) At worst, consultants are denounced as "hustlers and con men," as Joe Napolitan put it.[1] Consultants bristle at the slightest mention of any unfavorable press, blaming the criticism on the politicians they work for. As media consultant Michael Kaye expressed it:

> People don't like politicians. So no matter how skillfully a political consultant like me does his work, I am a bad guy. I am a packager. I am a manipulator. Now, is it because of what I do, or is it the product that I sell?

Yet widespread doubt about the work of consultants has a basis more thoughtful than Kaye's analysis suggests. That basis is a deep concern for the health and well-being of the democratic process. What consultants seem to forget is that their work cannot be evaluated solely within the context of their profession. "Is this artful media?" or "Is this an effective piece of direct mail?" or "Did this action by a political consultant help to elect candidate X?" are legitimate questions and necessary ones for any judgment of a particular consultant's worth. But the ultimate standard by which the *profession* of political consulting is judged cannot merely be success in electing or defeating candidates. There are much more vital considerations of ethics and democracy to ponder, because electoral politics is the foundation of any democratic society, and important actors in the political sphere must necessarily be the subject of special scrutiny.

...[T]o provide that scrutiny and to offer an informed discussion of the consequences of the consultant's trade and his new campaign technology. While an observer can reasonably conclude ... that most politicians have been fairly well served by their election professionals, it simply does not follow that the public and the political system have been equal beneficiaries. As the influence of consultants has grown, some very disquieting questions have begun to loom large. Influence peddling, all kinds of financial misconduct, shameful acts of deception and trickery, and improprieties with former clients who are in public office are only a few of the compromising and unethical practices found in far too many consultants' portfolios. At the root of some of the worst offenses is a profit motive unrestrained by ties to party, ideology, or ideals. Sadly, the truth is much as political columnist Jack Germond suggests: "Philosophy and party don't motivate most of the political consultants. Money does, partially, and there is a lot of money to be made if you're any good."

As distressing as they are, the ethical concerns fade by comparison to the democratic effects wrought by consultants. Political professionals and their techniques have helped homogenize American politics, added significantly to campaign costs, lengthened campaigns, and narrowed the focus of elections. Consultants have emphasized personality and gimmickry over issues, often exploiting emotional and negative themes rather than encouraging rational discussion. They have sought candidates who fit their technologies more than the requirements of office and have given an extra boost to candidates who are more skilled at electioneering than governing. They have encouraged candidates' own worst instincts to blow with the prevailing winds of public opinion. Consultants have even consciously increased nonvoting on occasion and meddled in the politics of other countries.

These activities have not occurred in a vacuum. The rules of the political game have been altered dramatically, with consultants clearly benefiting from the changes. The decline of the political parties and the establishment of a radically different system of campaign finance are foremost among the developments that consultants have turned to their advantage. For example, as a direct consequence of the diminution of party strength, a diminution to which consultants have themselves contributed and, in some cases, cheered, consultants have replaced party leaders in key campaign roles.

Yet the power flow from party leaders to political consultants does not have to continue, nor must unethical practices remain unchecked. Consultants and their apologists quite naturally can see no system better than the current one, and they will always have a ready excuse for distasteful doings in their profession. But those who lament the recent technological changes in electioneering have only to look to one of the major parties to see the path of renewal that these same new campaign technologies have made possible. A revitalized national and state Republican party organization, fueled by the marvels consultants had previously harnessed for themselves and monopolized, has provided

the model that can tame consultant abuses and develop a healthier, party-based electoral system in the future. This auspicious development and its considerable potential for good will be the object of special examination later....

IMAGES AND ROLES OF POLITICAL CONSULTANTS

The term "political consultant" is bandied about so loosely that any discourse on the subject must begin by attempting to define it. A *political consultant* is a campaign professional who is engaged primarily in the provision of advice and services (such as polling, media creation and production, and direct-mail fund raising) to candidates, their campaigns, and other political committees. Broadly the title can adorn almost any paid staffer on even the most minor of campaigns. Here, however, we shall concentrate on the relatively small and elite corps of interstate political consultants who usually work on many campaigns simultaneously and have served hundreds of campaigns in their careers. They are the sellers, and often the creators, of advanced campaign technology and technique.

There are basically two kinds of consultants. A *generalist* consultant advises a candidate on most or all phases of his campaign and coordinates most or all aspects of the technology employed by the campaign. A *specialist* consultant concentrates on one or two aspects of the campaign and peddles expertise in one or two technological specialties. While almost all of the early consultants were generalists, most consultants today are specialists (who nevertheless often advertise themselves as generalists).

Whether generalist or specialist, the consultant's primary role is the same: to provide services to campaigns. A consultant is hired to conduct a series of public opinion surveys or create a precinct organization or orchestrate a direct-mail fund-raising effort. The secondary roles played by consultants, however, are sometimes more intriguing and just as substantive as the provision of technological services. There is, for example, the "expert" role, a position accorded the consultant by the campaign staff and the candidate because of his wide experience and masterful reputation.

(In many campaigns the consultant probably has more influence, and his every word is weighed more carefully than his actual experience or his degree of involvement with the campaign can justify.) Even though he may only visit the campaign once a month or talk with campaign officials weekly, the political professional frequently becomes the grand strategist, designing and supervising the "game plan," orchestrating the press, and selecting the candidate's issues.

Because of the respect he is given as "the expert," the consultant more often than not also seems to assume the role of the candidate's confidant. As media consultant Douglas Bailey has suggested, "Most candidates are hiring outside consultants because within the campaign and within their circle of friends, they don't have anyone whom they feel has the experience or the savvy to satisfy their need for reassurance that they're doing it right or that they can win."

Another media professional, Robert Goodman (who produced advertisements for George Bush's 1980 Republican presidential bid), emphasizes the psychological aspects of the consultant's tour of duty:

George Bush said to me after four hours with him one day at his house, "Are you a psychiatrist or a filmmaker?" We're really into psychiatry.... It is incumbent upon the media guy to really look at the candidate and try to lead him past those personality landmines that will destroy him if he doesn't loosen up and do his thing.

These roles are hardly the only ones in the consultant's repertoire. He often finds himself a trusted postelection adviser when his clients win public office. Most significantly, and regrettably, he and his technological wares are "party pinch hitters," substituting for the weakened parties in a variety of ways.

A BRIEF HISTORY OF POLITICAL CONSULTING

There have always been political consultants in one form or another in American politics, but the campaign professionals of earlier eras were strategists without benefit of the campaign technologies so standard today. Usually, too, consultants were tied to one or a few candidates, or perhaps to a state or local party organization. Before consulting became a full-time profession, lawyers were often assigned campaign management chores since they had a flexible work schedule as well as the personal finances and community contacts to do the job properly.[2] The old-time press agent, usually a newspaperman familiar with the locale,[3] was also a crucial and influential figure in campaign organization. But in most cases these lawyers and press agents were only functionaries when compared to party leaders and organization bosses who wielded far greater authority in political matters.

On a separate track, one supported by the business community, the profession of public relations was developing. As Stanley Kelley, Jr. has stated, "Business was, and is still, the public relation man's most important patron."[4] Businessmen saw image making as a way to counter a rising tide of business criticism. The federal government followed in close pursuit of public relations professionals, expanding their role considerably during the New Deal. State and local governments, charities, religions, and colleges in succession all saw the "P.R. promise."

Dan Nimmo has called political consultants the "direct descendants" of the public relations professionals,[5] and the growth of both groups is clearly related to some similar phenomena, especially the revolution in mass media communications. Yet political consulting has causes all its own. The decline of the political parties has created opportunities for consultants and the tools of their trade. New means of financing campaigns, telling the candidate's story, and getting the candidate's voters to the polls became necessary as the parties' power waned. The new campaign techniques and the development of air travel, television, and the computer combined to give consultants the substitutes candidates desired. The fact that these techniques quickly became too complex for laymen to grasp easily—consultants themselves were forced to specialize to keep up with changes—and the acknowledged American need for, and trust in, experts, made professionals that much more attractive. Even if false, the belief that consultants' tricks could somehow bring order out of the chaos of a campaign was enormously reassuring to a candidate. And rising campaign costs (and expenditure and contribution limitations) have placed a premium on the wise use of every campaign dollar. All of these alterations of the political map seemed powerful arguments for hiring political consultants, who gradually became an unquestioned essential for serious campaigns. Everyone now needs them if only because everyone else has them.

The consulting movement coalesced first in California.[6] The state's traditionally anemic party system was weakened further in the twentieth century by the addition of new social welfare programs, a broadened civil service system, and a sprawling suburban shift from the central cities matched by the influx of hundreds of thousands of migrants from the East, Midwest, and South. The sheer growth in the size of the electorate made organizing difficult (and redistricting an even more wrenching and enveloping process). Finally, California was in the forefront of the popular initiative and referendum movement, and had an exceptionally long ballot and a multiplicity of elections.

It was during an initiative campaign, in fact, that modern political consultants first had a major effect.[7] In 1933 the California legislature passed a bill authorizing a flood control and irrigation development in northern California (called the Central Valley Project), which the Pacific Gas and Electric Company (PG&E) believed to be a threat to private power. The utility promptly launched a ballot initiative to reverse the decision. The project's proponents hastily enlisted Clem Whitaker, a Sacramento newsman and press agent, and Leone Smith Baxter, a public relations specialist, to mastermind a campaign to defeat PG&E's initiative. On a limited budget of $39,000, and using radio and newspaper appeals, Whitaker and Baxter managed to save the Central Valley Project.

Not only did PG&E hold no grudge, it actually put Whitaker and Baxter on annual retainer! The two consultants incorporated themselves (as Campaigns, Inc., and later as Whitaker and Baxter Campaigns) and eventually married as well.[8] There were two decades of smooth sailing for the firm, operating out of San Francisco,

and the lack of extensive competition[9] enabled it to post a 90 percent success rate in seventy-five major campaigns. Eventually, rival California consultants (such as Republicans Stuart Spencer and Bill Roberts and Democrats Don Bradley, Joseph Cerrell, and Sanford Weiner) came to the fore and reduced Whitaker and Baxter's edge and win-loss record.[10]

By the early 1950s it had become obvious that political professionals were playing an increasingly important part in electoral politics, so much so that Neil Staebler, then chairman of Michigan's Democratic party, alarmed a congressional committee with his prediction that "... elections will increasingly become contests not between candidates but between great advertising firms."[11]

While Staebler's vision seems a bit exaggerated even today, he was surely right in suggesting a role for consultants far beyond their relatively limited involvement in some statewide and national races in 1952. Political scientist Alexander Heard's survey of state party committees in 1956–1957 showed remarkable growth in a short time. Democratic state party committees in fifteen states and GOP committees in eighteen states employed public relations firms at some point during those years, and in many cases a high proportion of the committees' funds was spent for retainers.[12] Of the 130 public relations firms he contacted, 60 percent had had some kind of political account between 1952 and 1957, and forty firms in fifteen states reported that they could assume complete responsibility for a campaign.

Two decades later political consultants had become a campaign standard across the United States, and not just for major national and statewide contests. State races for lesser offices and U.S. House seats, and elections for local posts and even judicial offices, frequently had the services of one or more consultants. For example, a 1972–1973 survey indicated that 168 of 208 candidates running for state office had hired at least one political professional: sixty-one of sixty-seven U.S. Senate candidates, thirty-eight of forty-two gubernatorial candidates, thirty of thirty-seven attorney general contenders, and even nineteen of thirty-one and twenty of thirty-two aspirants for secretary of state and state treasurer.[13] Most politicians seeking major office attract a small committee of consultants. A *National Journal* review of sixty-seven opposed campaigns for U.S. Senate in 1970 revealed that sixty-two had an advertising firm, twenty-four had a pollster, and twenty secured help from some sort of campaign management firm.[14] Just five candidates made do with no consultants.

Consultants, moreover, rarely miss an opportunity to expand their domain. The judicial field in California is a classic illustration. In Orange County a judge seeking another term was defeated in 1940, and none ever lost again until 1978 when four county judges were beaten simultaneously. Sitting judges became understandably nervous and sought professional assistance. Joseph Cerrell and Associates, which had never done a judicial campaign until 1978, suddenly had nine at once. The agency's candidates, all incumbents up for reelection, made a clean sweep (at $7,500 apiece). Flushed with success, Cerrell sponsored a conference on Judicial Campaigning in 1979, designed for judges of the superior and municipal courts. For a $100 registration fee a judge would be treated to sessions on topics such as "Campaigning with Dignity: Maintaining the Judicial Image."

The number of consultants has skyrocketed along with the demand for their services. As late as 1960 there were relatively few full-time professionals in the field; twenty years later there are hundreds—thousands if local advertising agency executives specializing in politics are counted. In addition, they handle a great deal besides candidates' campaigns. Referenda, initiatives, bond issues, and political action committees (PACs) sustain many firms. Some consultants enjoy overseas work in foreign campaigns or specialize in primary and convention nomination battles as well as general elections. Today the average modern professional manages more campaigns in a year than his predecessors did in a lifetime....

End Notes

1. Napolitan, *The Election Game and How to Win It*, p. 11.
2. W. E. Barnes in *The San Francisco Examiner*, July 25, 1979.
3. Stanley Kelley, Jr., *Professional Public Relations and Political Power* (Baltimore: Johns Hopkins, 1956), pp. 26–30; see also pp. 9–25, 31–38.
4. Ibid., p. 13.
5. Dan Nimmo, *The Political Persuaders: The Techniques of Modern Election Campaigns* (Englewood Cliffs, N.J.: Prentice-Hall, 1970), p. 35.
6. Ibid., pp. 35–37.
7. Barnes in *The San Francisco Examiner.*
8. See Kelley, *Professional Public Relations and Political Power*, pp. 39–66, for a history of the Whitaker and Baxter firm.
9. Baus and Ross of Los Angeles, a rival consulting firm started by one of Whitaker-Baxter's former employees, provided what competition existed. Both firms primarily handled Republicans.
10. Nimmo, *The Political Persuaders*, p. 36, n. 2d. Whitaker and Baxter has now effectively withdrawn from candidate campaigns.
11. Hearings before the Special Committee to Investigate Campaign Expenditures, 1952, House of Representatives, 82nd Congress, 2nd session, p. 76: as quoted in Kelley, *Professional Public Relations and Political Power*, p. 2.
12. Alexander Heard, *The Costs of Democracy* (Chapel Hill: University of North Carolina, 1960), pp. 415–477. Heard notes that his totals were probably understated because of the limitations of his survey.
13. Robert Agranoff, (ed.) *The New Style in Election Campaigns* (2nd ed.) (Boston: Holbrook Press, 1976), p. 8. See also David Rosenbloom, *The Election Men: Professional Campaign Managers and American Democracy* (New York: Quadrangle, 1973). Rosenbloom indicates a 650 percent growth rate in consulting firms overall between 1952 and 1970, an 842 percent increase in consultant involvement in U.S. House of Representatives contests, and a 300 percent increase in their employment for local elections.
14. See *National Journal*, September 26, 1970, pp. 2084–2085.

42

News That Matters

Shanto Iyengar and
Donald Kinder

Not so very long ago, television was "nothing but a gleam in the entrepreneurial eye" (Weaver 1975, 81).[1] No longer. In just four decades, it has become a comfortable and easy habit, a settled and central institution. As television has moved to the center of American life, TV news has become Americans' single most important source of information about political affairs. The purpose of our effort has been to provide a systematic examination of this new relationship. ... [W]e summarize our principal results and position them within the context of the broader literature on mass communication and politics. We argue that, for good or ill, television news has become a regular participant in the American political process. Finally, as a means of assessing the normative implications of our results for a democratic society, we discuss the ways in which television news conveys unusual and distinctive views of politics—views that eventually become our own.

RECAPITULATION OF RESULTS

Agenda-setting

Americans' views of their society and nation are powerfully shaped by the stories that appear on the evening news. We found that people who were shown network broadcasts edited to draw attention to a particular problem assigned greater importance to that problem—greater importance than they themselves did before the experiment began, and greater importance than did people assigned to control conditions that emphasized different problems. Our subjects regarded the target problem as more important for the country, cared more about it, believed that government should do more about it, reported stronger feelings about it, and were much more likely to identify it as one of the country's most important problems. Such differences were apparent immediately after conclusion of the broadcasts one day later, and one week later. They emerged in experiments explicitly designed to test agenda-setting and in experiments designed with other purposes in mind; in sequential experiments that drew the viewer's attention to the problem each day for a week and in assemblage experiments that lasted but one hour; and for a broad array of problems: defense, pollution, arms control, civil rights, energy, social security, drugs, and education. Moreover, these experimental results were generally corroborated by our analysis of trends in network news coverage and national public opinion. That we found essentially the same result using different methods strengthens our conclusion that television news shapes the relative importance Americans attach to various national problems.

To our surprise, the basic agenda-setting effect was not generally enhanced by vivid presentations. If anything, dramatic accounts of personal travails chosen to illustrate national problems appear to undermine agenda-setting, particularly when viewers blame the victims for the troubles that have befallen them. We assume that vivid presentations may enhance agenda-setting, provided viewers regard the victims as innocent. For example, intimate, poignant film of Ethiopian children dying of starvation may drive home the meaning of famine in a way that written accounts cannot. Because such children may be widely understood to be blameless victims of a cruel fate, vivid presentations may add to the viewer's conviction that the African famine is a serious problem. Our results, however, showed only that stories of personal suffering, powerfully depicted, generally did not raise the priority viewers assigned to the target problems.

Our experiments showed that the position of a story in a broadcast did affect agenda-setting. Lead stories were generally more influential than nonlead stories. Our analysis of survey data showed that lead stories exerted a much more profound agenda-setting effect than nonlead stories. We suspect that viewers may simply pay more attention to the first story than to stories that appear later on and that disruptions in viewing are especially likely to occur at home. An alternative explanation of the lead story advantage is that the public may perceive lead stories as being particularly newsworthy. Certainly the networks claim to select the lead story on these grounds.

Television news is, of course, not the only source of information people draw on when thinking about the nation's problems. Another is personal experience. Using both experimental and national survey data, we found that people who encountered problems in their everyday lives were more inclined to see these problems as important for the country as a whole than were individuals not so affected. In particular, we found that blacks attached more importance to civil rights than did whites and that the elderly attached more importance to the viability of the social security system than did the young. When people think of themselves as members of a victimized group, they appear to see their own problems as serious and legitimate ones for the country.

Our special interest in personal predicaments was in the possibility that they might serve as predisposing factors making viewers more vulnerable to a particular news agenda. For the most part, that is just what we found. News coverage of civil rights was more influential among blacks than among whites; coverage of unemployment proved more influential among the unemployed than among the employed; and coverage of the possible bankruptcy of the social security system was a more compelling message for the elderly than for the young. The general point here is that television news appears to be most powerful when it corroborates personal experience, conferring social reinforcement and political legitimacy on the problems and struggles of ordinary life.

Overall, we see our results on agenda-setting as a vindication of Lippmann's observations of more than a half-century ago. Although Lippmann was writing with newspapers in mind, his analysis is nevertheless highly relevant to the place of television news in contemporary American society. His observation that citizens must depend on others for their news about national and world affairs—a world they cannot touch themselves—is amply confirmed here. What we have done is to begin to uncover the various and specific ways that television news determines the citizen's conception of the "mystery off there."

Priming

While our agenda-setting results contribute to a long-standing tradition inaugurated by Lippmann and sustained by others, our results in the matter of priming offer a more original perspective. Priming presumes that when evaluating complex political phenomena, people do not take into account all that they know—they cannot, even if they are motivated to do so. Instead, they consider what comes to mind, those bits and pieces of political memory that are accessible. Television news, we supposed, might be a powerful determinant of what springs to mind and what is forgotten or ignored. Through priming (drawing attention to some aspects of political life at the expense of others) television news might help to set the terms by which political judgments are reached and political choices made.

Our results support this claim handsomely. When primed by television news stories that focus on national defense, people judge the president largely by how well he has provided, as they see it, for the nation's defense; when primed by stories about inflation, people evaluate the president by how he has managed, in their view, to keep prices down; and so on. According to a variety of tests, priming is both powerful and pervasive: it emerges in a number of independent tests for arms control, civil rights, defense, inflation, unemployment, and energy; for a Democratic president (Carter) as well as for a Republican one (Reagan); in different experimental arrangements; in response to good news as well as to bad; and in analyses that estimate priming while controlling for the possibility of projection. All this suggests that television news does indeed shape the standards by which presidential performance is measured.

Because our experiments manipulated the attention paid to major national problems, we expected that viewers' judgments of overall presidential performance would be primed more effectively than would assessments of presidential character, whose determinants we assumed were more diverse, an intermixing of the political and the personal. This expectation was confirmed. We also expected that priming would be more pronounced in viewers' assessments of the president's competence than in assessments of his integrity, on the grounds that success or failure in such areas as national defense, inflation, arms control, and the like would reflect more on the president's competence than on his integrity. This expectation was supported in every detail in the case of President Carter but sharply and consistently violated in the case of President Reagan. This unanticipated result suggests that the public may be most susceptible to priming on those aspects of the president's character that are most open to debate. For President Carter, it was a question of competence—was he up to the demands of the job? For President Reagan, it was more a question of trust—did he care for the welfare of all Americans? At a more general level, the aspects of presidential character that the public takes seriously may be determined by the broader political context. Flagrant scandal may underscore trust and integrity, while runaway

inflation may feed anxieties about competence and leadership. Should this be so, it would be a case of priming on a historical scale, with potentially historical consequences.

We further found that the power of television news to shape the standards by which presidents are judged is greater when stories focus on the president, and less when stories focus attention elsewhere. When coverage implied that the president was responsible for causing a problem or for solving it, the priming effect increased. When coverage implied that forces and agents other than the president were responsible for the problem, the priming effect diminished. These effects were particularly apparent for problems relatively new to the American political agenda, for which public understanding is perhaps less solidly formed and therefore more susceptible to the way that television news frames the matter of responsibility.

Our final pair of experiments demonstrate that the networks' agenda also primes the choices voters make. First, voters who were shown local news coverage that emphasized the state of the economy, the president's economic policies, and the implications of such policies for the impending midterm elections, relied heavily on their assessments of economic conditions when deciding which congressional candidate to support. In contrast, voters who watched local broadcasts devoted to the congressional candidates themselves—their positions on policy questions, group endorsements, or personal backgrounds—assigned great importance to these qualities in their choices. These results show that television news (*local* television news in this case) can alter the grounds on which elections are contested. Depending on the interests and resources of local television stations, congressional elections can either be a referendum on the president's economic performance, or purely a local contest between two distinct candidates.

The second experiment moved to the presidential level by reconstructing the intensive coverage lavished upon the Iranian hostage crisis in the closing days of the 1980 presidential campaign. The results suggested, in line with the priming hypothesis, that such coverage encouraged viewers to cast their votes on the basis of President Carter's performance on foreign affairs.

Because Carter was widely perceived as ineffectual in his dealings with foreign countries, priming in this case may have dealt a final and fatal blow to the President's reelection chances, transforming an election that appeared breathtakingly close on Saturday into a decisive Republican victory on Tuesday.

MINIMAL EFFECTS REVISITED

Our results imply that television news has become an imposing authority, one that shapes the American public's political conceptions in pervasive ways. This conclusion seems to contradict the minimal effects verdict reached by most empirical research on the political consequences of mass media. How can this discrepancy be understood?

Serious and systematic empirical research on mass media and American politics began in the 1930s, motivated both by the spread of fascism abroad and by what many took to be the sinister proliferation of radio at home. But in a brilliant study of the 1940 presidential election described in *The People's Choice*, Lazarsfeld, Berelson, and Gaudet[2] (1948) concluded that media simply strengthen the predispositions that were already in place prior to the campaign. Meanwhile, an extensive and well-controlled series of experimental studies undertaken during World War II found that films designed to indoctrinate new draftees failed rather spectacularly (Hovland, Lumsdaine, and Sheffield 1949).[3] The avalanche of research on political persuasion that soon followed these path-breaking and ambitious efforts drove home the same point again and again: while propaganda reinforces the public's preferences it does not, and perhaps cannot, change them.

Political persuasion is difficult to achieve, but agenda-setting and priming are apparently pervasive. According to our results, television news clearly and decisively influences the priorities that people attach to various national problems, and the considerations they take into account as they evaluate political leaders or choose between candidates for public office. Had we been interested in studying persuasion, we would have designed other experiments and would have written another book. More likely, we would have written no book at all, since we probably would have

had little new to say. That is, had our television news experiments set out to convert Democrats to Republicans, or pro-choice advocates to pro-life advocates, we strongly suspect that the results would have demonstrated yet more evidence in support of minimal effects. Our results on priming in the final days of the 1980 presidential election suggest that persuasion *is* possible, but only under very special circumstances: (1) large numbers of voters remain uncommitted in the closing days of the campaign; (2) late-breaking political events attract considerable media coverage and focus attention on a single aspect of the national condition; and (3) the political developments decisively favor one candidate over the other. But as a general matter, the power of television news—and mass communication in general—appears to rest not on persuasion but on commanding the public's attention (agenda-setting) and defining criteria underlying the public's judgments (priming).

We do not mean to suggest that television's power to set the public agenda and to prime citizens' political choices is unlimited. In fact, our studies suggest clear limits to television's power, which must be kept in mind as we try to decipher the broader significance of our findings.

One limitation is that the agenda-setting effects detected in our experiments were generally confined to the particular problem featured in the edited newscasts. Stories about energy affected beliefs about the importance of energy and energy alone, stories about defense affected beliefs about defense alone, and so on. Such specificity may reflect both the way that the networks typically package the news—in tight, self-contained bundles (Weaver 1972)[4]—and the way that most Americans think about politics, innocent of broad ideological frameworks that might link one national problem with another (Converse 1964; Kinder 1983).[5] Whatever its cause, the specificity of agenda-setting serves to constrain and channel television's influence. Because of the specific nature of the agenda-setting effect, Americans are unlikely to be swept away by any coherent vision of the country's problems. More likely, they will be pushed and pulled in various directions as discrete problems emerge, rise to prominence, and eventually fade away.

Second, Americans are not without informational resources of their own. We found that agenda-setting is weakened among those viewers who are most deeply engaged in public life, presumably because their priorities are more firmly anchored. Because their opinions about the national condition are stronger, they are buffeted less by day-to-day fluctuations in the networks' agendas. We also found that priming is weakened among those who, in effect, are not ready to be primed, by virtue of their partisanship or their tacit theories about national problems. Democrats confronted with news about "Republican" problems, like Republicans confronted with "Democratic" problems, or like viewers whose understanding of national problems is either poorly worked out or does not include links between the president and the problem are, as a consequence, less vulnerable to priming. Television news defines political reality more completely for some Americans than for others.

There is a final and perhaps most important point to make regarding limitations on the power of television news. Each of our experiments on agenda-setting manipulated attention paid to problems that could all plausibly be regarded as relevant to the national interest, each widely understood as having the potential to affect millions of Americans seriously and adversely. Our hunch—unfortunately not tested—is that our experiments could not create concern over *implausible* problems. Had we inserted news stories portraying the discrimination faced by left-handers we very much doubt that viewers would suddenly put aside their worries about unemployment, defense, and environmental degradation. Nor do we think that television news could long sustain a story that was radically at odds with other credible sources of information. In the midst of booming prosperity, could the networks convince Americans that the economy was actually in a shambles? Or, turning the question around, in the depths of a severe recession, could the networks convince the public that times were good? We don't think so, though again we have little direct evidence. We believe that the networks can neither create national problems where there are none nor conceal problems that actually exist. What television news does, instead, is alter the priorities Americans attach to a circumscribed set of problems, all of which are plausible contenders for public concern.

In a parallel way, our experiments on priming reveal that the news reorders the importance viewers attach to various *plausible* standards of political evaluation: our experiments were not designed to test whether network news could induce viewers to apply trivial or irrelevant standards of evaluation to presidents or political candidates. We can only guess that had such experiments been conducted, they would demonstrate that television news cannot induce voters to abandon the traditional standards of evaluation.

In summary, television news shapes the priorities Americans attach to various national problems and the standards they apply to the performance of their government and the qualifications of their leaders. Although subject to limitations (television news cannot create priorities or standards out of thin air) television's power to shape political priorities is nonetheless formidable, as we will see shortly. This view clashes with the romantic ideal of the democratic citizen: one who is informed, skeptical, deeply engaged in public affairs, and thoughtful about the state of the nation and the quality of its leadership. But we know from other evidence that this vision is hopelessly idealistic; in fact, Americans pay casual and intermittent attention to public affairs and are often astonishingly ignorant of the details of contemporary politics (Kinder and Sears 1985).[6]

No doubt a portion of this indifference and ignorance can be attributed to candidates and government officials who practice evasion and deceit, and to the mass media (and especially television news), which operate all too often as if the average American were seven years old. But some of the indifference must be traced to the minor place accorded politics in everyday life. It seems to us highly unreasonable to demand of average citizens that they carefully and skeptically examine news presentations. If politics is ordinarily subordinate to the demands and activities of earning a living, raising a family, and forming and maintaining friendships, then citizens should hardly be expected to spend much of their time and energy each day grappling with the flow of news. How then do Americans "understand" politics?

The answer is that we muddle through. Faced with the enormous complexity and uncertainty of the political world, possessed of neither the motivation nor the wits to optimize, we strike various compromises. We resort to cognitive shortcuts (Tversky and Kahneman 1974)[7] and settle for acceptable solutions (Simon 1955).[8] As a consequence of such compromises, our judgments are often creatures of circumstance. What we think about the federal deficit, turmoil in Latin America, or the performance of our president depends less on what we know in some complete sense and more on what happens to come to mind.

The general moral here is that judgment and choice are inevitably shaped by considerations that are, however briefly, accessible. And when it comes to political judgment and choice, no institution yet devised can compete with television news in determining which considerations come to light and which remain in darkness.

POLITICAL RAMIFICATIONS

Although it was not our purpose to investigate the political ramifications of agenda-setting and priming directly, we nevertheless feel obliged to spell out what we take them to be. In doing so, we are in effect making explicit the assumptions that motivated our research. We undertook the various investigations reported here under the assumption that *if* television news could be shown to be a major force in shaping the viewing public's conception of national life, the political ramifications would be portentous. With the results now in, we believe that through agenda-setting and priming, television news affects the American political process in at last three important ways: first, by determining which problems the government must take up and which it can safely ignore; second, by facilitating or undermining an incumbent president's capacity to govern, and third, by intruding, sometimes dramatically and decisively, upon campaigns and elections.

The Government's Agenda

If television news influences the priorities Americans attach to national problems, and if such priorities eventually shape governmental decision-making, our results on agenda-setting become important for what they reveal about the formation of public policy. The essential question, then, is whether policy makers heed instruction from the general public in selecting which problems to consider and which to ignore.

We believe that public opinion does influence the governmental political agenda. We also agree with V. O. Key,[9] however, that although public opinion influences the focus and direction of government policy, such influence is sharply limited:

> The articulation between government and opinion is relatively loose. Parallelism between action and opinion tends not to be precise in matters of detail; it prevails rather with respect to broad purpose. And in the correlation of purpose and action time lags may occur between the crystallization of a sense of mass purpose and its fulfillment in public action. Yet in the long run, majority purpose and public action tend to be brought into harmony (1961, 553).

The "harmonizing" of government policy and public opinion is loose, and sometimes occurs very gradually, partly because ordinary Americans are indifferent to and uninformed about the details of policy, and partly because of the successful intervention of organized interests whose preferences depart from those of the unorganized public (Edelman 1964; McConnell 1966; Schattschneider 1960).[10] Nevertheless, the national government does appear to respond, if slowly and imperfectly, to the public's wishes (e.g., Burstein 1979; Burstein and Freudenburg 1978; Page and Shapiro 1983; Verba and Nie 1972; Weissberg 1976).[11] Thus, television news must assume a significant role in the intricate process by which citizens' inchoate goals and concerns eventually become government policy.

Presidential Power

Television news may also influence an incumbent president's capacity to govern. As Neustadt (1960)[12] proposed and others have shown (Kernell 1986; Rivers and Rose 1985),[13] presidential power derives partly from public approval. A president who is admired by the people tends to be powerful in Washington. The proliferation of opinion polls has accentuated this connection. Of course, public approval is not the only factor affecting a president's success. But other things being equal, the Congress, the governmental bureaucracy, world leaders, the private sector, and the executive branch itself all become more accommodating to a president who is riding high with the public. As television news shapes the criteria by which the president's performance is measured, so may it indirectly contribute to a president's power.

This point has not escaped presidents and their advisers. Without exception, presidents in the television age have assiduously sought to control the criteria by which they are viewed and evaluated. From the careful staging of news conferences to the manufacturing of pseudoevents, "making news" and "going public" have become essential presidential activities (Kernell 1986). Our findings suggest that presidents would be foolish to do otherwise. To the extent that the president succeeds in focusing public attention on his accomplishments while distracting the public from his mistakes, he contributes to his popularity and, eventually, to the influence he can exercise over national policy.

The Electoral Process

Finally, our results suggest that by priming some considerations and ignoring others, television news can shift the grounds on which campaigns are contested. Priming may therefore determine who takes office—and with what mandate—and who is sent home. Moreover, election results do matter in tangible ways: elected officials pursue policies that are broadly consistent with the interests of their core political constituencies (e.g., Bunce 1981; Cameron 1977; Hibbs 1977).[14] Consequently, insofar as television news contributes, if unwittingly, to the success of one candidate over another, the results on priming we have uncovered here are politically important.

It seems clear to us that television news has become a major force in the American political process. The problems that government chooses to tackle, the president's power over the focus and direction of national policy, and the real and tangible consequences of elections are all affected by the glare of the television camera. Less clear is whether this influence is necessarily undesirable. Whether, as many maintain, television threatens public opinion and menaces democratic government would seem to turn on the question of how faithfully the pictures and stories that appear on the news each night portray what of real consequence is actually happening in the world.

End Notes

1. P. H. Weaver, "Newspaper News and Television News," in *Media Agenda-Setting in a Presidential Election*, eds. D. Cater and R. Adler (New York: Praeger, 1975).
2. P. F. Lazarsfeld, B. Berelson, and H. Gaudet, *The People's Choice* (2nd ed.), (New York: Columbia University Press, 1948).
3. C. I. Hovland, A. Lumsdaine, and F. Sheffield, *Experiments on Mass Communication* (Princeton, N.J.: Princeton University Press, 1949).
4. P. H. Weaver, "Is Television News Biased?" *The Public Interest*, 26 (1972), 57–74.
5. P. E. Converse, "Belief Systems in Mass Publics," in *Ideology and Discontent*, ed. D. E. Apter (New York: Free Press, 1964); D. R. Kinder, "Diversity and Complexity in American Public Opinion," in *The State of the Discipline*, ed. A. Finifter (Washington, D. C.: APSA, 1983).
6. D. R. Kinder and D. O. Sears, "Public Opinion and Political Behavior," in *Handbook of Social Psychology*, Vol. 2 (3rd ed.), eds. G. Lindzey and E. Aronson (New York: Random House, 1985).
7. A. Tversky and D. Kahneman, "Judgement under Uncertainty: Heuristics and Biases," *Science*, 185 (1974), 1124–1131.
8. H. A. Simon, "A Behavioral Model of Rational Choice," *Quarterly Journal of Economics*, 69 (1955), 99–118.
9. V. O. Key, *Public Opinion and American Democracy* (New York: Knopf, 1961).
10. M. Edelman, *The Symbolic Uses of Politics* (Urbana: University of Illinois Press, 1964); G. McConnell, *Private Power and American Democracy* (New York: Random House, 1966); E. E. Schattschneider, *The Semi-Sovereign People* (New York: Holt, 1960).

11. P. Burstein, "Public Opinion, Demonstrations, and the Passage of Anti-Discrimination Legislation," *Public Opinion Quarterly* 43 (1979), 157–172; P. Burstein and W. Freudenburg, "Changing Public Policy: The Impact of Public Opinion, Anti-War Demonstrations, and War Costs on Senate Voting on Vietnam War Motions," *American Journal of Sociology*, 84 (1978), 99–122; B. I. Page and R. P. Shapiro, "Effects of Public Opinion on Policy," *American Political Science Review*, 77 (1983), 175–190; S. Verba and N. H. Nie, *Participation in America: Political Democracy and Social Equality* (Chicago: Harper Collins, 1972); R. Weissberg, *Public Opinion and Popular Government* (Englewood Cliffs, N.J.: Prentice-Hall, 1976).

12. R. E. Neustadt, *Presidential Power: The Politics of Leadership* (New York: Wiley, 1960).
13. S. Kernell, *Going Public* (Washington, D.C.: CQ Press, 1986); D. Rivers and N. L. Rose, "Passing the President's Program: Public Opinion and Presidential Influence in Congress," *American Journal of Political Science*, 29 (1985), 183–196.
14. V. Bunce, *Do Leaders Make a Difference?* (Princeton, N.J.: Princeton University Press, 1981); D. R. Cameron, "The Expansion of the Public Economy," *American Political Science Review*, 72 (1977), 1243–1261; D. A. Hibbs, "Political Parties and Macroeconomic Performance," *American Political Science Review*, 71 (1977), 1467–1487.

43

Processing Politics: Learning from Television in the Internet Age

Doris Graber

THE "NEW" TELEVISION AUDIENCES

What kinds of programming preferences will the television journalists of the next few decades have to satisfy? Answering that question requires discussion of the major changes in attitudes toward political information between the baby boomer generation and their parents, on one hand, and the Internet generation, on the other. The early twenty-first century will belong to the Generation Xers, born in the 1960s and 1970s, and their offspring, who were immersed in televised information from infancy onward. While it is always hazardous to project generational changes, it seems quite likely that the children of GenXers, raised in the age of audiovisual plenty, will continue the trends in audiovisual information-gathering set in motion by their parents and grandparents. What do studies of GenXers tell us about their choices of political information and their preferred information delivery systems?

GenXers have spent more time watching the world unfold on audiovisual monitors than in any

From Doris Graber, *Processing Politics: Learning from Television in the Internet Age* (Chicago, IL: The University of Chicago Press, 2001), pp. 161–169.

other waking-hours activity. They have learned from infancy on to prize the creation of virtual reality that visual presentations make possible. GenXers like a great deal of control over their information supply, rather than patiently watching what newscasters have assembled for them in a newscast. GenXers are not intimidated by the technologies that need to be mastered to get information from multiple sources. As table 43.1 shows, three out of four GenXers like to skip television stories at will, and two-thirds enjoy selecting additional information for stories of their choice. Many relish having hundreds of different news sources at their fingertips. They also are perpetual surfers who move quickly from program to program unless a presentation truly engages them. When it comes to political information, half indicate that they want instant, round-the-clock access to news at times of their choosing.

GenXers like to participate in shaping their information menu. Half of them, according to table 43.1, enjoy assembling their own television programs, picking and choosing among stories. They also demand interactivity. This is the "talking back to your television" concept that first surfaced in the 1960s. But, above all, GenXers are niche viewers. They want to limit their news consumption, including news about politics, to the information that interests them most. They resist being told what information they ought to consume. That means that they skip stories they do not like and are eager to get more information about preferred stories at the punch of a button or the click of a computer mouse. Modern

technologies make it possible to indulge all of these preferences. The supply of political information has grown exponentially, thanks to cable television, the Internet, and a bevy of new digital television channels. Viewers are able to collect these riches at will.

Even though studies of generational changes in interest show that curiosity about some aspects of politics has diminished, GenXers retain an appetite for political news. More than half claim high interest in news about their local communities and their state, and nearly half say they are interested in news about the entire country.

Table 43.2 shows the types of programs in which GenXers claim to be "very interested." These programs should therefore be priorities for information suppliers, as long as expressed interests continue to be corroborated by audience statistics. Local community events rank at the top of news preferences for all generational groups. In fact, 45 percent of GenXers watched local news regularly in 2000 compared to 17 percent who watched network news (Pew 2000b). Events in one's state of residence are second, and news about the country ranks third. At the turn of the twenty-first century, average Americans, including GenXers, by and large, are most interested in politics close to the grassroots. When news focuses on events abroad rather than events at home, interest drops sharply. Only 23 percent of GenXers express keen interest in international news—on a par with their interest in news about consumer products and about entertainment and celebrities. Interest in day-to-day reports about

TABLE 43.1   Interest in Technological Innovations by Generation (%)

Type of Innovation	GenXers	Parents	Grandparents
Skip TV stories at will, as in newspapers	74	69	49
Click button for more information on story	66	61	38
Select news mix (politics/sports/weather)	54	53	32
Design program from story menu	50	49	27
Have Instant access to news any time	50	45	30
Choose from 100+ channels	43	33	14

Source: Excerpted from News in the Next Century 1996, 67.

TABLE 43.2 News Interests by Generation (%)			
News Topic	Generation X (18–29)	Boomers (30–49)	50 + and Older
Local community, hometown	59	71	67
State, place of residence	53	63	57
U.S., country as a whole	47	55	64
Weather	45	51	59
Health or fitness	34	33	37
Sports	29	22	23
Other countries, the world	23	18	29
Consumer products	23	24	25
Entertainment, movies, TV, celebrities	23	12	9
Computers/technology	18	20	11
Religion	17	19	29
Politics and government	11	23	36
Business, stock market	6	14	17

Source: Adapted from News in the Next Century 1996, 49.

the minutiae of politics and government in the nation ranks near the bottom, with a mere 11 percent of the GenXers—compared to 23 percent of their parents and 36 percent of their grandparents—saying they are "very interested."

Overall, the numbers in table 43.2 are encouraging for observers who are worried that young Americans are alienated from politics because they read and watch and listen less to the kind of political fare preferred by prior generations. If we use the grandparent generation represented in table 43.2 as a point of departure, rather than the parents of GenXers who were stirred by the turbulent sixties, the intergenerational drop in interest for local, state, and international news is below 10 percent. The sharpest drops—as high as 25 percent—come in national news, especially Beltway gossip. That suggests that Beltway gossip should shrink in favor of the types of local news that audiences find relevant to their lives. If the news supply becomes genuinely attuned to the changing needs and desires of news audiences and if the quality of the stories improves, it is quite likely that the numbers of viewers of political news will rise again.

In an age where the accuracy of audience research has reached new heights, journalists should have no trouble ascertaining continuously what types of stories will attract their viewers. Research tools to assess audience needs and capabilities include depth interviews, skillfully run focus groups, and various psychological and psycho-physiological tests, such as heart rate and galvanic skin response measures and checks of eye and other facial movements. Psychographic models, which were developed to segment audiences for marketing or analysis purposes, have pioneered many analytical techniques for scientific segmentation. These techniques use responses to a battery of questions in order to identify people with similar interests (Wells 1974; Myers 1996). The seminal work... that has shed light on the real nature of information-processing is also a major resource for producing audience-friendly program designs. The journalism community, schooled in social-scientific procedures through "precision journalism" training, is already familiar with many of these tools.

While progress in judging the audience's preferences has been great in some areas, it has lagged in others. For instance, few audience analyses appraise the knowledge base that particular audiences bring to political information. If this were done more frequently, journalists would be less likely to overestimate what audiences know and might recall to round out the sketchy information presented in news stories. Reporters would then be more likely to provide adequate contexts for news stories. When reporters write serious stories, they all too often tailor them to suit their own tastes, forgetting that their audiences' information backgrounds are generally far more limited. Stories about the need for reforming the welfare system, for example, convey little meaning when viewers are unfamiliar with the nature of the critical problems in the existing system.

NICHE PROGRAMMING: ADVANTAGES AND DISADVANTAGES

New digital technologies make it ever easier to satisfy the Internet generation's demand for news offerings that meet the special interests of various audience sectors. As has been true for radio, where the audience realms of giant stations splintered into tiny, specialized fiefdoms, so the audience realms of giant television networks are splintering into increasingly smaller configurations. While older viewers, especially women, have remained among the most loyal network television fans, younger viewers across the demographic spectrum are moving elsewhere (Pew 2000b). Television journalists therefore are less concerned about developing programs that please large, heterogeneous audiences, which previously forced them to offer much television fare pegged to the lowest common denominator. The trend toward narrowcasting began with the emergence of cable television. It has progressed to the digital technology stage, which allows a single television channel to carry multiple programs simultaneously.

The Internet has further extended the possibilities for niche programming. It allows people to select, at times and places of their choosing, from a seemingly endless array of multiple types of political information available worldwide. Even when Internet messages are substantively or technically flawed, they nonetheless diversify the political information pool—and the opportunities for glimpsing diverse views—far beyond past boundaries. Jürgen Habermas's (1989) funeral oration for the public sphere may have been premature after all. While economic constraints and lack of technical skills will prevent the vast majority of the world's people from using the Internet for the foreseeable future, these constraints are shrinking in technologically developed countries, where the first generation raised in the computer age is taking the helm (Pew 1998c, 2000b).

Television diversification has followed two distinct paths. The established television networks have chosen to address their offerings to selected demographic groups splintered along cleavages of age, gender, and ethnicity. For example, CBS has targeted older Americans, while Fox has aimed for a younger crowd. Some networks direct programming toward African Americans, and others target Spanish-speaking Latinos. Cable channels, by contrast, have ignored explicit demographics and have concentrated instead on interest fields, such as science, history, cooking, or mechanics.

Threats to Democracy

Narrowcasting does raise concerns about the viability of American democracy. If citizens do not drink from the same well of information, will they splinter into communication ghettoes? Will interactions diminish sharply among people whose backgrounds and matching preferences vary? Evidence of increasing fragmentation along various interest, lifestyle, age, income, religion, and ethnicity cleavage lines is mounting. A 1998 survey of audiences for entertainment shows, for example, showed that African Americans were flocking to newly available shows featuring African-American actors, while Caucasian Americans watched shows oriented toward white audiences. Fifty-one percent of African Americans followed crime news very closely in 2000 compared to 27 percent of whites and 32 percent of Hispanics. Figures for health news are 45 percent, 27 percent, and 29 percent, respectively (Pew 2000b). In the 1970s and 1980s, when fewer narrowly targeted choices were available, audience self-segregation along demographic lines was much less common (Sterngold 1998). As channel capacity grows, niche programming tends to progress into niche-within-niche offerings that make the splinter audiences ever tinier. They may be more satisfied by these specialized programs but also more disconnected from others in their community whose interests differ.

Niche programming may also be socially dangerous because it supports the Internet generation's penchant to limit their information diet to their special interest topics, creating a nation of people who know more and more about less and less. It may also mean that much of the public largely ignores entire areas of politics to which they gave at least passive attention in the past. Large numbers of people may be tempted to ignore civic information entirely if specialized news channels offer alternative program choices in competition with broadcasts of civic events, which most of the audience finds boring. Audience tallies show that this does happen (Pew 2000b). Attention to major political broadcasts, such as presidential addresses, declined sharply when other programs became available simultaneously.

Overall, the trends evident at the start of the twenty-first century do not bear out the nightmarish vision of large numbers of people isolating themselves from public affairs. The vast majority of citizens, including the Internet generation, have continued to attend to more general information sources, even when they devote substantial time to narrow-cast fare (Pew 2000b). Moreover, many of the news choice options on different programs are like peas in a pod, often low-intellectual-calorie peas at that. Such programs do restore some commonality to the political information supply, but they waste the chance for diversifying it.

Whenever major national events have loomed, such as key decisions in the impeachment case against President Clinton, viewing levels for general news programs have risen sharply. For example, on 19 December 1998, when the House of Representatives voted to impeach the president, CNN news scored its highest single-day rating of the year. Other broadcast outlets reported similar audience peaks, although these were below the levels of attention lavished a few years earlier on the verdict in football legend O.J. Simpson's murder trial or the events connected to the accidental death of the widely cherished Diana, Princess of Wales. However, CBS, which covered a major football game (New York Jets versus Buffalo Bills), attracted more than 12 million viewers on the day of the Clinton impeachment vote, surpassing the audience levels of all political news programs combined.

The Shrinking Scope of News

If news production is audience driven, will news offerings supply the political information that the public needs? For example, lack of interest among viewers has been cited as a major reason for the sharp reduction in the number of stories dealing with events outside the United States following the end of the cold war. ...[F]ocus group data...suggest that citizens will continue to demand political information about the broad range of issues that they deem salient to their lives. But citizens' interests do not necessarily encompass all the issues that elites deem important for average citizens. This portends a shrinking of the scope of news for individual citizens, though less severely than some observers fear, depending on the skill of journalists in clarifying the relevancy of seemingly remote issues.

The idea of allowing consumers of political news to guide the choice of information presented to them for immediate attention has been partially implemented already by print, television, and radio outlets in the United States that follow the tenets of "public" (or "civic") journalism. The staffs of papers like the *Charlotte Observer* in North Carolina and the *Wichita Eagle* in Kansas try to ascertain the interests of their readers through devices such as polls, focus groups, or town meetings. They then prepare stories that cover these concerns in exceptional depth. For instance, television programs can show how other communities have dealt with particular problems and provide guidelines for making fact-based comparisons between the local and the remote situations. Advocates of this type of journalism believe that it restores the role of the media as the mobilizer of civic action and the voice of public opinion. Journalists respect the public's choices, rather than derogating them. Opponents, who are plentiful and include prominent mainline journalists, argue that public journalism abandons the press's hallowed leadership role in setting the civic agenda, that it shamelessly panders to shallow public tastes, and that it leads to neglectful and dangerous silence about many important issues (Schudson 1998).

Leaving aside the question whether journalists know better than ordinary citizens what information belongs on the civic agenda, we do need to ask the "to what avail" question. If journalists supply information that is unwanted and largely ignored, while covering areas of strong demand sparingly, what is accomplished? It amounts to preaching to an empty church. If people do not want much international news but crave local news, shouldn't the demands of the mass audience be heeded, especially when specialized media, tailored to the preferences of elites, are available? A public that is exposed to political information that is of little interest is unlikely to be motivated to political thinking and action. "[I]t is not an informed public ... with the motivation or frame of reference or capacity to act in a democracy" (Schudson 1995, 26–27).

Regardless of what journalists do, in the end it is the audience that determines whether or not the content will lead to civic enlightenment and political participation. Attempts to force-feed audiences with news they do not care about are apt to fail when the audiences have alternative program choices (Entman 1989). However, it is within the grasp of journalists, as well as the political leaders who are their sources, to whet the public's appetite for important news stories. If it can be made clear that the story is, indeed, important and relevant to the audience's concerns and if story presentation is appealing, sizable audiences will be attracted. The presidency and other visible public offices have often served as the bully pulpit that can draw nationwide attention to important stories.

References

ENTMAN, ROBERT M. 1989. *Democracy without citizens: Media and the decay of American politics.* New York: Oxford University Press.

HABERMAS, JÜRGEN. 1989. The public sphere: An encyclopedia article. In *Critical theory and society: A reader*, edited by Stephen E. Bronner and Douglas M. Kellner. New York: Routledge.

MIFFLIN, LAWRIE. 1998a. As band of channels grows, niche programs will boom. *New York Times*, 28 December.

MYERS, JAMES H. 1996. *Segmentation and positioning for strategic marketing decisions.* Chicago: American Marketing Association.

Pew Research Center for the People and the Press.

———. 1998c. Online newcomers more middlebrow, less work-oriented. Available at http://www.people-press.org/tech98sum.htm.

———. 2000b. Media report. Available at http://www.people-press.org/media00rpt.htm.

SCHUDSON, MICHAEL. 1995. *The power of news.* Cambridge: Harvard University Press.

———. 1998. The public journalism movement and its problems. In *The politics of news: The news of politics*, edited by Doris Graber, Denis McQuall, and Pippa Norris. Washington, D.C.: CQ Press.

STERNGOLD, JAMES. 1998. A racial divide widens on network TV. *New York Times*, 29 December.

WELLS, WILLIAM D. 1974. *Life style and psychographics.* Chicago: American Marketing Association.

PART FIVE

Making Public Policy

44

The Structure and Context of Policy Making

Stella Z. Theodoulou

In Part One, it was made clear that if policy study theorists agree on nothing else, they tend to agree that there is a series of activities that take place during policy making; however, there is considerable disagreement on whether these activities take place in a sequence, with a certain activity taking place at one particular point and another activity occurring at a subsequent point of the process. Many textbooks on policy making take the "stages heuristic" approach, thus grouping activities into a sequence of stages, although in the real world there tends to be overlap and a blurring of these stages. In this chapter, the policy process will be discussed by looking at what we believe has to occur in three distinct phases of the policy process; the phases being Pre decision, Decision, and Post decision (see Figure 44.1). This allows us to utilize a structure that acknowledges first the complexity of the policy process and second that certain activities such as agenda setting and implementation have to occur. It also allows the reader

to integrate the various frameworks, theories, and models found in the literature so as to understand what happens when public policy is made.

Pre-decision Phase

During this phase, problems are defined and placed upon the agenda, and a policy is formulated to deal with that initially identified problem.

PROBLEM IDENTIFICATION: This is the very beginning of policy making. Some societal issues are generally recognized as policy problems; however, there are many issues that are not recognized as policy problems and seem to be ignored because they are considered to be issues that are private in nature. The question for us to ask is, When and how does an issue become a policy problem? This necessitates that we accept that policy actions do not just occur to address an issue that is troublesome to society. Policy actions

FIGURE 44.1 Public Policy Process Phases and Stages

are direct responses to an issue that policy actors have identified and defined as a problem that must be addressed. There might be agreement on what the issue is, but there is often disagreement as to why or in what way that issue is a problem and consequently disagreement on what policy action should occur. Crucial to problem definition is perception. In general, an issue will be defined as a public problem if it is perceived as representing a publically intolerable social or individual incongruity that cannot be allowed to continue. If at one point in time an issue is perceived to be a public problem, it does not always mean it will be perceived that way. The way that policy actors evaluate and assess an issue can change, as can societal beliefs surrounding that issue. All political systems face an overwhelming number of issues that have public consequences and thus can be considered as problems; however, their saliency will vary over time. For example, unemployment is always going to be an issue of concern; however, in stable or prosperous economic periods, it is less salient and thus not high on the agenda for policy action. Ideological perspectives are also crucial to understanding how policy actors perceive the seriousness of an issue and why it is or is not a problem of public concern. This often leads to heated debate over what should and what should not be considered a public problem and what policy action should be taken to remedy it. The fact that most issues are multifaceted exacerbates the disagreements. It is extremely rare that an issue will immediately be perceived and defined as a public problem by all policy actors and then proceed quickly to the policy agenda stage.

Rochefort and Cobb argue that there are a number of factors influencing how policy actors identify and define public policy problems.[1] The first factor is causality, which requires an understanding of who is responsible and what factors led to the issue being a problem. This will dictate whether the issue is seen as a private or public problem. The second factor is the severity of the problem. This requires policy actors to look at who bears the cost of the issue; the greater the number affected, the more likely an issue will be viewed as a problem. The third factor is incidence or frequency of an issue occurring. Policy actors' awareness of why an issue might be becoming, or is, a problem. The fourth factor is proximity; this refers to how close an issue affects an actor's personal social reality. The closer it affects, the more likely the actor will identify the issue as a problem. Crisis represents the last factor influencing the way policy actors identify and define policy problems. Defining what a crisis is is in itself problematic. In general, a crisis is when a large number of policy actors perceive an issue to be severe and immediate and to impact both individuals and society as a whole and thus action must be taken by government. There are times when policy makers will claim a crisis so as to elevate a problem on the agenda when in reality no crisis exists.[2] A real crisis is the most serious problem a society faces and often cuts across any differences as to whether a problem really exists.

For the most part, there is rarely immediate consensus amongst policy actors as to what constitutes a policy problem and what problems should be dealt with. Often what needs to occur is that an issue needs to gain the public's attention.

The greater the scope of an issue, the greater the attention of the public; scope can be defined as the number of individuals affected by an issue. The more individuals affected by an issue, the more likely a society will view the issue as a problem for the government to deal with. Conversely, if an issue affects only a few individuals or cuts across a small segment of society, it's unlikely it will be defined as a policy problem that requires action. Once again, perception is important in defining whether the number of individuals or segments of society affected justifies action being taken. In addition to the scope of an issue, the cost associated with an issue will also affect public attention. Cost is defined as the negative ramifications that result from an issue or problem. The longer a problem goes unmet, the higher the cost. As in the case of scope, perception is crucial to defining the associated cost of any one issue or problem.

But what if an issue is not clearly identified as a problem? It does not necessarily mean that the issue never gets on the agenda. Sometimes, issues not defined as problems will demand policy action through the agenda-setting process, which allows us to understand why some issues move onto the agenda while others are ignored.

AGENDA SETTING. The agenda-setting process is a multifaceted and complex process. In order to be able to discuss how the issue agenda is set, we must determine exactly what is meant by the term "agenda." Generally, the issue agenda is the list of subjects or problems to which governmental and nongovernmental policy actors are paying serious attention at any given point in time.[3] Agenda setting is the narrowing of the set of issues that the policy actors will focus on and address. There are different types of agendas. They can be highly general, such as a list of items that occupy the attention of the president, or they can be highly specialized, such as the agendas of congressional subcommittees.

To recap, there is a good chance that issue will move on to the agenda because it is perceived to be a problem. How policy makers define the problem will affect what action will be taken to address the problem. Thus, agenda setting begins when decision makers recognize a problem, feel the need to address it, and start to search for a solution.

The literature provides a number of different agenda-setting models that offer opposing analytical frameworks; however, for the most part these models pose similar questions. In many ways, the answers each agenda-setting model provides to these questions often complement and overlap each other.[4] All agenda-setting models are, in one way or another, asking how issues become problems and how they move or do not move onto the agenda. Within these overarching questions, there are subsets of questions that theorists concern themselves with. For example, why do some issues have a high amount of attention and priority while other issues of similar significance for society languish and receive less attention, why do some issues seem so important and then disappear from the agenda, and what are the interactions and roles of the various institutional and noninstitutional policy actors in the process? The answers to these questions are provided by many of the theories of the policy process that are concerned with how policy change occurs.

As discussed in an earlier chapter, the Multiple Streams model advanced by John Kingdon views the policy process as the interplay of multiple streams. Issues emerge on the agenda through the interplay of a number of dynamics. Kingdon views agenda setting as a garbage can where the coupling of the active streams with solutions, participants, and choice opportunities occurs.[5] According to Cobb and Elder, agendas can be classified into two main types.[6] The first such agenda is the systemic agenda; this can be viewed as the public agenda and covers all issues that are generally recognized to deserve public attention and are matters within the government's legitimate jurisdiction. An example of such a matter would be poverty. The second type of agenda is the institutional agenda; this can be viewed as the policy-making agenda and involves all issues explicitly up for active and serious consideration by the authoritative decision makers; for example, actual congressional bills.[7] The institutional agenda is less abstract and narrower in scope than the systemic agenda, and the priorities of both do not necessarily correspond. Often there is considerable discrepancy between the two agendas.

The "normal" agenda sequence is for issues to arrive on the systemic agenda before they are put onto the institutional agenda. This can be characterized as the instigating element that stimulates the agenda-setting process, and it occurs if the issue is identified and seen as a costly problem for a particular population within society. If not, then an issue will not be considered for policy action and move to the institutional agenda. For Cobb and Elder, the catalysts or events that move issues from the systemic to the institutional agenda should be viewed as triggering devices. In order for a catalyst such as an international crisis to act as a trigger, it must draw the attention of the public and policy makers. Crucial for a catalyst to become a triggering device is the interaction of four factors: scope, which refers to the number of people affected; intensity, which is the extent to which an event concerns the public; the duration of an event; and resources, which is simply what is at stake.

A key problem for policy makers and other involved policy actors is to ensure that the lag time between an issue moving from the systemic agenda and on to the institutional agenda is not too great; if it is, the issue could fall apart and prove critical to the political system. The viability of a political system is a function of its ability to cope with the lag between these two agendas. It is also important to note that both agendas have their own sets of biases and are therefore subject to conflict.

Once an issue or problem is on the agenda and there is the perception that the problem must be addressed, solutions must be formulated. Public policies do not just appear; they have to be created or designed. Formulation can occur prior to agenda setting or after the agenda is set. Kingdon focuses on the role of broad-based policy communities that over time may sometimes develop a consensus on a solution to a particular problem. When the problem becomes more salient, a solution is then already available. [8]

POLICY FORMULATION. Policy formulation is the creation of relevant and supportable courses of action for dealing with specific problems within the institutional agenda and does not always result in the adoption of policy.[9] Because a problem or issue arrives on the agenda, it does not necessarily mean that the government will act

effectively to resolve it.[10] Formulation takes place before legislation is enacted and theoretically ends once the policy is implemented. However, in reality, formulation often becomes reformulation because once a policy is implemented and then evaluated, it is often redesigned to address inadequacies either politically or policy-wise. This, then, is the iterative nature of formulation. The policy process itself is also iterative in nature.

Implicit in formulation is bargaining and compromise. Often, the policy that emerges is the one that has the most support from the relevant policy-making actors. In the real world of policy making, there are various competing policy actors each designing and promoting different solutions for solving the same problem. Another reality is that formulation can occur over a long period of time and with it comes a continuous process of coalition building behind certain policy proposals. A final reality as stated earlier is the recognition that formulation does not necessarily result in adoption, even though the expected result of policy formulation is that it is a solution to a problem.

A number of instruments and tools are at the disposal of policy makers when they formulate policy. Deborah Stone and a number of other authors have offered instrument classification schemes.[11] The classification schemes may vary but most have in common the assumption that policy instruments are mechanisms by which government seeks to alter the behavior of specified target populations and are meant to achieve policy goals. Instruments should have a focus of activity, a method by which they deliver the intervention to the problem, and an understanding of the level of administrative action the policy requires. When choosing from the various proposed solutions, policy makers should take into account political, technical, and administrative feasibility, available resources to implement, and the receptivity of the population who will most be impacted by the solution.

Policy formulation involves multiple policy actors and this is one of the difficulties in formulating solutions to problems. From the previous readings, the various policy actors involved in policy making are identified as institutional and noninstitutional. It should be noted, however, that some policy actors are more important than others and that there are very few rules guiding how to formulate the "best" solution.[12] B. Guy Peters argues that this absence of rules is responsible in part for the complexity of formulation.[13] The absence of rules and the presence of multiple policy actors who vary in their importance combine to ensure that formulation is fraught with political and policy difficulties.

Policy makers are not monolithic or neutral and so most often policy solutions are the result of a battle between groups of policy makers pushing their alternative over others. This battle by which alternative policy proposals are examined and assessed is theoretically the product of **policy analysis**.

Policy analysis as a term was first used by Charles Lindblom in 1958 to describe a type of quantitative analysis involving incremental comparisons in which nonquantitative methods are included in the recognition of values and policy.[14] Over the years, it has come to be defined in other ways. The different ways can be categorized as being either one of two approaches: analysis for policy or analysis of existing policy.[15] Many policy scientists would argue analysis for policy involves the use of reason and evidence to allow decision makers to choose the "best" policy from a number of alternatives. Policy analysis is not an exact science as there is no guarantee that it ensures chosen solutions are in the best interest of the public or even if they will solve the problem they were enacted for. Theoretically, policy analysis should help decision makers make more intelligent, more ethical, more effective, and more efficient choices. We can find such policy analysts on legislative staffs, in think tanks, in consulting firms, in nonprofit organizations, and in universities.

Analysis of existing policy is concerned with either how policy is made, why, when, and for whom or is interested in describing a policy in terms of its content and relationship to other policies. Factors such as effectiveness, feasibility (both political and economic), and equity must be included in the analysis. Common to both approaches is that they must be systematic and organized so that either the feasibility of public policy alternatives as possible policy solutions can be evaluated or the usefulness of an existing policy or program can be determined.

Most practical policy analysis is based on the work of Patton and Sawicki, MacRae and Wilde, and Eugene Bardach.[16] Such authors seem to agree that policy analysis involves a sequence of activities that must be carried out for effective analysis.[17] Preferably each step is linked to the next, and if the sequence is dramatically broken, then the likelihood of the analysis being flawed greatly increases. The sequence is illustrated in Figure 44.2. At each step, certain activities must be undertaken in order to move successfully to the next step. Also at the completion of each step, the analyst should review to see if the activities of the current step relate basically to what was done in the previous steps. The objective of any piece of policy analysis is the development of alternatives (policy proposals) that can be judged as to how well they meet the problem as it is identified and understood. Policy analysis provides a thread that connects the activities of the pre-decisional phase.

Crucial to either approach to policy analysis is the assessment of the feasibility of the policy that is being considered or that has already been enacted. Feasibility is most commonly based on the cost, both political and financial; the capability to be carried out; the capacity to actually undertake it; and the consequence or political outcome, either intended or unintended. Policy formulation is as complex as agenda setting and should be understood as never-ending even

FIGURE 44.2   Policy Analysis Steps

Source: Adapted from C. Patton and D. Sawicki, *Basic Methods of Policy Analysis and Planning*, Englewood Cliffs: Prentice Hall, 1986.

when a policy is successfully adopted. The nature of a problem will affect how solutions are formulated as well as what solution is finally adopted as policy.

To recap, the pre-decision stage of the policy process leads to the identification of a problem, agenda setting, and the formulation of potential policy solutions. Once alternative solutions have been generated, some kind of governmental decision is required as to what type of action will be taken. In short, a decision will be made to adopt a course of policy action.

The Decision Phase

POLICY ADOPTION.   Policy adoption is the act of choosing which policy alternative will be preferred course of action to meet the problem. It is the process by which alternatives are politically explored, debated, and negotiated and actions are taken to promote a specific solution over others. This requires, in many instances, bargaining and compromise among the policy actors and groups with the power and authority to make policy decisions. Key to bargaining and compromise is whether an alternative is politically feasible. Political feasibility in this instance is not necessarily whether it's the best or correct policy to solve a problem but whether it has a consensus of support from the key policy actors and groups surrounding the issue. James Anderson posits that institutional policy actors have to take into account certain factors that act as decision criteria for whether they support adoption of a specific policy alternative. Among these factors are their values, political party affiliation, constituency interests, and deference to policy, political, and administrative authorities.

In sum, policy adoption is the formal approval of a policy solution by institutional policy actors. When a legislature adopts a proposal and passes it into law or policy, it is referred to as policy legitimation. Legislation is only one means of adoption; policy adoption may also be achieved through regulations, executive orders, executive agreements, judicial action, and approval of referendum or initiatives. To conclude that policy adoption is limited to institutional policy actors would be wrong. It is true that any policy that is

adopted will be subject to the institutional process it has to come out of; however, common to all policy adoption is that its process develops within and across a wide spectrum of arenas, such as the public, the executive, the legislative, and the political arena. In such arenas, the debate is shaped and formed and eventually influences what alternative action is adopted and in some instances that no action be adopted. Often, what emerges and is adopted is the policy that is the most practical and feasible because policy adoption is subject to the influence of both institutional and noninstitutional policy actors who are at work in various arenas.

Policy adoption is the activity that occurs in the decision phase; once it happens, the process moves into the post-decisional phase, which includes the stages of implementation, evaluation, and policy termination or change.

Post-decisional Phase

POLICY IMPLEMENTATION.   Policy implementation starts after the decision to adopt a particular course of action is made and ends successfully when the goals sought by the policy are achieved and the costs are within reasonable expectations. Thus, policy implementation can be defined as the directed change that follows a policy adoption. Often, a decision by government to "do something" is seen by the general public as the end of the matter. However, in practice, the policy decision that emerges from the formulation and adoption stages sets off a long and complex chain— the policy implementation process—where any multitude of things can go wrong, including, for example, judicial constraints, abandonment by the public, and resistance by those who must alter their patterns of behavior so as to comply with the policy.[18]

Policy implementation should be viewed as the intervening stage between the desire for change and actual problem change. It does not matter how well a policy is designed; its propensity for achieving its goals will depend on how it is implemented. Moreover, there is a tendency for policy implementation to become largely bureaucratic and rule laden.[19] Thus, it is not uncommon for the original policy to be distorted, for the original goals to be forgotten, and for those responsible for implementation to substitute their own objectives as they implement policies. Thus, public policies often fail to have their intended effects due to the dynamics of the implementation process. Policies also fail if they are not well designed. Often, the policy that is formulated and adopted is a tradeoff between what is feasible and acceptable and thus will get the necessary support to be adopted; sometimes, this means that it will not "solve" the problem it's designed for because it does not adequately address the problem because in doing so it might alienate consensus building. Also crucial to policy implementation is the adopted policy must assign the appropriate implementing agency and instruments so as to alter the target population's behavior. Among the factors shaping implementation success are statutory compliance, bureaucratic accountability, accomplishment of statutory goals, accomplishment of goals at the local level, an improvement in political climate, and learning so that policy improves over time.[20]

Early scholars of implementation such as Derthick, Bardach, and Pressman and Wildavsky came to the conclusion after studying particular case studies that problems consistently existed in the way policies and programs were executed because of unforeseen or unrecognized problems during implementation.[21] It is from these early case studies that two theoretical approaches to policy implementation studies emerged; the top-down perspective and the bottom-up perspective.[22]

A top-down approach views policy implementation as planning, hierarchy, and control and is based on the assumptions that statutory language is complete and applicable and that implementation is an administrative function. The bottom-up perspective assumes that statutes are incomplete. The focus is on the critical role played by the network of policy actors given the responsibility of policy implementation; the local-level administrators and elected officials who have close ties to interest groups and other individuals who have an interest in the policy.[23]

Over the years, a number of theorists have argued that policy implementation should not be seen solely as top-down or bottom-up and have attempted to provide models which synthesize the two approaches. One such theorist is Richard Matland, who provides in a reading that follows what he labels the ambiguity-conflict model.[24] For Matland, the crucial elements that explain policy implementation success or failure are the level of ambiguity of a policy's goals, the level of ambiguity of the ways and means to achieve the policy goals, and the level of policy conflict.[25]

It is interesting to note that many of the originating authors of a top-down approach, such as Wildavsky and Sabatier, have altered their perspective on a strict adherence to the model. For example, in a later collaboration with Giandomenico Majone, Wildavsky argues policy implementation should be seen as evolution.[26] They conclude that it is shaped by the original policy making from which it springs; therefore, policies consist of a variety of goals, ideas, and dispositions, each connected in some disarray. Sabatier has, in a number of later publications, acknowledged that the bottom-up approach has methodological advantages over the top-down approach and that the approach taken will vary depending on whether dominant legislation structures the implementation process.[27]

The literature on implementation attempts to build "perfect" models of implementation that outline the conditions that must be met for successful actualization of policy.[28] One can also find in the literature various perspectives as to what implementation involves. Political scientists may differ in their perceptions but all agree that implementation is, in many respects, an opaque phenomenon, as its most consequential characteristics are difficult to detect and as it is a pliant process that can undergo rapid transformation.

Just as there are different types of agendas, different types of implementation can also occur.[29] The first such type is programmed implementation, which tries to eliminate or control the problems and pitfalls that await implementation by thorough, explicit programming of implementation procedures. Programmed implementation places high value on clarity and rationality and rests on the assumption that the problems that plague implementation are the result of ambiguities of policy goals; the involvement of an excessive number of policy actors; overlapping jurisdictions of authorities; misperceived interests; and conflicts. The second type of implementation that can occur is adaptive implementation, which tries to improve the process by allowing for adjustments to the original policy mandate as events unfold. In contrast to programmed implementation, clarity and specification are seen as barriers to implementation, for they produce rigidity in the face of shifting political realities.

The last type of implementation that can occur is premeditated nonimplementation: behavior deliberately aimed at preventing implementation from occurring. Such behavior ensures that the policy will never be more than partially accomplished. Usually, because of the multidimensional nature of the policy process, implementation is a combination of the programmed and adaptive types, though premeditated nonimplementation often occurs because policy goals and objectives are vague.

When asking who is responsible for implementation, one should realize that it is not the focus of policy makers, who are, in reality, only moderately interested in it. Their level of interest is dictated by the fact that they perceive implementation to be too costly—politically, time wise, and electorally; and too low in visibility and never living up to its promises. Thus, the major actor in implementation is the bureaucracy; indeed, implementation can be viewed as the bureaucratization of policy.

Once a policy is implemented, the discussion demonstrates, there are so many pitfalls and implementation is only sometimes successful; therefore, it is important that decision makers go back to evaluate the original policy. More often than not policies and the programs they create often fail to achieve their intended effects and have unintended outcomes.

POLICY EVALUATION. Increasingly elected officials, policy makers, community leaders, bureaucrats, and the public at large want to know what policies work and what ones are not working, and why. Within the policy literature, a number of perspectives on what evaluation exactly is can be found. We believe policy evaluation can be defined as a process by which general judgments about quality, goal attainment, program effectiveness, impact, and costs can be.[30] It is done after

the policy or program has been implemented and evaluators must be clear on the goals of the policy or program. The main purpose of evaluation is to gather information about a particular program's performance so as to assist in the decision to continue, change, or terminate that program.

In the 1960s and 1970s, concern with evaluation intensified and a variety of evaluation models or frameworks emerged. Many of these models fuse theoretic and practical guidelines for conducting a program or policy evaluation. As time passed, policy scientists have adapted many of the models to deal with changing contexts and needs. In the real world, policy evaluators will often use more than one model to evaluate a program.[31]

Many authors view evaluation as a three-stage sequence: planning, data gathering, and dissemination. Theodoulou and Kofinis in their reading "The Assessment of Executed Policy Solutions" indicate that in each stage, a series of essential activities take place.[32] It is important to understand what evaluation is and how and who does it. Evaluation if done correctly and without bias can be essential, for it often tells policy makers what is working, what does not work, and what the unintended and intended impacts are; this in turn should lead to the changing or termination of a policy or program.

POLICY CHANGE OR TERMINATION. As discussed, policy evaluation can demonstrate that a policy or program is not achieving its intended objectives and in some circumstances produces unintended impacts. Occasionally, it may result in policy change, and sometimes, although it is rare, policies are terminated completely. It is, however, more common for change to occur rather than policy termination.[33] In real-world dynamics, political and economic realities can also force policy evolution. Change does not necessarily have to be comprehensive, it can be and most often is incremental in nature.

Up until the 1980s, a survey of the policy literature demonstrates that for many authors analysis ended with policy evaluation and the acknowledgment that feedback from evaluation was cycled into policy-making activities.[34] It was generally argued that feedback could lead to policy reformulation and reimplementation.

Policy change is simply modification of existing policy and for many policy scientists, the policy cycle is an ongoing dynamic process with policy constantly evolving. Policies are reshaped over time and evolve through change. Such change can be referred to as policy succession.[35] In the Theodoulou and Kofinis reading, "Policy Change and Termination" the reasons why policy change occurs and the form that it takes are discussed. They and several other authors argue that there are discernable patterns of policy change.[36] As with other stages of the policy process, policy change is complex and subject to real-world dynamics.

On those rare occasions when decision makers decide to end a policy, much of the analysis is on particular case studies. From these examples it is clear that termination is not easy to accomplish and often political and economic realities prevent more policies or programs from being terminated.[37] There are several reasons why a policy may be terminated; however, it is clear that unless the political environment is conducive to the ending of a policy, termination will simply not occur. Termination of a policy does not always mean that the policy disappears; it can mean that but often it might mean a particular part of a policy or program is ended, the entity given implementation responsibility will be eliminated, or implementation will be subsumed by another entity.[38] Often the type of termination and the prospects for its success will be dependent on the consensus that has built within the political environment and the decision makers' approach to termination.[39]

THE CONTEXT OF POLICY MAKING

Like so much of politics, the process of policy making cannot be divorced from the context in which it happens. To understand why we get the type of policy that we do, we should realize that more important than political processes are the underlying conditions within a nation.[40] Policy is determined by realities as opposed to advocacy coalitions. Realities can be defined as historic and geographical conditions, social and economic composition, and mass political behavior. The policy process is a funnel through which realities are sifted, the filter being political institutions and elites. Problems are defined and policy formulated through policy makers' capacity to influence realities.

Another way to define realities would be to see them as a number of individual or subcontexts coming into play.[41] The first such individual subcontext is the history of past policies. In short, the policy history in a specific issue area is an important contextual limit on new policy options because policy changes take place in a context provided by past policies. Environmental factors form the second subcontext. From the environment come demands for policy action, support for both the overall political system and individual policy proposals, and limitations on what policy makers can do. The environmental subcontext is a composite of cultural, demographic, economic, social, and ideological factors. Common values and beliefs help to determine the demands made on policy makers, and if such values and beliefs are commonly held, then greater public acceptance for policies can be won by decision makers. Public opinion lays the boundaries and direction of policy while the social system attunes policy makers to the social forces that are salient in terms of both demands and supports. The interaction and interrelationship between the political arena and the economic system are a given. Those who possess economic power through their control of economic resources also possess undeniable political power, which raises their demands and support for policies to a level of priority. The institutional subcontext, which involves both the formal governmental institutions and structural arrangements of the system, also affects the formulation, implementation, and substance of public policies. A further subcontext affecting policy debates in all areas is the ideological conflict between liberals and conservatives over the nature of governmental action. The level and type of government intervention is the framework of all policy.

A final subcontext is the budgetary process, for few public policies can be implemented without public expenditure. In turn, public expenditure cannot take place unless governments raise finance through taxation charges or through borrowing. This fact of life is the basis for the complicated political process of deciding resource allocation, which in turn gives rise to an equally complex process of bargaining and compromise between government and groups within society. One need only listen to CNN or other network news to recognize the pressure put upon government by various societal groups to spend more or less public money on a particular policy area. The demand for spending is eternal, although the willingness to pay for it through taxation is not. Some authors argue that, on top of this, the process cannot ignore ideological concerns and economic theory.[42]

The budgetary process is a highly politicized one in which bargains are struck, targets are not met, deviations are made, and large numbers of policy actors are involved. Additionally, it is heavily influenced by the need to control public sector borrowing requirements and the deficit.[43] Authors such as Heclo and Wildvsky note the importance of the "political climate" over spending policies.[44]

CONCLUSION

The discussion here has tried to outline what the literature commonly perceives to be the main stages of activity within the policy process. It is not the intention to suggest that the only way to view the process is as a sequential cycle, as the stages heuristic model of policy making does. Rather, the use of stages of activity can be seen as a way of managing and acknowledging that a series of activities need to take place when policy is made. The simplest way to view the process is to view a policy as a decision and that events occur prior to the decision being made and also occur after the decision is made. Given the complexity and fluidity of the real world, it is useful to understand the activities that need to happen for a policy decision to occur, and that when looking at these activities or as we and others refer to them as stages of the policy process that we view them through a variety of different theories and models. Ultimately, policy making is a complex endeavor that involves struggle and accommodation among many policy actors. Ultimately, decisions will be made and differences among

competing interests resolved by authoritative decision makers in a process of accommodation, bargaining, and compromise.

End Notes

1. D. A. Rochefort and R. W. Cobb, "Problem Identification: An Emerging Perspective," in D. A. Rochefort and R. W. Cobb, *The Politics of Problem Definition* (Lawrence, K.S.: Kansas University Press, 1994), pp. 15–20.
2. *Ibid*. Rochefort and Cobb, p. 20.
3. James E. Anderson, *Public Policymaking* (Boston: Houghton Mifflin, 1986), Chapter 3; Lawrence G. Brewster, *The Public Agenda* (New York: St Martin's Press, 1984), pp. 1–12; Robert Eyestone, *From Social Issues to Public Policy* (New York: Wiley, 1978), Chapter 1.
4. W. Parsons, *Public Policy: An Introduction to the Theory and Practice of Policy Analysis* (Aldershot, U.K.: Edward Elgar, 1995), pp. 184–207.
5. This is a modification of the model described by Cohen and others, "A Garbage Can Model of Organizational Choice," *Administrative Science Quarterly*, 17 (March 1972), pp. 1–25.
6. See Roger W. Cobb and Charles D. Elder "Issues and Agendas" (this reader, part 5, reading 47).
7. *Ibid*. Cobb and Elder, "Issues and Agendas" (this reader, part 2, reading 47).
8. John Kingdon, *Agendas, Alternatives, and Public Policies* (New York: Longman, 2003).
9. James E. Anderson, *Public Policymaking* (Boston: Houghton Mifflin, 1986), p. 93.
10. Peter Bachrach and Morton S. Baratz refer to this as nondecisions, *Power and Poverty* (New York: Oxford University Press, 1970), p. 44.
11. D. Stone, *Policy Paradox and Political Reason* (Glenview: Scott Foresman, 1988); A. L. Schneider and H. Ingram, *Policy Design for Democracy* (Lawrence, K.S.: University of Kansas Press, 1997); and J. E. Anderson, *Public Policymaking* (4th ed.) (Boston: Houghton Mifflin, 2000), pp. 233–244.
12. James E. Anderson, *Public Policymaking* (Boston: Houghton Mifflin, 1986), pp. 94–98.
13. B. Guy Peters, *American Public Policy: Promise and Performance* (Chappaqua: Chatham House, 1999), pp. 59–67.

14. C. Lindblom, "The 'Science' of Muddling Through," *Public Administration Review*, 19 (Spring 1959), pp. 79–88.

15. I. Gordon, J. Lewis and K. Young, "Perspectives on Policy Analysis," *Public Administration Bulletin*, 25 (August 1977), pp. 26–35.

16. D. MacRae and T. Wilde, *Policy Analysis for Public Decisions* (Belmont, CA: Wadsworth, 1985), pp. 7–11; C. Patton and D. Sawicki, *Basic Methods of Policy Analysis* (Englewood Cliffs, N.J.: Prentice Hall, 1986), p. 35; E. Bardach, *A Practical Guide for Policy Analysis* (Chatham: Chatham House, 2000), pp. 20–26.

17. C. Patton and D. Sawicki, *Basic Methods of Policy Analysis* (Englewood Cliffs, N.J.: Prentice Hall, 1986), p. 29.

18. L. A. Gunn, "Why Is Implementation So Difficult?" *Management Services in Government* 33, no. 4 (November 1978), 169–176.

19. Anthony Downs, *Inside Bureaucracy* (Boston: Little, Brown, 1967).

20. Richard Matland (this reader, part 5, reading 51).

21. Martha Derthick, "Defeat at Ft. Lincoln," *The Public Interest*, 20 (Summer 1970), pp. 3–39; J.L. Pressman and A. Wildavsky, *Implementation* (Berkeley: University of California Press, 1994); E. Bardach, *The Implementation Game: What Happens After a Bill Becomes a Law* (Cambridge, M.A.: MIT Press, 1977).

22. *Ibid*. Matland.

23. Richard Ellmore, "Backward Mapping: Implementation Research and Policy Decision," *Political Science Quarterly*, 94 (Winter 1979), pp. 606–616. Also, Paul A. Sabatier, "Top-Down and Bottom-Up Approaches to Implementation Research: A Critical Analysis and Suggested Synthesis," *Journal of Public Policy* 6, no. 1 (1986), pp. 22–48.

24. *Ibid*. Matland

25. *Ibid*. Matland.

26. Giandomenico, Majone and Aaron Wildavsky, "Implementation as Evolution" in *Implementation* (3rd ed.) (Berkeley: University of California Press, 1984), pp. 163–180, eds. Jeffrey Pressman and Aaron Wildavsky.

27. Paul Sabatier, "Top-Down and Bottom-Up Approaches to Implementation Research: A Critical Analysis and Suggested Synthesis," *Journal of Public Policy* 6, no. 1 (January–March 1986), p. 37.

28. Brian Hogwood and others, *Policy Analysis for the Real World* (Oxford: Oxford University Press, 1984), pp. 199–206. These authors draw upon several writers on implementation to list ten preconditions that have to be satisfied for successful implementation.

29. Paul Berman, "Thinking about Programmed and Adaptive Implementation," in *Why Policies Succeed or Fail*, (Newbury Park, Calif.: Sage, 1980), eds. Helen Ingram and Dean Mann.

30. C. Weiss, *Evaluation: Methods for Studying Programs and Policies* (2nd ed.) (Upper Saddle River, N.J.: Prentice Hall, 1998).

31. J. R. Sanders, *The Program Evaluation Standards* (Thousand Oaks, CA: Sage, 1994), pp. 8–12.

32. Essential Activities in the Evaluation Process:- Identification of goals and objectives of the program/policy in such a way to make measurement possible; Comprehension of Mission Statement or noting absence of on; Construction of analytic model of what program/policy is expected to achieve, this includes a set of theoretical propositions about means–end relationships; Development of a research design to distinguish actual program/policy goals from what are actually achieved; Collection of data or actual measurement; Analysis and interpretation of data.

33. M.E. Rushefsky, *Public Policy in The United States* (Belmont: Wadsworth, 1990), p. 16.

34. R. Haverman, "Policy Evaluation Research After Twenty Years," *Policy Studies Journal* 16, no. 2 (Winter 1987), pp. 191–218; M. J. Dubnick and B. A. Bardes, *Thinking About Public Policy* (New York: Wiley, 1983), p. 203.

35. B. Guy Peters, *American Public Policy* (Washington, D.C.: CQ Press, 2009), pp. 100–161.

36. *Ibid*. Peters, pp. 161–163.

37. Peter DeLeon, "A Theory of Policy Termination," in *The Policy Cycle* (Beverly Hills: Sage, 1978), pp. 173–202.

38. J.P. Lester and J. Stewart Jr., *Public Policy: An Evolutionary Approach* (2nd ed.) (Belmont: Wadsworth, 2000), pp. 156–157.

39. R. Behn, "How to Terminate a Public Policy: A Dozen Hints for the Would be Terminator," *Policy Analysis* 4, no. 3 (Summer 1978), pp. 393–413.

40. R. Hofferbert, *The Study of Public Policy* (Indianapolis: Bobbs Merrill, 1974).

41. This discussion of the institutional, historical, and environmental contexts draws extensively

upon the work of Clarke E. Cochran and others, *American Public Policy* (4th ed.) (New York: St. Martin's Press, 1993), Chapter 1; and James Anderson and others, *Public Policy and Politics in America* (Monterey: Brooks/Cole, 1984), pp. 7–16.

42. See L. Pliatzky, *Getting and Spending: Public Expenditure, Employment and Inflation* (2nd ed.) (Oxford: Basil Blackwell, 1984).

43. Irene S. Rubin, *The Politics of Public Budgeting* (2nd ed.) (Chatham, N.J.: Chatham House, 1993), pp. 1–6; 10–20.

44. Hugh Heclo and Aaron Wildavsky, *The Private Government of Public Money* (2nd ed.) (London: Macmillan, 1981), pp. 35–36.

Suggested Further Reading

ALBAEK, E, "Why All This Evaluation? Theoretical Notes and Empirical Observations on the Functions and Growth of Evaluation," *Canadian Journal of Program Evaluation* 11, no. 2 (August 1996), pp. 1–34.

ALBAEK, E, "Knowledge, Interests, and the Many Meanings of Evaluation: A Developmental Perspective," *Scandinavian Journal of Social Welfare,* 7 (April 1998), pp. 94–98.

BARDACH, Eugene, *The Implementation Game: What Happens After a Bill Becomes a Law.* Cambridge, M.A.: MIT Press, 1977.

———. *A Practical Guide For Policy Analysis: The Eightfold Path to More Effective Problem Solving.* Washington, D.C.: CQ Press, 2005.

BERMAN, PAUL. "Thinking About Programmed and Adaptive Implementation: Matching Strategies to Situations." In *Why Policies Succeed or Fail*, ed. Helen Ingram and Dean Mann, pp. 205–227. Beverly Hills, CA: Sage, 1980.

BINGHAM, RICHARD D. and CLAIRE FELBINGER. *Evaluation in Practice: A Methodological Approach.* N.Y.: Seven Bridges Press, 2002.

BREWER, GARRY D. and DELEON, PETER. *The Foundations of Policy Analysis.* Homewood, I.L.: Dorsey Press, 1983.

BREWER, G.D. "Termination: Hard Choices, Harder Question." *Public Administration Review* 38, no. 4 (July/August 1978), pp. 338–344.

DANIELS, M.R. *Terminating Public Programs: An American Paradox.* New York: M.E. Sharpe, 1997.

EULAU, HEINZ. "The Workshop: The Place of Policy Analysis in Political Science: Five Perspectives."

American Journal of Political Science, 23 (May 1977), pp. 415–433.

FERMAN, BARBARA. "When Failure Is Success: Implementation and Madisonian Government." In *Implementation and the Policy Process: Opening Up the Black Box,* ed. Dennis Palumbo and Donald Calista, pp. 39–50. Westport, C.T.: Greenwood Press, 1990.

FITZPATRICK, JODY L., SANDERS, JAMES R., and WORTHEN, BLAINE. *Program Evaluation: Alternative Approaches and Practical Guidelines.* Boston, M.A.: Pearson, 2004.

FRANTZ, J.E. "Reviving and Revising a Termination Model," *Policy Sciences,* 25 (May 1992), pp. 175–189.

GOOGIN, MALCOLM, BOWMAN, ANN O'M., LESTER, JAMES, and O'TOOLE JR., LAURENCE. *Implementation Theory and Practice: Towards a Third Generation.* Glenview, I.L.: Scott, Foresman/Little Brown, 1990.

R. HAVERMAN, "Policy Evaluation Research After Twenty Years," *Policy Studies Journal* 16, no. 2 (Winter 1987), pp. 191–218.

HJERN, BENNY. "Implementation Research: The Link Gone Missing." *Journal of Public Policy,* 2 (August 1982), pp. 301–308.

HJERN, BENNY, and HULL, CHRIS. "Implementation Research as Empirical Constitutionalism." *European Journal of Political Research,* 10 (June 1983), pp. 105–115.

INGRAM, HELEN M. and SCHNEIDER, A.L. "Policy Analysis for Democracy." In *The Oxford Handbook of Public Policy,* eds. Michael Moran, Martin Rein, and Robert E. Goodin, pp. 169–189. New York: Oxford University Press, 2006.

JAMES, THOMAS E. and JORGENSEN, PAUL D. "Policy Knowledge, Policy formulation, and Change: Revisiting a Foundational Question." *Policy Studies Journal* 37, no. 1 (February 2009), pp. 141–162.

LIPSKY, MICHAEL. "Street Level Bureaucracy and the Analysis of Urban Reform." *Urban Affairs Quarterly,* 6 (June 1971), pp. 391–409.

MAJONE, GIANDOMENICO. "Agenda Setting." In *The Oxford Handbook of Public Policy,* eds. Michael Moran, Martin Rein, and Robert E. Goodin, pp. 228–250. New York: Oxford University Press, 2006.

MAJONE, GIANDOMENICO and WILDAVSKY, AARON. "Implementation as Evolution." In *Implementation,* eds. Jeffrey Pressman and Aaron Wildavsky. Berkeley, CA: University of California Press, 1979.

MARK, M.M., HENRY, G.T., and JULNES, G. "Toward an Integrative Framework for Evaluation Practice." *American Journal of Evaluation,* 20 (June 1999), pp. 177–198.

MATLAND, RICHARD. "Synthesizing the Implementation Literature: The Ambiguity-Conflict Model of Policy Implementation." *Journal of Public Administration Research and Theory,* 5 (April 1995), pp. 145–174.

MAZMANIAN, DANIEL, and SABATIER, PAUL. *Implementation and Public Policy.* Glendale, I.L.: Scott, Foresman, 1983.

MUNGER, MICHAEL. *Analyzing Policy: Choices, Conflicts, and Practices.* New York: W.W. Norton, 2000.

NACHIMAS, D. *Public Policy Evaluation: Approaches and Methods.* New York: St. Martin's Press, 1979).

NAKAMURA, ROBERT and SMALLWOOD, FRANK. *The Politics of Policy Implementation.* New York: St. Martin's, 1980.

NEIMAN MAX and STAMBOUGH, STEPHEN J. "Rational Choice Theory and the Evaluation of Public Policy." *Policy Studies Journal,* 26, no. 3 (September 1998), pp. 449–465.

O'TOOLE JR., LAURENCE J. "Rational Choice and Policy Implementation: Implications for Interorganizational Network Management." *American Review of Public Administration,* 25 (March 1995), pp. 43–57.

———. "Research on Policy Implementation: Assessments and Prospects." *Journal of Public Administration Research and Theory,* 20 (April 2000), pp. 263–288.

PRESSMAN, JEFFREY and WILDAVSKY, AARON. *Implementation: How Great Expectations in Washington Are Dashed in Oakland.* Berkeley, CA: University of California Press, 1973.

RADIN, BERYL. *Beyond Machiavelli: Policy Analysis Comes of Age.* Washington, D.C.: Georgetown University Press, 2000.

SHULOCK, NANCY. "The Paradox of Policy Analysis: If It Is Not Used, Why Do We Produce So Much of It?" *Journal of Policy Analysis and Management,* 18 (Spring 1997), pp. 226–244.

SYLVIA, R.D., SYLVIA, K.M., and GUNN, E.M. *Program Planning and Evaluation for the Public Manager* (2nd ed.). Prospect Heights: Waveland Press, 1997.

WEISS, C. *Evaluation: Methods for Studying Programs and Policies* (2nd ed.). Upper Saddle River, N.J.: Prentice Hall, 1998.

WEIMER, DAVID and VINING, AIDAN. *Policy Analysis: Concepts and Practice.* Upper Saddle River, N.J.: Prentice Hall, 2005.

WILSON, RICHARD. "Policy Analysis as Policy Advice." In *The Oxford Handbook of Public Policy,* eds. Michael Moran, Martin Rein, and Robert E. Goodin, pp. 152–168. New York: Oxford University Press.

WOOD, B. DAN and DOAN, ALESHA. "The Politics of Problem Definition: Applying and Testing Threshold Models." *American Journal of Political Science,* 47 (October 2003), pp. 640–653.

WOOD, B. DAN and VEDLITZ, ARNOLD. "Issue Definition, Information Processing, and the Politics of Global Warming." *American Journal of Political Science,* 51 (July 2007), pp. 552–568.

YANOW, D. *Conducting Interpretive Policy Analysis.* Newbury Park, CA: Sage, 2000.

45

Causal Stories as Problem Definition

Deborah A. Stone

Men do not think they know a thing till they have grasped the "why" of it (which is to grasp its primary cause).

Aristotle's Physica, Book II

Aristotle's treatise on causes speaks to a fundamental human instinct to search for the cause of any problem. We often think we have defined a problem when we have described its causes. Policy debate is dominated by the notion that to solve a problem, one must find its root cause or causes; treating the symptoms is not enough. Analysis of causes is so much taken for granted that it is scarcely mentioned in policy analysis textbooks. What most scholars have to say about causal analysis is that it is difficult, that policy problems are complex, and that we often lack a good understanding of underlying causal processes. But they are unanimous in their belief that one cannot solve a problem without first finding its underlying cause or causes.

The effort to define a problem by identifying the causes of bad conditions rests on a certain conception of cause. In this conception, any problem has deep or primary causes that can be found if one only looks hard enough and does enough careful research. Causes are objective and can, in principle, be proved by scientific research. We speak of suspected causes and true causes as though once a true cause is found, suspected causes are off the hook and the true cause, like the convicted criminal, bears some known

relationship to the problem. Once "the" cause is identified, policy should seek to eliminate it, modify it, reduce it, suppress it, or neutralize it, thereby eliminating or reducing the problem.

Causal reasoning in the polis is something quite different from this mechanistic model. In politics, we look for causes not only to understand how the world works but to assign responsibility for problems. Once we think we know the cause of a problem, we use the knowledge to prevent people from causing the problem, to make them compensate other people for bearing the problem, and to punish them for having caused suffering. To identify a cause in the polis is to place burdens on one set of people instead of another. It is also to tell a story in which one set of people are oppressors and another are victims.

In the polis, causal stories are strategically crafted with symbols and numbers and then asserted by political actors who try to make their versions the basis of policy choices. Causal stories are essential political instruments for shaping alliances and for settling the distribution of benefits and costs.

CAUSAL STORIES AS PROBLEM DEFINITION

We have two primary frameworks for interpreting the world: the natural and the social. In the natural world, we understand occurrences to be

From Deborah Stone, *Policy Paradox: The Art of Political Decision Making* (New York: W.W. Norton and Co., 1997), pp. 188–209.

"undirected, unoriented, unanimated, unguided, 'purely physical.'"[1] There may be natural determinants—the clash of a cold front and a warm front causes a storm—but there is no willful intention behind the occurrences (at least not without invoking a purposeful God). The natural world is the realm of fate and accident, and we believe we have an adequate understanding of causation when we can describe the sequence of events by which one thing leads to another.

In the social world we understand events to be the result of will, usually human but perhaps animal. The social world is the realm of control and intent. We usually think we have an adequate understanding of causation when we can identify the purposes or motives of a person or group and link those purposes to their actions. Because we understand causation in the social sphere as related to purpose, we believe that influence works. Coaxing, flattering, bribing, and threatening make sense as efforts to change the course of events, and it is possible to conceive of preventing things from happening in the first place. In the natural world, influence has no place. We laugh at those who would bring rain with their dances or sweet-talk their computer into compliance. In the natural world, the best we can do is to mitigate effects.

In everyday discourse, as Erving Goffman points out, we use the term causality to refer to both "the blind effect of nature and intended effect of man, the first seen as an infinitely extended chain of caused and causing effects and the second something that somehow begins with a mental decision."[2] Yet in policy and politics, the distinction between actions that have purpose, will, or motivation and those that do not is crucial. So, too, is the distinction between effects that are intended and those that are not, since we know all too well that our purposeful actions may have unintended consequences.

These two distinctions—between action and consequences and between purpose and lack of purpose—can be used to create a framework for describing the causal stories used in politics. Each section of Table 45.1 contains a type of causal story commonly asserted in policy argument. The types are rough categories with fuzzy boundaries, not clear dichotomies. Once you recognize the different types, though, you can analyze how political actors strategically represent issues by framing them as different types of causal stories, or metaphorically, by pushing them around from one box to another.

In the upper right box are *accidental causes*. These include natural disasters such as floods, earthquakes, droughts, and hurricanes. Here, too, goes anything our culture understands as belonging to the realm of fate—perhaps personal looks, some aspects of health, a person's good fortune to have bet the right lottery number or purchased a company's stock just before a takeover bid. Here we might also put machines that run amok—the car that careens out of control or the CAT scanner that crushes its captive patient. These phenomena are devoid of purpose, either in their actions or consequences. In fact, one cannot properly speak of actions here, but only of occurrences. This is the realm of accident and fate. Politically, this is a good place to retreat if one is being charged with responsibility, because no one is responsible in the realm of fate.

At the opposite pole politically are *intentional causes* (in the lower left section). Asserting a story of intentional cause is the most powerful offensive position to take, because it lays the blame directly at someone's feet, and because it casts someone as willfully or knowingly causing harm. In this kind of story, problems or harms are understood as direct consequences of willful human action. Either someone acted in order to bring about the consequences, or someone acted with full knowledge of what the consequences would be. When the consequences are perceived as good, this is the domain we know as rational action. But when the consequences of purposeful human action are perceived as bad, we have stories of oppressors and victims. One interpretation of immigration policy, for example, holds that the plight—and to some extent the sheer presence—of illegal immigrants is directly traceable to deliberate decisions on the part of American legislators and bureaucrats. Many politicians support permissive immigration rules for agricultural workers and other very low wage industries, and the Immigration and Naturalization Service accommodates the needs of employers by being

TABLE 45.1	Types of Causal Theories with Examples	

| | Consequences | |
Actions	Intended	Unintended
Unguided	MECHANICAL CAUSE	ACCIDENTAL CAUSE
	intervening agent(s)	nature
	brainwashed people	weather
	machines that perform as designed, but cause harm	earthquakes
		machines that run amok
Purposeful	INTENTIONAL CAUSE	INADVERTENT CAUSE
	oppression	intervening conditions
	conspiracies that work	unforeseen side effects
	programs that work as intended, but cause harm	avoidable ignorance carelessness
		omission

lax in enforcing the law. Yet many of these same politicians, such as California's governor Pete Wilson, accuse illegal immigrants of flouting the law and of taking social aid they don't deserve, when in fact (the interpretation goes), American recruitment and underpayment of illegal workers is the cause of whatever problems illegal immigrants generate.[3]

In this box also belong conspiracy stories. Here, the argument is that problems are the result of deliberate but concealed human action. For example, congressional hearings in 1994 developed the line of argument that smoking-related disease and death was due not so much to personal choices about smoking as to tobacco companies' deliberate efforts to conceal scientific evidence about the dangers of smoking. Cigarette manufacturers advertised and promoted smoking, knowing full well that nicotine is addictive and that smoking is a health hazard.[4]

In the lower right section are *inadvertent causes*, or the unintended consequences of willed human action. (Actions often have good side effects, but I will ignore these, since politics is usually concerned with problems.) One type of story here is the tale of harmful side effects of well-intentioned policy. Here, the consequences are predictable but still unforeseen. Proponents of free markets and deregulation often tell such stories, whose gist is that knowledgeable economists could have predicted why government interference with markets would fail. Rent control, for example, is intended to make housing affordable but drives landlords out of the market by restricting their income, reduces rental housing stock, and raises the price of remaining housing.[5] Minimum wage laws are passed by softhearted politicians who want to protect the standard of living of low-wage workers, but any first-year student of economics knows that if the cost of hiring workers goes up, employers will hire fewer of them, and so higher unemployment will result.[6] The larger, more general, argument that governments inevitably make things worse when they interfere with private markets is an example of what Albert Hirschman calls "the perversity thesis," and as he notes, this is a common pattern of conservative argument against social change, whether the change is increasing voting participation, redistributing income, or expanding the welfare state.[7]

The story of inadvertent cause is a common interpretation of poverty, malnutrition, and disease. Accordingly, the poor don't realize how important it is to get an education or save money; the elderly don't understand how important it is to eat a balanced diet even if they are not hungry;

and the sick don't understand that overeating leads to diabetes and heart disease. Inadvertence here is ignorance. Ordinary people do not understand the harmful consequences of their willful actions, even though the consequences are predictable by experts. These stories are soft (liberal) versions of "blaming the victim:" if the person with the problem only became more informed and changed his or her behavior, the problem would not exist. (A conservative version of blaming the victim is intentional causation: the victim actually chooses to have the problem. Many people, so the story goes, calculate the economic returns of working versus the returns from welfare, and choose to go on AFDC, and thus to remain poor.)

Another type of inadvertence is carelessness or recklessness. Problems in occupational safety and health are often explained in this rubric, although carelessness is alternately attributed to labor or management. In management's version, workers understand the dangers of machines or chemicals but decline to use protective gear and safety devices because their tasks are easier, more comfortable, or faster without the precautions. In labor's version, management understands the hazards, but does not monitor equipment conscientiously or provide safety gear, hoping it can keep productivity up without any undue mishaps. And in a more radical labor version, management knowingly stints on safety in the interests of profits, a conscious trade-off that pushes the problem into the sphere of intent.

In the upper left section are *mechanical causes*, which include things that have no will of their own but are designed, programmed, or trained by humans to produce certain consequences. The idea of mechanical cause is that somebody acts purposefully, but their will is carried out through other people, through machines, or through "automatic" social procedures and routines. Their purposeful actions are guided only indirectly, through an intervening agent. When, for example, a policy or program is implemented by subordinates who rigidly follow orders and fail to exercise their own discretion, problems might be understood as the result of humans acting like automatons.

In mechanical cause, the exact nature of human guidance or control is then at issue.

Often, a fight about the cause of a problem is a debate about whether certain people are acting out of their own will or mechanically carrying out the will of others. To return to the example of malnutrition, a liberal causal story rests on unintended consequences of purposeful action: malnourished people do not know how to eat a proper diet. A conservative story rests on intended consequences of purposeful action: malnourished people knowingly choose to spend their food money on beer and junk food. And a radical causal story rests on indirect control: food processors and advertisers, in their quest for profits, manipulate people into eating junk food and unbalanced diets.

If the nature of human control over other humans is problematic, so is human control over machines. After a chemical leak at its plant in West Virginia, Union Carbide officials immediately blamed a computer for their delay in notifying local authorities. The computer had erroneously predicted that a toxic gas cloud would not leave the plant site. This was a story of accidental breakdown. Then the president of the company that produced the computer safety system said the computer had never been programmed to detect the toxin in the cloud, aldicarb oxime. "The computer worked exactly the way it was supposed to," he affirmed, changing the story to pure mechanism. He revealed that his company could have provided a more expensive safety system that would have detected the leak, predicted the flow of the cloud, and automatically notified local authorities, but Union Carbide had ordered only the "basic model."[8] With this information, it began to look like Union Carbide had intentionally stinted on safety, deliberately choosing not to buy a more comprehensive safety system while knowing that some hazards would not be prevented.

By the end of the week, the Union Carbide story had grown hopelessly complex. The injuries from the leak could be traced to a tank that wasn't designed to hold aldicarb oxime, faulty meters on another tank, defective safety valves, weak gaskets, pipes too small for the job, mistaken transmission of steam to the tank, failure of control room operators to notice pressure and temperature gauges, failure of the computer to detect the spreading gas cloud, failure of executives to purchase a program that could detect the chemical, and failure of government to regulate the chemical industry.[9]

The Union Carbide incident suggests a type of causal story far more complex than can be contained in the table. The ideas of accidental, mechanical, intentional, and inadvertent causes all conjure up images of a single actor, a single action, and a direct result. This underlying image remains even when the ideas are applied to corporations, agencies, and large groups, or to sequences of identifiable actions and results. Many policy problems—the toxic hazard problem notable among them—require a more complex model of cause to offer any satisfying explanation. There is a wide variety of such models, but let me paint three broad types.

One type might be called complex systems.[10] This model holds that the social systems necessary to solve modern problems are inherently complex. Today's technological systems, such as chemical production, involve parts that serve multiple functions, juxtaposition of different environments (say, high and low temperatures), complicated feedback loops, multiple human decision-makers, and interactions between different parts of a system. In such complex interactive systems, it is impossible to anticipate all possible events and effects, so failure or accident is inevitable. Failures also involve so many components and people that it is impossible to attribute blame in any fashion consistent with our cultural norm that responsibility presupposes control.

A second type of complex cause might be called institutional. This model envisions a social problem as caused by a web of large, longstanding organizations with ingrained patterns of behavior. The problem of cost overruns and "gold plating" in weapons acquisition—symbolized by $91 screws and $630 toilet seats—has been explained in these terms. The armed services operate with a basic drive to "have the edge in operational performance" over the other side. They believe that it pays to develop the best-quality weapons during peacetime because Congress will certainly authorize high-quantity production during wars. The different service branches gain by colluding for overall increases in the defense budget rather than competing with each other for a fixed pie. The services also gain by colluding with industry contractors to push programs through Congress on the basis of low initial cost estimates and coming back later for increased appropriations once there have been sunk costs. As one analyst says, "the causes of gold plating in its broadest sense are rooted in the institutional interests and professional outlooks of the military."[11]

A third type of complex cause might be called historical. Quite similar to institutional explanations, this model holds that social patterns tend to reproduce themselves. People with power and resources to stop a problem benefit from the social organization and resource distribution that keeps them in power, and so maintain these patterns through control over selection of elites and socialization of both elites and non-elites. People who are victimized by a problem do not seek political change because they do not see the problem as changeable, do not believe they could bring about change, and need the material resources for survival provided by the status quo.[12]

In politics, ironically, models of complex cause often function like accidental or natural cause. They postulate a kind of innocence, because no identifiable actor can exert control over the whole system or web of interactions. Without overarching control, there can be no purpose—and no responsibility. Complex causal explanations are not very useful in politics, precisely because they do not offer a single locus of control, a plausible candidate to take responsibility for a problem, or a point of leverage to fix a problem. Hence one of the biggest tensions between social science and real-world politics: social scientists tend to see complex causes of social problems, while in politics, people search for immediate and simple causes.

In politics, causal theories are neither right nor wrong, nor are they mutually exclusive. They are ideas about causation, and policy politics involves strategically portraying issues so that they fit one causal idea or another. The different sides in an issue act as if they are trying to find the "true" cause, but they are always struggling to influence which idea is selected to guide policy. Political conflicts over causal stories are therefore more than empirical claims about sequences of events. They are fights about the possibility of control and the assignment of responsibility. ...

CAUSAL STRATEGIES IN PROBLEM DEFINITION

1. Show that the problem is caused by an accident of nature.
2. Show that a problem formerly interpreted as accident is really the result of human agency.
3. Show that the effects of an action were secretly intended by the actor.
4. Show that the low-probability effects of an action were accepted as a calculated risk by the actor.
5. Show that the cause of the problem is so complex that only large-scale policy changes at the social level can alter the cause.

End Notes

1. Erving Goffman, *Frame Analysis* (New York: Harper & Row, 1974), p. 22.
2. Ibid., p. 23.
3. Peter Shuck, "The Message of 187," *The American Prospect*, no. 21 (Winter 1995): 85–92.
4. Philip J. Hilts, "Scientists Say Cigarette Company Suppressed Findings on Nicotine," *New York Times*, Apr. 29, 1994, A1; and Alix M. Freedman and Laurie P. Cohen, "How Cigarette Makers Keep Health Question 'Open' Year After Year," *Wall Street Journal* Feb. 11, 1993, p. A1, A6.
5. William Tucker, *Zoning, Rent Control, and Affordable Housing* (Washington, D.C., Cato Institute, 1991).
6. For the story and a critique, see David Card and Alan Kruger, *Myth and Measurement* (Princeton: Princeton University Press, 1995).
7. Albert O. Hirschman, *The Rhetoric of Reaction* (Cambridge: Harvard University Press, 1991), chap. 2.
8. David E. Sanger, "Carbide Computer Could Not Track Gas That Escaped," *New York Times*, Aug. 14, 1985, pp. 1, 18.
9. See, in addition to the Sanger article in the previous note, Stuart Diamond, "Carbide Blames a Faulty Design for Toxic Leak," *New York Times*, Aug. 13, 1985, pp. A1, B8, and "Chemical Pipe Size Called Key Safety Factor," *New York Times*, Aug. 14, 1985, p. A19; and Robert E. Taylor, "Carbide Tank Wasn't Designed to Hold Chemicals that Leaked," *Wall Street Journal*, Aug. 16, 1985, p. 2.
10. For an excellent statement and exploration of this theory, see Charles Perrow, *Normal Accidents* (New York: Basic Books, 1984).
11. Robert J. Art, "Restructuring the Military-Industrial Complex: Arms Control in Institutional Perspective," *Public Policy* 22, no. 4 (Fall 1974): 423–59. A more theoretical version of institutional causation can be found in Douglas C. North, *Institutions, Institutional Change, and Economic Performance* (Cambridge, England: Cambridge University Press, 1990).
12. An excellent example of this type of argument is Joshua Cohen and Joel Rogers' explanation of how capitalist democracy reproduces itself, in their *On Democracy* (Harmondsworth, England: Penguin, 1983), chap. 3; see also Arthur Stinchcombe, *Constructing Social Theories* (New York: Harcourt Brace, and World, 1968), pp. 101–30.

46

Issues and Agendas

Roger W. Cobb and
Charles D. Elder

...An issue is a conflict between two or more identifiable groups over procedural or substantive matters relating to the distribution of positions or resources. Generally, there are four means by which issues are created. The most common method is the manufacturing of an issue by one or more of the contending parties who perceive an unfavorable bias in the distribution of positions or resources. For example, in 1950 truckers in Pennsylvania thought the railroads had an inherent advantage in carrying freight over long distances and sought to create an issue to redress this imbalance.[1] Such initiators are labeled "readjustors."

Another form of issue creation can be traced to a person or group who manufacture an issue for their own gain; for example, individuals who want to run for public office and are looking for an issue to advance their cause. Such individuals may be labeled "exploiters." As Herbert Blumer has written:

The gaining of sympathizers or members rarely occurs through a mere combination of a pre-established appeal and a pre-established individual psychological bent on which it is brought to bear. Instead the prospective sympathizer has to be aroused, nurtured and directed.[2]

Hans Toch echoes a similar sentiment when he writes:

People are brought into social movements through the skills of leaders and agitators rather than because of pre-existing problems.... Appeals seem to originate with people who are primarily interested in other ends than the solution of the problems of potential members.[3]

Another means of issue initiation is through an unanticipated event. Such events could be called "circumstantial reactors." Examples include the development of an oil slick off the California coast near Santa Barbara in early 1969 that led to a reconsideration of the whole question of offshore drilling regulations. Other examples are the assassination of President Kennedy, which led to the gun control issue, and Eisenhower's heart attack in the mid-1950's, which raised the question of presidential disability.

Issues can be generated by persons or groups who have no positions or resources to gain for themselves. Often, they merely acquire a psychological sense of well-being for doing what they believe is in the public interest. These initiators might be called "do-gooders." The efforts to support Biafran relief programs fall in this category.

The above categories are not mutually exclusive, as an individual or group may have more than one motive for a particular action. For example, some people supported civil rights legislation because they felt it was humanitarian, while others supported it because they sought personal or collective gains.

Triggering Devices

At least two classes of triggering mechanisms, or unforeseen events, help shape issues that will be defined by the initiators. These can be subdivided into internal and external events that correspond to the domestic and foreign spheres.

Within the internal subdivision, there are five types of triggering devices. The first is a natural catastrophe, such as a mine cave-in, air inversion, flooding, and fire. The second is an unanticipated human event, such as a spontaneous riot, assassination of public officials, air hijackings, and murder of private individuals. The third is a technological change in the environment that creates heretofore undiscussed questions. It might involve mass transportation, air and water pollution, or air travel congestion. The fourth category is an actual imbalance, or bias, in the distribution of resources leading to such things as civil rights protest and union strikes.[4] A fifth type is ecological change, such as population explosion and black migration to Northern cities.

There are four types of external trigger mechanisms. The first is an act of war or military violence involving the United States as a direct combatant. Examples include the Vietnam war, the Pueblo seizure, and the dropping of atomic bombs on Hiroshima. The second category includes innovations in weapons technology involving such things as arms control, the Hotline between the Kremlin and the White House, and the deployment of an anti-ballistic system. The third type is an international conflict in which the United States is not a direct combatant, such as the conflicts in the Middle East and the Congo. The final category involves changing world alignment patterns that may affect American membership in the United Nations, troop commitments in the North Atlantic Treaty Organization, and the American role in the Organization of American States.

Issue Initiation and Trigger Mechanisms

The formation of an issue is dependent on the dynamic interplay between the initiator and the trigger device. This can be seen in the following diagram:

For example, a mine disaster itself does not create an issue. Many times in the past such an event has occurred with no ameliorative action. A link must be made between a grievance (or a triggering event) and an initiator who converts the problem into an issue for a private or a public reason.

In a system perspective, the inputs consist of the initiator and the event, or triggering mechanism, that transform the problem into an issue. ...

AGENDAS: WHAT ARE THEY?

In general terms, we have identified two basic types of political agendas. The first of these is the systemic agenda for political controversy. *The systemic agenda consists of all issues that are commonly perceived by members of the political community as meriting public attention and as involving matters within the legitimate jurisdiction of existing governmental authority.* Every local, state, and national political community will have a systemic agenda. The systemic agenda of the larger community may subsume items from the systemic agendas of subsidiary communities, but the two agendas will not necessarily correspond. For example, the systemic agenda of Boston may include items on the national agenda of controversy, such as pollution and crime in the streets, but will also include such items as the need for a new sports arena.

There are three prerequisites for an issue to obtain access to the systemic agenda:

(1) widespread attention or at least awareness; (2) shared concern of a sizeable portion of the public that some type of action is required; and (3) a shared perception that the matter is an appropriate concern of some governmental unit and falls within the bounds of its authority. The terms "shared concern" and "shared perception" refer to the prevailing climate of opinion, which will be conditioned by the dominant norms, values, and ideology of a community. An issue requires the recognition of only a major portion of the polity, not the entire citizenry.

For an item or an issue to acquire public recognition, its supporters must have either access to the mass media or the resources necessary to reach people. They may require more than money and manpower; often the use of action rhetoric is essential. For example, use of terms such as *communist-inspired* or *anti-American* is a useful verbal ploy in attracting a larger audience than the original adherents of a cause.

In addition to gaining popular recognition, the issue must be perceived by a large number of people as both being subject to remedial action and requiring such action. In other words, action must be considered not only possible, but also necessary for the resolution of the issue. To foster such popular conviction, the mobilization of a significant number of groups or persons will normally be required.

Often, the fate of an issue in gaining systemic agenda status will hinge on whether or not it can be defined as being within the purview of legitimate governmental action. Perhaps one of the most devastating tactics that may be used to prevent an issue from reaching the systemic agenda is to deny that it falls within the bounds of governmental authority. For example, equal access to public accommodations was kept off the systemic agenda for some time because opponents successfully argued that the grievance fell outside the proper bounds of governmental authority.

The second type of agenda is the institutional, governmental, or formal agenda, which may be defined as *that set of items explicitly up for the active and serious consideration of authoritative decision-makers.* Therefore, any set of items up before any governmental body at the local, state, or national level will constitute an institutional agenda.

Two clarifications are in order regarding key terms in the above definition of a formal agenda. "Explicitly" refers to an issue involving action or policy alternatives or involving simply the identification of a problem requiring some action. An example of the former would be a proposal to raise the minimum wage to a specific level per hour. An illustration of the latter would be a reconsideration of certain restrictive loan practices of savings and loan institutions in the ghetto.

"Active and serious" are used to distinguish formal agenda items from what might be called "pseudo-agenda items." By pseudo-agenda, we mean any form of registering or acknowledging a demand without explicitly considering its merit. Decision-makers will often use such an agenda to assuage frustrations of constituency groups and to avoid political ramifications of a failure to acknowledge the demand. This typically occurs in a legislature where bills are placed in the hopper to placate some groups of activists with no real chance of action being taken.

Policy-makers will participate in the building of both systemic and institutional agendas. However, the natures of the two agendas are substantially different. The systemic agenda will be composed of fairly abstract and general items that do little more than identify a problem area. It will not necessarily suggest either the alternatives available or the means of coping with the problem. For example, it might include a vague item like "ending discrimination."

An institutional agenda will tend to be more specific, concrete, and limited in the number of items. It will identify, at least implicitly, those facets of a problem that are to be seriously considered by a decision-making body. An example would be a city council's consideration of alternative forms of local taxation for the support of public schools. It is possible for an item to get onto the formal agenda without having been a part of the systemic agenda. Each year, Congress considers many private bills of little social import or concern. However, it is unlikely that any issue involving substantial social consequences will gain standing on a governmental agenda unless it has first attained systemic agenda status.

Content of Formal Agendas

Formal agenda items can be divided into two major categories: *old items* and *new items*. *Old items* are those that have action alternatives delineated. They are predefined in most instances, except in specific cases (for example, the issue may not be whether workers will receive a 5 percent or a 10 percent raise, but whether they will get a raise at all).

There are two agenda components under the general heading of *old items*. Habitual items include those that come up for regular review. Examples would be budget items such as personnel pay and fights between existing agencies for a larger slice of the federal budget.

Recurrent items are those that occur with some periodicity, but need not appear at regular intervals. Examples would include governmental reorganization and regulation arising from a concern for efficiency or economy or both, rules changes in the legislature (for example, the filibuster in the Senate), Congressional reform, tariff items, tax reform, and social security increases or extensions.

The second general heading, *new items,* refers to those components that have no predetermined definitions, but are flexible in their interpretation or development. The first subdivision would include automatic or spontaneous issues appearing as an action or reaction of a key decision-maker in a specific situation. Examples include public employee or major industry strikes with a substantial impact on the economy or our military strength, the steel crisis under President Truman during the Korean War, foreign policy crises (e.g., Korea, Cuba, and the Dominican Republic), and innovations in foreign policy (e.g., American entrance into the United Nations, the test ban treaty, and the nuclear proliferation treaty).

A second component of *new items* is channeled items, those issues channeled to the agenda by the mobilization of mass support or by the activation of significant public groups (e.g., unions). Examples of issues with mass support include the civil rights issues of the 1960's and the gun control issue. Illustrations of issues backed by significant public groups include the Taft-Hartley repeal effort and the farm parity program.

An issue need not be static or confined to one category throughout its existence. At any point in time, it may be redefined. An example of a dynamic issue is the Vietnam policy. Initially, it became a spontaneous issue when President Eisenhower committed several hundred advisers in the late 1950's. The issue of expanded commitment became recurrent under Presidents Kennedy and Johnson. By 1963, the dispute appeared on the docket with great regularity. It continued in this form until opposition to the war—a channelized item begun by peace groups—raised the question of the legitimacy of American involvement. The peace groups expanded concern with American involvement until it became the policy stance of a major presidential candidate in 1968.

The Form of an Institutional Agenda

The explicit form of the formal agenda may be found in the calendar of authoritative decision-making bodies such as legislatures, high courts, or regulatory agencies.[5] Unless an item appears on some docket, it will not be considered to be an agenda item. Agenda composition will vary over time. However, recurrent or habitual items will be the most numerous. They tend to receive priority from the decision-makers, who constantly find that their time is limited and that their agenda is overloaded. Spontaneous, or automatic, items take precedence over channeled items, so it is very difficult to get new issues on the agenda. Decision-makers presume that older problems warrant more attention because of their longevity and the greater familiarity officials have with them.

DIFFERENTIAL ACCESS TO INSTITUTIONAL GATEKEEPERS

The content of a formal agenda will tend to reflect structural and institutional biases found within the system. These biases arise from differential resources among individuals and groups and concomitant differences in access. For an issue to attain agenda status, it must command the support of at least some key decision-makers, for they are the ultimate guardians of the formal agenda.

Political leaders are active participants in the agenda-building process, not simply impartial arbiters of issue disputes. As Bauer, Pool, and Dexter note:

> Congress is not a passive body, registering already-existent public views forced on its attention by public pressures. Congress, second only to the president, is, rather the major institution for initiating and creating political issues and projecting them into a national civic debate.[6]

The strategic location of these leaders assures them of media visibility when they want to promote an issue and places them in an excellent position to bargain with other decision-makers over formal agenda content. Because they have fairly direct control over what will appear on the formal agenda and considerable freedom to choose among the plethora of issues competing for attention, they can insist that an issue of concern to them be considered in return for agreement to consider an issue that is salient to another decision-maker or set of decision-makers.

It is easy then to understand why access to one or more key officials is so important to political groups. As one commentator noted,

> The development and improvement of such access is a common denominator of the tactics of all of them, frequently leading to efforts to exclude competing groups from equivalent access or to set up new decision points access to which can be monopolized by a particular group.[7]

Some groups have a greater ease of access than others, and are thus more likely to get their demands placed on an agenda.

This differential responsiveness arises from a variety of factors. First, the decision-maker may be indebted to a particular group or identify himself as a member of that group. Second, some groups have more resources than others or are better able to mobilize their resources. Third, some groups are located so strategically in the social or economic structure of society that their interests cannot be ignored (for example, big business and agriculture). Fourth, some groups (such as doctors, lawyers and church leaders) are held in greater esteem by the public than others and thus can command greater access to decision-makers. As a consequence, certain groups are more likely than others to receive attention from decision-makers when they come up with new demands. Farmers have an inherent advantage over many other groups in obtaining action on their needs because there are many decision-makers who identify themselves with farm groups and because agriculture occupies a pivotal position in the American economy.

A group may encounter different types of responses from different levels or branches of the government. When the National Association for the Advancement of Colored People first started to press its demands, it focused on the Congress and the presidency, but received no support. However, the group was much more effective when it focused on a judicial strategy of making gains in civil rights through a series of court cases. Thus, differential responsiveness may result from the type of governmental unit petitioned as well as from differences among groups themselves.

Political parties also play an important part in translating issues into agenda items.[8] To assure support, they will often seek out and identify themselves with issues that are salient to large portions of the populace. Typically, these issues are identified in the party platform in general terms and with considerable ambiguity. However, as Truman notes:

> The significance of preparing a platform lies primarily in the evidence that the negotiations provide concerning what groups will have access to the developing national party organization. ... Interest group leaders are aware that the real settlement of the issues they are concerned with ... will take place later; in the platform, they seek tentative assurance of a voice in that settlement. To maximize this assurance, political interest groups normally seek recognition in the platforms of both major parties.[9]

Certainly recognition on a party platform is at least indicative of an issue attaining standing on the systemic agenda of political controversy.[10]

The media can also play a very important role in elevating issues to the systemic agenda and increasing their chances of receiving formal agenda consideration. Certain personages in the media can act as opinion leaders in bringing publicity to a particular issue. Examples of individuals who have gained a larger audience for a dispute include Walter Lippmann, Jack Anderson, and Drew Pearson. Individuals who have acquired an audience simply by constantly appearing in the news can also publicize an issue. Ralph Nader has a ready-made constituency stemming from his many attacks on various inefficient and unscrupulous business practices.

DIFFERENTIAL LEGITIMACY

While most observers grant that there are inequalities in access to decisionmakers, they argue that the existence of multiple points of access owing to different levels and branches of government has the net effect of insuring widespread contacts. Further, the existence of dispersed inequalities (that is, the fact that groups having great resources in one area may not have comparable resources in other areas) supposedly assures that no group will be without political influence in some areas. However, this argument fails to consider the relatively stable pattern of differential legitimacy accorded various social groupings. Differences in accessibility to decision-makers are a function of the relative legitimacy of various groups. For example, a proposal advanced by a group of businessmen to improve traffic flows into the downtown business area is more likely to receive the attention of decision-makers than a counterproposal by ghetto residents to develop more extensive and effective mass transit systems.

The problem confronted by any newly formed group is often how to legitimize the group and the interest represented rather than how to legitimize a particular issue position. The legitimacy of the group will be greatly enhanced by the status and community standing of its members. In other words, people without resources (for example, lower-income groups) will have greater difficulty attaining legitimacy than their higher-income counterparts. For example, the anti-war movement initially promoted by student groups who traditionally have little political standing received little public support until more socially prominent persons and groups entered the fray on their behalf (for example, business groups, military leaders, clergymen, and senators).

Even if an issue is promoted by a group that is perceived to be legitimate, its appearance on a formal agenda may be problematic owing to cultural constraints on the range of issues that are considered legitimate topics for governmental action. Any institutional agenda will be restricted by the prevailing popular sentiment as to what constitutes appropriate matters for governmental attention. For example, federal aid to education was long considered by many to be an inappropriate area for federal governmental action, a fact that precluded active and serious consideration of the merits of the issue for decades. Legitimizing issues that are considered outside of the governmental realm is difficult and normally takes a long time. The net effect of this is that new demands of particularly disadvantaged or deprived groups are the least likely to receive attention on either the systemic agenda of controversy or the institutional agenda. ...

End Notes

1. For a case study of this conflict, see Andrew Hacker, "Pressure Politics in Pennsylvania: The Truckers vs. The Railroads," in Alan Westin. (ed.), *The Uses of Power: 7 Cases in American Politics* (New York: Harcourt, 1962), pp. 323–76.
2. Herbert Blumer, "Collective Behavior," in J. B. Gittler (ed.), *Review of Sociology* (New York: Wiley, 1957), 148.
3. Hans Toch, *The Psychology of Social Movements* (Indianapolis: Bobbs-Merrill, 1965), 87.
4. Here the focus is on *actual* maldistribution of resources. A *perceived* maldistribution is covered by the "readjustor" type of issue initiator.
5. Calendars normally provide predefined agendas for both the legislature and the court. However, most legislatures have some procedure to allow items to be entered on the agenda at the request of one decision-maker without going through the normal procedures of agenda specification. For example, in the Congress, this procedure involves the private calendar. That calendar will

be excluded from our analysis, which focuses on the public and union calendars, where most issues of public import will be found.

6. Raymond Bauer, Ithiel Pool and Lewis Dexter, *American Business and Public Policy* (New York: Atherton Press, 1963), p. 478.

7. David Truman, *The Governmental Process* (New York: Knopf, 1964), p. 264.

8. See, for example, Everett C. Ladd, Jr., *American Political Parties* (New York: W. W. Norton and Company, 1970).

9. Truman, *op. cit.*, p. 285.

10. Significant differences in the platforms of the two major parties may portend a major alteration in the national systemic agenda. This change may be realized through what Key called "a critical election." Certainly a critical, or realigning, election may be taken as an indicator of a major shift in the systemic agenda. See V. O. Key, *Politics, Parties and Pressure Groups*. 5th ed. (New York: Thomas Crowell Company, 1964), pp. 520–36.

47

New Research on Agendas in the Policy Process

Barry Pump

... The literature on agenda setting has matured from developing concepts to analyzing the underpinnings of those concepts. This represents an important development in advancing scholars' understanding of the policy process. Researchers now have a firmer foundation for testing hypotheses about agenda setting. Greater precision about the mechanisms of agenda setting and policy change also help to foster more comparative studies, so general patterns can be discerned regardless of institutional specifics.

Richer descriptions of the policy process have advanced knowledge of how policy entrepreneurs and officials set the agenda. Boscarino (2009) demonstrates how advocacy organizations search out problems to which to attach their preferred solutions. Liu et al. (2009) demonstrate how attention can differ across institutional venues. And Liu, Lindquist, Vedlitz, and Vincent (2010) show that local policymaking adds different contours to the current understandings, finding that coalition- and consensus-building influenced the policy process more than adversarial politics and public opinion. A renewed appreciation for the importance of venue on the agenda setting process is just one way richer descriptions have improved existing research.

Deeper theorizing about how bounded rationality produces policy punctuations has also emerged in the last two years. This theorizing has

From Barry Pump, "Beyond Metaphors: New Research on Agendas in the Policy Process," *Policy studies Journal*, Vol. 39, No. 1, April 2011, pp. 1–12.

focused on institutional friction and information processing (Baumgartner et al., 2009; Workman et al., 2009). The increasing costs of policymaking activity as policy works its way through the process can mean inputs build up to critical thresholds and then cause a flurry of activity as policy makers act to catch up. How information is processed by political institutions also matters in the formulation of policies. This deeper theorizing has also included how the bureaucracy is prepared to send signals to political masters. May et al. (2008) focus on how the bureaucracy pays attention to policy issues and how that affects to what the bureaucracy pays attention. This increased attention to the bureaucracy advances the literature on agenda setting to include even more relevant players.

The bureaucracy is a critical component in understanding the linkages between policy subsystems, and how transboundary policy problems are addressed by connected policymaking institutions. Scholars have recently started moving beyond subsystems to describe how policymakers make sense of the complex issues confronting them. Jochim and May (2010) and Jones and Jenkins-Smith (2009) advance policy scholars' understanding of how to think about these problems that connect several, previously insulated subsystems. For Jochim and May (2010), subsystems are linked by similar ideas, interests and institutions. For Jones and Jenkins-Smith (2009), public opinion is the glue that positions these subsystems in relation to one another.

While this new line of thinking about policymaking remains to be fleshed out, one element of it is clear: the problems facing policymaking communities are increasingly complex, and crises are often the greatest catalysts of transboundary policymaking. Boin (2009) and Lagadec (2009) argue that as crises increase in complexity, there is a new era of policymaking as a result. Modernization, Boin notes, has created "highways for failure" because of the complexity of networked systems (2009, p. 370). Flexibility in policymaking seems to be one way of averting catastrophe.

Yet, there is reason to doubt that widespread crises and interconnected policy regimes actually produce tightly-knit policymaking communities. May et al. (2009a,b) find that the disruption of

the 9/11 terrorist attacks did not dramatically affect significant portions of the subsystems attendant to issues now grouped as "homeland security," such as food safety. Their work forces scholars, again, to consider various nuances of subsystem dynamics. While transportation security subsystems were affected by 9/11, the food safety subsystem was not, despite the reorganization of both into the Department of Homeland Security. Theories of the policy process now have to include the possibility that widespread exogenous shocks produce differentiated policymaking processes.

For all the progress and increased richness in the study of the agenda setting process, however, there remain gaps. Some of the gaps relate to how agenda setting matters to policy adoption, and then, implementation. Other concerns relate to how to operationalize the mechanisms of agenda change. For example, do the president's speeches really count as informative signals to the bureaucracy? Finally, how does agenda setting affect the durability of the legislation enacted?

Howlett (2009) makes the case that many policy scholars have inadequately accounted for the sequence in which policymaking events occur. New Institutionalists, then, are neglecting what American Political Development scholars can bring to the research table analytically: a focus on the role of time. Howlett (2009) argues that instead of focusing on path dependency and increasing returns, policy scholars should view events in the policy process as a series of reactions that do not necessarily produce "lock in" of certain patterns but may in fact reverse earlier events. So while Howlett's critique extends to both New Institutionalists and APD scholars, it nevertheless presses all researchers to take time and the sequence of events seriously.

The role of time is particularly important when looking at the durability of legislation. Patashnik (2008) examines major reform efforts, and discovers that instead of increasing returns to a way of doing business, policy can destroy previous interests opposed to reform—remaking the landscape. His conclusions take aim at both the punctuated equilibrium model of policy change and other models of institutional design as well. For example, Patashnik examines the role of outside interest groups and their downstream effects, unlike those who only look at policy entrepreneurs. The limitations of punctuated equilibrium models is also apparent. Reform efforts, Patashnik finds, can vary in pace and across parts of a subsystem. And punctuations themselves differ in size and import. Studies like Patashnik's are rare at this point, but reflect where implementation research is headed.

There seems to be endless variation in the politics of agenda setting and downstream developments. This variation poses a challenge to analysts seeking a way to create general predictive models of individual and organizational behavior. The challenges of complex problems and the often sclerotic nature of bureaucracy only add to the challenges. As a result, the policy process literature seems stuck between "grand theories that are not helpful and helpful theories that are not grand" (Weimer, 2008, 493).

Another potential challenge may be embedded in the literature analyzed above. The complexity of policy problems, the role of information in the policy process, and the speed at which problems change (think of the exponential rise in mean temperatures indicating climate change) all point to a reevaluation of existing theories of the policy process. Is the natural state of policymaking really slow, incremental change given how quickly problems arise and demand attention? Are rapid periods of change really interesting departures from the norm? Or will the changing nature of problems and issues lead to a changed policy process approach that reflects nearly continuous change? In science and policy studies alike there is a heightened interest in entropy, chaos, and complex adaptive systems as a way of approaching the challenge of continual change (see Bardach, 2008).

It is unclear, however, whether existing frameworks are inadequate to the task of addressing such a problem. System-wide agenda space will always be a scarce commodity and how policymakers' attention to problems shifts focus is a central question in all extant theories, especially punctuated equilibrium theories of policy change. Periods of instability and change will always happen because of agenda scarcity. It is impossible for legislators and presidents to maintain concentration

on all issues at once. It is unclear how other theories deal with the reality of the serial processing of policy problems, even when complex problems change and demand attention frequently.

The research over the last two years, however, seems to make clear that there are plenty of opportunities for firming up scholars' understanding of the precise dynamics of agenda setting. Future efforts at doing so will have to be holistic in their accounts—taking full account of the roles and relationships between legislative actors as well as the bureaucracy and interest groups. Future efforts will have to address variation across and within subsystems, since some parts of policy change may move at different paces than others. They will also have to carefully track differences in policymaking according to varying venues. And finally, increasingly complex problems often prompt efforts at overarching regimes to make sense of related issues. Future research will have to investigate how regimes, as a unit of analysis, add to understanding of linked policymaking across subsystem boundaries.

The scholarship on the politics of agenda setting seems to have hit a second stage in its development. From grand theories of the policy process, recent research has narrowed the field to tractable questions. While questions about operationalization will remain, researchers appear to have moved away from metaphors and examples toward richer descriptions of activity that examine the underpinnings of the policy process.

References

BARDACH, EUGENE. 2008. "Policy Dynamics." In *The Oxford Handbook of Public Policy*, eds. Michael Moran, Martin Rein, and Robert E. Goodin. New York: Oxford University Press, 336–66.

BAUMGARTNER, FRANK R., CHRISTIAN BREUNIG, CHRISTOFFER GREEN-PEDERSEN, BRYAN D. JONES, PETER B. MORTENSEN, MICHIEL NUYTEMANS, and STEFAAN WALGRAVE. 2009. "Punctuated Equilibrium in Comparative Perspective." *American Journal of Political Science* 53 (3): 603–20.

BAUMGARTNER, FRANK R., and BRYAN D. JONES. 1993. *Agendas and Instability in American Politics.* Chicago: The University of Chicago Press.

BOIN, ARJEN. 2009. "The New World of Crises and Crisis Management: Implications for Policymaking and Research." *Review of Policy Research* 26 (4): 367–77.

BOSCARINO, JESSICA E. 2009. "Surfing for Problems: Advocacy Group Strategy in U.S. Forestry Policy." *The Policy Studies Journal* 37 (3): 415–34.

GIVEL, MICHAEL. 2010. "The Evolution of the Theoretical Foundations of Punctuated Equilibrium Theory in Public Policy." *Review of Policy Research* 27 (2): 187–98.

HOWLETT, MICHAEL. 2009. "Process Sequencing Policy Dynamics: Beyond Homeostatis and Path Dependency." *Journal of Public Policy* 29 (3): 241–62.

JOCHIM, ASHLEY E., and Peter J. May. 2010. "Beyond Subsystems: Policy Regimes and Governance." *The Policy Studies Journal* 38 (2): 303–27.

JONES, MICHAEL D., and HANK C. JENKINS-SMITH. 2009. "Trans-Subsystem Dynamics: Policy Topography, Mass Opinion, and Policy Change." *The Policy Studies Journal* 37 (1): 37–58.

KINGDON, JOHN W. 2003. *Agendas, Alternatives, and Public Policies*, 2nd ed., New York: Longman.

LAGADEC, PATRICK. 2009. "A New Cosmology of Risks and Crises: Time for a Radical Shift in Paradigm and Practice." *Review of Policy Research* 26 (4): 473–86.

LIU, XINSHENG, ERIC LINDQUIST, AND ARNOLD VEDLITZ. 2009. "Explaining Media and Congressional Attention to Global Climate Change, 1969–2005: An Empirical Test of Agenda-Setting Theory." *Political Research Quarterly* 20 (5): 1–15.

LIU, XINSHENG, ERIC LINDQUIST, ARNOLD VEDLITZ, and KENNETH VINCENT. 2010. "Understanding Local Policymaking: Policy Elites' Perceptions of Local Agenda Setting and Alternative Policy Selection." *The Policy Studies Journal* 38 (1): 69–91.

MAY, PETER J., SAMUEL WORKMAN, and BRYAN D. JONES. 2008. "Organizing Attention: Responses of the Bureaucracy to Agenda Disruption." *Journal of Public Administration Research and Theory* 18: 517–41.

MAY, PETER J., JOSHUA SAPOTICHNE, and SAMUEL WORKMAN. 2009a. "Widespread Policy Disruption and Interest Mobilization." *The Policy Studies Journal* 37 (4): 793–815.

———. 2009b. "Widespread Policy Disruption: Terrorism, Public Risks, and Homeland Security." *The Policy Studies Journal* 37 (2): 171–94.

PATASHNIK, ERIC M. 2008. *Reforms at Risk: What Happens after Major Policy Changes are Enacted.* Princeton, NJ: Princeton University Press.

SIMON, HERBERT A. 1983. *Reason in Human Affairs.* Stanford, CA: Stanford University Press.

WEIMER, DAVID L. 2008. "Theories of and in the Policy Process." *The Policy Studies Journal* 36 (4): 489–95.

WORKMAN, SAMUEL, BRYAN D. JONES, and ASHLEY E. JOCHIM. 2009. "Information Processing and Policy Dynamics." *The Policy Studies Journal* 37 (1): 75–92.

48

Policy Analysis - A Multidisciplinary Framework

William N. Dunn

Policy analysis is partly *descriptive*. It relies on traditional social science disciplines to describe and explain the causes and consequences of policies. But it is also *normative,* a term that refers to value judgments about what *ought* to be, in contrast to descriptive statements about what *is*.[1] To investigate problems of efficiency and fairness, policy analysis draws on normative economics and decision analysis as well as ethics and other branches of social and political philosophy-all of which are about what *ought* to be. This normative orientation stems from the fact that analyzing policies demands that we choose among desired consequences (ends) and preferred courses of action (means). The choice of ends and means requires continuing trade-offs among competing values of efficiency, equity, security, liberty, and democracy.[2] The importance of normative reasoning in policy analysis was well stated by a former undersecretary in the Department of Housing and Urban Development: "Our problem is not to do what is right. Our problem is to know what is right."[3]

POLICY-RELEVANT INFORMATION

Policy analysis is designed to provide policy-relevant information about five types of questions:

- *Policy problems.* What is the problem for which a potential solution is sought? Is global warming a human-made consequence of aircraft and motor vehicle emissions? Or is global warming a consequence of periodic fluctuations in the temperature of the atmosphere? What alternatives are available to mitigate global warming? What are the potential outcomes of these alternatives and what is their value or utility?
- *Expected policy outcomes.* What are the expected outcomes of policies designed to reduce harmful emissions? Because periodic natural fluctuations are difficult or impossible to control, what is the likelihood that emissions can be reduced by raising the price of gasoline and diesel fuel, compared with requiring that aircraft and motor vehicles use biofuels?
- *Preferred policies.* Which policies should be chosen, considering not only their expected outcomes in reducing harmful emissions, but also the value of reduced emissions in terms of economic costs and benefits? Should distributional criteria involving environmental justice be used along with criteria of economic efficiency?
- *Observed policy outcomes.* What policy outcomes are observed, as distinguished from the outcomes expected before a preferred policy is implemented? Did the preferred policy actually result in reduced emissions? Were other factors such as political opposition to governmental regulation responsible for the limited achievement of emissions targets?

From William N. Dunn, *Public Policy Analysis*, 5th ed. (Boston, Mass.; Pearson, pp. 4–14)

• *Policy performance.* To what extent do observed policy outcomes contribute to the reduction of global warming through emissions controls? What are the benefits and costs of government regulation to present and future generations?

Answers to these questions yield five types of information, which are *policy-informational components*. These components are shown as rectangles in Figure 48.1.[4]

A *policy problem* is an unrealized need, value, or opportunity for improvement attainable through public action.[5] Knowledge of what problem to solve requires information about a problem's antecedent conditions (e.g., school dropouts as an antecedent condition of unemployment), as well as information about values (e.g., safe schools or a living wage) whose achievement may lead to the problem's solution. Information about policy problems plays a critical role in policy analysis, because the way a problem is

defined shapes the search for available solutions. Inadequate or faulty information may result in a fatal error: defining the wrong Problem.[6]

Expected policy outcomes are likely consequences of one or more policy alternatives designed to solve a problem. Information about the circumstances that gave rise to a problem is essential for producing information about expected policy outcomes. Such information is often insufficient, however, because the past does not repeat itself completely, and the values that shape behavior may change in the future. For this reason, information about expected policy outcomes is not "given" by the existing situation. To produce such information may require creativity, insight, and the use of tacit knowledge.[7]

A *preferred policy* is a potential solution to a problem. To select a preferred policy, it is necessary to have information about expected policy outcomes as well as information about the value or utility of these expected outcomes. Another

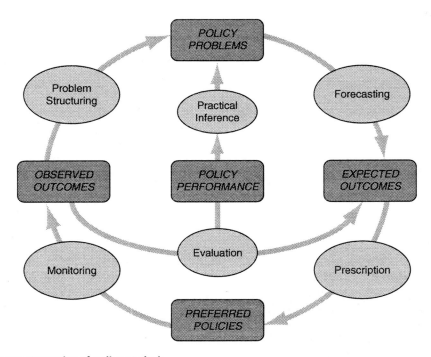

FIGURE 48.1 Forms strategies of policy analysis

way to say this is that factual as well as value premises are required for policy prescriptions. Fact alone-for example, the fact that one policy produces more of some quantity than another-do not justify the choice of a preferred policy. Factual premises must be joined with value premises involving efficiency, equality, security, democracy, or some other value.

An *observed policy outcome* is a present or past consequence of implementing a preferred policy. It is sometimes unclear whether an outcome is actually an effect of a policy, because some effects are not *policy* outcomes; many outcomes are the result of other, extra-policy factors. It is important to recognize that the consequences of action cannot be fully stated or known in advance, which means that many consequences are neither anticipated nor intended. Fortunately, information about such consequences can be produced *ex post* (after policies have been implemented), not only *ex ante* (before policies are implemented).

Policy performance is the degree to which an observed policy outcome contributes to the solution of a problem. In practice, policy performance is never perfect. Problems are rarely "solved"; most often, problems are resolved, reformulated, and *even* "unsolved."[8] To know whether a problem has been solved, resolved, reformulated, or unsolved requires information about observed policy outcomes, as well as information about the extent to which these outcomes contribute to the opportunities for improvement that gave rise to a problem.

POLICY-INFORMATIONAL TRANSFORMATIONS

The five types of policy-relevant information are interdependent. The arrows connecting each pair of components represent *policy-informational transformations*, whereby one type of information is changed into another, so that the creation of information at any point depends on information produced in an adjacent phase. Information about policy performance, for example, depends on the transformation of prior information about observed policy outcomes. The reason for this dependence is that any assessment of how well a policy achieves its objectives assumes that

we already have reliable information about the outcomes of that policy. The other types of policy-relevant information are dependent in the same way.

Information about policy problems is a special case. Information about policy problems usually includes some problem elements-for example, potential solutions or expected outcomes-and excludes others. What is included or excluded affects which policies are eventually prescribed, which values are appropriate as criteria of policy performance, and which potentially predictable outcomes warrant or do not warrant attention. At the risk of being overly repetitious, it is worth stressing again that a fatal error of policy analysis is a type III error-defining the wrong problem. [9]

POLICY-ANALYTIC METHODS

The five types of policy-relevant information are produced and transformed by using policy-analytic methods. All methods involve judgments of different kinds:[10] judgments to accept or reject an explanation, to affirm or dispute the rightness of an action, to prescribe or not prescribe a policy, to accept or reject a prediction, and to formulate a problem in one way rather than another.

In policy analysis, these procedures have special names:

- *Problem structuring*. Problem-structuring methods are employed to produce information about which problem to solve.
- *Forecasting*. Forecasting methods are used to produce information about expected policy outcomes.... An example of a simple forecasting tool is the Goeller Scorecard-Monitoring and Forecasting Technological Impacts. Scorecards, which are based on the judgments of experts, are particularly useful in identifying expected outcomes of science and technology policies .
- *Prescription*. Methods of prescription are employed to create information about preferred policies. An example of a prescriptive method is the spreadsheet. The spreadsheet goes beyond the identification of expected policy outcomes by expressing consequences in terms of monetary benefits

and costs. Benefit-cost analysis and other methods of prescription are presented in Chapter 5.

- *Monitoring.* Methods of monitoring are employed to produce information about observed policy outcomes. The scorecard is a simple method for monitoring observed policy outcomes as well as for forecasting expected policy outcomes.
- *Evaluation.* Evaluation methods are used to produce information about the value or utility of observed policy outcomes and their contributions to policy performance. The spreadsheet may be used for evaluation as well as prescription.

The first method, problem structuring, is about the other methods. For this reason, it is a *meta-method* (method of methods). In the course of structuring a problem, analysts typically experience a "troubled, perplexed, trying situation, where the difficulty is, as it were, spread throughout the entire situation, infecting it as a whole."[11] *Problem situations* are not problems; problems are representations of problem situations: Hence, problems are not "out there" in the world, but they stem from the interaction of thought and external environments. Imagine a graph showing the growth of defense expenditures as a percentage of gross domestic product. The graph represents a problem situation, not a problem, because one analyst will *see* the graph as evidence of increasing national security (more of the budget is allocated to defense), while another interprets the graph as an indication of a declining budget for social welfare (less of the budget can be allocated to social services). Problem structuring, a procedure for testing different representations of a problem situation, is the central guidance system of policy analysis.

Policy-analytic methods are interdependent. It is not possible to use one method without first having used others. Thus, although it is possible to monitor past policies without forecasting their future consequences, it is usually not possible to forecast policies without first monitoring them.[12] Similarly, analysts can monitor policy outcomes without evaluating them, but it is not possible to evaluate an outcome without first establishing that it is an outcome in the first place. Finally, to select a preferred policy requires that analysts have already monitored, evaluated, and forecasted outcomes.[13] This is yet one more way of saying that policy prescription is based on factual as well as value premises.

Figure 48.1 supplied a framework for integrating methods from different policy-relevant disciplines. Some methods are used solely or primarily in some disciplines, and not others. Program evaluation, for example, employs monitoring to investigate whether a policy is causally relevant to an observed policy outcome. Although program evaluation has made extensive use of interrupted time-series analysis, regression discontinuity analysis, causal modeling, and other techniques associated with the design and analysis of field experiments,[14] implementation research within political science has not. Instead, implementation researchers have relied mainly on techniques of case study analysis.[15] Another example comes from forecasting. Although forecasting is central to both economics and systems analysis, economics has drawn almost exclusively on econometric techniques. Systems analysis has made greater use of qualitative forecasting techniques for synthesizing expert judgment, for example, the Delphi technique.[16]

FOUR STRATEGIES OF ANALYSIS

Relationships among policy-informational components, policy-analytic methods, and policy-informational transformations provide a basis for contrasting four strategies of policy analysis (Figure 48.2).

PROSPECTIVE AND RETROSPECTIVE ANALYSIS

Prospective policy analysis involves the production and transformation of information *before* policy actions are taken. This strategy of *ex ante* analysis, shown as the right half of Figure 48.2, typifies the operating styles of economists, systems analysts, operations researchers, and decision analysts.

The prospective strategy is what Williams means by policy *analysis*.[17] Policy analysis is

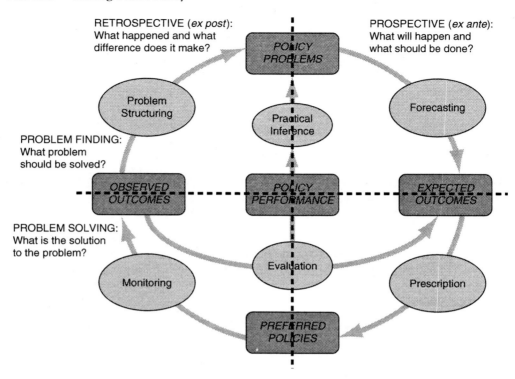

RETROSPECTIVE (*ex post*):
What happened and what
difference does it make?

PROSPECTIVE (*ex ante*):
What will happen and
what should be done?

PROBLEM FINDING:
What problem
should be solved?

PROBLEM SOLVING:
What is the solution
to the problem?

FIGURE 48.2 The process of integrated analysis

"a means of synthesizing information to draw from it policy alternatives and preferences stated in comparable, predicted quantitative and qualitative terms as a basis or guide for policy decisions; conceptually, it does not include the *gathering* of information [emphasis in original]." Policy *research,* by contrast, refers to "all studies using scientific methodologies to describe phenomena and/or determine relationships among them." Prospective analysis often creates wide gaps between preferred solutions and actual efforts to implement them. Perhaps no more than 10 percent of the work actually required to achieve a desired set of policy outcomes is carried out *before* policies are implemented: "It *is* not that we have too many good analytic solutions to problems. It is, rather, that we have more good solutions than we have appropriate actions."[18]

Retrospective policy analysis is displayed as the left half of Figure 48.2. This strategy of *ex post* analysis involves the production and transformation of information *after* policies have been

implemented. Retrospective analysis characterizes the operating styles of three groups of analysts:

• *Discipline-oriented analysts.* This group, composed mainly of political scientists, economists, and sociologists, seeks to develop and test discipline-based theories that describe the causes and consequences of policies. This group is not concerned with the identification of specific policy goals or with distinctions between "policy" variables that are subject to policy manipulation and those that are not.[19] For example, the analysis of the effects of party competition on government expenditures provides no information about specific policy goals; nor is party competition a .variable that policy makers can manipulate to change public expenditures.

• *Problem-oriented analysts.* This group, again composed mainly of political scientists, economists, and sociologists, seeks to describe the causes and consequences of policies. Problem-oriented analysts, however; are less concerned with the development and testing of theories believed to be important in social science disciplines than with identifying variables that may explain a problem. Problem-oriented analysts are not overly concerned with specific goals and objectives, primarily because the practical problems they analyze are usually general in nature. For example, the analysis of aggregate data on the effects of gender, ethnicity, and social inequality on national achievement test scores provides information that helps explain a problem (e.g., inadequate test performance) but does not provide information about policy variables that can be manipulated.

- *Applications-oriented analysts.* A third group includes applied economists, applied sociologists, applied psychologists, and applied anthropologists, as well as analysts from professions such as public administration, social work, and evaluation research. This group also seeks to describe the causes and consequences of public policies and programs and is not concerned with the development and testing of discipline-based theories. This group is concerned not only with manipulable policy variables but also with the identification of specific policy goals and objectives. Information about specific goals and objectives provides a basis for monitoring and evaluating outcomes and impacts of policies. For example, applications-oriented analysts may address early childhood reading readiness programs that can be manipulated in order to achieve higher scores on reading tests.

The operating styles of the three groups reflect their characteristic strengths and limitations. Discipline-oriented as well as problem-oriented analysts seldom produce information that is directly useful to policy makers. Even when problem-oriented analysts investigate important problems such as educational opportunity, energy conservation, crime control, or national security, the resultant information is often *macronegative*.

Macronegative information describes the basic (or "root") causes and consequences of policies, usually by employing aggregate data to show why policies do *not* work. By contrast, *micropositive* information shows what policies and programs *do* work under specified conditions.[20] It is of little practical value to policy makers to know that the crime rate is higher in urban than rural areas, but it is practically important to know that a specific form of gun control reduces the commission of serious crimes or that intensive police patrolling is a deterrent.

Even when applications-oriented analysts provide micropositive information, they may find it difficult to communicate with practitioners of *ex ante* policy analysis, who in most cases are professional economists. In agency settings, *ex ante* analysts, whose job, it is to find optimally efficient solutions, often have limited access to information about policy outcomes produced through retrospective analysis. For their part, practitioners of *ex ante* analysis often fail to specify in sufficient detail the kinds of policy-relevant information that will be most useful for monitoring, evaluating, and implementing their recommendations. Often, the intended outcomes of a policy are so vague that "almost any evaluation of it may be regarded as irrelevant because it missed the 'problem' toward which the policy was directed."[21] Legislators, for example, usually formulate problems in general terms in order to gain acceptance, forestall opposition, or maintain neutrality.

Contrasts among the operating styles of policy analysts suggest that discipline-oriented and problem-oriented analysis are inherently less useful than applications-oriented analysis-that retrospective *(ex post)* analysis as a whole is perhaps less effective in solving problems than prospective *(ex ante)* analysis. Although this conclusion may have merit from the point of view of policy makers who want advice on what actions to take, it overlooks several important benefits of retrospective analysis. Retrospective analysis, whatever its shortcomings, places primary emphasis on the results of action and is not content with information about expected policy outcomes, as is the case with prospective analysis. Discipline-oriented and problem-oriented analysis may offer new frameworks for understanding policy-making processes, challenging conventional formulations of problems, questioning social and economic myths, and shaping the climate of opinion in a community or society. Retrospective analysis, however, "has been most important in its impact on intellectual priorities and understandings, and not nearly so effective in offering solutions for specific political problems."[22]

DESCRIPTIVE AND NORMATIVE ANALYSIS

Figure 48.2 also captures another important contrast, the distinction between descriptive and normative strategies of policy analysis. Descriptive policy analysis parallels *descriptive decision theory,* which refers to a set of logically consistent propositions that describe or explain action.[23] Descriptive decision theories may be tested against observations obtained through monitoring and forecasting. Descriptive theories, models, and conceptual frameworks originate for the most part in political science, sociology, and economics. The main function of these theories, models, and frameworks is to explain, understand, and predict policies by identifying patterns of causality. The principal function of approaches to monitoring such as field experimentation is to establish the approximate validity of causal inferences relating policies to their presumed outcomes.[24] In Figure 48.2, the descriptive form of policy analysis can be visualized as an axis moving from the lower left (monitoring) to the upper right (forecasting).

Normative policy analysis parallels *normative decision theory,* which refers to a set of logically consistent propositions that evaluate or prescribe action.[25] In Figure 48.2, the normative strategy of policy analysis can be visualized as an axis running from the lower right (prescription) to upper left (evaluation). Different kinds of information are required to test normative and descriptive decision theories. Methods of evaluation and prescription provide information about policy performance and preferred policies, for example, policies that have been or will be optimally efficient because benefits outweigh costs or optimally equitable because those most in need are made better off. One of the most important

features of normative policy analysis *is* that its propositions rest on disagreements about values such as efficiency, equity, responsiveness, liberty, and security.

PROBLEM FINDING AND PROBLEM SOLVING

The upper and lower halves of Figure 48.2 provide another important distinction. The upper half points to methods that are designed for *problem finding,* whereas the lower designates methods for *problem solving.* The problem-finding strategy has to do with the discovery of elements that go into the definition of problems, and not to their solution. How well do we understand the problem? Who are the most important *stakeholders* who affect and are affected by the problem? Have the appropriate objectives been identified? Which alternatives are available to achieve objectives? Which uncertain events should be taken into account? Are we solving the "right" problem rather than the "wrong" one?

Problem-solving methods, located in the lower half of Figure 48.2, are designed to solve rather than find problems. The problem-solving strategy is primarily technical in nature, in contrast to problem finding, which is more conceptual. Problem-solving methods such as econometrics are useful in answering questions about policy causation, statistical estimation, and optimization. How much of the variance in a policy outcome is explained by one or more independent variables? What is the probability of obtaining a coefficient as large as that obtained? Another problem-solving method is benefit-cost analysis. What are the net benefits of different policies? What is their expected utility or payoff?

SEGMENTED AND INTEGRATED ANALYSIS

Integrated policy analysis links the four strategies of analysis displayed in Figure 48.2. Retrospective and prospective strategies are joined in one continuous process. Descriptive and normative strategies are also linked, as are methods designed to find as well as solve problems.

Practically speaking, this means that policy analysts bridge the several main pillars of multidisciplinary policy analysis, especially economics and political science. Today, this need is not being properly met by specialized social science disciplines, which tend to practice *segmented policy analysis.* The job of bridging segmented disciplines to convert intellectual knowledge into practical knowledge is carried out by multidisciplinary professions including public administration, planning, management, and policy analysis. The American Society for Public Administration (ASPA), the National Association of Schools of Public Affairs and Administration (NASPAA), the American Planning Association (APA), the International Association of Schools and Institutes of Administration (IASIA), the Academy of Management (AM), the Operations Research Society of America (ORSA), and the Association for Public Policy and Management (APPAM) are organizations that represent these professions. So far, these professions have been more open to the disciplines of economics and political science than those disciplines have been open to them, notwithstanding a consensus among policy scholars and practitioners that the substance and methods of these and other disciplines are essential for producing policy-relevant information.

In summary, the framework for integrated policy analysis (Figure 48.1) helps examine the assumptions, strengths, and limitations of methods employed in disciplines that tend to be overly segmented and excessively specialized to be useful in practical problem solving. The framework identifies and relates major elements of policy analysis-policy-informational components, policy-analytic methods, and policy-informational transformations-enabling us to see the particular roles performed by methods of problem structuring, monitoring, evaluation, forecasting, and prescription. The framework (Figure 48.2) identifies different strategies of policy analysis: prospective *(ex ante)* and retrospective *(ex post),* descriptive and normative, and problem finding and problem solving. ,The framework integrates these strategies of analysis and explains why we have defined policy analysis as a problem-solving discipline that links social science theories, methods, and substantive findings to solve practical problems.

End Notes

1. One classic statement of the difference between positive and normative knowledge in economics is Nlilton Friedman, *Essays in Positive Economics* (Chicago, IL: University of Chicago Press, 1953). This same positive-normative distinction is present throughout the social sciences.
2. Deborah Stone, *Policy Paradox: The Art of Political Decision Making,* rev ed. (New York: W. W. Norton, 2001).
3. Robert C. Wood, "Foreword" to *The Study of Policy Formation,* ed. Raymond A. Bauer and Kenneth J. Gergen (New York: Free Press, 1968), p. v. Wood is quoting President Lyndon Johnson.
4. The framework was originally suggested by Walter Wallace, *The Logic of Science in Sociology* (Chicago: AIdine Books, 1971). Wallace's framework addresses research methodology in sociology, whereas Figure 48.1 addresses the methodology of policy-analysis.
5. Compare James A. Anderson, *Public Policymaking; An Introduction,* 7th ed. (Boston, MA: Wadsworth, 2011); Charles O. Jones, *An Introduction to the Study of Public Policy,* 2d ed. (North Scituate, MA: Duxbury Press, 1977), p. 15; and David Dery, *Problem Definition in Policy Analysis* (Lawrence: University of Kansas Press, 1984).
6. Defining the wrong problem is a type ill error, as contrasted with type I and type II errors committed when the level of statistical significance *(alpha)* is set too high or too low in testing the null hypothesis. An early statement of this contrast is Ian 1. Mitroff and Thomas R. Featheringham, "On Systematic Problem Solving and the Error of the Third Kind," *Behavioral Sciences* 19, no. 6 (1974): 383–93.
7. Dror, *Ventures in Policy Sciences;* Sir Geoffrey Vickers, *The Art of Judgment: A Study of Policy Making* (New York: Basic Books, 1965); and C. West Churchman, *The Design of Inquiring Systems; Basic Concepts ofSystems and Organization* (New York: Basic Books, 1971).
8. Russell L. Ackoff, "Beyond Problem Solving," *Generdf Systems* 19 (1974): 237–39.
9. Type I and type II errors are also known as false positives and false negatives. Other sources on

type III errors include A. W. Kimball, "Errors of the Third Kind in Statistical Consulting," *Journal of the American Statistical Association* 52 (1957): 133–42; Howard Raitfa, *Decision Analysis* (Reading, 1\1A: AddisonWesley, 1968), p. 264; and Ian I. Mitroff, *The Subjective Side of Science* (New York: Elsevier, 1974).

10. Joho O'Shaughnessy, *Inquiry and Decision* (London: George Allen & Unwin, 1972).

11. John Dewey, *How We Think* (Boston, MA: D.C. Heath and Company, 1933), p. 108. The original statement of the difference between a problem and a problem situation is attributable to philosophical pragmatists including Charles Sanders Peirce.

12. An exception is predictions made on the basis of expert judgment. The explanation of a policy is not necessary for predicting its future consequences. Strictly speaking, a prediction is a causal inference, whereas a projection, extrapolation, or "rational forecast" is not.

13. Causation may be assumed but not understood. Recipes claim only that a desired result is a consequence of action. Joseph L. Bower, "Descriptive Decision Theory from the 'Administrative' Viewpoint," in *The Study of Policy Formation,* ed. Bauer and Gergen, p. 10. _____:"

14. See, for example, William R. Shadish, Thomas D. Cook, and Donald T. Campbell, *Experimental and Quasi-Experimental Designs for Generalized Causal Inference* (Boston, MA: Houghton Mifflin, 2002).

15. Paul A. Sabatier and Hank C. Jenkins-Smith, "The Advocacy Coalition Framework: An Assessment," in *Theories of the Policy Process,* ed. P. A. Sabatier (Boulder, CO: Westview Press, 1999), pp. 117-66.

16. See Chapter 5.

17. Walter Williams, *Social Policy Research and Analysis: The Experience in the Federal Social Agencies* (New York: American Elsevier, 1971), p. 8.

18. Graham T. Allison, *Essence of Decision: Explaining the Cuban Missile Crisis* (Boston, MA: Little, Brown, 1971), pp. 267–68.

19. James S. Coleman, "Problems of Conceptualization and Measurement in Studying Policy Impacts," in *Public·Policy Evaluation,* ed. Kenneth M. Dolbeare Beverly Hills and London: Sage Publications, p. 25.

20. Williams, *Social Policy Research and Analysis,* p. 8.

21. Ibid. p. 13; and Alice Rivlin, *Systematic Thinking for Social Action* (Washington, DC: Brookings, 1971).

22. Janet A. Weiss, "Using Social Science for Social Policy, *Policy Studies journal* 4, (Spring 1976): 237.

28. Bower, "Descriptive Decision Theory," p. 104.

24. See Thomas D. Cook and Donald T. Campbell, *Quasi-Experimentation: Design and Analysis Issues (or Field Settings* {Boston, MA: Houghton Mifflin, 1979}; Shadish, Cook, and Campbell, *Experimental and Quasi-Experimental Designs for Generalized Causal Inference.*

25. Bower, "Descriptive Decision Theory," pp. 104–05.

49

Synthesizing the Implementation Literature

Richard E. Matland

... As implementation research evolved, two schools of thought developed as to the most effective method for studying and describing implementation: top-down and bottom-up. Top-down theorists see policy designers as the central actors and concentrate their attention on factors that can be manipulated at the central level. Bottom-up theorists emphasize target groups and service deliverers, arguing policy really is made at the local level. Most reviewers now agree that some convergence of these two perspectives, tying the macrolevel variables of the top-down models to the microlevel variables "bottom-uppers" consider, is necessary for the field to develop. This article reviews the two major implementation schools and previous attempts to synthesize the literature. The ambiguity-conflict model then is presented as an alternative model for reconciling the existing findings on implementation.

TOP-DOWN, BOTTOM-UP, AND ATTEMPTS TO COMBINE THEM

Top-Down Models

Top-down models (Van Meter and Van Horn 1975; Mazmanian and Sabatier 1981; 1983; 1989) see implementation as concern with the degree to which the actions of implementing officials and target groups coincide with the goals embodied in an authoritative decision. Mazmanian and Sabatier (1983, 20) define implementation as "The carrying out of a basic policy decision, usually incorporated in a statute but which can also take the form of important executive orders or court decisions ..." The starting point is the authoritative decision; as the name implies, centrally located actors are seen as most relevant to producing the desired effects.

In the most fully developed top-down model, Mazmanian and Sabatier (1989) present three general sets of factors (tractability of the problem, ability of statute to structure implementation, and nonstatutory variables affecting implementation) which they argue determine the probability of successful implementation. These factors then are developed into a set of sixteen independent variables that are hypothesized to influence goal compliance. The complexity of their model points to one of the more striking problems and recurrent criticisms of implementation research—the lack of parsimony.

Top-downers have exhibited a strong desire to develop generalizable policy advice. This requires finding consistent, recognizable patterns in behavior across different policy areas. Belief that such patterns exist and the desire to give advice

From Richard Matland, "Synthesizing the Implementation Literature: The Ambiguity-Conflict Model of Policy Implemention," *Journal of Public Administration Research and Theory* (April 1995), pp. 145–174.

has given the top-down view a highly prescriptive bent and has led to a concentration on variables that can be manipulated at the central level. Common top-down advice is: Make policy goals clear and consistent (Van Meter and Van Horn 1975; Mazmanian and Sabatier 1983); minimize the number of actors (Pressman and Wildavsky 1973); limit the extent of change necessary (Van Meter and Van Horn 1975; Mazmanian and Sabatier 1983); and place implementation responsibility in an agency sympathetic with the policy's goals (Van Meter and Van Horn 1975; Sabatier 1986).

Top-downers meet three sets of criticisms. First, top-down models take the statutory language as their starting point. This fails to consider the significance of actions taken earlier in the policy-making process. Winter (1985 and 1986) notes that many implementation barriers are found in the initial stages of the policy-making process and to understand policy implementation these processes must be studied carefully. Nakamura and Smallwood (1980) argue that the policy-formation process gives implementers important cues about intensity of demands, and about the size, stability, and degree of consensus among those pushing for change. An analysis that takes policy as given and does not consider its past history might miss vital connections. By concentrating on the statutory language, top-downers may fail to consider broader public objectives. O'Toole (1989) argues that a top-down analysis of wastewater treatment would find that privately managed facilities are superior because they are built more quickly, they are less expensive to build, and they provide approximately the same quality of waste treatment as publicly owned facilities. When broader issues such as affirmative action, compliance with Davis-Bacon labor laws, use and development of innovative technology, and local government autonomy and accountability are considered, publicly owned and operated facilities score much higher.

Second, top-downers have been accused of seeing implementation as a purely administrative process and either ignoring the political aspects or trying to eliminate them (Berman 1978; Hoppe, van de Graaf, and van Dijk 1985; Baier, March, and Saetren 1986). For example, the call for clear, explicit, and consistent goals contradicts

much of what is known about how legislation is passed. Passage of legislation often requires ambiguous language and contradictory goals to hold together a passing coalition. The top-down emphasis on clarity, rule promulgation, and monitoring brings to mind the Weberian bureaucrat making independent decisions based on merit and technical criteria, free from political influence. It is, however, rarely possible to separate politics from administration. Attempts to insulate an inherently political subject matter from politics do not necessarily lead to apolitical actions. They instead may lead directly to policy failure.

Finally, top-down models have been criticized for their exclusive emphasis on the statute framers as key actors. This criticism has two primary variants. One argues from a normative perspective that local service deliverers have expertise and knowledge of the true problems; therefore, they are in a better position to propose purposeful policy. Top-down models, however, see local actors as impediments to successful implementation, agents whose shirking behavior needs to be controlled. The second variant argues from a positive perspective that discretion for street-level bureaucrats is inevitably so great that it is simply unrealistic to expect policy designers to be able to control the actions of these agents. That service deliverers ultimately determine policy is a major tenet of bottom-up models.

Bottom-Up Models

Bottom-uppers, such as Berman (1978 and 1980); Hjern and Porter (1981); Hjern (1982); Hjern and Hull (1982); Hull and Hjern (1987); and Lipsky (1978) argue that a more realistic understanding of implementation can be gained by looking at a policy from the view of the target population and the service deliverers. Policy implementation occurs on two levels (Berman 1978). At the macroimplementation level, centrally located actors devise a government program; at the microimplementation level, local organizations react to the macrolevel plans, develop their own programs, and implement them. Berman argues that most implementation problems stem from the interaction of a policy with the microlevel institutional setting. Central planners only indirectly can influence microlevel factors. Therefore, there is wide variation in how the same national policy is implemented at the local level. Contextual factors within the implementing environment can completely dominate rules created at the top of the implementing pyramid, and policy designers will be unable to control the process. Under these conditions, according to the bottom-uppers, if local level implementers are not given the freedom to adapt the program to local conditions it is likely to fail (Palumbo, Maynard-Moody, and Wright 1984).

Bottom-uppers argue that the goals, strategies, activities, and contacts of the actors involved in the microimplementation process must be understood in order to understand implementation. It is at the microlevel that policy directly affects people. The influence of policy on the action of street-level bureaucrats must be evaluated in order to predict that policy's effect (Weatherley and Lipsky 1978). Because implementation arises from the interaction of policy and setting, it is unrealistic to expect the development of a simple or single theory of implementation that is "context free" (Maynard-Moody, Musheno, and Palumbo 1990).

The most extensive empirical work within the bottom-up tradition has been that of Benny Hjern (1982) and his colleagues (Hjern and Hull 1985; Hull and Hjern 1987). Hjern's strategy is to study a policy problem, asking microlevel actors about their goals, activities, problems, and contacts. This technique enables Hjern to map a network that identifies the relevant implementation structure for a specific policy at the local, regional, and national levels, and allows him to evaluate the significance of government programs vis-à-vis other influences such as markets. It also enables him to see strategic coalitions as well as unintended effects of policy and the dynamic nature of policy implementation. Hjern finds that central initiatives are poorly adapted to local conditions. Program success depends in large part on the skills of individuals in the local implementation structure who can adapt policy to local conditions; it depends only to a limited degree on central activities.

While top-downers have a strong desire to present prescriptive advice, bottom-uppers have placed more emphasis on describing what

factors have caused difficulty in reaching stated goals. The strongly inductive nature of this research combined with results finding most of the relevant factors varying from site to site has led to few explicit policy recommendations. The primary policy recommendation from researchers within this tradition is for a flexible strategy that allows for adaptation to local difficulties and contextual factors (Maynard-Moody, Musheno, and Palumbo 1990). Some researchers have suggested that policy changes should be consonant with the values of implementing agents (Berman 1978).

Two criticisms of bottom-up models appear with some consistency—one normative, one methodological. The normative criticism is that, in a democratic system, policy control should be exercised by actors whose power derives from their accountability to sovereign voters through their elected representatives. The authority of local service deliverers does not derive from this base of power. Decentralization should occur within a context of central control. Street-level bureaucrats *do* have great discretion in their interactions with clients. To proceed from this fact to theorize that because such flexibility exists it should serve as the basis for designing policy, however, is to turn the role of theory on its head (Linder and Peters 1987). It effectively equates description with prescription. Flexibility and autonomy might be appropriate when the goals of the policy formulators and implementers are the same, but if they differ greatly, flexibility and autonomy may lead to policies which result in lower performance on official goals. Classic organizational theory is rife with examples of agents subordinating the goals of their principals and concentrating on their own subgoals (March and Simon 1958; Merton 1957; Michels 1949; Selznick 1949).

The second criticism is that the bottom-up methodology overemphasizes the level of local autonomy. Hjern's methodology relies on perceptions; therefore, indirect effects and the effects actors are unconscious of are not registered. Variations in actions can be explained largely by local level differences, yet all actions may fall within a limited range where the borders are set by centrally determined policy. While central actors do not act in detail or intervene in specific cases, they can structure the goals and strategies of those participants who are active. The institutional structure, the available resources, and the access to an implementing arena may be determined centrally and substantially can affect policy outcomes. Sabatier (1986) notes that a bottom-up analysis of environmental regulations in the United States would find that central government authorities play only a limited role. Most suits are brought by environmental interest organizations on behalf of individuals. Yet the decision to give individuals standing and the right to sue for collective damages under classaction suits is a crucial factor that was decided by policy designers when they framed the policy. By giving these actors access, the central policy designers structured the actions that occurred later.

Combinations of the Two Perspectives: Previous Attempts

Limited number of attempts have been made to combine these two major perspectives and other perspectives on implementation. One group of researchers has proposed different ways of combining the two formats within the same model and another group has searched for conditions under which one approach is more appropriate than the other.

Elmore's concept of forward and backward mapping (1982 and 1985) is an early attempt to combine top-down and bottomup perspectives. Elmore argues that policy designers should choose policy instruments based on the incentive structure of target groups. Forward mapping consists of stating precise policy objectives, elaborating detailed means-ends schemes, and specifying explicit outcome criteria by which to judge policy at each stage. Backward mapping consists of stating precisely the behavior to be changed at the lowest level, describing a set of operations that can insure the change, and repeating the procedure upwards by steps until the central level is reached. By using backward mapping, policy designers may find more appropriate tools than those initially chosen. This process insures consideration of the micro-implementers' and target groups' interpretations of the policy problem and possible solutions.

Elmore's approach is a useful suggestion for policy designers; micro implementers' and target groups' views must be considered in planning an implementation strategy. On the other hand, it is not a theoretical model in the traditional sense. Sellitz, Wrightsman, and Cook (1976, 16) define theory as a "set of concepts plus the interrelationships that are assumed to exist among those concepts." The consequences that logically follow from the relationships posed in the theory should be testable hypotheses. Elmore's model has no predictions as to generalized behavior. No specific interrelationships are hypothesized; effectively there are no hypotheses to test. As a tool, Elmore's discussion is useful; as a theory, however, it lacks explanatory power.

Sabatier (1986; 1988; 1991; Sabatier and Pelkey 1987) has moved away from the top-down perspective, which he helped develop, and toward a combined perspective. He now argues that policy needs to be analyzed in cycles of more than ten years. The longer time allows for an opportunity to consider policy learning, a concept emphasized by Sabatier. Policies operate within parameters most easily identified by using a top-down approach. These parameters include socioeconomic conditions, legal instruments, and the basic government structure. These remain relatively stable over long periods of time. Within this structure, however, substantial actions occur. Sabatier argues that advocacy coalitions should be the main unit of analysis in the study of these actions. Advocacy coalitions are groups of policy advocates from differing organizations, both public and private, who share the same set of beliefs and goals. These groups attempt to have their views of policy problems, solutions, and legitimate actors accepted. Sabatier urges the use of Hjern's networking methodology to develop a mapping of these advocacy coalitions.

Sabatier's proposal represents a legitimate method for studying public policy. When examining a broad policy area over a long period of time, however, the question of whether this is actually studying implementation becomes a relevant concern. Sabatier's definition of implementation (see p. 146) does not appear to be about the same process. A policy field followed over many years can change so radically that it bears little resemblance to its initial form. If implementation research is to retain a meaningful definition, it should be tied to a specific policy rather than to all actions in a policy field.[1]

Goggin et al. (1990) present a communications model of intergovernmental policy implementation that sees state implementers at the nexus of a series of communication channels. They describe three clusters of variables that affect state implementation: inducements and constraints from the top (the federal level), inducements and constraints from the bottom (state and local levels), and state-specific factors defined as decisional outcomes and state capacity. Elements of the two major models are considered by including signals from both the top and the bottom. The communication model also emphasizes that signals are perceived differently, distortions occur, and contextual conditions can affect the interpretation of signals.

Some authors prefer to discuss when a model is appropriately applied rather than to try to build a combined model. Dunsire (1978) and Saetren (1983) argue that the two perspectives should apply to different times in the implementation process. Top-down perspectives are more appropriate in the early planning stages, but a bottom-up view is more appropriate in later evaluation stages.

Berman (1980) argues that an implementation plan should be developed using either the top-down or bottom-up approach depending on a set of parameters that describes the policy context. He argues that these situational parameters are dimensions that the implementation designer cannot influence. They include scope of change, validity of technology, goal conflict, institutional setting, and environmental stability. Berman suggests that when change is incremental, technology is certain, environment is stable, goal conflict is low, and institutional setting is tightly coupled, an implementation plan should follow the tenets of the top-down model. He convincingly argues that when a viable solution already exists, efforts should be concentrated on making sure that solution is used. Therefore a top-down strategy is appropriate. Berman suggests further that major policy changes involving uncertain technology—with goal conflicts and an unstable and loosely coupled environment—should be built around a bottom-up framework. This argument is less convincing. Part of the confusion

lies in the distinction between a descriptive and a prescriptive model. It virtually is certain that when major policy changes are implemented where technology is uncertain and goal conflict high, bargaining *necessarily* occurs and adjustments are made. As a description of the process, many factors emphasized in bottom-up models are relevant. A prescription that suggests these conditions should lead to the delegation of autonomy to microlevel implementers, however, makes implementation feasibility the sole criterion on which to evaluate implementation plans. Linder and Peters (1987) argue that while feasibility is an important consideration, other political, economic, or ethical criteria may lead to a desire for a more centrally directed policy. For example, instituting or expanding civil rights to a new sector of the populace is a policy that probably exhibits most of the conditions in which Berman recommends a bottom-up strategy. Nevertheless, a policy with strong central steering may be preferred as the most effective way to assure actions consistent with policy objectives. Berman argues that choosing a top-down strategy can lead to resistance, disregard, and pro forma compliance. Such dangers certainly do exist. Choosing a bottom-up strategy, however, may lead to cooptation and pursuit of individual goals that run contrary to the policy objectives, and these are often more objectionable.

In synthesizing the two implementation models I have chosen to develop a model that explains when the two approaches are most appropriate rather than to develop a model that combines both simultaneously. I believe this is the most fruitful approach to synthesis for both theoreticians and practitioners. Until now, implementation studies have tended to present long lists of variables that may affect implementation. The conditions under which these variables are important and the reasons we should expect them to be important have been ignored to a large degree or have been treated superficially. This has given us a field overflowing with diagrams and flow charts with a prodigious number of variables. Synthesis that merely combines ten variables considered by the top-downers with ten variables considered by the bottom-uppers, without exploring the theoretical relationship between them, is likely to exacerbate the problem. I have chosen, therefore, to concentrate on a more limited set of variables and to explore their theoretical implications more fully.

Structuring implementation research and bringing some closure to the topic is likely to be even more important for policy designers. While many factors may be relevant and more accurate decisions could be made if all factors were considered, even readily available information isn't considered when decisions are made (Feldman and March 1981). Therefore, while it is proper to remind policy designers to consider all relevant factors, a much greater service is rendered if policy designers are given an adequate description of the implementation process that directs them to the variables of greatest importance and to the factors on which to focus their scarce resources should their search processes be limited, as they inevitably are.

WHAT IS SUCCESSFUL IMPLEMENTATION?

Before turning to model exposition, a proper definition of *successful implementation* should be discussed. Policy can be defined as the programmatic activities formulated in response to an authoritative decision. These activities are the policy designer's plans for carrying out the wishes expressed by a legitimating organization, be it a legislature, a judicial agent, or an executive body. The pivotal question is whether attention should be focused on fidelity to the designer's plan or on the general consequences of the implementation actions when determining success? Disagreements between top-down and bottom-up theorists have at their very base disagreements over this question. Top-down theorists desire to measure success in terms of specific outcomes tied directly to the statutes that are the source of a program. Bottom-up theorists prefer a much broader evaluation, in which a program leading to "positive effects" can be labeled a success (Palumbo, Maynard-Moody, and Wright 1984).

The failure to specify what is meant by *successful implementation* causes considerable confusion. Ingram and Schneider (1990) note several plausible definitions of successful implementation. Among these are: agencies comply with the directives of the statues; agencies are held accountable for reaching specific indicators of success; goals of the statute are achieved; local goals are achieved, or there is an improvement in the political climate around the program. In determining which of these definitions is appropriate, the decision hinges on whether the statutory designer's values should be accorded a normative value greater than those of other actors, especially local actors. If the policy designers' desires do have a superior value, then the bottom-uppers' measure of success is inappropriate. This assertion is grounded in democratic theory. Statutory designers derive their power by being elected or by receiving a mandate from duly elected officials. This mandate can be revoked through electoral disapproval by sovereign voters. The street-level bureaucrat has no such base of power. Clearly, discretionary power exists at the local level, but this power is based on the inability to control actions. Street-level bureaucrats do have legitimate claims to power based on their expertise, but this power claim does not have the same moral quality as claims based on powers bestowed by a sovereign citizenry. It is therefore legitimate to measure implementation success in terms of its ability to execute faithfully the goals and means present in the statutory mandate.

This proposal quickly runs into difficulties, however, when specific policies are considered. Statutory mandates often are exceedingly vague. They do not incorporate specific goals and they fail to provide reasonable yardsticks with which to measure policy results. Broader evaluation standards need to be used when significant ambiguity exists regarding the specific goals of a policy.[2] These can range over a broad set of plausible measures. For example, efficiency gains and economic growth may be used in one case, whereas enhanced support of the political system may be valid in another. Increased understanding and alleviation of local problems are two measures of success that frequently are likely to be relevant.

To recapitulate, when policy goals explicitly have been stated, then, based on democratic theory, the statutory designers' values have a superior value. In such instances the correct standard of implementation success is loyalty to the prescribed goals. When a policy does not have explicitly stated goals, the choice of a standard becomes more difficult, and more general societal norms and values come into play....

A COMPREHENSIVE IMPLEMENTATION MODEL: EXPOSITION OF THE FOUR PERSPECTIVES

In reviewing proposals for remedying implementation failure O'Toole (1986) found that the literature makes contradictory recommendations. I believe this occurs because the underlying antecedent characteristics of a policy are analyzed insufficiently. The factors that help implement policy under one set of conditions exacerbate already existing problems under another. Previous theoretical work has failed to identify the conditions under which policy recommendations will be effective.[3] The conflict-ambiguity matrix presented in exhibit 1 is an initial step toward sorting out various useful recommendations in the literature.

Each box in exhibit 1 presents the type of implementation process, the central principle determining outcomes for this type of implementation, and an example of a policy that fits this category.[4] The four cells in the conflict-ambiguity matrix are reviewed below. The following aspects

CONFLICT

		Low	High
AMBIGUITY	**Low**	*Administrative Implementation* Resources Example: Smallpox erradication	*Political Implementation* Power Example: Busing
	High	*Experimental Implementation* Contextual Conditions Example: Headstart	*Symbolic Implementation* Coalition Strength Example: Community action agencies

EXHIBIT 1 Ambiguity-Conflict Matrix: Policy Implementation Processes

are discussed for each perspective: the central principle describing the factor expected to have the greatest influence on the implementation outcome; a description of the implementation process with special emphasis of the implications of policy ambiguity and conflict; a discussion of the expected pitfalls; and the appropriateness of top-down or bottom-up approaches as a description of the process.

Administrative Implementation: Low Policy Ambiguity and Low Policy Conflict

In decision-making theory, choice opportunities where ambiguity and conflict are low provide the prerequisite conditions for a rational decision-making process. Goals are given and a technology (means) for solving the existing problem is known. Simon (1960) called decisions of this type "programmed decisions." The central principle in administrative implementation is *outcomes are determined by resources*. The desired outcome is virtually assured, given that *sufficient resources* are appropriated for the program.

The implementation process can be compared to a machine. At the top of the machine is a central authority. This authority has information, resources, and sanction capabilities to help enact the desired policy. Information flows from the top down. Implementation is ordered in a hierarchical manner with each underlying link receiving orders from the level above. The policy is spelled out explicitly at each level, and at each link in the chain actors have a clear idea of their responsibilities and tasks. The paradigm invoked is Weberian bureaucrats loyally carrying out their appointed duties.

Low levels of ambiguity mean it is clear which actors are to be active in implementation. As the actors are stable over time, they develop standard operating procedures to expedite their work. The transparency of the technology makes clear which resources are required, and resource procurement is built into the implementation process. The system therefore is relatively closed to outside influence. The isolation from environmental factors, along with the programmed nature of policy, results in relatively uniform outcomes at the microlevel across many settings.

Etzioni (1961) describes three types of mechanisms for gaining compliance from an actor: normative, coercive, and remunerative. A normative mechanism induces compliance through reference to a mutually held goal or to the legitimacy of the person requesting action (for example, a superior in a hierarchy). A coercive mechanism threatens sanctions for failing to comply with a request for action. A remunerative mechanism includes sufficient incentives, often additional resources, to make the desired course of action attractive to the agent. For administrative implementation, where levels of conflict are low, normative compliance mechanisms are generally sufficient. The orders given are perceived as legitimate, and there is little controversy that might lead to subversion. Remunerative mechanisms may be used, especially for pulling in outside resources, but most actions are induced through normative mechanisms. In those few cases where coercive mechanisms are needed, they can be expected to be effective since means are clear and easily monitored.

Since a technology for dealing with the problem exists, implementation activities are concerned primarily with getting the technology in place and functioning. They often consist of a set of rules that structures discretion so as to insure the preferred outcomes. Implementation failure occurs because of technical problems: the machine sputters. Problems occur because of misunderstanding, poor coordination, insufficient resources, insufficient time to use the correct technology, or lack of an effective monitoring strategy to control and sanction deviant behavior.

As messages pass through a communication network, they tend to get distorted. Even when the message appears clear to the sender, it may fail to be comprehended fully due to cognitive limitations of the receiver. In addition, cognitive dissonance may lead to selective perception. Pressman and Wildavsky (1973) calculate the probability of successful implementation as less than 50 percent if an order is followed with 90 percent accuracy after going through six hierarchical levels. If orders are comprehended with less than 90 percent accuracy, the probability of success will fall even faster.

This description of the implementation process closely parallels those found in traditional top-down approaches. Top-down models are descended from old public administration models, and the Wilsonian tradition, which defined administration as separate from politics, is effective in these cases. When a policy is characterized by a high degree of consensus and the means for reaching the policy goal are known, the implementation process becomes dominated by technocratic questions of compliance and follow-up. An example of such a policy is the World Health Organization's (WHO) program to eliminate smallpox. The means—mass vaccination and quarantine—and goals—eradication of smallpox—were clear. As the program developed, standard operating procedures were established to decrease discretion and increase efficiency. Success was determined largely by the level of resources available and the efficiency of the program developed to implement the policy. The difference between WHO's program to eradicate smallpox and the U.S. program to contain tuberculosis show strikingly the crucial role that resources play for administrative policies. In the case of smallpox, there were sufficient resources to continue active implementation until the disease was eliminated completely. In the case of tuberculosis, existing policy led to a decreasing number of cases and appeared to have effective control over tuberculosis into the early 1980s. At that time federal funding was cut off. The consequence of that action has been both a resurgence of tuberculosis in the 1990s and the appearance of a drug-resistant strain of tuberculosis.

Kelman (1984) describes how he developed an implementation plan for the Emergency Energy Assistance program.[5] This program was to take effect in case of a new energy crisis. The policy theory was to allow market prices on energy, tax the windfall profits of energy companies, and recycle the money back to citizens via an emergency energy rebate. The rebate portion of the program was both clear and nonconflictual, and therefore it fit the administrative implementation paradigm. Nevertheless, difficulties existed with implementation. This program required substantial new capacity; virtually all adult citizens in the United States would need to be identified and to have checks mailed to them, all in a short time. There were many obstacles: finding an agency with the expertise and capacity to process tremendous numbers of cases quickly (i.e., a problem of sufficient resources); combining several different lists to develop one complete list of eligible recipients (coordination problems); and providing citizens access throughout the country to file complaints in case of oversight (resource problems). Kelman, using the implementation literature as a guide, revised the initial plans, which called for state agencies to provide lists of recipients. Noting the great difficulties involved in getting 150 different agencies to provide data on short notice, he devised a plan that gave full responsibility to the Internal Revenue Service (IRS) and based the identification of recipients on IRS records. Placing the primary responsibility for the program with the IRS helped to minimize possible coordination problems and enabled policy designers to take advantage of IRS's capacity to train large numbers of employees quickly. IRS also had the necessary expertise to quickly process applications and to deal with consumer complaints. According to Kelman, IRS support was relatively easy to enlist because of its loyalty to the congressional mandate, a promise of resources, and an opportunity for the IRS to improve its image by giving people money rather than taking money away from them. Kelman's discussion is instructive: it indicates that the problems that arise under conditions of low ambiguity and low conflict are primarily technical, and it shows that, even for policies with low levels of conflict and ambiguity, an implementation plan can require substantial effort.

Political Implementation: Low Policy Ambiguity and High Policy Conflict

Low ambiguity and high conflict are typical of political models of decision making (Allison 1971; Halperin 1974; Elmore 1978).[6] Actors have clearly defined goals, but dissension occurs because these clearly defined goals are incompatible. Equally conflictual battles can occur over means. It is often precisely in the designing of the implementation policy that conflicts develop and vigorous battles erupt. The central principle in political implementation is that *implementation outcomes are decided by power*. In some cases one actor or a coalition of actors have sufficient

power to force their will on other participants. In other cases actors resort to bargaining to reach an agreement.

For policies of this type, compliance is not automatically forthcoming. While there is an explicit policy, essential resources are controlled by skeptical actors outside the implementing organization or by actors actively opposed to the proposed policy. Often both conditions exist. Such a system is more open to influences from the environment than from administrative implementation. The implementation program consists of securing the compliance of actors whose resources are vital to policy success and ensuring that the process is not thwarted by opponents of the policy. Since some of the actors whose cooperation is required may disagree with the policy goals, successful implementation depends on either having sufficient power to force one's will on the other participants or having sufficient resources to be able to bargain an agreement on means. Coercive and remunerative mechanisms will predominate.

Coercive mechanisms are most effective when the desired outcomes are easily monitored and the coercing principal controls a resource essential to the agent. This point is made convincingly by Durant (1984) in his study of two controversies involving the Tennessee Valley Authority (TVA) and the Environmental Protection Agency (EPA). He found that where the sanctions available to the EPA threatened the central mission of the TVA, compliance was quickly forthcoming. In the case where the controversy did not threaten the central mission of the TVA and the sanctions seemed less onerous, several years were spent arguing and litigating before the TVA finally complied.

The greater the implementer's authority to require agent action, the more likely it is that agents will comply with the principal's requests. Agents, however, often are not in a direct line relationship with the implementer, and coercive mechanisms fail to bring about compliance. Many actors have independent bases of power and can refuse to participate without having their own missions threatened. Even where there are relatively strong sanction opportunities (such as federal grants to states and local entities) states and municipalities exhibit a surprising degree of independence (Ingram 1977). Under these conditions, activities are directed toward reaching a negotiated agreement on actions. Agreement on goals is unnecessary, agreement on actions is sufficient. Many bargaining techniques commonly found in the legislative forum reappear. Disputes are resolved through side payments, logrolling, oversight, or ambiguity. Questions that cannot be resolved can be buried in ambiguous text and left for later resolution.

The opposing sides of a policy question previously may have done battle at the policy adoption stage. The shift of forum, however, can result in a change in the balance of power. A legislative coalition often consists of actors whose support is fleeting. Supporters agree to vote for a policy on the basis of logrolling, in response to political pressure, or simply because it appears to be a sensible policy. Many of these supporters have little interest in the implementation stage. Even among those with an active interest the rewards from oversight are limited and likely to lead to only sporadic activities (Mayhew 1974; Ogul 1976). This venue shift can result in the nonimplementation of policy. This view is borne out by the regulation literature, which finds industries more successful at influencing the implementation phase than the legislative phase of policy (Stigler 1971; Joskow and Noll 1981).

The description of the policy process proposed by the newer top-down models comes closest to capturing the essence of the implementation process under these conditions. The traditional public administration models and the earliest top-down models took an administrative view of what is essentially a political problem; they failed to identify the sources of implementation barriers. The more sophisticated top-down models, which were developed partially in response to the failings of standard public administration teachings, emphasize political factors. Among the political factors built into Mazmanian and Sabatier's model (1989) are general public support, support from upper-level political leaders, resources and support from relevant constituency groups, and the commitment of implementing officials.

The bottom-up argument, that policies are decided at the microlevel, fails because it does not take account of the considerable forces and power that can be brought to bear upon an issue when it is unambiguously and explicitly formulated. School integration through busing is an example of a highly contentious yet unambiguous issue implemented by central authorities, with local officials looking on with little power to halt actions. While local authorities may disagree, sometimes vehemently, with the means that are used, the central authorities (i.e., the courts) have sufficient power to force their plan on the other participants. Low ambiguity insures that monitoring of compliance is relatively easy; attempts at subversion are likely to be caught and swiftly punished.

Experimental Implementation: High Policy Ambiguity and Low Policy Conflict

If a policy exhibits a high level of ambiguity and low level of conflict, outcomes will depend largely on which actors are active and most involved. The central principle driving this type of implementation is that *contextual conditions dominate the process.* Outcomes depend heavily on the resources and actors present in the microimplementing environment. These are likely to vary strongly from site to site, therefore broad variations in outcomes will occur. In decision-making terms, this type of implementation condition closely parallels a "garbage can" process with streams of actors, problems, solutions, and choice opportunities combining to produce outcomes that are hard to predict. The conditions that are required for a choice opportunity to develop into a garbage can are problematic preferences (ambiguous goals); uncertain technology (no predefined correct behavior); and fluid participation (actors vary over time) (Cohen, March, and Olsen 1972; March and Olsen 1976 and 1986). By definition, experimental implementation defines cases where preferences are problematic and technology is uncertain. The crucial element is: Which participants are active and what is their intensity of participation? Participants' level of activity in a choice situation depends on the intensity of their feelings, the number of other demands on their time, their physical proximity to the place where decisions are made, and a host of other variables.

As a result of policy ambiguity, the implemented program differs from site to site. The constellation of actors participating, the pressures on the actors, the perceptions of what the policy is, the available resources, and possible programmatic activities vary widely across policy settings. The lack of conflict is likely to open the arena for a large number of actors to participate and to provide those who have intense interests, or substantial slack resources, with an opportunity to mold policy significantly. The opportunities are excellent for bureaucratic entrepreneurs to create policies to deal with local needs.

This process is more open to environmental influences than are other forms of implementation. Program mutations arise as different organizations implement different policies in different environments. These mutations can be seen as natural experiments, and it is important for policy designers to actively use them to enhance their knowledge of change processes within the policy area, with a strong emphasis on formative evaluations (Mohr 1988). For policies that have clear goals, it is possible to carry out and use summative evaluations that explicitly state whether the policy has reached its appointed goal. For policies with unclear goals, it is far more useful to use formative evaluations that describe the process and describe the way outcomes are arrived at without an explicit stamp of approval or disapproval.

Policies where both goals and means are unclear naturally fall into the category of experimental implementation. In addition, policies with clear and widely supported goals but with unclear means of implementation take on experimental characteristics. For many policies the goals are agreed upon and known, yet the means of reaching these goals is unknown. Implementing policies of this type can be technology-forcing and can lead to the development of entirely new capabilities. Nakamura and Smallwood (1980) point to the Clean Air Act of 1970 as a prime example of a case where the technology did not exist before the policy was passed; it developed quickly in response to the Act. Biomedical research is another example where technology doesn't exist but policy is widely supported. On the other hand, ambiguous policies can breed limited accountability and can lead to the creation of minifiefdoms with

leaders pursuing their own interests. These may have little, if any, connection to the public interest.

The emphasis on seeing each iteration of a policy as an experiment is important when one evaluates possible pitfalls to the implementation process. More important than a *successful* outcome is one that produces learning.[7] Policies operate in areas where there is insufficient knowledge to institute programmed implementation or of how elements in the policy environment are causally connected. Ambiguity should be seen as an opportunity to learn both new means and new goals. Two pitfalls must be avoided. First, the process should not be forced into an artificially constrained form. Programs demanding conformity are likely to meet with superficial compliance efforts from local implementers. In addition, demanding uniformity when processes are poorly understood robs us of vital information and limits the street-level bureaucrats' use of their knowledge as a resource. Since uniformity is to be discouraged, development of effective compliance monitoring mechanisms is of limited relevance. Second, the process requires a conscious realization that learning is the goal. If there are fifty sites with fifty differing results, but the information is neither gathered nor compared, then learning is likely to occur in a random pattern. Evaluation and feedback are vital components of effective learning.

The bottom-up description of the policy implementation process is superior to the top-down in describing conditions in this category. The emphasis on the opportunities available to local-level actors appears most appropriate. Tolerance for ambiguity is much greater in bottom-up than in top-down models. The top-down models emphasize command, control, and uniformity and fail to take into account the diversity inherent in much implementation that occurs.

Headstart is an excellent example of experimental implementation. It officially was approved in March 1965 and was to begin in the summer of 1965. The Office of Economic Opportunity (OEO) had barely three months to prepare, far too short a time to develop any type of comprehensive plan. The central administration had only the most general notion of what the goals of a preschool program for disadvantaged children should be. At the same time, Sargent Shriver III, the director of the OEO, had a serious problem in that he was unable to spend all of his budget. These factors combined to produce a situation in which virtually all proposals for summer school programs were approved. There was a cornucopia of proposals, and Headstart meant many different things for its first several iterations. Over time, as information was gathered, the program became more structured, but at the start few attempts were made to steer it from the top. The meaning of Headstart in those early stages was dependent almost exclusively on which actors were involved at the microlevel and what resources they had at their disposal.

Symbolic Implementation: High Policy Ambiguity and High Policy Conflict

It may seem implausible that a policy can have high levels of ambiguity and yet be conflictual. As was noted earlier, many scholars suggest making a policy more ambiguous to diminish conflict. Nevertheless, policies do exist that appropriately are characterized as having both high levels of ambiguity and high levels of conflict. Policies that invoke highly salient symbols often produce high levels of conflict even when the policy is vague.[8] Symbolic policies play an important role in confirming new goals, in reaffirming a commitment to old goals, or in emphasizing important values and principles (Olsen 1970). The high level of conflict is important, because it structures the way resolutions are developed. The high level of ambiguity results in outcomes that vary across sites. The central principle is that local level *coalitional strength* determines the outcome. The policy course is determined by the coalition of actors at the local level who control the available resources.

For policy with only a referential goal, differing perspectives will develop as to how to translate the abstract goal into instrumental actions. The inherent ambiguity leads to a proliferation of interpretations. Competition ensues over the correct "vision." Actors see their interests tied to a specific policy definition, and therefore similar competing coalitions are likely to form at differing sites. The strength of these actors will vary across the possible sites. Contextual conditions at the local level affect outcomes through their effect on coalition strength. Variations in coalition strength and dominant coalition make-up manifest themselves in differing programs in different localities. Outcomes are bounded and less differentiated than for cases of experimental implementation, because opposition coalitions are able to put effective limits on policy even when they cannot determine its content. Nevertheless, substantial variation is expected, with coalition strength at the local level being of central importance in determining the policy outcome.

Professions are likely to play an especially important role for symbolic policies. Professional training provides a strong set of norms as to legitimate activities and effective problem-solving actions. When faced with a vague referential goal and an ambiguous program of action, actors with professional training are likely to step in quickly with proposals grounded in their professions. Professions with competing claims over an area and different standard programs for attacking problems often form the core of competing coalitions. For example, a youth employment program may have an official goal of improving opportunities for disadvantaged youths. This policy has a referential goal that may include any of the following sub-goals: decreased crime, increased educational opportunities, increased income, and provision of on-the-job training. Among actors with different training, there are substantially different proposals for implementing this policy. Their implementation battles are likely to be long and bitter.

Policies aimed at redistributing power or goods are perhaps the most obvious examples of programs that fall under this category. Policy goals often provide little information to a policy designer about how to proceed, yet the symbols are sufficient to create significant opposition before any plans are promulgated. The Community Action Agencies (CAA) established as part of the War on Poverty are a prime example of a symbolic policy. The stated goal of the CAA was to facilitate local citizenry empowerment. What this meant was unclear to virtually all participants. Despite great ambiguity, the CAA generated considerable controversy and animosity, often precisely because the policy was ambiguous and there was a fear of what the policy implied for existing relationships.

Symbolic implementation policies are conflictual, therefore they exhibit similarities to political implementation. Actors are intensely involved, and disagreements are resolved through coercion or bargaining; problem solving or persuasion are used to a limited degree only. Any actor's influence is tied to the strength of the coalition of which she is part. Symbolic implementation *differs* from political implementation in that coalitional strength at the microlevel, not at the macrolevel, determines the implementation outcome. This difference occurs because of a high ambiguity level. When a policy has a referent goal and ambiguous means it is solidly in the symbolic quadrant. As the ambiguity level decreases the policy moves upward, toward the political implementation quadrant. A decrease in ambiguity, either through explicit goals or a crystallization of discussion around a limited number of possible means, would provide central level actors an increased opportunity to assert some control and influence. When the policy is very clear, the macrolevel actors are able to exert considerable control, and this becomes a case of political implementation.

When dealing with cases of symbolic implementation, identifying the competing factions at the local level, along with the microlevel contextual factors that affect the strengths of the competing factions, is central to accurate explanations of policy outcomes. Neither the top-down nor bottom-up models appear entirely appropriate in describing the implementation process when there is substantial conflict and an ambiguous policy. The macroimplementers who are so prominent in the top-down models see their powers diminish. Policy ambiguity makes it difficult for the macroimplementers to monitor activities, and it is much more difficult to structure actions at the local level. Nevertheless, centrally located actors do constitute an important influence through provision of resources and incentives and through focusing attention on an issue area. Because of the higher level of conflict, the process is likely to be highly political, but it will be dominated by local actors. The bottom-uppers are correct in that the local actors are paramount, but their models do not emphasize the strongly political nature of the interactions.

CONCLUSION

I noted at the outset that the implementation literature suffers from a lack of theoretical structure. By drawing on the organizational theory literature, considering how ambiguity and conflict affect policy implementation, and combining these factors into the ambiguity/conflict model, this article provides a more theoretically grounded approach to implementation. By studying a policy's level of conflict and ambiguity, testable predictions can be made as to how the implementation process will unfold.

Traditional top-down models, based on the public administration tradition, present an accurate description of the implementation process when policy is clear and conflict is low. The recommendations found in this literature provide a useful set of heuristics in promulgating an implementation plan. Because there is a clear policy, macroimplementation planners wield considerable influence. Bottom-up models provide an accurate description of the implementation process when policy is ambiguous and conflict is low. The expectation is that conditions at the micro-implementation level dominate and should be encouraged to vary. Under conditions identified as political implementation, where conflict is high and ambiguity is low, the newer top-down models—which emphasize the importance of structuring access and providing resources with a conscious concern for the heavily politicized atmosphere that attends such policies—provide an important starting point. When there is substantial conflict and an ambiguous policy, both models have some relevancy. Microlevel actors dominate the process, but actions are highly political as emphasized by top-down models.

One implicit concern underlying this model is that ambiguity should not be seen as a flaw in a policy. Despite its being blamed often for implementation failure, ambiguity can be useful. Ambiguity can ease agreement both at the legitimation and the formulation stage. It provides an opportunity to learn new methods, technologies, and goals. Widespread variation provides an abundance of knowledge which should be actively nurtured. Ambiguity should be viewed neither as an evil nor as a good. It should be seen as a characteristic of a policy, without imbuing it with any normative value.

Finally, while I have argued that under certain conditions it is most appropriate to hold either a top-down or a bottom-up perspective, it is important to recognize that both schools contain kernels of truth relevant in any implementation situation. For example, central authorities inevitably influence policy implementation through decisions on funding and jurisdiction, even when policies are vague and conflict is low. It is also clear that policies are almost never self-executing. A microimplementation process occurs, even for purely technical questions with all the characteristics of administrative implementation. This model provides a description for the policy designer pondering where the most important problems are likely to lie. For the researcher it provides a map to those elements expected to most greatly influence policy outcomes.

End Notes

1. It should be noted that Sabatier doesn't see his advocacy coalition model as an implementation model; he sees it as a broader approach to studying public policy.
2. Ingram and Schneider (1990) provide a discussion of the conditions under which various alternative definitions of successful implementation are appropriate.
3. For an important exception within the regulatory field see Gormley (1986).
4. In exhibit 1, ambiguity and conflict are presented as dichotomous; this is strictly to simplify the exposition. The theoretical constructs are continuous. As a policy gradually moves across a dimension, for example from low to high conflict, the implementation process is expected increasingly to show the characteristics of the paradigm being moved toward and decreasingly to show the characteristics of the paradigm being moved away from. There is no tipping point at which a slight move up or down causes a radical shift from one type of implementation to another.
5. While this program was never implemented, his discussion is very instructive on how implementation plans are developed.
6. By calling this *political* implementation I am not implying that other types of implementation do not have political elements, any more so than calling the previous category administrative implies that it is the only category with administrative elements. The term is merely meant to emphasize that this type of policy is expected to prominently exhibit bargaining and other activities associated with the bureaucratic politics tradition of decision making.
7. See Ingram and Schneider (1990) for a similar argument in discussing a grass roots approach to statutory design.
8. Traditionally, symbolic politics has been associated with nonimplementation of policy (Edelman 1964 and 1977). The typical example is a policy that receives substantial exposure at the adoption stage, but that ultimately has little substantive effect. While that tradition is important, it ultimately is very confining. Symbolic politics is almost always tied to substantive failure. A considerably richer understanding of the effects of symbols on politics can be produced if policies are defined as symbolic *before* they have been implemented.

References

ALLISON, GRAHAM. 1971. *Essence of Decision: Explaining the Cuban Missle Crisis.* Boston, Mass.: Little,Brown.

BAIER,VICKI; March, J.G.; and SAETREN, H. 1986. "Implementation and Ambiguity." *Scandinavian Journal of Management Studies* 2: 197–212.

BERMAN, PAUL. 1978. "The Study of Macro-and Micro-Implementation. "*Public Policy* 26: 2: 157–84.

BERMAN, PAUL. 1980. "Thinking about Programmed and Adaptive Implementation: Matching Strategies to Situations." In H. Ingram and D. Mann, eds. *Why Policies Succeed or Fail.* Beverly Hills, Calif.: Sage.

COHEN, MICHAEL D.; MARCH, JAMES; and OLSEN, JOHAN P. 1972. "A Garbage Can Model of Organizational Choice." *Administrative Science Quarterly* 17: 1–25.

DAHRENDORF, RALF. 1958. "Towards a Theory of Social Conflict." *Journal of Conflict Resolution* 2: 2: 170–83.

DUNSIRE, ANDREW. 1978. *Implementation in a Bureaucracy.* Oxford: Martin Roberson.

DURANT, ROBERT F. 1984. "EPA, TVA and Pollution Control: Implications for a Theory of Regulatory

Policy Implementation." *Public Administration Review* 44: 3: 305–15.

EDELMAN, MURRAY S. 1964. The Symbolic Use of Politics. Champaign: University of Illinois Press.

EDELMAN, MURRAY S. 1977. *Political Language: Words That Succeed and Policies That Fail.* New York: Academic Press.

ELMORE, RICHARD F. 1978. "Organizational Models of Social Program Implementation." *Public Policy* 26: 2: 185–226.

ELMORE, RICHARD F. 1982. "Backward Mapping: Implementation Research and Policy Decisions." In Walter L. Williams, ed. *Studying Implementation: Methodological and Administrative Issues.* Chatham, N.J.: Chatham Publishing.

ELMORE, RICHARD F. 1985 "Forward and Backward Mapping." In K. Hanfand T. Toonen, eds. *Policy Implementation in Federal and Unitary Systems.* Dordrecht: Martinus Nijhoff.

ETZIONI, AMITAI. 1961. *Complex Organizations: A Sociological Reader.* New York: Holt, Rinehart, and Winston.

FELDMAN, MARTHA S., and MARCH, JAMES G. 1981. "Information in Organizations as Signal and Symbols." *Administrative Science Quarterly* 26: 171–86.

GOGGIN, MALCOLM L.; BOWMAN, ANN; LESTER, JAMES P.; and O'TOOLE, LAURENCE J., Jr. 1990. *Implementation Theory and Practice: Toward a Third Generation.* Glenview, Ill.: Scott, Foresman/ Little, Brown.

GORMLEY, WILLIAM T., Jr. 1986. "Regulatory Issue Networks in a Federal System." *Polity* 17: 2: 595–620.

HALPERIN, MORTEN H. 1974. *Bureaucratic Politics and Foreign Policy.* Washington, D.C.: Brookings.

HJERN, BENNY. 1982. "Implementation Research- The Link Gone Missing." *Journal of Public Policy* 2: 3: 301–08.

HJERN, BENNY, AND HULL, Chris. 1982. "Implementation Research as Empirical Constitutionalism." *European Journal of Political Research* 10: 2: 105–16.

HJERN, BENNY, and HULL, CHRIS. 1985. "Small Firm Employment Creation: An Assistance Structure Explanation." In K. Hanfand T. Toonen, eds. *Policy Implementation in Federal and Unitary Systems. Dordrecht: 'Martinus Nijhoff.*

HJERN, BENNY, and PORTER, DAVID. 1981. "Implementation Structures: A New Unit of Administrative Analysis." *Organization Studies* 2: 211–27.

HOPPE, ROBERT; VAN DE GRAAF, HENK; and VAN DIJK, ASJE. 1985 "Implementation as Design Problem: Problem Tractability, Policy Theory, and Feasibility Testing." Paper presented at meeting of the International Political Science Association, Paris, July.

HULL, CHRIS, and HJERN, BENNY. 1987. *Helping Small Firms Grow: An Implementation Approach.* London: Croom Helm.

INGRAM, HELEN. 1977. "Policy Implementation through Bargaining: Federal Grants in Aid." *Public Policy* 25: 4: 499–526.

INGRAM, HELEN, and SCHNEIDER, ANNE. 1990. "Improving Implementation Through Framing Smarter Statutes." *Journal of Public Policy* 10: 1: 67–88.

JONES, CHARLES. 1975. *Clean Air: The Politics and Unpolitics of Air Pollution Control.* Pittsburgh: University of Pittsburgh Press.

JOSKOW, PAUL L., and NOLL, ROGER C. 1985. "Regulation in Theory and Practice: An Overview." In G. Fromm, ed. *Studies in Public Regulation.* Cambridge, Mass.: MIT Press.

KELMAN, STEVEN. 1984. "Using Implementation Research to Solve Implementation Problems: The Case of Energy Emergency Assistance." *Journal of Policy Analysis and Management* 4: 1: 75–91.

LAVE, CHARLES A., and March, James G. 1975. *An Introduction to Models in the Social Sciences.* New York: Harper & Row.

LINDER, STEPHEN H., and PETERS, B. GUY. 1987. "A Design Perspective on Policy Implementation: The Fallacies of Misplaced Prescription." *Policy Studies Review* 6: 3: 459–75.

LIPSKY, MICHAEL. 1978. "Standing the Study of Policy Implementation on Its Head." In Walter D. Burnham and Martha Weinberg, eds. *American Politics and Public Policy.* Cam-Mass.: MIT Press.

LOWI, THEODORE J. 1979. *The End of Liberalism.* New York: Norton.

LUCE, DUNCAN R., and RAIFFA, HOWARD. 1957. *Games and Decisions.* New York: Wiley.

McLAUGHLIN, MILBREY WALLIN. 1987 "Learning From Experience: Lessons From Policy Implementation. "Educational Evaluation and Policy Analysis 9: 2: 171–78.

MARCH, JAMES G., and OLSEN, JOHAN P. 1976. *Ambiguity and Choice in Organizations.* Oslo: Universitetsforlaget.

MARCH, JAMES G., and OLSEN, JOHAN P. 1986. "Garbage Can Models of Decision Making in Organizations. "In James G. March and Roger Weissinger-Baylon, eds. *Ambiguity and Command: Organizational Perspectives on Military Decision Making.* Cambridge, Mass.: Ballinger.

MARCH, JAMES G., and SIMON, HERBERT A. 1958. *Organizations.* New York: Wiley.

MAYHEW, DAVID R. 1974. *Congress: The Electoral Connection.* New Haven, Conn.: Yale University Press.

MAYNARD-MOODY, STEVEN; MUSHENO, MICHAEL; and PALUMBO, DENNIS. 1990. "Streetwise Social Policy: Resolving the Dilemma of Street Level Influence and Successful Implementation." *Western Political Quarterly* 43: 4: 833–48.

MAZMANIAN, DANIEL, and SABATIER, PAUL A.1983. *Implementation and Public Policy.* Glenview, Ill.: Scott, Foresman.

MAZMANIAN, DANIEL, and SABATIER, PAUL A. 1989. *Implementation and Public Policy,* rev. ed. Latham, Md.: University Press of America.

MAZMANIAN, DANIEL, and SABATIER, PAUL A., eds. 1981. *Effective Policy Implementation.* Lexington, Mass.: Lexington Books.

MERTON, ROBERT K. 1957. *Social Theory and Social Structure,* 2d ed. Glencoe, Ill.: Free Press.

MICHELS, ROBERT. 1949. *Political Parties.* Glencoe, Ill.: Free Press.

MOHR, LAWRENCE B. 1988. *Impact Analysis for Program Evaluation.* Chicago: Dorsey.

NAKAMURA, ROBERT T., and SMALLWOOD, FRANK. 1980. *The Politics of Policy Implementation.* NewYork: St.Martin's.

OFFERDAL, AUDUN. 1984. "Implementation and Politics, or: Whether It Is a Successor a Failure." (in Norwegian) *Statsviteren,* Nr. 2–3.

OGUL, MORRIS S. 1976. *Congress Oversees The Executive.* Pittsburgh: University of Pittsburgh Press.

OLSEN, JOHAN P. 1970. "Local Budgeting-Decision-Making or Ritual Act?" *Scandinavian Political Studies* 5: 85–118.

O'TOOLE, LAURENCE, Jr. 1986. "Policy Recommendations for Multi-Actor Implementation: An Assessment of the Field." *Journal of Public Policy* 6: 2: 181–210.

O'TOOLE, LAURENCE, Jr. 1989. "Goal Multiplicity in the Implementation Setting: Subtle Impacts and The Case of Waste-water Treatment Privatization." *Policy Studies Journal* 18:1:1–20.

PALUMBO, DENNISJ.; MAYNARD-MOODY, STEVEN; and WRIGHT, PAULA. 1984. "Measuring Degrees of Successful Implementation." *Evaluation Review* 8: 1: 45–74.

PRESSMAN, JEFFREY, and WILDAVSKY, AARON. 1973. *Implementation.* Berkeley: University of California Press.

RAIFFA, HOWARD. 1970. *Decision Analysis.* Reading, Mass.: Addison-Wesley.

REGAN, PRISCILLA M. 1984. "Personal Information Policies in the United States and Britain: The Dilemma of Implementation Considerations." *Journal of Public Policy* 4: 1: 19–38.

SABATIER, PAUL A. 1986. "Top-Down and Bottom-Up Approaches to Implementation Research: A Critical Analysis and Suggested Synthesis." *Journal of Public Policy* 6: 1: 21–48.

SABATIER, PAUL A. 1988. "An Advocacy Coalition Frame-work of Policy Change and the Role of Policy-Oriented Learning Therein." *Policy Sciences* 21: 3: 129–68.

SABATIER, PAUL A. 1991 "Towards Better Theories of the Policy Process." PS: Political Science and Politics 24: 2: 147–56

SABATIER, PAUL A., and PELKEY, NEIL. 1987. "Incorporating Multiple Actors and Guidance Instruments into Models of Regulatory Policy-making: An Advocacy Coalition Framework." *Administration and Society* 19: 2: 236–63.

SAETREN, HARALD. 1983. *The Implementation of Public Policy.* (in Norwegian) Oslo: Universitetsforlaget.

SELLITZ, CLAIRE; WRIGHTSMAN, LAWRENCE S.; and COOK, STUART W. 1976. *Research Methods in Social Relations,* 3d ed. New York: Holt, Rinehart, and Winston.

SELZNICK, PHILIP. 1949. *TVA and the Grassroots.* Berkeley: University of California Press.

SIMON, HERBERT A. 1960. *The New Science of Management Decision.* New York: Harper.

STIGLER, GEORGE. 1971. "The Economics of Regulation." *Bell Journal of Regulation* 2: 3–21.

TUKEY, JOHN. 1962. "The Future of Data Analysis." *Annals of Mathematical Statistics* 33: 1: 13–14.

VAN HOM, CARL E. 1987. "Applied Implementation Research." Paper presented at Midwest Political Science Association Meeting, Chicago.

VAN METER, DONALD S., and VAN HOM, CARL E. 1975. "The Policy Implementation Process: A Conceptual Frame-work." *Administration and Society* 6: 4: 445–88.

WEATHERLEY, RICHARD, and LIPSKY, MICHAEL. 1977. "Street-Level Bureaucrats and Institutional Innovation: Implementing Special Education Reform." *Harvard Educational Review* 47: 170–96.

WINTER, SOEREN. 1985. "Implementation Barriers." (in Danish) *Politica* 17: 4: 467–87.

WINTER, SOEREN. 1986 "How Policy-Making Affects Implementation: The Decentralization of the Danish Disablement Pension Administration." *Scandinavian Political Studies* 9: 4: 361–85.

50

The Assessment of Executed Policy Solutions

Stella Z. Theodoulou and C. Kofinis

Concerns over accountability, efficiency, and effectiveness in policymaking are intensifying at all levels. Elected officials, policy makers, community leaders, bureaucrats, and the public at large want to know what policies work and what ones are not working, and why. More often than not policies and the programs they create often fail to achieve their intended effects and have unintended outcomes. The purpose of evaluation is to determine whether an implemented program is doing what it is supposed to. If it is, then evaluation will assess how well it is achieving its intended objectives and goals. If the program or policy is not performing well, evaluation will determine what effects the program is having. Through evaluation we can determine whether a policy's effects are intended or unintended and whether the results are positive or negative benefits for the target population and society as a whole.

Over the years evaluation has become more common place, although it is not new for governments to assess whether their programs are cost effective and are achieving desired benefits. For example, in the Roman Empire, it was common to alter tax policies in response to fluctuations in revenues. This was an early form of policy evaluation. American policy makers became more concerned with judging the effects of policies in the 1960s with the advent of the War on Poverty programs. From this point in time American policy makers became more concerned with whether the different welfare and anti poverty programs were having the effect they were supposed to and whether tax dollars were being spent efficiently and effectively. From the late 1960s, requirements for program evaluation were written into almost all federal programs.[1]

Subsequently, Congress established evaluating organizations such as the Congressional Budget Office and The General Accounting Office. Funding support for such organizations has varied with each subsequent presidential administration. For example, the Reagan administration made deep budgetary cuts that affected the federal government's ability to conduct program evaluation.[2]

In this chapter we will identify the different types and approaches to evaluation, discuss the process of evaluation, identify who carries out evaluation, and the obstacles that face evaluators. The chapter's objective is to offer readers a brief, simple, and clear introduction to program or policy evaluation. It is not intended to point the reader to any one approach or type of evaluation over another. Rather the reader should understand that the best evaluation is the one which meets the needs of the program or policy that is being evaluated. We begin by distinguishing program evaluation from other related forms of assessment activity.

From Stella Z. Theodoulou and Chris Kofinis, *The Art of the Game: Understanding American Public Policy Making* (Belmont: Wadsworth, 2001).

What Is Policy Evaluation?

Policy evaluation consists of reviewing an implemented policy to see if it is doing what was mandated. The consequences of such policies programs are determined by describing their impacts, or by looking at whether they have succeeded or failed according to a set of established standards.[3] Within the field of public policy a number of perspectives as to what evaluation exactly is can be found. The first perspective defines evaluation as the assessment of whether a set of activities implemented under a specific policy has achieved a given set of objectives. Thus, overall policy effectiveness is assessed.[4] A second perspective defines evaluation as any effort that renders a judgement about program quality.[5] The third perspective defines evaluation as information gathering for the purposes of making decisions about the future of a program.[6] A final perspective found in the literature views evaluation as the use of scientific methods to determine how successful implementation and its outcomes have been.[7]

The General Accounting Office (GAO) defines program evaluation as the provision of sound information about what programs are actually delivering, how they are managed, and the extent to which they are cost-effective.[8] For our purposes none of these definitions are necessarily unacceptable. We believe policy evaluation can be better defined as a process by which general judgments about quality, goal attainment, program effectiveness, impact, and costs can be determined.

What differentiates policy evaluation from other informal types of assessment is, first, its focus on outcomes or consequences.[9] Next, evaluation is done post implementation. In other words the program must have been implemented for a certain period of time. Third, the goals of the policy or program are provided to the evaluators. The main purpose of evaluation is to gather information about a particular program's performance so as to assist in the decision to continue, change, or terminate.

The Usefulness of Evaluation

One way that programs or policies may be assessed in terms of their accountability is through formal evaluation. Thus, the real value of program or policy evaluation is that it allows for accountability to be measured empirically. Conducting an evaluation allows policy makers to be provided with accurate information on key policy questions that arise from the implementation of any policy or program. Such information is of course provided by an evaluation study within a given set of real world constraints, such as time, budget, ethical considerations, and policy restrictions. The usefulness of conducting an evaluation study of a program or policy is that it provides information to policy makers on whether the policy or program in question is achieving its stated goal and at what costs these are being achieved. The effects of a program or policy will also be ascertained and if the evaluation is conducted correctly policy makers will be able to determine whether those effects are intended or unintended. Of course, policy makers want to know if programs are being administered and managed in the most efficient, accountable, and effective manner. An evaluation study can determine if this is true or not. Evaluation is also useful because it can eventually stimulate change. Finally, the utility of conducting an evaluation is that it can discover flaws in a program that policy designers were never aware of in the abstract.

TYPES OF POLICY EVALUATION

There are a variety of models or frameworks that fuse theoretical content with practical guidelines for conducting a program or policy evaluation. Most models arose in the 1960s and 1970s and were early attempts to conceptualize what evaluation was and how it should be conducted. Thus, they offer varying understandings as to the goals of an evaluation, the role of the evaluator, the scope of an evaluation, as well as how it is organized and conducted. Subsequent practitioners have taken the models and adapted them to changing times, contexts, and needs. Often two or more models will be used in conjunction with each other. The result is that there are several different types of evaluation models that vary in complexity.[10] There are, however, four types that are most commonly applied: Process Evaluation, Outcome Evaluation, Impact evaluation, and Cost-Benefit Analysis.

PROCESS EVALUATION. This type focuses on the concrete concerns of program implementation. It assesses how a program or policy is being delivered to target populations or how it is being managed and run by administrators. A process evaluation should address the following:

- determine why a program or policy is performing at current levels
- identify any problems
- develop solutions to the problems
- improve program performance by recommending
- how solutions should be implemented and evaluat once carried out.

With this type of evaluation the focus is not on whether the program is meeting specified goals, but is solely to develop recommendations to improve to implementation procedures. This type of evaluation is best suited to the needs of program managers and has the objective of helping managers overcome barriers to achieving the goals of the program policy being implemented.

OUTCOME EVALUATION. This type focuses on the degree to which a policy is achieving its intended objectives with regards to the target population. It is concerned with outputs and whether the policy is producing the intended results. This can lead to assessment of effectiveness, including cost. Outcome evaluation is not well suited to the needs of program level managers because it does not provide operational guidelines on how to improve the implementation of the program. Rather it is best suited to the needs of policy designers because it identifies whether there is consistency between policy outputs and program intent. An outcome evaluation must determine the following:

- legislative intent
- program goals
- program elements and indicators
- measures of indicators
- program outcomes and outcome valences (Whether they are positive or negative).

IMPACT EVALUATION. This type focuses on whether a program is having an impact on he

intended target population. The major difference between an impact evaluation and an outcome evaluation is that the latter are solely concerned with whether the program or policy's goals and objectives are being achieved. In comparison the impact evaluation is concerned with assessing whether the target population is being affected in any way by the introduction and implementation of the policy. There is also concern with the impact of the program on the original problem being addressed. The benefit of an impact evaluation is it is suited to the needs of both program level managers and policy designers, for it is important for both to ascertain whether target populations are appropriately receiving delivery of a program. A successful impact evaluation must help to identify the following:

- theoretical goals of the program/policy
- the actual goals
- the program or policy objectives
- program or policy results and whether they are intended, unintended, positive or negative in effect.

COST-BENEFIT ANALYSIS. This type of evaluation focuses on calculating the net balance of the benefits and costs of a program. Essentially, cost benefit analysis is a method with which to evaluate and assess the effectiveness of a policy's costs, benefits, and outcomes. Evaluators identify and quantify both the negative costs and positive benefits in order to determine the net benefit. For many it is a controversial evaluation technique because of the difficulty of applying it to the public sector. It ignores qualitative concerns at the expense of quantitative information. For example, if we take a cost benefit analysis approach to assessing certain policy issue areas, it is sometimes easier in certain issue areas to calculate the immediate real dollar costs then the tangible benefits. For certain types of programs such as education or the environment, one could argue that the real benefits do not materialize for years or decades. Hence a cost benefit analysis may evaluate a program for being inefficient in terms of monetary expenditures when it may in fact be effective in realizing its long term goals and in delivering benefits that in the long term far exceed the dollar costs. There are simply some things, such as quality of life, that cannot be quantified. If used alone, cost benefit analysis can color discussion on whether a program or policy is successful or not. It is most useful as a tool in conjunction with one of the other types of evaluation.

How Policy Is Evaluated

Evaluation of policy is fairly complex and includes initial activities that must be undertaken to ensure the success of the overall evaluation. Intrinsic to this success is the duty of the evaluator to communicate findings and conclusions to the client. Evaluation can be viewed as a three-stage sequence: planning, data gathering, and dissemination. Across these three stages a series of essential activities must take place (see Box 50.1).

Stages in the Evaluation Process

STAGE ONE - PLANNING.   This stage consists of three steps. Step one is familiarity with the program. Step two is deciding the focus of the evaluation, and step three is developing evaluation measures. In step one evaluators must become aware and familiar with the actual program or policy being evaluated. This can be accomplished through the evaluator asking him or herself a series of questions. The first question attempts to clarify the goals and objectives of a program or policy. This is not always easy to do since the legislative mandate for the policy may have ambiguously expressed goals, or multiple goals, or conflicting goals. Next, the evaluator must determine the relationship of the program being evaluated to other similar programs. Third, the evaluator must identify the major stakeholders in and the target populations of the program.

Stakeholders are individuals, agencies, or groups who hold stakes in the outcome of the evaluation. Target populations are those whom the policy affects. Non target groups should also be considered because they may potentially be affected by the policy.[12] Finally, the evaluator must learn the ongoing and recent history of the program. Once all of these questions have been answered then the evaluator can move on to the next activity in the planning stage.

In step two of the planning stage evaluators must decide what they are actually assessing. Specifically what is the focus of the evaluation? Is

BOX 50.1
Essential Activities in the Evaluation Process

- Identification of goals and objectives of the program/policy in such a way to make measurement possible

- Comprehension of Mission Statement or noting absence of one

- Construction of analytic model of what program/policy is expected to achieve, this includes a set of theoretical propositions about means-end relationships

- Development of a research design to distinguish actual program/policy goals from what are actually achieved

- Collection of data or actual measurement

- Analysis and interpretation of data

Sylvia, Sylvia and Gunn argue that we can ensure that an evaluation is being planned correctly by running a ten-point checklist:[11]

1. Is the program experimental or is it ongoing?
2. Who is the audience?
3. Are the measures, indicators and the design appropriate for the needs of the audience?
4. Are you interested in outcome or impact?
5. What is the purpose of the evaluation?
6. Are we trying to build theoretical knowledge or in seeing if maximum service is provided?
7. How will the study affect funding of the program?
8. Can we realistically produce a valid design given our resources?
9. Are we measuring what we are supposed to?
10. What am I doing, how am I doing it, and who cares what I tell them?

it the policy's impact, is it its outcomes, is it the costs and benefits, or is it the way the policy is being delivered? Once the focus is decided upon then the evaluator can conduct step three which is the development of measures for the focus. Such measures should include estimating the cost of the policy, in both dollar and non dollar terms.

STAGE TWO - DATA GATHERING. Two types of data must be collected by evaluators. First, data must be collected that allows for the program's overall configuration and structure to be better understood. Thus, information on how the program is delivered, to whom, and how many clients are served must be gathered. The second type of data gathering deals with the degree to which program goals and objectives are being achieved. The evaluator must also collect data on other effects, both intended and unintended, that can be attributed to the policy. How data is gathered will be determined by the evaluator's decision to apply quantitative or qualitative methods. Quantitative methods refer to a range of techniques that involve the use of statistics and statistical analysis for systematically gathering and analyzing information. Qualitative methods are aimed at understanding underlying behavior through comprehending how and why certain actions are taken by implementers, clients, and target populations. Box 50.2 highlights the differences between quantitative and qualitative methods of analysis.

There is no essential agreement on which type of analysis to utilize. Often the best way to determine which methods to apply is to look at the program's size and scope, the intended audience for the evaluation, the program's goals, the evaluator's own skills, and the resources available to conduct the evaluation. Once the methods have been determined, the evaluator must develop the research design and confirm the instruments (data collection devices) that will be applied (see Box 50.3). Research designs can be seen as strategies that can help the evaluator to improve the validity and reliability of the evaluation. Designs must be rigorous so as to avoid validity or reliability threats but must also be appropriately applicable to the complexity and needs of the program. Once a research instrument is selected and data gathered the evaluator may use a number of statistical techniques to analyze and interpret the data. Such techniques allow the evaluator to determine the potential associations or correlations of the variables under analysis.

STAGE THREE - DISSEMINATION. The final stage involves the dissemination of the findings of the evaluation to those who commissioned the evaluation, specifically the client. In some cases evaluation findings are also forwarded to stakeholders, target groups, or the public at large. The goal of any evaluation is to provide useful information. Usefulness depends upon a number of factors, including timeliness, accuracy, and completeness. All evaluation reports should report assumptions as well as real indicators which affect data interpretation. In sum, every evaluation will include the perceptions and assumptions that the evaluator derives from the assessment. Additionally,

---

BOX 50.2
Differences Between Qualitative and Quantitative Analysis

Quantitative	Qualitative
Counting	Interpreting
Measuring	Experiencing
Confirming	Understanding
Determining	Arguing
Testing	Exploring
Observing	Experiencing
Finding what is real	Exploring Multiple realities

BOX 50.3
Research Instruments

Quantitative Method	Qualitative Method
Subject Knowledge Tests	Case Studies
Attitude Surveys	Personal Interviews
Samples	Personal Observations

there should be alternative explanations for all observed outcomes, the separation of fact from opinion, and the findings should be clear and unambiguous. Finally, an evaluation should, when appropriate, include recommendations for the policy's continuation, change or termination.

Another dimension critical to effective dissemination is the relationship between the evaluator and the client. Clients in many ways can influence an evaluation study's outcome by bringing pressure to bear. For example, a client may have already made up his or her mind about the program and may pressure the evaluator to produce an assessment a predetermined finding. In response to such concerns, professional organizations in recent years have clarified the rights and responsibilities of evaluators in publishing standards and guiding principles for program evaluation practitioners.[13] The standards are principles rather than rules that evaluators should adhere to. They simply highlight what are acceptable and unacceptable practices. Thus, they are a benchmark for practitioners. Inevitably evaluators must decide for themselves what practices are ethical and justifiable.

Who Evaluates?

The choice for any agency or group that wishes to be evaluated is who should conduct the evaluation. In many ways this is the most critical decision in the evaluation process. The choice is between internal and external evaluators. Neither choice is inherently better then the other. The key to who should be used as an evaluator depends upon the needs of the organization that is commissioning the evaluation study. Both types of evaluators have their strengths and weaknesses. Internal evaluators have an overall advantage of being familiar with the program, the organization, the actors, and the target population. This can save time in the planning stage of the study. However, it can also prove to be a disadvantage in that internal evaluators, because of their ties to the organization, might be "too, close" to identify problems, to place blame, or recommend major changes or termination.

External evaluators are individuals who have no internal connection or ties to the organization being evaluated. They are perceived as "outsiders." External evaluators are often used when the evaluation is authorized by an entity other than the organization itself. For example, if the City of Los Angeles wanted to evaluate the Los Angeles Police Department, it would be an authorizing entity outside of the organization being evaluated. In this case it is more than likely the city would use external evaluators on the assumption that external evaluators would provide objective information because they have no vested interest or agenda to fulfill. The major advantage of external evaluation is that it is perceived to be impartial because evaluators supposedly have no stake in the outcome of the evaluation. This is particularly useful when controversial programs or policies are being assessed. A further strength of utilizing external evaluators is that they are usually professional consultants who are trained in the requisite skills and methods of evaluation techniques. In the past this was undoubtedly true. Recently, however, many individuals working in the public sector are educated in administration and management programs that train students in both policy analysis and program evaluation and are capable of conducting an evaluation.

The major disadvantage of opting for an external evaluation is cost, in both money and time. Some would also argue that it can prove costly in terms of organizational politics because of its potentially disruptive nature. A further disadvantage could be that external evaluators also have an agenda. For instance, they may wish to please the client in order to secure future jobs. This is potentially a dilemma. However, in theory professional ethics ensure that evaluators, although mindful of client needs, should stay true to their impartiality. Another weakness of utilizing external evaluators is they may face resistance from within the organization and between actors and other stakeholders who might have a vested interest in the outcome of the evaluation.

In conclusion it is interesting to consider two general laws formulated by James Q. Wilson, which put into perspective concerns about the evaluation process.[14] Wilson's first law is that all policy interventions in social problems produce the intended effect—if the research is carried

BOX 50.4
Validity Types

Internal Validity	External Validity	Programmatic Validity
• Does evaluation measure what it intends?	• Can findings be generalized?	• Does evaluation generate information that is useful to program officials?
• Requires correct identification and measuring of program goals	• Can findings be replicated?	• Requires designing an evaluation acceptable to all audiences

out by those implementing the policy or by their friends. Wilson's second law is that no policy intervention in social problems produces the intended effects—if the research is carried out by independent third parties, especially those skeptical of the policy. Wilson's two laws help explain just how difficult the evaluation process is.

Obstacles and Problems in Evaluation and Utilization of Evaluation Research

There are several factors that pose serious problems during the evaluation of a policy.[15] The first factor that clearly causes problems in any evaluation is ambiguity in the specification of the objectives and goals of a policy. It is common for objectives and goals to be sometimes unclear or equivocal and this can cloud the assessment of whether the goals and objectives have been met. A second problem can occur when objectives have been stated, but there is no clearly defined way to measure the success of the objective. A third problem is the presence of side effects from other policies that interact with the program being evaluated. In essence the problem is how to weigh outside factors relative to the operation of the program being evaluated. A fourth problem is that the necessary data is often not available, or if it is available, it is not in a suitable state for the purposes of the study. Fifth, the politics of the situation will often interfere with the evaluation process. For example, there may be resistance by administrators or other policy actors to an evaluation being conducted or to its findings. A sixth problem is determining if sufficient resources are being allocated to conduct the most appropriate type of evaluation. Finally,

the need for validity can prove to be a problem for evaluators.

There are three broad categories of validity that evaluators must be concerned with: internal, external, and programmatic. Box 50.4 highlights each of these factors in achieving a valid design. If evaluators do not pay close attention to such factors in the formulation and conduct of an evaluation then the very findings of the evaluation will be invalidated. The obstacles to validity are numerous and range from elements within the environment to methodological errors by the evaluator.[16]

Overall, obstacles to evaluation are important factors that can prevent successful evaluation and hinder the evaluator's recommendations being utilized by policy makers. Quite often, because of contextual factors, human factors, or technical factors, decision makers may be prevented from utilizing the results of the study. Contextual factors involve factors within the environment which will be affected in unacceptable ways if decision makers act on the recommendations of the evaluation. Technical factors refer to the problems caused by methodological considerations. Human factors are obstacles posed by the personality and psychological profile of the decision makers, evaluators, the client, and other internal actors. In reality, evaluation is fraught with problems and weaknesses.

Summary

In this chapter, we have discussed what policy evaluation is, how it is carried out, who does it, the problems that may be encountered and the obstacles to the utilization of recommendations made by program or policy evaluation studies. Over the past thirty years, policy evaluation has attracted considerable interest among policy makers at all levels in the public sector. It is important to remember that evaluation is essential, for it often tells policy makers what is working and what does not work.

End Notes

1. R. Haverman, "Policy Evaluation Research After Twenty Years," Policy Studies Journal 16, no.2 (winter 1987), pp. 191–218.
2. M.E. Rushefsky, Public Policy in The United States, (Belmont: Wadsworth, 1990), p. 16.
3. M. J. Dubnick and B. A. Bardes, Thinking About Public Policy (New York: Wiley,1983), p.203.
4. J. S. Wholey et al, Federal Evaluation Policy (Washington, D.C.: The Urban Institute, 1970), p.15.
5. R. Haveman, "Policy Evaluation Research After Twenty Years," Policy Studies Journal 16, no. 2 (Winter 1987), pp. 191–218.
6. R. D. Bingham and C. L. Felbinger, Evaluation in Practice: A Methodological Approach (New York: Longman, 1989), p. 4.
7. Ibid. p. 3.
8. General Accounting Office, Federal Evaluation Issues (Washington, D.C.: GAO, 1989), p. 4.
9. F. G. Caro, ed. Readings in Evaluation Research, 2nd ed. (New York: Russell Sage Foundation, 1977), p. 6.
10. J. R. Sanders, The Program Evaluation Standards (Thousand Oaks: Sage, 1994), pp. 8–12.
11. R. D. Sylvia, K. M. Sylvia and E. M. Gunn, Program Planning and Evaluation for the Public Manager 2nd ed. (Prospect Heights: Waveland Press, 1997), pp. 171–174.
12. E. R. House, Evaluating with Validity (Thousand Oaks: Sage, 1980), pp. 20–33.
13. J. R. Sanders, The Program Evaluation Standards (Thousand Oaks: Sage, 1994), pp. 8–12.
14. J. Q. Wilson, "On Pettigrew and Armor," The Public Interest 30 (Winter 1973), pp. 132–134.
15. B. W. Hogwood and L. A. Gunn, Policy Analysis for the Real World (New York: Oxford University Press, 1984), pp. 220–227.
16. R. D. Sylvia, K. M. Sylvia and E. M. Gunn, Program Planning and Evaluation for the Public Manager 2nd ed. (Prospect Heights: Waveland Press, 1997), pp. 117–127.

51

Policy Change and Termination

Stella Z. Theodoulou and C. Kofinis

Once a policy has been implemented, it becomes prey to all sorts of political realities and dynamics that constantly affect and shape how the policy is viewed as time passes. Interest groups mobilize, target groups complain, funding fluctuates, and sometimes there are legal challenges. Such real-world dynamics force policies to evolve and change. Under certain circumstances policies can also just end. One of the natural consequences of evaluating policies or the programs they create is that sometimes decision makers act upon the evaluation findings and force change, although...this

From Stella Z. Theodoulou and Cris Koffinis, *The Art of the Game* (Belmont: Wadsworth, 2004), pp. 201–210.

is not always the case. Policy does not always change radically because many political actors and much of the public may not support rapid change. We should also realize that sometimes policies remain essentially the same. There are various factors that can account for the absence of policy change. Among these factors are favorable evaluations, lack of evaluation, or extensive political support strong enough to overcome unfavorable evaluations.

In spite of wide acknowledgment of the effects of real-world dynamics, until recently, political scientists paid little attention to this stage of the policy cycle.[1] For many the stages-heuristic approach ended with policy evaluation. Some authors suggested that as part of the evaluation stage feedback occurred. This in turn allowed policies to be simply reformulated and reimplemented. With the addition of the change and termination stages, the feedback process has been encompassed and formalized into the stages-heuristic approach.

During the policy change and termination stages, policies are assessed, sometimes change occurs, and sometimes, although it is rare, policies are terminated completely. More often than not, changes to policies will occur rather than outright policy termination.[2]

POLICY CHANGE DEFINED

When a policy is replaced or modified in some respect or repealed in parts, then policy change has occurred. Policies are rarely maintained exactly as adopted. Change inevitably starts to occur as soon as a policy is implemented because of the intrinsic ambiguity of legislation. Thus, policies are constantly evolving and the policy cycle is an ongoing dynamic process. Policies are formulated, adopted, implemented, evaluated, reformulated, and reimplemented, and the cycle continues. Why is this the case? It is because when policies are designed they have as their goal the solving of a particular problem or the achievement of specific objectives. Whether objectives are achieved or not, policy makers will respond by altering or modifying the original policy. ... For example, antipoverty policies today are very different in many aspects than

they were in the 1960s. Whether the evolution is good or bad is not relevant to our discussion; what is germane is the fact that these policies have been reshaped over time and have evolved through change. Such change can be referred to as policy succession.[3] Policy succession can essentially be realized as taking one of the following three forms:

1. Modification of existing practices
2. Enactment of new legislative statutes
3. Major shifts in goals and direction of objectives

REASONS FOR CHANGE

There are eleven factors that can account for policy change. First, there might be changes in societal dynamics that force a policy to change to meet new conditions or facets of the same problem. Second, new policies may contradict or invalidate an existing policy. Third, a policy is challenged constitutionally or lawsuits are pursued against it. Fourth, technological changes alter a policy's feasibility or relevance. Fifth, new discoveries or revelations alter public support for the policy. Sixth, economic and political conditions change, thereby altering the environment in which the policy operates. Seventh, elections bring into office officials with very different ideological agendas and interpretations of what a particular policy should or should not be doing. Eighth, the problem is solved, thereby negating the need for the policy. Ninth, those implementing may lack the skills to manage the policy effectively. Tenth, once implemented a policy may show its defects and weaknesses. Finally, target groups simply refuse to comply with or they mobilize strongly against the policy.

Hogwood and Gunn suggest adding three further reasons for change to the policy cycle.[4] They argue that there are relatively few new areas of policy making in which modern governments can become involved. Thus, most new policies will overlap with or be extensions of existing policies and programs. This seems to reconfirm Charles Lindblom's classic characterization of American policy making as being incremental in nature.[5] The authors also contend that because of inadequacies or unintended effects, existing policies create conditions necessitating change. Finally, Hogwood and Gunn believe that changing policy is easier than terminating policy. Economic conditions may change and certain policies may be considered unnecessary, wasteful, or inappropriate; however, there will always be groups that support such policies. Therefore, politically it is easier to modify them than end them.

PATTERNS OF POLICY CHANGE

Policy change may follow several patterns. The most common patterns of policy change are listed below:[6]

Linear Change

With linear change, one policy is replaced with another or the location of an existing policy is changed. For example, the Aid to Dependent Children Act was replaced with Aid to Families with Dependent Children (AFDC). An additional example would be the conversion of the 1973 Comprehensive Employment and Training Act into the 1982 Job Partnership Training Act.

Consolidation Change

This type of change combines two or more programs with similar goals and objectives into a single new policy. When several environmental regulatory programs are fused or rolled together under one general policy consolidation has occurred. For example, under the 1992 Energy Policy Act several environmental regulatory programs were joined together.

Split Change

Split change divides an agency that is responsible for a particular policy or program into smaller organizational units, each of which are responsible for part of the original policy. Examples include the splitting of the Atomic Energy Commission in 1974 into two new agencies, the Nuclear Regulatory Agency and the Energy Research Development Agency, and the splitting of the Immigration and Naturalization Service into service and enforcement branches.

Nonlinear Change

This type of change reflects drastic or major policy change. It usually comes about because new social conditions develop, there are technological advances, or simply because political office holders desire change for ideological reasons. An example is the Clinton administration's reversal of the "gag rule," which forbade family-planning clinics from discussing abortion with their clients. A more recent example would be the 2001 Patriot Act which by some standards is a dramatic expansion of government powers in the areas of law enforcement and domestic security.

IMPLEMENTING POLICY CHANGE

The implementation of policy change is complex and often uncertain. Any policy change must go through the usual policymaking process. Each stage presents new difficulties for policy makers because established organizations, target groups, and stakeholders firmly entrench themselves in the process, attempting to block or control any changes. This extension of the policy cycle reflects how the policy process does not simply begin or end but is continually evolving. Figure 51.1 outlines the process of policy change throughout the policy cycle. It highlights the complexity of policy change at each stage of the cycle.

UNDERSTANDING WHY POLICY CHANGE OCCURS

The reasons for policy change have previously been discussed, but understanding why major changes in policy occur in the United States can best be understood through the use of policy change frameworks. There are three major frameworks that can be found within the literature: the cyclical thesis, the evolutionary or policy learning thesis, and the backlash or zigzag thesis.

As stated earlier in regard to policy implementation and evaluation, there is no single framework that can best explain policy change over time. Rather, each framework should be applied to specific policy areas to see whether change in a particular policy reflects policy learning, shifts in national mood, or transferal of benefits to new target populations.